Classics in Scientific Management

A BOOK OF READINGS

Classics in Scientific Management

A BOOK OF READINGS

Donald Del Mar
Rodger D. Collons

THE UNIVERSITY OF ALABAMA PRESS
University, Alabama

LIBRARY OF CONGRESS CATALOGING IN PUBLICATION DATA

Main entry under title:
Classics in scientific management.

Includes index.
1. Industrial management--Addresses, essays, lectures. 2. Industrial management--United States--Addresses, essays, lectures. I. Del Mar, Donald. II. Collons, Rodger D.
HD21.C64 658.4 75-20471
ISBN 0-8173-8701-3

MANUFACTURED IN THE UNITED STATES OF AMERICA

Contents

APPENDIX

Preface

Newton once noted that if he had seen a little farther than others, it was because he stood upon the shoulders of giants. We as students of management often fail to grasp as we read the latest articles and texts in our fields the indebtedness of the author to the pioneers of yesteryear, many of whom have long passed from the scene. We too often erroneously conclude that this concept or that, is straight from the brow of Jove, when with sufficient persistence and an historian's eye we may very well find that what the author said or did, knowingly or not, was to add at best another stone to the house of understanding.

The materials for this volume come primarily from a little known source--the Taylor Society Bulletins.[1] The Bulletins, originally published under the title "Bulletin of the Society to Promote the Science of Management" were issued about six times a year from 1914 to 1934 except for two years during World War I. After the first World War the name of the Society and its bulletin was changed to honor Frederick W. Taylor who had died in 1915 and whose widow had graciously offered some financial support for the Society's activities after the War. Except for a few articles, for example, Mary P. Follett's, "The Illusion of Final Authority," most have never reappeared in print since the time of their appearance in the Bulletins. A number of articles originally published in other magazines appeared as reprints in the Bulletins.

The editors chose to limit the material to a few sources on several grounds. First, there was, in their judgment, more than sufficient material of historical importance to make up a book of readings for students of management thought. Secondly, the Bulletins of the Taylor Society alone with its policy of reprinting what to the Bulletin's editor represented the best of management literature contained the widest spectrum of ideas and thoughts of any publication of the period. They include the early writings of many of the acknowledged pioneers of management thought as well as many more whose names have long been forgotten but whose writings and ideas are echoed in many of today's scholarly renditions. Thirdly, the editors are of the opinion that the revolutionary--evolutionary philosophy which captivated the thoughts of such pioneers as Taylor, the Gilbreths, Gantt, Barth, Dennison, Follett, William Green, Hopf, Mayo, Sheldon, Person, and Urwick were not generally understood by most practitioners of the period as well as the students of management thought since. The artificial "straw schools" set up by the academicians as a mechanism for analysis has not, in our opinion, aided in getting at the essence of the philosophy of scientific management. That is, paraphrasing Taylor, the problems of management can and should be approached scientifically.

---

[1]That these bulletins were not widely distributed is attested by the fact that only thirteen Universities in the United States claim to have a complete set while the over-whelming majority have none.

The text is shorter than the editors would have liked, but there is always a problem in convincing publishers of the merits of a larger volume. To partially correct this shortcoming an index to the Taylor Society Bulletins and a summary of the origin and aims of some of the early management societies originally published by the A.S.M.E. are included as appendices.

Introduction

The last two decades of the nineteenth century saw the rapid emergence of many giant enterprises in which professional managers were increasingly hired to operate. The administrative and financial model for these corporations came from the American railroads who like the textile industry of England provided the impetus to these respective countries to jump the economic chasm between an agriculturally dominated society and an industrially dominated one. Until the development of dependable all-weather transportations there was a limit placed on the size and density of population for those areas where, if other requirements necessary for industrial conversion were present, would industrialize on a large scale. Foodstuffs, for a large concentrated population, raw materials from afar, workers, and the development of channels of distributing the finished product were made possible by the development of transportation including railroads, steamship lines, the telegraph and later the telephone.

Industry, heretofore, had been dominated financially and economically by the family--entrepreneur--proprietorship--partnership where the supervisor had daily access to the owner-manager for his problems of production or sales. With the emergence of the corporation such immediate close contacts with the "ultimate" source of authority were no longer possible. With complexity of administration the flow of information up and down the chain of command of the impersonal entity known as the organization became a major problem.

These large, and some not-so-large but growing companies, although of increasing economic importance from 1850 onward, constituted the untypical American business enterprise in size and form. From 1880 to 1890 there was an increase in the number of businesses from 750,000 to 1,100,000.[1] Only a small percentage of those firms were large, incorporated, and had the many level bureaucratic hierarchy which comes to mind when discussing big businesses. Nevertheless these firms constituted the new form from the standpoint of organizational structure and financing and pioneered many of the "new" methods of management which later became accepted by managers in general. It is from this group of firms that many of the management pioneers emerged with their zest for new and better ways of solving the myriad complexities of organization and production facing their companies.

Most manufacturing firms before 1875 concentrated on manufacturing and sold their output to wholesalers, commission merchants, and jobbers who in turn would distribute the output via retailers and peddlers to the ultimate user. Control over volume sold, customer service needs, advertising, prices, discounts, and quality at the point of sales produced problems such that by 1910 many firms found it necessary and/or desirable to set up their own distribution organizations. Firms which first switched from dependence upon wholesalers and jobbers included the makers of agricultural machinery, sewing machines, carriages, typewriters, electrical machinery, and perishable goods producers such as meat products and other foods.[2]

Although machinery and mechanisms were widely employed they were for the most part crude and unsophisticated by today's standards. Industry in the nineteenth century was primarily, as it had always been before that time, labor intensive. With the success of the "agricultural revolution" rural America, east of the Mississippi and north of Virginia provided some of the muscle for those new industries. The other primary source which fueled American industrilization was immigration.

This influx of immigrants totaling 14 millions in the period 1860-1900 reached a peak in the decade 1900-1910. This was a major source of cheap, uneducated, and unskilled labor that lined up at the factory gates eager to work and apprehensive as to what they would find. Businesses through this period were increasing in number and size under the triple stimulus of an ever-growing and increasingly urban-oriented market, financial institutions designed to provide the means for expansion, and a generally cooperative attitude on the part of government.

Emphasis was on the production of things at the lowest possible cost. Little concern was shown for the possible long-run effects of waste for the land of plenty yielded more with the expenditure of little effort. Increases in output were achieved by constructing larger factories, installing more and more machinery and hiring more workers. Labor availability and cost tended to vary with changes in the economic tides of the country. Each tightening of the labor market, whether from increasing labor demands or a slowing-down of the foreign influx stimulated the drift toward mechanization.

The tools which formerly had marked their owner as an artisan now, except for the true craftsman, became the tools of industry and the intimacy of the small shops, as George describes it,[3] was snuffed out by the smokestacks of big factories. Strangers worked side-by-side often unable to communicate because of their inability to speak the other's tongue. The smell and sights of the farm, forest, or sea was being replaced by the sound, sight, and smell of a thousand wheels and shafts whirling on pedestal and hanger distributing the force of central power to the numerous noisy machines over which their tenders labored to feed them in an acrid atmosphere of smoldering belting, open fires, dripping lubricants, and infrequently washed bodies. This was a far cry from what most of these workers for wages had ever dreamed of, or had experienced. The closeness and darkness of the factory with the heat in summer, cold in winter, noise and smell, where the loss of an arm in open, unguarded machines was often preceded with an inquiry as to whether the machine was damaged, in which a man labored twelve or more hours a day with someone else's tools extracted a cost far beyond that of mere physical exertion. These then were the industrial serfs that had and would continue to build the basic industries of America and would at a later date demand their due.

The task of combining and coordinating the factors of production once performed by the owner-manager was, as previously noted, except for small enterprises was now being done by hired managers. The maintenance of their position, whether foreman or superintendent was dependent upon their success in extracting the maximum efficiency from the inputs of materials, labor, and machines.

The foreman's job included the selection, placement, and wage determination of new hands and the promotion, rewards, and the firing of old ones. This task as well as others was carried out on the basis of experience, guesswork, rules-of-thumb, and intuition. If the employee had any voice in these matters it was a very small one and that this encouraged them to try to beat the system was undeniable. At the same time the company sought to extract the last ounce of output from both worker and machine.

It was under conditions such as these that Frederick W. Taylor started to develop an approach to the problems of management which was to be later eternalized under the name "Scientific Management" by Louis Brandeis.

It is the development of the basic ideas espoused by Taylor and other promulgators of "the gospel of efficiency" and their subsequent refinement and enlargement by others that constitutes the theme of this readings book. It is hoped by the editors that the student, when reading these selections will place himself in the proper temporal economic, political, and social philosophical framework. Reflect if he will upon the meaning and implications of those thoughts in light of what is claimed to be "new" today. And if he concludes that the new science of management is not so new after all, it should occasion no great surprise.

---

[1]Thomas C. Cochran, "Basic History of American Business," (2nd ed). New York: D. Van Nostrand, Inc., 1968, pp. 59-85.

[2]Alfred D. Chandler, Jr., "The Coming of Big Business," in C. Vann Woodward, ed. The Comparative Approach to American History. New York: Basic Books, 1968, pp. 220-235.

[3]Claude S. George, Jr., "The History of Management Thought," (2nd ed.). Englewood Cliffs: Prentice Hall, 1972.

PART ONE

THE TAYLOR SOCIETY

This introductory section contains but three selections; "The Work and Aims of the Taylor Society" by Percy S. Brown, "The Social Meaning of Good Management" by Mary Van Kleeck, and an editorial by Joseph Hart entitled "Arbitrary Management on the Defensive." It seems most fitting to open this volume with a brief history of the society which furnished a forum for so many early practitioners and theorists in the field of management.

The origin and lineage of the Society as traced by Percy Brown is historically significant in that the scientific study of management, primarily industrial management, was perceived to be a part of the larger field of engineering. The incorporators of the new Society to Promote the Science of Management were practitioners of the art--the engineer-executives. The philosophy they promulgated reflected their engineering outlook and their spirit of public service. To them the entire range of management problems was their game open to scientific inquiry and they welcomed to membership "all who have become convinced that the business men of tomorrow must have the engineer mind."[1]

Mr. Brown was at the time he wrote this article Works Manager of Corona Typewriter Company and President of the Taylor Society. As Brown's article notes the Society was organized by members of the A.S.M.E. who were very much interested in finding a forum form which topics of primary concern to managing and managers could be presented and discussed. To dispell any notion that these individuals were disgruntled with the A.S.M.E. we need but to quote F. B. and L. M. Gilbreth:

> "We can state without question that the Taylor Society was not founded because of dissatisfaction with the attitude of the American Society of Mechanical Engineers toward management. . . . There was no feeling of criticism toward the American Society of Mechanical Engineers; no desire to withdraw from the Society, in any way or in any sense, and so far as we know, all members of the original group were, always have been and are at present enthusiastic and loyal members of the American Society of Mechanical Engineers."[2]

The origin, organization, and objectives of some of the other early management oriented organizations is given in the appendices of this volume.

Van Kleeck's "The Social Meaning of Good Management" is included to indicate the high level of enthusiasm, dedication, and the idealistic outlook that characterized so many members of the Society and the scientific management movement. At times it seems that they saw themselves as a part of an efficiency crusade. This same effervescence of enthusiasm, generally associated with youth movements, came primarily from a group composed of middle aged engineer-managers who were daily engaged in the practice of management and academicians and public servants.

The third selection by Joseph Hart, written in 1925, provides a measure of the progress in change in attitude, scope, and goals that had taken place in the intervening years since Towne's paper before the A.S.M.E. in 1886. It also serves the purpose of suggesting that scientific management is improperly a term for a "system" or a period of time but is an evolutionary management spirit that can be summarized by the word progress.

The society's open acceptance of criticism, the recognition of the need for change, the willingness to test new ideas, and a general lack of smuggness and pettiness seems most refreshing when compared to many of today's "professional" society meetings. The recognition of a public duty and the idea of an intellectual challenge to solve industrial problems seems somewhat out of focus in today's world of managerial slots and grey flannel suits. This may be due to the fact that academicians were a small fraction of those who participated at that time while the opposite is true today. The willingness to accept the comfortable, a second best position, or leave it to others attitude was not a part of this crusading spirit which drove these warriors onward up the hill toward the edifice of efficiency.

---

[1]This seems to have a familiar ring to it when one reads University Catalogs describing the objectives of our Masters of Business Administration Programs.

[2]L. P. Alford, "Ten Years Progress in Management," A.S.M.E. 1922, p. 1287.

THE WORK AND AIMS OF THE TAYLOR SOCIETY[1]

An Open Forum for Open Minds Seeking by Methods of Science the Solution of Industrial Problems

By Percy S. Brown

It was among engineer-trained executives that consciousness of the management problem first began to find expression in what has come to be known as "the management movement." During the '80s the development of big-scale industry was under way and brought with it problems centering about the supervision and control of operations. The analytic engineer-mind first perceived and attacked the problem. In 1886 Henry R. Towne clearly set forth its nature in the famous paper before the American Society of Mechanical Engineers, The Engineer as Economist, and for nearly a decade thereafter meetings of the American Society of Mechanical Engineers and technical engineering journals offered the only forum for study and discussion of the management problem, in which there was a growing interest. This was a natural center for the beginning of interest in management. The problem had been created by big-scale enterprises utilizing labor-saving machinery under division of labor, and it was one of learning how to manage the use of machines--of production. It was not then a problem of selling, for America was uncovering abundant new resources, population was increasing rapidly, purchasing power was increasing more rapidly, and there was a continuing sellers' market. The management problem first took the form of complications in the utilization of machinery, and it was inevitable that the first group to be challenged by it should consist of the very men who were inventing and installing equipment, and endeavoring to teach industry how to manage it.

Origin and Lineage of Taylor Society

But all engineering sciences were growing rapidly during this period, and by 1910 the American Society of Mechanical Engineers was confronted by the problem of settling the scope which its resources and facilities would permit its work to take. It was decided that the greater service would be rendered by emphasizing pure engineering, and consequently study and discussion of management found its opportunity restricted.

There being no other forum, a small group of about a dozen members of the A.S.M.E., led by such men as James M. Dodge, Frank B. Gilbreth, Robert T. Kent, Conrad Lauer, Carl G. Barth, Morris L. Cooke and H. K. Hathaway, began to meet regularly for continued, more intensive, discussion of management. There was at the beginning no formal organization of a "society," but in the winter of 1910-11 the organization was made formal and the Society to Promote the Science of Management came into being. This formal organization was stimulated by the marked general increase of interest in management caused by testimony concerning the achievements of scientific management at the Eastern Rate Case Hearings, and more particularly by the fear that, because of the sensational nature of the testimony concerning results, there would be a grand rush by industry to "get efficient quickly," and the very engineering technique which had brought the results would be neglected and eventually lost. The group decided that it was a service obligation for them to strengthen their position as defenders of the engineering point of view.

The Society to Promote the Science of Management continued to hold meetings of a more formal nature, and in December, 1914, began the publication of a periodical bulletin. The quality of its discussions and published articles attracted some attention and caused a gradual and unsensational increase in membership, so that by the outbreak of the war, in 1917, the membership was something over 100. No campaign for membership increase was undertaken, the policy being to preserve the homogeneity of point of view and technical approach towards management problems, and to let membership increase be the result of natural attraction of like-minded executives and engineers.

During the war nearly all the members became absorbed in one way or another into the war machine, and the society became quiescent. But immediately after the Armistice activity was resumed and on a larger scale. Perceiving the magnitude of the industrial problems which would inevitably result from maladjustments left by the war, and believing it had something to contribute to the solution of those problems by emphasis of the engineering approach, whatever the area of the field of management in which the problems might arise, the society organized deliberately for larger service, established a New York office with a full-time executive, and, in honor of the pioneer of engineer-executives who had died in 1915, changed its name to the Taylor Society. Since that time its membership has gradually increased to some 800.

Purpose and Range of Interest

The above account of the origin and lineage of the Taylor Society is important, as it makes more understandable the purpose and methods of the society. In the first place, it is the descendant in direct line of that group of engineer-executives--such as Henry R. Towne, Oberlin Smith, James M. Dodge and Frederick W. Taylor--who first perceived the emergence of a management problem in American industry. In the second place, it inherited from that group and cherishes the engineering point of view and method of attack on management and other social problems. In the third place, descended from men who had been trained as scientists and who valued the search for truth for its own sake, it is without ulterior motive or special interest, and is not afraid to consider any problem within the scope of its general interest, and particularly to consider all facts, whatever their source, bearing upon any problem which falls within its field. These three things, I believe, together with certain features of organization and methods of work resulting from them, are the outstanding characteristics of the Taylor Society.

Faithful to these traditions, it has fearlessly searched for, appraised, and put on record the most progressive and noteworthy thought and practice with respect to every phase of management which has assumed importance as changing industrial conditions have defined importance. Its first inquiries were concerned with production, for on a sellers' market that was then the important problem of management, and the Taylor Society believes that fundamentally and in the long run production will always be the most critical management problem. But when complications of big-scale industry caused industrial relations to become a problem of outstanding importance, the society considered it in a characteristic manner. It was the Taylor Society which promptly gave such progressive thinkers as Robert Valentine and Robert Wolf a forum, and which more recently established real contact between psychologists and industry. And when the buyers' market generated by the war came upon American industry, the Taylor Society promptly made inquiry into two phases of management which emerged as of major importance--general control and selling. Nowhere are there to be found records of more searching inquiry and more fruitful suggestions concerning the function and technique of coordination and the function and technique of selling than in the published bulletins of the Society.

What may result from the engineering method of approach to such a problem as that of industrial relations? That method, distinguished by insistence upon ascertainment and measurement of all the facts pertinent to any problem, as applied to the problem of industrial relations has unmistakably established two conclusions: that the human element is as real a factor in management as is the mechanical and cannot be disregarded in any adequate system of management; and that the regard for the human element in any system of management must itself be upon a factual and not an emotional basis. Too many of the studies of industrial relations during the past ten years have been dominated by emotionalism and have resulted in ill-considered methods of personnel management. In too many instances personnel management has been assumed to be something separate from operating management, and personnel departments have been plastered onto instead of incorporated into operating organizations. Fortunately most of these mushroom-growth personnel departments were eliminated by the depression following the war, and industry is now able to approach its problem of industrial relations anew along those sounder lines which make good or bad industrial relations a function of good or bad policies and methods of operating management. It is in the process of engineering its policies and methods of operating that an enterprise is engineering its conditions of human relations. This was noted recently by Miss Mary Van Kleeck, of the Russell Sage Foundation, in the following words:

> My experience began with what is called the human element in industry, and I saw it first outside the shop in the community. In the lives of wage-earners, particularly women in industry, I saw the effects of long hours of work, unemployment and low wages. In the search for remedies I was led back into the causes of these conditions in the shop itself, and nowhere did I find so many questions in process of being answered as in the Taylor Society. Not the final answer but the process of discovering the answers was for me the big contribution of this group . . .My interest in the Taylor Society is not directed toward challenging the technical engineer to give attention to problems of human relations. I am not worried about that, because if he

> is a good engineer he cannot fail to contribute to human relations. I am concerned rather with the other end of the story. I am eager to have those people who see in the community the present disastrous results of industrial organization realize how the art of management in the shop can fundamentally change those social conditions in the community. The Taylor Society can thus interpret management to the group who are seeking to construct a better community.

Engineering Point of View

This faithfulness to ancestry has imposed upon the Taylor Society certain restrictions which it has recognized and accepted. In the first place, insistence upon the engineering point of view and method of attack upon problems has permitted only modest growth in membership, for executives whose background is that of frontier conditions--American industry is just emerging from frontier conditions--come slowly to appreciate the engineering point of view and methods. Yet it is interesting that the membership of the Society is today made up chiefly of executives who have not had engineering training and have not been concerned with what are generally regarded as engineering responsibilities. That means, of course, that the mental attitude identified by the term engineering is independent of particular training, and it means also that an increasing number of American executives are developing the habit of approaching their problems in an engineering fashion.

That the engineering point of view and technique should gradually appeal to an increasing number of manufacturing executives was to be expected. But it is somewhat surprising to find that its march has been so rapid as to excite the interest even of executives of merchandising enterprises. The organization under the inspired leadership of A. L. Filene, the Boston merchant, of such an enterprise as the Retail Research Association a dozen years ago was a venture in organizing for an engineering attack on problems of retail management. And recently E. A. Filene, the other of the two sons of Wm. Filene's Sons Company, has in his book, The Way Out, specifically declared the necessity of the engineering method in solving our industrial problems. I cannot refrain from quoting the following:

> American business has reached its last frontier . . . As society develops the pioneer must be succeeded by the engineer . . .The business men of tomorrow must have the engineer-mind. We would better turn our energies to the urgent job of substituting the engineer-mind for the pioneer-mind in the American business of the future.

That is exactly what the forebears of the Taylor Society saw, and what the Taylor Society has made it a mission to persuade American industry to see.

Definite Philosophy

Again this faithfulness to ancestry has imposed limitations in growth for the reason that the engineering point of view demands the acceptance of a definite philosophy and technique of management. One cannot have the engineering mind and fail to systematize his thought and methods. Therefore the Taylor Society has accepted, in a liberal way, the only philosophy of management which research has yet enabled industry to formulate--the Taylor philosophy. It is either that or no unifying system of thought--no one has formulated an alternative. Therefore, although subscription to the Taylor philosophy is not a condition of membership, the very fact of the Society's acceptance of a governing system of thought in its investigations of management problems, and in its appraisal of management experiments, is a deterrent to rapid and spectacular increase of membership. Some executives do not desire to accept consciously, however tentatively, any system of thinking; and particularly some do not desire to be identified with the Taylor philosophy because of failure to perceive its essential nature and separate that from incidents of controversy during the early days of its formulation. The Taylor Society recognizes all of this, accepts the consequences of temporary restrictions, and goes seriously on its way, for it is "bullish" on the value of the engineering point of view and its ultimate acceptance by American industry, and on the spiritual and intellectual strength which comes from guidance by a definite system of thinking which contains within itself the principles of adaptability to changing conditions and the requirements of new information.

Methods--Possible

The characteristics of the Taylor Society which have been described naturally influence its organization and methods of work, and cause them to be different from the organization and methods of other societies having a similar and equally worthy purpose. The operations of a management society may be distinguished in the large by the manner in which it combines and emphasizes certain possible elemental operations. The most important of these elemental operations are as follows:

A. Investigation

1. Genuinely scientific research through a staff of paid experts.
2. Group organizations of the membership for comparison of experiences.
3. Discovery, discussion and appraisal of the results of significant research and experiments by specialized research organizations and progressive industrial enterprises.

B. Service to Members

1. Meetings

a. Carefully organized programs featuring selected advanced ideas and practices.
b. Carefully organized programs featuring general participation of members and comparison of their experiences.

2. Publications

a. Containing selected and edited material derived from meetings of the type Bla and similar materal from other sources.
b. Containing articles reflecting records of general membership experience derives from meeting of the type Blb.

3. Advisory and Information Service

a. Information related to particular problems rendered to members in response to inquiries by correspondence and personal interview.

4. Miscellaneous Service

Such as assistance in securing particular types of personnel for member's organizations, introductions for those on tours of inspection, etc.

C. Public Service

1. Promotion of and participation in programs of a public nature, involving management problems, undertaken for the public welfare.

It is obvious that to perform all these operations adequately would require large resources and a considerable executive staff, and no management society finds itself in that happy position. So the problem of organization and methods consists of choosing and emphasizing elemental operations such as those enumerated above.

Methods--Adopted

Because of its moderate size and limited resources the Taylor Society has had to choose carefully. The choosing has been influenced also, obviously, by the society's origin, antecedents and point of view.

In general it has chosen to apply its limited resources to the fields of investigation and service to members rather than to the commercial phase of increase of membership with corresponding neglect of the investigation and service activities.

With respect to investigation it has recognized the impossibility of expensive genuine research through a staff of its own. It has emphasized, in the work of the national society, the discovery, discussion and appraisal of the researches of specialized research organizations and the experiments of progressive enterprises. On the other hand the investigation involved in comparison of experiences of members is emphasized in the work of constituent regional sections.

This is reflected in the programs of meetings and in the BULLETIN OF THE TAYLOR SOCIETY. The meetings of the national society feature the presentation and discussion of new and progressive ideas and practices, whether by members or non-members, and the Bulletin features articles of a similar nature. The more frequent meetings of a regional section, on the other hand, emphasize the consideration of problems, practices and experiences common to the membership of the particular section.

The advisory and information service is an experiment and time will be required for members to learn to use it and for the society to learn how to render the service. But it is growing slowly; members of all classes--old and young, engineers, and executives--are utilizing the executive staff of the society as a center of information bearing on their problems. As the fund of information which members may tap increases in quality and quantity--and the very nature of the operations of the central office of the society causes it to increase--members will more and more utilize such facilities of the society.

The society has not hesitated to cooperate with others in programs motivated by the desire for improvement of social conditions where such improvement has involved problems of management. A noteworthy instance was the publication of Horace B. Drury's study of the three-shift system in the steel industry, a study the influence of which, combined with the influence of other similar studies, brought about a significant change in management methods in the steel industry. Another instance of international public service was the acceptance by the Taylor Society of detail labors involved in the organization of the effective contribution of the Committee on American Participation to the Prague International Management Congress in 1924.

The Taylor Society is interested in advancing sound thinking concerning the management problem throughout its entire range, in promoting understanding of established principles and discovery of new principles, and in assisting its membership to the command of an engineering technique of investigation and a flexible technique of management derived by that method of investigation. It welcomes to membership all who have become convinced that "the business men of tomorrow must have the engineer-mind."

---

[1]Bulletin of the Taylor Society, June, 1925; Reprinted from "Science in Modern Industry" Vol CXIX of the Annals of the Academy of Political and Social Science, May, 1925.

THE SOCIAL MEANING OF GOOD MANAGEMENT

I shall limit my remarks to an attempt to show the significance of the Taylor Society in my own experience. This I do, not as a means of enlightening any of you, but in the hope of stimulating each of you to evaluate once more the meaning of the Society.

I was keenly interested in the discussion at the morning session in which, as in previous meetings, several speakers talked about "the new recognition" of "the human element in industry." They seemed to think that this was lacking in the first formulation of the principles of scientific management.

I should like to turn the subject completely around. My own experience began with what is called the human element in industry, and I saw it at first outside the shop in the community. In the lives of wage-earners, particularly women in industry, I saw the effects of long hours of work, unemployment, and low wages. In the search for remedies, I was led back into the causes of these conditions in the shop itself, and nowhere did I find so many questions in process of being answered as in the Taylor Society. Not the final answer but the process of discovering the answers was for me the big contribution of this group.

Those answers did not relate merely to what is called the human element in industry, conceived as a separate problem in a different compartment of the manager's desk. My interest in the contribution of scientific management to the social problems in the lives of wage earners was not solely in its emphasis upon personnel relations, but in the technical organization of industry as it affects wage earners. The constructive imagination which can spend seventeen years studying the art of cutting metals is the imagination which can make industry and all its results in human lives harmonize with our ideals for the community. That kind of constructive imagination, though it may deal with one technical problem, will not fail to envisage the whole significance of industrial management. Nor will it be content merely to increase profits. The philosophy and the procedure which it represents will ultimately build a shop whose influence in the community will be social in the best sense, because the shop and all its human relations are built on sound principles.

Therefore, my interest in the Taylor Society is not directed toward challenging the technical engineer to give attention to problems of human relations. I am not worried about that, because if he is a good engineer he cannot fail to contribute to human relations. I am concerned rather with the other end of the story. I am eager to have those people who see in the community the present disastrous results of industrial organization realize how the art of management in the shop can fundamentally change those social conditions in the community. The Taylor Society can thus interpret management to the group who are seeking to construct a better community. Membership in the Taylor

Society means an opportunity to share in that interpretation.

I can illustrate in another way what membership in the Taylor Society means. I have in my mind a picture of the Taylor Society in session. A valiant member rises with tilted spear to advance upon the rest of us. He has discovered a new idea which was lacking in Mr. Taylor's formulation of principles. He hurls his challenge. I see members of the old guard sitting on the front row, and I observe over the collar the tip of a smile. The smile means: "If this young man will think a little more deeply, he will find his idea already formulated in scientific management, but we won't tell him so." For this is what the Taylor Society is for. It makes just one claim upon its members--the claim to understanding by each member for himself. To the man who asks, "What shall I get out of membership in the Taylor Society?" the answer is simply "a challenge to think for yourself and to test your thinking in actual practice." Membership in the Taylor Society does not mean simply paying dues in order to receive a bulletin and to share in other attractive perquisites of an ordinary society. It means a readiness to accept a challenge presented in the discovery and formulation of principles of management which have a lasting value because they stimulate the conflict of ideas.

Abstract of remarks by Mary Van Kleeck, of the Russell Sage Foundation, at the dinner of the annual business meeting of the Taylor Society, December 4, 1924.

Arbitrary Management on the Defensive [1]

What Science in Management Means to the Worker

Traditional, rule-of-thumb management in industry made a fatal slip, back in 1881 or 1882, when the authorities of the Midvale steel plant, Philadelphia, permitted a young gang boss to organize his responsibilities after a fashion of his own. When Frederick W. Taylor was permitted to substitute his early beginnings in scientific analysis and organization for the older rule-of-thumb processes, industry all over the country, all over the world, indeed, should have seen that this was the beginning of the end for arbitrary rule everywhere. There was, after that--there is, now, no permanent stopping place for the scientific analyst until every item of every process in industry is understood and approved by the most adequate intelligence that humanity can produce. And arbitrary, rule-of-thumb management, wherever it persists, waits, on the defensive, the coming of the scientist.

Workers long believed that the whole incidence of the Taylor System was directed to the increase of the employer's profits. For this reason they opposed the system in many places. They should have understood--they have since found out--that traditional methods, attitudes and relationships have never specifically favored the worker.

It may even be that industrial management was first induced to accept the Taylor idea because it seemed to promise increased profits, at small additional outlay. If so, here is another proof that business men sometimes buy either more or less than they agree to pay for. Management should have been forewarned that science is not likely to give up, at any arbitrary wish or command, an unfinished task.

Those early analyses had to do with physical factors involved in specific operations. Management relished this and the workers did not--for the most part. But in those days science had no technique with which to probe any of the other processes involved in industrial operations. And, anyhow, the establishment of the scientific ideal with respect to objective factors and in the elimination of obvious wastes was not an undesirable first step. Waste serves no good purpose; and management must learn to respect science, since, in the long run, the impact of the new method will be most severely felt on the side of management.

The intervening years have provided a new technique. Analysis is now rapidly passing over from the consideration of the old physical processes to the uncovering of those many intimate moral and emotional factors which under all conditions of industry implicate the worker in his work and which help to determine, not alone his present effectiveness in his present work, but also his wider relationships to his whole environment and, therefore, his ultimate effectiveness in the industrial order and his human significance in and to the community which supports and is supported by industry. This new technique is that extension of the psychiatric approach which is coming to be called industrial psychology.

At the December, 1924, meetings of the Taylor Society, in New York City, the significance of this wider analysis was set forth by Dr. Elton Mayo, in an address on The Basis of Industrial Psychology.

It is impossible to summarize that address here. It appears in full in the December number of the Taylor Society Bulletin. The spirit of it--its promise for the future of the workers and the standpoint of the emotional release of the workers and the humanization of the whole industrial complex--may be found in the following single quotation:

"Taylor confined his attention, upon the whole, to the problem of irrelevant synthesis or mistaken coordination in our muscular apparatus; there is urgent need to extend this inquiry to discover what irrelevant syntheses of emotions and ideas are imposed upon workers by indifferent education and unsuitable conditions of work. I use the term 'worker' here to include proprietors and managers as well as machine operators."

The address was characterized by one of the hearers who took part in the discussion as "the most important message ever delivered to industry in America." As applied to the content of this particular address, the statement may be an exaggeration; but as applied to its import, it was but a simple statement of fact. Arbitrary, rule-of-thumb industrial management is more and more on the defensive. When the management engineer and the industrial psychiatrist have finished their work, every rule-of-thumb cranny in the industrial world will have been cleaned and swept; every traditional and arbitrary management will have been discharged; and industry will have become, under the direction of intelligence and good will, the effective and human means by which the community provides for its inclusive economic needs and desires.

PART TWO

FREDERICK WINSLOW TAYLOR (1859-1915)

To each identifiable stage in the development of an art or science there becomes associated with it a few names whose mention, at a later time, serves to capsulize for the audience the philosophical essence of that period. That the philosophy and concepts were not necessarily promulgated or subscribed to by these persons is important to both the scholar and the student of management. Often, however, this is overlooked or ignored in our haste and compulsion to categorize philosophies and to tuck each into a distinct "intellectual cubby-hole," i.e. a school of thought. The intellectual mischief done by our seemingly impulsive instinct for categorizing and "cubby-holing" is compounded by having these inaccuracies handed down to successive generations of students by professors performing from yellowed notes saved from their school days or who have not taken the time to do their homework. This later group includes many of the so called human relations disciples who, just as the charlatans and exploiters of the mechanics of the "scientific management school" before them mistook the more easily understood mechanics for its philosophy.

The editors hold, despite the arguments of others including the editors of Engineering Magazine[1] who claim that Henry Towne was unquestionably the pioneer of scientific management, that if the mantle of "Father of Scientific Management" is to be bestowed upon one individual, that individual would be Taylor. The breath and depth of Taylor's contributions, however much they were inspired by Towne's writings and association, were greater than the contributions of Towne and more basic to much of the work by other noteworthy contributors and influencers such as Lawrence Gantt, Carl Barth, Henry Dennison, and Frank and Lillian Gilbreth. Secondly, the criticism that Taylor and his associates did not develop a systematic body of knowledge although true, begs the question as to who has. Another criticism, closely related to the preceding one and also essentially true was that Taylor was primarily concerned with the operating level and not with the work of managers. This is more of an observation than a valid criticism when one observes that Fayol having read and studied the work of Taylor and his associates concluded in the end that he had no basic disagreement with scientific management and that his contribution was complementary to that of Taylor and not a refutation or criticism as such--including Taylor's controversial functional foremanship.[2] In today's systems jargon, Taylor contributed at a different (lower) level in the hierarchy of systems and subsystems. Thirdly, it might be observed that there tends to be in the development of any movement that the "easier," in this case the more mechanistic aspects, are first set forth while the more difficult and sophisticated aspects tend to follow. We find this today in the area of operations management.

To appreciate and properly evaluate the contributions of individuals it is necessary to consider what they wrote and said and the time and environment in which they performed. A deeper insight into their impact upon their contemporaries can be gotten if one can see the "whole man." This unfortunately is difficult to do since most evaluations by these contemporaries are not preserved. That these intellectual assessments may be biased and overstated is beside the point. What seems historically important is that there was sufficient evidence in their eyes regarding someone's contributions to warrant their publicly acknowledging it. A second source of information that may add to the intellectual tapestry of the man is his private correspondence. Unlike most published works and speeches they are generally less formal, less structured and more revealing as to the author's basic philosophy and character, and thus his impact upon his contemporaries.

Such is the conclusion reached by the editors regarding Frederick Winslow Taylor, his contemporaries, his followers and his philosophical disciples and the "Scientific Management School." With these thoughts in mind we chose for Part Two, eight relatively short selections.

The first two selections are personal letters written by Taylor. The topic of the first letter is profit sharing--the panacea for motivating workers held then as now by academicians and practitioners alike as well as labor leaders and workers--most who fail to recognize its shortcomings and/or perceive it as a one-way street. The second letter to Morris Cooke gives a measure of Taylor's intellectual curiosity, the scope of his scientific inquiry and his persistency in applying the scientific method to the various phenomenon under his investigation.

In the third selection on government efficiency Taylor notes what many people inside and out of government fail to grasp--the mental organizational philosophy of the "typical bureaucrat." Some of the many reasons why Presidential Commissions investigating inefficiency in government fall short of their goals is clearly recognized in this article.

Oliver Sheldon's article includes a synthesis of his own observations regarding Taylor and the philosophy he fathered. This is interwoven with his review of Frank Copley's biography of Taylor. In a few pages Sheldon attempts to capsulize for the reader the essence of the man and the philosophy--a task which took Copley some nine hundred pages. His succinct observations on the origin, evolution and objectives of Scientific Management should aid in dispelling some of the confusion that has grown up around the movement.

Copley's article, as footnoted, was originally submitted as a letter to the Editor with the objective of dispelling what Copley considered a false impression being spread regarding Taylor's attitude toward trade unions. As in Sheldon's article we get a glimpse of Taylor's concern for treating the third party, i.e. the public, fairly by recognizing their existence in any wage negotiation. This we seem to often to forget today.

Lyndalls Urwick's "On Industrial Esperanto" is a succinct discussion of the nature and problems arising from the development and implementation of scientific management here and abroad. The article is a defense of the scientific philosophy against those who say for various reasons that they do not believe in it or are overly critical of scientific management without really understanding the movement.

It seems only fitting to close this part with a word of advice by Taylor (1909) to the students of management at the University of Illinois. Like most such addresses "success" is somewhat lengthy, however, its totally redeeming feature is its simplicity, forthrightness, and its "drive it home" approach which characterized so much of Taylor's work. What student after having read Taylor's words on common sense, character, and integrity can but reflect at a later time on his contributions to the betterment of mankind?

---

[1]Industrial Management, The Engineering Magazine, LXI (1921), p. 232.

[2]See for example: Charles de Freminville, Henri Fayol, Taylor Society Bulletin, February 1927. (This article is included in a later section of this book.)

PROFIT SHARING[1]

Why It Will Not Solve The Difficulties Between Capital And Labor. A Personal Letter Written By The Late Frederick Winslow Taylor

August 22, 1912.

Mr. George Elbert Taylor
Calumet Club
267 Fifth Avenue
New York City

My dear Mr. Taylor:

I have read through your plan for profit sharing with the very greatest of interest, and I want to congratulate you upon the most complete and thorough way in which you have thought out every detail of your scheme, as well as upon the lucid and most interesting way in which you have described every feature of it. You have certainly presented the most carefully thought out and elaborated scheme of profit sharing that has ever come to my attention.

Since receiving your paper, I have again given a great deal of thought to the whole subject, and wind up where I started, with the firm conviction that the satisfactory and final solution of the difficulties between employers and employees will not be made through profit sharing. I beg to quote you from a paper on "A Piece Rate System," written by me in 1895, as follows, on profit sharing:

> "Co-operation, or profit sharing, has entered the mind of every student of the subject as one of the possible and most attractive solutions of the problem; and there have been certain instances, both in England and France, of at least a partial success of co-operative experiments.
>
> "So far as I know, however, these trials have been made either in small towns, remote from the manufacturing centres, or in industries which in many respects are not subject to ordinary manufacturing conditions.
>
> "Co-operative experiments have failed, and I think, are generally destined to fail, for several reasons, the first and most important of which is, that no form of co-operation has yet been devised in which each individual is allowed free scope for his personal ambition. Personal ambition always has been and will remain a more powerful incentive to exertion than a desire for the general welfare. A few misplaced drones, who do the loafing and share equally in the profit with the rest, under co-operation are sure to drag the better men down towards their level.
>
> "The second and almost equally strong reason for failure lies in the remoteness of the reward. The average workman (I don't say all men) cannot look forward to a profit which is six months or a year away. The nice time which they are sure to have today, if they take things easily, proves more attractive than hard work, with a possible reward to be shared with others six months later.
>
> "Other and formidable difficulties in the path of co-operation are, the equitable division of the profits, and the fact,

> while workmen are always ready to share the profits, they are neither able nor willing to share the losses. Further than this, in many cases, it is neither right nor just that they share either in the profits or the losses, since these may be due in great part to causes entirely beyond their influence or control, and to which they do not contribute."

I quote this as giving merely a bird's eye view of my study of profit sharing. No single element touched upon by me in these few words is at all satisfactorily treated, and yet I still retain the same views that I had when this was written in 1895.

There are a number of elements which I have not touched upon in this quotation, and which in my judgment form the very essence of the objection to profit sharing. The first of these is that so far as I am able to find out, capital is not, on the average, generally speaking, receiving at the present time more than its fair share of the joint return given to capital and labor. And the eyes of the laboring people are continually directed to the wrong spot when they are focussed upon the great and unjust rewards which capital is now receiving.

I feel very certain that one of the greatest misfortunes under which laboring people now are suffering, is that they are not correctly informed on this very subject. One of the most illuminating articles that I have ever read appeared in the June Atlantic Monthly, and was written by Mr. Chas. Norman Fay. It begins on Page 758. I am sending you an extra copy of this number, which I have procured. The apparently reliable statistics given towards the end of this paper constitute, to my mind, its very great value, and show, for instance, that if the entire reward which now goes to capital were divided equally among all the working people of the country, the average head of the family could receive an addition of only 60 cents a day to his wages.

That means that if the entire reward now received by capital were divided equally among all the people in the United States, each individual would receive only 13 cents a day.

Now I have not the slightest idea that the ordinary mechanic or employee of a company knows the facts in this case. He is under the impression, as I was to a large extent, that capital received entirely too large a share of the joint product of capital and labor. (This of course is true, and true beyond the slightest doubt, in the case of certain aggregations of capital throughout the country, but is the exceedingly rare exception and not the rule.) Now, if the reward which capital is receiving is so small that if all of it went to the working people there would only be an increase of 60 cents to the head of each family, we certainly cannot look in this direction for much greater prosperity to the working man.

I have felt sure, both from my personal practical observation, and from everything that I can read on the subject, that the only true hope for an increase in prosperity to the working people lies in an increase in the productivity of every working man, throughout the country. Whether this increase comes through greater personal efficiency, through a better order of co-operation, through the introduction of labor saving machinery, or from whatever source, it is to the increase of productivity of the whole mass of our people that the working people must look for an increase in their prosperity.

This I conceive to be at the root of the whole labor problem, and it seems to me that it is of the very first importance that the laboring people of the country should be brought to understand this fundamental fact. They are now—through labor leaders, through the press, through public opinion—taught to believe that there is something radically wrong with the division of the surplus earnings, and that if they only got their fair share of the joint product of capital and labor, everything in the world would be couleur de rose for them.

Now, as to profit sharing. If profit sharing would result in so stimulating the workmen who come under it that each one would very materially increase his daily output, say double his productivity, then I should look to profit sharing as the cure for the present troubles. My judgment and observation and study of men leads me to the conclusion, however, that profit sharing, while it would induce workmen to become slightly more productive, would not have the effect of greatly increasing the average output of the individual. This has been the history of practically all profit sharing institutions up to date. It has not greatly stimulated the output of the individual.

And the fundamental reason for this lies in the fact that the human animal is so constituted that he looks upon his own immediate individual welfare and happiness and ease and comfort as of vastly more importance than the welfare of his fellow beings. The only way to get a large output from the individual is to let him have, in plain sight and in the immediate future, a personal reward to him which shall be proportional in a way to the exertions and endeavor which he puts forth; so that the profit which the men receive under profit sharing, and which comes to them only at the end of the year, or say every six months, is not a sufficient stimulus to affect them materially in their every day work. This reward is too remote.

I have seen this fact illustrated in so many different ways that to me it has come to be an absolute certainty. The average workman, for example, cannot look forward for more than three weeks to a month for a reward. His reward must come to him at shorter intervals even than this, if he is to be stimulated to greater endeavor. As the character of the individual becomes less formed and weaker, this period must be made shorter and shorter. In my book on "Shop Management," I have referred to the case of a lot of girls who were inspecting bicycle balls. (See pages 85-91, Harper edition). We found distinctly that unless these girls were informed every half hour as to whether they were keeping up properly with their work, they would become entirely indifferent and fall away behind; not just lapse off a little, but they would completely collapse in most cases. This of course is at the extreme lower limit in this respect, but in principle this practically true of all laboring people.

It is for this reason that the contract system, even, does not in any way compare with the scheme of daily giving a carefully measured task to each workman. To get much of any large return from working men, you must give a short task, to the end of which the workman can look with ease, and against which he can measure himself throughout every hour in the day.

And you cannot do both; that is, give the workman an extra large reward day by day, and then also give him a large share of the profits at the end of the year. Let us therefore use the total profit which the workman is to receive in the way which will most increase his productivity.

Now, under scientific management we deliberately plan to increase the workman's wages, or his profit, to the extent of from 35 to 100 per cent each year. By giving him this extra profit day by day, as a reward for accomplishing the tasks laid before him, instead of giving it to him at the end of the year, and also by giving him the help and co-operation of the many men who are working jointly with him on the management side, it is possible on an average to more than double the output of each working man. If the same profit, that is, a profit of from 30 to 100 per cent on his wages, were offered to the working man through the profit sharing scheme and given to him at the end of the year in the form of dividends, my judgment and observation is that it would not increase his productivity to the extent of 10 per cent. And that is my main reason for not favoring the profit sharing scheme. I am exceedingly desirous that the condition of the working man should be bettered. In fact, I am devoting my whole life to this cause. But I am profoundly convinced that the road towards prosperity does not lie in any better scheme for dividing the joint product of capital and labor than those which now exist, but that it does lie in a great number of schemes for greatly increasing the productivity of the average working man, so that my whole time and attention is given to the promotion of schemes which have this for their main object.

Yours very sincerely,

P. S. One more thought in this matter. The only way to make the world happier in a material way is to increase the riches of the world, that is, the material things which are useful to man; and all of these come from two sources only—from what is produced by the earth, or comes up out of the ground, and what is produced by man. An important fact to bear in mind is that more than nineteen-twentieths of all the wealth produced in the world is consumed by the poor people, and not by what are called rich people.

Any increase, therefore, in productivity of the individual simply increases the wealth of the world to that extent, and nineteen-twentieths of this increase goes straight to the poor people.

F. W. T.

---

[1]Bulletin of the Taylor Society, December, 1916.

PERSONAL HISTORY [1]

Some Interesting Facts and Comments About His Early Training and Later Pastimes, By The Founder of Scientific Management.

A Personal Letter.

December 2, 1910

Mr. Morris L. Cooke,
Boston, Mass.

My dear Mr. Cooke:--

In answer to your letter asking for facts in my personal history, I can hardly think of any with which you are not already familiar.

The two years of school in France and Germany, then a year and a half travel in Italy, Switzerland, Norway, England, France, Germany, Austria, etc., (all of which I disapprove for a young boy), then a return to the healthy out-of-door life of Germantown, than which I believe there is nothing finer in the world, in which sport is the leading idea, with education a long way back, second. Then two years of really very hard study, coupled with athletics, at Exeter, and what I look back upon as perhaps the very best experience of my early life, namely, the very severe Exeter discipline, in which no excuse was taken for any delinquency whatever, and in which every boy had to toe the mark in all respects.

At that time one half of the scholars at Exeter were dropped each year (they have again returned to the old Exeter idea, in which one quarter of the boys were dropped). It was the wrong side of the Exeter training, however, which ruined my eyes and left me no other alternative than working as a workman for the four years following 1874. At that time the great ambition of all boys at Exeter was to be at the head of the class in studies, and the competition was so severe that all of those who were not very brilliant had to work away late into the night in order to get there. It was this competition that broke my eyes down, and it would be also noted that the three other men who led the class before I did also broke down and had to leave Exeter, on account of poor health.

The very best training I had was in the early years of apprenticeship in the pattern shop, when I was under a workman of extraordinary ability, coupled with fine character. I there learned appreciation, respect and admiration for the everyday working mechanic.

Throughout my apprenticeship, of course, I had my eye on the bad industrial conditions which prevailed at the time, and gave a good deal of time and thought to some possible remedy for them. It was this that led me to go to a very much larger company, the Midvale Steel Works, in 1878. I think you know my whole history there; starting from a laborer, getting first into the time office, then back on to the machine as gang boss, etc., etc. Throughout my early days at Midvale I found myself very much short of a scientific education, and began by taking a home study course in mathematics and physics, which was given by the scientific professors at Harvard University. After getting all that I could by correspondence in this way, I then went to the professors at Stevens Institute, and asked them for proper text books, etc., and this started my home study course at Stevens.

About two years and a half after this time, namely, in June, 1883, I graduated as M. E. from Stevens, without however, having been there except for the purpose of passing all of the entrance exminations and finally one after another of the examinations required throughout the course.

You will realize that my time was greatly shortened in getting through Stevens from the fact that I was able to pass in languages--French and German--and in history, etc., right off at the start, owing to my experience abroad and to general reading, etc. So that this left me much less actual work to do than the other boys, and enabled me to get through in two years and a half, while I was at the same time carrying on my duties as foreman, master mechanic, chief draftsman, and chief engineer, successively, at Midvale.

You will probably realize that with me investigation, or rather invention, is a mental dissipation, that it is a very great amusement, rather than a labor, and that if I followed my personal inclinations I would be very likely to give the greater part of my time to this sort of thing. I realize, however, that no man has the right to do very much of this kind of work. This is of course especially true when you are doing it with other people's money, and all through my engineering life I had to keep my conscience in very active service to prevent me from devoting too much time to this end of the business, and not enough to the less interesting, but vital, end of every day management and economy, etc.

No one knows better than you that all the theories, fine or otherwise, which we have evolved as to the principles of scientfic management, etc., have come after the fact and not before. Neither I nor any man of our group who has been chiefly instrumental in developing scientific management did so as the result of any preconceived theory. We first evolved the remedy for some existing trouble, and later found out what the theory was that was back of the trouble; and I am not quite sure that some of our group fully understand the weight of this theory, even now.

One of the reasons why I am giving a lot of my time and thought to the growing of grass is that it is an innocent outlet to my tendency to dissipation in the speculative field, in which no one is hurt except myself. Any money that I choose to put in it, or any time, is at my own expense, and even if no results follow no company is hurt. In properly sizing up myself, I believe that the only strong quality which I have is the ability to wait for any length of time, and to keep on working, whether results come or not. This I think is the result of years of habit. I believe that I used to be excessively impatient for immediate results in everything that I went into.

In some grass experiments which you speak of, what I am trying to do is to be able to tell any man in any part of the United States how he can manufacture soil out of raw materials which are purchasable on the market, and which can be reduplicated in any part of the country, rather than to try to tell a man to take some native soil right around him and grow grass in it.

It is absolutely impossible to describe a soil which is in existence so that a man can reduplicate it. You must build up the soil synthetically in order to be able to describe it. And these experiments are chiefly devoted to finding a synthetically built soil which will grow grass better than any soil has in the past. I think I have already reached this, and will far exceed anything that has ever been done in the past, before the experiments are through.

In addition to this, another experiment is going on, which may prove of great value or not, namely, the idea of handing up from a reservoir of water underground the necessary food in solution and the needed water supply to the roots of the plant, so that even in a drought or in the hottest of our Philadelphia summers, grass will stay green all the time, and flourish, where now even with the heaviest of artificial watering it cannot get through some of our summers.

You realize, of course, that in these grass experiments I am experimenting only with the most delicate and difficult of the finer varieties of grass; such grasses as are fit for putting greens, and which it is almost impossible to grow at all under any circumstances in the climate of Philadelphia.

Another part of the experiments in grasses is that in the past, particularly the finer grass seeds, there was no known way of germinating with uniform success. In my experiments I have found a way to germinate properly four to five times as many, at least, as could be done under the old conditions; namely, I manufacture an artificial soil in which the seeds are germinated, and treat the seeds throughout the germinating period in a definite scientific way.

The grass growing problem is really a very large one when it is treated from a scientific standpoint, and I find it an intensely interesting one. I have already made probably 800 or 900 experiments, and expect to make a great many more. I have succeeded in getting the Agricultural Depattment at Washington very much interested, and they are going to cooperate with me to a very considerable extent. But one of the first things that I found out was that grass needs air all the time at its roots; and it needs air even more than it does water and nourishment. If you exclude the air from the roots in summer time for five days, you will entirely kill the tender varieties of grass, whereas it will do without water for a long time, and revive; and also without nourishment for a good while.

A rather spectacular part of my experiment is that I have succeeded in growing a grass which was planted in the fall, in the month of November, and which went from the first of June till the first of September without having a drop of rain or other artificial moisture come to it from above. A glass cover was put over it to keep the rain water off, and it received its water supply from the water reservoir below, through the lifting sands which soaked the water up from the reservoir and passed it on up to the roots.

We experimented with lifting sands from all parts of the country, and finally succeeded in finding sand of a particular grain composition, which will lift water as high as 48 inches from a water reservoir below, and hand it over to the grass roots.

Some ordinary sands will lift water only half an inch, some not at all, others all the way between this and 48 inches, depending upon the grain composition of the sands.

The years which Mrs. Taylor and I spent away from Philadelphia were at the time very trying ones, as we both lived in very narrow quarters, in a single room most of the time, and yet we both look upon this period as the most developing perhaps of our lives. We were obliged to mingle with people from all parts of the country and as a result we found the finest kind of men and women living in all ranks of society, and in the smallest and most out of the way places. We both value this experience, because of the enlarged sympathies which it gave us for our own kind.

You of course know yourself the nature of the work involved in systematizing. It involves a mingling of war and peace, of hard blows and tact, which give one rather a trying life, and I can assure you that this was no less true in the past than it is now. It was a life full of disappointments in many respects and yet full of great satisfaction whenever results were accomplished.

Yours very sincerely,

Dictated by F. W. T. but not revised.

---

[1]Bulletin of the Taylor Society, December, 1916.

GOVERNMENT EFFICIENCY

By Frederick Winslow Taylor.

It may be said, on the whole, that the quality of the work done by government employes is good, not superlatively so, but on the whole good.

For example, while we have not been leaders in the development of our army and navy equipment, and in the development of army and navy tactics, etc., still we have followed closely in the wake of the leaders. For example, we did not invent the Dreadnought, nor the torpedo boat, nor the dirigible torpedo, nor were we the first to make high power steel guns, but we have been quick in following after the best of the foreign nations in choosing our equipment.

When, however, we come to consider the quantity of service which is rendered by our government employes, we find quite the reverse. It can in fact be safely said that the average government employe does not do more than one-third to one-half of a proper day's work. The reason for this contradictory state of affairs is not far to seek. The quality of the service must be good, because on the whole our people are accustomed to seeing and possessing the best equipment. We are a nation who believe in first-class things, and the quality of the results produced by government employes can be seen and appreciated by the people.

From this fact has grown up the feeling almost universal among government employes, that to make a blunder is fatal, or at least very serious, because a mistake or a blunder will be recorded against the employe and remembered throughout his career. However efficient and energetic and employe may have been in doing his work, this will not atone for his having made a blunder. Consequently, splendid positive constructive results, brought about by a government employe, count for less than freedom from errors. In a very great number of cases the government employe fully realizes that in case he does a particularly original or especially efficient piece of work for the government, those who are over him will insist that the credit for his accomplishment shall be theirs, and in many cases instead of commending and rewarding the man, jealousy on their part leads them to persecute him. Thus "play safe" is the rule in the government service, even if you accomplish little or nothing. Yet nothing in industrial life is more true than that the man who never makes mistakes never accomplishes anything.

On the other hand, when it comes to the quantity of work done by each employe, the public (that is, the whole people) has as yet had no definite standard for measuring the work of its public servants. And in fact, in a general way it may be said that the people of our country realize that most government employes are inefficient (exactly how greatly ineffecient they do not know), and that they have come to look upon this as perhaps the normal state of affairs. We would all like to have the highest possible standard of efficiency for our public servants, but a hundred years of experience have shown us that they are almost universally inefficient, and we have come to look upon this condition as irremediable.

There have been, indeed, fundamental reasons why government employes should be inefficient, instead of efficient. Throughout civil life, 19 out of 20 employes realize that in order to succeed they must render a quality and quantity of service which will enable them to compete with a large number of other men who are at all times ready to take their positions in case they fail to make good. Thus they fully realize that it is only through their own personal accomplishment, through each day doing a big day's work and doing it right, that they can hold their jobs and have the hope of advancement. In government service, however, it has been almost universal that the employe has received his position mainly through the influence which he has been able to bring to bear upon the men at the top. The employment has been given as a reward for political services, and the men have held their jobs more through political pull and influence than through merit. In civil life almost every employe feels that the permanent tenure of his job, as well as his advancement, depends upon his ability to continually render full and efficient service to his employer. Few of the government employes (even those under civil service rules) feel any fear of losing their jobs on account of not doing a full day's work. They almost all realize the importance of not making any serious blunder, but providing they make no serious mistakes they feel that they can do only a fraction of a day's work, without danger of losing their jobs.

Even in spite of civil service examinations, this still remains substantially true, that certainly the greater number of government employes look to influence to keep their jobs rather than to their own merit. Even when the government employes have ceased their own political activity in the direction of getting votes for their party, and doing similar party work, still they realize that political pull is more important for their success than turning out a large day's work.

The government as an employer is looked upon in a totally different light from the private employer. Government employ is looked upon as a crib at which vast numbers of men are to be fed. The Congressman in whose districts government work goes on; the labor leaders who claim to be able to deliver the labor vote; large numbers of workmen, and in many cases the government officials-- even those high in rank-- unite in adopting the view that the principal function of government employment is to provide work for their henchmen, their friends, and their political allies. By many of these men government employment is viewed almost entirely from this stanpoint, so that the more men they can get in the government employ and the higher the wages that these men are paid, the better they are satisfied. All hands, however, realize that the American people will not tolerate a sloppy quality of work, so that in spite of the fundamental lack of interest in the results obtained, a fairly good quality of work is insisted upon. This mental attitude still represents the survival of the old "spoils system" in which practically the whole people acquiesce, in the conviction that "to the victor belong the spoils." This mental attitude on the part of the great majority of those connected with government work represents the largest obstacle to government efficiency. And the principal problem before any administration which attempts to obtain government efficiency will be that of changing this mental attitude, shared by practically all government employes.

In the past there has been very little inducement for those superintendents and managers who believe in a large and full day's work to go into government employ, and with very rare exceptions every man who has undertaken to bring about efficiency in large numbers of public employes has failed and has ended by deeply regretting that he ever had anything to do with the whole problem of getting a fair day's work out of government employes. Even under what may be looked upon as a reform administration, that for example of President Roosevelt, we have the notable instance of Mr. Stillings, who went into the government Printing Office with President Roosevelt's entire approval, and who made great changes, practically all tending toward increased efficiency. He dismissed hundreds of incompetents, hundreds of loafers, from the Printing Office and was in a fair way, if time had been given him, to make a reasonably efficient establishment out of the Printing Bureau, which had been nothing less than a public scandal. The discharged employes, the labor leaders, and many politicians in Washington (some in Congress), and even some high up in the Senate, however, united in opposing the good work of Stillings and, during the campaign for the election of Mr. Taft for the Presidency, they took advantage of certain blunders which Mr. Stillings had made to drive him out of the government employ. And this in spite of the fact that the errors and mistakes which he had made were not equal to one-thousandth part of the good which he had accomplished. It can be safely said that Stillings' dismissal was the direct result of the supposed political necessity of electing Mr. Taft to office. Stillings was sacrificed to the good of this cause. It must be understood, however, that Mr. Taft had nothing whatever to do with Mr. Stillings' dismissal, and it is doubtful even whether he was aware of it. At any rate, this is not an arraignment of any individual but of the supposed necessities of our system.

Now, with object lessons of this sort before them, there is very little inducement for strong and earnest men to undertake the type of fight which is necessary in order to secure a fair day's work from government employes. The government official who attempts to insist upon a full, proper day's work from the employes who are under him, goes at this undertaking with the certainty that he will have the bitter enmity of the public officials high and low, and that whatever promises he may have received from those who are over him, he is likely to share the fate of Mr. Stillings, and many others who have made this attempt. Any attempt at efficiency is looked upon by the place holders and their backers as an assault upon their personal rights,and is fought by all parties with bitterness. Man after man who has come into the high places in government employ, and who has fully realized the gross inefficiency of government employes and been possessed with an earnest desire to reform, has weakened when he realized the tremendous uphill fight ahead of him, with the prospect that when the next Congressional or national election came he would be made a sacrifice for the necessity of obtaining votes. This has led him to give up any great effort towards increased efficiency, and to turn his energies into other channels.

Government efficiency will never be brought about until the prevailing mental attitude of government employes has been radically changed; and the great problem is how this great change is to be brought about. In facing this problem, the first fact which must be approached is that a great mental revolution of this sort will of necessity demand a large amount of time. It is not a question of producing physical changes, but rather of working a great mental revolution in large numbers of men, and any such change demands time, and a large amount of time.

It is absolutely useless to attack this system until our Chief Executive Officer shall be deadly in earnest in this attainment of efficiency, and I think it can be said that no President, up to Mr. Taft's administration, has had government efficiency as a serious problem before him. No government employe who looks back at what has happened in the past, however high up he may be, will in the future want to tackle this great problem of efficiency without the backing of the President of the United States, and without the certainty that the President of the United States will guard all those who are engaged in the earnest effort to increase government efficiency from political attacks, and that he will place government efficiency above the getting of votes, either at the time of a Congressional or national election. I believe this is the very first requirement in the attainment of efficiency, that the President shall place it above and beyond politics.

In the case of my personal friends, who have been asked to assist in obtaining government efficiency under Mr. Taft's administration, knowing the treatment that was meted out to Mr. Stillings, for example, they have invariably undertaken this service for the government with very great reluctance, even under the administration of Mr. Taft, whom we all believe to be earnestly seeking for government efficiency. They have all been afraid that when the time came for getting votes, that such pressure would be brought upon the administration through the labor leaders, through the political leaders, through all government employes, and through Congressmen, Senators, and even some members of the Cabinet, that even to a man of Mr. Taft's sterling qualities it might appear to be of less importance to sacrifice the man who was engaged in promoting efficiency rather than to lose votes at the election.

First, then, be sure that the President of the United States is solidly behind this government. Not only this, but it is almost a necessity that the President should have some advisor close to him in whom he will have complete confidence as far as this efficiency problem is concerned. There is no question that Mr. Taft earnestly desires economy and efficiency in government administration, and yet no fixed or settled policy has been followed during his administration. So those men who are working for efficiency are constantly left in doubt as to whether they will ultimately receive the backing of the President or not. For example, in the War Department, under General Crozier, the Chief of Ordnance, the principles of scientific management have been adopted as the standard, and for two years and a half to three years this Department has been working with great energy and success in introducing these principles. During this same period, however, the Navy Department have been carefully hunting down every element of scientific management which was installed in the Navy Yards, and completely wiping it off the slate.

And both of these occurrences have gone on with the knowledge of the President. This can be accounted for only by the fact that the President himself has no fixed or settled policy as to the means to be taken in accomplishing efficiency. And why should he, when he has in his Cabinet not a single man with whom industrial efficiency has been a life study? It would seem that under any President who really wants efficiency, one cabinet officer should be chosen whose chief interest will be that of obtaining governmental efficiency, and who will be able to properly post the President as to the steps to be taken and unify the action of the administration throughout all of the governmental departments.

The greatest emphasis should be laid upon the fact that, in order to obtain results, it is necessary to begin at the top, with the thorough co-operation of the President and his Cabinet. And, bearing in mind that four years is a short time in which to effect changes which are well worth while, it seems almost a necessity to begin work in the early part of a Presidential administration; that is, unless the President is to be re-elected, because history indicates the fact that a change of administration almost always marks a very material change in the governmental policies, even though the two succeeding Presidents may belong to the same party. History shows that too frequently the President himself, and in a large number of cases the Cabinet officers, think it necessary for their own personal success that they should openly and avowedly greatly modify the policy of their predecessors. In order to brand the achievements during their own administration with their own names, they find it necessary to discredit the accomplishment of those who went before them.

Having then laid the proper foundation, through obtaining the backing of the Chief Executive and his officers, the important question is, what steps shall be taken to produce efficiency. Our answer to this is that, in the government departments, one should follow the same procedure as is followed in the organization of industrial companies. Under the older systems of management which are in common use, it has been necessary in order to obtain the best results in management, to secure the services of some one or more men of very exceptional, in fact extraordinary, ability; and the personality of these uncommon men has been relied upon largely to bring about results. Such men through their personal knowledge, through that knowledge and special ability which they carry in their own heads and which dies with them, and through their personal magnetism and energy, control and guide the men under them. Under the older system of management, in which the problem of obtaining greater efficiency is put up directly to the men, the function of the manager lay chiefly in persuading men largely through personal influence, to do better for their employer than they had in the past. Under scientific management, fortunately for the possibility of progress in governmental employ, the personality of the few men or the man at the top is far less important than under the older management. This necessity of securing a very-high-class man has in the past made any great progress almost impossible under government employ, because the highest class civilians have greatly hesitated to accept government employment, owing to the fact that politics have played in the past such a large part.

They recognized that the difficulty of playing the political game in addition to their own specialty of bringing about greater efficiency was too large an undertaking, and have almost invariably preferred private to public employment. So the impossibility of getting these great leaders or captains of industry to enter government employ, in itself made it impossible to achieve any great amount of efficiency.

The process of building up an efficient management under the principles of scientific management is radically different from the older type. Under scientific management, personal influence counts for far less than the other elements. The scientific study of what should constitute a proper day's work for each government employe becomes the element of perhaps the greatest importance, and this study can be made by men of very ordinary calibre. It calls for honesty on the part of the time student, and continued hard work, but not the extraordinary qualities demanded of the old type "captain of industry." It places the development of the science of doing each kind of work far above any man or men, and makes it possible for a number of ordinary men when co-operating with the aid of science, to far outstrip the individual leaders of the past.

This study of the duties of each individual government employe and of the proper time required to perform those duties, evidently involves a very large amount of continuous, plodding work. Fortunately, however, the results from this analysis of duties and of the time required to perform those duties, begin to show almost immediately, and present the foundation for obtaining important economies in the government service. When it is shown, for example, that the clerical work to be performed by a man in a given position in the government can be done in an hour and a half a day, whereas he now takes the whole day, this fact alone points the road towards economy. To use the expression in common use, in scientific management, each employe is given his daily task to perform, and the determination of this daily task really lays the foundation for government efficiency.

This system has a very great advantage over the older system, in that many hundreds of men can work at the same time in widely scattered locations in laying this foundation for efficiency; whereas, under the old plan, where personal influence counted, the work of the usual man was of necessity confined to a small group of men under him. Without doubt a central planning department should be established, in which the governmental standards for a proper day's work, etc., should be recorded and distributed to the local planning departments.

Under the older system of management, it has been usual to start at an entirely different point, that is, by introducing a system of cost records, showing the expense of performing each class of work, etc., and acting on this idea President Taft has established his "Commission on Economy and Efficiency," of which Dr. Cleveland is the head. I do not wish in any way to deprecate or belittle the use of a system of cost records of this sort. The establishing of a budget for the United States Government in a way similar to that which is made out for the English Government should be in immense help both to the executive departments and to Congress in carrying on the governmental work; but what I want to emphasize is that this leads only in the most indirect way to efficiency.

It does not produce efficiency. An accounting system at the best is a signboard which points out inefficiency. It is a hand, indicating "This is an especially inefficient spot." Now we all of us know that practically all of the activities of the United States government are carried on in an inefficient way, that is, as far as quantity of work is concerned, not in quality; so that in the government work at least, we now need no accounting system to point to the fact that the work is inefficient.

On the other hand, as the work grows more and more efficient, then the accounting system becomes more desirable to point out and equalize inequalities between different departments and in different localities.

My advice, therefore, is to begin by setting up the great standards of efficiency to which the various men in government employ should rise. With these tasks established for each position, it become possible, automatically and rapidly to weed out the drones and the inefficient men, or change men from positions for which they are not well suited to other positions for which the are well adapted. The discharge of an employe or his promotion or his change of position is no longer, under scientific management, a question of opinion of some man who is over him, it is a question of recorded fact. The man is unable to accomplish his daily task, and therefore must make room for some man who is.

This system, then, in this way makes for very rapid progress. It is clear, however, that in the application of this new test for filling and holding governmental positions, the old idea of influence, pull and friendship must entirely disappear, and it will be useless for any administration to go after real efficiency in government service unless they are willing to disregard absolutely this political influence which even now plays the most important part in government service. The moment those at the top cease giving attention to the backing and to the pull of the government employe, that moment will the employe himself start to change his mental attitude towards his own work, and he will realize that his success must in the future depend upon his own efforts, and not on what some on else can do for him.

The Civil Service examinations and rules have done an immense amount in keeping men out of the government service who were utterly unfitted for their jobs. In no sense do I advocate any relaxing of the Civil Service requirements. It is very unfortunate, however, that no Civil Service examination has been devised which will indicate whether the applicant has the moral qualities required for his job, whether he has integrity, grit, energy, perseverance, etc. Of necessity the Civil Service rules are limited, one may say, to the mental qualifications. The need, therefore, in government service is some way by which the other much needed qualities can be recognized and have their proper weight in the selection and in the retention of a candidate. It should at least be possible at all times for the government to discharge peremptorily a man who lacks energy, determination, and the moral qualities necessary to obtain results in his particular job.

The moment political influence ceases, and when those high up in government office or employ cease to consider in the least the political qualifications of government employes, it will become comparatively easy to promote men who show especially fine qualities other than intellectual, and in the same way get rid of those who lack these qualities. Emphasis, however, must be laid upon the fact that there is no hope whatever of obtaining any great increase in efficiency unless the managing heads of the various departments and the important leading men who are under them look upon their government positions practically as their life's work. If they contemplate the probability of going out of government employ every four years and making room for a man of some other political complexion, or for some one who has rendered the incoming administration important political service, then no great or lasting progress can be made in government efficiency. We have before us two object lessons which illustrate, in a very remarkable way, the necessity for premanency in government positions. These object lessons are presented by the two most important manufacturing or engineering departments of the government, namely, the Ordnance Department of the Army, which controls the manufacture of the guns, ammunition, munitions of war, and supplies of all kinds for the Army; and the Navy Yards, which perform a similar function for the Navy.

At the head of each of thses Departments we have, individually, an unusually fine set of men. It should be made perfectly clear to the public that, as a class, our naval officers represent a magnificent body of picked men, who are devoted to the government service, who are self-sacrificing, and who in their duties at sea are an uncommonly efficient and hard-working set of men. Too large a part of our people look upon our naval officers as rather ornamental men who fill easy berths. This is far from the truth. It would be difficult to find a more devoted, hard-working and upright set of men than compose a great body of the officers of our Navy. The writer has been fortunate in having been placed in close, intimate contact with numbers of these men for many years, because he was engaged in the Midvale Steel Works, in the Bethlehem Steel Works and Cramps Ship Yard, in the manufacture of the materials from which our big guns, armor plate, ships and the machinery in them, were manufactured, and in his whole personal experience he never met a single naval officer with whom there was even the slightest suspicion of corruption or in fact of anything but the highest motives. The same is equally true of our army officers. The writer has had more to do with the officers in the manufacturing department of the government, that is, the Ordnance Department, than with the line officers, but with all of these men his experience has been the same as with naval officers, namely, that they represent the highest type of American citizens. The criticism, then, which is being made of the Navy, as well as against the Army, is one of system and methods, and not of the personnel.

The schemes of management in all of our navy yards has involved bringing on shore for from one to three years all naval officers, and placing them in command of the navy yards as a whole; also of placing the detailed management of each of the shops, and even the subdivision of the shops under naval officers, who come directly from sea duty. It is no reflection on these naval officers to say that these men, who are admirably trained and suited to their work on board battleships, are utterly untrained and unfit to manage the industrial work which goes on in the navy yard. Any one of these naval officers would recognize the complete unfitness of, we will say, the best manager of a large machine shop to take command of a battleship, and yet without hesitation these men, who have been trained to the command of battleships, assume all of the responsibilities of the manager of a machine shop. Thus, it is perfectly clear that for success in managing any one of the large manufacturing departments of the navy yards, the man must make it his life's work, and must have been especially educated and trained to it, just as he should be especially educated and trained to the management of the battleship.

In many respects, also, the training which the naval officers receive at sea largely unfits them to be at the head of an industrial establishment. The kind of discipline which must be maintained on shipboard, the methods which must be used there in directing the 800 or 1,000 men on a battleship, are almost directly opposed to the methods which must be used in the management of the men of a machine shop. Their habits of mind and the whole education which they have received in handling men at sea actually unfits them for handling men in civilian life, and this makes it almost impossible for them to learn very much about the management of a shop even in the two or three years during which they are detailed to this work. For this reason, while our navy yards have been in the past officered and commanded both in gross and in detail, nominally by naval officers, they have really been managed and run by the civilian foremen and quartermen, etc., who in our navy yards are distinctly the cheap second, third and fourth class men. And it must be said that it is next to impossible to get a really first-class foreman to accept service under naval officers in our navy yards.

Again, the fact should be emphasized that this is no reflection upon the individual character of our naval officers, but it marks the great, and, I suppose, essential difference in the types of management necessary for success in civilian life and in military life.

It may be said, then, of thses naval officers, that they come to their jobs in the navy yards knowing practically nothing about their work, and that they leave their jobs in nine cases out of ten, after two or three years of service, with almost no knowledge of industrial work. Shore duty for men is an incident. Their real life's work and their ambitions and hopes for success, lie at sea; and very properly they look upon their shore duty in most cases chiefly as their opportunity to make the acquaintance of their families and get in touch with the life of the country. They themselves realize the impossibility of becoming skillful in more than one profession, and practically do not make the attempt.

These cheap civilians who are really in command of our navy yards, unfortunately, have no interest whatever in promoting efficiency. In fact, they join with the workmen in the yard, and are universally backed up in this by the labor unions, in trying to make employment in the yards for the largest possible number of workmen, and in many, if not most cases, they assist the workmen in seeing to it that each man does a small day's work, instead of a large day's work, thus making room for more employes.

The Ordnance Department of the Army, on the other hand, presents a totally different object lesson. In this Department, the officers are selected from the line of the Army by competitive examinations, and they enter this Department expecting to devote their lives to the industrial problems rather than to the military problems; that is, to the scientific study of the design and manufacture of the implements of war, which becomes mainly an industrial problem. Thus the mental attitude of these officers differes entirely from that of the navy officers. Their ambitions lie towards promoting efficiency in manufacture. The present organization of this Department offers an ideal opportunity for the development and selection of men well suited to their work. At the end of every three or four years (?) the young officers are obliged to go back to the line of the Army for a year's work, and unless they have made good in their work as manufacturers or designers they are not again taken into the Ordnance Department. On the other hand, if they themselves find that they are unfitted to work of this character, they can voluntarily return to the line. This insures the gradual selection of men especially picked for the manufacturing duties, and this primarily accounts for the fact that the work of the Ordnance Department under the Secretary of War, with General Crozier at its head, represents the only case in which government shops and government employes are able to successfully compete, as far as the cost of manufacture as well as accuracy and finish of the work is concerned, with corresponding manufacturing companies in civil life.

If should be emphasized again that the same general calibre of men as those of the Navy, so that the utter failure of the Navy, the fact that the navy yards become a bywork and a laughing stock in industrial life, is not due to a difference in the naval officer from the army officer, but is due to the difference of the systems in vogue in the two, and until we have permanent managers in our navy yards there is no hope whatever of any great increase in efficiency. This again illustrates the fact that you must lay your foundation by beginning with the men at the top, not with those at the bottom.

---

[1]Bulletin of the Taylor Society, December, 1916. (A hitherto unpublished article written probably in 1911.)

TAYLOR THE CREATIVE LEADER[1]

A Review of Copley's "Frederick W. Taylor" Which is a Critical Analysis of Taylor's Contribution to the Problem of Human Welfare

By Oliver Sheldon

"The history of the world is but the Biography of great men," said Carlyle. "For, as I take it, Universal History, the history of what man has accomplished in this world, is at bottom the history of the Great Men who have worked here." In that work of the world every man has his share, and more intriguing than any novel, more emboldening than any romance are the stories of the share which this man or that man has taken. "We cannot look, however imperfectly, upon a great man, without gaining something by him," continued Carlyle; and Frederick Taylor himself echoed the same thought,--"I think no book is more stimulating than the history of a devoted and successful life."

This thought of Frederick Taylor is mine as I read Frederick Taylor's own life.

I turn over the last pages of this book, and, as I read of that simple grave on a hill, above the Schuylkill River, I try to sieze upon my main impression. Through many pages I have followed the growth of a man and of a movement. I have seen childhood, youth and manhood; work and pleasure; difficulty and success; home life and public life, in the story of one man. I stand where this buoyant, restless, indomitable stream runs into the inscrutable sea, and I look back. I trace it from its source in Germantown. I see it widening and deepening as it flows through Midvale and Bethlehem and anon the pleasant greenery of Boxly, till it meets the incoming tide. I try to weld my chasing thoughts into some unifying impression, and it is this--that, in the intimacy which these pages have afforded me, I have been treading a pathway in the rare company of the man who hewed it out--a footpath broadening into a highway which leads on further than the lights of this mortal city of mine. I see a man building a road, and the road outstrips all sight. Some men are great, for the fruits of their work are spread for all the world to applaud. Frederick Taylor is great, for the fruits of his work have yet to be garnered. The potentiality of it all is what strikes me most. The greatness of a man is normally associated with the movement in which he played a leading part. Great as was Frederick Taylor, greater still is the movement of thought which he has inspired.

I have seen a purposeful and tenacious mind toiling, through the hard school of experiment and the clanging uproar of day-to-day living, towards a philosophy of which it was not yet aware; I have seen it boldly developing systems which gave that philosophy an actual, workable life; I have seen it pounce upon the various facets of that philosophy, as the light glinted from the stony surface of reality and revealed a principle; I have seen each facet, each principle fitted into its place, like the pieces of a mosaic pavement--and the philosophy is greater even than the thought of him who pieced the stones together. As the philosophy of

Rousseau, in the body politic, was greater than Rousseau, so is the philosophy of Taylor, in the body industrial, greater than Taylor. It is, indeed, the privilege of great men, the pioneers and builders of human thought and progress, to be immersed in the movements which they have originated or furthered.

It is well, however, that we should, from time to time, fight our way back to the original work and constructive effort of those who have done outstanding service in any field of progress, that we may know and admire the source of that which we inherit. For, if a great movement is greater than the life of any who served it, yet does such a life inform the movement with something tangible, and bring it within the compass of every day affairs. No great movement but has its great men, and in their lives are hidden the keys which open the doors of understanding. Philosophies are intangible; men are real. The life of the man brings the philosophy closer to the things we know, gives it substance, makes personal the impersonal. And truly the life of Frederick Taylor, while opening a wonderful vista, in the very ruggedness of its story makes the philosophy essentially work-a-day.

Mr. Copley has achieved a remarkable work. He has faithfully and pituresquely recorded the life of Frederick Taylor, yet at the same time has presented like a panorama, the growth of a philosophy, of which Frederick Taylor was the leading artisan. While he traces the life of Taylor to that stone memorial on a hill, which stands for all that mortal frame endured and conquered, he makes us see the contribution of Taylor to human thought as a stage from which the curtain is but half withdrawn. Of the life, the tale is told; but of the philosophy, the play has barely begun. In this, Mr. Copley has succeeded in an immensely difficult task. Rarely has a man, either in fact or in popular thought, been so closely associated with a movement, as was Frederick Taylor with Scientific Management. Rarely has a man lived to see the growth of definite principles out of his own groping experiments as Frederick Taylor saw the principles of Scientific Management emerging from his work at Midvale and Bethlehem. Rarely has a man lived to bear upon his own shoulders both the praise and the execration accorded to a new movement of thought, as Taylor in his own lifetime did. Rarely have the name of a man and the name of a movement been so readily interchangeable and in fact so actually interchanged as the names of Frederick Taylor and Scientific Management. Yet, in spite of the close and personal relation between the man and the movement, Mr. Copley has succeeded, while treating the man and his work as a whole, in distinguishing between the two, and leaving us distinct impressions of each. The sun of the man has sunk to its inevitable setting, but the sun of his philosophy has but barely broken the clouds in its dawning. To write the biography of such a man is no easy task. It cannot be just the bare record of a man's life and what he did. It must give that, and more, for what he did was not something which ended with himself. The task of the biographer was not only to tell a life-story, but to relate that story to what was yet to follow,--to trace the fleeting life to its premature close, whilst its philosophy was waxing to its springtide. This Mr. Copley has achieved with singular success. He has given us a living picture, with all its lights and shadows, of Taylor, the man; and a wise survey of what Taylor aimed at and achieved, and how his life-work swelled into a mode of thought, which we believe is destined to redirect the whole trend of industrial progress. If the words spoken by a certain gentleman are true of the man--"What Mr. Taylor did was to go out into the works and start a revolution"--they are true also of what Mr. Taylor's philosophy will yet achieve in the whole fabric of industry.

To those who, like myself, have studied Scientific Management from afar, who have not had the opportunity of coming into touch with its pioneers, who have not experienced the rough-and-tumble of its youthful encounters, this book comes as an illuminating story. It has rendered the whole thought of Scientific Management far more intimate and personal. It has clothed it with human form, and brought all the kaleidescopic thought, activity and experiments back to the thought of a man strolling across the sloping lawns, beside the herbaceous borders, under the rose arches and between the box hedges of a garden. This philosophy which I have studied and endeavoured to apply is not now something abstract and theoretical; it is very human. It is a delightfully living medley of time studies and weird golf clubs, of planning rooms and forceful epithets, of minute experiments and amateur theatricals, of tool rooms and of "my little intellectual friend," Putmut the cat. I am glad to think that the chief exponent of Scientific Management was a brilliant tennis-player, a fine gymnast, captain of his Exeter baseball team, and, later on in life, a most stimulating father to two lads. It puts a complexion of Scientific Management which makes me believe in it all the more. It is no longer something imposed on the world out of an ethereal void, but something that has welled up from the work of a man who made his daily trip to the factory and, at night, read aloud "The Lure of the Labrador Wild" to his family. . .

Indeed, Frederick Taylor seems to have been more normally human in many ways than most men who have left their imprint in history. No man of whom it can be said--and by a lady too--that he "never seemed more of a gentleman than when he was swearing," and who can come out with such sweeping statements as "All Germans are liars," and "You can't introduce economical methods by sitting up and howling," can but be held as a human among humans. He found public speaking a stumbling block; he wrote with difficulty; mental agility was not his strong point; his swearing, when necessary, was forcible--all features of the people one meets in the day's march. His home life was wholly delightful. His relations with his adopted children--now stern, now mischievous, now tender--tell us of a man to whom fame brought no pride. "He was kept humble by his knowledge of the ability he did not have and the things he did not know. There was much that was wistful in his attitude towards men who spoke familarly of things upon which he felt he had no light." Despite the strain of his work, despite the opposition he encountered, and despite the increasing reputation which brought him scores of visitors and shoals of correspondence, this man, of whom things both laudatory and damnatory were spoken with unusual vigour, retained a character singularly free from the faults which are associated with fame. Nothing from this outside world could break the serenity of his home. No reports or rumours could disturb the openness of his hospitality, the sociability of his nature, or his loyalty to and thoughtfulness for his friends. It is not to be wondered at, therefore, that those who visited him should, having come to see the leader of a new movement, have left, admiring not only an able thinker but a manly character. Thus, Mr. Brandeis wrote:

> I quickly recognized that in Mr. Taylor I had met a really great man--great not only in mental capacity, but in character, and that his accomplishments were due to this fortunate combination of ability and character.

And, Rudolph Blakenburg expresses the same dual charm of the man in the eloquent words he delivered at the Taylor Memorial Meeting:

> Mr. Taylor was to me a paradox. On one hand we find his rugged intellect blasting its way through layer after layer of conventions formed by generations of prejudice, tradition and ignorance until he became recognized as perhaps the world's foremost industrial leader. When truth was at stake, he was resourceful, robust and tireless. The problem once even dimly visioned he pursued with the zest of a hunter until he conquered. On the other hand, those whose contacts with him were, like my own, only casual and who went to him as converts, rather than to be converted, could harldy sense his power. He was born and bred to a gentle manner. His sweet smile and courtly bearing were only the surface indications of an innate and broad spreading sympathy and kindliness. He knew he had much to give and he gave it with a generosity which knew no limits.

Mr. Copley has been both faithful and wise in including in this book so much of Mr. Taylor's personal life, as distinct from his work. Character, indeed, plays a leading part in the achievements of a man; how much, I fancy, we sometimes underestimate. Brandeis glimpsed how much the character of Taylor had contributed to Taylor's life-work. Perhaps others in his day would have viewed Scientific Management in a different light had they known the character of the man behind it. How alien to Taylor's character was much that they attribute to Scientific Management! How contrary to Taylor's ethics were some of the motives attributed to the man whom they knew only through the second-hand channels of books, newspapers, rumours and experiences of others! A downright man, true; an outspoken, often brusque man, true; a strict, exacting, imperious man at times, true; a man, who having suffered, was perhaps a little intolerant, perhaps a little stinging, true; an impatient, tactless man, maybe. "But, however much he might irritate men, they had a habit of saying: 'Well, you know where you stand with the doggone cuss, anyway'"--and that sentiment is not a tribute either to a great thinker or a great scientist and inventor, but to a commanding character,--a character which flamed with enthusiasm and courage, and bore honesty and a meticulous regard and respect for justice emblazoned on its shield. It was open to men to question Taylor's abilities, if they could find a cranny wherein to fire a shaft, but none could gainsay either the qualities and motives he brought to his work, or the charm and friendliness he displayed openhandedly in his home. Here, indeed, was a man, a chip of common manhood, a wholehearted liver of life.

Like all men who have set in motion or furthered great mental revolutions in the world, however, Taylor brought to his work, not only a high character but also a truly remarkable mental ability. Primarily, his mind had in the highest degree those qualities which we associate with the scientist--critical, inquisitive, thorough, painstaking, logical, tenacious, persistent, constructive. He had preeminently the scientist's passion for truth, the scientist's reliance only on those facts which, by endless experiment and testing, are proved to be true.

> His reputation (said Henry L. Gantt) does not depend upon the fact that he designed and built the most successful big stream hammer in the world, or that he developed a method of treating tool steel that trebled its cutting power, or that he determined the laws of cutting metals, or even that he was the father of scientific management. These were incidents in his career, and only the logical results of his methods. At an early date, he realized how much of the world's work was based on precedent or opinion, and undertook to base all his actions on knowledge and fact.

In other words, his chief claim to fame, as indeed it was the chief attribute of his mind, was his use of the scientific method and his elaboration of a science for everyday practical things. He was not only a supremely scientific man, but he was bold enough to apply his scientific mind to things for which it was little thought a science could or should exist. As Mr. Copley points out, he thus anticipated a subsequent prophecy made by Mr. H. G. Wells, when he wrote, in one of those delightfully interpolated reflections with which he is wont to add to the fascination of his novels:

> When the intellectual history of this time comes to be written, nothing, I think, will stand out more strinkingly than the empty gulf in quality between the superb and richly fruitful scienfitic investigations that are going on, and the general thought of other educated sections of the community. I do not mean that scientific men are, as a whole, a class of supermen, dealing with and thinking about everything in a way altogether better than the common run of humanity, but in their field they think and work with an intensity, an integrity, a breadth, boldness, patience, thoroughness and faithfulness--excepting only a few artists--which puts their works out of all comparison with any other human activity. . . . . In these particular directions the human mind has achieved a new and higher quality of attitude and gesture, a veracity, a self-detachment, and self-abnegating vigor of criticism that tend to spread out and must ultimately spread out to every other human affair.

Taylor himself realized something of the novelty of his work in this sense, when, in 1912, he said: "A very serious objection has been made to the use of the word science in this connection (that of management). I am much amused to find that this objection comes chiefly from the professors of this country. They resent the use of the word science for anything so trivial as the ordinary, everyday affairs of life."

Taylor, indeed, must rank among the greatest of scientists for, not only did he prove himself an incomparable exponent of the scientific method, but he built, on the basis of his research, a new science, and a science in a new field, far from the laboratories of the universities, where the clangour and smoke of factories strike the air, and men dig and shovel and carry and draw. He made everyday things the subject of thought, and thereby raised them. He lifted the toilsome task of the labourer out of the ruck and muck and "lit it up with a ray from the realm of pure intellect." High tribute, indeed, was it to receive from such a man as Le Chatelier, professor of chemistry in the Sorbonne, the words, "I was somewhat ashamed to find the science of a practical man infinitely more developed than my own. . . "

It is strange to think that this man, who began his work in industry on the floor of the Midvale machine shop, who moved from clerk of the shop to work as a machinist, who then became gang boss in charge of the lathes and subsequently became foreman, chief draughtsman and chief engineer successively--this man, who, in his early days, worked from 6:30 to 5:10, who often volunteered to work on Sundays as well as overtime on week days, whose drawings William Sellers flung in the fire, who stopped the daily beer and whiskey wagon driving into the Midvale works--this man, who fought his way from the lowest and lived his life among the hard knocks and rough-and-tumble of the factory, should have, in such surroundings and as a part of such a life, brought to bear on his work a mind so scientific that it has come to command the respect of the whole world of science.

What Taylor achieved, however, could not have been won by a scientific mind alone. There were other mental qualities which contributed to this success. Of these, I should place foremost his determination, persistency, thoroughness, tenacity, and above all, enthusiasm. These are qualities, of course, common to most successful men who have encountered opposition in the pursuit of their ideals. Yet, recurring again, as they do, in the life of Taylor, one cannot but marvel as, at every turn in his life, they loom into prominence. One can quote from this book instance after instance where Taylor, had he been of poorer clay, would have taken the easier road. It may seem a barren field of battle in which to try such highly tempered weapons as Taylor's persistency and thoroughness--this machine shop at Midvale, for example. Yet the story of Taylor's struggle with his men, ending, as it did, in a most solid hold upon them, reads like the yarn of an Arctic explorer. Only infinite determination, inexhaustible enthusiasm and unyielding persistency could have climbed the obstacles which were laid in his path. It was the same throughout his life. Nothing was impossible, if it were necessary. Few men would have won the degree of M.E. when occupied, in the whole-hearted way he was, in the work-a-day toil of the shops. Few men--to take a more domestic incident--would have planned the removal of old box hedges with the thoroughness and disregard for precedent and prejudice with which he undertook it. "We were told," wrote Taylor, "not only by the former owner of the place, but by all the gardeners and landscape architects whom we consulted, that it was an impossibility." Yet, he set to work in his own scientific way to solve this 'impossibility', as he had solved many another greater one; and, later, one might have seen box hedge-rows in huge wooden crates, pulled by horses, running along a wooden track, to their new destination. Where others had failed, Taylor succeeded. It was characteristic of Taylor's whole attitude to things that wanted doing,--whether it was to increase the cutting speed of steel, to ensure the proper care of belting, to learn the content of the shoveler's task, or to elaborate functional foremanship in the Bethlehem machine shops. In big things and small things, there was always the same undaunted persistency and thoroughness, kept going by an enthusiasm, which not only made him a supreme optimist, but drew others along with him. "Why, he would have filled up a corpse with enthusiasm, if only the corpse could hear," said a Midvale executive. His whole work, viewed from this angle, was indeed, little short of amazing. For years, industry had revolved in the same old way; then, the youth Taylor enters Midvale, and within ten years, not by any great display of mental genius or brilliant discovery, but by sheer drive and tenacity and enthusiasm, coupled with an unfailing belief in and use of the scientific method, this man, between the ages of 22 and 32, set the whole establishment buzzing along lines which had hitherto hardly been imagined. As an example of mental intensity, I know few achievements, whatever the field, to equal it.

In reviewing the mental attributes of Frederick Taylor, moreover, one cannot but refer to those other qualities which formed, as it were, the complement to those we have already noticed. I mean his intensely logical mind, his genius for detail, and his boldness in construction. These were the qualities which enabled him to found his constructive work on fully analyzed bases of fact. In speaking of Taylor's work at Midvale, Carl Barth says:

> He constantly investigated tools and other small appliances that gave minor trouble or fell short of giving entire satisfaction, and in discovering the cause of their shortcomings, was able to effect highly-desirable improvements. Many of these improvements probably could easily have been made by anyone else who had taken the trouble Taylor did to investigate. The basis of it lay in the fact that it was Taylor's genius to recognize the importance of trifles.

To Taylor, nothing was too small or insignificant. It was the little motions, the little adjustments, the little elements which were the basis of his whole philosophy. He realized to the full that, for the average man, invention itself was a question of studying the detail.

> It is thoroughly illegitimate, he said, for the average man to start out to make a radically new machine, or method or process, new from the bottom up, or to do things most of which have not already been done in the past. Legitimate invention should be always preceded by a complete study of the field to see what other people have already done.

What Taylor meant by a "complete study" may have differed from what his hearers interpreted it to mean, but to him it meant a study so exhaustive that every detail was laid bare before his microscopic eye. Perhaps what

Mr. Copley has entitled, "A Tale of Shoveling," is the supreme example of this Taylor genius for detail, though the work which led up to his discovery of high-speed steel is an equally striking illustration.

> Now, gentlemen (said Taylor in giving evidence before the Special Committee of the House of Representatives in 1911-12) shoveling is a great science compared with pig-iron handling. . . . Under the old system you would call in a first rate shoveler and say, "See here, Pat, how much ought you to take on at one shovel load?" And if a couple of fellows agreed, you would say that's about the right load and let it go at that. But under scientific management absolutely every element in the work of every man in your establishment, sooner or later, becomes the subject of exact, precise, scientific investigation and knowledge to replace the old "I believe so" and "I guess so." Every motion, every small fact becomes the subject of careful, scientific investigation.

Taylor was speaking out of his experience. In describing the method of Scientific Management, he was emphasizing that application to detail which was one of the distinguishing features of his own genius.

As is often the way, this capacity for detail was part and parcel of a highly logical mind. The successive steps which Taylor took in the expansion of his system form a singular picture of lucid, constructive thinking. It is an entire misconception to believe that Scientific Management originated as a theory and that certain mechanisms were subsequently devised for the application of the theory. The story is wholly the reverse. By the singular efforts of a shop foreman to solve his practical shop problems, certain mechanisms were designed and applied, which one by one led on to other mechanisms, each one requiring a further one, till what had grown as need arose became recognized as a system. The system being recognized, there came the final stage of deducing from the specific mechanisms those principles which seemed to be of general application; and thus in the end came a philosophy. It was the logical thinking of Taylor which made the various mechanisms fit into a system. The detailed investigation of machine operations and handling times came first; from this, it was possible to deduce standard methods of operation. Standard methods of operation required, for their continuous performance, standard conditions of working. There were devised, consequently, such mechanisms of management as the Tool Room. But this divided the worker from his implements and materials. A condition of obtaining standard output was the delivery of "the right materials and the right tools in the right condition to the right man at the right machine with the right instructions at the right time." This inevitably led to the development of planning. But how to get the worker to operate correctly? The only way was to supply detailed written instructions; and, in order to have those instructions scrupulously observed, to devise a wage-system which would provide extra wages for following the instructions. Thus, in a series of consequential stages, Taylor came to his functional organization,--looking back, a remarkable feat of logical thinking. As Dr. Person said, when, under his direction the Amos Tuck School made

Scientific Management the basis of its instruction in management--"We found that the Taylor System was the only system of management which was coherent and logical, and therefore was teachable."

Of the further quality of inventiveness which Taylor possessed, there is little need to speak. His inventiveness was implicit in his spirit of scientific enquiry. His inventions were not born of revolutionary genius, but of the naked truths which his minute investigations brought to light. His famous steam hammer,--of which Gantt said, "I do not know of any more daring piece of engineering construction"--was not the outcome of what Mr. Copley calls "an egotistic desire to be original, to do great and glorious things," but rather was it the logical consequence of a long and painstaking survey of other steam hammers and of what a steam hammer ought to be and do. But I do not dwell on this, for Taylor's inventive work was due to attributes which we have already discussed.

That there were flaws in Taylor's mental equipment will be readily understood. His abilities were outstandingly those of what we have come to call the "engineering" type of mind--the mind which "works for the solution of a single technical or engineering problem and is concerned with the determination of the solution rather than the application of that solution to practical activities." As an executive, it cannot be doubted that, despite a high order of ability in management, he had serious defects,--the defects of a man who has thought far ahead of the practice, and is impatient that the practice should catch up; the defects of a man who has probed to the very truth of things and is careless of aught but the truth; the defects of a man who followed where logic led him, and was scornful of the roundabout way of reaching a conclusion. I think too, we must class among his defects his antipathy (if the word is not too strong) to the "academic" and the "humanities." It is a common fault of practical men, though most successful practical men, unknowingly perhaps, are already possessed of those qualities which real culture furnishes. "Real culture," says Mr. Copley, "is that which widens one's sympathies and thus is the cure for egotism or the inability to see oneself and one's work in proper relation to the universe." That is as good a definition as I have heard, and it is true to say that, in many respects, Taylor stood in need of no such cure. But, here and there in his life, one can see how this refinement of culture was lacking. He had great difficulty in formulating the philosophy of his achievements. None of his published works completely portray the essence of his philosophy. There was just lacking that breadth of perspective as a permanent attribute of the man. In flashes it came; within himself, inchoate and uncrystallized, it was there; but it was not a lasting light which he could turn on at will to reveal the inwardness of his life work. That others, who have taken upon themselves leading parts in the subsequent work of Scientific Management, have been university men, replete with the qualities which that training provides, is evidence that a movement so broad and so revolutionary has need of and can find niches for every type of mind.

To dwell upon the flaws in a mental armoury so commanding as that of Taylor is, however, to pick holes in the sky. I have left little enough space to consider what great things it is that Taylor has contributed to the progress of the world, and to what particular end he himself considered his work had contributed.

Too little emphasis has, in general, been laid--an omission which this Life amply rectifies--upon the motive which caused Taylor to start upon and continued to inspire him in the work he achieved. Again and again, throughout his life, in terms which are absolutely unmistakable, Taylor testified to the one main purpose which dominated his work. In 1912, when referring to his first steps in developing his system, he said: "My whole object was to remove the cause of antagonism between the boss and the men who worked under him; to try to make both sides friends in the place of tactical enemies." The same thought is uppermost when, in 1914, in reply to certain criticisms, he wrote: "I cannot agree with you that there is a conflict in the interests of capital and labor. I firmly believe that their interests are strictly mutual, and that it is practicable to settle by careful scientific investigation the proper award that labor should receive for the work which it renders."

It is usual to speak of Scientific Management as a powerful lever in the elimination of waste, as the means best calculated to arrive at effective management, and as a sound set of principles to govern the development of an organization. But that was not the primary point of view which Taylor took, though the "engineer" within him could not but be gratified by such results. To Taylor, his system of management was primarily a means to eliminate the cause of friction between management and men. He held the old type of management responsible for the chaotic condition of industry in its "humanics." He drove to the heart ot it, and determined not merely to effect a cure, but to remove the cause. We should regard Scientific Management, therefore, as preeminently a plan to solve the great social problem of industry, and secure an enduring industrial peace. It is for that reason, prime amongst others, that I regard the philosophy of Scientific Management (and, indeed, many of the mechanisms which Taylor introduced to put his philosophy into practice) as among the greatest of modern contributions to the progress of our social economy. It is not simply and solely a means to greater output and efficiency; still less is it a means to greater profits for the individual business. Primarily, its object is to remove the cause of strife and promote peace. Its field of service is not limited to this or that business; it is not even bounded by the confines of industry. Its service is to the world.

It is strange that, with this motive and object inspiring the work of its founder, Scientific Management should have been so strenuously attacked for its effect upon the worker. It has been accused of making men into machines, of creating narrow specialists in place of all-around operatives, of creating and furthering the monotony and consequent fatigue of the workers' life, of reducing the chances of a "square deal," of dispensing with the need for skilled workers, of over-working men and causing physical ills, of destroying initiative, inventiveness and ingenuity, of aiming to do away with unions, and of robbing the worker of his legitimate earnings. By far the most formidable attacks upon Scientific Management have been from this angle. Yet Taylor himself said, "It appears to me that the effect of the system upon the workman is in the end the most important element in the whole problem," upon which Mr. Copley comments. "He regarded the reduction of labor costs as <u>very</u> important, and he regarded the increasing of wages as <u>very</u> important.

But it was his deliberate opinion that the most important feature of any system must be its effect upon the workman's character." Of this fundamental purpose in Taylor's work his opponents, and perhaps some of his supporters and followers, have been neglectful. If for no other reasons, the writing of this book would be well worth while, for its reminder to us that the main object of Scientific Management, in the conception of its greatest protagonist and exponent, was to better the human side, the "humanics" of industry.

There is, even amongst the most progressive employers, a tendency to think that the solution of the great human troubles of industry is not a matter for scientific research or for scientific administration. They fancy that it is a question of the heart rather than of the brain, thereby omitting to realize that the one is essential to the interpretation of the other. They often quite properly set up Employment or Personnel departments, but fail to realize that, though one may segregate in special units of the organization certain specific activities affecting the workers, one cannot by any means, divorce the broad problems of industrial relations from the day-to-day management. For management is essentially a daily relationship with the workers; these relations constitute the main problem of management. Any remedy must resolve itself into an improvement of the management. Any study of the causes of the problem must be a study of the methods of management. This is, indeed, fundamental to Taylor's philosophy. He would claim that the contribution of industry to social welfare is to be judged, not merely by the presence or absence of employment and welfare work, but by the extent to which all the work of management is motivated by and conduces to sound industrial relations. He would, I surmise, strongly deprecate the conception, which arises even in the best regulated industries, that managerial efficiency is something alien from the proper care of labor and from the study and practice of means to achieve a lasting settlement and industrial strife. On the contrary, he would claim that these things are possible only through scientific management, and that, in the individual factory, the burden of attaining these objects rests mainly on the shoulders of those who organize and manage the production and distribution of goods, and only in a certain specialized degree on those who specifically are charged with the care of the workers' welfare. The Labour problem, in fact, is not an isolated problem, to be dealt with by units not directly responsible for production and distribution, to be studied by organizations divorced from the daily planning and execution of work, but rather one aspect, and the main aspect, of the whole work of managing a business scientifically. The conception that responsibility for promoting sound industrial relations can be allocated to one specific unit, that such work calls for specialized capacities and is aimed at objects of only secondary importance to other units in the organization, is wholly opposed to Taylor principles. The object of Scientific Management and organization is the betterment of labor conditions and the promotion of peace; the whole organization is indeed a personnel department. The development of sound labor policy is, in fact, synonymous with sound organizing and management.

It is on this ground that Scientific Management, as a great movement may rightly claim to be serving, not just this or that particular business, but the whole world of industry and the social and economic life of the community. It is not just a means to greater efficiency, in the sense of producing more goods, but a profound contribution to bettering the life of the community.

> I have been devoting my whole time (said Taylor) and almost every cent of money which I can spare from my income, to promoting the cause of Scientific Management; and my object in this work is primarily, I may say almost entirely, that of securing a larger measure of prosperity and happiness for the working people. I am, of course, and ought to be, interested in the material welfare of the companies who are using Scientific Management; but if the results of my work were merely to increase the dividends and prosperity of the manufacturing companies, I certainly should not devote my time to this object. Scientific Management is for me, then, primarily a means of bettering the condition of the working people.

Listen again to the significant words which Dean Sabine, of Harvard's Graduate School of Applied Science, addressed to Taylor:

> While listening to you and even more in thinking it over since I left you, I am persuaded that you are on the track of the only reasonable solution of a great sociologial problem. The systematization and standardization of work has a bearing far beyond the organization of a particular business or industry. I do not believe that you are a socialist any more than I am, but you are preparing data for the solution of a problem on which socialistic and cooperative movements have time after time been wrecked.

Far too little has been heard and far too little account taken of the possible contribution of management, scientifically conducted, to what one may call the sociological problem of industry. Some of the greatest minds have striven with the problem of Capital and Labor, as if these alone constituted the body of industry. Modern sociological and economic thought has yet to realize that Management is a third partner, whose position renders it an authoritative partner; that neither panaceas nor changes in heart, neither socialistic programmes nor experiments in cooperative working and governance will singly bring about a redirection of social progress, but rather the application to industry of the analytical and synthetical methods of science, by a body of management inspired by right-minded motives and viewing its work, in the day-to-day control of its shops and factories and warehouses, as highly constructive work in the building of a new order and the development of a new spirit in industry.

Consideration of Taylor's motive automatically tells us what was his conception of Scientific Management. To him, it was a philosophy, not a set of mechanisms or a hide-bound system. "The essence of modern scientific management," he said, "consists in the application of certain broad, general principles, and the particular way in which these principles are applied is a matter of entirely subordinate detail."

And again, he said, "In its essence, Scientific Management involves a complete mental revolution"--on the part of the men and of the management. To this broad vision of Scientific Management he held throughout. In later years, when efficiency became a craze, and efficiency societies spring up like mushrooms in a night, he maintained his same attitude--that Scientific Management was not essentially any of these things, but was "something that varied as it was adapted to particular cases, <u>but always involved a mental revolution of employer and employee toward their work and toward each other</u>." To Taylor, Scientific Management was a journey to an ideal, a course which led to some ultimate condition. It was not a static system, but a dynamic philosophy. "Scientific Management," he said, "fundamentally consists of . . . . a certain philosophy which can be applied in many ways," and philosophy is purposeless without an ideal, and fruitless save as it serves to move life forward towards that ideal. One of our dangers is to regard Scientific Management as something we have "installed," when the essential consideration is whether our management and our men have achieved that mental revolution which makes any set of mechanisms living and permanent. In a phrase, this "complete mental revolution" consists of "recognizing as essential the substitution of exact scientific investigation and knowledge for the old individual judgment or opinion in all matters relating to the work done in the establishment." The Taylor ideal was a condition of industry where its daily tasks had been subjected to the reign of law, scientifically established, and equally binding on management and men. Towards this ideal his work was one long, consistent struggle. What was, indeed, the core of his work at Bethlehem? "Essentially, it was this: that the government of the Bethlehem Company cease to be capricious, arbitrary, despotic; that every man in the establishment, high and low, submit himself to law." "The gist of the matter is," wrote Taylor, "that Scientific Management demands that the acts of the men and movements of all these men and elements shall be regulated according to clearly defined scientific rules and formulae."

The most significant feature in Taylor's efforts to reach this ideal, however, is the fact that his main difficulty lay with the management rather than the men. Despite his early tussle with the men of Midvale, the main combats of his life were with those in the management. In some instances he encountered direct opposition; in others he had to face the perhaps even more difficult problem of the man who enthused over Scientific Management for others, but was himself not in need of its medicine. "It took over two years," said James M. Dodge, "for our organization to surrender fully, and so change our mental attitude that we became really receptive. I mean by this that I found no difficulty at all in having the heads of various departments agree that the introduction of the Taylor system would be most desirable, but in each case it was for everybody else in the establishment but entirely unnecessary for him." Taylor's own difficulties at Bethlehem and those of his associates in other plants afford ample evidence of the toilsome task it was to bring about in the various managements that "mental revolution" which he himself postulated as the essence of Scientific Management. Yet it was only to be expected, and remains still one of the major problems of his followers. For, upon management Taylor threw a greater burden;

he made operative efficiency a problem which was up to the management. Moreover he demanded that management should subject itself to the reign of law which was the outcome of his scientific investigations, and further demanded that the petty despotisms of the old-time foremen and managers should be broken down, their work scientifically organized, and their positions rendered rather that of teachers than of driving masters. It was only human, perhaps, that these innovations should be opposed, and the "mental revolution" a very slow grinding of the wheels. Conservatism and inertia are the property of no class, and Taylor had too many sad experiences with managers to escape this fact. "It was his mature judgment," says Mr. Copley, "that the philosophy of 'initiative and incentive' was, in the main, the lazy manager's philosophy; the management could talk as it pleased about the workmen being supposed to be expert in their trade, but the real reason for putting the details up to the workmen was likely to be that the management was disinclined to assume the duties, burdens and responsibilities that naturally belonged to it."

Yet, it was true in Taylor's own work and is true today that efficiency must begin at the top. The workers cannot transfer their skill to a management which is not ready to receive and use it, nor can they single-handed standardize the conditions of their work. The development of efficiency is primarily a task of management, and efficiency is primarily a question of efficiency in those who direct and control the work of others. "Scientific labor can exist only as scientific management creates it. There is no labor that is scientific that is not the product of long arduous study with the methods of the laboratory," said Mr. Ernest H. Abbott in a singularly discerning statement. Management has yet to measure itself up to the standard which this ideal presents. It has yet to appreciate its responsibilities and the vast intricacy of its task. Whilst it continues to fall short, waste is the difference between what management is and what it should be. Of all documents perhaps the report of the Committee on Elimination of Waste in Industry is the strongest condemnation of the old-time management. It publicly places the main responsibility for waste on management. It is both a condemnation and a challenge. The philosophy of Taylor alone points the way to greater efficiency and it is upon management that the main responsibility must lie for bringing it about. General Crozier singled out as the feature which distinguished the scientific from other principles of management "the amount of administrative energy which is devoted to it," and by that energy alone is the herculean task of attaining the highest efficiency to be completed. Even amongst the managements which are definitely in sympathy with the underlying principles of Scientific Management, there is often a certain hesitation in putting any system based on those principles into operation, on the score of expense. Taylor himself, in fact, was often accused of "making the money fly." The tendency of most manufacturers, especially in times of depression, is to keep a very tight grip on the expenses ledger. Any system of scientific management, however, by throwing a greater burden on the management and by insisting that management shall work scientifically and not by arbitrary "rule-of-thumb" methods, necessarily involves, in most cases, an increase in the number of purely brain-workers over the number required under any non-scientific system. "The belief is almost universal among manufacturers," writes Taylor, in "Shop Management," "that for economy the number of brain workers, or non-producers, as they are called, should be as small as possible in proportion to the number of producers, i.e., those who actually work with their hands." And again, he wrote, "It has been my observation that there is no definite relation of any kind in the ratio of overhead expenses to direct expenses in the prosperity of a company. . . . I have found, however, that those companies which are managed in the very best way and which are earning the largest dividends in relation to their competitors, have the largest ratio of overhead expense in relation to direct expense. . . . As a general rule, I can say that the more men you can have working efficiently in the management, that is, on the management side, the greater will be your economy. No greater mistake can be made than to assume that economy is realized by cutting down the so-called overhead expense. Just the opposite is true in the very best managed companies." Mr. Copley's comment on this extract--that Taylor was a voice crying in the wilderness--is apt indeed, and is still largely true.

Management as a corporate body in industry has yet to see itself in its right perspective. It has yet to appreciate that business is progressing beyond the stage where it was a game of chance, a selfish, crazy tussle with capricious fortune, with alternating profits and losses, and is gathering speed towards an order of industry where the motive is that of social service and the methods of capable of scientific determination and regularized control. Progress towards this ideal is overwhelmingly dependent upon the energy, concentration and genius of management. Management will be called upon for a far higher standard of ability, a far higher concept of its duties and its relationships with the workers and the community, and a far higher development of its technique. It must bring more brainwork to bear on its task, more ethical considerations to fashion its motives and objectives. Perhaps the essence of what this deepening and widening of the sphere of management involves may be put in a phrase--that management is tending and must further tend to become a profession. The practise of a profession presupposes several things: firstly, a codified and proven body of knowledge, or, a science; secondly, a skill in the application of that knowledge, or, an art; thirdly a progressive enlargement and intensification of the knowledge, or in fact the constant use of the scientific method; fourthly, a standard by which efficiency in the practice of the profession may be assessed; fifthly, a motive which places first the good of the community. If then, these be the conditions of a profession, management, as Taylor conceived it, and as the industrial world is now slowly coming to conceive it, is indeed a profession in embryo. It is the task of management--as skill comes to replace chance and luck, as more and more thought and research expands knowledge, as definite criteria of efficiency become possible for its various branches, and as the element of social service drives out the false domination of petty autocracy--to develop itself into a profession, with professional standards and ethics.

To this end all Taylor's philosophy leads us; towards this ideal, the idealist in him constantly strove. "It is the promotion of harmony between employers and their workmen that is my chief interest," he said. And again; "All our inventions are meant to contribute to human happiness."

Above all men, perhaps, Taylor exemplified the new management to which his vision and work gave birth--a management directed by a social motive, yet operating by severely practical and scientific means.

This book tells us of Taylor's own life and work, but in the few years since he died, the outcome of his work has been a universal stirring of management to an appreciation of its responsibilities. Consciously or unconsciously, this new movement has been inspired by his teaching and leadership. Scientific Management has come to be recognized as a philosophy which is applicable, not only to shop management, but also to every activity of a business, from accountancy to selling, and, further, to every corporate enterprise, whether it be a manufacturing concern, a professional society, or a municipal organization. His principles have spread, like a great flame over all the world. His published works have been translated into every language, from English to Chinese, from Russian to Spanish. Both the French and Soviet Russian governments have given his principles official recognition. From Vienna to Paris, Paris to London, and London to New York, the work he began is being carried on by his followers.

Bringing into the very shops of industry the quality of thought which is normally the attribute of the hermit of the laboratory and study; working in happy cooperation with other pioneers--his friends one and all, whose devotion to him was only equalled by his friendship and respect for them;--gilding his work with the rare gleams of far-looking visions, and buoying it ever on the tide of a high motive and objective; delving deep into the caverns of truth in the work-a-day things of life, and pressing fearlessly forward where the light of truth led him--Frederick Taylor set on its path a movement which, when the time comes to see it in its proper perspective, will have been found to have given a redirection to our social progress. At a time when industry was reaping the shrivelled harvest of low ideals and selfish, unlightened management he brought to it the fertile seed of high ideals and unselfish, enlightened management. "He injected the concept," in the words of Dr. Person, "that a business should exist for social service, that its purposes can be defined, its objectives planned and scheduled, detailed execution be so controlled as to contribute most economically to the final result, and that the final result can be a productivity of useful things so shared as to increase the comfort and promote the happiness of all concerned." Wherever Scientific Management is the philosophy governing the conduct of any enterprise, there will Frederick Taylor's spirit--and, as he would wish it, the spirit of his associates--be found still working. The day, indeed, cannot be far distant when Scientific Management will come to be recognized as a great social movement, not only by those in industry who are the immediate objects of its service, but by all that commonwealth which industry itself serves.

It was time that the life of Frederick Taylor should be written and published to the world, for, if he was a generation ahead of his time, that generation is now with us. He blazed the trail; we put foot upon a more royal highway. No more inspiriting message could come to us than this story--so faithfully told, so intimate yet so heroic and portentous--of the life of him who has been named, in a significantly mingled title,--a mingling of the man and the mission, the family and the world, the sowing and the fruit, the present and the henceforward, the mortal frame and the imperishable legacy, the body that fails and the thought that prevails--"The Father of Scientific Management."

---

[1]*Bulletin of the Taylor Society*, February, 1924.

TAYLOR AND TRADE UNIONS[1]

By Frank B. Copley

I had thought that the attitude of Frederick W. Taylor toward labor unions was easy to read in the biography of Mr. Taylor I had the honor of preparing. It would appear, however, that some of the reviewers have not fully understood Mr. Taylor in this connection; perhaps you will grant me space for a statement designed to settle this matter finally.

As an example of the lack of understanding to which I refer, I may take Mr. John A. Fitch's review which, prepared for the Machinists' Monthly Journal was reprinted in the Taylor Society Bulletin for June, 1925. In view of Mr. Fitch's evident appreciation of many phases of Mr. Taylor's personality and work, and in view also of Mr. Fitch's generous references to the part played by me as Mr. Taylor's biographer, it may seem ungracious of me to find fault with some of his statements. As a matter of fact, Mr. Fitch's review, in the main, appealed to me very much, and I would not venture to question any of his statements did I not feel that my object of clearing up Mr. Taylor's attitude toward labor unions has no little importance.

Mr. Fitch says that Taylor had "no formula for the defense of the workers against the 'fool' employer." Surely Taylor not only did have such a formula, but it was exactly the same as Mr. Fitch's; namely, labor unionism. This, I think, must clearly appear when due weight is given to Taylor's utterances in this connection. For example, in "A Piece-Rate System," presented at a meeting of the American Society of Mechanical Engineers in 1895, he said:

> The labor unions--particularly the trades unions of England--have rendered a great service not only to their members, but to the world, in shortening the hours of labor and in modifying the hardships and improving the conditions of wage-workers. . .
>
> When employers herd their men together in classes, pay all of each class the same wages, and offer none of them any inducements to work harder or do better work than the average the only remedy for the men lies in combination; and frequently the only possible answer to encroachments on the part of their employers is a strike.

Mr. Fitch again says:

> Taylor and his associates did not try very hard to understand the trade unionists. They appeared to be quite unconscious of the basic historical facts that have made labor movements inevitable, and seemed to think of it as a superfluous and irritating interference with the process of sound industrial management.

I find that these statements, at least as they relate to Taylor apart from his associates, start out to be very inaccurate and wind up by being quite accurate. That Taylor did not try to understand trade unionists and was unconscious of the historical facts that have made labor movements inevitable, is, I am sure, disproved by the quotation from "A Piece-Rate System" I have here presented. But that Taylor came to think of the labor unions he encountered in his day as a superfluous and irritating interference with the process of sound industrial management, there can be no possible doubt whatever.

I remember that when I saw him in the summer of 1912 he was, you might say, uncommonly irritated with labor unions. He pitched into them with all the enthusiasm of which his nature was capable--and the Lord knows that was plenty! Well, seeing that he was a human being who had not yet attained to one hundred per cent sanctification, you couldn't feel so terribly shocked. Organized labor's campaign against all things Taylor was then in full cry--and, take it from your old uncle, it was no soft, pretty, plaintive cry, but the cry of those who were out for blood and weren't overly particular how they got it. What had Fred Taylor done to bring this thing upon him? The evidence is that the warfare against him was due solely to the efforts being made to introduce more or less of his management principles and methods into the navy yards and the army's manufacturing arsenals. Now, the management he sought to introduce into these government establishments is set forth in detail in the Taylor biography, and the interference of organized labor with this management is there also to be read. Can any disinterested person examine this record without concluding that the management was, on the whole, pretty sound and that the interference would have been found quite superfluous and irritating even by a less earnest, intense, and peppery person than Fred Taylor?

But what I want to make emphatic here is that when I saw him in that summer of 1912 (my business with him was to obtain material for a magazine article), he was just as vehemently and picturesquely enthusiastic in whacking what he called "damn fool" and "hog" employers as he was in thumping the then existing chiefs of the American Federation of Labor. And he then made it exceedingly plain that his remedy or "formula" for the hopelessly hoggish employer was the big, striking stick of unionism.

You may remember the incident in Henry Adams' autobiography where the author told a certain member of the President's cabinet that it had been charged that he, the cabinet member, had not been very tactful in his dealings with Congress. "A Congressman," replied the official, "is a hog; you can't use tact with a hog; you have to take a stick and beat him over the snout." That illustrates Taylor's idea very well in connection with hog employers, and brings us to the essence of his attitude toward labor unions.

He found that the unions of his time were seldom organized for cooperation with employers, but in the main were big-stick, fighting organizations. As such they were very useful indeed for workers who had to deal with selfish and greedy employers. By precisely the same token (as well as by such other tokens as their restriction of output and opposition to the principle of the worker's being paid individually in accordance with his production) he was positive that the unions of his time had no place under scientific management.

It will be observed that I have been careful to speak only of the unions of Taylor's time. In this I am but following Taylor's own limitation, as will be seen by this extract from a letter of his (written in 1911) which was quoted by me in the biography (pp. 413 and 414, vol. II), the italics here being mine:

> You realize, of course, that I am not opposed to labor unions. Their proper field *as they now exist* is, I feel, outside of scientific management. I am sure that labor unions (active unions, at least) *as they are now constituted* would serously interfere with the progress of scientific management.

Taylor, in fine, did not oppose labor unionism under scientific management because of the principle of the thing by itself considered, but because of the particular ways in which he found labor unions conducted. In the letter from which I have just quoted he added: "I can conceive of a union that would be most helpful to scientific management, but I have not yet seen this union."

At the same time, he had the vision to realize that such a union would come. In the course of a discussion before the A.S.M.E., he said:

> I think the time will come when trades-unionists will realize that their true and permanent road toward prosperity lies in so educating themselves that they will be able and willing to do more work in return for larger pay, rather than in fighting to do less work for the same pay or the same work for larger pay.

There is evidence that such trades unions are now, ten years after Taylor's death, coming into being. In the same number of the Taylor Society *Bulletin* containing Mr. Fitch's review of the Taylor biography there is a review by Mr. Ordway Tead of "The Women's Garment Workers: A History of the International Ladies' Garment Workers' Union," by Dr. Louis Levine. We here read that this union has subscribed to these principles among others:

> Acceptance by the union of a share in responsibility for getting production.
>
> Use of guaranteed weekly pay rates; but use of payment incentives for work done above a defined standard.
>
> Definitions of fair minimum standards of amounts of work on a basis of careful study of jobs, determination of amounts to take place under joint agreement.

Mr. Tead comments:

> All this represents, of course, a virtual reversal in policy from that of many unions on questions of measured production, use of scientific methods to discover fair amounts of work, willingness to allow the better workmen to earn more than the union scale--in fact, the whole cooperative emphasis in the matter of production.

It is true that the principle of collective bargaining is here retained as regards the guaranteed weekly pay rates, and that the employees have their joint "look-in" as regards the determination of minimum standards of production. And, as Mr. Fitch correctly points out, Taylor in his last years stood against collective bargaining and joint employee action of any kind. Personally I think that this stand showed Taylor's tendency to concentrate on economic considerations to the neglect, not of ethical considerations, but of political. Mr. Robert B. Wolf has said that "no matter how skillfully the management determines the one best way, it ceases to be the one best way if the workman does not want to do it that way." As I see it, determining the best way pertains to ecnomics, while getting the worker to want to do it that way pertains to politics. And I take it that politics never can be wholly excluded in the affairs of human beings, so that the management engineer must be both an economist and a politician. I judge, for example, that Mr. Wolf is a very fine politician, indeed. This aside, it is to beobserved that Taylor did not assume his extreme stand against collective action by employees until after it had become plain to him that most of the then labor chiefs were resolved on decorating a sour-apple tree with his shotriddled body without pausing to find out what he really was up to. His extreme stand, I take it, was largely the reaction of his intense nature to labor's extreme stand; and surely with such a handsome modification of labor's old attitude as is represented by the principles subscribed to by the Ladies' Garment Workers' Union he would have hailed it as a union with which he <u>could</u> cooperate and modified his own attitude accordingly.

This much is certain, that the idea should perish that Taylor, like a regular old Bourbon of a capitalist-employer, presented a hard-boiled countenance to all kinds of labor unions and labor unionists. Actually there was not a leading unionist of his day he did not seek to convert. True, he was not his own best converter; but to me, at all events, there was an element of pathos in his warm regard for such labor unionists as William B. Wilson and John Tobin who, mind you, never spoke a single word in favor of his work, but simply refrained from condemming it.

Just one more statement in Mr. Fitch's review which I think needs correcting in justness to Mr. Taylor. I quote:

> . . . he [Taylor] fell into errors of various sorts, and often contradicted himself. For example, he declared in his "Principles" that scientific management has as its "very foundation" the idea that the interests of employer and employee "are one and the same." He thought that the question of the rate of wages could be reduced to a scientific formula, no more to be bargained over than the question of the hour for the sun to rise. But he forgot these theories in the face of concrete realities. When he was promoted to a foremanship over the machinists with whom he had formerly worked, he "told them plainly that he was now working on the side of the management"--a thing that could hardly be said to exist apart or different from the "side of labor," if the principle of identity of interests as confidently set forth above was true.

This implies that when, in 1879 at the age of twenty-three, Fred Taylor became a boss over those Midvale machinists, he had got his theory of scientific management already worked out in his head. Surely Fred Taylor's biography was written in vain if it did not make plain that when he began his career as a boss he was as guiltless of any theory of scientific management as the legislature of Tennessee is guiltless of any thoery of evolution. Instead of Taylor's forgetting, "in the face of concrete realities," his theory that the interests of employer and employee are one and the same, it was the concrete realities he encountered throughout his many years as manager and engineer that finally led to his forming the theory. And this leads me to quote once more from Mr. Tead's review of Dr. Levine's book:

> Indeed, if its present program carries on, this union will go down in history as among the very first of those within the fold of the American Federation of Labor to realize that its prosperity and the industry's prosperity are inseparable, and that all the union can do to strengthen the industry will in turn strengthen it.

Is it too much to call this a very strong labor endorsement of the very principle or theory that Taylor said lay at the very foundation of scientific management? And is it not probable that the endorsement also was arrived at, not in spite of concrete realities, but in consequence of them?

One of Taylor's objections to collective bargaining was that a wage is not necessarily a just one simply because it is agreed upon by employer and employees in conference--such a wage, by making necessary an increased price of the product, might very well be unjust to the third party, the whole people, or that element which at the last analysis gives employment to capital, management, and labor alike. Taylor saw, in fact, that the unions of his day often forced up prices by their wage demands; and he feared that any form of collective bargaining would throw the door open to this unionism. But here, now, is a union enlightened enough to see that its prosperity is bound up with that of the industry. Well, then, such a union may be depended upon to recognize that it cannot exact wages which make necessary prices that are discouraging to consumption; and here, as sure as you are born, is more evidence that Taylorism and unionism are not necessarily incompatibles, but may derive great support, the one from the other.

---

[1] Bulletin of the Taylor Society, August, 1925. (Although this article was a letter to the Editor, because of the importance of the content it has been given the form and place of an editorial (original footnote)).

AN INDUSTRIAL ESPERANTO[1]

By L. Urwick
Director, International Management Institute, Geneva

Under the title, "The Industrial Tower of Babel," which appeared in the August 1, 1928, number of the Labour Magazine, Mr. R. M. Fox reviewed the Congress of the International Association for the Study and Improvement of Human Relations and Conditions in Industry, which took place at Cambridge in July. As he rightly observed "the keynote of the Congress was to be found in the declaration that work is a social function, industry is a science." Apparently this point of departure met with his approval. On the other hand, he was critical of those who believed in scientific management. He did not seem to appreciate that Taylor was the first man to insist to the world that industry is a science, that the only hope of the dispassionate study of work as a social function lies with those who would apply the definition, the intellectual methods, and the ethical standards which inspire scientific workers.

Much early mythology still centers round the work of F. W. Taylor. The founder of scientific management, as is the case with nearly all great and original thinkers, was hugely misrepresented in the days when his work first attracted public attention. He was particularly distorted by a large number of unscrupulous people who advertised themselves as "efficiency engineers" in order to exploit the goodwill attaching to his ideas. Since they had no conception of the underlying principles on which those ideas were based, they were guilty of many crimes both against the employers who consulted them, and against the workers in those factories with which they were permitted to experiment.

It is, therefore, not surprising that the trade union world in the United States should have reacted sharply against what it described as "Taylorism." Over several successive years the annual congress of the American Federation of Labor passed the strongest possible resolutions on the subject, which contained such phrases as "the hideous and tyrannical so-called Taylor system." This chain of events was naturally well known to trade union leaders in England. A feeling grew up among the workers that scientific management was something hard and ruthless, and that their sole concern with it was to oppose it with might and main.

The fact is that the question of scientific management has been confused with the various matters at issue between labor and capital. With that great controversy it has, properly considered, nothing directly to do. As a trade union representative from Vienna pointed out at the Cambridge Conference: "Whatever may be the ultimate political organization of industry, there will always be human problems arising from the employment of persons." Unless we are prepared to scrap the whole of our modern machinery of production, in which case we should have to cut down our population by more than two-thirds, we must contemplate a state of society in which there are those whose function it is to plan and to direct, and those whose function it is to carry out these plans and directions.

The same consideration applies to our political, educational, recreational, and other forms of social organization. As F. W. Taylor himself constantly insisted, scientific management is not a system. It does not consist of a particular series of methods and devices. It is an attitude of mind, a method of approach to all those problems which arise from the employment of persons, whoever happens to be in control, or whatever the purpose in view. It is as applicable to a government department, a church, a football club, or to the international administration of a trade union as it is to the conduct of a factory under the control of a limited liability company.

It differs from the older conceptions of management in this, that it approaches all such problems afresh, with the methods, the standards, and the intellectual technique of the scientist. It endeavors to secure that every decision is arrived at, not as the result of rule of thumb, guesswork, or personal emotion, but by a careful collection, balancing, measurement, and test of <u>all</u> the available facts bearing on the point at issue.

The methods of science are analysis, definition, measurement, and proof. The scientist forms tentative conclusions by means of experiment, and is constantly engaged in adjusting these conclusions in the light of fresh hypotheses or of fresh groups of facts. Where they stand this searching test they issue in the formation of principles and laws. As will presently be recognized, more particularly by the workers, it was F. W. Taylor who first insisted on this great principle, that the confusion of modern industrial administration can only be solved in the light of principles, evolved by the methods of thought which have inspired the triumphs of modern discovery in the material sciences.

Inevitably, Taylor's work was tentative and incomplete--as the work of Darwin in biology has been rounded out by later workers in the same field. Experimental psychologists of the English school have rightly called attention to the importance of individual rhythms and the necessity of modifying the conception of the "one best way" in the light of more recent discoveries. Taylor himself would have welcomed such discoveries. He even envisaged developments in experimental psychology which have taken place since his day. "There is one science," he writes, "to which insufficient attention has been given, the science of human motives."

Similarly in the United States, the technique which he applied specially to the problems of machine production, has been carried over into the field of industrial relations. The results in many factories in the increased comfort, welfare, and contentment of the workers have been noted by the Mackenzie Commission, and by many trade union observers.

Those who have made the closest study of his underlying philosophy are the most convinced that the faults of expression and the ignorant and piecemeal attempts to apply his methods which brought his work into temporary disrepute with the American trade unions in no way represented the fine social idealism and underlying vision of the man himself. It is true that in his later years he was critical of the trade unions. He was a human being. And in the confusion of immediate controversy they had covered with obloquy the work and the ideas to which he had given his life and his fortune.

This is being realized by ever increasing numbers of persons in all branches of the labor movement. For some years past, leaders of the American trade unions have taken note of two important facts. In the first place it is just in those factories where Taylor's principles are most thoroughly understood, that they find the strongest support for the doctrine of high wages. Secondly, it is there, too, that they find the greatest willingness to co-operate in working out experiments in industrial relations.

The past and present presidents of the American Federation of Labor have declared roundly in favor of scientific methods of production and the elimination of waste. At a recent conference a representative of the printers described how his union had established its own consultants in scientific management. When an employer said that he could not pay the union rates, they sent a representative along to advise him on the better management of his plant.

The same is true of England. It is not the employers who are indifferent to labor and its developing status who are most interested in scientific management. It is the Renolds and the Rowntrees--the men who are most willing to accord full recognition to trade unionism and to co-operate with its leaders in working out in practice those measures by which the workers may collaborate critically and creatively, and take a growing part in the running of industry.

Many of the leaders of the Labour Party appreciate this. Mr. Bevin's signature appears under the report of the Mackenzie Commission. Mr. Pugh recently said at a conference at the Guildhall: "Rationalization involves scientific management, a much misunderstood term. This does not mean the regimentation of labor, a sort of goose-step to the time of the machine; it means the science of good management, good government in industry, applied to the workshop, winning the co-operation of labor for the elimination of waste in human effort, material, and organization, and in getting the best results in productive enterprises and services. Combined with this is the acceptance of the principle that in the science of good management, cutting down wages and extending hours of labor is the last and not the first resource."

Turning to the left wing, it may be noticed that one of the first actions of the U.S.S.R. was to establish in Moscow an institution for the study of F. W. Taylor's work, and of the developments which have flowed from it. Is any further evidence needed that the science of management is not integral with the present political organization of industry, an employers' dodge to be dismissed with a shrug, but is something essential to any form of effort in which men must co-operate?

But the prejudice remains. Many workers seem to be totally unaware that the chief motive which drive Taylor to try to evolve a new approach to questions of industrial management was the disgust of a sympathetic and sensitive man at the bullying methods which were the common currency of foremanship in the American machine shop of the '80's. To say, as has been said, that Taylor desired "to remove all initiative, all thought, all criticism from the workshop," and to "degrade the worker into a productive machine" is preposterously wide of the mark. One wonders how many of his critics have studied the standard biography of the great reformer.

Now, this prejudice is important. Because it blinds some of the ablest minds in the labor movement to the strongest line of attack against many of the inequalities and injustices under which the workers suffer, an attack on the obsolete methods of management which give rise to them. Moreover, it prevents a proper understanding between the worker groups and those groups of managers and technicians who, economically, should be in sympathy with them. Collaboration is a social fact. It will remain a social fact whoever owns the industrial capital of the country, or on whatever system our industry is organized. Today, co-operative societies, municipal undertakings, and government departments have their problems of management, no less than capitalistic undertakings. They can only be solved with the consent and willing co-operation of all concerned.

But men cannot collaborate, they cannot even negotiate or discuss a question intelligently together unless the words they use have the same meaning for all of them. An effort to introduce a common language into the industrial babel is probably the most important problem which now confronts the world. The only progress which has ever been achieved in this direction has been in the established sciences. In mathematics, physics, and chemistry, men of different races and different social status can speak together on their problems of common interest. Because they have used the intellectual technique of the investigator--analysis, definition, measurement, and proof--they have established a currency for the rapid and easy exchange of ideas in the search for truth. There is no other path by which we can march to the solution of our industrial and social difficulties.

When, therefore, representatives of the workers say that "they do not believe in scientific management," when they misrepresent the essential work which F. W. Taylor performed--the application to industrial problems of the scientific intellectual technique--what they are really saying is this:

"We do not believe in definition. We do not want analysis. We abhor measurement. We are indifferent to proof." They are shutting the door on the only real hope, the progressive discovery of truth. They are denying at the start any possibility of collaboration, because they will not use the intellectual methods by which alone the verbal instruments of collaboration can be forged. They leave the manager and technician feeling like a Darwinian biologist trying to talk to a fundamentalist from Dayton.

---

[1] *Bulletin of the Taylor Society*, June, 1929. First printed in Labour Magazine, October, 1928.

SUCCESS [1]

A Lecture to Young Men Entering Business

By Frederick Winslow Taylor

I want to speak to you on success; success for the ordinary man, not success for the genius or the unusual man. I do not doubt that among you there are many geniuses, and those among you who are geniuses will more than likely be a law unto themselves. I should not, however, advise any one very strongly to start out to be a genius. The genius is usually an indirect product, not a direct one. What I have in mind, then, is to try to be of some help to the ordinary, every-day engineer in obtaining success.

The young man, up to the time that he leaves college, is chiefly engaged in absorbing and assimilating knowledge for his own use. The moment he leaves college he begins directly the opposite, namely, using what knowledge he has for the benefit of others.

Up to the time that the young man leaves college practically all those around him have been serving him. His parents have been supporting, guiding and disciplining; his teachers have been helping him to get an education. The moment he leaves college, however, he begins his life's work of serving others.

Now I use this word "serving" advisedly. It gives the exact shade of meaning which I wish to convey. Practically every man engaged in active, useful work is engaged in serving someone else, and this is equally true of the president of the company and the office boy. Everyone is serving someone else.

The work of the young man until he leaves college has been that of getting an education. There are, however, three by-products of this process of getting an education, either of which, for success in life, is more important than the education itself. These by-products are common-sense; character; and integrity.

Let me tell you what I mean by these words. Of course they cannot be completely defined in a few or even in many sentences, but briefly, common-sense is the ability to decide as to the relative importance of things,--the ability to select from among the several possible lines of action which lie before you the one act which is best, the one act which will yield the largest return.

Character is the ability to control yourself, body and mind; the ability to do those things which your common-sense tells you you ought to do; the ability above all to do things which are disagreeable, which you do not like. It takes but little character to do difficult things if you like them. It takes a lot of character to do things which are tiresome, monotonous and unpleasant.

By integrity I do not mean merely the kind of integrity which will keep a man out of jail. I mean that straightforward honesty of purpose which makes a man truthful, not only to others but with himself; which makes a man high-minded, gives him high aspirations and high ideals.

Now, I wish to emphasize the fact that each of these three by-products counts for far more in success than the more brilliant and interesting qualities of intellect, knowledge and mental attainments.

During the process of getting an education your success has depended mainly upon yourself, and this will, of course, remain true at all times. It is clear, however, that during your life-work of serving other people, your success must also depend to a large extent upon your ability to please the man you are serving, and you will do this by serving him his way, not yours; by doing the things which he wants, not the things which you want.

For success, then, let me give one simple piece of advice beyond all others. Every day, year in and year out, each man should ask himself, over and over again, two questions. First, "What is the name of the man I am now working for?" and having answered this definitely, then, "What ought I to do in the interest of the company that I am working for?" Not, "What are the duties of the position that I am filling?" Not, "What did I agree to do when I came here?" Not, "What should I do for my own best interest?" but, plainly and simply, "What does this man want me to do?"

Perhaps these two questions sound very much alike, but let me assure you that there is a vast difference between the two. The question, "What does this man want me to do?" implies that you propose leaving this decision to him. The question, "What ought I to do for the interest of the company?" implies that you propose making this decision yourself, and it should be clear to you that if you expect to please the man whom you are serving you must leave this most important decision to him.

Bearing in mind, then, that your success will depend mainly upon your ability to please the man whom you are serving, it becomes of the greatest importance to know exactly what will please him, and I am sure that you will find certain general principles of use in making this decision.

When I was about to begin to serve my apprenticeship, an old gentleman who had been very successful sent for me to come to see him. He lived some 20 or 30 miles away, and said that he had something very important to tell me. What he had to say took but three or four sentences. He said, "If you want success in your work, do what I say.

If your employer wants you to start work at 7 o'clock in the morning, always be there at ten minutes before seven. If he wants you to stay until 6 o'clock at night, always stay until ten minutes past six. Now, if you haven't sense enough to know what I mean by this, you haven't sense enough to succeed, anyway."

He also said, "Let me tell you one more thing. Whatever happens, however badly you may be treated, however much you may be abused, never give up your job until you have taken 48 hours to think it over; and if possible don't talk back to the man who is over you until you have time to cool off."

Now, in the first of these recommendations there is a broad and general principle involved which is not altogether apparent on the surface. At least, it took me several years to grasp fully what the old man meant when he said, "If your employer wants you to start work at 7 o'clock in the morning, always be there at ten minutes of seven."

There are two ways of giving orders, and in all cases the young man must use his common-sense and a small amount of brains to decide in which of these two ways the order has been given. The first of these ways is, "Take that chair in your left hand. Carry it over into the corner and lean it against the wall." The second of these ways is, "That chair wants to be put away. Go and do it." Now, when a man tells you precisely and exactly and minutely what he wants you to do, it is because he wants you to do just that, and nothing else. When, however, as is the case in perhaps nine times out of ten, a man gives the second type of order, then he expects you not only to do what he says but perhaps also to do a little better than he says, and in giving the man you are serving a little more than he expects lies more than in anything else the key to rapid success.

Throughout life it is the small, unexpected, unasked-for acts of courtesy and kindness that give especial pleasure. It is the little gift, the small piece of uncalled-for generosity, that charms, makes life worth living--and remember, your employer is no exception to the rest of mankind in his appreciation of this.

Quite a large proportion of young men set out deliberately to do barely enough to satisfy their employer,--in fact, many of them would feel happy to do as little as they can and still satisfy their employer. Another set of men propose to do just what their employer wants. They, however, are at all times exceedingly careful to guard their own rights and not to give a single thing in the way of service that they are not paid for. About one man, however, in twenty takes the real, quick road to success. He makes up his mind deliberately that in all cases he will not only give his employer all that he wants, but that he will surprise him with something unexpected, something beyond what his employer has any right to ask or expect, and it is astonishing how fast this line of action leads to success.

To do this, then, it is perfectly clear that as a foundation the decision of what you are to do must rest in all cases with your employer, and not with yourself. This seems exceedingly simple, and yet most men, if they ever learn it, learn it by having it pounded into them.

Let me tell you how it was pounded into me. I was foreman of a machine shop more than half of the work in which was that of repairing and maintaining the machinery in a large steel works. Of course my chief interest and hope in life was that of doing some great thing for the benefit of the works that I was in. My head was full of wonderful and great projects to simplify the processes, to design new machines, to revolutionize the methods of the whole establishment. It is needless to say that 99 out of 100 of these projects were impracticable, and that very few of them ever came to anything, but I was devoting every minute of my spare time, at home and on Sunday, and entirely too much of my time in the works, to developing these wonderful and great projects. Now the superintendent of the works, who had been a warm friend of mine for years, wanted me to keep all of the machines going with the minimum loss of time, and kept telling me this over and over again. I, however, knew much better than he what was for the interests of the works. I did not daily ask myself, "What does this man want me to do?" but I daily told myself just what I ought to be doing. He stood this as long as he could (which was a great deal longer than he ought to have stood it) and finally came into my office one day and swore at me like a pirate. This had never happened before, and I, of course, at once made up my mind that I should get right out; wouldn't stand any such treatment. I, however, remembered my early advice, and waited 48 hours before doing anything. By that time I had very greatly cooled off, but for two or three weeks at regular intervals my friend, the superintendent, repeated this process of damning me up and down hill, until he finally beat it into my dumb head that I was there to serve him and not to work in the interests of the company according to my own ideas, when these conflicted with his; and from that time forward I made quite rapid progress toward success.

What your employer wants is results, not reasons. He wants you to _get there_, and he is not interested in your explanation of why you failed to get there. There is one saying which we have all used since childhood, and which has had no little part in the failure of unsuccessful men. We have all of us said, "I have done the best that I know how; no one could expect any more of me." Now, whenever a man fails to get the result that his employer asks for he should feel intense chagrin and disappointment, instead of feeling satisfied because he has done the "best he knows how." What we are in the world for is to learn continually to do better than we know how. And be sure that in 99 out of 100 cases your employer has very little interest in hearing that you have done the "best you know how," when you have failed.

Andrew Carnegie came back from England one summer and found that one of his superintendents had made an unusually large profit in his plant. He wrote this man a check for $15,000 as a gift. Another of his superintendents had lost money, and when this man started to explain to Mr. Carnegie the reasons for this loss, Carnegie said, "Oh, John, don't bother about telling me any reasons. One single reason is good enough. Just tell me that you are a _____ _____ fool--that'll do."

Now, this sounds brutal, and yet it forcibly expresses the mental attitude shared by perhaps the majority of employers when they are given reasons instead of results. Let me tell you how this fact was driven home in my case.

A workman came up to my house in the middle of the night to tell me that a valve had broken and shut down one of the large departments in the works. I took the earliest train at 6 o'clock down into Philadelphia, hired a carriage and drove all over the city to every dealer who might possibly have the valve on hand, and also to all the establishments who were users of this kind of valve. I failed, however, to find it in Philadelphia. About noon, I returned to the works, feeling very well satisfied that I had left no stone unturned in my hunt for the valve. I started to explain to the superintendent just how thoroughly I had done my work, when he turned on me.

"Do you mean to say that you haven't got that valve?"

"Yes, sir."

"Damn you, get out of this and get that valve!"

So I went to New York and got the valve.

Not reasons, but results, are wanted.

There, however, is one exception to the rule that you should do just what your employer wants. You, of course, must do nothing mean or dishonest for your employer. If your employer wants you to do anything of this sort, get a new employer.

But what I want particularly to call your attention to is, that in almost all cases success is due not to the brilliant qualities, but to the plain, ordinary, homely virtues--to grit, determination, perserverance; to the willingness and the character required to do ordinary, disagreeable things; to the ability to take a licking and come up smiling, over and over again.

I think I am through now with personal illustrations. I have tried to emphasize the fact that success, character, common-sense and integrity count, and that the most important idea should be that of serving the man who is over you his way, not yours; and that this lies, generally speaking, in giving him not only what he wants but also giving him a little extra present of some kind, in doing something for him which he has no right either to ask or expect.

In an engineering establishment there were ten or fifteen young college men who were all trying to work up into good positions. Among them there was one man of no especial ability. He didn't do especially well at college, although he was an ordinary scholar. He appears to have been endowed, however, with fully the ordinary amount of common-sense. At any rate, he saw an opportunity for advancement which the other young men failed to see.

Most of the departments of the works ran night and day, so that every Saturday night and Sunday urgent repairs were required to keep the place running. Naturally, the work of making these repairs was in no way sought for by these young college fellows. They all had something much more interesting to do on Sunday--either choir practice or lawn tennis or social engagements of some kind. So that the superintendent in charge of repairs had a hard time to get the men whom he wanted to work hard, and chiefly on Sunday. One of these young college men, however, went to the repair superintendent, and told him that he didn't mind Sunday work at all--in fact, he rather liked it. He said he had served his apprenticeship as a machinist, and didn't mind being called upon at any time. This was such a new experience to the repair superintendent that he sent for him to come in on the following Sunday. He did so well that he kept him at work practically every Sunday throughout the year, and also quite frequently all of Saturday night, and, contrary to what usually happened, he never had any kicks or complaints from this young man. All of this man's friends, however, laughed at him and remonstrated with him for being so foolish as to take much more than his share of Sunday work. This was particularly true of the rest of the college fellows. His parents, his social friends, also told him that he was nothing but a fool to work in this way. However, by the end of a year practically every superintendent throughout the establishment wanted this young man in his department, and as a result he was promoted with great rapidity. At the end of two or three years all of the other college graduates were wondering why this man, who really was not as smart as some of them, was given all the promotion, all of the good jobs, all of the best positions.

In another establishment a young man, also a college graduate, had worked up to be at the head of one of the departments. A drain which ran underneath this mill became clogged up. He sent his best foreman and gang of men to clean it out. After they had tried to do it with jointed rods of all kinds, they failed, and reported to him that the only thing to do was to dig down, break open the drain, and clean out the obstruction. Now this drain was some twenty or thirty feet below the mill, and ran underneath the foundations, which made it extremely difficult to dig, and certainly involved the loss of several days in the operation of the mill. This young man made up his mind that the drain must be cleaned, so he took off all of his clothes, put on over-alls, tied shoes on to his elbows, shoes on to his knees, and leather pads on to his hips to keep from getting cut in the drain, and then crawled in through the black slime and muck of the drain. Time and again he had to turn his nose up into the arch of the drain to keep from drowning. After about 100 yards, however, he reached the obstruction, pulled it down, and when the water had partly subsided backed out the same way that he had come in. He was covered with slime perhaps half an inch thick, all over, which had to be scraped off with a scraper, and his skin was black for a week or two where the dirt had soaked in. He was, of course, very much laughed at, and finally the anecdote was told as a good joke at a meeting of the Board of Directors. The President of the company, however, realized that this was just the kind of joke that his company appreciated. He realized that the company had been saved perhaps one or two thousand dollars in profits by the grit of this young man. It was the first time it had been called to the President's attention.

A few weeks afterward the President sent for him to come to his office and said, "I have tried to get the oil out of the cylinders of our steam hammers. I know that you are not in the hammer department. Are you able to keep the oil out of those cylinders?" "Yes, sir, providing you will give me the necessary authority to do it." The President wrote him a letter, stating that he had authority to discharge anyone who disobeyed the orders of this young man in the matter of keeping the oil out of the cylinders, and armed with this letter he returned to the works, and appointed a hammer-man on day shift and one on night shift, for each hammer, part of whose duty it was to see that no oil got into the cylinder of his hammer. He showed him the President's letter and told him that if any oil was found in the cylinder of a steam hammer on his shift he would discharge him, whether he put it there, allowed it to get there, or not. In addition to this, he chained up the various inlets to the cylinder and locked them with heavy padlocks, so as to make it difficult to get at the cylinders to oil them. Before starting to do this, however, he wrote a letter to the President of the Company, telling him that he believed it was a mistaken policy to keep the oil out of the cylinders; that it was his personal conviction that the cylinders would cut without oil and be ruined. The President answered that he had had a steam engine in one of his other establishments running for some twenty years without any oil in the cylinder, and that he would therefore take the personal responsibility of the matter himself.

About three or four months later the company paid a bill of many thousands of dollars to have the cylinders of its steam hammers rebored. They had almost all cut for lack of oil.

This young man, however, had proved by these two incidents, first, that he had common-sense enough to recognize the fact that his employer wanted him above all things to save money; second, that he had the grit and pluck required to do disagreeable things; and third, that he could obey orders even if he personally disagreed with the policy; and these incidents marked the starting point in the career of one of our most successful engineers and managers.

In the spring of 1900 a large company decided to exhibit a big machine in the Paris Exhibition. It was so late, however, when they came to this conclusion that the machines of most of their competitors were already in the exhibition. They, however, were able to obtain space, and it was of course necessary to have the machine in operation at the earliest possible minute. There were a great many young college graduates in the employ of this company. Many of them wanted to go over with the exhibit, and have charge of it, and were fairly well equipped in that they had a certain knowledge of French. It, of course, was of the greatest importance to select men who would be sure to get the machine going in the shortest space of time, and these young college men were surprised to find that two young men were chosen, neither of whom had a college education, both of whom, however, had shown their resourcefulness and their ability to "get there." Many of those in the company, however, were greatly surprised at their appointment, because neither of them spoke one word of French.

These young men arrived in Paris ahead of their machine, and found that a large proportion of the machines which had arrived in their department were still unpacked, and far from being set up, because the rules of the Exhibition required that all of the work done in the Exhibition should be done by official employees, official masons, bricklayers, carpenters, etc. These men saw clearly that if they waited their turn it would be well on into the summer before their machine would be up, so they bought a car-load of bricks, mortar, shovels, etc., for building foundations and had them consigned to themselves in the Exhibition. When the car arrived they pinched it opposite their materials themselves, and unloaded all the building materials at night. The next day there was great horror in the Exhibition when these men were found digging their own foundation and preparing to build it themselves. There was, however, no rule which prevented the exhibitors from doing any work which they themselves saw fit, so the officials of the Exhibition could not interfere with their getting the foundation up. The foundation was done by the time the machine arrived, and at the same time that the machine came into the works they had another car sent in, with rigging materials, tackle, etc., for unloading it. They again pinched their car with rigging materials and their car with their machine into the exhibit opposite their space, and unloaded their 20-ton machine, with the help of one or two other laborers and exhibitors whom they were able to get with them. They placed the machine on its foundation, put up their counter shaft, and had it running before many of the machines which were in the Exhibition before they had started from America.

These young men, who did not speak a word of French, and who were not college educated, fully justified their choice. I received a letter a few days ago from one of them, stating that he had just finished building a works which had cost $600,000, which he had completed in a year and a quarter, and that he was about to begin another works of the same kind which he hoped would be done in eight months. The other of the two young men is at the head of a very successful selling force.

Now, as an illustration of what plain, every-day persistence will do, many years ago, when I was foreman of a machine shop, there was a young man at the head of one of the rather unimportant departments who had been dropped from Annapolis. He didn't have brains and scholarship enough to keep up with his class. My chief business at the head of this department was that of making repairs, and keeping the place running, and all of the heads of the other departments came to me one after another with their breakdowns. They were all in a hurry, and I had to use my best judgment in deciding which repair was of the greatest importance. This young Annapolis failure came into my office one day and explained that he had to have a certain repair made right away. "Well, I'm sorry, but I can't do it. There are a lot of things that are ahead of you."

"Well, what are they?"

"Oh, I haven't time to go all over it, I'm too busy."

He said, "Won't you tell me what other repairs are ahead of mine?"

"No, I haven't time. I'll make your repair as soon as I have a chance."

"Well, what machine are you going to put my broken piece on to repair it?"

"On to the slotter."

"Well, what work is ahead of that slotter?"

"Oh, I can't tell you, I have too many other things on hand."

So my friend went out of my office, walked all of the way across the works, about a quarter of a mile, to the central office, found the superintendent of the company and placed before him a piece of paper for his signature, which read:

"Mr. Taylor. Please tell Mr._______ what pieces of work will go in the slotter in advance of his breakdown. I am desirous of having Mr. _____'s work done as soon as possible."

He walked all the way back again to my office and gave me that piece of paper. I, of course, wrote at once the names of the parts which were ahead of his. He again walked back to the central office and again returned to my office, with a second paper, reading:

"Mr. Taylor. Please do work on the slotter in the following order," stating exactly the time which his work came on. He practiced this same scheme on me enough times for me to find that it paid better to drop all work when he came in the office and answer his questions, rather than to waste time in finally having to write the whole thing out.

Now this quality of persistence certainly is not a very brilliant one, and surely requires comparatively little brains, and yet it was just that quality which has placed this young man at the head of a works employing some 5,000 men.

Brilliant suggestions as to new, great and revolutionary changes and improvements are the last things that your employer wants. He has enough of these at all times to last him for years. He is not looking for some one to tell him what to do. He is looking for some one to carry out the plain, simple, every-day, much needed improvements which are always in sight.

Let me give you an illustration of the fact that one simple idea is enough to last a successful man a life-time. During the Centennial Exhibition, held in Philadelphia in 1876, I left my apprenticeship to take charge of a lot of New England machines that were exhibited. One day an old gentleman came into my exhibit, and I saw at once by the questions which he asked that he was a fine mechanic. I took every pains to explain our machines and tried to sell him some. After a while he sat down and asked me to sit alongside of him. He said:

"What is your idea for success in life?"

I said I didn't know, that I had no particular idea.

"Why," he said, "you must have something that you are working for."

I said: "Yes, sir, I am working to get to be a machinist and earn $2.50 a day."

"Oh, no," he said, "I don't mean that. When I was your age and before I was out of my apprenticeship, I had made up my mind just what I was going to do. I decided that I was going to learn how to do work just a little more accurately than any of the other apprentices around me, and when I had succeeded in doing this, then I decided that I would learn to do it still more accurately than I had done before. Throughout my whole life that has been my one idea. I have never cared so much about the rapidity of the work--although I worked about as fast as other people--but I have always been determined to do a little better work than anyone else around. That is what I am still aiming at today--to do better work next year than I am doing this year." He said, "I suppose you know who I am?"

"No."

"I am 'Old Man Sharpe,' at the head of the Brown & Sharpe Company of Providence, R. I."

Now this simple idea has been enough to build up and keep through two generations the great Brown and Sharpe Company at the head of all the companies in this country who are doing accurate work, and probably no finer work, on the whole, is done in any company throughout the world.

Remember that the kind of engineering that is most wanted is that which saves money; that your employer is first of all in business to make money, not to do great and brilliant things, and he wants you to help him in making money, rather than in doing great and brilliant things.

In a large establishment which had enlarged very rapidly, but without a plan which was originally carefully laid out, it became a matter of the greatest difficulty to lay out tracks which were capable of taking care of the traffic, incoming and outgoing, and also between the various departments. The problem of locating these tracks was given in succession to the three best engineers in the establishment, men who were finely educated and experienced engineers. Now laying out tracks is a distinctly monotonous and uninteresting piece of work, with no glory in it whatever, and whether each of these men did their best or not, at any rate they one after another gave up the problem, and said that the buildings were so located that it was practically impossible to make a proper lay-out of the tracks.

In the drafting room was a young man who had merely an ordinary school education, in fact, very little of that even, who was working making cheap drawings, tracings, etc. He saw these men try the problem one after another and give it up, and after they were through he applied to the superintendent for permission to tackle the track problem. The superintendent said, "Why certainly, my boy, go right ahead. Do what you can." In about three months this young man had laid out the tracks so as to solve the traction problem in a complete and satisfactory way. And this is the incident that started a man on his upward career who I am sure you would all recognize as certainly the combined engineer and machinist who has made the largest pecuniary success of anyone in this country.

In another establishment it became necessary to add a number of additional furnaces to the melting department. The flues leading to the chimney of this department were so located that it was very difficult to build a new chimney which should have sufficient capacity to run the old plus the new furnaces without tearing down the old chimney and locating the new one in its place. This would necessarily involve a loss of at least one or two months in time. It appeared to be impossible to add to the height of the present chimney, because, years before, its foundation had sunk unevenly, and the chimney was leaning over so far to one side that its centre of gravity was barely within its base.

There was one young engineer, however, who realizing the seriousness of a stoppage of two months, proposed to build another chimney, on top of the first one, leaning back in the other direction, thus bringing the centre of gravity of the new chimney raised to twice its height back over the centre of the foundation. He carried out this work without even stopping the furnaces for a day. He raised a false sheet iron chimney above where the workmen were building all the time, so that they could build the new chimney with the smoke continually coming out of the top of the old one.

Now, neither laying out tracks nor adding to the top of an old chimney are very brilliant or original feats of engineering, and yet they marked the important events which led to the success of two great engineers.

There is one rock upon which many a bright and ingenious man has stranded, and perhaps the greatest temptation to the engineer who loves his profession is that of indulging his inventive faculty. Many of our brightest men practically spend their lives in worrying over the great improvements and inventions which they have in their minds, and they squander all of their own and their friends' money in trying to make them successful in a moneyed way after they have been perfected. Now for the average man no invention can be looked upon as a legitimate invention which is not an improvement on mechanism or processes or appliances which are already in existence, and which are successful. It is thoroughly illegitimate for the average man to start out to make a radically new machine, or method, or process, new from the bottom up, to do things which have already been done in the past. Legitimate invention should always be preceded by a complete study of the field to see what other people have already done. Then some one or more defects should be clearly recognized and analyzed, and it is entirely legitimate for an engineer to use his ingenuity and his inventive faculty in remedying these defects, and in adding his remedy to the existing elements of the machine or the process which have already been found to work well. Any other invention than this should be looked upon as illegitimate, since it is almost sure to waste the money of your employer, as well as your own, and to result in partial, if not complete, disaster. Throughout the manufacturing world there exists a proper and legitimate suspicion and dislike for the man who is forever coming forward with new and radical improvements and inventions. Let me give you one illustration of legitimate invention.

There was a machine, a large number of which were in common use, and of which there were many designs and types used all over the world. This machine was of such a nature that it battered itself to pieces. Almost all of its parts broke. There was a young engineer who had many of these machines to use in his manufacturing department, and who decided to try to build a machine that would not batter itself to pieces. He spent one or two years in collecting, from all over the world, data about the various machines that had been designed, until he found instances in which some one of the parts of each of the various machines of different designs had never broken. He then copied the design of each of the parts which had not broken, collecting one element from one machine, another from another, another from a third, etc. There was, however, one portion of the machine of which he could find no single instance of a design which had not, at some time or other, broken. He devoted his special energy and ingenuity to the study of this element, and finally evolved what he believed to be a principle which would prevent it from breaking. He then constructed a machine containing all of the parts already existing which had not broken, plus the one of his own design, and patent, which he believed would not break, and as a result obtained a machine which lasted for many years without a single break-down--the first instance of its kind in the history of that art. And this furnishes an illustration of what may be called thoroughly legitimate invention.

Don't kick, certainly don't kick unless you are sure of accomplishing your result. Your kick, in perhaps nine cases out of ten, will result merely in aggravating your employer, whether it is just or unjust, and your common-sense should tell you that it is foolish to aggravate him unless some good is to come of it.

William Sellers ranked undoubtedly in his time as the most noted engineer in this country. It was my good fortune to work under him for several years. During this time I was badly treated by one of the superintendents who was over me. I stood it for a long time, and then decided to go to Mr. Sellers about it. He listened and agreed with what I told him, and then turned to me, almost laughing, and said, "Do you know that all of this impresses me with the fact that you are still a very young man? Long before you reach my age you will have found that you have to eat a bushel of dirt, and you will go right ahead and eat your dirt until it really seriously interferes with your digestion."

Does all of this sound humdrum and commonplace? Yes, it does, but remember that I have been trying to point out the implements and methods which are to be used in obtaining success, and that implements and methods are almost always commonplace. But back of this each engineer should have, at all times, the hope, the ambition, the determination, to do great things; to do things which shall leave the world the better for his having lived in it; to do things which shall bring him into the front rank of his profession; and then to take at least one or two forward steps in his chosen line of work. It is the pleasure, the joy and the delight in doing this, more than anything else, that leads us to become engineers and that keeps us cheerfully at work, in spite of repeated disappointments.

In your desire to do great things, however, do not try for the impossible. Let your common-sense guide and control your ambition. Don't try for perpetual motion; don't look for a diamond mine in the coal fields of Indiana; don't make a machine to fly to the moon; but keep your eyes wide open all the time to see and clearly recognize defects in the machines, apparatus and methods that are immediately around you, and in the line of your regular duties; in those machines and processes which you understand best, not in someone's else field that you don't understand.

Next, clearly define this defect and if possible describe it in words. Then use your ingenuity to find the simplest possible remedy for it.

And lastly, your common-sense to see how, under existing conditions, the remedy can be applied with profit to your employer.

And if conditions prevent your doing it this year, then do it next year; and if not next year, then five years from now. Have patience and grit, and don't give it up.

Now, as I here have laid so much stress on common-sense and character as factors in success, it may well be asked where education comes in. I will tell you.

Young college men who work in any first-class establishment soon find that many of the workmen who cannot talk grammatically, men who chew tobacco, slouch along the street with greasy overalls on, who hardly look up, who are scarcely willing to speak to you politely as you pass them, are intellectually as clear as they are. That is what a young college man can learn through one year's work in a shop.

I remember very distinctly the perfectly astonishing awakening at the end of six months of my apprenticeship, when I discovered that the three other men who were with me in the pattern shop were all smarter than I was. Now when a young man gets it clearly in his head that he is made of the same kind of clay, physically as well as mentally, as these other men, then he finds that his only hope of outstripping them in the race lies in getting a better education--in _knowing_ more than they do.

But your knowledge will avail you nothing without energy, grit, pluck, determination, ability to stick to it, character.

Of all the habits and principles which make for success in a young man, the most useful is the determination to do and to do right all those things which come his way each day, whether they are agreeable or disagreeable; and the ability to do this is best acquired through long practice in doggedly doing, along with that which is agreeable, a lot of things which are tiresome and monotonous, going out of your way, if necessary, to find them.

---

[1]_Bulletin of the Taylor Society_, April, 1926. This lecture was prepared by Mr. Taylor for presentation to the students of the College of Engineering of the University of Illinois in Urbana, February 18, 1909, though delivered first to students of the College of Engineering of the University of Cincinnati on his way to Illinois. Later it was presented at various other engineering schools. It has never before been published in a form available for general reference, although numerous excerpts may be found in Copley's "Frederick W. Taylor."

PART THREE

SCIENTIFIC MANAGEMENT--EXPLANATIONS AND EVALUATIONS OF THE MOVEMENT

The selections in this part are being presented in chronological order of their appearance in the Bulletins as an aid in seeing the historical picture of the scientific management movement unfold.

Horace Drury's "Scientific Management and Progress" is a thumb nail historical sketch of the conditions leading up to the beginnings of the scientific management movement in the 1880's. The growing importance of industry as a source of employment, the great immigrations from Europe, the disappearance of the frontier, the development of organized labor are discussed in relation to their effects on the role of management. Of special historical interest and importance is Drury's criticisms regarding scientific management as well as his defense of the movement against its critics. He concludes his discussion with some most timely observations as to the necessary changes in scientific management if it is to remain viable. Among his recommendations is that employers must think of the employee of tomorrow as being cultured, possessing intellectual power and initiative, and being brought up in the exercise of freedom and judgment rather than being the dumb ox of Taylor's pig iron handlers. Lastly the time of individual self expression in industry is seen, by the author, as being just around the corner.

The second article, "Positive Contributions of Scientific Management" by Henry Farquhar succinctly puts forth the many contributions of scientific management so familiar to the production manager and the industrial engineer. Topics of discussion include the employement of equipment, labor, material control and routing. Other topics discussed include quality control, customer service, the human factor in industry industrial peace, working conditions, training, individual initiative, labor turnover, and "a spirit of cooperation and confidence, and a feeling of security." These later topics include many observations that should help quell the fires of rightness indignation from the human relationist concerning scientific management's mechanistic philosophy. Note the date--October 1919.

The article "On the Contribution of Scientific Management to Industrial Problems" by H. S. Person, first published in Brotherhood of Locomotive Engineer's Journal beginning with a philosophical note that the time has not come for a definite statement regarding the contribution of scientific management nor may it ever come for the industrial problems are continuously changing and with each change scientific management has something new to contribute. Interestingly a contemporary discussion of what is now referred to as the systems concept is put forth with the interweaving of the "mechanism of scientific management and industrial relations." The author notes that the major contribution of scientific management at this time (1923) is to the solution of the problem of industrial relations. Hopefully but wrong is the writer's closing prediction that "the day is not far distant when organized labor will be the principle proponent of scientific management."

Henry Kendall's article "A Decade's Development in Management" covers much of the ground noted by Person. It treatment of the industrial relations problem is much more detailed in that he outlines what to him is the basis of sound industrial relations. Among the topics included are the need for employment stability, adequate wages, employee voice in management and the opportunity of the worker to advance. Another section of the article deals with the topic of scientific management and selling. The discussion of the topic includes the need for a scientific study of the product and the market, the need for a sales budget, and a scientific approach to advertising. The regular demise of companies due in part to poor marketing policies should be sufficient to recommend the article for its elementary treatment of some of the basics.

A second article by Henry Farquhar, "A Critical Analysis of Scientific Management" starts with an historical survey of some of the contributions of scientific management. This introduction is followed by a systematic critique of the movement and its contributions. This critique is organized under such topics as: neglected opportunities, labor, inadequate analysis, and the failure to get the message accepted. Among his list of suggested problem areas which should occupy the attention of managers in the future are, production, distribution, finance and general administration. The article is the essence of constructiveness in that it indicates the accomplishments of the movement, compares these accomplishments with an idealized standard noting the major short comings, suggests areas of improvements and ends with an acknowledged need for managerial soul searching and their cooperation with organized labor if the movement is to be successful.

The sixth article by Irving Fisher "Scientific Management Made Clear" is included as a capsulized historical essay on the scientific management movement. Like the preceding article by Farquhar it is both a survey of history and a critique. The historical notes, many of which are by now familiar to the reader, are more detailed and numerous than those provided in the previous article. In his essay Fisher provides numerous short quotes from Copley's biography of Taylor to support his theme as to what scientific management is.

An interesting tabulation of the chronological development of scientific management up to 1931 is set forth in a second article by H. S. Person, then managing director of the Taylor Society. The paper is an excerpt of a much larger paper the author presented at the World Social Economic Congress held in August of 1931.

The last article selected for inclusion in Part III is by Sanford Thompson, then President of the Taylor Society, entitled "The Influence of Scientific Management." The essay based on questionnaires sent to five hundred American firms sought to determine the extent to which scientific management was then being employed by American firms. A strikingly contemporary observation concludes the writer's article--"Finally, it must be recognized that it is a national duty to provide at least a subsistence wage to all who desire it. This is a social responsibility which must be solved by the scientific method." Althoug the times (1932) were those of economic depression the recognition of a social responsibility of that magnitude seems more a product of an economy of affluence than one of depression it does provide an historical note regarding the evolution of the social obligations that must be faced by an integrated, interdependent social/economic order.

SCIENTIFIC MANAGEMENT AND PROGRESS[1]

A Discussion of How Far Scientific Management is Coping With Present Day Industrial Problems and What is the Outlook for the Future

By Horace B. Drury

The object of this paper is to explain what scientific management is; to note in what respects and how admirably it has fitted in with the industrial movements of the past thirty-five years; and then to search for any adjustments which the system may be asked to make if it is to be in full accord with the world of tomorrow. The scientific management which we are to consider this morning originated in the eighties. It was the answer, however, to industrial conditions which began to take definite shape soon after the close of our Civil War. The million soldiers who had been engaged on the northern side in that great struggle were, after their release, a great factor in peopling the agricultural west, and swelling the labor force of a manufacturing east. More important, five millions of immigrants flocked to the United States during the two decades 1860 to 1880, and another five millions in the single decade 1880-1890. This occupation of our public domain closed the frontier safety valve for turbulent or ambitious spirits, and brought the east, for the first time in its history, face to face with a serious labor problem.

The manufacturing industries into which the nation's surplus energy then turned had, before the middle of the century, been scarcely a promise. But by 1870, the number of wage earners had already increased from less than one million to more than two millions. By 1890, the new army had reached a total of four and a quarter millions; while the capital invested had grown from scarcely more than a half billion in 1850 to six and one-half billions in 1890. That is, less than one-twelfth of the capital invested in manufactures in 1890 had originated earlier than 1850. The two periods of great gain were the Civil War decade, and, more especially, the eighties. From 1880 to 1890, the number of wage earners in this country increased by one and a half millions, a growth twice as great as in any preceding decade, and fifty per cent greater than that which was to mark the nineties. The gain in capital during the eighties was three and three quarters billion dollars, or more than three times as great as in any preceding decade, and greater by about half a billion than the advance that was to be made between 1890 and 1900.

Even more phenomenal and significant than the expansion of manufacturing was that revolution in method known as the introduction of large scale production. Government reports and general opinion unite in placing the date for this transformation at about 1880. In the iron and steel industry the movement was well under way in the seventies, but in a greater number of industries the apex was reached in the eighties.

Neither before nor after this period was there anything like as rapid a swing towards concentration, perhaps not even after 1900. It is remembered that the first trusts were also formed at this time, the Standard Oil Trust in 1879, and the first sugar and whisky trusts in 1887. In short, for the first time in American history it had now become common for large numbers of workmen to be employed under one management.

Another aspect of industry, significant in its bearings upon the origin of scientific management, was the new foreign element employed in the shops. The year 1882 was to mark the flood tide of a great wave of immigration, the 789,000 who came in that year setting a record which had never before been rivaled, and which was not again to be equaled for twenty years. Very nearly one-third of all the persons engaged in manufacturing, mechanical, and mining pursuits were already in 1880 natives of foreign countries, with the greatest immigration yet to come. The foreigners were mostly unskilled laborers, occupying the lower places in the industrial scheme, and that rapid shift in the source of immigration from northwestern to southeastern Europe, later to be so noticeable, had already begun.

It is seen, in short, that by 1880 or shortly after, most of the industrial problems of our time were on hand, and in that initial period when they were the most likely to do mischief, and to excite alarm. The rapid elimination of the frontier, which was to be practically complete before the end of the decade, was already beginning to confine ambitious workmen to subordinate positions in the east. The rapid increase in the size of many industrial plants was separating the employer from his employees. The foreign third of the workmen, many of them newly arrived immigrants, were not capable of ready cooperation with their employers, even had other conditions been favorable.

The resultant of these new forces was, on the one hand, the beginning of the modern labor movement. Prior to the Civil War, there had been in this country no union movement of other than transitory importance. Unions began to become influential in the latter part of the Civil War period, and, barring a few years of depression following the crisis of 1873, their membership steadily increased in numbers and influence. Especially after 1878 a period of growth set in, many of the unions finally merging themselves in the Knights of Labor, which by 1886 claimed 600,000 members. The first strikes of national importance which the country had ever had were the violent and widespread railroad strikes of 1877. During the eighties the losses arising from strikes increased rapidly, reaching a climax in 1886. The few years prior to 1886 constituted, indeed, the greatest strike period in our history. Since 1886, the number of strikes has not kept pace with the growth of population, much less with the growth of industry. But more important than the strikes of this period was the chronic disloyalty and inefficiency which marked the daily activity of thousands of workmen. The lack of contact and sympathy between employer and employee had weakened and perverted the entire industrial system. Limitation of output, soldiering, carelessness, these were the first fruits of the new large scale employment, and they constituted a problem which caused worry on all sides.

The other great development of the period, but one which was not to be at first so noticeable, was the creation of scientific management.

The system which now bears this name started as the personal reaction of the late Dr. Frederick Winslow Taylor to the above described labor spirit. Taylor was born of upper-class American stock five years before the outbreak of the Civil War. As a boy he had been educated in France, Germany, and Italy, and prepared to enter Harvard. Trouble with his eyes, however, prevented his continuance in college, and we find him during four years of his youth working out apprenticeships in a small Philadelphia shop as pattern maker and machinist. He entered one of the new large scale establishments, the Midvale Steel Company, as a laborer in 1878. From laborer he successively rose through the positions of clerk, journeyman machinist, gang boss, foreman, and chief draughtsman until he finally became chief engineer. It was when he became gang boss in 1880 that Taylor first determined to discover by scientific methods how long it should take each man to do each given piece of work; and it was in the fall of 1882, shortly after he had been elevated to the position of foreman, that he started to put the first features of scientific management into operation.

Before proceeding to an analysis of the principles of scientific management, let us first perfect our idea of Taylor by noting the other outstanding features of his life. In 1889, Taylor left the Midvale Steel Company in order to apply his ideas in a wider field. For three years he served a corporation operating large pulp mills in Maine, and then he attempted in various parts of the country a reorganization of industrial plants. This involved a variety of manufacturing, structural, and engineering work. His most celebrated personal undertakings were in connection with the plant of the Bethlehem Steel Company between 1898 and 1901. By 1901, Taylor had acquired a fortune which enabled him to retire from work for pay.

Dr. Taylor took the degree of mechanical engineer from Stevens Institute of Technology in 1883. In 1906, he served as President of the American Society of Mechanical Engineers. Besides his writings on management, he contributed to this society several notable papers on mechanical subjects of which the greatest was his president's address in 1906 on "The Art of Cutting Metals." He took out about one hundred patents, his greatest invention being the discovery between 1898 and 1900, jointly with Mr. Maunsel White, of the Taylor-White high-speed steel. He was honored by the University of Pennsylvania with the degree of Doctor of Science in 1906, and was claimed as a friend by some of the highest officers of the navy, and by prominent engineers, manufacturers, and public men. Dr. Taylor died March 21, 1915.

To return now to the youthful Taylor of 1880, and his beginnings of scientific management. Taylor's observation had been that his neighbors in the Midvale shops failed to produce more than about one-third of a good day's work. Wages were on a piece-work basis, and the men were afraid to let the management guess how large a product they could really turn out because it might mean a cut. This tendency on the part of the workmen had resulted in a war between Taylor, the gang-boss, who was trying to induce the men to work faster, and the workmen under him, who were determined that by fair means or foul they would avoid working faster. As a result of this struggle, life to Taylor had become hardly worth living. Accordingly, shortly after he was given the greater authority of foreman, he determined to work out some system of management by which the interests of the workmen and of the management would be made the same.

The basic principle of the scientific management which he evolved is that the management shall determine very carefully just how much work a man ought to do, and on the other hand, that the man should then be offered a premium sufficient to induce him to perform the task. From this simple idea all of scientific management has grown, and to this idea most of it may still be reduced. The classic illustration of the scientific determination of the task was Taylor's twenty-six year study in the field of cutting metals. The regular method is to make a study of every element entering into a job; and then add together the times which it takes to perform the necessary elements, to find the time required to perform the entire job. A margin of safety is ordinarily left, to cover delays. The stop watch is the instrument ordinarily used in making the time studies.

The methods by which men are induced to perform the task are Taylor's differential rate--and, among later developments, Gantt's task and bonus system, and other special bonus or premium systems. The amount of reward to the workmen varies considerably, but most often amounts to twenty or thirty per cent higher wages than they have been accustomed to earn. Such a reward is usually sufficient to induce workmen to attain the tasks laid out for them, and the tasks can often be so set as to increase production one hundred per cent or more.

It is not to be supposed, however, that scientific management is based upon the overspeeding of workmen. The goal is reached largely through a more perfect utilization of machinery and tools, the elimination of actual idleness or wasted motions on the part of the men, the withdrawal from a job of operations that can more fittingly be performed some place else, and only to a very limited extent by means of speeding up. It is primarily the interest, the loyalty, the obedience of workmen that scientific management strives for; and for this obedience the management does not hesitate to pay a substantial price.

This method of inducing workmen to do their best constitutes historically, the most fundamental and essential aspect of scientific management. It is, however, by no means, the system's only feature. It was very early discovered that in order to set tasks properly the management had to learn a great deal about the work, and, when it knew a great deal about the work, it could commonly introduce improved methods of performing it. So planning rooms developed, motion studies were made, instruction cards drawn up, employees trained, tools and equipment standardized at high quality. Much of the increased output under scientific management springs from the methodical and exact way in which these features have been worked out. This second story of scientific management is today almost as important as the first.

A third notable characteristic of scientific management is what is known as functional foremanship. In order that the management might discharge creditably its greatly increased responsibility, it became necessary not only to increase its numerical strength, but to split up the duties of management among as many as eight different authorities. These are given such names as gang boss, speed boss, inspector, repair boss, order of work or route clerk, instruction card clerk, time and cost clerk, and shop disciplinarian.

A capacity in scientific management and its leaders to expand Taylor's original program and adjust itself to the needs of industry appeared very early. As the system was first thought out and practiced by Dr. Taylor it had a certain inflexibility amounting almost to impracticability. And especially was this true of the methods which he used in pushing the system. It is no secret that Dr. Taylor was not himself very much of a manager. Persistence and genius he had without end. But he was not an adept at judging men, or tactful or conciliatory in his method of approach. Even for his friends he was a hard task-master, and his entrance into a new plant would stir things up from the bottom. He insisted, too, that reorganization be thoroughgoing and complete, according to what often seemed a preconceived notion.

These characteristics were partly due, doubtless, to the fact that Dr. Taylor himself had comparatively little experience with the introduction of his own system. Besides his deep interest in scientific management, Taylor gave a considerable portion of his time to other matters. He was an inventor of no mean ability, and took much pains with scientific investigations, as, for instance, that into the cutting of metals. Taylor did not work what most men would regard as a full day, but came late and went home early. And finally, he retired from active service in 1901, at the age of forty-five, fourteen years before his death, and scarcely twenty years after getting started seriously in work. No wonder that he did not accomplish everything, and that much was left to be developed by others.

Among the first friends of Taylor to improve upon his methods was Henry L. Gantt. Gantt is what Taylor never was--a skillful manager. He has carried through such undertakings as the reorganization of the Remington Typewriter Company, the concern which makes Remington, Monarch, and Smith-Premier typewriters, and many other concerns almost equally large and well-known. Gantt gets along well with the people whom he has to manage, bends his course to suit the exigencies of a situation, and aims at important practical savings. He regards every factory as a law unto itself. His scientific management is not one mould, which all factory organizations must be warped to fit; but, as he sees it, there are as many distinct scientific managements as there are different shops. Gantt's work, however, is only one illustration of what has been done to a greater or less degree by all the close friends and followers of Taylor. Scientific management is the joint product of many minds, working under the inspiration of a dominant personality.

The results obtained under scientific management have been such as to attract the attention of a wide public, and to win support in many and important quarters. As before indicated, it seems probable that on many kinds of work, the increased output of employees runs well up to one hundred per cent; while there are instances of increases of two hundred per cent and more. In other instances, of course, the gains are much more moderate. The prestige of the system among engineers and with the public has been heightened by the support of men like Henry R. Towne, James M. Dodge, and Frederick W. Taylor, all past presidents of the American Society of Mechanical Engineers, and Louis D. Brandeis, Justice of the Supreme Court; and by the space given to discussions of the system in leading technical and popular journals and in the writings of leading thinkers. Its standing in the manufacturing world has been assured by its adoption in such representative plants as that of the Pullman Company, the Yale & Towne Manufacturing Company, the Union Typewriter Company, the Remington Arms Company, the Government arsenals, and, in the old days, the Bethlehem Steel Company and the Santa Fe Railway. Some tens of thousands of workmen are already working under it in a fairly complete form; while it is safe to say that the influence of the system has spread in one way or another into almost all the industrial plants of the country.

In spite of this rapid growth in favor, there nevertheless remain some very powerful and persistent antagonists. When Charles M. Schwab obtained control of the Bethlehem Steel Company in 1901, this company's position as a center of scientific management activity, which up to that had been without a parallel, was promptly destroyed. While much of the system was in fact retained, all allegiance to it was emphatically disowned. It is not surprising that in this and numerous other places scientific management has met with opposition on the part of employers. The idea of one man does not take precedence over the ideas of a thousand other men without meeting constant challenge, especially when it is the province of the other thousand to decide the issue.

The only opposition which may be regarded as really serious, however, is the opposition of organized labor. The reports of the American Federation of Labor show that their first period of rapid growth occurred following 1898 and prior to 1904. In these years the membership of the Federation leaped by one great bound from 275,000 in 1898 to 1,675,000 in 1904. But following 1904, for a period of five years the Federation lost ground, so that in 1909 the membership was about one-eighth less than it had been in 1904. This check seems to have been imposed partly by a hostile attitude assumed by the courts, but more especially by a policy of antagonism on the part of great corporations and powerful employers' associations. Professor Commons, writing in 1908, declared that "the unions have practically disappeared from the trusts, and are disappearing from the large corporations as they grow large enough to specialize minutely their labor." Naturally the unions began to give their attention to the matter of the obstructive forces, and to form plans for defending themselves. In the words of Professor Carlton, writing in 1910-11, "bitter opposition and adverse judicial decisions may force even conservative unions to adopt other methods and policies than those utilized during the last two or three decades."

It was just at this juncture that for the first time a blaze of publicity was thrown around scientific management. In the fall of 1910 and the spring of 1911, the now Justice Brandeis conducted before the Interstate Commerce Commission his famous defence of the eastern shippers against a proposed advance of railroad rates. Brandeis' main argument was that the railroads would not need to increase rates if they would introduce scientific management. In a few weeks, the entire country was inquiring as to what this scientific management was, and organized labor was confronted by the necessity of taking a stand with reference to the new development.

The labor leaders very quickly and very properly decided that the growth of scientific management presented a danger to their organization. The main reason why we have labor unions as at present organized is because of the existence of laboring classes, whose manner of life, education, and interests are enough at variance with those of the employing classes, so that the former crave a special protection. Were there no sharp divergence of interest or sympathy, it would not be necessary to build up class solidarity, to insist on organized action, or to extend systematic aid and protection to the otherwise isolated worker.

It was, however, a postulate laid down by Dr. Taylor that there is no natural clash between employer and employee. Both, he would say, are interested primarily in greater production. Taylor believed that he had devised a system that would substitute a scientific for a contentious division of the product. Employers should not be organized in employers' associations and workmen in labor organizations for the purpose of battle. But all should be partners, work in harmony, and settle their relationships according to scientific truth. Recognizing no divergence of interest, Taylor, therefore, would have the management itself look out for the laboring man.

To Taylor and his followers, moreover, the spirit of the unions seemed unfavorable to industrial progress. Taylor was interested in greater production, in introducing better methods, in progress; whereas the union membership is made up largely of that middle class of people who are conservative, suspicious of change, and somewhat hard to reason with. In particular, the workingman has been suspicious of the introduction of machinery, of increases in output, of speeding up. Partly unjust, these suspicions have been; but they were a big factor in preventing Taylor and the unions from working as partners in a common cause.

The outcome in scientific management plants of this unfavorable sentiment towards trade unions has been that the latter have almost invariably had the worst of it. Taylor testified before the Industrial Relations Commission in 1914 that members of labor unions had left in large numbers at Midvale, Bethlehem, Tabor Link-Belt, and to a certain extent in every company where he had ever been. It is easy to see why unions could not put up much of a fight in shops operating under such a system. In so far as it centralizes skill, scientific management takes from the workmen that bond of common craft knowledge, which tends to make brothers of the men engaged in a trade. Since it pays on an individual or efficiency basis, and promotes the more able men to fill positions as functional foremen, scientific management appeals to personal ambition, rather than to class solidarity, and makes less sharp the line of cleavage between management and men. As it voluntarily pays higher wages than the men could win through force, scientific management weakens the main motive for organization, and makes the employees hesitate to compromise themselves with their employers. In short, scientific management did not need to lay itself out to any noticeable extent in order practically to rid itself of trade union connection.

Scientific management was not extensive enough in 1904-1909 to have been any important factor in the temporary checking of trade unionism which then occured. Its spirit, however, was one with the spirit of the great corporations which were making themselves independent of unions. Its spirit was the very essence of centralized power, of managerial self-sufficiency, of workingman subordination. Against its winning persuasiveness the outside labor union could hurl itself in vain.

It was not to the workingman, however, that organized labor was to make its appeal. A million or two men are not sufficient to control the industrial world. But a million or two voters are not to be neglected. It was in the political arena, therefore, that organized labor was to show its greatest strength; and it was to Congress that labor went for aid in its contention with scientific management.

Congress happened to have a very direct concern in scientific management, inasmuch as the system was being introduced in the government arsenals, and was later to be proposed for other departments,--as the post office. On its floors, therefore, ever since 1911, bills and resolutions in great number have been introduced calling for investigations or prohibiting the continuance of the system. In particular, riders attached funds for the making of time studies or the payment of bonuses.

The first victory for labor was won in March, 1915, when the House forced the Senate's unwilling consent to provisions in both the army and navy appropriation bills forbidding the use of funds for either of the purposes just mentioned. The shaft failed to hit the mark, though, as it developed that the condemned devices were financed through the fortifications appropriation, and not through the army or navy appropriations. In the 1915-16 session of Congress the fight was therefore taken up again with renewed vigor, and riders withholding funds for time studies and bonuses were attached to the fortifications, army, navy, post office, and sundry civil appropriation bills. All these measures went into operation last July, and had the important effect of suspending bonus payments at the Watertown arsenal, the one point where the Government had extensively introduced scientific management, and also preventing, for the year at least, the installation of scientific management in the other branches of the federal service covered by the bills. A yet more substantial victory, however, is the goal of labor. The Tavenner Bill, introduced and fought over last session, and on the calendar for consideration next session, would permanently forbid by statute the use of time-measuring devices on, or the payment of bonuses to, any employee of the United States Government, declaring any such act a misdemeanor punishable by fine or imprisonment. The Van Dyke Bill, which now rests in the hands of the Committee on Post Offices and Post Roads, contains similar provisions, but applies to the post office only.

Such tactics on the part of the labor men, and the response being made by Congress, seem to be, and, we believe, are, both unjust and a menace to the future progress of the country. Yet it is not hard to see how the situation arose; nor is it impossible to find weaknesses in scientific management itself which invited such attack. It is true that the arguments presented to Congress were pitifully weak. The two counts against scientific management are first that it involves overwork; and second, that to have one's motions timed by a stop watch is degrading. But neither government commission nor critical private investigator has been able to unearth any extended instances of overwork. Even so watchful a critic as the late Professor Hoxie testified that he had "a strong impression that scientific management workers, in general, are not overspeeded." And as for the stop watch, the real objection, surely, cannot be to the thing itself; but only to some peril that it is felt will grow out of it. But what this peril is, is usually not very clearly indicated.

Yet underneath these surface arguments, there exists a real clash involving fundamental principles. We are called to witness a struggle, which it would be folly to try to evade, and which is bound to continue until both scientific management itself, and the general character of our national life will have been profoundly affected. Taylor himself never regarded scientific management as perfect or complete. We may, therefore, without prejudice to him, or his work, inquire into those aspects of his system which are at the real root of the present controversy, and which the world of tomorrow probably will not accept, save in modified form.

In the first place, and of most importance, the confidence which the system places in the unselfishness and public spirit of the management is excessive. Not that managements may not, and have not, in notable instances, possessed great virtue. But there is no reason to suppose that those particular organizations known as industrial corporations can be made so universally and fundamentally superior to city councils, labor unions, churches, chambers of commerce, etc., that they alone of all organizations should be allowed to go their way unchecked, unwatched, possessing the complete and unchallenged confidence of the public, of labor, of the government. Taylor was eminently right in urging managements to assume this high character; and one of the most hopeful signs of the time is the noble way in which they have responded. But should not the pre-eminence which any management enjoys in this respect rest upon the voluntary recognition of its achievements and character, rather than upon a pious insistence that organizations of employees or of outsiders must refrain from passing an opinion upon matters so out of their sphere? That would not be a popular attitude if assumed by the president of the United States. Even a bank cashier, though selected for his integrity, does not refuse to have his accounts examined.

In the second place, the principle of Dr. Taylor that the management should acquire and sum up in itself _all_ the skill and science required in industry is an ideal that is likely to fall increasingly short of realization. In no shop has scientific management yet succeeded in placing _all_ of the work on the task basis, though sometimes this end is fairly closely approached. Not even in the best and most widely praised shops is the time allowed for the work so scientifically correct, that the men take no thought of limiting their output a little on the easier jobs. Yet time study based on existing methods is the least serious of the tasks which scientific management has obligated itself to accomplish. How likely, then, is it that when it comes to devising entirely new methods of work, the small group of men in a shop known as the management will be able themselves to hit upon all of the best features. As industry increases in complexity, and as the laboring man grows in education and intelligence, we may be sure that a time will come when the laboring man will know more about many things than the management possibly can. Hence this system's vision of an industry animated almost altogether from the top may turn out to be considerably distorted.

In the third place, scientific management has relied too largely upon the daily wage as an all powerful link binding a man with ties of loyalty to his employer. Pay is undoubtedly the one most important relationship that needs careful treatment in order to insure the loyalty of employees. But it is by no means the only factor. Much of the best work of the world in science, in government, in art has been done for small pay. Even in business the British man of affairs is apt to be as much influenced by the hope of a peerage, as by that of large profits; the American financier as much by the love of playing the game as by the pleasure of disposing of the proceeds. It is to be hoped, therefore, that managers may acquire greater skill in analyzing human motives, and be able to control various additional forces that lead men to labor.

In the fourth place, scientific management has given only superficial attention to the important topic of fatigue.

There is a widespread impression that, in addition to what has already been noted, scientific management has been yet more careless in its estimate of the worth of workmen; that it has ignored much of their humanity, and consciously and inexcusably been indifferent to their welfare. There is much gross exaggeration in this. Dr. Taylor once declared: "The interest of every man who is in any way engaged in scientific management, in the introduction of the principles of scientific management, must be first the welfare of the working man. That must be the object. It is inconceivable that a man should devote his time and his life to this sort of thing for the sake of making more money for a whole lot of manufacturers." As far as Dr. Taylor's own actions were concerned, his life put the stamp of sincerity upon these words. And it is equally true of most of the other men active in introducing scientific management that they have been kindly and even magnanimously disposed towards labor.

Yet, as Mr. Robert G. Valentine has well said, many of the impressions which Taylor conveyed in describing his ideas did violence to his real spirit. He used to speak, for instance, of pig-iron handlers at Bethlehem as having the mentality of the ox; and designate whole classes of workmen as being analagous to the dray horse, or the grocery-wagon horse; while others were of the trotter class. Such language did Dr. Taylor and his cause immeasurable harm. Yet he had no thought of insult. In later life he would in like manner swear before classes at Harvard; though probably he had genuine respect both for the institution and the students. It was merely his picturesque and forceful mode of expression, schooled as he was in the ways of the shop.

Possibly, however, it should be put down as one of the weaknesses of scientific management that it takes workmen too much as they are, forgetting that a larger social program might conceivably make of them quite different and better men.

While we therefore believe that certain aspects of scientific management are not ideal, this is not to be regarded as an adverse criticism of Dr. Taylor, or his work. If only we recall the conditions under which scientific management was originated, we are compelled to forgive and even praise the course which Taylor followed.

Take workmen as Taylor knew them about 1880, and a paternalistic system was eminently fitting. Strangers in a new country, ignorant of its institutions, crude and stolid in intellectual development, they were not fit for self government. The employers of this time, moreover, had to fill a more responsible and independent position in the nation's industry than ever before or since. It was in the initial stages of a new and large-scale production, when resources were being exploited, new fields of manufacture opened up, foreign markets conquered. In such a period of transition and construction, the business enterpriser is the all important director of the country's activities. Even able employees have little higher responsibility. The great questions to be decided are whether an industry should be created, or perhaps discontinued; whether the people employed should be skilled or unskilled, or whether machinery should displace labor. On such matters the employees concerned cannot, of course, pass unbiassed judgment. What industry needed was a pliable working class, who would fit in readily with the shifting programs of capitalist and enterpriser. Lucky the workman who could secure a benevolent employer. And lucky the manufacturer who could secure humble, foreign workmen, unbound by tradition, and not self-assertive.

Likewise, when we remember Taylor's situation, we cannot blame him for refusing to allow much place for the initiative of workmen. Many of the workmen were of the class just described; and most of the balance lacked that specific training which might otherwise have made their cooperation of value. The graduates of the new engineering education were in the eighties but a thin leaven in a great world; while it was to be many years before the schools were to plan an industrial education for the masses. But even had they been trained, the workmen of Taylor's time were filled with a suspicion of efficiency that made them more interested in limiting output than in increasing it, in blocking the introduction of machinery and improved methods rather than in assisting in this work. These conditions, we believe, account for and excuse the rigid control, the too-sharp separation of planning from performing, and the insistence upon a rather blind obedience to directions which has characterized scientific management.

Again, the earlier relations which had prevailed between employers and employees may be cited as an explanation of Taylor's failure to develop any thoroughly socialized system of drawing out loyalty. Scientific management was started in order to displace a warfare which had developed between management and men. And in combatting and overcoming this warfare, the system necessarily took a part of its own character from it. The spirit of the men had so long been steeped in antagonism, that there was practically only one appeal that could be made to them. The central principle in the science of management therefore became the forging of a very tight and somewaht mechanical grip upon employees, through a skillful regulation of their pay. It is, however, to the great credit of Taylor and his associates that they progressively gave more and more attention to the spirit of the shop, and dwelt less heavily upon the earlier mechanical devices.

This justification, which we have just been making, of the attitude assumed by scientific management in times past, does not, however, affect our judgment that, in the future a more democratic control and a more widely diffused responsibility will have to prevail. Certain basic changes now taking place in our social and economic institutions will eventually render obsolete many practices once thought necessary.

The chief of these changes, and the one which will have the greatest import for scientific management, will be a transformation in the working population. Any group of people who presume to outline a program for the future which does not take into account the rise of an employee class quite different in character from that which formerly filled our shops will be making a grave mistake. The whole trend of our modern spirit is in the direction of a sharp uplift of the mass of mankind. Our original human nature is going to blossom into a very different kind of manhood and womanhood under the greater opportunities which are not being thrown open.

The accomplishment of such a transformation is the goal of the progressive political movement, which gave up its independent life only because it had won control of one, if not both, political parties. The elevation of the ordinary man is the program of the modern social movement,--which dominates the public schools, the churches, the universities, and the Y. M. C. A., and finds its expression throughout the literature of the time. It is this spirit which has borne fruit in the reform of taxation, in the fight against privilege, in the founding of all sorts of civic institutions, but first and pre-eminently in the expansion of popular education.

We must think of the employee of tomorrow, then, as the graduate of a technical or trade school, if not of a university. We must think of him as a man or woman of culture, of intellectual power, of initiative, a person nourished from youth in the exercise of freedom and judgment. Trained in science, and polished by a varied experience, he will be no more like Taylor's pig-iron handlers, or the typical workman of yesterday than vapor is like a solid or a liquid. In short, the human material with which the science of management purports to deal will have been changed. And when the subject matter of a science changes so must the science also.

In keeping with this new environment, we must therefore anticipate a new scientific management. It will have to be somewhat different, first of all, in method. The ideal of securing individual efficiency through restraint and command will have to give way, some time, before the more efficient program of opening the way for individual self-expression. Not that no one should lay out tasks for others; or that vast numbers of workers should not make their methods conform closely to one most efficient standard. An opera singer may fittingly follow the directions of her managers as to routes of travel and concert dates; a great engineer or builder may conform in detail to specifications drawn up by others. The point is that, while an individual does many things that others plan, he should have some things to plan himself. That is what a man is for. To neglect to utilize and develop the unique originating, choosing, and adapting power with which every individual is more or less endowed is to waste the earth's greatest resource for which the growing complexity of industry and the arts will ever make greater demands. Besides, to deprive men of the opportunity to create is inhuman, degrading, and destructive for the individual, the ruination of pleasure in work, of romance and achievement in life.

Scientific management will also have to clothe itself in a somewhat different spirit. That agelong impulse towards democracy that first humbled kings, and later liberated and enfranchised serfs, is still in full swing; and can stop short of nothing but complete social and individual emancipation. The storm that has risen around scientific management has largely grown out of a notion that the system was trying to block this movement. But we need not fear that such an interpretation of the system can be maintained. The age that rushes to give the vote to women on this side of the water, and hesitates in time of national peril to conscript labor on the other side will not tolerate any system of management which does not give praise to the man who works, thrust upon him respect and opportunity, give heed to his sentiments, acknowledge his fellowship, ask for his cooperation. Whatever smacks of any other feeling in scientific management is a product of the past, and like it will have to be left behind.

The fathers of our revolutionary period, it is worth while to remember, were not greatly injured by the policies of Great Britain. For years after the revolution they continued to buy mostly from England, and to use much the same trade routes as it had been the policy of the mother country to prescribe. Their burden of taxation was only increased by independence, their protection diminished. But the founders of our nation would not tolerate the shadow of subordination to Great Britain. It was the spirit rather than the acts of the imperical government which inflamed American opinion and led to the longest and most fateful struggle in our history. So let us take heed of the continuation of independent spirit among the masses, even the immigrant masses of today. Let us be thankful that the spirit of our country's past is not dead, and let us bend before it, work with it, utilize it. Not money alone, but self-respect, responsibility, partnership, is the birthright of American labor. Not only the reality of these things, but out and out, thoroughgoing recognition must be maintained.

Now these things have not been overlooked altogether by Dr. Taylor's associates. The most interesting development in the field of scientific management at present is the start that is being made in the direction of such Twentieth Century ideals. The recognition of the humanity of employees, of the importance of the social life of an industrial organization, is possibly nowhere more complete than in the Clothcraft Shops of the Joseph & Feiss Company, Cleveland. In a paper on "Personal Relationship as a Basis of Scientific Management," written by Richard A. Feiss, the manager, as well as in various descriptions of the Clothcraft Shops given by other persons, it would appear that we have here an unusual example of a socialized, industrial undertaking. Among the institutions of the factory are a choral club, with membership upwards of two hundred, a factory orchestra, and leagues for baseball, quoits, captain ball, and other sports. During the winter, the different divisions of the shops give parties, at which entertainment is furnished by the employees and their families. Members of the firm, as well as all others, attend these parties, and a democratic spirit prevails. On regular days dancing is a feature in the woman's recreation room, and there are dining rooms where every employee has his own seat.

One of the highest officials of the Joseph & Feiss Company is their Employment and Service Director. It is, among other things, the duty of this lady and her department to develop an organization spirit, and to facilitate among the employees the development of a democratic expression of personal and public opinion. The department itself comes in contact every day with about one-fifth of the Clothcraft employees; and all cases where direct conference with the management would be beneficial are immediately referred to it. The interest of the firm in its employees extends also to their families and their homes, as the Employment and Service Department has instituted the practice of home calls. One effect of these visits and of the company's careful medical advice has been the practical elimination of tuberculosis. A net effect of the entire social and individual program has been the development of an *esprit de corps* which has been remarked by all observers.

The road to advancement in these shops, moreover, is not only open to all employees, but every possible aid and encouragement is given. Practically all positions in the organization, both clerical and executive, are filled by those whose abilities have raised them from the ranks. The plant has reading rooms, and a branch of the city public library. Information is furnished employees concerning special classes in the schools. The management believes in encouraging to the utmost individual education and development.

The significant thing about the Clothcraft Shops, however, is not these things taken by themselves, but the fact that the shops are operated under scientific management, the features described being regarded not only as consistent with, but essential to, a thoroughgoing application of Taylor's principles.

Another plant widely regarded as characterized by an advanced spirit in the place accorded to the men, and also for many years in sympathy with the Taylor movement, is the German-American Button Company, of Rochester, headed by Mr. Henry T. Noyes. Mr. Noyes has a wide vision of the change in spirit that is taking place in industry, and regards the old way as a survival of feudalistic class distinctions. In particular, the distinction between office and factory is a relic of the old disdain with which a leisure class formerly regarded the laboring class. Conditions as to hours of work and treatment in the German-American Button Company are identical for office and factory. Even in ringing in and out on coming to and leaving work, officers, office, and factory have followed the same routine.

Mr. Noyes counts on his employees' taking part in the life of the business through regular department and other meetings. Practically all the foremen have risen from the ranks. None of these features are found to be inconsistent with the use of the stop watch. Nor has the latter device prevented the development of the most cordial relations between management and men. Even the Italians of the second generation are welcomed into the fellowship as full Americans.

These illustrations are advanced not because the shops described are necessarily superior to anything that might be reviewed outside of scientific management; but because the honor and attention which great numbers of the followers of Taylor are giving to this kind of thing shows in which direction the tide of scientific management is setting. We do not say that the spirit in these shops is perfect, or that they are an exact prototype of what will later be universal. On the contrary, we are very doubtful about some of their policies. But do they not in fact show that scientific management is striding towards a more humanized and socialized system, a real science of human relations?

The last point which we wish to make is the important one that, in spite of any elements in scientific management which the future may show to have been ephemeral, there is in the original spirit of Taylor, a principle or two that is valid not only for his time but for all time. The changes taking place and to take place in the outer aspects of scientific management have not and will not carry it away from these principles. They may be given as two in number: first, science in industry; and second, harmony in industrial relations.

The science at which Dr. Taylor so skillfully worked was, as he himself used to insist, never complete. With every change in social institutions, the human side of it will have to be recast; with every advance in invention and industrial technique, the mechanical side of it will tend to become obsolete. Yet the vision of a science in industry has taken possession of some dozen of the leaders of American industry, and by them is being passed on to numerous factories, until it is to be hoped that it will reach ultimately the humblest of American workingmen.

The harmony which Dr. Taylor tried to establish ignored several important forces, which his training had not permitted him to understand. His quest for harmony led through conflict, passion, and disappointment to death itself. Yet Taylor's vision will not be forgotten, nor will the effect of his effort be lost. In many factories the relations between employers and men have been ameliorated. And his ideal to consolidate and unify the conduct of American business will live.

Mr. George D. Babcock has defined scientific management as "that kind of management which conducts a business or affairs by standards established by facts or truths gained through systematic observation, experiment, or reasoning." Concretely put, this involves, first, the scientific laying out of tasks; second, a just system of rewards for those who successfully cooperate; third, the scientific study of methods; and fourth, the organization of all work according to a functionalized or specialized division of authority. The more one reflects over these principles, the more evident it becomes that the industry of the future will have to be built upon some such general basis.

It will be the task of human engineering to see that the standards set up under scientific management become increasingly more scientific, taking into account the real natures of both materials and men. It will be the task of public opinion to see that industry becomes progressively more vitalized and more democratic.

---

[1]*Bulletin of the Taylor Society*, November, 1916. An address given before the first Congress of Human Engineering, held under the auspices of the Ohio State University College of Engineering, October 6-8, 1916.

POSITIVE CONTRIBUTIONS OF SCIENTIFIC MANAGEMENT[1]

The Elimination of Some Losses Characteristic of Present-day Manufacture

By Henry H. Farquhar

I. Introduction

Today, when present and impending conditions are trying men's souls and forcing a weighing in the balance of their past achievements of so many directions, it seems appropriate and important to make at least a partial appraisement of the contributions of scientific management to the field of industrial problems. It may be well, however, at the start to look back briefly over the successive stages of its development in order to arrive more fairly at a true estimate of its present value, and to enable a correct forecast of its potential worth as a means for the adjustment of present and future social and economic problems.

As long as the early discussions and the evolution of the science were confined within the bounds of the American Society of Mechanical Engineers, the public knew little of what was taking place. This was as it should have been, for the early papers which stimulated discussion and really crystallized and forced the concrete statement of principles and methods, later served as the substantiation of the most potent claim of scientific managers--namely that scientific management is not a *theory* evolved on paper by a more or less practical dreamer, but is the result, tho as yet imperfectly expressed, of carefully worked out solutions evolved by far-sighted and eminently practical managers and engineers to meet everyday problems. Such theory as has been developed was preceded long years by sound practice.

With the Eastern Rate Case hearings in 1911, however, came the second stage, the public awakening; and immediately succeeding it came a flood of popular articles, extravagant claims, and vehement denials. There was a mad scramble on the part of various owners of industries (possessing a lamentable lack of understanding as to what this new movement really was) to secure this "panacea," and of course an equally eager readiness on the part of incompetent and frequently unscrupulous charlatans to supply the demand. It is safe to say that had not such abundant evidence of the real value of the fundamental *principles*, properly applied, been available during this period, the inevitable reaction would have been much more severe and of much longer duration. The fact that it was not is only another tribute to the (possibly unconscious) farsightedness of the real leaders in the movement.

For there is no question that the reaction is largely past and that we are now in the third stage. This does not mean, however, that there is not still a tremendous amount of misunderstanding as to the real significance of the movement, or even a considerable amount of active opposition. The third stage is again clearly reflected in the literature on the subject. The popular matter has dropped out pretty completely and has been replaced by an already large and constantly growing number of articles dealing, on the one hand with concrete illustrations and explanations of the actual workings of the system or of parts of it, and on the other hand with frequently altogether healthy and well-intentioned, tho unfortunately not always well-informed, attempts to appraise its true economic significance. The active and open opponents, failing to find proof of the fulfillment of their dire prophecies as to the ill effects on the workman and the heartlessness of it all, have largely been driven to a less outspoken if more insidious activity, unwittingly furnishing tremendous arguments for the extension of what they sought to kill through measures forced on misinformed legislators in a vain attempt to stop the inevitable. And incidentally, those of the Taylor persuasion--upon witnessing the constant putting forth, by those either ignorant of or actually opposed to the Taylor System as such, of "new" and brilliant ideas in management, incorporated long since in the practices of that group--may be pardoned for an unseemly chuckle up their sleeves at the rapid and irresistible spread of the principles and methods for which they have long stood. Not only in current trade journals laying no claim to being scientific management disciples, but also in the practices of many managers, some of whom at least lay claim to being exactly the reverse, is this tendency most noticeable. Only upon coming in more or less close contact with numerous plants is that fact brought home so forcibly.

We may say, therefore, that the sensational and propagandist period is past, that the foisting of halfbaked "efficiency" schemes on an unsuspecting and overeager public is rapidly passing (altho there are still, unfortunately, too many managers who give less attention to the selection of an industrial adviser than they give to the purchase of a new machine), and that the skeptical stage--the "my business is different" attitude--is gradually passing with the constant addition of new lines of industry to the list of scientifically managed plants, and that we are now in a period of healthy growth accompanied by a much more sympathetic and truer understanding of the fundamental nature of the principles and problems involved. "Scientific management" has comfortably taken its place among the things which are here to stay.

It is perhaps a little early to attempt to judge of many of the economic problems raised by scientific management--the smoke of battle is yet a little too pungent, and we are not yet sufficiently removed from its beginning to enable us to get a true perspective of the movement as a whole. Whereas in the past, however, it has been necessary to speculate as to its probable effects on this or that phase of the problems presented, and even tho we may still justifiably concern ourselves in this manner with the numerous as yet unsolved questions, we can now, nevertheless, get a much clearer perspective than has been possible heretofore and perhaps more profitably focus our attention on the positive aspects and accomplishments in certain directions, realizing that it is no longer theory but facts with which we are dealing. If the writer succeeded in crystallizing a few of the accounts on the debit side of our balance sheet by bringing together some of the concrete economic losses already eliminated or or alleviated by scientific management, it may perhaps make easier our minds as to the state of the science as a whole.

In considering the effects of scientific management from the standpoint of its positive contributions to industry we may take up first the mechanical phase--the more purely impersonal aspects--divorced so far as possible from considerations of its direct effect on the individual, leaving the human factor as the last and most important topic. The two are to a certain extent interactive, yet sufficiently distinct to warrant separate treatment.

II. The Mechanical or Impersonal Aspects

A. Increased Production

Turning first then to the effects of scientific management on industry as such, as exemplified by those establishments directly affected by it, by far the most striking single fact is the increase in production it has effected with the same equipment and personnel. This has occurred in many cases to such an extent as to be almost unbelievable. Ten, twenty, thirty per cent increases are the rule, and an output twice or even three times as great as had formerly been secured is not uncommon. And these results have not been uniformly secured, as might be supposed, from plants that were near the lower level of efficiency before the development of the system was started. On the contrary, in many cases the standard of production was comparatively high, and I know of one case where the production was increased over 60 per cent in a plant which from every standpoint was previously generally considered to be absolutely the most efficient of its kind in the country. The desire for increased production is often, indeed, one of the minor causes for the management's determination to have scientific management--too often the output is greater than ever before and yet the firm through other causes is losing money, or conditions are unsatisfactory in other respects. But in just that same plant when scientific management is developed, the output is almost sure to increase--incidentally as it were.

Increase in production has been the cry of economists for centuries, and for centuries they have had their cry answered--at least partially. For it is the exception where, take any industry you will, with the constant substitution of new and improved labor saving machinery and equipment the output has not been very largely increased over what it formerly was. Our industrial highway is strewn with the corpses of those individuals who would not or could not keep abreast of these improvements.

Such increases, however, altho they may enable the individual to survive, may not and often do not wholly satisfy economic demands. They are brought about by the substitution of new machines for those already in use, oftentimes long before the latter have earned their keep. I heard of a case where recently in one department, new machines costing thousands of dollars and having been in use less than one year, were scrapped to make way for new and supposedly superior machines.

The increase in production brought about through scientific management, however, is of a fundamentally different nature. True, the scientific manager does not tolerate obviously antiquated machinery, but he does not tolerate inefficient machinery of any kind, and it is just here that his real economic contribution comes in. With him it is not a case primarily of increase in production through new machines; it is first and foremost a case of increase through getting the most out of existing equipment and personnel. Only after present means are brought to their highest productiveness may the question as to whether new equipment is justifiable be satisfactorily determined. With the present mania for new equipment, we may well inquire whether, in very many cases, these changes do not impose an added rather than a lessened burden on the consumer. If a proper charge for such rapid obsolescence as well as a regular charge for depreciation were figured into the expected cost resulting from the contemplated "improvement," and particularly if this expected cost were compared not with present costs with existing equipment, but with what those costs should be, it is safe to say that many new machines would go unbought, that many firms would avoid bankruptcy, and that the owners as well as the buying public would profit thereby. It is just here that the line between the two kinds of increases may be sharply drawn, which brings us to the consideration of the financial aspect of the question.

B. Decreased Cost

For all practical purposes the consumptive capacity of mankind as a whole may be considered to be unlimited. Yet not infrequently there has occurred a state of so-called "overproduction" in one or more widely consumed lines of commodities. This apparently anomalous state of affairs will be found, upon analysis, to be due not to overproduction as such--not to a simple cessation of demand because of satiated desire--but to a conviction on the part of the consuming public, that at that price under existing conditions the commodity in question no longer yields the demanded return for money invested in it. What was formerly exchanged for this commodity now goes elsewhere where the equivalency is considered to be more attractive. Lower your price on this one commodity, however, and see what happens;--the balance of equivalency just established is again disturbed, the commodity now immediately represents a relative increase in return, those articles which before replaced it are now themselves replaced by it, and we get back at least to the original state of demand with possibly an added demand. Continue to lower the price, and this commodity will continue to edge its way into favor, constantly disturbing the balance and in constantly widening circles continuing to replace other articles which we deem, in comparison, as of lesser utility.

It would then seem clear that a simple increase in production without at the same time a decrease in unit cost (and therefore, in the long run, in selling price) cannot of itself in the great majority of cases be considered an economic gain and may at times lead to a direct economic loss--overproduction. Furthermore, a simple increase in production with an accompanying decrease in a cost which, due to inefficiency in management, was hitherto higher than it should reasonably have been as judged by modern standards, may not and usually does not wholly satisfy economic demands. It is only erasing the negative and getting back to par, as it were, but failing to add a plus.

Where the increase in production and the decrease in already satisfactory cost go hand in hand, however, our gain is direct and indisputable.

It was for this reason that the distinction above was drawn, and it is on this ground that scientific management may lay just claim to a more favorable economic judgment than the prevalent increase in production brought about through new equipment which may not be economically justifiable. With its insistence on present efficiency before new equipment is permitted, which with its accurate cost system furnishes a basis for determining the effectiveness of contemplated substitutions, scientific management has a very much firmer foundation upon which to rest its claim. It of course has also the absolute reduction in cost in addition.

Of the various means by which scientific management increases production and decreases cost, some--such as the selection, fitting and training of the workers, the reducing of labor turnover, absences, lates, etc., the determining and securing of a proper day's work and the paying of a correspondingly increased wage--are distinct economic gains in themselves. These will be discussed under the human factors. Others, however, must be considered simply as the elements which go to form the most outstanding contribution of scientific management under this head--decreased cost--and as such several merit discussion here.

1. The Use of Equipment. Closely connected with the question of new equipment referred to above, is that of the full utilization of that now on hand, using the term in its widest sense to include all facilities of production.

A certain amount of idleness of equipment is of course unavoidable. That it should be even one-half of what it unquestionably is, however, is a striking commentary on the lack of foresightedness of many managements. The encouraging feature about it, however, is that a large proportion of idleness can be prevented and that a few progressive managers are informing themselves and taking effective steps to remedy the evil. Less encouraging is the fact that the extent and seriousness of the losses through idle equipment are seldom appreciated by the manager until it is brought forcibly, even violently, to his attention through cold figures. In comparatively few plants is a record of machine time regularly and systematically kept, and in still fewer instances is the effort made to determine in each case the exact cause of idleness upon which to base intelligent remedies. If, as advocated by Mr. Gantt, each manager could be shown that during the last two months a certain group of machines was idle say 40 per cent of the time, and that this idleness was distributed as follows:

Total Idleness		40%
Unavoidable breakdowns.		3%
Avoidable breakdowns		12
Lack of work at machines		15
Lack of orders for product	0	
Lack of materials	4	
Unbalanced equipment	6	
Poor planning	5	
Lack of help		10

and if in addition the money loss from each cause could be shown, measures to reduce the idleness would follow almost as a matter of course. Nothing is more common than an abundance of room in what was previously a very much crowded and overburdened department after steps have been taken to balance, rearrange, standardize and maintain equipment, and it is not unusual to hear of a whole contemplated addition to a plant being found entirely unnecessary and consequently abandoned upon the presentation of such statistics as those cited above--a direct saving of usually thousands of dollars, to say nothing of the avoidance of actual loss (through decreased production or increased costs) which many times occurs with an enlargement of plant.

Just why such conditions exist it is hard to say. Attention to such matters should be one of the main duties of the manager. And with a table such as the above, he would soon make them his principal duty. Yet, even under present conditions, it seems so much easier to order new equipment, blame the seller for such slow deliveries that our production is held up, and overlook the fact that by the aid of such facts the way out lies right under our noses. The answer probably lies somewhere between our natural aversion to real thought and planning, and the fact that the prevalent forms of organization keep the manager so hemmed around with ordinary routine that he is left no time in which to conceive and execute manifest reforms. The exception principle in management emphasized by Mr. Taylor, merits a much wider application on the part of most of our executives.

2. The Use of Labor. Unlike an idle machine, there is of course no such thing as an absolutely idle man permitted in any plant, yet a man who, before thoro time study and planning might be considered to be extremely busy--as indeed he might be, tho perhaps inefficiently so--in the light of highly systematized working conditions would be thought of as having been previously very ineffectually employed. The term "idle" is becoming a relative one. In general, except as the human element, to be discussed, enters here, the same conditions as pointed out for idle equipment are applicable in this case, and for the present the two may be considered as of like nature and effect. Taken together they constitute the most tangible field for reducing costs.

3. Material Control. The stores system in a scientifically managed plant is typical of the minute control designed to be exercised over all departments of the work. It is designed to cover the four factors covering the efficiency of material use: Quality, Quantity, Time, and Cost, and great care is taken to maintain the proper balance between these four interdependent variables so that their resultant effect will be the best for any given case, all things considered.

It is not the purpose of this general review to go into a description of either the methods or the exact results of the various means by which modern management's economic contributions are made. To do so, even for the present topic, would require volumes. Only the broader features can be briefly touched upon. In general it may be said that the principal losses in the materials field occur on the one hand through oversupply, and on the other through undersupply; and curious as it may seem, losses from both sources occur most often in the same plant.

It is the exception where the cost of installation of the stores system does not pay for itself by immediate savings effected, and in many cases these savings arise largely through the elimination of surplus stock and useless varieties, and through the effecting a more rapid turnover. In fact, reports as to the amounts of junk disposed of in various plants upon the development of the stores system would be almost unbelievable to one who has not had first hand contact with this work, were it not for the records supporting the statements. Tons and tons of supplies--ordered by the foreman for the expected rush which did not materialize, parts lost or rejected in process, duplicate orders uncaught, "rainy day" and spoiled parts cached by the workman, wrong material delivered and not sent back, parts for discontinued products, and fantastic variations from standard--all accumulate in the storerooms or at various odd places (including valuable working space) throughout the plant, until a detailed study of production requirements leads to a wholesale housecleaning. Immediately and almost invariably, the inventory of stores which it is necessary to keep on hand is decreased, releasing idle capital. This capital invested in turn becomes more productive through more rapid use.

The experience of the Watertown Arsenal where, upon the development of the system, the savings in one year resulting from the use of surplus stock amounted to $122,789.61 is typical of many, many plants in this respect. Similar instances could be multiplied almost indefinitely.

Looking behind such conditions we readily see not only the general disorganization and lack of knowledge thus typified, but also the large amount of capital tied up, the inevitable depreciation and deterioration of stock, and the general interference with the flow of work in productive processing. Add to this the elimination of the generally rapidly disappearing annual or semiannual shutdown for inventory taking, and the sources of the large savings become apparent.

Similarly, lack of the proper material at the right time is frequently the cause of expensive delays, postponed delivery dates and even loss of trade. Here again a certain amount of lost motion is unavoidable; but that four-fifths of the current inconveniences and losses experienced in material handling can be eliminated by detailed knowledge and proper planning is proved by those scientifically managed plants which have systematically attacked and regulated stores problems.

4. Routing. The decreasing of costs through the full utilization of equipment, of men, and of materials has been discussed. Another of the means by which this reduction is secured is the broader use and correlation of the business as a whole, including both the physical layout and the administrative control of the various component parts of the business.

Just what is meant by this topic, as well as its significance, may be illustrated by an example. In modern or scientific management a factory is looked upon from the strictly production standpoint as comparable to an automatic machine. Just why this conception is necessary may be seen from considering a compound full automatic consisting of five successive components, A, B, C, D, and E. As a piece is completed in any one of these parts, it is automatically swung around to be further processed in the next, and obviously that next must be free of its previous piece and ready to receive the new. Properly to set up such a machine of course requires detailed knowledge of and strictest attention to the time element for each head.

Now, a great many plants are being run today without an appreciation of the fact that the various departments of the plant as a whole are exactly analogous to the various parts of the automatic machine. The result is very much like the result would be if the automatic were set up either by one man who lacked or disregarded knowledge of all parts except that he was working on at the time, or by two men working independently without the knowledge of what the other had done, was doing or expected to do. In the case of the machine its various parts simply must be correlated and brought into proper synchronism by one man or by concerted action if by more than one; the same thing is less obvious but equally true in the case of the interdependent departments of the manufacturing plant if equally satisfactory results are to be expected. The "set up" and regulation of the various departments of most factories is an exceedingly complex and technical undertaking commonly defined by the term "routing," and not for a moment can any one foreman be allowed to run his department as he sees fit regardless of its relation to other departments and to the business as a whole. Hence the insistence in scientific management on a somewhat elaborate Planning Department, or at least on a central control of all activities which in any way have an interacting effect, and conscious and constant effort is put forth to secure this central control. As perhaps the finest example of the practical application of what has here been incompletely described, reference is made to the work of G. D. Babcock in the plant of the H. H. Franklin Manufacturing Company. Suffice it here to emphasize the point that such control is the cardinal aim of every scientific manager, more or less perfectly realized in the best shops and secured through the systematic collection of all relevant information and through the practical application of this knowledge through measures collectively known technically as "control." This control is established through the proper use of such measures as standardization, time study, logical layout, careful routing of work and first-piece inspection, uneconomic symbols, the Order of Work and the Bulletin Board or its equivalent--all mechanisms which, in one form or another have become integral parts of modern management.

5. _The Regularizing of Production_. Perhaps nowhere better than in the elimination of seasonal production and its attendant evils is the fact illustrated that what is of permanent benefit to the management also benefits the workmen, and _vice versa_. It would in fact in this case be difficult to say to whom the larger benefit accrues--to capital and the consumer through full and continuous use of a minimum of plant, equipment and personnel, or to the body of employees through fulltime employment and regular wages. Operation under conditions of seasonal fluctuations is a direct economic waste to the community, and that in very many cases it is not an unpreventable waste has been amply proved by those industries which have attacked and eliminated the evil. It would of course be folly in this case as in so many others to claim any monopoly of effort along this line for scientific management plants--the case simply illustrates what may be accomplished along so many lines by what scientific management does make it a _definite policy_ to do: a policy of conscious and continuous _taking thought_ of the numerous economic and social factors which make for permanent success.

C. Improvement in or Maintenance of Quality

Next to increased output and decreased cost, the question of quality of output deserves attention, for obviously, while in cases improvement in quality may be justified even with decreased production and increased costs, the reverse would infrequently be the case.

That the increases in production under scientific management have not been secured at the expense of quality would seem proved, if proof were needed, by the permanence both of those increases and of the firms which have secured them, and will be questioned by no one acquainted with the facts. As a minimum, the maintenance, at least of the engineer's "good-enough-is-best" quality, must be the first concern of those who expect fully and permanently to benefit by modern methods of management. It has remained largely for the time study man and the instructor, supported by proper quality bonus and thorough inspection, however, to prove that as between speed and quality there is not only no intrinsic irreconcilability, but indeed that with intelligent handling an improvement in quality usually accompanies increase in speed. Just why this is so may be left largely to the psychologist--we are here dealing simply with the abundantly proved fact.

D. Speedy Production and Accurate Delivery

It must never be forgotten that any industry, to remain in operation, must produce a profit. When it ceases to do so it loses the support of the investor and must perish. As a corollary to this it must be borne in mind that investments in plant, in materials, and in labor become bills receivable only when the finished product is shipped from the factory door. This shipment date then becomes one of the vital points of contact between seller and buyer--the earliest point ordinarily at which <u>expense</u> becomes convertible into <u>profit</u>.

The quoting of a minimum time necessary for delivery after the receipt of the order and the strict adherence to the specified delivery date are two commonly unappreciated factors in business success. From the buyer's standpoint they are outranked in importance only by quality, and oftentimes not even by that quite frequently intangible and relative characteristic. As between two reputable firms whose selling prices are not at too wide variance, the duration and definiteness of the time for delivery become governing considerations, and not infrequently indeed delivery outweights both quality and price. The firm which, on a basis of knowledge and through the systematic measures of control discussed above, can accurately predict and rigidly maintain delivery dates is not only in an enviable position from the buyer's standpoint but may claim a distinct contribution to itself, to the buying public, and to the community at large.

For every cessation of processing operations for lack of material, every delay due to machine breakdowns, every loss of production due to discontented or absent workmen--every interference with high production from whatever cause in our factory--is an economic loss; every failure to meet scheduled and attainable delivery dates (regardless of whether thereby the purchaser's schedule is also upset for in any event <u>our</u> turnover is less rapid than it should be and our costs must be higher than they should be)--every performance below a standard which, as gauged by current and freely available modern practice, may be reasonably expected and justifiably demanded, is an economic loss which must ultimately be paid for by the consumer.

The quickening of production and the consequent increase in rapidity of turnover, the informed and detailed control of work in process, and, resulting from these, the quoting of a quick and dependable delivery date--these factors characteristic of properly managed plants together constitute a decided antidote to the tendency for ever increasing costs of living.

E. The Power and Stimulus of Knowledge

As a final consideration under the industrial or nonhuman aspects of the discussion must be mentioned, partially by way of summary, the numberous factors which considered as a whole form the possibly less tangible but nevertheless eminently comforting features of operation under scientific management. I refer to the confidence, the sense of security, the power and stimulus, the aplomb which spring from the knowledge that we have real control of our business through the ordered regulation of its activities according to adequate knowledge and best practice--one of those by-products of Scientific Management which are often of such transcendent importance.

There is something immensely stimulating about it all, something akin to the inspiration and confidence we feel when in the presence of a man who is a master of his subject and whose opinions and actions we know are based on thoro knowledge and thoro understanding. Who has not experienced the enthusiasm which comes with the final solution of an inticate problem; who has not experienced the stimulus of directing interdependent forces in perfect confidence toward a solution which, be what it may, we know must be the proper one because arrived at through absolute adherence to natural law. In the one case it is the enthusiam of the chemist when he knows he has ferreted out a new element; in the other it is the confidence and the power of the master at his work.

This enthusiasm, this stimulus is nowhere more infectious than in industry. Striking proof of this is afforded by the avidity with which the "efficiency" gospel has been bandied back and forth between adherents and opponents during the eight or nine years it has been public property, and by the readiness with which very many of the largest and most progressive firms in the country have accepted and successfully applied the principles of modern management. It is fortunate that this is so, for in the search for and utilization of better methods wherever found lies the hope of American industry. The metal working industry generally has been tremendously spurred forward not only by the development of high speed steel, but also by the example of those plants which have not been content with being forced to adopt this means of increased production but which have voluntarily followed this measure up with others of far-reaching importance, and who have thereby postponed in their cases the time of diminishing returns. Tho lacking the same stimulus, there are increasing signs that the textile and other industries are shortly due for a less revolutionary yet none the less peremptory awakening. They also must catch up with the, as yet, comparatively few examples of advanced management among them.

The fear of the power of knowledge even more than that of the power of capital may well cause competitors to demand forthwith a balance sheet of knowledge. Tho capital is needed to put knowledge to work and to keep it there, capital without knowledge is likely quickly to disappear in competition with those who possess both. Knowledge without capital is a stronger asset than is capital without knowledge, for knowledge may be capitalized while capital cannot be educated. We may well pause to consider our probable future status when our competitor and not ourselves is one who knows how long work should take; who knows the capacity of each machine, of each department, and of his plant as a whole, and who takes measures to see that these various factors are properly balanced; who has worked out, standardized and reduced to permanent form the best methods of performing work; who really knows costs (as far as from their very nature they may be known) and knows at how low a figure he can sell in dull times and still make a profit or secure more work to keep his organization and plant intact even at no profit, and who knows when he does quote a specified selling price whether he is losing money on the sale or not. We may well consider our relative positions when he is the one who knows that there is no inherent inconsistency between wages plus and cost minus, because he knows, appreciates and acts on the fact that "maximum prosperity for the employer, coupled with maximum prosperity for the employee ought to be two leading objects of management." Such a competitor, we know, really _controls_ his business and has a check on its efficiency--we are but alchemists, he is the chemist of industry.

III. The Human Factor

Just as increased production may be frowned upon if unaccompanied by decreased cost of the product and either of these may be censured if, thereby, quality is allowed to suffer, so none of these accomplishments can be recommended or tolerated if at the same time labor--the human element--be not kept in satisfactory adjustment and correspondingly benefited.

Important tho it be for the country at large that we have high production and low costs, that we establish a strong industrial basis, it is of greater importance that while we are making _things_ we do not forget that our first and infinitely more important duty is the making of _men_--of good citizens.

Scientific management has from the first been a storm center around which questions of labor have raged. Because of its effects in so many particulars on human relations it must continue to be so.

Time and space might profitably be given to showing how, in the evolution of scientific management, more and more emphasis has been placed on the necessity of maintaining just human relations and of promoting the best interests of all concerned; how the very structure of the mechanism itself is designed to safeguard, to increase and to satisfy those interests; how its very nature is such that, so far from militating against those interests, it is vitally dependent for its very continuance on a proper maintenance of them. Certainly such considerations must prove of vital interest and concern to anyone who deplores and looks beyond the present troubled days. Profitable and interesting as such a story might be, however, I believe it to be still more profitable and pertinent to summarize, even somewhat categorically, some of the specific accomplishments known personally or through reliable authority which show in concrete cases the embodiment in actual practice of the theory and principles of scientific management. A theory may be ever so beautiful in the abstract; to judge of its soundness we must examine its results in practice.

Before turning to the discussion of concrete cases, it should be remembered that in considering the relations between industry as such and the individual, one is dealing with questions of tremendous significance and complexity. Many of the unsatisfactory conditions under which we work today are heritages of an age long past, just as many of the more satisfactory conditions today are in turn the successors to those once less satisfactory. The massing of workers, the economic dependence of the employee on the employer, the specialization of processes and the minute subdivision of labor, the aggregation and power of capital--the problems and ills of the individual arising through such factors have not, as is sometimes intimated, been brought on _by_ scientific management; they are inherited problems and abuses with which, in common with other agencies, scientific management must deal. There is and can be no panacea for industrial ills--industry is not such a static thing as to make possible any such consummation. No movement can be justly judged from this standpoint--it must be judged according to the vigor and success with which it attacks and solves or ameliorates such unsatisfactory conditions as it may encounter under given circumstances. In the case of scientific management then, our inquiry must be, not whether it has completely solved partially unsolvable problems, but whether it is entitled as its exponents claim to be ranked as a movement which, as a cardinal principle makes a vigorous attack upon these problems a definite part of its policy, and which is in fact, perhaps more than any other one agency contributing in a substantial degree to their satisfactory adjustment. It is from this standpoint that the following discussion is offered.

A. Industrial Peace

It would be impossible to say to what one feature the freedom from "labor trouble" characteristic of plants operating under scientific management has been most due. Certainly no one feature in itself has brought this about, and probably not any one feature has been most potent, for high wages is by no means everything for which the workman looks to the management. The absence of labor unrest is due undoubtedly to a combination of causes--to increased personal individual production and improvement in quality with the resulting personal satisfaction; to high wages unaccompanied by overexertion; to individual and impartial opportunity, assistance, recognition and reward; to an adequate machinery for the speedy adjustment of grievances; to conditions of work, of pay and of opportunity measurably better than the labor union in neighboring plants of the same type has been able to obtain and at the same time to absence of ultra "welfare work" and similar measures which smack too much of paternalism and which tend, the workers feel, unduly to lighten the weight of their pay envelope. It is due to a spirit of cooperation--the "mental revolution" which is such a vital part of scientific management--to fair dealing, to a proper work environment, to a spirit of democracy, and to a feeling on the part of the employee that his best interest is being and will be looked after. It is due in fact, to the various factors discussed above and yet to be discussed considered collectively--it is inclusive of them all.

Summarize the causes as we may, however, the fact remains that in scientifically managed plants there has been remarkable freedom from the turbulent and distressing manifestations of industrial maladjustment characteristic of the last four years. It would be too much to expect that they entirely escape the epidemic of industrial unrest, but it is extremely significant that so far as is known through broad inquiry, such disturbances as have occurred have been of an altogether minor character, quickly and satisfactorily adjusted.

This fact is of preeminent important at the present time. It is unquestionably <u>the greatest</u> contribution of scientific management--all the more so because secured, not as industrial "peace" was secured during the latter period of the war by governmental <u>suppression</u> of the disturbance of industrial conditions by either labor or capital, but by <u>cooperation</u>, justice, and fair dealing.

B. High Wages

It has sometimes been claimed that, in the cases of certain profit sharing and other measures, daily wages have been depressed below the market rate in the exact ratio in which profits were to be shared. Whether the claim is well founded does not concern us here. So far as the writer knows, this accusation has never been laid at the door of Scientific Management. That it is not likely with justice ever to be is due to the dependent relation between daily wages and output. Starting with a current base rate of pay and the normal amount and quality of work customarily delivered by the operatives for that pay, scientific management first takes measures by which that production or that quality, or both, may be increased. Having thus provided the possibility of higher and better production, it then offers, as a matter of justice as well as of necessity, a correspondingly increased incentive for its accomplishment, payable at once regardless of whether or not during any given period a profit is made on the business as a whole. Each is necessary to maintain the other, and the increased wage is solely dependent on and must follow immediately, not precede, increased output.

Increases in the earnings of operatives working under scientific management are too common and well known to need repetition here. Bonus percentages, above the prevailing market rate of wages, vary from 20 percent to 40 percent or higher depending on the character of work, and on the average are earned on from perhaps 70 percent to 90 percent of the jobs worked upon.

That the more progressive managers are beginning to question the prevalent empirical bases of wage determination and to seek for a more satisfactory basis is evidenced by an attempt on the part of several of them to reduce to formulae the effects of various factors previously wholly neglected or only empirically estimated. Thus

Babcock takes into account the following factors:

1. Rate of production.
2. Cost of living.
3. Number of processes workman can do.
4. Years of connected service.
5. Fixed charges rate per hour which man has chance to modify.
6. Percentage of premium earned.
7. Late or absence record.
8. Spoiled work.
9. Percentage of time under task.
10. Cooperation and conduct.

Such an attempt shows careful consideration of one of the three most important things for which the workman looks to the management: wages, conditions, opportunity.

Since the present paper is designedly little more than a synopis of conditions as they are, it would be inappropriate to prolong it into a discussion of the various interesting social and economic aspects of scientific management as related to the wage question as a whole. It must suffice here to emphasize the undoubted fact that scientific management is leading the way both in the actual payment of wages higher than the general market level and in attacking some of the deeper fundamental phases of the problem.

C. Proper Working Hours

Mr. Taylor was one of the first to recognize and to prove the fact that overlong working hours are not conducive to high output, and that in very many cases hours of work may be sharply decreased _up to a certain point_ and output increased simultaneously, this point having to be scientifically determined for each class of work. The policy of reducing excessive working hours offhand, and of continuing thereafter to reduce them to a point not inconsistent with maximum gross output, has been consistently followed by his associates, and scientifically managed factories as a body today are operating under at least as short hours as any other group of plants, while excessive hours on the part of any of them are unknown.

When one stops to consider it, it does seem rather remarkable, not to say significant, that scientific management presents such a unifrom history of simultaneous increase in output, increase in quality, increase in wages, decrease in working hours and decrease in costs in those plants where it has been developed. Such is its record, nevertheless, in dozens of applications. It has ceased to be a novelty and is now the expected thing.

D. Conditions of Work as Related to the Health and Well-Being of the Workers

Looked at from a perfectly cold-blooded standpoint the return on the investment in the upkeep of the efficiency of the human machine exceeds that on the investment in the upkeep of the mechanical product.

A moment's reflection will show why this must be so, for under proper conditions the human mind and heart delivers a plus which the inanimate machine is incapable of. From the entirely personal, selfish financial aspect, then, there can be no question that the very best condition for the employee is the very best condition for the owner of the business. And by the word "best" is here meant what is really best for the workman in the long run: wages neither too low nor too high, hours neither too long nor too short, general treatment neither too degrading through neglect or abuse nor too emasculating through ingratiation or paternalism.

From the purely economic standpoint, furthermore, this condition is equally true. It is economically wrong to allow the human machine to work under unsocial conditions of long hours, low wages, poor working conditions, unfair competition and lack of free scope for the proper exercise of one's individual abilities, because under such unsocial conditions best results are not obtainable from human beings. A prematurely incapacitated workman, much more than an inefficiently employed one, is a direct financial loss to the industry and a direct economic loss to the community.

But it is particularly the social and ethical aspects of the question which I wish to emphasize. That the owners and managers of plants under scientific management recognize and capitalize that source of additional personal profit is true; that they consciously consider their economic obligations may or may not be true; but that they primarily and continuously have the best interests of their people at heart, not from any ulterior motives but because they are that sort of person, I believe can be doubted by no one who will take the trouble to visit them and their employees. They would otherwise never have achieved scientific management--for scientific management is distinctly a thing to be achieved; it cannot be purchased and it cannot be had or maintained without this attitude.

One would naturally expect, therefore, to find in such plants satisfactory conditions as regards accidents, health and sanitation, the speedy and impartial adjustment of grievances, and comfortable working conditions generally. The providing of such necessities follows almost as a matter of course. In addition are found also in varying degrees of completeness rest and recreation rooms, playgrounds, libraries, lunch rooms where necessary operated at cost, first aid hospitals, etc., on an unpretentious scale according to strict utility. Such measures, if initiated upon actual need and if properly regulated, are appreciated by the employees and express the good will of the firm toward them. Then, as a step further, there are the mutual benefit societies and insurance and retirement funds which were initiated by Mr. Taylor very early in his work and which are very characteristic of plants following his lead as well as of many others at the present time.

There is another phase of this question, however, which is of much greater importance than most of the measures enumerated in that it affects the workman during his entire working hours while he is at the machine and for his entire life as a productive member of society. While it is important to provide means for caring for him during temporary sickness or disability and after he has ceased to be productive, it is at least equally important that his period of usefulness be safeguarded and prolonged through attention to his daily work. This is accomplished through the determination of "the best day's work that a man could do, year in and year out and still thrive under." The object of time study is just this--the determination of a proper day's work which, through allowance for rest and necessary delays, the workman may do year in and year out and thrive under. The setting of a task either too high or too low is equally shortsighted, since the object for which the study is made is thereby defeated. As a vital part of the determination of such a task is the investigation of the tiring effect on a workman for each class of work, investigations commonly described today by the term "fatigue study."

It is significant that the first "fatigue study" ever conducted in a really thorough and scientific manner, so far as the writer's records show, was performed over thirty years ago by Mr. Taylor as a part of his determination of a proper day's work. Indeed, so far ahead of the time was he that, except as embodied in the routine of current time study according to the methods he and his associates developed and insisted upon, these early researches seem until very recently to have been generally overlooked until the admirable work of the British Health of Munition Workers Committee served again to emphasize their importance.

And in closing the discussion of this topic, it may be stated that, in spite of the oft-expressed fears on the part of various estimable gentlemen that the so-called "speeding up" would result to the immediate or ultimate detriment of the worker, no authentic case of anything but beneficial results has been brought to light.

E. Selection, Fitting and Training

It would be difficult to overestimate the advantage both to the individual and to the nation of a condition where each person could be engaged, under conditions satisfactory to him, upon work for which he is naturally best fitted. The misfits in industry are the causes of a direct loss of thousands of dollars annually, and of a loss of initiative impossible to appraise and of far greater importance. In the first place it is an economic waste to hire a workman who is not fitted for the work in hand. This waste is not always avoidable or even to be avoided under all circumstances, however. In the second place, after a man is hired he must be quickly trained to his full productiveness or transferred without delay to work on which this will be possible. He must in the third place, both for his own sake and for that of the management, be taught to do several different operations if possible (see Babcock's formula, item 3, page 24 above), and finally in the fourth place he must be given an opportunity to measure up to his full abilities as he proves, by careful and impartial records, that he can assume increasing responsibilities. It is a direct loss to employ a man on work for which he is not fitted or to fail to take advantage to his full ability. The human scrap heap of discouraged, discontented and worn out men is but a sorry return for our modern industrial system.

If we believe that "for each man some line (of work) can be found in which he is first class," it imposes upon us the duty of acting in conformity with our belief. In addition it is sound business. Committed from early days to a policy of "scientifically selecting, training, teaching, and developing the workman," in plants adhering to this principle it is the customary thing, therefore, to find operatives who are now doing excellent work in their third, fourth, or even fifth trial after having previously been unsuccessful at work for which even they originally thought they were best fitted. We naturally expect to find, and do actually find, numerous cases of promotion from the ranks. Starting with the original functional foreman inappropriately called the disciplinarian, now developed into the modern functionalized Employee's Department (known variously also as the Personnel Department, the Labor Department, the Employment Department, etc.), there is set up not only a means for bringing to pass such conditions as those described above, but also a means to establish and maintain a more intimate personal touch between management and men, and to modify or counteract the tendencies on the part of the foremen and the production officials generally to press for high production regardless of the best interests always of the individual, and on the part of the employees to go to the other extreme. This department is so constituted that it sits in judgment over the employee on the one hand and the management on the other--acting as buffer, as it were, between the two. The very recent widespread adoption of this safety valve is a decided step in the right direction and has far-reaching possibilities in capable hands.

F. Free Scope for Individual Initiative and Opportunity for Advancement

"Democracy in industry" has been defined as existing where conditions are such as described in the above title. Whether we agree that this is a sufficiently comprehensive viewpoint or not, certainly this degree of "industrial democracy" should constitute the minimum for which we should strive, and is necessary for true progress. And yet even this amount is extremely difficult to obtain in modern industry, even with the best intentions in the world. Opportunity may be abundant, yet there are so many unmeasurable elements to be considered in determining advancement--so many questions of judgment and of personality and of circumstance. The best one may do is to do the best he can, in fair-mindedness and in impartiality.

Monotony, where monotony exists (for there is ample evidence that many for whom in their "deadly monotonous" tasks we are prone to feel compassion, do not at all envy us with our larger responsibilities), is due not so much to the unvarying repetition of recurrent operations as to the accompanying feeling that the work holds no future possibilities. Introduce the possibility and the probability of a more attractive future, and the humdrum task becomes but a stepping stone, seen in its proper relation to the whole scheme of things and eminently serviceable and satisfactory as a present means. The belief that each of us has a marshal's baton in his knapsack is no less stimulating today than it was in Napoleon's time, and the conviction that we have reached a positions of status is no less deadening.

Difficult as it is, therefore, it is nevertheless vitally important that the channels of advancement be kept open and that every incentive and opportunity be given a man for bettering his position. As possibly the most effective avenue through which this is accomplished in scientific management, is functional foremanship. The requisites of the customary "line" foreman are so numerous and of such a nature as to preclude from that position all but the rather exceptionally gifted workman. Functional foremanship, by dividing among several foremen the duties ordinarily expected of the one, introduces greater opportunity for the man of limited or specialized talent and at the same time does not lessen the demand for those of greater or more balanced capabilities.

For the most part, since this topic is so closely allied to the preceding one where the provision for definitely teaching and guiding the employees was discussed, little additional emphasis is needed here. Before passing on, however, a prevalent fallacy in regard to the limitations placed on personality in these plants should be noted. The idea is frequently expressed that in working under highly standardized conditions and with detailed instruction and supervision from above in regard to methods, there can be little chance for the exercise for one's individuality.

I belive it has been conclusively demonstrated in practice that scientific management is decidedly a _dynamic_ movement, governed not by inflexible methods and case-hardened mechanisms, but solely by _principles_. There have certainly been new developments from time to time sufficient to prove that there is a ready acceptance and adoption of better ways immediately they are proved. But, here is the point, they must be _proved_; for it is no less a waste to be constantly upsetting carefully worked out methods upon the insistence of those who, because they have not first mastered present ways, have little right to an opinion at all as to thier relative efficiency, than it is to refuse to adopt new and better ways when they are found. We do not and it is right that we should not let a novice tamper with a new and delicate mechanism until he has proved that he has mastered it.

The complaint to this extent, therefore, is well founded. It is not individuality and initiative run wild, however, which is really constructive; it is intelligently applied individuality, and prerequisite to this is an understanding of things as they are and why they are so. Founded on laws based so far as possible on _fact_ from whatever competent source obtained, and administered through a democratic form of organization which draws its various functionaries from the ranks of the workman, scientific management embodies "management sharing" on a basis and to a degree infrequently encountered in industry today.

G. Reduction of Labor Turnover

It is unnecessary to review either the extent or the evil effects of undue labor turnover. Much has been written on the subject, recent experience has made us familiar with its prevalence, and but brief discussion is necessary here.

Much of the restlessness in industry is curable. It is due to the existence of unsatisfactory conditions in just those features of management discussed in the preceding topics--to low wages, to long hours, to poor working conditions, to lack of proper selection, fitting, and training, and to a conviction on the part of the employee that for him his present job in his present place offers no future. Naturally, therefore, with the removal of the causes in any particular place the evil itself largely disappears. This has been the experience in numberless plants which have adopted advanced measures more or less completely, and the testimony to this effect is in nowise limited to the particular group of industries we are here considering. The simple fact that their adoption with the accompanying low labor turnover are characteristic of scientific management plants to a high degree, as is proved by their records, is what primarily concerns us at present. Although the amount of turnover has increased probably without exception during the last three years, it has noticeably been kept within bounds, comparatively, in plants of this type. Upon the introduction of labor-saving devices and methods where increase in sales has been insufficient to enable the retention of the whole previous force, the policy has been adopted of securing an eventual net reduction in personnel, through filling the places of those who voluntarily leave, from the ranks of the resultant force trained, as before mentioned, to perform several different operations.

H. A Spirit of Cooperation and Confidence, and a Feeling of Security

As a result of all of the positive products of advanced management enumerated above come the last and most important of them all. Indeed so important is the spirit of cooperation and confidence and the feeling of security on the part of the whole personnel that nothing should be allowed to undermine them; for without them, although a certain *efficiency* may be obtained, true *scientific management* is impossible.

Cooperation may be obtained only by securing the confidence of those with whom we deal, and this confidence in turn results only when each man feels secure in the belief that he is in the best possible place for him and that he need have no fear for the future as long as he fully plays his own part.

Needless to say a feeling of security is not engendered by rate cutting, by low wages, by long hours and poor working conditions; it does not spring from paternalism nor from leaving in the hands of the foreman--the most directly interested party--the arbitrary power of promotion, reprimand, demotion or discharge with the often resulting nepotism and favoritism, not to say despotism. A sense of security is not furthered through a feeling on the part of the operative that not only is his training, development and guidance neglected by the management, but that even though he may try hard himself, there is yet little chance for him to secure just recognition. An overemphasis of the profit motive does not lead him to feel that he wil not some day be forced to choose between the employer and his own self respect or his own best interests. Security does not accompany such conditions.

Confidence and an open mind is not established through haphazard methods of manufacture (for which the capable workman at heart has a profound if respectful digust); low wages and high costs, which he knows are unnecessary, do not impel respect for the management, when he knows they are caused by the nonuse or the misuse of equipment, of labor and of materials which he sees about him and which he knows it is the management's responsibility to remedy. Industrial strife does not inspire in the workman confidence in a management which, as he knows, usually brings it on through shortsighted or selfish dealings. No great respect for the ability of his leaders is awakened when he realizes that they know less about what constitutes a proper day's work and how to bring it to pass than he does--when, in other words, the leader knows less in this respect than the led. Only when the management really assumes its full share of the work and the responsibility may his confidence be secured.

And only through making this security and this confidence an actual fact has scientific management been able to produce what it so highly prizes and what it has so remarkably obtained--true cooperation.

We may thus distinguish several marked characteristics and accomplishments of Scientific Management. The first is its stability--the fact that it has progressed through the stages of novelty and exploitation to that of permanence. The second is its marked contributions to purely economic factors such as increased production and decreased cost, improvement in quality, a more rapid capital turnover and the stimulus to industry in general resulting from the sound foundation of knowledge on which it is based. The third is its equally striking but far more important contributions to the field of human industrial relations in the success with which it has maintained industrial peace, increased wages, improved working conditions, established proper employment and training facilities, stimulated and provided for a larger individual opportunity, reduced labor turnover and secured true cooperation between management and men.

Such are some of the notable constructive accomplishments of the science of management in the field of industry during the thirty years or less of its development.

---

[1]Bulletin of the Taylor Society, October, 1919. Reprinted from the Quarterly Journal of Economics, XXXIII: 466-503, May, 1919.

ON THE CONTRIBUTION OF SCIENTIFIC MANAGEMENT TO INDUSTRIAL PROBLEMS[1]

By H. S. Person

The time has not come for a definite statement of the contribution of scientific management; in fact, that time may never come, for industrial problems are continually changing and with each change scientific management has something new to contribute. It is today contributing more to the solution of industrial problems than at any time in the past, and it seems certain that a decade from now the evidence of its influence will be still greater. Such are the facts, although one can count on the fingers of one's hands the plants which may properly be called scientific management plants; for it has in one fashion or another penetrated industry, not only in the United States but in every industrial country, inspiring here a new mental attitude, there a new plant policy and in another place new methods of operation--in the majority of instances without identification as scientific management.

For, although there has been much opposition to scientific management, among executives as well as workers, that opposition has on the whole been superficial; superficial in that it has really been directed against the man Taylor, his incidental observations and his methods of exposition, rather than against the substance of his philosophy of management and even his system. At the same time that some managers and workers have damned Taylor and scientific management, industry has been coming little by little to his mental attitude, his philosophy of industrial management, and has even approved and adopted now one and now another of the elements of his system--provided it was not labeled scientific management.

It should be borne in mind that no one prior to Taylor had enunciated a logical and comprehensive philosophy of management, and devised a system of operations to give any managerial philosophy and body to principles a concrete expression; therefore any theories and mechanisms of management existent today which conform to those of Taylor, may be attributed to the influence of his exposition. It should be borne in mind also that Taylor too modestly declared that the elements of his system were not original with him; that he had merely taken them from here and there, put them together into a purposeful relationship and given them a new meaning. We say that the Wright brothers invented the aeroplane, but when we examine the parts of the original aeroplane separately we find nothing which did not exist before; what the Wright brothers did invent was a new combination which would accomplish a new purpose. So it was with Taylor's discovery or invention or formulation of scientific management.

The fundamental element of Taylor's philosophy of management is that the solution of the problems of management must rest on a factual basis and that tradition, guess and prejudice must be eliminated. That is an axiom of industry today, although practice has too little accompanied preachment. Perhaps the next most fundamental element of his philosophy is that the factual basis must be determined by utilization of all the apparatus of investigation furnished by science (hence the name scientific management), and today as never before industry is using the approved methods of science, experimental and statistical. Another element of Taylor's philosophy, derived by his scientific investigation of his problems, is that when a large number of people are working together at specialized tasks for the accomplishment of a common purpose, these specialized tasks group into two grand divisions each of which requires a special temperament and skill. One is the group of specialized tasks pertaining to planning and preparation; the other the group of tasks pertaining to detail execution. For the segregation of the first of these groups he devised the planning room, where what, how, and when should be taken care of; and today in industry an establishment without a planning room is very much of a back number. Organized labor has been known in some of its controversies to make much of the point that the particular employer is so inefficient in management as not to have a planning room, with the result that jobs do not come through regularly, materials are not always available, and in general there is "unemployment within employment." There are even signs that workers are coming to recognize the value of the stop watch as an instrument of investigation "when properly used;" and one of my most interesting experiences was the appearance in my office one morning of an industrial engineer and a secretary of a local, inquiring if the Taylor Society could furnish a stop watch--they "had been looking all over the city for one;" were "in a hurry to make some investigations in order to confront employers at a conference with facts." Leaders and advisers of organized labor, in sufficient number to be significant, are coming to the point of view that the establishment of a standard time in which an operation may be performed will eliminate one of the guesses on which wage rates are based, with a consequent nearer approach to stability of conditions, rates and workers' income.

One might write at length concerning the manner in which and the extent to which the Taylor philosophy has influenced managerial and labor thinking, and Taylor methods have been incorporated into production systems. But it is not necessary; the reader can prove the point for himself. He has but to reread Taylor's "Shop Management," recall the actual changes which he has observed come into production methods, and put the two together.

The Taylor principles and system of management, as first presented, were concerned principally with shop management; it is natural therefore that their greatest contribution should have been towards better factory management. But not less significant, although at present less extensive, has been their contribution towards better management of an enterprise as a whole; better definition of the purpose and policy of an enterprise and better coordination of the major departments--selling, production and finance.

For it has occurred to some managerial minds that the problems of the enterprise as a whole are similar in broad outline to the problems of the shop, but on a greater scale. Just as shop management may bring specific orders, jobs, workers, machines and materials into a harmonious and economical relationship, mutually profitable to employers and workers, so the management of the enterprise as a whole may bring orders in mass, workers in mass, materials in mass, and equipment in mass into a similar harmonious and economical relationship, mutually profitable. The decisions pertaining to the enterprise as a whole, like the decisions pertaining merely to the factory, should and may have a factual basis; that factual basis should and may to a considerable extent be determined by the methods of science; even the major specialized tasks of management of the enterprise as a whole may be grouped into two grand divisions--planning and preparation on the one hand, and execution on the other. There should and may be a super-planning room for the enterprise. Therefore the development of sales engineering and market analysis, the formulation of budgets, master plans and schedules of sales, finance and production, and consolidated reports of departmental progress to check against these plans; just as in the shop there are now schedules and progress reports. It is the application of the principles of scientific management along these major lines as well as in detail, which has permitted certain firms to go through the recent depression with 98 per cent of normal sales, processing, and consequently employment of workers.

Now this is a matter of utmost importance. Wise managers and wise workers should strive for stabilization of the operations of an enterprise. It is not sufficient merely to stabilize the operations of the shop <u>when there are orders</u> (this is what scientific management in its early developments has accomplished); it is even more essential to stabilize the business and assure a <u>predetermined regular flow of orders</u> (which is what scientific management in its later developments is accomplishing in a number of enterprises). This is true for several reasons, two of which stand out; regularity of employment and income to workers and of profits to employers is more essential to human comfort than mere occasional economy resulting in occasional high wages and high profits; also regularity of orders, processing and employment has a great deal to do with detail economy, high wages and good profits. Scientific management has reached into the field of general management as a matter of necessity--it was inevitable. For as soon as it had taught managers how to develop the shop management of least waste, with its better wages and better profits, it realized that this management is dependent upon continuous performance; therefore, with the vision and persistence of Taylor, his managerial descendents have not hesitated to carry their principles into the field of general administration. If the reader should make two lists of enterprises, one of plants in competitive industries which have maintained reasonably regular operations and employment during the depression, and another of plants which are generally identified as Taylor plants, he would be astonished at the similarity of the two lists.

Scientific management has made its influence felt on a still higher plane. The present administration of the Department of Commerce has been endeavoring in many new ways to assist American industry. One was the appointment of a committee to investigate the extent of and the reasons for waste in American industry. The report of the Committee on Elimination of Waste in Industry is considered a most important public document; it was hailed by organized labor as one of the most important documents in their interest ever published--for it publicly placed the chief responsibility for waste on management. That committee was composed largely of Taylor engineers, its point of view was entirely Taylor, and the standards by which it judged waste were the standards, simon-pure, of scientific management. The present campaign of the Department of Commerce for simplified commercial practice (standardization of products within a trade) is the application in a large way of the good old scientific management principle of standardization of the products of the individual shop as an individual measure of economy.

The outstanding contribution which scientific management is now making, is to the solution of the problem of industrial relations. There have been advanced during the past four or five years many theories concerning the problem of industrial relations, nearly all of which have not and could not find practical expression; there have been many specific things attempted which have proved insufficient because they have not taken into consideration fundamental facts of human nature and of industry; now there is evident a tendency to turn for solution to the one thing which in individual plants has shown a large measure of success--management on a factual basis; in other words, scientific management.

There are many, both workers and managers, who believe that the only practicable means of settling industrial disputes is through strikes, lock-outs, jockeying in conference, temporary compromises, and so on, even though they recognize that these things are wasteful and costly to both sides. But there are others, both workers and managers in increasing number, who feel that the number of controversies would be materially reduced, if all the essential, indisputable facts concerning the situation which have given rise to a dispute could be laid on the table in negotiation, or even informally reviewed by representatives of both parties before the stage of formal controversy and negotiation is reached. When leaders of the two sides to a potential serious controversy approach each other with this common mental attitude, begin to consider the details which have contributed to the unfavorable situation, endeavor to get at the real facts, inquire into the conditions of the business and of the management, and finally attempt to formulate constructive remediable measures, it is found that these remediable measures have to do with the administration and management of the enterprise, and are in spirit and in technique essentially identical with scientific management.

For "industrial relations" connotes relations in the conduct of enterprise; relations with respect to policies, plans and their execution. These relations pertain to no one thing, but to everything in the enterprise; they are found in no one spot, but everywhere in the enterprise. They are as long, as broad and as deep as is management. The problem of industrial relations is a problem, the problem, of management. A personnel department may perform many useful specialized functions; but it should always be borne in mind that everyone in the enterprise is responsible for a personnel function; that the entire enterprise is the real personnel department. Problems of industrial relations arise out of the policies adopted by owners and general management; out of the nature of general plans and schedules; out of the detail plans, schedules and standards established by the planning room; out of the conditions of work, nature of the equipment, and nature and adequacy of the materials provided; out of the conditions of employment and the wage rates which are established; out of the mental attitudes and specific conduct of executives and foremen. The diagnosis of a situation which offers a potential controversy must be a diagnosis of the methods of management; the remedy must be practical measures for improvement of the management; and those practical measures which most frequently improve the management in such a way as to remove the unsatisfactory conditions, are found to be measures which express the principles of scientific management.

In this connection I should like to call attention to a most illuminating book--Common's "Industrial Government." It is a report on the new, forward-looking measures developed by some eighteen plants conspicuous for their attempts to solve their problems of industrial relations. They are plants which represent the progressive movement in management--and nearly every one is either an avowed Taylor plant or a plant which represents the spirit of scientific management.

It is my own conviction that at some future time, when the development of scientific management can be reviewed in proper perspective, its greatest contribution to the solution of industrial problems will be discovered to have been this: That at a time when American industry was dominated by ideals which made management but a game of chance, of trading in natural resources, growing markets, materials, equipment, processes, workers and equities, with now profit and now loss--that in the midst of an industrial society with such ideals, Taylor injected the concept that a business should exist for social service, that its purposes can be defined, its objectives planned and scheduled, detailed execution be so controlled as to contribute most economically to the final result, and that the final result can be a productivity of useful things so shared as to increase the comfort and promote the happiness of all concerned. In short, the Taylor philosophy of management first gave logical and coherent expression to the ideal that business should be an aggregate of processing enterprises instead of an aggregate of speculative enterprise, and his system of management pointed the way to the technical accomplishment of that ideal.

Most of our industrial problems are the consequences of conduct which expressed the point of view that business is a speculative enterprise, a point of view which has by no means disappeared. The remedy is to substitute conduct which expresses the point of view that business is a measurable, controllable processing to meet a social need. To the extent that such a substitution is made will industrial society increase its demands upon scientific management.

I believe the day is not far distant when organized labor will be the principal proponent of scientific management. It will insist that the enterprises in which it participates shall cease to be speculative and shall become stabilized processing activities; and when it has so insisted, and has been countered with inquiry as to how that is to be accomplished, it will--whether it uses the term or not--recommend the methods of scientific management.

---

[1] Bulletin of the Taylor Society, June, 1923. Reprinted from Brotherhood of Locomotive Engineer's Journal.

A DECADE'S DEVELOPMENT IN MANAGEMENT

TRENDS AND RESULTS OF SCIENTIFIC MANAGEMENT[1]

By Henry P. Kendall

It has been suggested that I consider this evening the difference between unsystematized, systematized and scientific management, reviewing from the point of view of ten years later, so to speak, the subject-matter of an earlier address. Something worth while might be gained by reconsideration of that subject, for even in these days there are consultants and practitioners--ostensibly of scientific management--who confuse systematized and scientific management; but I have reconsidered that address and prefer to let it stand as it is. The distinction there drawn still holds good, even for the scientific management of today, which is both more extensive and more intensive in its application.

The point of view of the earlier address was that of production management, while tonight I shall consider principally other fields of the application of scientific management. But let there be no misunderstanding; scientific production management is no less important than it was ten years ago--it is more important. Consideration of developments during the past decade calls for emphasis upon the new phases, but that does not mean that one considers the earlier phase of development of less importance either absolutely or relatively. If we have learned that scientific management in the shop requires also its application, for instance, in sales and personnel management, we have also learned that scientific management in sales, personnel or any other phase of management is conditioned on even more scientific management in the shop. Do not assume that Taylor was unaware of this; he stuck to his last, but he was aware of the necessity of other lasts. I recall that a small group of us were once querying him at Rockland, Maine, and one of us asked him why he had not turned his attention to personnel, sales and other aspects of business. He said he felt his life would be too short to attempt demonstration of the application of his point of view to those fields; that the most and best he could do was to make a thorough demonstration in the field of production management; that others on the basis of that demonstration could carry the demonstration into other fields of management.

I do not propose to consider tonight the tendency of scientific management during the past decade to extend laterally--to other plants and to other industries than those of its earlier application--its quantitative development. I am more interested in its development vertically, qualitatively--to more phases of management. Business has been becoming more complicated and exacting, has demanded more intelligence and clear, straight thinking, and has required more of the scientific approach to its problems in every phase of management.

Business has become conscious of a swinging through a cycle. A tremendous pressure on production came immediately before the war, and was intensified during the war and in the secondary inflation that followed. Then came a drop in business--the near-depression which for many industries was a real depression--which put a test on the principles of scientific management. Both the rise and the fall of demand and of production applied very unusual tests to this form of management: how could it provide control in a time of expansion and--much more important--what would be the effect of the larger overhead in scientific management when it came to curtailing, to trying to show black ink figures on 65 and 60 and 55 per cent of normal production?

We are faced today with anywhere from 15 to 30 per cent more productive capacity than we can utilize, because of the war expansion, lessened exports, and a timid domestic market. Costs are high; wages are at a new high level because of the war and show no tendency to decline. It has been the tendency in past depressions for wages to run along on a level even after depression has set in, although earnings will follow fairly closely the line of depression.

This new production capacity, the new standard of what industrial managers think is the normal output of their plants, has put an added pressure on the production organization for economies and lowered costs, the like of which we have not seen for years. It has likewise put a pressure on the sales organization for greater volume, new products and new markets. It has put a pressure on the financial, accounting and controlling organizations for exact knowledge of internal and external conditions, by which they can establish policies and lay out their courses. At no other time have the exactions been so great in that respect.

How has scientific management aided both in expansion and in contraction of business under these conditions? I propose to consider these questions with respect to _first_, manufacturing; _second_, industrial relations; _third_, selling and _fourth_, control. What have been the outstanding tendencies and results?

I. DEVELOPMENTS IN MANUFACTURING PROBLEMS

A. Plant Location

The engineering, the scientific point of view which Taylor inspired in management has put new emphasis on the importance of studying the plant, both location and construction. Traditions have been departed from more in the last few years than ever before. The high freight rates and the importance of being near either the sales market or the raw material market have made new studies necessary in the geographical location of plants. High freight rates, social legislation in the northern states, and the drift of the center of population and of purchasing power steadily westward have affected, for instance, the textile industry; and there has resulteda tendency to study scientifically the problem of location with respect to long-time policy. Many mills are moving south; some even to the west. Paper mills have a similar problem with respect to supply of wood pulp. The paper mills of Wisconsin, where it is estimated there are but eight years of pulp wood left, the Main Mills and New Hampshire mills have a problem and in consequence there is an unceasing tendency to develop in Canada to be adjacent to raw materials.

The power problem resulting from the high price of coal and the danger of interruption of the coal supply, the problem of labor supply and cost, the cost of living, the cost of owning homes--all of these facts have been given new study with relation to the location of mills and of plants.

B. Plant Construction

There has been a departure from tradition in the buildings, even in such an industry as cotton manufacturing, which has the tradition of years back of it. The history of progress in cotton mill machinery gives 1887 as the last time when any improvement of consequence in textile machinery was made. Cotton mill buildings until a very few years ago were similarly built according to an early standard. Within the last few years departures have been made. One textile firm studied the flow of the work and, departing from traditions, put in mechanical and gravity conveyors--an adaptation of the Ford idea to cotton manufacturing for the first time.

Recently a hat company in Connecticut felt that they needed to put themselves in a strong competitive position with the best equipped plant possible. They made very careful studies and decided that instead of revamping their present buildings, they would build an absolutely new plant, requiring a large investment, although their present equipment is quite up to the standard of their competitors. They employed production and mechanical engineers and mill architects who are working together to produce the very best plant possible.

In modern plant design new consideration is being given to the comfort of the workers. The war strengthened the position of labor and created an additional incentive for employers to turn more than ever before to a study of the labor situation within their own plants and of general labor tendencies; and the more enlightened managers show, in their building design, greater consideration for the comfort and the pleasure of their employees at work. Recently I visited the new plant of the President of this Society, and was surprised and pleased to see the amount of floor space which he had deemed it wise to give to the comfort and recreation of the employees. Engineers are thinking in those terms now for almost the first time.

C. Machinery and Equipment

I have not very much to say about machinery and general equipment except that high wages and keen competition are giving a new impetus to a study of labor-saving machinery and its economical arrangement and utilization, and to mechanical and gravity means of internal transportation. The increasing use of machinery has been one of the most conspicuous aspects of the development of manufacturing during the past half century; the most noteworthy feature of the past decade has been simply a more intense development due to more intense competition and ever increasing costs. The constant effort to substitute labor-saving equipment for labor has far-reaching effects. One concern found that the introduction of new equipment at one point in processing so influenced the volume of flow at that point as to necessitate adjustment through new or additional equipment at other points and an intensive study of the methods of operating and of handling material.

D. Purchasing and Materials Control

The scientific attitude towards management problems has given impetus to the study of the operating problem, and this phase of management has made a good deal of progress in the last ten years. And in purchasing a closer relationship between stores control and purchasing has been generally recognized.

One of the companies in which I am interested set up for a goal a few years ago a stores or inventory turnover of six times a year, as against the best previous practice of perhaps three or four times. That was accompanied by a closer relationship between purchasing and stores, a study of materials, of markets, of times of delivery, and of business conditions in the industries from which we purchased. We have been meeting that six times turnover for about two years. It released $50,000 of working capital for uses related to an expanding volume of sales. What does that sort of thing mean if carried out as successfully, or more so, in for instance a concern like the General Electric Company, which advertises to sell 420,000 different articles and carries in stock between 4,000,000 and 5,000,000.

A large company may find economies in setting up a special research and statistical department. One of the largest industrial companies--which I regard as the best managed large industry in this country--has within the last two years added an economist from one of our big universities to its staff. The comptroller of that company told me that while he had not expected to get any good from the studies of that economist until he had been there a year or two, in his first six months he made studies in fundamental tendencies in commodity prices, and the suggestions that he made to their purchasing department had already saved them several hundred thousand dollars.

Industry is not always willing to take the advice of such specialists, as the following statement from a large rubber company suggests:

> It would seem right to say that our statistical researches have not always been adopted. An example of this was the last coal strike in 1922. We presented studies showing that a sharp rise in bituminous coal prices in the past has always taken place when surplus stocks reached 20,000,000 tons, and we predicted that this point would be reached July 1st, 1922. This forecast was within 15 days of being correct. Prices began to rise sharply on July 15th, 1922 with the result that we paid around six and seven dollars for our supplies for the months of August, September, October and November. We have completed studies on the present outlook on coal and our people have adopted our recommendations not fully but about eighty per cent. This study shows that there will be a strike on April 1st, or if not, there will be an interruption of production. The coal stocks are around 65,000,000 tons, so that about June 10th, 1924 the 20,000,000 tons surplus mark will be reached, prices will rise sharply and will continue at high levels until production

is resumed and there are surplus stocks of 30,000,000 tons. This production follows our forecast in October that the time to contract for winter supplies of bituminous coal would be just before President Coolidge's message to Congress or about fifteen days after. This prediction proved correct information on coal. Our executives have adopted this suggestion and we now have in our storage yards 15,000 tons of coal.

1. Joint Research in Purchasing

Statistical research has been accelerated a good deal in the last ten years--both by companies themselves and by organizations. The Retail Research Association, established seven years ago for the benefit of certain non-competing dry goods department stores, with a membership of seventeen companies, is studying their organizations, methods and sources of supply, and is now running on a budget of $500,000 a year. It represents the purchases for sales that amount to $225,000,000 a year. Recently there has been formed in Boston a Manufacturers' Research Association, with a staff paid by assessment among a membership of twelve non-competitive manufacturing establishments, which is making the same kind of close analytical study of the different phases of management. Each member of this association has claimed to have saved at least the cost of the participation, and some of the concerns after less than a year's operation have saved it many times over. We have not reached the end of what analysis and thought, team work and exchange of ideas will do on the purchasing problem alone.

E. Time Study and Wage Systems

With respect to the efficiency of the workers, time study has been made a matter of fairly common practice, due to Taylor's efforts. Contrary to the opinion of a good many, time study has two distinct functions; first, to find the best way of doing a thing; and, second, to determine the proper elapsed time for doing it, as a basis for some form of incentive wage and for the better control of routing.

The particular method of wage payment is not important, but I think that in the past few years there has been a tendency towards a policy of some form of wage payment which has a relation to performance. The non-financial incentive methods of Robert Wolf and the development of the Bedaux system indicate that profitable study can still be made and is being made with respect to methods of wage payment.

F. Planning Room Control

Centralized control through the planning room is becoming more extensive and more intensive--more precise and effective because of the statistical knowledge which the chief executive now gets. I had considerable apprehension after the war as to what would happen when we were forced to curtail, whether we could cut down the overhead of planning room and functional management when we had a declining market. I have answered that question for myself conclusively.

In one of our plants which was affected by the aftermath of the war, so that its output dropped to one-third and was only by sales pressure brought up to 55 per cent, we were able to make necessary economies without cutting into the vitals of our control organization and to show eventually black figures on 55 to 60 per cent of normal output. I am satisfied that we could not have approached that control, that definite predetermined efficiency and cost without the Taylor methods.

In another plant we had somewhat similar conditions. I was pleased the other day, on receiving the figures, to learn that although because of competitive conditions, they had been able to operate on only 71 per cent of normal volume this last year, they had showed a profit of 13.3 per cent of net sales--in a highly competitive market and on a very close profit margin. Facts of that kind convince me not only of the efficacy of Taylor principles and their application, but of the importance of following them in bad as well as good times.

II. INDUSTRIAL RELATIONS

The belief of a good many that labor had had its day during the war, and that after the war the employers would have their day and the open shop would be established pretty generally throughout the country, has not proved sound. Notwithstanding certain setbacks, labor unions have increased in number; their treasuries and their strength have increased. The United States follows in many respects the same evolution as that of the older civilizations, and while we may not have to look forward to labor government in this country as is the case now in England, nevertheless it is very significant that labor has become stronger in negotiations relative to wages and conditions of work. We find that wages are from 100 to 110 per cent higher than the pre-war level, and the cost of living is only 62 or 63 per cent higher. Hours have been shortened. The worker has a better standard of living. He has more leisure. He is more of a student of economics.

I was interested four or five years ago in carrying on some negotiations with a labor union. The employers in the particular industry were gathered around a table, ready for negotiation with the usual horse-trading point of view. In came the executive committee of the union, and the secretary in a very businesslike way opened up a briefcase and said: "Gentlemen, the cost of living has advanced so and so, according to the figures published so and so, found on such and such a page of the Bureau of Labor statistics; wages in our industry have advanced only so and so. Now, gentlemen, let's get together and discuss our wages in the light of the cost of living." The employer group was completely taken off its feet, and before the next meeting they had an economist working out some of the facts. Things have taken a new turn.

A. The Basis of Sound Industrial Relations

One evidence of this new turn is the additional attention industry is giving to the question: What are the essential things that must be done to make labor contented? Whether you are for the open shop or whether you believe that labor ought to organize, and prefer to deal with organized labor, there are certain things which I think have been demonstrated as essential to sound industrial relations:

First: The worker wants security in his job. Whiting Williams and other men who have lived intimately with him have ascertained that his chief horror is the danger of losing his job.

Second: He wants an adequate wage, adequate as measured in commodity value.

Third: He wants a voice, individually or collectively or both, in the determining of conditions which immediately surround and affect him.

Fourth: He wants to be under the right kind of a foreman.

Fifth: The more ambitious worker wants an opportunity to raise himself by his own efforts into work of higher responsibility and higher earning capacity.

What have been the tendencies in scientific management to meet these desires?

1. Stability of Employment

I was listening the other day in our Research Association in Boston to a man who was advocating unemployment insurance. He said he had looked into it and it really would not cost as much as he had thought it would cost, because 60 per cent of his employees had worked less than a year in his plant. That interested me and I thought I would like to see, not for the purpose of unemployment insurance but for information, what the figures are in two of our plants--one of them the Plimpton Press at Norwood where, so far as we know, we were one of the earliest to functionalize employment and personnel. This plant was moved from Boston and established in Norwood twenty-six years ago; it has a normal working force of 721. I found that 4½ per cent of the force had worked there twenty-five years, 11½ per cent twenty years; 20 per cent fifteen years; 33 per cent ten years; 53 per cent five years; 64 per cent four years; 74½ per cent three years; 80 per cent two years; and 88 per cent more than one year. Part of that is due to a determined effort on the part of the company to stabilize employment in what is a seasonal industry. This has been done in two ways: one, by bringing in work that can be done, even at a loss, during the winter and the dull season; the other, by training in gradually high school and college students to help in the school book work at the peak season before the schools open.

The labor turnover, exclusive of that group of people who come in from school in the summer and go back to school in the fall, is interesting, too. Although the plant employs a large number of women and girls for whom turnover is normally higher than for men, the turnover in 1919 was 46 per cent; in 1920 52 per cent; in 1921 13½ per cent; in 1922, 15 1/3 per cent; and in 1923, 14½ per cent.

I turned to another concern, in which we really did not have effective personnel work until 1918. During these six years of operation I got the figures. In this plant, 56 per cent have been there five years; 62 per cent, four years; and 73 per cent, two years--though here also quite a number of workers are girls and women.

While our works manager was getting out those figures he gave me some others which illustrate that stability of employment develops a feeling on the part of the workers that they are part of the concern.

They talk about "our plant" and they become more and more experienced. In one department where the workers are machine tenders, where there has been no change in wage method--a flat hourly rate--there has been this last year, traceable the works manager thinks to just this growing feeling of proprietary interest, an increase of 11½ per cent in the man-hour product from that department for the year. Now, mind you, that is just a machine tending job where the speed or rather the output is determined by the machines and the increase comes in less lost time.

In another department in the same plant which is entirely hand work, there used to be a very low rate of production. They had a poor foreman and bad conditions. They got a better type of foreman, corrected working conditions and reduced labor turnover. The men were still on a weekly wage with no financial incentive, but the output measured in terms of pounds per man-hour increased from 113 in 1913 to 143 in 1920, 285 in 1922, and 378 in 1923.

I have been very much interested in the first joint efforts so far as I know in this country for the employers in an industry to accept unemployment as management's responsibility and to provide for it as a charge on industry. The Chicago Industrial Federation of Clothing Manufacturers and the local organization of the Amalgamated Clothing Workers of America have worked out a plan by which the workers are assessed 1½ per cent of their wages and the company contributes a like amount, so that during the dull seasons workers are guaranteed for four or five weeks, I think it is, 40 per cent of their wages. This is a much saner method, it seems to me, of attacking the problem of stabilizing employment than the English method of having it done through the government.

2. Adequate Wages

Taylor early enunciated the fact that low wages are not necessarily economical. In fact, he went so far as to say they are uneconomical. I think those of us who have been practitioners in that school hold that belief. It is the labor cost per unit that is important, not the wage.

Higher wages and higher earnings accompanied by low costs depend on stability of employment, freedom from labor turnover and precise control. Some illustrations of what is being done on those lines have already been given.

3. A Voice in Management

I have not yet found any employee who wants to sit on the board of directors, who feels that he can contribute to the general financial policy or the general sales policy. But workers everywhere have a lot of concern about that which immediately affects them.

The development of the works committee to capitalize in the manufacturing problems of the company the latent intelligence of the workers has been given new impetus. Works committees, like well organized employment and personnel departments, serve to form lines of communication: outlets for letting grievances out of the worker's system, and for expressing his aspirations.

Take again the labor unions. There is a growth unmistakably in the demand for collective bargaining. I am familiar with its development community.

Revamping the physical and the human side of the cotton mills in the South is a fascinating story and a problem in itself. I have been interested in a couple of these mills for six or seven years. We have improved conditions a little relatively--in the long run not very much--but the friendliness that crops out as you walk through the mill and the village is very different from what it was on my first visit--when no one looked up, when it was not regarded as safe to be in the mill village after dark. A trip now to those mills is a veritable spiritual uplift.

B. Psychology and Industrial Relations

The subject of industrial relations must not be left without mention of a new measuring device which management is using--the psychological test. There are four essentials which an employer wishes to know about an applicant for work. First, his general intelligence and ability. Now it doesn't need to be high. It is a mistake to put into a blind alley job a person of intelligence beyond the need of that work. Second, his habits of industry: how hard does the man or girl like to work? The idea of everybody being ambitious is, beyond certain levels, an exploted theory. I have tried to advance men into positions of greater responsibility and have them come back to me and say: "We don't want the extra money and the extra responsibility. We are happy at doing this job at that wage level and we would rather do it because we are happier doing it and it is less wear and tear on us." Third, his interests, What does he like to do? What gives him the most pleasure in doing? Fourth, his personality. How does he get along with people? How does his executive capacity or his willingness to follow fit him for the job?

Not all of these qualities can be tested, but in my paper of ten years ago I raised the query if psychology applied in the selection of workers by the development of the Binet test or something of the kind might not help in reducing misfits of square pegs in round holes. Because of that query and the interest in it, I have been looking into what applied psychology has done. I was interested in following the work of Walter Dill Scott and the psychologists whom he brought together in determining the rating tests for the classification of the draft army. He frankly admitted to me that these tests were very hastily put together; they accomplished something but were just a beginning in showing the possibilities of tests.

The General Electric Company in West Lynn has been going somewhat extensively into tests for the selection of workers because they were faced with the necessity of reducing their labor costs. One of their operations involves the preparation of jewels for the parts of a meter. They purchase sapphires from the size of a peanut to the size of a walnut. They cannot use another stone which it is very hard to tell from a sapphire. The Company engaged, at a considerable expense, George Kountz of Tiffany's to come up and show them how they could differentiate this sapphire from white jade by optical methods, but they were not always sure of the optical refraction, because it changed with impurities. So they tried to train girls to do that work. Now they do all of that in the printing trades with the old strongly established conservative unions, for the most part under pretty intelligent and able leadership. I believe that in some way those who are compelled by necessity to deal with labor unions or who wish to, have got to find a better basis of working than they have had in order to insure against industrial disputes. It is quite possible to have strikeless eras, I believe. An understanding of the background of unionism, of the abuses and grievances upon which the unions have thrived, of their underlying philosophy and traditions, is essential in dealing with them. In some unions in industries where the unions are strong and can curtail output and limit apprenticeship, it is a vital thing for the manufacturers to insure their future source of supply of labor, and the easiest way in such cases is by cooperation with the unions. On the other hand, in non-union plants, it seems to me it is essential to keep the organization free from grievances and from unrest, and to develop through shop committees and other methods responsible leadership, so that if those plants are taken over at any time by the unions you have a responsible body who have confidence in the concern and are not going to be stampeded by a Bolshevik agitator. That to my mind is the insurance that one should secure in operating a non-union plant.

4. The Right Kind of Foremen

When the history of the operations in France is written, a large part of the credit will go to the lieutenants and second lieutenants, the men who lived close to their men, who helped them in their troubles, who were there personally when they went over into "No Man's Land." And so to the foremen in industry. I think that industry by and large gives too little attention to the importance of the foreman. It is the foreman who represents the point of view and the personality of the company to the men, and there is nothing that is such a cause of grievance among employees as a foreman who is unfair, disagreeable, surly and ever faultfinding. Provision of proper foremanship is one of management's major tasks.

5. The Opportunity to Advance

It is pretty deadening for an ambitious, intelligent fellow, working away at one machine all the time, with a growing family, trying to pay for a house, wanting his children to go to high school and to get into an industrial stratum better than his own, to feel that he is hemmed around and limited in his sphere. He cannot be a contented workman. You have got to have a contented workman. Workers must have the opportunity to rise by their own efforts, their own intelligence and industry. That opportunity can come only through a well functioning employment and personnel department and the spirit of the plant back of it to teach and develop all ambitious employees. Corporation schools, vocational training in the plants and all that sort of thing have been a reflection of this consciousness on the part of employers.

There is a chain of candy stores that use as their slogan, "Happiness in Every Bag." I like to paraphrase that by saying, "Happiness in Every Shop." And that will mean happiness in the homes and in the sorting by girls who take these little precious jewels and toss them up in their hands and feel the weight of them--the specific gravity is about 3.8 and 4.2 respectively--and drop the sapphires into one place and the white jade into another and they do it more accurately than could be done by the Kountz method of optical refraction. They have arranged the selection of these girls by tests designed to test their coordination between vision and tactile sense, and these tests are working out quite accurately.

The general manager said he had some startling examples of the value of these tests, and though startling examples are not significant, this example is very interesting. One of his foremen wanted a girl for a certain job. Of two applicants turned over to him by the employment department for review he picked out Susie as the girl that he wanted. The tests for their adaptability to that particular kind of a job had said conclusively that Jennie was the girl. The general manager saw his chance to test the value--not conclusive at all--of this foreman's judgment and of the test; so both girls were hired and put to work. In thirty days Jennie, whom the test said was the better adapted, was doing twice the work of the other girl.

They have not compelled the old employees to subject themselves to the tests, but they offer to give them tests with the privilege on the part of the old employee of having the result of the test buried if he wishes it. Forty of these older employees told the management that they would like to be tested to see if they were not round pegs in square holes. Those forty were tested for their adaptability for different kinds of work, since various exacting jobs at the General Electric Company call for different attributes. As a result of these tests each of the forty had his position changed, and without exception each one of the forty increased his earning capacity by quite a little after he had reached his stride in his new job.

These are just indications that the psychologist, while he has not yet scratched the surface of industry, has a real contribution to make to industry in cutting down the percentage of failures, in reducing labor turnover, and in increasing the contentment of the employee by getting him into the job which he can do well.

III. SCIENTIFIC MANAGEMENT AND SELLING

During the war the industrial battle line lay within the production man. Now the sales managers have been moved up to the front. Their's is the fight and they have taken up the weapons of the production man. What have been the results of the application of the engineering point of view to sales management? It has meant an analytical study of the market as never before. It has meant an analytical study of the products as never before. It has meant a study of trade channels, the development and adaptation of new products for old existing markets, the development of new markets for old products.

In my previous paper I used as an illustration the work that had been done in improving a razor blade by much the same method that Taylor developed high speed tool steel. It was an indication of the forward looking point of view of that company. Patents on that particular kind of razor ran out last year. This might have been a matter of considerable concern to a good many companies, but for several years previous they had been perfecting an improvement, studying their market and arranging their sales campaign so that when the patent ran out the volume would not be impaired. Their planning was so well done that they not only maintained their old volume, but had to build a new plant to meet the increased volume.

A. The Study of the Product

Frequently some simple idea is the one which capitalizes the best. The other day I was shown rubber overshoes, or galoshes as we call them up in our part of the country, with a fastening that has been for a number of years familiar on tobacco pouches. You pull it down and your shoe is open. A simple thought, a simple application, but what has it meant to an industry in which this year has been especially bad because we haven't had any occasion to wear galoshes? An officer of that concern stated that they have been so overwhelmed with sales prospects that it looked as though they couldn't catch up for three years and the thing has hardly got out on the market.

The leather and shoe business has been particularly bad. We feel it especially in New England. A new sales manager who had no previous experience in the shoe business came into one of our New England shoe concerns a while ago and started in on an analytical, statistical study of the facts of the business. He found that they were spending a lot of money advertising their shoes, that they were operating a lot of retail stores which handled their trade-marked shoes exclusively, but they were dependent still for a large part of their output on shoes without their trademark, sold to jobbers on the jobber's specifications--which is the way the shoe business is very largely done. Not being hampered by the traditions of the industry, this sales manager started in to ascertain the facts of the business. He found that there were 150 styles or combinations which they made for jobbers on which they could make a profit. He advocated what seemed to the entire organization the dangerous decision to decline to make anything except those 150 styles and combinations, and to offer those to jobbers with the retail price and the name of the company, not the jobber, stamped on the bottom. It was hard to convince the organization, but he got his way, and that plan worked out. So far as I know that is the only shoe concern that has gone through this year without decreasing its production and without showing red ink figures. It was a formulation of a sales policy based on securing the facts of the business.

B. The Study of the Market

There has gradually grown a new conception of market problems which is evidenced by the desire to get at the real facts instead of going ahead on hunches. I have forgotten who it was who said that one of the seven deadly sins is the preconceived idea; certainly the experience of all of us in preconceived ideas, both as to management methods and as to selling, has cost us a lot of money. But the last few years have shown many interesting analytical and statistical studies.

I have a letter from the statistician of one of the large and conspicuously successful rubber tire companies. He uses for his sales department many statistics outside his business. From the returns from the Federal Income Tax a while ago he learned how many people receive salaries of $1,000 a year, how many $2,000, etc. Then he found out how many automobiles of various prices were owned, and how many were owned by people who kept two automobiles. His figures showed a surprising number of automobiles owned by people who couldn't afford to keep an automobile.

What were the conclusions? Roughly that there was a large part of the purchasing public who had to buy tires, who have automobiles that they can not really afford, hence have to buy a very cheap tire. So this concern started out to make a certain part of its output of those cheap tires which they knew from their statistical evidence were going to be purchased. On account of this sales policy they had just the edge on many other manufacturers.

C. The Evolution of Merchandising

The sales manager today is thinking more and more of merchandising his product. This is a new conception in selling. I was interested in the gradual evolution in the thinking of our own salesmen in one business that I am interested in, as revealed in a sales conference I attended in the Middle West this year. In all the discussions those salesmen were impressed with the fact that they must not only sell the jobber but also must think how to get the stuff from the jobber to the retailer and how to get it off the retailer's shelves. And they were all thinking in terms of merchandising the product so that it passed right straight through. We have been working for years to get out sales force thinking in those terms and it was extremely interesting to have it come out.

D. The Sales Budget

The outstanding tendencies, as I see it, in sales and distribution of the last few years are the use of statistics and the development of the sales budget. I was interested in an article describing what the Dennison Company had done after the war in studying their sales problem, with a view particularly of bringing sales and production capacity into a balanced relationship. They are one of the few concerns that came through the war and the aftermath of the war with practically no lessening in sales volume. The Walworth Manufacturing Company has made somewhat similar studies and has tied it up with the business cycle and with the curves of statistical organizations, and has budgeted its sales in advance. An article published in the Taylor Society <u>Bulletin</u> showed that in 1922 the twelve months sales volume was almost exactly what the budget had provided.

I had a personal experience that interested me recently. A year ago in November I had to take over a little business in which a certain community where I lived was interested, which was going to be sold through a receivership sale and might become a nuisance to us all. Not wanting to fuss with that business, I thought the best thing for me to do was to focus any experience and ability we had in industrial management right on that little business, organize it as though it were a little industry, tighten up all the loose ends and then turn the general financial supervision over to my assistant. We spent some time in its reorganization and among other things had made an itemized budget twelve months in advance. In fact this was made out before we got the business to find out whether we were buying a business which could make money or not, since it had been losing money up to that time. A careful budget of sales expectancy month by month, twelve months in advance from last November, and of expenses, departmentalized and divided with ample provisions for everything, showed that we could make perhaps a few thousand on the present basis of operation.

The manager of this establishment had never had any experience of that kind at all, and he and his accounting crew began to watch that budget. It became a non-financial incentive, and if they beat the budget they could not wait to get me the news of it.

That budget swung one side or another each month, but on the twelfth month it came out within $14.00 of its expectancy. That is just a coincidence, but so was Howard Coonley's twelve months budget which came out almost exactly. But it shows how the budget tells the story. We have the budgetary control in each enterprise that I am mixed up in--each budget for each plant made by its separate crew--and the accuracy with which they come out is almost uncanny.

E. Joint Research

In selling as in purchasing problems there are many opportunities for joint research. Those of you who adopt the policy that I have always adopted, of not hiring salesmen from competitors but training your own, know that you cannot always pick the right man, and you have to make an investment--and quite an investment--in many before you discover that they cannot be fitted for your work. The insurance companies have done much along this line, and since we are all poor prospects as insurance customers, insurance salesmen have certainly been well trained. But the insurance companies got together a cooperative fund which they placed at the disposal of the Carnegie Institute in Pittsburg for making studies covering the testing, selection and training of salesmen. I have understood that the insurance companies have gained a good deal from that, and that the Equitable, under their vice-president who was brought in from a teaching position in psychology, has had exceedingly good results. In the retail field, the Comptrollers' Congress, associated with the National Drygoods Association, has been one of the chief agencies in helping the retail drygoods stores develop sound selling methods.

F. Scientific Advertising

Statistical and research work is tremendously important in advertising, for advertising as a tool for selling has become ever more important. Advertising poorly done is tremendously expensive. The two great developments in advertising in the past few years, it seems to me, have been the tendency to truth, and the development of skill in making tests of advertising effectiveness.

One friend, a psychologist, who has given a good deal of thought and study to the effectiveness of advertising copy developed a series of tests of the efficacy of advertising matter. He applied his tests to the advertising copy of twenty large concerns, and then compared his conclusions with the actual performance of this copy, and he found his tests were 80 per cent accurate as to the effectiveness of the different kinds of copy. He is now making a study, with the aid of these tests, for a concern which during the first quarter of this year spent $35,000 in advertising a product which they had been selling for some time, but secured only $1,000 increase in sales. Now they have turned to see what applied psychology can tell them about that advertising material, so that they will get, if possible, 80 per cent of success instead of a fraction of nothing. If the validity of this method of testing copy can be established, it is going to increase sales efficiency.

I think we are going to see a gradual evolution in advertising. The way advertising is done now on a commission basis makes the advertising firms who have the greatest talent practically unwilling to give advertising advice or service to the man who does not have a large enough appropriation to give the agency a very real return. So the man who has from five to ten thousand dollars to spend on advertising--which he might spend very readily and fruitfully if properly advised--has no place to go to buy skill. I wonder if eventually advertising agencies and advertising advisors are not going to be on tap much as doctors and lawyers are, so that the moderate sized concern with a relatively small appropriation can get good advice in making that tool of selling more effective.

This sales and advertising drive, with advertising playing a larger and larger part in the cost of selling, together with the tendency of manufacturing to get low costs through quantity production seems to my mind to be pointing inevitably toward the larger consolidation of industry in this country. That tendency has already started in the textile industry. It is going on at a rapid pace in the automobile industry. Today 95 per cent of all the automobiles in the country are manufactured by thirteen concerns, and it is my guess that two or three years from now there will be fewer automobile concerns than there are today. I have seen the same tendency in rubber goods, in shoes and leather, in metal working, in woolen manufacture, and so on; and I think that with over-production, the keen competition for volume with the lowering cost is putting a premium on the best managed concerns. All this puts upon those who represent this school of management more and more of a burden to prepare for the problems that come with consolidation.

III. CONTROL

There is just one other phase of management which I want to speak of, and that is the development in the clerical, statistical, accounting and control end of business. In the old days and today the unsystematized form of management gets off its balance sheet of assets and liabilities once a year. The systematized form of management gets off its profit and loss and balance sheets four times a year or monthly. But about all they know about it is a simple analysis of sales and production and costs. Today an accurate, current and dependable cost system in the hands of the sales manager is absolutely essential to help him in his strategy. There are times when he has got to have the courage to take work at cost when the other fellow does not dare to, but he must know it is cost and not below cost. The executives in business today want not only internal statistics for their internal management; budget control of sales, manufacturing and purchasing require that they have external statistics such as the tendencies of raw materials in the market, the variable demands of markets for commodities, the availability of financial and technical resources and changes in these; the availability of workers, restrictions or regulations imposed by government, and so on. The growth of the big statistical organizations is an evidence of the importance that people are attaching to this need of business.

As I foresee the tendency of business, competition for a great many industries is and will be very keen in the next two or three years--a life and death struggle for volume. There is going to be a tendency to consolidation through the failure of the poorer managed concerns. The one-man type of establishment with its low overhead will always continue, and in many cases will be a thorn in the flesh of the larger concerns. But one is not safe without taking a long look to the future; and in the long run, there is a premium put on scientific management. The larger concern of the future will need superior production methods to produce a dependable product and a dependable service at costs lower than its competitors; it will need superior selling methods to guage the market, select proper channels of distribution and to search out and sell the consumer; it must have superior control methods--master plans, budgets, schedules of operation for a considerable period ahead, and detail independent schedules for selling, production and finance. The concern of the future needs to continue the development of the art and science of management. And if we are not going to have labor troubles and the economic waste of bad industrial relations, we must take a broad point of view in the handling of the human equation. With the broadening authority that comes from the growth of industrial enterprises there comes also a greater opportunity and a greater responsibility for making those enterprises agencies not only in producing and distributing their physical product better and more cheaply, but also in giving a wider opportunity for health, happiness, education, and progress for the many people employed and the communities which they support. In our organizations we try to feel that responsibility and are trying day by day to put more "happiness in every shop."

---

[1] _Bulletin of the Taylor Society_, April, 1924. An address before the Taylor Society, New York, January 24, 1924.

A CRITICAL ANALYSIS OF SCIENTIFIC MANAGEMENT[1]

Its Accomplishments, Shortcomings, and Future Obligations

By H. H. Farquhar
Assistant Professor of Industrial Management,
Harvard Graduate School of Business Administration

In presenting this paper I find myself in the accustomed position of being "between the devil and the deep sea." I am peculiarly fortunate in that I am constantly being admonished as regards the Taylor philosophy of management by two groups--by one for being too "liberal," by the other for being too "orthodox"! I hope that the friendly protests I constantly receive from these groups have at least resulted in a balanced viewpoint. The following discussion is offered not primarily as a representative of any group, but as the personal observations of one who, in preparing this paper, desires to be neither modernist nor fundamentalist.

I. SOME PREVALENT MISUNDERSTANDINGS OF SCIENTIFIC MANAGEMENT

It is a little curious in view of the very considerable literature on the subject that the movement that we are discussing continues to be so persistently misunderstood. I believe we cannot do better than turn back occasionally to the fundamentals as expressed in the writings of Taylor in an effort to clear up not only what Scientific Management is _not_, but also to see what is the real essence of its philosophy. Mr. Taylor has constantly emphasized, for instance, that it is _not_ any "system" or efficiency device or a new scheme of paying men, or time study, or functional foremanship; that "the mechanism . . . must not be mistaken for the true essence or underlying philosophy" because "precisely the same mechanism will in one case produce disastrous results and in another the most beneficient;" that "Scientific Management is _not_ a theory" but that "it is the practical result of a long evolution." He constantly combatted the serious and persistent misunderstanding that Scientific Management may be bought, or copied, and installed in a business in much the same fashion that a new process for making steel may be--a misunderstanding for which, as will be discussed later, I am afraid some of our own practices have been partially to blame. Mr. Taylor says: "The essence of Scientific Management consists in the application of certain broad, general principles, and the particular way in which these principles are applied is a matter of entirely subordinate detail."

Another fallacious idea for which no in particular seems to be to blame (unless it be what Sheldon has called Scientific Management's "profligate pursuer, 'efficiency'") is that all one needs do to have Scientific Management is to introduce some sort of incentive payment scheme. Taylor's followers, largely without avail, have constantly reiterated his position on this point, as for instance, when he says: "Under Scientific Management the particular pay system adopted is of minor consequence, and in many of our establishments we have six different pay systems all going on at the same time . . . ." He furthermore emphasized the "paramount importance" of standardization as a basis of incentive payment.

So much very briefly for some of the things which Scientific Management is not. Although Mr. Taylor emphasized the fact that the theory and philosophy was given almost no attention until long after its development in numerous industries, it is rather significant that of all who have attempted to tell of what this movement really consists, we still turn back to Mr. Taylor for the most complete and convincing description of its theory and principles. It is important to note that his very first effort was to harmonize the interests of the workmen and the management; he gives this as the first objective he had in mind when he was made foreman at Midvale.

The importance in which he held the matter of mutuality of interest is made clear when he says: "Scientific Management has for its very foundation the firm conviction that the true interests of the two (employee and employer) are one and the same; that prosperity for the employee cannot exist through a long term of years unless it is accompanied by prosperity for the employer, and vice versa."

As against these quotations from Mr. Taylor it is interesting to see what organized labor has to say in this connection: "It is not the mission of industrial groups to clash and struggle against each other . . . . Industry must organize for service . . . for justice to all who participate."

In its essence, then, Taylor conceived the movement which he started to involve a "complete mental revolution on the part of the working man . . . and on the part of those on the management's side . . . both as to their duty to cooperate in producing the largest possible surplus and as to the necessity of substituting exact scientific knowledge for opinion . . ."

He summarized the duties of the management in his four well-known "Principles": (1) the development of a science, (2) the scientific selection and development of the workmen, (3) the hearty cooperation with the men, and (4) the division of work and of responsibility between the management and the men.

As a result of Mr. Taylor's vision expressed in these excerpts, and in the light of the best development of these principles in practice today, I believe that we can briefly summarize some of the significant viewpoints which distinguish this movement. I believe there is coming to be a better understanding that Scientific Management rests upon the viewpoints:

1. That business is organic, no part of which can function to best advantage until all parts function to good advantage;

2. That thorough standardization and scientific methods throughout the whole business are necessary for organic control, that management must be based so far as possible on facts, and that ignorance leads to more harm than does malice;

3. That the interests of the employer and employee are mutual; that, as Mr. Taylor says, the principal object of management should be

to secure the maximum prosperity for employer and employee; that this viewpoint requires a change in mental attitude and a belief that employees cannot be tricked or driven into working efficiently, but that they must be carefully selected, trained in their jobs and fitted to the highest class of work of which they are capable, and that they be promoted on merit;

4. That the management must take the lead in bringing about proper conditions and mutual helpfulness;

5. That lasting development must come from within the organization; that Scientific Management cannot be "installed" from without; that outside assistance is often desirable, but that any outsider can do absolutely nothing unless the heart of the management is in the work, because the success rests absolutely on the management; that Scientific Management cannot remove the need of big men, but can make a little manager bigger and add permanence to the business.

6. That development must be democratic; that the road to opportunity must be kept open; that promotion must rest on proved ability backed by adequate records; and that sound methods will bring pressure to bear upon the management for the proper exercise of its functions;

7. That development must be based on principles, consciously, continuously and consistently enforced through <u>sound</u> <u>methods</u>.

Scientific Management is not "simply common sense"; neither is it simply the scientific method applied to the management of industry. Both of these definitions leave out of account the "mental revolution" and the mutuality of interest so constantly stressed by the founder of the movement. I believe "Scientific Management" at its best comes pretty close to being the golden rule made operative in industry through the scientific method.

II. POSITIVE CONTRIBUTIONS OF SCIENTIFIC MANAGEMENT

In setting down as impartially as I can what I believe to be the principal contributions of Scientific Management at the present time, it would, of course, be folly to claim any monopoly of effort along constructive lines for the movement as a whole or for any business operating under its principles. These cases are simply illustrations of what may be accomplished along so many lines, by a policy of conscious and continuous taking thought of the numerous economic and social factors which make for permanent success, and of coordinating these elements into a rounded, balanced management.

A. Original Contributions

The outstanding accomplishments of Mr. Taylor and his associates are well known and require only a reference. His revolutionary invention of high speed steel has had a profound effect on all metal-cutting establishments; as a result of long investigation we have the standard shapes of tools which are in everyday use in all well-run shops today, the marvelous slide rules devised by Mr. Barth, and the modern automatic tool grinder. As part of his early work also came the standardization of belting care and maintenance which constitutes best practice up to the present time. The present sharp line which well-run plants draw between planning and performance is a direct outgrowth of his later work. His instructional or functional form of organization, found in such wide use today, is a direct heritage from his early insistence on making the work of the management more effective. Over thirty years ago he devised a cost system which, with slight modifications, has not suffered in comparison with the best along this line that we have at the present.

Some of the significant contributions, as outlined in a paper by the present writer in 1919, will be briefly summarized, but reference must be made to that paper for a more extended discussion of each of these contributions than is possible here.

1. The Mechanical or Impersonal Aspects

a. Increased Production

By far the most striking single fact as regards the results of Scientific Management is the very considerable increase in production it has effected with the same equipment and personnel. And this result has not been always secured, as might be assumed, from plants that were near the lower level of efficiency before the development took place.

Of the various means by which Scientific Management increases production and decreases cost, some--such as the selection, fitting and training of the workers, the reducing of labor turnover, absences, lates, etc., the determining and securing of a proper day's work and the paying of a correspondingly increased wage--are distinct economic gains in themselves. These will be indicated under the human factors. Others, however, only indirectly related to questions of personnel relationship, merit mention here. Among the most important of these are:

(1) The more effective utilization of equipment, a use greatly stimulated by Mr. Gantt's admirable idleness charts showing as accurately as may be the cost of each different kind of idleness;

(2) The more effective use of labor through scientific man and job analysis and the devising of better methods of work;

(3) The strict regulation of materials through simplification and standardization, and through methods of control of material activities;

(4) More accurate routing, including both the physical layout and the administrative control of work in process; and finally,

(5) The regulation of industry. Perhaps nowhere better than in the elimination of seasonal production and its attendant evils is the fact illustrated that what is of permanent benefit to the management also benefits the workmen, and vice versa. That seasonal variation in many cases is not an unpreventable waste has been amply proved by those industries which have attacked and eliminated the evil.

b. Improvement in or Maintenance of Quality

Scientific Management has pretty conclusively shown that as between speed and quality there is not only no intrinsic irreconcilability, but indeed that with intelligent handling an improvement in quality has usually accompanied increased speed. Just why this is so may be left largely to the psychologists--we are dealing simply with the abundantly proved fact.

c. Speedy Production and Accurate Delivery

The firm which can accurately predict and rigidly maintain delivery dates is not only in an enviable position from the buyer's standpoint, but may claim a distinct contribution to itself, to the buying public, and to the community at large. This control, characteristic of the properly managed plants, constitutes a decided antidote to the tendency for ever-increasing costs of living.

d. The Power and Stimulus of Knowledge

As a final consideration under the industrial or non-human aspects comes the confidence, the sense of security, the power and stimulus which spring from the knowledge that we have real control of our business through the ordered regulation of its activities according to adequate knowledge and best practice.

2. The Human Factor

Important though it be for the country at large that we have high production and low costs, that we establish a strong industrial basis, it is of greater importance that while we are making _things_ we do not forget that our first and infinitely more important duty is the making of _men_--making good citizens.

a. Industrial Peace

The fact seems to be that in scientifically managed plants there has been remarkable freedom from the turbulent and distressing manifestations of industrial maladjustments characteristic of the last few years. This absence of labor trouble is due undoubtedly to a combination of causes; to a spirit of cooperation--the "mental revolution" which is such a vital part of Scientific Management; to fair dealing; to a proper work environment; to a spirit of democracy, to increased individual production; to high wages unaccompanied by over-exertion; and to a feeling on the part of the employee that his best interest is being and will be looked after. It is due indeed to all these factors; it is inclusive of them all.

This fact is of pre-eminent importance at the present time. The bringing about of industrial peace in its establishments is unquestionably _the greatest_ contribution of Scientific Management.

b. High Wages

Increases in the earnings of operatives working under Scientific Management are too common and well known to need repetition.

c. Proper Working Hours

Mr. Taylor was one of the first to recognize and to prove the fact that overlong working hours are not conducive to high output, and that in very many cases hours of work may be sharply decreased up to a certain point and output increased simultaneously.

d. Conditions of Work as Related to the Health and Well-Being of the Worker

Looked at from the entirely personal, selfish, financial aspect, there can be no question that the very best condition of the employee is the very best condition for the owner of the business. That the owners and managers of plants under Scientific Management primarily and continuously have the best interests of their people at heart--not from any ulterior motives, however, but because they are "that sort of person"--I believe can be doubted by no one who will take the trouble to visit them and their employees.

There is another phase of this question, however, which is of much greater importance in that it affects the workman during his entire life as a productive member of society. This is the determination, through time study and allowances for rest and necessary delays, of "the best day's work that a man could do, year in and year out and still thrive under." It is significant that the first "fatigue study" ever conducted in a really scientific manner, so far as the writer's records show, was performed over thirty years ago by Mr. Taylor as a part of his determination of a proper day's work.

In closing the discussion of this particular topic, it may be stated that, in spite of the oft-expressed fears that the so-called "speeding-up" would result to the immediate or ultimate detriment of the worker, no authentic case of anything but beneficial results of high individual production has been brought to light.

e. Selection, Fitting and Training

It would be difficult to overestimate the advantage both to the individual and to the nation of a condition where each person could be engaged, under conditions satisfactory to him, upon work for which he is naturally best fitted.

In plants run under Scientific Management, committed as they are from early days to a policy of "scientifically selecting, training, teaching, and developing the workman," it is the customary thing to find operatives who are now doing excellent work on their third, fourth, or even fifth trial after having previously been unsuccessful at work for which even they originally thought they were best fitted. We naturally expect to find, and do actually find, numerous cases of promotion from the ranks.

f. Free Scope for Individual Initiative and Opportunity for Advancement

The criticism has been made that in working under the highly standardized conditions and detailed instructions that Scientific Management insists upon, there can be little chance for the exercise of one's individuality. This accusation is true in that we do not let a novice tamper with a new and delicately built mechanism until he proves that he has mastered it.

It is not individuality and initiative run wild which is really constructive; it is intelligently applied individuality, and prerequisite to this is an understanding of things as they are and how they have come to be what they are.

So far from killing the right kind of initiative, Scientific Management plants are promoting individual initiative in the truest and highest sense--the initiative of the enlightened type of workman. The oft-quoted criticism that under Scientific Management the worker's job is monotonous, overlooks the fact that monotony is due not so much to the unvarying repetition of recurrent operations, as to the accompanying feeling that the work holds no future possibilities. The consistent policy of promotion from the ranks has done much to make every workman feel that he has a marshal's baton in his knapsack. Instructional (or functional) foremanship opens up avenues for advancement to others than the exceptionally gifted workman.

g. Reduction of Labor Turnover

Much of the restlessness in industry is curable. It is caused by the existence of unsatisfactory conditions in just those features of management discussed in the preceding topics--too low wages, long hours, poor working conditions, lack of proper selection, fitting and training, and to a conviction on the part of the employee that for him his present job in his present place offers no future. Naturally, therefore, with the removal of the causes in any particular place the evil itself largely disappears. This has been the experience in numberless plants which have adopted advanced measures more or less completely.

h. Spirit of Cooperation and Confidence and Feeling of Security

As a result of all of the positive products of advanced management enumerated above come the last and most important of them all. Indeed, so important are the spirit of cooperation and confidence and the feeling of security on the part of the whole personnel that nothing should be allowed to undermine them; for without them, although a certain _efficiency_ may be obtained, _true Scientific Management_ is impossible.

Cooperation may be obtained only be securing the _confidence_ of those with whom we deal, and this confidence in turn results only when each man feels _secure_ in the belief that he is in the best possible place for him and that he need have no fear for the future so long as he fully plays his own part. Only when the management really assumes its full share of the work and the responsibility may his confidence be secured. And only through making this security and this confidence an actual fact has Scientific Management been able to produce what it so highly prized and what it has so remarkably obtained--true cooperation.

B. Refinements in Technique

There are some significant advances which have been made during the last few years which can be referred to only briefly. Since progress has been rapid and widespread, the following list of accomplishments must necessarily be incomplete.

1. Cost Methods

Mr. Taylor's early work set up admirable means for the collection of costs and the distribution of overhead expenses. Mr. Gantt emphasized strongly the desirability of ascertaining that part of expense of operation which was due to idleness of various causes. The result has been that in the last few years much attention has been given to the establishment of "standard costs" or standard rates for overhead distribution. In fact, I question whether the pendulum has not swung too far in this direction in that the actual cost is too often disregarded by simply taking the difference between actual and standard directly to Profit and Loss. I feel that Mr. Taylor himself would have heartily approved of setting up a normal or standard overhead rate, but that he would have most emphatically condemned our using the resulting theoretical cost figures alone without being able to compare them with the facts--the actual cost of the product, including all expense of turning that product out.

2. Organization

What seems to me to be one of the really significant developments is that made by the Joseph & Feiss Company in functional organization. Among other valuable features, this organization is tied absolutely to the cost classification so that the expense of performing each function is definitely tied to the man responsible for that function. It is hoped that this matter will be the subject of a future paper before the Society.

3. Fatigue

The publication in 1917 of Merrick's articles on "Time Study for Rate Setting" (followed later in book form), with the fatigue allowances presented, can by no means be overlooked as a distinct addition and extension of Mr. Taylor's pioneer work in the study of rest and delay allowances.

4. Executive Reports

Much remains to be done in the field of executive reports, both as to subject matter, form, and period of time covered. There are two noteworthy developments which must be mentioned here: one, the admirable administrative guide called the "Progress Chart," devised by Mr. Gantt; the other, the advanced thinking presented in a paper entitled "A Technique for the Chief Executive" presented to the Society in 1921 by John Williams.

5. Control

We are familiar, of course, with the refinements of control worked out by Mr. Barth and Mr. Babcock at the H. H. Franklin Manufacturing Company. I am not sure that the latter gentlemen has not at the Holt Manufacturing Company out-Babcocked himself in securing a degree of control that seems to come pretty close to the ultimate goal. With Mr. Babcock's permission I quote from a statement on this subject which he gave me under date of December 29, 1923:

> A significant fact which should be noted in connection with the results of scientific management at this plant is the absolute control and regularity with which our product is produced. For a period of 496 working days, starting with March 13, 1922, up to the present time, our shops have not failed in one instance to bring through exactly the number of units of product which were scheduled to be finished on each of the 496 working days.

6. Adaption of Methods

As is pointed out later, one of the most serious shortcomings of which we as a group are guilty is an over-readiness to accept as suitable, under a wide diversity of conditions, methods which have proved satisfactory in one or more instances. I am glad, however, to record the fact that a distinct advance has been made in the last two or three years; first, in analyzing the particular situation in hand, and second, in devising methods to meet that situation.

C. Application to Broader Fields

This record would be incomplete without referring even very briefly to the significant extension of Taylor principles to fields outside of production proper. Probably as fine an example of Scientific Management as we have today is to be found in the non-selling departments of the Jordan Marsh Company of Boston, Mass. Should the members of this Society have an opportunity to investigate that development I am sure that they would be struck with the extent to which the principles, and even the detailed methods, with which they are familiar in a factory, have been applied to a department store. The work which has reached such a high plane in this firm is being extended in several other similar establishments. Similarly, the managements of general offices in manufacturing plants, and banks, etc., particularly as regards layout and office procedure, are being reorganized in several instances in accordance with the principles found so effective in the factory.

It would be impossible in the space available to give due praise to the splendid development of the principles and methods which such firms as the Dennison Manufacturing Company, and the Joseph & Feiss Company have made in the selling ends of the business. I believe the leadership which a few of these firms is showing in the field of distribution is destined to have a profound affect on American industry.

A significant line of development also is experienced in the maintenance department of a large eastern mill. Gratifying savings in cost of actual repairs as well as freedom from breakdowns have been made through careful inspection, through standardization and advanced planning of all maintenance work so far as it can be foreseen, through elementary time study, and through the payment of bonus.

Reference should here be made to the widespread adoption of budgets and quotas as simply an extension of the general principle laid down in "Shop Management" of setting up standards and of measuring actual performance (whatever form it may take) against such standards.

Reference has been made to the early efforts of Scientific Management plants to regularize production. It is gratifying to note that these attempts have been followed up and extended to cover the span of the business cycle.

Following the extension of the principles of Scientific Management to the selling end of several businesses, has come the effort, as yet scarcely under way but destined to receive increasing attention, to raise the level one stage higher by extending the same principles to the control of the total activities of the business. This attempt to coordinate sales, production and finance, coming to be known as "master planning for balanced management," is occupying much attention today in progressive firms.

D. General Influence on Industry

Mr. Taylor as early as 1895 said:

> This system of management will be adopted by but few establishments, in the near future at least, since its really successful application . . . . involves such thorough organization that . . . . but few manufacturers will care to go to this trouble until they are forced to . . . .

Although this prophesy regarding the number of establishments has been borne out, nevertheless the influence of Taylor philosophy on industry has been tremendous. Many organizations which would be very loath to admit it, show unmistakably the influence of this movement. The growth in numbers of really scientifically managed plants has been slow, but what is of much more importance, there has been a growth, and this growth has been entirely healthy and permanent.

1. Although some other "philosophies" of management can claim many more original converts, nevertheless the plants which have really achieved true Scientific Management almost without exception are running along as merrily today as they were five, ten, or twenty years ago, while the examples of these other systems existing today are exceedingly rare. The object lesson of this permanence resting upon thorough conversion has not been without its effect on industry generally.

2. This permanence is particularly striking in view of the readjustment period since the war. The present writer raised the question just prior to the depression as to whether the methods or even the principles of Scientific Management would not have to be very closely scrutinized and possibly materially modified during the coming years of a declining market. Rather extensive investigation, both personally and through correspondence, has revealed the gratifying fact that these

principles have in no way been found wanting, and that is most cases not only the principles but the methods used have stood up together with altogether healthy refinements and modifications made to adapt them to changed business conditions.

3. Scientific Management has affected industry generally by pointing out the only known method of attempting even a partially satisfactory solution of wage problems, that is, by making a sharp distinction between the amount of work and the amount of pay for that work. Only through a determination of a standard output may industry be assured against a disproportionate increase in the cost of living due to possible decreased production with increased wages.

4. Another significant influence has been the lesson pointed out so forcibly that it is the little things which produce profits. Seldom can dividends be paid out of revolutionary inventions--they must ordinarily come through constant attention to what someone has called the "tremendous trifles."

5. Possibly the greatest effect, although as yet not very widespread, is the emphasis which Scientific Management has placed on the responsibilities of the management as against those of the workman. It has been shown conclusively, I believe, that it is the management's duty to bring about thorough standardization and accurate planning and control before asking the workman through an incentive method of payment to exert himself toward increased production.

6. Finally, the general acceptance on the part of the average manager of the desirability and place of the scientific method in the management of business has been particularly noticeable during the last few years. It is true that many managers still shy at the word "science," and it is true that we have as yet barely scratched the surface in the application of the scientific method to industry, particularly as regards departments other than the shop; but the entering wedge has been driven, and as Professor Sederholm of Finland has said:

> . . . . Industry . . . . has not yet advanced beyond the Mesozoic stage, but the time will soon come when people will regard shops without a planning department of sufficient size, shops where hundreds of laborers are managed by half a dozen engineers and foremen, with the same wonder as is felt by us when we look at the skeleton of a *Diplodocus Carnegie* with its gigantic body and almost microscopical brain.

III. NEGLECTED OPPORTUNITIES

It has previously been stated that it would be improper to claim for the Scientific Management movement any monopoly of effort and accomplishment along many of the various lines indicated previously, although this movement has always been at the front of new developments. In considering what seem to me to be some of our neglected opportunities, I wish also to state that Scientific Management as such must not be blamed because it has not completely solved partially unsolvable problems. It must be remembered that many of the unsatisfactory conditions under which we work today are heritages of an age long past. The problems and ills of the individual due to the massing of workers, the economic dependence of the employee on the employer, the specialization of process and the minute subdivision of labor have not, as is sometimes intimated, been brought on by Scientific Management. They are inherited problems and abuses with which, in common with other agencies, Scientific Management must deal. The following queries are therefore raised, as to whether Scientific Management has made as aggressive an attack on these bigger problems as it might have. The attempt will be made to deal only with those features which we can remedy or at least strongly ameliorate, and which, therefore, will be of concern to any group interested in the future of the movement.

A. The Art as Distinct from the Science of Management

Oliver Sheldon has forcibly brought out the distinction between "operative sciences," which embody standards of procedure with respect to different kinds of processing, the "managerial sciences" or the sciences of putting these standards into operation, and the general administration of an enterprise. He further brings out very clearly the fact that while there may be a considerable managerial science, there is without question much in management that must remain an art. There must still be required the skilful exercise of human faculty, since there can be no science, for instance, of cooperation--cooperation rests not on scientific but on ethical principles. I believe Sheldon has done a real service in putting this viewpoint before the Society and that because we have not sufficiently recognized these distinctions in practice, we have fallen into a number of serious errors.

I wonder whether we have given sufficient weight to the question of personality in management; I wonder whether we have not tended a little too strongly to establish scientific methods, to tie these together into a logical "system," and to rely on this oftentimes beautifully designed machine to accomplish our objects, forgetting that such a system, just as is the case with any other system or mechanism, requires human direction and control?

I wonder if we have sufficiently realized that, in order to live up to Mr. Taylor's ideals, the need of real leadership is even more necessary than under the older types of management; I wonder whether on the contrary there has not been a tendency to employ too cheap clerks at certain strategic positions in the organization, trusting that the carefully outlined procedure would make up for their lack of leadership and personality?

I wonder whether, with our admirably proper insistence on considering each individual as an individual, we have not obscured the possibility of making that individual and his fellows more productive and more contented through recognizing the psychological benefits to be gained through group dealings?

I wonder whether we have considered the question of fatigue from a too coolly scientific viewpoint?

B. Labor

Many of us feel that it is unfortunate that Mr. Taylor expressed himself so frequently and so forcibly on the question of soldiering, and that he emphasized the profit motive on the part of the workman almost to the exclusion of other instincts and motives in life in which at heart he knew every workman is interested. This attitude on the part of the leader I fear has been too largely inherited by his followers. I believe it is true that the average American workman is not inherently lazy, but on the contrary is delighted to put forth his best efforts in production and in cooperation where he can be even reasonably assured that the management is doing its own part and that it really has his best interests at heart. Have we had the dollar so firmly fixed before our own eyes that we have assumed that the workman is similarly constituted, overlooking the workman's pride in workmanship, his logical desire to retain what he considers to be his own tools of livelihood. . . his trade secrets . . . and his desire to be a regular fellow in his own group? I wonder if we have sufficiently remembered Mr. Taylor's admonition:

> The principles of Scientific Management must rest upon justice to both sides, and it is not Scientific Management until both sides are satisfied and happy.
>
> Now if the mechanism . . . of Scientific Management . . . is used by unscrupulous people, it is not then used under Scientific Management; it may do a durned lot of harm.

Can we honestly say with Mr. Taylor:

> . . . if the results of my work were merely to increase the dividends of the manufacturing companies, I certainly should not devote my time to this object. Scientific Management is for me, then, primarily a means of bettering the condition of the working people.

I wonder whether we have sufficiently realized that to get real cooperation on the part of all of our people it is desirable to give them the psychological appeal of at least some stock ownership in the enterprise? Experience has proved that stock ownership by the employee has a tremendously beneficial effect upon the management. Incidentally, I wonder whether we have considered also our obligation to the public at large, whether Mr. Taylor's comment given below does not apply with considerable force even today:

> Most of us see only two parties to the transaction, the workmen and their employers. We overlook the third great party, the whole people, the consumers, who buy the product of the first two and who ultimately pay both the wages of the workmen and the profits of the employers.
>
> The rights of the people are . . . greater than those of either employer or employee.

C. Organized Labor

Scientific Management has to date neglected its opportunities and obligations to organized labor. There are many indications that organized labor's attitude and cooperation with managers in the application of the principles of Scientific Management have changed for the better. We should, however, show more readiness to meet organized labor half-way in a constructive program, and also aid by combating in a helpful non-antagonistic spirit the uneconomic practices on the part of some labor leaders. I believe there are great possibilities for cooperation, but they imply a prime obligation on our part of absolute straightforwardness and friendly instruction in the high principles for which we stand. It also places upon organized labor a prime obligation of recognizing that all men are not created mentally, mechanically or productively equal, and of allowing individual liberty to produce up to individual ability.

Mr. Taylor's attitude towards organized labor has been misunderstood by most people. For his views we can turn to his own writings:

> . . . in many establishments under the ordinary system, collective bargaining has become and is in my judgment an absolute necessity.
>
> . . . there is no reason on earth why there should not be collective bargaining, under Scientific Management just as under the older type, if the men want it.
>
> . . . I have not the slightest objection, and never had had, to collective bargaining, but I merely say that under the principles of Scientific Management that necessity has never come before me.

D. Lack of Adequate Analysis

What I shall have to say under this topic will be largely destructive criticism. It is offered merely as having possible value for future analysis.

It seems rather an anomaly to charge against engineers and scientific managers, above all things a lack of analysis, yet I feel that this is one of the most serious criticisms to be leveled against most of us who attempt to follow the technique of Mr. Taylor. I believe it is partially due to the fact that we are so intent upon following him that we do not always stop to realize that he himself would undoubtedly have disapproved under present conditions numerous things which we have done and have left undone in his name.

Our most serious failure is neglecting sufficiently to analyze the particular sales, production and financial problems of the particular business before attempting to apply methods for more effective management. The fact that practically all groups particularly interested in industrial management have done likewise does not by any means excuse us who have the reputation for possessing a scientific, analytical method of attack. I refer specifically to an analysis of the general type of industry (assembly or continuous); to the present size of the business; to the competitive state of the business; to the character of the personnel as regards the skill required on the part of the management and the workmen, and the general "intelligence level" of this personnel; to the traditions and type of management, i. e. whether autocratic or democratic, its policy as regards promotion from the ranks, and the mental and spiritual development and coordination of personnel; to the degree of quality required in the various operations and in the finished product; to the existing degree of departmentalization, and the possibility of modifying present arrangements in this respect.

All of these factors and many more, I submit, must be carefully analyzed before even the general type, much less the details of production control most suitable to the particular circumstances, can be determined. I believe we should not have quite so much argument as to whether centralized or decentralized management is better if we confined our arguments to a particular plant of a particular size, because the question of the proper degree of centralized as against decentralized control is very considerably one of size and departmental arrangement. Similarly, the types of organization, the questions of degree of functionalization, are scarcely things to be scrapped over in general but only as regards a particular situation. We have had too much of a tendency to impose our pet mechanisms promiscuously on plants of widely different character, just as was so long ago the custom with certain persons to sell family medicines good for all diseases. As a result, individual businesses have had to cast off these unsuitable mechanisms (mechanisms perfectly good in themselves when used under the right conditions) with the result that in more than one case I have in mind not only the mechanisms but even the principles for which we stand have become discredited.

Is it not still true that as Robert G. Valentine said in 1915:

> A great deal of the Scientific Management in use at the present day, whether in sales, finance, production or personnel, is similar to the situation in which a great deal of money might be spent in curing of flat foot a person who had some disease of the bone which might lead to amputation. This lack of coordination is an excellent illustration of one of the basic inefficiencies which permeates the world today.

It becomes so easy to let good enough alone, to use outworn mechanisms and to hold to outgrown notions. As Alexander Meiklejohn says:

> . . . The bane of a democracy is the man of easy solutions . . . such a man is a pest when there is thinking to be done. He does not need to think; he knows. He does not need to experiment; he has already found out. His father has told him, or his party, or his common sense, or his church.

It is a pleasure to quote Carl G. Barth:

> . . . the fact so often laid stress upon by Mr. Taylor himself . . . that while the principles of his system of management were essential, yes even perhaps as immutable as the laws of nature, the detail mechanisms he had to date developed for the attainment of the results aimed at, were necessarily subject to continual, if not continuous, growth and change. He laid such stress on this as to express

> the opinion that not a single one of his details, either paper forms or mechanical contrivances, would be in use ten years after he handed them over to myself and my co-workers.
>
> Because Mr. Taylor invariably insisted upon the use of such forms and contrivances as had been developed . . . up to a certain time, until the members of a new organization should have become thoroughly familiar with these, his "system" undeservedly got the reputation of being an uncompromising and rigid code . . . .
>
> . . . Whenever a workman had learned to obtain results known to be possible by an implicit following of . . . instructions, Mr. Taylor even insisted on a special reward being given him for any suggestion that would lead to improved instructions and better results.
>
> Mr. Taylor's whole spirit was that of continued progress, <u>but by evolution only and not by revolution</u> . . . . .

It is in this spirit that progress must be made.

E. Our Failure to Get Our Message Accepted

It is folly to delude ourselves into believing that the message which we have been preaching for thirty years has reached the average or even the high-grade manager. The apparent salability of various "efficiency systems" and incentive payment plans, dressed up in new and attractive clothes but as a matter of fact violating the very basic principles of sound management which we have been proclaiming, would seem to testify to our failure to impress the average manager of industry.

Believing as firmly as we do in the fundamentals of the industrial philosophy initiated by Mr. Taylor, why have our mechanisms and methods received so much attention at the expense of the basic principles? Why have we failed to make management and men realize the mutuality of interest existing between employer and employee; to bring the management to a realization of its own responsibility as against that of the workman; to make the manager know that before he is justified in an appeal to the workman through incentive payment or any other measures to give forth the best he has, he, the manager, must first do his full share in standardization, planning and the providing of proper working conditions? Is this condition due partly to complacency, or to a lack of aggressiveness or persuasive powers on our part?

To be sure, it is sometimes difficult to get some managements to assume their just share of the work and the responsibility, and Taylor himself had his share of this difficulty. That the development of his principles of management would necessarily be slow, was foreseen by Mr. Taylor as early as 1895, and he emphasized the very necessity of slow development. Yet I find most managers are willing to do their share when it is made clear to them of what their share really consists. I wonder how much of our failure to impress the manager and to secure the progress we desire is because we have given more thought to training the workman than we have to training the management?

Much of the disregard of what I believe to be fundamentally sound principles of industrial relationship as laid down by Mr. Taylor has been due to a lingering prejudice against the name "Taylor" and to a reaction of scepticism connected in the linking of the terms "scientific" and "management."

Undoubtedly also our message has not been more fully absorbed because, as Taylor himself has pointed out, the easy way is usually more attractive to the average manager. Short-cuts are particularly tempting. It is due also to the fact that we have been talking calculus much of the time when the manager is still struggling with elementary algebra.

Primarily, however, I believe it is a case of psychology. Mr. Taylor himself was not noted for his tact and appreciation of the psychological elements in human affairs, and I am afraid that we have tended to forget certain principles of mass as well as of individual psychology. I am afraid that we have too often given the impression to the manager that nothing which he has or does is worth much, that we have asked him as well as his workmen to "lose face" by expecting that he "back up" on matters which he cannot do without losing status, as well as by failing to give credit for good work and good suggestions where credit is due.

We must admit that some who are least sound in their principles and least scientific in their work have been better missionaries than we have. Impossible programs are proposed in the name of Scientific Management, and when these superficial substitutes are sold it adds to the doubt and distrust of intelligent management as regards the whole movement.

On the whole, however, as has been intimated before, I have found recently a very deep interest in really scientific methods of management and a much more open-minded and receptive attitude generally in any effort to really take advantage of what Mr. Taylor has given the world. For this we very largely have to thank the splendid constructive work of this Society under exceptionally able leadership. I am not preaching pessimism and discouragement therefore, but exactly the reverse, for I believe we are on the threshold of a development along lines which we believe will far surpass anything in the past. But the extent to which we can take pride in this growth and its permanency, and the extent to which we will be relieved of the present necessity of denying responsibility for attempted short-cuts, which have no part in our philosophy but which nevertheless reflect back upon us, will depend upon the extent to which we first formulate and then secure the acceptance of the fundamental and underlying principles of this whole movement--the mutuality of interest of all parties, standardization as a basis of good management, the primary duty of the management to assume its full share of the work and responsibility; realizing that unless we ourselves emphasize these fundamentals we must not be surprised if others mistake the mechanisms for the essence. We are very directly the custodians of an industrial philosophy which is distinctly a "quality product"; upon us devolves the obligation of keeping faith with and proclaiming the ideals of its founder. Is it not possible for us to get our message across so that administration can distinguish the sound from the superficial?

IV. OBLIGATIONS AND FUTURE PROBLEMS

Some of the outstanding problems which must occupy our attention in the future will be outlined very briefly.

A. Production

One of the biggest problems ahead I believe is that of securing suitable foremen. Under the rapidly increasing complexity of modern business, in spite of the unquestioned advantages in attempting to meet problems of organization through instructional foremanship, there is going to be increasing difficulty in securing and training the right type of foreman. Not only the mechanical and managerial duties of securing maximum production at minimum cost, but also the increasing realization of the importance of the foreman from the industrial relations standpoint, is constantly emphasizing the necessity of training high grade men for these key positions.

I believe that with restriction of immigration the question of the better utilization of such unskilled labor as we can secure, and particularly the devising of labor-saving equipment and methods to make up for an inadequate supply of common labor, deserves intensive study.

I feel that the question of fatigue must be given additional attention for the proper determination of rest and delay allowances. There is needed here the combined efforts of the production man, the industrial physicial and the practical psychologist.

As regards mechanisms, the period of competition which we are entering will force the development of effective and more expeditious means of control, and new mechanisms of real value will undoubtedly continue to be devised. Simply to mention one such apparatus, we find need today of more adequate methods of determining the order of work and thereby securing a better machine and departmental balance, in plants doing a miscellaneous jobbing or made-to-order business. Closely related to this is the need of further intensive study of lot sizes.

B. Distribution

The importance of cutting down as far as possible the extremely high expenses of selling must not fail to receive more intensive study than is generally given it today. There are to be sure a few pioneer firms which are making real headway, but any one firm or group of firms can have but limited effect except by way of example on this truly national problem.

In a report of the Joint Committee on the Agricultural Industry, it is shown that of each $1.00 spent for many articles in the United States in 1921, less than $.50 in many cases represents the cost of the finished product ready to sell. The conclusion of the Commission is that we have outgrown our whole distribution system. The insistence of immediate service in every case where it is at all practicable has made manufacturing to order practically a thing of the past. The problem confronts us as to the means by which the increasing cost of production and warehousing pending the customer's demand is to be met, and to what extent field assembly plants can relieve the situation.

C. Finance and General Administration

A further standardization and simplification of materials, and of varieties and finish of product, needs the detailed attention of factory executives.

Questions of seasonal industry, continuity of employment, unemployment insurance, service bonus and pension systems, and the general coralling of the business cycle, must continue to be studied in a scientific manner.

Industrial relations problems must continue to be investigated in a sympathetic manner. Since these problems probably cannot be permanently solved, it is therefore incumbent upon us to devise more adequate means for adjusting differences currently as they occur.

Our relations with organized labor, which has shown a very much more open-minded attitude toward the Scientific Management movement during the last few years, must be fostered. I believe one of our great duties is to minimize those seemingly irreconcilable points of differences which may remain, and to co-operate in the solution of common problems. We have an excellent opportunity to help in persuading organized labor that it is its duty to allow and persuade the individual to produce up to his individual ability. In order to secure that organized labor must have confidence in our motives as respects both the group and the individual.

The following striking excerpts from the Resolutions of the American Federation of Labor have the ring of sincerity:

"Industry must organize to govern itself . . . . It must bring order to itself constructively or it will have an order thrust upon it . . . .

"It is not the mission of industrial groups to clash and struggle against each other.

"Facts must take the place of opinion and selfish interest.

"Labor stands ready for participation in this tremendous development."

Are we willing to help them?

We as a Society have not, I feel, utilized as we might the many educational institutions which are giving courses on management. I believe that in a few years the profession of management will be generally recognized, and that our future managers will be expected to have had training in this, as in other professions. It is our obligation to see that the part which the schools of business plan in this training is based on thorough understanding of what really constitutes sound management.

A prime educational duty before us is to foster the increasing readiness on the part of the banker to look beyond the balance sheet. It is only through a wider dissemination of truly scientific and broad-minded methods of industrial management that we may hope to secure united action in bringing about more enlightened administration of national and international affairs.

Related to this subject is that of the measurement of management. We have yet barely scratched the surface in this respect, and although the measurement of the art part of the management can never be exact, yet that part which is scientific has not yet had applied to it satisfactory yardsticks. In this connection the general question of executive reports needs further study.

One of the really big questions we must face in the future is that of getting back more nearly, not to the one-man organization itself, but to the essence of it so far as coordination, control and personal touch go. The manager in one-man organizations has many advantages in these respects over the manager of large plants. As soon as a manager is forced to sub-divide his duties and departmentalize his plant, he loses much in control which he formerly held. Recognizing that this specialization is necessary in large establishments, it then becomes a matter of prime importance to set up some means by which this unified control and personal touch may be restored.

Finally as regards our responsibilities as managers, I wish to quote the manager of one large establishment--an establishment to which we commonly refer as being one of the very finest examples of the application of Taylor principles and methods of management. In reply to my question as to the probable future trend of developments in his plant, he writes:

> The most important development in our management methods in the near future will probably be improvement in management itself. We have an idea that in general the efficiency of the management is less at the present time than the efficiency of labor.

---

[1] *Bulletin of the Taylor Society*, February, 1924. A paper presented at a meeting of the Taylor Society, New York, January 24, 1924.

SCIENTIFIC MANAGEMENT MADE CLEAR[1]

Copley's Story of its Genesis and Development More Informing than any Set of Generalizations

By Irving Fisher
Professor of Political Economy, Yale University

It may seem strange that so technical a subject as that of shop management could give anyone a thrill. But Copley's Life of Taylor thrilled me as much as Robinson Crusoe did when I was a boy. This is not altogether because of Copley's sprightly way of writing. There was a very dramatic quality in the life of Taylor as a great pioneer--lonely, persevering, unappreciated, cruelly frustrated, and yet increasingly triumphant. There is also something thrilling in the thought that Taylor's work has only just begun; that his life work consisted not so much in directly saving millions of dollars to the people of his generation as in demonstrating the possibility of saving billions more in future generations--to say nothing of the more intangible benefits.

As the story of Taylor's life is the story of "The Taylor System," I shall review that system as traced in Copley's book rather than write a conventional review of the book as a book, and I shall quote liberally from Copley in the double hope of affording representative samples for some of my readers who cannot or will not read the two volumes; and of enticing others, as I was enticed, to do that very thing.

It is altogether likely that Taylor would never have been the Taylor we now know had it not been for the accident of weak eyes. Except for this he would have gone to college and, in all probability, entered a conventional profession. Certainly he never would have begun at the bottom of the ladder and entered a machine shop as an apprentice. But that is what he did do in 1874 at the age of eighteen. It was young Taylor's own idea, when he could not go to college, to enter industry. Though he could have been supported by his well-to-do father, he chose to cast his lot with workingmen and take voluntarily the hard knocks which that involved.

Frederick Taylor brought to his work a native ability inherited from an unusual ancestry. He put science into the machine shop because he brought to the shop a scientific mind. Given this unusual combination, given Taylor and the shop, the result which followed was as inevitable as any chemical reaction.

A Genetic Exposition of Scientific Management

In telling us the story of what Taylor did to the machine shop, Copley draws the clearest picture of scientific management which has ever been drawn. There are various reasons why his picture is so much clearer than any other. Besides his vivid method of presentation and the fact that he has two volumes in which to elaborate it, there is the still more important fact that a genetic exposition of scientific management, such as a biography requires, is far more instructive than any set of generalizations. To trace the genesis of anything helps us understand it, and this is particularly true of scientific management.

After all, there is, perhaps, nothing qualitatively distinctive in scientific management. Anyone prejudiced against it could exclaim, after reading Taylor's generalized formulae, "That is nothing new. I've always believed in 'science,' 'harmony,' 'cooperation,' 'maximum output,' and 'efficiency,' the things which according to Taylor constitute his system," and then go smugly on his way, missing the point entirely.

Only recently I read a criticism of scientific management by a scholar who had faithfully read Taylor's books, and yet had failed utterly and ludicrously to catch the elusive vision.

But no one can read Copley's account of the actual evolution of scientific management without obtaining a lively sense of its profound value, simply because he sees it grow, and can measure the contrast between the beginning and the end.

Its progress, however, was always painfully slow. There were few sudden jumps in invention or discovery. Taylor's genius was the proverbial capacity for taking infinite pains.

> An egotistic desire to be original, to do great and glorious things, to be revolutionary, is notoriously a weakness of youth. If Taylor himself really came to do great things, it was just because the desire to do them was early knocked out of him. Beginning in the management field with no desire other than that of adding his humble improvement to what had been found good, he followed a strictly evolutionary course throughout. [Volume I, page 196.]

Ultimately he had the satisfaction of seeing his ideas triumph and command the admiration of all who grasped them.

> "It is my belief," says Mr. Charles L. Holmes, "that in a man's life he has only one great experience, and my great experience was meeting Mr. Taylor." [Volume I, page 375.]

Mr. Copley tells us that scores of men ascribe their development to some contact with Taylor. Justice Brandeis of the Supreme Court says;

> "I quickly recognized that in Mr. Taylor I had met a really great man--great not only in mental capacity, but in character." [Volume II, page 371.]

Milestones of Progress

The chief periods in Taylor's unique career were: (1) the years spent as an apprentice in the Enterprise Hydraulic Works in Philadelphia [1874-1878], (2) those spent as an employee of the Midvale Steel Company [1878-1890], (3) those at the Bethlehem Steel Co. [1898-1901], (4) the remainder of his life [1901-1915] when he played the part of unpaid missionary or teacher of scientific management.

The second period, the twelve years spent at Midvale, with William Sellers, was the most active period of Taylor's life. The four years before going there were years of unconscious preparation for what followed, while after leaving Midvale his life was spent in applying and expanding what he had discovered there.

Of those twelve full years at Midvale, Copley writes:

> Going to Midvale when he was twenty-two , he packed into those twelve years of his young manhood an aggregate of achievements which, without exaggeration, can be called exceptional. While he was acquiring the expertness at tennis that enabled him to win with Clark the doubles championship of the United States in 1881, he had begun the study at night that qualified him for the degree of M. E. he obtained at Stevens in 1883. From 1878 on to about 1881 he resorted to every method he could think of to force his men to increase their production; then came his time-study, metal-cutting, and belting investigations, and the years of wearing struggle to build up a system and develop an organization that would facilitate the establishment and maintenance of his scientifically determined standards. In the meantime he met the claims of friendship, won a wife, and established a home of his own. In 1883 and 1884 he designed and superintended the construction of a new machine shop having many novel features. In 1886, two years after his marriage, he joined the A.S.M.E., became an attentive student of its papers, and prepared one of his own (on the use of gas in open-hearth furnaces). As a master mechanic and chief engineer he became responsible for all repairs and maintenance throughout the works. And all along he poured out his ingenuity in the invention, not only of management devices, but of purely mechanical; this latter form culminating in the designing, apparently in the latter part of 1889, of his great and revolutionary steam hammer. [Volume I, page 332.]
>
> But the most remarkable part of it is this:. . . . he developed, single-handed, a system of shop management the like of which never had been known before, and despite the opposition his radically new ways were bound to arouse, put the thing into effect with such success that he brought the entire works around to it. [Volume I, pg. 117.]

After these Midvale days, Taylor's most notable work was [1898-1901] with the Bethlehem Steel [formerly Iron] Company, where he, with Maunsel White, discovered "high speed steel."

After this, i.e., beginning in 1901, Taylor stopped working for money. He had accumulated a fortune, though only a trifle compared with the fortunes he had made and continued to make for his fellowmen.

In 1910 when the railways were asking for increased rates, Taylor and his ideas came into the limelight because Louis Brandeis, now Justice of the United States Supreme Court, brought forward eleven witnesses to show that by means of Taylor's "Scientific Management," the railways could so reduce their costs as to gain more than by their proposed increase in rates.

This publicity was overdone and, as Taylor feared it would, it damaged as much as helped the movement, especially by encouraging charlatans to rush into the field of "efficiency engineering." Like any other counterfeits, they have often been mistaken for the genuine article.

To Stop "Soldiering"

We may trace the beginnings of Taylor's study in trying to stop the universal "soldiering," or shirking of workmen.

Taylor was convinced through his life that practically all workmen in industry, except the few under scientific management, soldiered.

He confesses that as a workman, he himself "soldiered" with the rest. In fact, he sympathized with them, under the circumstances. Nor did he ever lose their point of view or regard them as solely to blame.

It was because of his loathing of soldiering, or the system causing it, and of his persistent efforts to find some way to stop it that he was led, step by step, to what is now called the Taylor System.

As soon as he became gang boss, he sought to stop soldiering. At that time the only way he could think of was by instilling fear. That was the traditional way and Taylor simply sought to make this fear-method more frightful.

But Taylor did not find it easy to make workmen work against their wills. They tried every possible way to circumvent him, even sabotage, and often nearly persuaded the management that Taylor was responsible for these "accidents" because he drove both man and machine too fast.

Almost anyone but Taylor would have failed utterly, but he knew, from his own experience as a workman, that the soldiering was genuine and the "accidents" a sham, while the management knew, from Taylor's antecedents and character, that he was to be depended upon. He was indefatigable and undaunted even by frequent threats against his life.

He threatened in his turn. He also tried fines. Sometimes in justice, he had to fine himself for misplacing tools or otherwise breaking his own rules.

> This spectacle of his fining himself provided amusement for the entire establishment; but it was an early example of his principle of one law for all, high and low, and the lesson of it was not lost. [Volume 1, page 172.]

But neither threats, cursing, fines, firing men, hiring others nor teaching them the trade succeeded, at first, in overcoming the sullen resistance of his men. Ultimately, however, after three years, they got sick of being fined, their opposition broke down, and they promised to do a fair day's work and did.

He had succeeded "in doubling the output of the men on the whole." But he was far from satisfied.

> "It is a horrid life for any man to live, not to be able to look any workman in the face all day long without seeing hostility there, and feeling that every man around you is your virtual enemy." [Volume I, page 5.]

Yet he did not relinquish his faith in fear as a driving force, though he came to feel the urgent need of supplementing this force by other forces. He explored further, and it was this exploration which led to scientific management.

We may perhaps register as the second step in Taylor's progress, a reconsideration of the reasons for soldiering, a clearer diagnosis. Why, he asked, do workmen so generally want to shirk? If only workmen could be led to put more will into promoting instead of retarding the work of the shop!

Taylor became conscious of several reasons for soldiering. One was the almost universal ignorance, on the part of the employers, of what constitutes a day's work. Another was the fact that when men work in large groups, individual incentive is lost. A third reason was that the clumsy efforts of employers to remedy this by substituting piece rates for day rates proved self-defeating, for the instant the piece rates operated to increase daily earnings, the rates were cut. Then the workmen "become imbued with a grim determination to have no more cuts if soldiering can prevent it."

A Fair Day's Work

With this threefold diagnosis of the soldiering disease--ignorance of what constitutes a day's work, herding of workmen together, and rate cutting, not to mention other complications--Taylor set out first of all to discover, by scientific experiment, what constitutes a fair day's work in any concrete case.

His main idea was that, once the employer knows that a workman can do twice, three times, or four times what he actually does do, the higher standard can be insisted upon, and piece rates can be established which will not have to be cut.

Here entered the stop-watch idea which later became a chief target of criticism. Evidently the way to ascertain what labor can do is to measure the time it takes.

Taylor tells us that the stop-watch idea was first suggested in his school days at Exeter, when his mathematics professor, Wentworth, used this method for ascertaining what was the proper length of lesson to assign to his classes. He had each student raise his hand as soon as a certain problem was solved until just half had done so, and recorded this last or median time with a stop watch.

Little did "Bull" Wentworth, famous as the author of mathematical text books, realize that this idea, implanted in the fertile mind of one of his students, would play so vital a part in a future Taylor System and be the storm center of a raging controversy!

The next step was to make due preparation for such time studies. They must, Taylor saw, be done under standard conditions.

It was evident that a workman's speed must depend largely on his surroundings and equipment, and that time studies would be valueless unless the workman studied was first assured of a continuous and convenient supply of the material worked upon, with standard tools and machines, sufficient light, freedom from interruption and innumerable other preparations to secure the best conditions under which his work was to take place.

Clearly, preparation must precede time study; many of the half-informed "efficiency engineers" who have too often counterfeited Taylor's thorough work have made some of their worst blunders by attempting time studies prematurely.

So Taylor virtually turned his shop, or parts of it, into an industrial laboratory to set up the standard conditions for measuring a day's work. This measurement was accomplished by dint of thousands of careful experiments.

Transfer of Functions

In order to secure such laboratory conditions for his experiments, he found it necessary himself to arrange many details formerly left to the workingman. This transfer of function from worker to management proved to be one of the most essential elements in scientific management.

Instead of the workmen owning the tools they used, in all sorts, sizes, and degrees of repair, the management ultimately established a tool room with tools duly assorted after scientific tests to discover the best tools for each job. These tools were supplied as needed and were sharpened, repaired and replaced through the management.

For instance, Taylor's experiments disclosed the surprising fact that few shovellers know how to shovel, or even know what muscles to use or what size of shovel. His tests showed that a shovel holding 21½ pounds is ideal. This led to supplying different sized shovels for different materials to be shoveled instead of one shovel for all. Taylor was not content to accept the shovels then standard in trade. After his young assistant, Gantt, once reported that for a certain job no shovel big enough was on the market, Taylor said:

> "You would be damn fool enough, would you, to fix a task that would last perhaps for twenty years at 14½ pounds, when you know 21½ pounds can be done, rather than pay $1,000 for fifty shovels to be made?" [Volume II, page 72.]

Task and Bonus

After a day's work in, say, shovelling had been duly determined under certain conditions, the next step was to so remunerate the workman as to induce him to live up to the higher standards thus ascertained. This led to various sliding scale ideas, especially to the "Task and Bonus" (a suggestion of Gantt's). This is a system of payment by which every workmen doing his allotted task within the normal time should be paid a "bonus" of from 30 per cent to 100 per cent above current wage.

> All previous [plans for management] advocated the payment of ordinary wages to give workmen an incentive for doing more or better work, but Taylor paid such wages to induce workmen to accept the standards determined by the scientific method. [Volume I, page 409.]

Under the former plans the stimulus failed to work because of soldiering, and the employer was often none the wiser. Under the latter system, such deceit was impossible.

> It now should be recognized that here, coming into being was an entirely new thing in management, the "central idea" of which, as Taylor came to describe it, was this:

"a. To give each workman each day in advance a definite task, with detailed written instructions, and an exact time allowance for each element of the work.

"b. To pay extraordinarily high wages to those who perform their tasks in the allotted time, and ordinary wages to those who take more than their time allowance." [Volume I, pages 261-262.]

"We have found for economy that the record which is made up early on the morning of the day following the work, which shows how many men in each department failed to earn their bonus, is the most helpful record in promoting economy. It becomes possible, then, the day after bad work has been done by anybody, to chase it right home, either to the foreman, the teachers, the tool department, planning department, or to the workman himself, and prove right then and there to the men or the department just what they have done that is wrong." [Volume I, page 368.]

"Two-thirds of the moral effect, either of a reward or penalty, is lost by even a short postponement." [Volume I, page 318.]

One by-product of Taylor's measurement of work was to enable him definitely to buy and pay for work as such, not the workers' time.

Undoubtedly his suggestion that those clerks be permitted to go home when they had finished the daily tasks he proposed for them was found nothing less than sensational. [Volume I, page 451.]

Planning

Constant planning was necessary to control and maintain the standard laboratory conditions year in and year out.

This daily planning led to a planning room to schedule the work of each employee and machine.

Really it all comes down to the homely old adage: first plan your work, then work your plan. [Volume I, page 286.]

To "prepare" fully a shop in the first place, i.e., to place the machinery in the most effective way, to set up a tool room and planning room and to create other conditions such as would enable workmen to work at their best, often required a year or two for its accomplishment.

Taylor's Exception Principle

A well-planned shop will separate the routine from the exceptional. Many an employer is swamped by details because he does not make this separation. Through scientific management, 95 per cent of the mass of letters, reports, etc. (routine matters), never pass over the desk of the employer, so that his time may be devoted to the exceptional 5 per cent.

This daily planning of the work for each individual workman and the daily measurement of their accomplishments led at once to a sifting and selection, better fitting the various men to the various jobs.

> So that, under the plan which individualizes each workman, instead of brutally discharging the man or lowering his wages for failing to make good at once, he is given the time and the help required to make him proficient at his present job, or he is shifted to another class of work for which he is either mentally or physically better suited. [Principles of Scientific Management, page 70.]
>
> For each type of workman, some job can be found at which he is first class. [Volume I, page 180].

Functional Foremen

The vast increase in the functions of management required subdividing and more functions.

> What Taylor did as he found that he could not thoroughly discharge all of his foreman's duties was the most natural thing in the world: he employed assistants. And it was as he pursued this course that he developed a new type of organization . . . what is now termed the functional type of organization to distinguish it from the military type.
>
> It is permissible to call it new only in the sense that a difference in degree can amount to a difference in kind. [Volume I, pages 284-285.]
>
> All along he had been moving unconsciously--that is, wholly in natural response to the conditions he met with--in the direction of functional foremanship and its full development, the planning department, and at Bethlehem he became fully conscious of this thing as a definite principle. [Volume II, page 19.]

The difference between a country road and Broadway, between a dug-out and the Woolworth Tower is simply one of degree.

Barth's Slide Rule

Taylor soon discovered that even the simple problem involved numerous independent variables, and was therefore never really simple. In algebra even equations of one variable may tax the resources of the best mathematician. When two variables are involved, the complications are likely to be enormously multiplied.

But Taylor's problems almost always involved over half a dozen variables. It was Carl Barth to whom Taylor finally turned for mathematical help of a practical kind.

> One day while he was still helping to run the experimental lathe, Barth happened to see the plot on Gantt's desk, and was told by him that he had tried in vain for about six weeks to construct a mathematical formula to represent its curves. Unhesitatingly and abruptly, Barth declared: "I'll eat my hat if I can't work up an acceptable formula this evening and bring it in in the morning." [Volume II, page 32.]

Copley tells us that Barth did not have to eat his hat. The outcome was Barth's wonderful, famous slide rule.

> Magic instrument, that slide rule. By it the most complicated mathematical problems are solved in a minute. An abolisher of guess work, opinions, arguments, debates. A determiner of the law! [Volume II, page 35.]
>
> Writing to General William Crozier in 1909, Taylor, referring to Carl Barth, said: "He is one of the most brilliant minds I have ever met." [Volume II, page 26.]

The most startling discovery of Taylor's was the tremendous difference between the rule-of-thumb solutions of those "simple" problems of industry, solutions often accepted without question for generations, and the true scientific solution with the aid of experiment and of Barth's slide rule.

In one case there was a lively controversy, the slide rule indicating one course of action and "common sense" of the old rule-of-thumb operators a very different course. Both were tried, the result being that all agreed that "the slide rule knew what it was talking about."

We thus see that while Taylor set our merely to stop soldiering, he ended by creating a general system aiming to get the best not only out of workmen, but out of all elements involved in the problem.

Cost Accounting

Every part of Taylor's system required records. One of the most important of these was cost accounting. But he disapproved as "red tape" all records not actually made use of in management. He said:

> "I have known, for instance, cost keeping to go on in industrial establishments through a long term of years with all the expense incident to it, and upon investigation found that the owners and managers of the business were paying little or no attention to the costs which they figured out." [Volume II, page 376.]

> So he removed cost accounting from the general accounting department and placed it in the planning room, while at the same time tying up the cost accounting with the main books in the manner that since has become known as interlocking.
>
> Placing the cost accounting in the planning room, he made it a by-product of operations, and thus got his costs coincidently with the operations. That is to say, the papers and slips he designed to plan and control operations became the documents on which were based both the cost and production records. [Volume I, page 369.]
>
> In fact, the leading feature of Taylor's general accounting system would appear to be the unerring certainty with which it enables the manager to pick out the cause of any unusual cost or waste. [Volume I, page 365.]

Taylor's system made increased use of brains, and so increased, relatively, the "overhead," an increase justified many times over, Taylor found, by the decrease in running expenses.

The introduction of scientific management itself is, of course, an increase of overhead, and justifiable only as it is repaid with interest in decreased running expenses.

Specific Gains From Scientific Management

That scientific management pays richly is proved by the experience of those who have used it. There may be apparent exceptions due to undue haste or to following the advice of pseudo-experts. But real exceptions seem to be conspicuous by their absence.

Taylor's own verdict is:

> At least 50,000 workmen in the United States are now [1911] employed under this system; and they are receiving from thirty per cent to one hundred per cent higher wages daily than are paid the men of similar caliber with whom they are surrounded, while the companies employing them are more prosperous than ever before. In these companies the output, per man and per machine, has on an average, been doubled. During all these years there has never been a single strike among the men working under this system. In place of suspicious watchfulness and the more or less open warfare which characterizes the ordinary types of management, there is universally friendly cooperation between the management and the men. [Principles of Scientific Management, page 28.]

Many specific cases are given by Copley.

> The Watertown foundry had an order for a large number of molds for pack-saddle pommels. The first man put on this job made on an average of nine molds a day, and he backed up by the civilian foreman of the foundry, who was not in sympathy with Taylor methods, contended that this production was ample. A time study having been made of the job, a new man was put on it under the premium plan, and he made on an average of 24 molds a day. . . . And after all direct and overhead charges had been taken into consideration, it was shown that the cost of each mold to the Government had been reduced from $1.17 to 54 cents. [Volume II, page 345.]

These startling contrasts apply to every phase of the manager's problem. The truth is, both master and man have habitually guessed and bluffed. Under scientific management they can guess and bluff no longer.

In one case, after discharging workmen who continued soldiering, training others to take their places,

> ". . . we had within three months increased the output from 15 to 25 tires a day. This output went on, right on the same machine, increasing until three or four years later we had an output of 150 tires a day."
>
> The big jump in the production of this rolling machine came when the horsepower used in it was "immensely increased" and the men running it were put under Taylor's differential-rate system. [Volume I, page 316.]

Here is another example:

> Testifying in 1912 before that Special House Committee, Dr. Hollis Godfrey, who later became president of Philadelphia's Drexel Institute, said:
>
> "The first plant under scientific management with which I was connected was the Tabor Co. I had full opportunity there to see all books and figures, and nothing was more impressive to me than the fact that the Tabor Co., with approximately the same number of men and machines as were used under the old system, was turning out three times the production; that it was giving 73 per cent higher wages to workmen; that it had made 25 per cent reduction in the selling price of its machines; thereby producing so much saving to the consumer. Moreover, that this company, which had lost money before the introduction of scientific management, was now and had been making a good profit; that from the condition of a strike and inharmonious relations before the introduction of scientific management there had come about the friendliest feeling between management, working men and outsiders." [Volume II, page 185.]

On another type of industry, under the management of Mr. Feiss, afterward President of the Taylor Society, Copley comments:

> Only in a general way can we here indicate the outcome at that Cleveland clothing factory, with its eight or nine hundred men and women employees largely composed of immigrants from eastern and southern Europe, and the children of such immigrants. Hours reduced from 54 a week to an average of about 43 a week; productivity at the same time increased 43 per cent; wages increased on an average of 40 per cent. In 1910 the labor turnover had been 150.3 per cent (what is called a "good normal" for the clothing industry); in 1914 this turnover was 33.5 per cent. Scores of young men and women taught English at the factory, so that all might have a common medium of speech and thus really get to know and <u>understand</u> one another. A service department headed by a college woman of the highest type, and devoted largely to raising standards of living, so that all might have a vision inspiring them to learn and to earn. Hundreds of foreigners Americanized--taught not only our language, but our customs, our sports, our songs. [Volume II, page 448.]

The experience with Taylor's system under General Crozier, in the United States Arsenal at Watertown, showed extraordinary gains. As shown by an official report made in 1911:

> ". . . under the new system we accomplished 5.46 times as much work as under the old method of management." [Volume II, page 339.]
>
> "In the case of the 6-inch disappearing-gun carriages, the cost of direct labor was reduced from $10,239 to $6,949, and that of direct labor and other shop expenses from $10,263 to $8,956. [Volume II, page 337.]

Taylor believed that practically every ordinary, or rule-of-thumb, establishment was desperately in need of scientific management.

> "I am well within the limit, gentlemen, in saying [he testified in 1912] that not one machine in twenty in the average shop in this country is properly speeded. This may seem incredible, and yet I make the statement with a great deal of confidence. . ." [Volume I, page 249.]

Ball Bearings

> "The working hours were arbitrarily shortened in successive steps to 10 hours, 9½ and 8½ [the pay per day remaining the same], and with each shortening of the working day the output increased instead of diminished. . . In this case, however, a large part of the improvement was due to the scientific selection of the girls, rather than the shortening of the hours.

> There is, however, no question whatever that in this case merely shortening the hours also produced an increase in output." [Volume I, page 460.]
>
> "The final outcome of all the changes [was that] thirty-five girls did the work formerly done by one hundred and twenty. [And that] the accuracy of work at the higher speed was two-thirds greater than at the former slow speed." [Volume I, page 464.]

It is interesting to note that the girls first objected to the changes by which in the end they benefited so much.

This is one of several illustrations of the need of initiative of the management. Another was, as Taylor pointed out, that without this initiative of the management, the workers would never have discovered that the ideal shovel load is 21½ lbs.

Bricklaying

One of Taylor's followers, Gilbreth, made a striking application of scientific management ideas to bricklaying. He averaged, after his selected workmen had become skillful in his new methods, 350 bricks per man per hour; whereas the average speed of doing this work with the old methods was, in that section of the country, 120 bricks per man per hour.

Such cases of success as those just mentioned are doubtless star cases--above the average--but success is almost always marked, whenever the system is fairly tried as shown by an extensive study by C. B. Thompson.

The Steam Hammer

One by-product of scientific management is a crop of inventions of which Taylor made several.

His crowning achievement at Midvale in the strictly mechanical field was his invention of the steam hammer.

> He spent one or two years in collecting, from all over the world, data about the various machines that had been designed, until he found instances in which some one of the parts of each of the various machines of different designs had never broken. . . As a result he obtained a machine which lasted for many years without a single breakdown--the first instance of its kind in the history of that art. [Volume I, pages 197-198.]

High Speed Steel

But the chief example was Taylor's discovery of "high speed steel." His experiments proved that [contrary to all tradition] by heating the tool almost to its melting point and then cooling it with a blast of cold air, a much higher cutting speed could be gained than with a tool which had never been "over-heated."

> One engineer has referred to it as a discovery "which is, at a very conservative estimate, worth fifty million dollars per year to the machine industry of this country." We also read that "by means of these high-speed tools, the United States during the World War was able to turn out five times the munitions that [it otherwise] could have done in the same time. On the other hand, if Germany alone had possessed the secret of the modern steels no power could have withstood her." [Volume I, page xv.]

Indirect Benefits From Scientific Management

Besides direct material gains from scientific management, there are numerous indirect and less ponderable gains--peace and good will between employer and employee, initiative and ingenuity, self-respect, good habits and improved character.

The best way to secure good principles in men is to establish them firmly in good habits. Gantt said:

> "They [those working under scientific management] improve under it, both in honesty and efficiency, more than I have seen them do elsewhere. Realizing that substantial justice was being done and that to do their duty was to follow their own interest, it soon became a matter of habit with them." [Volume I, page 330. Quoted from Gantt.]
>
> "With almost certainty they begin to guide the rest of their lives according to principles and laws and to try to insist upon those around them doing the same." [Volume I, page 328. Quoted from Taylor.]
>
> A noted French engineer and steel manufacturer, who spent several weeks in the works of the Midvale Company in introducing a new branch of manufacture, stated before leaving that the one thing that had impressed him as most remarkable about the place was the fact that not only the foremen, but the workmen, were expected to and did in the main tell the truth in case of any blunder or carelessness, even when they had to suffer from it themselves. [Volume I, page 330.]

Thus, while Taylor was arriving primarily at the material welfare of workingmen, he reckoned among the benefits indirectly attained, the spiritual welfare and discipline in the homely virtues he himself practiced as well as preached.

Taylor stoutly defended his system from the charge that it narrowed the man and enslaved him to the machine.

> Thus if the operation of those machines became work calling for less skill in the sense that there was removed from it the planning element, it at the same time, as plain execution, became work requiring more skill; work requiring much greater manual and mental

> dexterity; work of a greatly improved technic; work calling for a decidedly higher order of these qualities of application and industry that lie at the root of all skill and knowledge and character progress. [Volume II, page 131.]

Not the least important results of scientific management were the shortening of the hours of the workers, the higher wages, and the increased incentive to work that comes when the man realizes that his efforts are being noticed and rewarded.

Taylor's chief emphasis, however, was always on the advantage _to the public_ of cheaper prices through increased production.

Using Past Experience

While in the end, Taylor's methods and results were almost always different from the ordinary methods and results, he invariably tried to begin where previous experience left off. He insisted on first finding out all that had been done before attempting to improve on it.

When, for instance, he set out to measure a day's work, "his first step was to look up all that had been written on the subject in English, German and French."

In this case he was misled, rather than helped, by some of his supposed clues obtained from previous experimenters. These had tried to measure human work in horse-power. Taylor wasted much time and effort in trying to get some useful human equivalent of horse-power, much to the amusement of Barth, who warned him of the futility of such a quest.

Although he never deviated from his rule of exhausting every available source of information as to what had already been done, he did come to see the folly of waiting to make sure he was _entirely_ right before he went ahead.

He not only never began far away from current practice, but deplored the idea of sudden breaks with tradition. He satirized such foolish innovating by supposing a surgeon teaching a younger man, and encouraging originality as follows:

> "Don't be hampered by any prejudices of the older surgeons. What we want is your initiative, your individuality. If you prefer a hatchet or an ax to cut off the bone, why chop away, chop away! Would this be what the modern surgeon would tell his apprentices? Not on your life!" [Volume I, page 193.]

The Essence of Scientific Management

What, then, is the essence of scientific management? P. T. Barnum, when asked what was the most wonderful thing about his "greatest show on earth," answered "that it pays!"

This is the most important thing about the Taylor System. In its sphere, and without any of the showman's exaggeration, the Taylor System is still industrially the greatest show on earth because it pays so handsomely, not only in cold cash, but in higher values as well.

If it were true that scientific management failed greatly to surpass the rule-of-thumb, its detractors would be right in claiming that it amounted to little except red tape.

It is the enormous difference which scientific management makes to output, wages, and profits, which marks it out as distinctive. "By their fruits ye shall know them."

We have already seen some of the extraordinary results of Taylor's work. We saw that productivity was commonly doubled, or tripled, or even quintupled.

Method Rather than Devices

The present question is what is there in method that lies behind these results? What is it which makes this enormous difference between the productivity under scientific management and that under ordinary management?

Is the real secret to be found in task and bonus, slide rule, stronger belting, for instance?

The answer, as Copley's book so clearly shows, is both Yes and No. Usually and incidentally, Yes; fundamentally, No.

If we must list the chief concrete aids to scientific management, we find then, according to Taylor, as follows:

> Time study, with the implements and methods for making it properly.
>
> Functional or divided foremanship and its superiority to the old-fashioned single foreman.
>
> The standardization of all tools and implements used in the trades, and also of the acts of movements of workmen for each class of work.
>
> The desirability of a planning room or department.
>
> The "exception principle" in management.
>
> The use of slide rules and similar time-saving implements.
>
> Instruction cards for the workman.
>
> The task idea in management, accompanied by a large bonus for the successful performance of the task.
>
> The "differential rate."
>
> Mnemonic systems for classifying manufactured products as well as implements used in manufacturing.
>
> A routing system.
>
> Modern cost system, etc., etc. [Principles of Scientific Management, pages 129-130.]

In more general terms, scientific management breaks down every task into five principal functions: planning, preparation, scheduling, production and inspection.

But those who seek the soul of scientific management in such devices or classifications are like those who seek the soul of religion in a particular ritual. The great secret of scientific management is not to be found here. Detailed devices might express the difference between any two unscientific systems. It might be fair so to describe the difference between Smith's and Jones' systems, but Taylor's system differs from Smith's and Jones' and everybody else's in this--that his methods were not simply favorites to which he took a fancy, but the result of painstaking scientific testing.

> The grand ends to which this system is all directed may be here defined as [1] the determination of best or standard ways, implements, and materials by scientific investigation and experimentation, and [2] a control so extensive and intensive as to provide for the maintenance of all standards in this way reached. [Volume I, page xvi.]

We might, then, define scientific management as management which makes enormously better results by substituting science for guess work. The one supreme criterion of whether an industrial method is scientific or not is found by asking "has that method been proved to be the best?"

Of course, scientific management, in the ideal sense, has never been attained; in fact, strictly speaking, it is unattainable. When Taylor was testifying in 1912 and was asked: "How many concerns to your knowledge use your system in its entirety?" his reply was: "In its entirety?--none, not one."

A Revolutionary Spirit

But even these attempts to formulate the elusive essence of scientific management are apt to be barren, meaningless, and even misleading to the novitiate. The precondition for substituting scientific management for other management is a willingness to forsake everything traditional if need be, that is, if scientific investigation so indicates. Only through such a "spirit meet for repentance" can the candidate for scientific management ever expect to find the straight and narrow path to industrial salvation.

> It actually was the fact that men to follow after him had to undergo a mental revolution singularly like that of a religious conversion. [Volume II, pages 124-5.]

Huxley, that great apostle of the scientific spirit, used to say that a scientific man must have a fanatical regard for the truth, that he must be ready to sit down before a fact and humbly accept it and all its implications.

That was Taylor's spirit, and history will accord to him the everlasting honor of being the first man in industry, or at any rate in industrial management, to exemplify and utilize that subtle scientific spirit which previously we associated with universities and laboratories.

When we speak of "men of science," we still think of such examples as Huxley, Darwin, Pasteur, Newton, Gibbs, Einstein. That being the case, some university professors quite naturally failed to recognize in Taylor a man of science. But the realm of science is constantly expanding, and in industry Taylor was its prophet and pioneer.

One consequence of this new apotheosis of science in industry was that when "the one best way" was discovered, scientific management paid homage to that one best way as the supreme law. In other systems the supreme law was the say-so of the boss. In the Taylor system the supreme law is the way scientifically proved to be best.

Reign of Law

Taylor is thus the lawgiver of industry. Before his day the government of industry was--in fact for the most part it still is--in the same primitive stage that political government was in before constitutional monarchies came into being. The say-so of the king was the only law. It followed that "the king could do no wrong." Contrast this old doctrine with England's constitutional monarchy today where the king is bound by the law as truly as are his "subjects"!

So it was that Taylor called the ordinary system the "military" system, a hierarchy of arbitrary power in which the head of the business, as captain of industry, simply subdivided the command among departments under lietenants, who still further subdivided it; as in an army a General's authority is subdivided among Colonels, Majors, Captains, etc. In such a system, each commander's word is the supreme law for those below him. In Taylor's system, on the other hand, every functionary was himself subject to the higher law of what had been proven best.

The following is quoted from the manuscript he prepared for his Harvard lectures, the italics being his:

> "You realize, of course, that the military type of management has been here entirely abandoned, and that each one of these functional foremen is king over his particular function; that is, *king over the particular class of acts which he understands, and which he directs*; and that not only all of the workmen throughout the place obey the orders of this functional foreman in his limited sphere, *but that every other functional foreman obeys his orders in this one respect*."
>
> "Thus we have a radically new, and what at first appears exceedingly confusing state of things, in which every man, foreman as well as workman, receives and obeys orders from many other men, and in the case of the various functional foremen they continually give orders in their own particular line to the very men from whom they are receiving orders in other lines. For this reason the work of the planning department represents an intricate mass of interwoven orders or directions, proceeding backward and forward between the men in charge of the various functions of management." [Volume I, page 290.]
>
> Actually there is only one master, one boss: namely, knowledge. [Volume I, page 291.]

Copley says of Taylor himself:

> Imperious as Caesar, *he was not dogmatic or arbitrary*. He did not pretend to be a lawmaker--Only a lawfinder.

> You had to do what he said, not just because he said it, but because he knew the best way; and you had to take his word for this only for the time being, or until the thing could be proved by its workings. If you could prove that yours was the best way, then he would adopt your way and feel very much obliged to you. Fequently, he took humble doses of his own imperious medicine. [Volume I, page 175.]

As the novelty of functional management impressed itself on Taylor he realized how hard it would be to convert others to it.

> The prepossession in favor of the military type was so strong with the managers and owners of Midvale that it was not until years after functional foremanship was in continual use in this shop that he dared to advocate it to his superior officers as the correct principle. [Volume I, page 304.]

Science vs. Tradition

Doubtless it might be answered that even the ordinary shop management has its laws or customs to which managers and men are subject. Granted that this is true, nevertheless, the law of tradition and the law of science are as different as night and day.

Practically never can we find "the one best way" by guessing or groping in the dark. One might as well try to predict the next eclipse by guessing. Yet tradition rules our lives more than any other force.

When, after hoary ages of tradition, science enters on the scene a battle royal is inevitable. It is therefore no accident that we find the conflict between science and tradition in the biographies of Copernicus, Galileo, Darwin or Pasteur as in Copley's biography of Taylor.

Such a conflict was inevitable. Taylor had to pay the price for disturbing the peace in industry--industry being sublimely unconscious of its shortcomings and unwilling to be reformed.

It might naturally be supposed that if scientific management is capable of enriching employer and employee to the extraordinary extent shown in Copley's account, it would be eagerly adopted by every business concern. The fact that this has not yet happened is sometimes made the basis of childlike argument to prove that there must be something radically wrong with it.

Even today scientific management has to fight is way. Copley's book will help enormously to smooth the path of the Taylor Society. But with the best of salesmanship, progress against the inertia of tradition will be slow.

Copley tells us of Taylor:

> In 1909 he wrote to a fellow worker in the field of industrial management: "I have found that any improvement of any kind is not only opposed, but aggressively and bitterly opposed, by the majority of men, and the reformer must usually tread a thorny path." [Volume I, page 416.]

Take for instance, the specific example of Taylor's discovery that a stream of water continually poured on the cutting edge of a tool would cool the tool so as to increase the speed of cutting 30 to 40 per cent.

A French scholar, on reading of this discovery, remarked "[This fact is] so easily verified that one is justified in being astonished that [it is] not known to everybody." Although this fact had been known to the public since 1884, Taylor wrote in 1906:

> So far as the writer knows no other shop [than Midvale] was similarly fitted up [with water supply for the machines] until that of the Bethlehem Steel Company in 1889, with the exception of a small steel works which was an offshoot in personnel from the Midvale Steel Company." [Volume I, page 242.]

The disinclination to change expresses itself in every sort of excuse for not changing. Taylor said:

> "It is a very curious fact that each individual manager looks upon his problem as the most difficult there is anywhere in the world, and as having little or no relation to any other problem of management. This is caused by the fact that each manager realizes the special difficulties which he has to face in his own problem, and fails to see that other managers are faced with equal difficulties.
>
> "For example, the man who is managing a simple type of company, in which the work is rather elementary, will say, 'Scientific management can very readily and very properly be applied to an elaborate company, in which there are a great many trades calling for especial skill, etc., but for my company, which is very simple in its nature, scientific management calls for too much red tape.' On the other hand, the manager who is at the head of an establishment calling for intricate work, and work of great variety, will state, 'Scientific management can very readily be applied to the simpler kinds of work, but my work is so intricate and difficult that it can never be reduced to anything like scientific laws of rules.'
>
> "I have hardly ever seen the manager who firmly believed at the outset that scientific management could be successfully applied to his particular work." [Volume II, page 363.]

Obstacles to Progress

All or most of the obstacles which impede progress may be included under the head of conservatism, but in the present case, we may conveniently distinguish six sub-divisions: laziness, ignorance, offended pride, offended special interests, labor prejudice, and false economic theories.

Laziness

Laziness in some degree may perhaps be said to be a universal human attribute. We all dislike the effort required to get out of a rut or habit.

> There still are many thousands of men and women who are so worried and generally upset when called upon to depart from a fixed routine ahat the only thing you can do do is to leave them to the routine or wean them away from it gradually. [Volume I, page 434.]

It takes gumption to make any change, and after it is made, every nerve must be stretched to keep the new system going full speed. One essential of the Taylor System is that everyone should do his utmost while the natural tendency is ever to play the slacker. It is the old conflict between our higher and lower natures. We like to see others try but seek to avoid the strain ourselves.

The following shows how insidious is the tendency to back-slide and take it easy.

> Though Midvale did not throw out Taylor's methods, it began, not long after he left there, to slough them off . . . For this sloughing or sagging, there is a ready explanation: no one at Midvale except Taylor himself was imbued with the philosophy that lay back of his methods and mechanisms. In his later years, Taylor came to see clearly that scientific management could not exist in any establishment until chief executives, planners, supervisors, and executors or operatives all had undergone the "complete mental revolution" involved. [Volume I, pages 339-340.]

To Taylor, laziness was a deadly sin. He disliked seeing anyone do less than his best. "What William James calls <u>the habit of inferiority to our full self</u>, was his special object of attack. The "one best way" seemed, in Taylor's mind, to stand out not as the top of a rounded hill, but as the sharp peak of a mountain.

He disapproved not only of lazy workmen but of lazy managers. He believed they often put details up to the workman not really because "they thought this the best way, but simply because "the management was disinclined to assume the duties, burdens and responsibilities that naturally belonged to it."

Ignorance

As an example of ignorance, we find the curious spectacle of a great captain of industry under the traditional "military" system, ruthlessly replacing scientific management by his own accustomed methods. Without, apparently, knowing or wanting to know exactly what it was which he was throwing away.

Taylor wrote to General Crozier in 1910:

> "I think it is quite remarkable that our system should have survived as well as it appears to have done at the Bethlehem Steel Company. I think I told you that the moment Schwab took charge of the Bethlehem Works in 1901, he ordered our whole system thrown out. He saw no use whatever in paying premiums for fast work; much less in having time study men and slide rule men, "supernumeraries," as he called them, in the works at all. His orders were obeyed, and the output of the large machine shop in the following month fell to about one-half of what it was before. _______ _______, who was then in command, ordered our system reinstated. He, however, did not tell Schwab that he had done so. On the contrary, he led Schwab to believe that our system had been entirely thrown out. In carrying out this deceit, for several years the use of our slide rules and time study, etc., was carried on in Bethlehem Works without Schwab's knowledge. The slide rules were operated in a room back of the kitchen, which Schwab never visited, and all of the slide rule, time study men, planners, etc., were carried on the payrolls as mechanics; that is, machinists who were supposed to be working in the shops. And it is only through an accident that this state of affairs was finally brought to Schwab's attention. The office of the large machine shop burnt down some years later, and destroyed all of the slide rules, and many of the time study records. During the year following this fire, the output of the machine shop necessarily fell off to a tremendous extent, because the mechanism for helping the workmen to do a big day's work was lacking. They attempted to guess at what was a proper day's work, as is done in other establishments under the old system of management, with the result that at the end of the year practically all of the head men connected with this department were discharged for incompetence, and a set of men inferior to them were put into their places to run the shop.
>
> "This led to the true facts being brought to Schwab's attention, and from that time forward the slide rules and time study men, and in fact all of the elements of our system of management were practiced openly in the shop." [Volume II, pages 160-161.]

Old-fashioned managers find it hard to realize the importance of any radical departure from the creed handed down to them. In one case, Taylor's recommendation that a higher priced workman be employed to do certain work was rejected because such pay for such work was unprecedented. The result was that the system failed to work until Taylor appealed directly to the company's chief executive. "Would you," he asked, "expect an engine to work with a broken connecting rod?"

Offended Pride

Quite naturally, although unreasonably, when any manager or foreman was asked to mend his ways, as prescribed by scientific management, he considered such request as a personal reflection on himself. It is hard for anyone to admit that he has been doing his work wrong all his life.

> Nine-tenths of his [Taylor's] troubles were with men in the management. As he extended his functional principle to management, it acted on the typical foremen or manager of his day "as the proverbial red rag on the bull." (Volume I, page 292.)

In one instance

> The superintendent was distinctly displeased when told that through the adoption of task management the output, with the same number of men and machines, could be more than doubled. He said that he believed that any such statement was mere boasting, absolutely false, and instead of inspiring him with confidence, he was disgusted that anyone should make such an impudent claim. (Principles of Scientific Management, page 98.)

The average man, once in a rut, wants to be let alone. When he is disturbed he finds innumerable grievances.

The men who most resented Taylor's innovations were, naturally, those nearest to him. They could not abide his being their teacher.

> He must needs be conscious of his power, and he manifested this consciousness in an insouciance which if you could not know what a modest man he was at bottom, you were likely to find more trying than outright boasting. (Volume II, page 21.)

Often, therefore, he found himself a prophet not without honor save in his own shop.

> Even when he (Taylor) in collaboration with Maunsel White, made the discovery (of high-speed steel), which was the sensation of the industrial world here and abroad and saved the company a prospective expenditure of at least a million dollars, none of the men high up in that company had sufficient pride in it to offer him a word of congratulation. (Volume II, page 78.)

In March, 1901, Taylor wrote the President of the Bethlehem company:

> "It is a curious psychological fact, and one for which the writer can find no explanation, that of all the parties who have visited the works and are acquainted with what has been done here, the only ones who have failed to congratulate the writer upon the results accomplished are, with one or two exceptions, the leading officers of the company." (Volume II, page 113.)

Offended Special Interests

Scientific management, by disclosing the truth, must needs expose many shortcomings which had previously been concealed. Every bluffer fears to have his negligence or incompetence revealed. Such people, whether managers or workmen, naturally oppose scientific management knowing that they will lose thereby their previous advantage from deception, or even lose their jobs.

Every innovation will expose someone who profited under the old regime. One of the most curious cases was when at Bethlehem, "Speedy" Taylor reduced the number of pig iron handlers so far that real estate agents feared he would disturb rental values of tenements!

Organized Labor

The opposition to Taylor thus far described was merely the natural spontaneous opposition of individuals. But we now come to an organized opposition, the most remarkable and regrettable of all.

Organized labor then as now represented the accumulated hostility of several generations of grievances against employers.

Between the two classes a great gulf was fixed. Anything originating with one side was suspect to the other. And the more grievances any labor group felt, the more its hostility to the Taylor System.

> Experience others have had in developing scientific management indicates that the difficulty of getting the workmen in any particular establishment to adopt the new methods always is in nice proportion to the lack of consideration that there has been shown them in the past. (Volume I, page 421.)

Labor leaders, in particular, charged as they were with the responsibility of leading in the fight of labor against "Capital," were active in opposing the introduction of the Taylor System.

Probably today millions of labor men think themselves opposed to Taylor's ideas, and scientific management.

This is remarkable because the individual workmen under scientific management soon come to realize that they are beneficiaries under the system. In particular they have higher wages by from 30 per cent to 100 per cent. The result is as already stated, that wherever the Taylor System has been established, strikes are practically unknown.

Yet history teaches that we often crucify our best friends. It will be recalled that Taylor's first efforts were aimed at breaking up soldiering, that the bitterness of that early fight convinced him of the need of a more thorough measurement of a fair day's work and that this study led to the discovery--for discovery seems to be the right name for it--of scientific management.

Antipathy of Unions

So fate decreed that Taylor's life quest to find a way of enlisting labor's enthusiastic cooperation ended by incurring their organized bitter opposition. Labor's reluctance to labor remained because entrenched in their traditions and organization.

Labor unions originated for the purpose of fighting employers rather than cooperating with them. They had capitalized the idea of soldiering in their mistaken dogma of limitation of output and had fortified that idea by the fallacious economic theory that the more we "make work," the higher wages will be and the less unemployment.

"Speedy" Taylor stood for speeding up industry. Organized labor stood for slowing it down. Taylor regarded the difference as irreconcilable, so long as labor adhered to doctrines contrary to his principles, such as limitation of output and equality of pay for good and bad workmen alike.

The union leaders feared that either the unions must destroy the Taylor System or the Taylor System would destroy the unions.

An interesting instance of the working out of this drama was at Mare Island, California, where Naval Constructor Evans, of his own initiative, introduced the Taylor System in the navy yard with the following results, before misguided labor leaders "got busy"!

> The lowest direct labor cost of retubing boilers at Mare Island had been $1,200 per boiler. When this work was "Taylorized", the cost per boiler was reduced to $400. Six or seven sailmakers were brought to do the work that previously had taken thirty. (Volume II, page 308.)

Three or four years later, after bitter political fighting, backed by labor unions, we read:

> Then came to Mare Island from Washington a party of six line officers to tear to shreds about everything Evans had done there during three and a half years to establish an efficient system. Under the regime that followed it was forbidden to keep any labor records. (Volume II, page 312.)

As soon as organized labor had declared war on scientific management, scientific management was under a cloud. Employers who used it tried to conceal the fact for fear of labor troubles and often do so today.

> In a letter written by him (Taylor) in July, 1912, to L. P. Alford, of the A. S. M. E. Sub-committee on Economic Administration, he, referring to this highly exceptional railway official, said:
> "Mr. _________used our methods for several years, while he was master mechanic of the side lines of the _______ R. R., with headquarters at ________. He did really a wonderful piece of work in getting all of the repairs of the locomotives made on piece work, some twenty different types of locomotives being repaired on the side lines. He showed me, in fact, several books containing some 120,000 different piece-work prices

> for repairing locomotives.
> "He came to see me about his work a number of times, and was most enthusiastic. When, however, the Congressional Committee wanted to get him to testify as to what he had done in this matter, he told me that if they forced him to come before them, he would be compelled to give them no information whatever. They subpoenaed him, and when he went there he denied that he ever had done anything in the line of scientific management whatever. He justified this to me by saying that if he had come out frankly before the committee and said just what he had done, that in the first place the people in his own railroad would have jumped on him; second, that lots of lines friendly to the ________line would have complained that their master mechanic acknowledged that there was good in scientific management; and third--and most important of all--that the unions in the ________R. R. would be very apt to antagonize him, and, as he said, 'It would take three years to recover from the harm that I would have done to by work by my testimony.'" (Volume II, pages 374-5.)

Congressional Investigation

One result of Taylor's fight with labor unions over Government work was a congressional investigation of the Taylor System under William B. Wilson, later Secretary of Labor, Congressmen John Q. Tilson and William C. Redfield.

Labor, unfortunately, seemed to have made up its mind, in advance, and the labor representative, presumably under instructions, really did not investigate.

> Mr. Redfield and Mr. Tilson spent hours in Taylor establishments, but Mr. Wilson, the labor representative, not a single minute. (Volume II, page 405.)

The object of the labor unions was to secure legislation throwing out the Taylor System in governmental workshops. This the Committee refused to recommend.

> Said the committee (House Labor Committee): "Your committee does not deem it advisable nor expedient to make any recommendations for legislation upon the subject at this time."(Volume II, page 349.)

Beyond this negative approval of the Taylor System, the Committee discreetly declined to go.

Their recommendation against legislation was, however, not successful in stemming the tide of opposition to the Taylor System.

> "The scheme was resorted to of attaching to appropriation bills this rider:
> "PROVIDED, That no part of the appropriations

made in this bill shall be available for the salary or pay of any officer, manager, superintendent, foreman, or other person having charge of the work of any employee of the United States Government while making or causing to be made, with a stop-watch or other time-measuring device, a time study of any job of any such employee between the starting and completion thereof of the movements of any such employee while engaged upon such work; nor shall any part of the appropriations made in this bill be available to pay any premium or bonus or cash reward to any employee in addition to his regular wages, except for suggestions resulting in improvements or economy in the operations of any Government plant; and no claim, for service performed by any person while violating this proviso shall be allowed."

The chief speaker for the proviso was Senator Henry Cabot Lodge, of Massachusetts, who made these astonishing remarks: "The very fact of a stop watch implies strain on every faculty, on every physical power, driving the heart and lungs and every muscle to the utmost possible point. . . ."

"The greatest disappointment of the whole debate to me is the disgusting demagogery of Lodge . . ."(Taylor in a letter to General Crozier, March 3, 1915, Volume II, pages 350-1.)

The adoption of this rider in 1915 was, politically, a great triumph for organized labor, and a crushing defeat for Taylor and his system. The whole episode of labor's hostility must nearly have broken his heart and may possibly have had something to do with his death, soon after. For his highest ambition was to help the laboring man.

Labor's False Economic Theory

It would be interesting to speculate on what might have happened had Taylor and Labor gotten together on the advantages of scientific management. It seems altogether likely that by this time the real income of labor, what they purchase with their money wages, would be double what it is.

In the end labor gains, and, as a class, gains the most from so-called "labor-saving devices," and scientific management is the greatest labor saving device in the world. Just as labor opposed the introduction of the machine loom because it would throw hand loom workers out of work, just as stage coach drivers opposed the railways, and teamsters opposed pipelines, so labor opposes scientific management. Yet in all such cases, labor really benefits, and benefits greatly through increased production. The scientific management which makes more shoes and clothes decreases the real cost of shoes and clothes; real wages consist partly in shoes and clothes. Scientific management which makes bricklaying more rapid makes the rents of brick houses more available; real wages consist partly of house shelter.

Had labor leaders been more far-sighted or clear sighted and joined in the task of convincing their followers that the true interests of labor lay in scientific management, labor unions today would have more prestige than they do and would not be playing so negative and obstructive a role. Labor unions have done much to prevent individual laborers from being imposed upon. The idea of organized labor is legitimate and wholesome. But in this case they have failed to serve their own ends.

In order to accomplish this, it would have been necessary for labor to abandon the two doctrines of limitation of output and equal pay for unequal work, and to have substituted the opposite, or Taylor, doctrines of maximum production and of a labor reward varying with individual productivity.

The transition from the former pair of doctrines to the latter pair means so tremendous a gain to labor that I cannot but believe that some day labor will receive the change gladly and organized labor will be leading the movement.

It will help enormously toward that end if once the make-work fallacy can be exploded in the minds of workingmen.

Fortunately the lessons of the war and of Russia since the war have not been altogether lost. The late Mr. Gompers has been quoted as saying, "Efficiency in industry is of paramount importance." Sometimes a labor union, in stigmatizing the management as inefficient and not sufficiently helpful to the workman, has sneeringly said,"Why, they haven't even a planning department!"

The mistake of organized labor was natural and inevitable because, after all, there is a grain of truth in the idea that speeding up production sometimes fails to help labor as it should.

Taylor Partly at Fault

It is altogether likely that Taylor was himself to blame for much of the antagonism he encountered. As Copley says:

> It is to be reported also that there are those who feel that if Taylor could have lived to witness the change in the attitude of many labor leaders since the World War, he would have modified his own attitude towards trades-unions.(Volume II, page 431.)

I think part of Taylor's opposition to unionism was due to confusing the idea of collective bargaining with the idea of unindividualized pay. A union could surely bargain in behalf of all its members without demanding equal pay for unequal work.

Labor unions could conceivably take the initiative in demanding scientific management. If we compare a baseball team to a corps of factory workers we note that they do not wait for the baseball manager to perfect their play nor seek in every way to avoid each man playing his best and, instead, do the least he can until driven by the manager!

As has been said, Taylor encountered more opposition from management than from labor, but management's opposition was purely individual and never came to a head in organized fashion as did labor's.

Not only has the laboring man seen rate-cutting take away piece rate incentive as fast as offered, virtually making the worker into a donkey following an ever receding bundle of hay, but he has seen scientific management constantly throwing people out of their jobs.

One can scarcely expect him to have faith that somehow, somewhere, these temporary disadvantages will more than be made up. Better a bird in the hand than two in the bush.

Taylor's system did obviate the hateful rate-cutting. To do that was one of his chief objects from the start. But it did not directly obviate their temporary unemployment; on the contrary it sometimes increased it.

Had Taylor added to his cardinal idea that piece rates once scientifically determined ought never to be cut (except under very extraordinary circumstances)a second cardinal idea that the same scientific management by which any workman should lose his job through no fault of his, should assume the responsibility of finding him another, one of the very greatest objections to his system in the minds of workingmen would have been removed.

Employers at Fault

Moreover, capital cannot throw the first stone at labor for believing in restriction of output. Has not capital often sought to corner the market and sometimes destroyed part of a crop which was a drug on the market? Has it not cried for "protection" from foreign competition? Curiously enough even Taylor was misled by the argument for "protection" while decrying the fact that workmen were misled by the basically similar fallacy regarding restricting their output.

One great stumbling block which alienated many labor men or labor sympathizers was the socialistic idea that labor is the sole producer, or, at any rate, deserves a much larger fraction of the product than he gets.

Taylor's practical answer was that squabbling over the division of spoils is a waste of time, in view of the possibility, under scientific management, of increasing everybody's share by increasing the total.

Taylor's Faith in Community of Interest

One of the most striking points which Copley brings out is Taylor's sublime and, I believe, well justified, faith that, in a very practical sense the antagonism of interest between employer and employee is more apparent than real.

> (Taylor) believed that greed arises from ignorance, from not knowing where your interests (i.e., ultimately and permanently) lie; and he believed he had started a movement destined to prove to employers as a class that greed does not pay . . . . . . that one cannot take advantage of the other without ultimate injury to the interests of both. (Volume II, page 424.)

That is, he believed, with David Harum, "it ain't a bad idea to be willin' to let the other feller make a dollar once'n a while." The employer should, in self interest, pay his employees well, and the laborer should, in self interest, help his employer earn handsome profits. Each affects the other so intimately that any attempt at over-reaching on either side does the over-reacher more harm than good because it reduces the total to be divided faster than it increases his share. That there is much truth in this idea, Taylor's experience proves. Accordingly he believed "that the cure of poverty lies not in a redistribution of wealth, but in an increased production."

Yet so intent are socialists on getting for labor a larger fraction that they oppose a system which gives it, they think, an unfairly small fraction even though it amounts to much more than labor ever got before.

Upton Sinclair inveighed against increasing pig-iron handlers' pay only 61 per cent, while the work they turned out had been increased 362 per cent. He thought their pay should have been increased 362 per cent.

> Taylor's reply to this young man (Sinclair) probably represents the most careful statement of his industrial philosophy he ever made . . . .
> "Doubtless some of those who like Mr. Upton Sinclair are especially interested in workingmen will complain because under scientific management the workman when he is shown how to do twice as much work as he formerly did is not paid twice his former wages, while others who are more interested in the dividends than the workmen, will complain that under this system the men receive much higher wages than they did before . . .
> "Mr. Sinclair sees but one man--the workman; he refuses to see that the great increase in output under scientific management is the result not only of the workman's effort but quite as much also of the study of pig-iron handling by the management and of the cooperation of teachers who help him and the organization which plans and measures his daily tasks, etc. . . ." (Volume II, pages 51-2.)

Taylor's Wage Principles

Other statements of Taylor's industrial philosophy merit quotation here:

> "Mr. Barth here has perhaps been the most efficient man of all the men who have been connected with scientific management in devising new methods for turning out work fast. I can remember--one or two--instances in which almost overnight he devised a method for turning out almost twenty times as much as had been turned out before with no greater effort to the workman. In that case you could not pay the workmen twenty times the wage. It would be absurd, would it not?" . . .(Testimony of Taylor, Vol. II, page 127.)
> "It is just and fair that men of the same general grade (when their all-round capacities are considered) should be paid about the same wages when they are all working

> to the best of their abilities. (It would be grossly unjust to other laborers, for instance, to pay this man 3.6 as high wages as other men of his general grade receive for an honest full day's work.)
> ". . .It is a significant fact that those workmen who have come under this system during the past thirty years have invariably been satisfied with their increase in pay while their employers have been equally pleased with their increase in dividends." (Vol. II, pages 53-4.)
> "And this third great party (the public) should be given its proper share of the gain . . .
> "In the past hundred years, for example, the greatest factor tending toward increasing the output and thereby the prosperity of the civilized world, has been the introduction of machinery to replace hand labor. And without doubt the greatest gain through this change has come to the whole people--the consumer."(Vol. II, page 52.)
> "The one element more than any other which differentiates civilized from uncivilized countries--prosperous from poverty-stricken peoples--is that the average man in the one is five or six times as productive as in the other." (Vol. II, page 54.)

Prerequisites of Scientific Management

Perhaps there should be added to the preceding formidable list of obstacles always standing in the way of scientific management the fact that its introduction, under the best of conditions, requires time and patience.

Even believers in it sometimes lose their enthusiasm when they learn that several years are often needed before scientific management can be developed.

> It is impossible to hurry it beyond a certain speed. The writer has over and over again warned those who contemplated making this change that it was a matter, even in a simple establishment, of from two to three years , and that in some cases it requires from four to five years.
> The first few changes which affect the workmen should be made exceedingly slowly, and only one workman at a time should be dealt with at the start. Until this single man has been thoroughly convinced that a great gain has come to him from the new method, no further change should be made. (Principles of Scientific Management, page 131.)

And after the system is set up its wheels creak at first and require readjustment.

> Again and again they would set their system going, only to have it fall down. Says one of these engineers with more force than elegance: "After every fall down, you

> pick the system up by the scruff of its neck, give it a kick, and it goes on again. And so it continues until one fine day, lo and behold! it proceeds as if by a miracle to work and keep working of its own accord." (Vol. II, page 183.)

To install genuine scientific management, the practical requisites seem to be

1. That the existing management should first "get religion" on the subject.
2. That they should employ one of more persons trained in the system.

The latter employee need not necessarily be given authority though Taylor always insisted on that. Possibly in pioneer days it was necessary; but today Gantt's idea seems more reasonable.

> If Taylor's slogan was "no responsibility, without authority," Gantt told you that as a consulting engineer he wanted neither responsibility nor authority; it was his method to have you come to him that he simply might advise you what to do. (Vol. II, page 23.)

Today there are only a few genuine scientific management experts available. As the demand grows the time will surely come when provision must be made for training such experts in large numbers.

Taylor and the Colleges

The universities or the technical schools are the natural places to look for solving this problem of training up a sufficient number of such men.

Just as other engineering training started in industry but had to be taken over by the universities, so management engineering must follow much the same course. And just as the universities now turn out annually thousands of engineers in other fields, so in this field of management engineering must they begin to supply the demand for basic training.

Taylor was reluctant to approve of this step when Professor Gay of Harvard first proposed it, and doubtless Taylor was right, at least to this extent, that in the education process the shop must be used as well as the training school. But this is also true in some degree, in other engineering--in fact in every occupation.

In his attitude toward university education, Taylor showed the usual limitations of a self made man.

> Now, it may be that, despite his scientific bent and his instinctive appreciation of the value of "book learning," he absorbed some of the prejudice against college folk that was general in American industry in his Midvale days. (Vol. I, page 125.)

In a letter to Miss Laura D. Gill, of Boston, member of a "Woman's College Committee, " he wrote:

> "I think that functional management should supersede both the committee organization by which some of our universities are managed, and the "benevolent tyrant" who runs the rest of them . . . . . ." (Vol. II, page 268.)

It will be a curious turn of the wheel of fate, if, as seems likely, Frederick W. Taylor's fame shall ultimately be kept alive in our great universities, most of all.

This is not saying that the present system of education does not deserve the particular rebukes administered to it by Taylor in his University of Pennsylvania address on Technical Education and in other statements, such as that just quoted.

But however great the shortcomings of our universities and technical schools (and they seem no greater than the shortcomings of our shops) they are the only known sources of systematic higher education and what the scientific management movement now needs is such systematic education.

Taylor's Shortcomings

Taylor, with all his acute consciousness of the shortcomings of academic institutions, was likewise conscious that he had shortcomings of his own, by virtue of not having the liberal training he criticised.

> With his friend Birge Harrison, the painter, or his friend Frank L. Babbott, a connoisseur, he would stand before a picture and ask for an explanation of what made it great. It was obvious that he groped for the laws governing this thing. He groped also for the laws governing intangible things like ethics and morals and religion. He groped for laws to which he had been obedient all his life, but which he could not formulate; his mind having been trained to deal almost exclusively with tangible things and tangible proof. He did not deny; he simply could not follow. . . He was kept humble by his knowledge of the ability he did not have and the things he did not know. There was much that was wistful in his attitude toward men who spoke familiarly of things upon which he felt he had no light. (Vol. II, pages 436-7.)

Psychology of Labor

The shortcoming which, I believe, chiefly handicapped him in his professional work was his failure to give due attention to that important intangible, labor psychology.

This criticism has often been made and has called forth vigorous defense from Taylor's friends who point out how thorough and intuitive was his knowledge of human nature and how uncanny he was in fixing the attention of workmen on what they were to get instead of on what they were to give.

Doubtless all this is true, but it is quite inadequate. It seems certain that Taylor regarded the material side as primary and the psychological as secondary. He never consciously and scientifically set out to produce mental contentment by endeavoring to satisfy due fundamental instincts of workmanship, self-respect, loyalty, etc.

Taylor realized, however, the existence of this field of study.

> There is another type of scientific investigation which has been referred to several times in this paper, and which should receive special attention, namely, the accurate study of the motives which influence men. (Principles of Scientific Management, page 119.)

That Taylor should explore this psychologic field with the same systematic thoroughness with which he explored the material side of the problem was scarcely to be expected, not only because his talents ran in a different direction, but because practical psychology, especially of "the subconscious mind," had in his day not developed very far.

Had Taylor lived a few years more, I have no doubt he would have welcomed and made systematic use of the important findings of Robert B. Wolf, who has, more than Taylor, stimulated workmen by non-monetary incentives such as by having them keep score on themselves by charts. Like Taylor, Wolf often obtained surprisingly great results.

Again, Taylor would doubtless have welcomed, and made use of "Golden Rule Nash's" ideas, one effect of which is to interest workmen in what they give as well as in what they get. Similarly he would have welcomed the revolutionary idea of Henry S. Dennison, by which those who actively manage an established business become the chief common stockholders or "partners" so that the rewards or penalties for the policy of a business accrue to those responsible for the policies--a principle quite analogous, though in a different field, to that of the "bonus" for workmen.

Such shortcomings as these in Taylor's original system are being remedied. His followers can best honor Taylor, not as some would have it, by following literally his exact procedures, but by adopting his truth-seeking, iconoclastic, ever-ready-to-improve spirit and by improving a little on him as he improved so much on his predecessors. The best way to honor a prophet is to be a prophet.

Some Other Ideas of Taylor

Taylor applied his very practical idea of making the workman's reward fit his individual performance in criticism of profit sharing for workmen. The fact that the system of profit sharing pools the workingman's interest instead of rewarding each in proportion to his efforts was, to him, a fatal objection.

Taylor had many other practical suggestions for industry aside from scientific management, strictly speaking. He believed that directors of a company ought not to be selected chiefly on the basis of their financial interest.

> "One man should be selected for his financial knowledge, another for his general knowledge of the subject of management, a third for his technical knowledge of the needs of the trade and general knowledge of the selling side of the business; a fourth perhaps for his legal knowledge and yet another for his engineering knowledge which should fit him to direct progress in this line . . ." (Vol. I, page 418.)

He believed financiers generally ill adapted to conduct industry in a sound way and for the best permanent interests of those concerned. He wrote to a friend:

> "Personally my experience has been so unsatisfactory with financiers that I never want to work for any of them. . . . .As a rule, financiers are looking merely for a turnover. They want to get in and out of their business quickly, and they have absolutely no pride of manufacture." (Vol. I, page 388.)

He believed any incumbent in a position should not try to make himself indispensable, but should train others to fill his place.

> "The writer is quite sure that in his own case, as a young man, no one element was of such assistance to him in obtaining new opportunities as the practice of invariably training another man to fill his position before asking for advancement!" (Vol. I, page 140.)

Though often accused of pace-making, which threatens the health of workers, he was, on the contrary, very solicitous for their health. The only pace he sought to make was that which was best for all concerned. As to the stop-watch myth, Taylor said:

> "Somehow there has come to be an impression . . . that for every workman who is working in the shop there are probably four or five men standing over him year in and year out with stop watches . . . .There are many workmen who never have a stop watch held on them. And probably the average man would not be timed for more than one day in his lifetime. So that probably one day of the workman's life would sum up the total of this terrible, nerve-racking strain which several of the men who have testified . . . . have complained of." (Vol. I, page 234.)

One of his ideas which, if generally adopted, would promote the health of women in industry he expressed as follows:

> "All young women," he wrote in the Principles (page 96), "should be given two consecutive days of rest (with pay) each month, to be taken whenever they may choose." (Vol. I, page 464.)

Taylor was one of the first men in industry to combat the drink evil systematically.

> It is said that as early as these Midvale days of his he predicted the triumph of prohibition, and that it would prevail not so much for moral reasons as economic . . .
> "In other cases we induced them to sign a pledge for a year, and time and time again, just before the year was up, we went to these men and induced them to sign again for a second and third year.
> "The result of this was that in a few years drunkenness was practically eliminated. (Vol. I, page 178-9.)

Creative Instinct

Although Taylor's main effort toward spurring on the workman was confined to arranging more effective financial rewards, it is interesting to note that his own motivation was not primarily that of a money maker.

Like the older economists who assumed the existence of "the economic man," a purely selfish being, Taylor assumed that his task was to appeal to selfishness. Yet both he and the economists belied the theory.

My own revered master in economics, Professor William Graham Sumner, built up his economics on the money-making instinct. Yet he himself was motivated primarily by the love of science for science's sake.

A similar incongruity is exhibited in the life of Taylor. He too founded his system primarily on the idea of the money-making motive. Yet he, like Sumner, was motivated quite otherwise.

> We believe, in fact, that his life's leitmotif is to be interpreted in terms of the counterplay in him of these two forces, the one impelling him to discover and invent, the other to make his discoveries and inventions serve the interest of society. And as we follow him through his life, we perchance may catch the echoes of a noble, if largely unconscious, self sacrifice born of this counterplay of forces. On the one hand, he longed for the peace and quiet of laboratory and study and the happy companionship of congenial souls; on the other hand he was impelled to go out and fight to bring things to pass, so that his innately gentle spirit got all scarred up. (Vol. I, page 44.)

> He seemed to count that day lost whose low descending sun viewed from his hand no novel action done. (Vol. I, page 333.)

The creative instinct was strong within him.

> "I think there is no greater pleasure to a man of inventive faculty than exercising this faculty." (Vol. I, page 426.)
> Looking back, he always found that the big thing was the accomplishment. (Vol. I, page 427.)

Taylor's last years were dedicated entirely to the work of spreading his gospel. He took no pay, but on the contrary paid salaries to young men to learn the system.

> When he left the Bethlehem Steel Company, he had accumulated a competency which sufficed to make him feel, with his prejudices against great wealth, that he no longer could afford to work for money. (Vol. I, page 393.)
> The shrewd Yankee in him came to recognize that few things would so much help him in promoting his cause as the knowledge, discreetly diffused, that in this educational work he had no money interest whatever. (Vol. II, page 167.)

Even when working at a lathe, Taylor was motivated by interest in the product. He said:

> "I worked the same hours as the other workmen, and I tell you it was the easiest and happiest year I have had since I got out of my apprenticeship--that year of going back and working on a lathe. I worked hard from the machinist's standpoint and harder than I had ever worked before in my life as a mechanic." (Vol. I, page 433.)

We may guess that his happiness in those years was not appreciably due to any bonus or piece rate or other appeal to his acquisitive instinct! Yet he never seemed clearly to realize that other workmen needed the same sort of interests in workmanship to be happy at work. Like everybody else they need to satisfy all the fundamental instincts of human nature. The Taylor System, after all, harps chiefly on one string, the instinct of self preservation. A complete life must satisfy many other instincts, such as the instincts of workmanship, self-respect, home making, reverence, loyalty and play. These are among the things men live by and not by bread alone. There is an example of workingmen attracted back to Bethlehem from Pittsburgh by the higher earnings they got under the Taylor system. But it is clear also to anyone who reads between the lines in Copley's vivid account of this incident that, combined with that money making motive, were the motives of workmanship and self-respect. Mr. Barth tells me of another case where non-monetary motives were uppermost.

> "While I was with the Link-Belt Co., a 'drill press hand' who had left for some trifling grievance, came back, giving me as his reason that the drill-press he had been given to run was so underspeeded that the fastest speed was not half enough, and that, having learned what constituted proper speeds, he could not stand it, day after day, to run so slow. Similarly a 'boring mill hand' who left because he had been transferred to the night gang, came back, giving as a reason that he could not stand hanging around the tool room for an hour or so to get a boring cutter made for every special job, after he had worked in a place where the cutter was always delivered to him beforehand. These are, I think, good early examples of the character building effect of scientific management."

Team Work

Taylor's dream was of harmonious team work between capital and labor.

> That indeed was the object of most of his luncheons and dinners--to bring workingmen and other men together, and so fill in the social chasm that usually exists between such men. (Vol. II, page 437.)
> The appeal to class consciousness and to class interests and the stirring up of class hatreds and class warfare was to him a thing accursed. (Vol. II, page 423.)

His ideals were the democratic ideals of Abraham Lincoln. He practiced and preached the simple conventional virtues. He biographer records the fact that he found in Taylor's youth "no problems of indiscretion" to embarrass him.

Many of Taylor's followers and admirers were also conspicuous altruists, including Barth, Cooke, and Brandeis, now of the Supreme Court, formerly "the people's lawyer."

Taylor's Swearing

His only vice was one of which he was proud--a virtue rather than a vice--to him, at least--and that was swearing. He made swearing a find art, believing, apparently, with army officers, that it was an important means of discipline. To that extent his system always remained a "military" one.

Psychologically, swearing is justified as an outlet for the emotion of anger. But in the ideal psychology no outlet is necessary since the emotion itself is absent. It is a sad commentary on the pent-up feelings among foremen and men that swearing is so common in industry. Were Taylor living and still studying his favorite problem of labor contentment he would surely be immensely impressed by the observation of "Golden Rule Nash" that under his regime swearing tends automatically to disappear simply because the inner feelings of resentment and irritation disappear with the observance of the golden rule.

Taylor Too Serious

Taylor took life seriously--very seriously indeed. Even his sports came to be regarded as a duty. He wrote:

> "For me, however, I find it many times exceedingly irksome to give up the intellectual work in which I am at the time very greatly interested, and go out onto a dreary golf links to spend two or three hours chasing after a golf ball. For me this medicine is frequently as bad as to go to the dentist; and yet when I once get out on the links and begin my exercise in the open air, somehow I lose my disgust and begin to cheer up and profit by the complete physical and mental change. Personally, I feel as if I need a guardian a good deal of the time, to lay out my day's work for me and keep me from doing too much of the nerve-racking kind." (Vol. I, page 454.)

Again we read:

> ". . With . . onerous golf duties, my time has been more than full." (Vol. II, page 391.)

He experimented with the best golf strokes and developed unheard of methods, which, judged by tradition, were far from "good form."

> It is said that the emotion aroused in a stranger by Taylor's stance and stroke at driving was as nothing compared to the emotion that followed when this same stance resulted, as it often did, in a 250-yard drive. (Vol. II, page 220.)

Taylor Personally

At home, however, Taylor really cast aside his business cares and even avoided talking shop with his family.

> He not only invariably shielded his wife from worry, but acted in every relation on the principle that is was for him to share his joys abundantly while he bore his troubles alone. (Vol. I, page 389.)

When once, in Maine, he tested a saddle horse for his wife--

> He rode the horse, not only in the side-saddle his wife was to use, but in the skirt borrowed from her. It is easy to imagine the awe with which the natives viewed this action by the city man; but, Lord bless you! appearances never concerned Fred Taylor. (Vol. I, page 374.)

When the war came its horror nearly crushed him. His life work had been constructive *par excellance*, while war was destructive *par excellance*. He wrote friends:

> "This war is inconceivably horrible. I am completely upset and unnerved by it, and can think of nothing else . . . ."
> "To me the whole thing is absolutely unthinkable. I lie awake at night worrying over it, . . ." (Vol. II, page 443.)

Like so many reformers he came to feel the weight of the whole universe on his shoulders. He could not bear to see things go wrong.

Seemingly his philosophy had one grave defect. Throughout his life he was inclined to take too much upon himself, to assume and to feel too great a responsibility. He did not leave enough up to God. (Vol. II, page 438.)

Taylor's Fame

Frederick W. Taylor has made a unique place for himself in history as one who bridged the gap between science and industry, between theory and practice. The world owes him at least undying fame for his accomplishment in replacing guesswork by science and thereby adding immensely to the wealth and welfare of all mankind. Some day even labor may canonize him as a patron saint.

---

[1] *Bulletin of the Taylor Society*, February, 1925.

A TABULAR PRESENTATION OF THE PRINCIPLES, TECHNIQUE AND CHRONOLOGICAL DEVELOPMENT OF SCIENTIFIC MANAGEMENT[1]

By H. S. Person
Managing Director, Taylor Society, New York

The table on the following pages is taken by permission from the paper by Dr. Person, "Scientific Management as a Philosophy and Technique of Progressive Industrial Stabilization," presented at the World Social Economic Congress held in Amsterdam, Holland, in August, under the auspices of the International Industrial Relations Association.

The sixty-four page paper from which it is taken was prepared as an answer to the question, "What has private industry developed in the nature of a basis for a technique of national and international planning if the latter should be proved to be desirable?"

The argument in the paper runs along three lines: (1) scientific management is a technique of stabilization of managerial situations; (2) its history is that of a compulsion, in order completely to stabilize any lesser area (e.g., production), to reach out and stabilize the influencing environment (e.g., sales); and (3) the best managed (most stabilized) private industries are now victims of an unstable economic environment, and are confronted by the necessity of stabilizing that environment through some form of collective control of industrial processes. The answer to this problem is application of scientific management on the collective plane; particularly the establishment for national industry of a research and planning unit which would work out a national budget of production matched to consumption, rendered voluntarily acceptable by the weight of controlling facts disclosed.

---

[1] *Bulletin of the Taylor Society*, October, 1931.

SCIENTIFIC MANAGEMENT IN PERSPECTIVE
As A Means of Achieving Progressive Stabilization

COLLECTIVE PRINCIPLES	MAJOR ITEMS OF TECHNIQUE IN INDIVIDUAL ENTERPRISE 1. Work-Place	2. Shop	3. Personnel
Research in its various forms is the approach to solution of all problems of management.	Engineering studies in design of equipment. Economic studies in size and output of machines. Methods study Time study Motion study Studies in behavior of materials Studies of skill	Studies of the relations of facilities and classes of skills available at the various work-places, and of the most effective co-ordination and proportioning of them under varying conditions of the kind and quantity of orders flowing into the shop.	Studies in mental and manual aptitudes Studies in personality requirements of various jobs Studies in emotional conditions and reactions Studies of group organizations
Standardization provides the basis of understanding necessary to co-operative effort, through formulation of purposes, policies, plans, projects, facilities, methods, conditions, etc., which become constant factors in planning and execution.	Specifications of Materials Machines Tools and apparatus Product Unit times Methods Jobs Conditions Wage rates Quality Quantity	Specifications covering co-ordination, proportioning and application of skills and facilities under various specified conditions of the kinds and quantities of work. Production schedules	Specifications of personality requirements for various jobs Specifications relating to hiring, promotion and discharge Specifications relating to training and sharing of information Specifications relating to personal and group relations

COLLECTIVE PRINCIPLES	MAJOR ITEMS OF TECHNIQUE IN INDIVIDUAL ENTERPRISE 1. Work-Place	2. Shop	3. Personnel
Control is effected by co-operative observance of the "Laws" inherent in the situation, discovered by research and made practical by formulation in terms of standards.	Provision of materials and tools Specification of jobs or operations Inspection of product Inspection of performance	Functional separation of planning and execution Classification of operations Analysis of orders Routing; the analysis of the sequence of operations on a job Scheduling or assignment of operations to various work-places in accordance with routing Inspection: products, results, costs	Systematic intelligent direction of conduct in accordance with specifications indicated above
Co-operation as a mental attitude is a condition of efficient common effort, and as a mode of conduct is the result of the formulation of standards of purpose, facility, method and relationship.	As a condition and as a result, co-operation is promoted by the combination of all factors in the total situation: understanding and acceptance of the common purpose; instruction and the understanding of details; acceptance and performance of complementary responsibilities; proper		

The order from left to right indicates roughly: (1) chronological development; (2) application to expanding managerial areas.

MAJOR ITEMS OF TECHNIQUE IN INDIVIDUAL ENTERPRISE			COLLECTIVE ENTERPRISE
4. Marketing	5. Finance	6. Gen. Administration	
Market analysis Quantitative Qualitative Studies of consumer demand Studies of the channels of distribution Studies in methods of selling Studies in sales promotion Studies of competition	Most of data required by this department are procured by other departments, e.g., costs Studies of market for capital Studies of customers' credits and collections Studies of prices of materials when purchasing is speculative instead of routine (e.g., cotton, rubber) Studies of financial ratios	Studies of the state and tendency of-- Industry generally The particular industry The particular enterprise Industrial forecasting Studies of managerial operating ratios All researches of all departments contribute to the information required by general administration	Scientific management has not been applied to the stabilization of industry on national and international planes, although experiments pointing in that direction have been initiated. These experiments, however, are not free from simultaneous experimentation in other fields of social organization.
Specifications Sales schedules Quotas: territorial commodity and personal Channels of distribution Methods of selling Prices Discounts Salaries and commissions	Specifications Standard costs Financial ratios	Specifications of Policy Projects Plans Master schedules Master budgets Operating ratios Ratios of relationship to the industry generally	

MAJOR ITEMS OF TECHNIQUE IN INDIVIDUAL ENTERPRISE			COLLECTIVE ENTERPRISE
4. Marketing	5. Finance	6. Gen. Administration	
Functional separation of planning and execution	Inspection of financial aspects of management in terms of various ratios	Inspection of: Conformity of operations to budgets and schedules Special attention to exceptional situations Prompt decisions concerning changes in purpose and policy	

selection, assignment and promotion of personnel; provision of adequate facilities; just sharing of the joint economic rewards; humane personal relations; steady provision of work to be done.

THE INFLUENCE OF SCIENTIFIC MANAGEMENT

BASED ON A QUESTIONNAIRE ADDRESSED TO FIVE HUNDRED AMERICAN FIRMS[1]

By Sanford E. Thompson
President of The Thompson & Lichtner Co. Inc., Boston,
and President of the Taylor Society

The amazing wealth of our nation which we are now dissipating so strenuously has been brought about through four lines of scientific development: power, mechanism, process and management. On the other hand, as the present depression has evidenced, we have individually and collectively sadly neglected the scientific development of investing, credit, finance, and distribution. In other words, we produce goods scientifically but we have developed no scientific means to see that they are properly consumed. There has been no Frederick W. Taylor of distribution and finance.

The analysis we are presenting this evening confines itself to the industrial field, but the past twenty years of progress in the industrial field has been so remarkable as to show the possibilities and necessity for broader developments to cover the entire range of individual and collective business and financial activities.

At the risk of beginning the evening with a "dry-as-dust" commentary, I wonder if I may be pardoned for reading to you a brief scientific treatment--perhaps too scientific for an audience of the calibre I see before me--of this problem of finance. This is a letter printed by "Industry" of the Associated Industries of Massachusetts under the caption of "Why the Depression": Following a brief paragraph analyzing Republican prosperity--this was written before the election--Mike Clark, a Tennessee farmer writes to his local newspaper from Holler Brook Junction:

"I have taken my own case for instance. I see my mistakes, and many others have acted likewise. I bought a Ford instead of a farm, and it is worn out, but the farm I figured on is still O.K. I invested in a Radio instead of a Cow, and the Radio gives static instead of milk.

"I am feeding five nice hounds, which answer to the names of Red, Redwing, Jake, Slobber and Bayrum, instead of five pigs. I had our piano tuned instead of our well cleaned out. I spent all of my cash in 1928, and used my credit in 1929, and traded up all my future wages in instalments in 1930; so hard times caught me in bad shape last fall.

"I am on the cash basis now but I ain't got no cash. I am tied to the end of my rope, and the man I am working for is busted on account of nobody won't pay him, and his cotton won't sell 'cause nobody won't buy no cotton clothes. All the gals wear slick, silky underwear right here in our own cotton patches. I had four dollars saved up for a rainy day, but it turned off dry and I spent the four dollars for two inner tubes.

"I tried hard to make both ends meet with a turnip patch, but when I got turnips ready to sell, everybody was selling turnips for nothing and the market was glutted. I am worried plum to the bone, and my wife's kinfolks are coming over next Tuesday to spend two weeks."

Let us now come down from the realms of high finance to our study of the influence of Scientific Management in American industry.

GENERAL CONCLUSIONS

To determine the influence of Scientific Management upon industry, questions were sent to a number of manufacturers of the progressive type all over the country. Answers regarding their organization and methods of management in production, accounting and marketing were received from representatives of the major lines of industry located in the various manufacturing states.

The returns from the study indicate not only an advance in scientific method but also the vital part played by Scientific Management in the remarkable stamina of so large a proportion of our industrial establishments in resisting the effects of the drastic reduction in output. I venture to say that if such a depression as this had occurred twenty years ago with the then existing methods of production, procedure, accounting, and budgetary control, the number of business failures would have been innumerable.

The returns show a remarkable adoption in practice of the fundamental principles first developed by Frederick W. Taylor in production and inventory control, incentives based on time study, and functional organization. Budgeting of sales, production, and operating costs, which has played so large a part in reducing the number of industrial failures during the depression, while distinctly less common than other phases of management is carried out by an appreciable majority of those replying to the questions. Marketing methods, on the other hand, are relatively backward in their various phases, although a large number of firms indicate scientific development in selling.

PRINCIPLES OF SCIENTIFIC MANAGEMENT

In planning an analysis to indicate the influence of Scientific Management upon American industry it is necessary as a premise to consider the fundamental principles.

> Frederick W. Taylor gave the four great underlying principles of management substantially as follows ("Principles of Scientific Management"): (1) Development of a true science to replace rule-of-thumb methods; (2) scientific selection of the personnel; (3) scientific education and development of the personnel, to insure the carrying out of scientific methods; (4) intimate friendly co-operation between the management and the men, dividing the responsibilities and work between them.
>
> These four principles in practice require: (1) The development of standards of methods and procedure; (2) the fitting of a man to his task; (3) the provision of means to encourage each man to best utilization of his ability; (4) an organization which

effectively controls and actuates the various phases of the business.

It is evident that these fundamentals apply not only to production but also to all phases of accounting, marketing, and organization. They also apply in principle to the conduct of business as a whole: the adoption of scientific methods of procedure planned in advance and then carried through to a definite goal by means of smooth running organization which eliminates the dire catastrophes which are now coincident with modern business.

To determine, however, the extent to which industry has progressed in these directions, it is necessary to find out whether these general principles are being followed. But since the answers to direct inquiries would be indefinite we must determine whether the specific procedures which are essential to scientific management are being operated. While prosecution of procedures does not prove conclusively that the spirit of the principles is being maintained, it is fair to assume--especially in view of the practical results which we know are being attained generally where the methods exist--that scientific methods tend to produce scientific management.

The agreement of the methods generally used in modern practice in the more scientific shops with those first enunciated by Taylor is so close that we may go back to Taylor for the basis of our present inquiry. Note that these methods now so general were actually non-existent before Taylor worked out the fundamentals in the 1880's and were scarcely further advanced when in 1911 he wrote "Shop Management."

The following is a summary of the chief "leading functions" as outlined by Taylor ("Shop Management"): (1) Analysis of all orders; (2) time study of hand work; (3) time study of machines; (4) balance of stores, or running inventories, of raw materials, stores and finished parts and balance of work ahead for men and machines; (5) promises of delivery, based on standard times and available men and machines; (6) standard methods of performance and standard tools and appliances; (7) maintenance of methods and of plant; (8) employment bureau; (9) pay department. These are the more important of Taylor's "functional elements" and assume an organization designed to supervise each.

Even without a survey such as we have conducted, it is evident from our knowledge of industry that these essentials of scientific management are in widespread use. But we also find many cases where orders are put into the shop in sequence of their receipt without regard to machine capacity; records of quantities of stores on hand in the heads of employes but not on paper; in a large percentage of establishments the omission of the most essential element in planning, _viz._, standard times in scheduling work; and we find piece rates set by guess and past performance.

I challenge the manager of any successful plant to deny not only that the elements enumerated are essential, but also that a large measure of his success in smoothness of operation, reduction in cost and maintenance of quality are due to the carrying through of these principles.

On the other hand, as regards marketing and distribution, we find on every side a confirmation of the findings in our study of the lamentable deficiency in the application of the basic principles, which are adaptable to these branches of industry. We find also in other phases of business--credit and finance--a still greater lack of elements of planning, control, and standardization.

The Survey

The returns from the survey conducted by the author indicate the status of scientific methods in industry. The principal divisions of the questionnaire were:

Production:	Running inventories or "balance-of-stores" Planning and control; Incentives and time study.
Accounting:	Cost accounting; Budgeting.
Organization:	Division of responsibility.
Marketing:	Compensation of salesmen; Quotas; Territorial assignment; Routing; Training of salesmen; Market analysis.

Certain other elements are also essential in scientific marketing such as merchandising and product analysis, but it is evident that the items enumerated all relate to the fundamental principles of scientific standardization, planning and control, and training of the personnel.

Accuracy of Returns

In laying out the plan for the questionnaire the writer first consulted a number of management engineers and former associates of Mr. Taylor, including Carl G. Barth, King Hathaway, Robert T. Kent, H. S. Person, Edward W. Clark, 3d, John H. Williams, Henry P. Kendall, Henry Post Dutton, John M. Carmody, William H. Leffingwell, Richard H. Lansburgh and G. E. Schulz. The series of questions was prepared in such a way as to permit a "Yes" or "No" answer, and with a covering letter was mailed to some 500 concerns. This relatively small number--of whom about 25 per cent replied, a satisfactory percentage--apparently gave returns that were quite representative of the class of firms replying. Since the returns were signed, confidentially, it was possible to guage their size and standing. The number of concerns is sufficient to be indicative.

On the other hand it is obvious that those replying, because interested in the review, are those operating under modern methods of management. Furthermore, an executive answering this type of inquiry naturally puts a high standard on his virtues and performance and interprets questions so as to present the best possible showing. In the study of the figures, therefore, it was clearly borne in mind that the principle conclusions must be based on relative percentages rather than upon actual figures. Admitting that the returns necessarily present a roseate picture as a whole, it is fair to assume that in relation to each other the findings may be accepted as fairly representative of American industry.

Production

Running Inventories. Some 95 per cent of those replying state that they maintain inventories on raw and on finished material; some 15 per cent fewer on material in process, while 30 per cent fewer apportion material to orders. These relative values are substantially what one would expect, although the percentages all appear high for industry as a whole. Inventory values are reflected in general accounts in the large majority of concerns.

Planning and Control. A large percentage of those replying, 82 per cent, maintain planning as a definite function either through a department or an individual. A larger percentage than this claim to take into account the capacity of the departments and the "choke" points when planning. Evidently, however, many did not appreciate the significance of this most important characteristic of planning or in fact of the use of standard times--which 77 per cent claim to use. From direct contacts which we have with plants all over the country we find a surprising ignorance even in large plants of the importance of using the time element in scheduling the work to the different departments. Even with this qualification on the accuracy of the returns we see what a remarkable hold the general principles of planning and control have attained in production management.

Incentives. Over three-fourths of those replying have an incentive type of wage payment, showing that there are still opportunities for real development. Two-thirds of the plants on incentive use straight piece work, and one-third some form of bonus or premium. A few (4 per cent) use day work standards; the balance straight day pay. The number of operatives on incentives in the plants which use incentive plans ranged from 15 to 100 per cent, with an average of 69 per cent. While more than two-thirds of those replying use a stop watch, a much smaller number utilize unit times for setting wage rates. Many still base their wage rates on past experience.

Accounting

About three-fourths of those replying state that they use either standard costs or job costs and about the same proportion say they tie in their costs with the general books. In 43 per cent of the replies the overhead is distributed by departments, and in about the same percentage by a per cent of labor costs. Fourteen per cent distribute by groups of products. Here again we note definite possibilities for improvement.

Budgets for expected sales, expected production and permissible operating costs are maintained in about two-thirds of the replies. Monthly or four-weekly profit and loss statements are reported by 90 per cent of those replying. This common practice, like most of the other features considered, has developed almost entirely during the last twenty years. Taylor worked out the basis of present accounting methods in the early 1890's.

Organization

Functional management, that is, the distribution of authority by function rather than entirely by line, is necessary properly to control the working of a business organization. Consequently the questions regarding special departments or functions under a sub-executive or specific individual on whole or part time are of special interest.

Of the firms replying some 90 per cent stated that they maintained such divisions in production and control. Almost two-thirds have time and methods study divisions; over 80 per cent carry repair and maintenance departments and about 70 per cent separate employment or service as a distinct function of management.

Marketing

While in production we find a preponderance of what may be termed scientific methods, in marketing we find a different picture. Unstandardized methods predominate. It is here that we find that nearly half of the companies pay straight salaries, most of them with expenses; about one-quarter pay commission with or without a drawing account; and the remainder pay salaries plus commission, or use both salaried and commissioned men.

A most striking feature of the returns is the preponderance of the plan of compensating solely on the basis of volume sold without regard to any other factors. Manufacturers apparently fail to realize that compensation on a basis only of volume sold, with no consideration of effort, balanced sales or profit, is akin to the antequated and obsolete payment in factories of uniform piece rates regardless of variation in the character of the operations.

In determination of quotas, in allocation of territory, in routing salesmen, and in utilizing the accumulation of knowledge regarding product demands, there also is marked deficiency in application of the scientific method of approach and its utilization in practice.

The unscientific methods of commission payment are striking--and it must be remembered further in all of this marketing tabulation as well as in production that there is an unavoidable weighting of the results on the high side. Four-fifths of the concerns which report commission payment pay on volume sold alone--only one-fifth considering profit or type of product. Considerably less than two-thirds set quotas. Only 25 per cent allot territories by definite rule, the large majority using judgment only. Again we find that the majority route their salesmen merely by total territory--only 7 per cent route salesmen by exact schedule.

In the selection of salesmen more than half select merely by references. More than three-quarters train simply by verbal instructions.

In the knowledge of markets the picture is somewhat better. Nearly two-thirds of those reporting think they have a fairly good idea of their markets and the proportion of the business which they themselves get.

The conclusion is obvious, however, that sales management in the majority of industrial concerns, even the larger and better managed ones, is markedly inferior to the management of production; and yet the dire need is evident, in this period of unbridled competition, for the most effective and profitable sales methods. Executives throughout the land are devoting their efforts chiefly to marketing problems. It would appear that there is an opportunity as yet unappreciated by many of them for profitable sales through more scientific methods of sales management.

General Progress

Marketing Progress. All in all, while it is evident that progress in the science of sales has been markedly less than that in production, the returns do indicate a definite progress and foreshadow a sound and rational advance. This is particularly certain if we examine what some individual concerns have accomplished in scientific sales development. A few have in fact attained a standard of practice equal to the highest developments in production lines. These accomplishments have resulted from the utilization of methods closely akin to those which have produced such outstanding results in production lines. In professional work carried on by our own organization, for example, we have adopted similar principles of analysis of the problems involved to those which have proved so satisfactory in other branches of management. Planning and control are as necessary in selling as in production. The introduction of salesman's compensation involves principles similar to those required for wage or salary compensation in the factory. Market analysis is based on a scientific examination of the needs of a situation and the simplest means of obtaining desired results.

Production Progress. The status of progress in production can be somewhat more closely defined. Viewing the picture as a whole on the basis of a general examination of returns rather than of computed values, it would appear that more than 75 per cent of the firms replying are working with a preponderance of scientific methods. Allowing for the measureable weighting in the returns which has been noted, we may estimate, I believe conservatively, that at least 50 per cent of the industrial production in the country is carried on by methods which in the main fall under the category of Scientific Management. In marketing the estimate would fall as low as 25 per cent. Many of these, of course, fall far short of the ideals of Frederick W. Taylor ("Principles of Scientific Management": Science, not rule of thumb; harmony, not discord; co-operation, not individualism; maximum output in place of restricted output; the development of each man to his greatest efficiency --and prosperity) but the accomplishments have been remarkable.

Development in Machines and Processes. In the introduction were mentioned other phases of scientific development which have taken place coincidently with the development of management. These are power, mechanization and process. The development of power has been chiefly dependent upon electrical progress, although oil and gas and coal have played their part, which in turn has involved the highest degree of scientific research.

The design of machines, made possible by power, has proceeded apace. Taylor used to say that up to the 1880's machines were built by guess with no computation of stresses. If a part broke, it was enlarged the next time. More recently machine development in certain industries, but by no means in all, has been elaborating automatic equipment which replaces manpower to a remarkable degree. Along with this we have scientific progress as distinct from cut and try methods along such lines as the art of metal cutting, following the pioneering researches of Taylor in high-speed steel beginning in the 1870's.

Process development has received less publicity than machine design but has played an important part. Research divisions are maintained as district departments in all large industrial concerns. Electrical and chemical and physical research have developed processes and new products which have had such marked effect upon our social as well as upon our business structure.

Influence of Scientific Developments Upon Business in General

We cannot close without looking at the broader business and social aspects of scientific development. Has the getting of wealth made us poor? Must we, as some would have us believe, drop all our philosophy of productivity? Must we, as some of our orators would tell you, dig our dirt with tea spoons? Shall we throw away our automatic machinery? Shall we adopt permanently the ca'canny policy of Great Britain to work slowly to make the work go 'round--a policy that in 1926 caused America to produce three and one-half times as much goods per man as Great Britain?

To answer this question let us examine the philosophy of increased unit production. Let us for simplicity assume a small, self-supporting territory. Let us suppose that the automobile manufacturer in this territory reduces the intrinsic cost and selling price of his automobile one-fourth. This throws, let us say, 1000 men out of employment. But the rest of the people in the community by saving 25 per cent on their car can purchase more of other goods. The men thrown out of the automobile factory will therefore obtain jobs in other places. And note this: every man by being able to buy more goods will raise his standard of living. This is what actually has been happening in the United States ever since its founding. And now we are told that we are reaching the limit of our consumptive capacity; we have no more absorption power. I tell you, friends, that this is the most dangerous possible philosophy irrespective of whatever social order we may develop. If we are to progress, if our $1,000 a year men are to become $4,000 a year men, we must continue to increase our unit productivity.

The Future for Scientific Management

But do not misunderstand me, I am talking about unit productivity and not about total production. We cannot absorb an unlimited quantity of shoes; we cannot eat more than a certain amount of food. We can absorb more automobiles, radios, and airplanes. We can use better houses, better clothes and more luxuries. It is evident as our productivity continues to increase that real satisfaction in life requires a broadening of our consumptive capacity through greater production of those things which make for higher development, physical, social and spiritual. To provide employment and purchasing power for all under such conditions involves creating greater opportunities in the so-called service industries and public services. With the greater leisure that should be at our disposal--not forced leisure as at present, but planned leisure--we shall have the time and opportunity for enjoying these broadened interests and activities.

We must have a bold stimulation of business activity in contrast to a policy of drifting toward lower levels. There are only two alternatives: either let matters take their course with only sufficient action to avoid banking collapse, or else, as we would do if war were declared, start industry through the immediate injection of the means to increase purchasing power among the rank and file of our people who are now suffering and in some instances dying. All of these things are a challenge to Scientific Management; to the extension of the science of management to the broader fields--not only to marketing, but to the analysis of the broader problems of distribution, credit and finance. Means will be found in the coming years for adjusting the volume and flow of goods to all consumers just as surely as it has been worked out in the factory from the old rule of thumb to the scientific control visualized by Frederick W. Taylor. Means will be found if our present social order is to survive for a control and scheduling of financial investments and credit. These things can be solved by the same type of scientific analysis which has produced such astounding results in production.

Finally, it must be recognized that it is a national duty to provide work at least a subsistence wage to _all_ who desire it. This is a social responsibility which must be solved by the scientific method.

Address before a meeting of the Taylor Society, New York, December 8, 1932.

---

[1] _Bulletin of the Taylor Society_, April, 1933.

PART FOUR

EVOLUTION OF THE SCIENTIFIC MANAGEMENT MOVEMENT

The articles in this section are, as in Part Three, arranged in chronological order of their appearance in print. Although the entire selection of articles in this book, in a very real sense, represents the evolution of the scientific management movement, the articles selected for this part were chosen for their distinct originality and pivotal characteristics.

The first two articles by Robert G. Valentine represent two of the first and finest on the subject of industrial relations. The writer's views on a need for an industrial audit, his belief in absolute democracy in group action, and his flirting with the concept of guaranteed yearly employment places these essays some decades ahead of their common acceptance.

The systems concept of business is clearly delineated in Person's description of the managerial job in his essay "The Manager, the Workman, and the Social Scientist." His advice for the building and maintenance of a viable business organization seems not entirely out of place in today's world--some fifty years since.

The fourth article, "Man Management: A New Profession in the Making" by Meyer Bloomfield is a succinct discussion of the then evolving function of personnel administration as distinct from, supportive of, and a part of the industrial relations department.

"Superstandards" by F. B. and L. M. Gilbreth is a timely reminder that the study of methodology should always precede the establishment or setting of standards of performance. It had been common practice, and it still regretably is, to accept current practice as acceptable and to establish a time standard for the task--thus foregoing the opportunity for improvement before the resulting standard becomes "institutionalized" by its acceptance by the workers. In the authors' words superstandards "retain all the value of a standard as to means of improvability, but is recognized as the embodiment of the One Best Way extant and a further step toward the discovery of the One Best Way available--at the time. The discussion covers the significance of superstandards from the managerial, economic, and psychological standpoints and its relationship to fatigue and skill.

In "Management as an Executive Function," Williams presents a summary of the findings of various writers on scientific management, psychology, and biology and argues that management is not as scientifically based as some would have us believe but best be perceived as being dichotomous--management as an executive function and management as a science. He notes that "however far management as a science may encroach upon management or administrations as an executive function through the development of facts bearing progressively upon problems as they arise, there will always be a plane on which the final determination must include things other than facts." He concludes by observing that the next step in the development of management is the incorporation of the findings of modern psychology and biology as a basis for dealing with the most complex problem faced by managers--man.

In "The Basis of Industrial Psychology" Elton Mayo supports William's contention regarding the need for psychology of the total situation as a firm foundation for the practice of management. Although much which Mayo discusses has been superseded by later investigations and experiments including those at Hawthorne it does serve the purpose of illustrating an early awareness of the problems arising from the individual as a member of a group in an industrial setting. An expression of regret and an appeal for investigations into industrial problems from a psychological point of view concludes his presentation.

"The Great Obsession" by Bruére is a plea to managers to avoid the problems besetting managers in other countries by affronting organized labor and opposing trade unions. He takes issue with Mayo's offered solution that to avoid a "class-war" you should make unionization unnecessary--you create open-shops. He argues the need to take into account the total situation and achieve what Follett calls "the plus values of conflict" by a process of integration of their interests and not the doing away of one by the other or the giving in of one to the other. The article is a rational argument to the obtaining of industrial peace in which both parties come out winners and no one loses.

In reply to Robert Bruére's article noted above; the article "A Supplement to 'The Great Stupidity'" by Elton Mayo was penned as an open letter to Mr. Bruére to "clarify" Mayo's viewpoint as to unions and the potential of "Class-warfare" between the owners of industry including managers and organized labor.

Ordway Tead's contributions "Purpose as a Psychological Factor in Management" is a further discussion of the problems arising out of management's employment of "scientific management" and the adverse reaction by labor--particularly organized labor after World War I. Tead approaches the problem through an analysis of the "purposes" or the objectives of the various groups in an industrial situation. In reply to a guery as to whether there is a solution to a situation where different groups having "opposing" objectives can be induced to modify their purposes enough to achieve "most of the pie" if not all, the author replies in the affirmative. In doing so he sets forth a number of principles upon which industrial peace is possible.

The Managing Director of the Taylor Society, H. S. Person makes one of his "scouting expeditions" into the need for researching the nature and methods of management in "Managements Concern in Research."

He proposes the employment of the scientific approach to problem identification and solution and a number of other research methods particularly applicable to the problems of management. He suggests the systematic accumulation and analysis of records concerning managerial plans, programs, and procedures on both the individual company level and by trade associations, cooperative research by firms having common problems, the use of professional research organizations, and support for research by higher education.

A succinct summary of the problems and progress of industrial psychology is presented in W. V. Bingham's article entitled "Industrial Psychology." Of particular interest to students of management should be his presentation of psychological problems of industry and the influence of psychology on American industry. These influences although slow in starting and in having an impact on the thinking and conduct of managers is shown to be substantial and increasing. In showing how this influence has been achieved the author notes that it was achieved through industry's response to psychology as a science, as a point of view that psychology pays, and as a method or approach to evaluating policy or plans.

SCIENTIFIC MANAGEMENT AND ORGANIZED LABOR [1]

The Functions of The Industrial Counselor-Possible Relations of Scientific Management and Labor Unions

By Robert G. Valentine

In beginning my work I had to adopt as a working hypothesis very distinct tentative beliefs. One working hypothesis I adopted was a belief in scientific management, and I claim to understand it very much as you do. The second hypothesis is a belief in absolute democracy in group action on matters. Without assenting to any particular form of association, I feel that in any community or in any group of people, where you do not find a sane quiet beginning towards group action, that group or that concern or those individuals are headed for trouble. And so in accepting the facts of our time as we find them, I believe in trade unionism as one distinct form of demorcratic development, despite all its imperfections and its monstrous economic fallacies.

Last Saturday I was called on the telephone by one of a firm of Buffalo lawyers, who asked if I knew anything about a text-book concern in Massachusetts. I told him I had no accurate information about it. He said, "Assuming what you have seen in the papers and what you know about it is all true, would you consider that firm financially sound at the present time?" I said, "Yes, sir."

Then, "Assuming also what you know about it, would you consider that firm or would you not consider that firm as sound in its methods of management and its processes of doing the work?" Knowing the concern to be what any of us would consider an up-to-date, clean-cut business concern, I said, "Yes; I should consider it perfectly solvent, both financially and as regards the way it works its processes."

Next I was asked, "Do you think that concern is industrially solvent, meaning that the relations between employers and employees in that concern, and of all the partners in that concern in any relations they have with each other and with their employees, and with outside labor forces of any kind, and with the management itself, are not only all fixed pretty soundly, but are developing in the right direction?" I replied, "From what I know of the concern I should not consider that concern industrially sound. I do consider it financially sound. I do consider it sound as to its plant and equipment and methods and processes of manufacture and operation, but not so on the side of human relations existing all throughout." The man inquiring then said, "That is what I wanted to know. I had some doubts about it myself; and we will look into it further now, from what you have said."

Now, to me it is significant that that type of question is rising. I want to place before you that same question in another form.

Imagine that a large industrial concern desires to issue new capital stock. The ordinary process is for it to go to its bankers. Bankers talk over the situation, and if they think generally well of the plan, they ask the industrial company to have its financial conditions certified to by an impartial disinterested concern of public accountants. Bankers also get, either from those accountants or directly through a firm of industrial engineers, a certificate as to the condition of the plant and the equipment. Those certificates appear in the prospectus of the new securities, and stand to the investing public as a mark of the care taken by the bankers before they lend their names to the flotation of the securities. It also assures the public that the concern did not have capital tied up in unnecessary stores; that its methods of storeskeeping were in keeping with economy.

The day is not far distant when the same bankers will demand a third certificate, in connection with any such transaction. The third certificate will testify to the industrial relations existing within the concern. It will be made by industrial counselors, and will certify as to the industrial relations existing in this concern. This concern may have a good bill of health on the first two points, and yet in the next six months they might have a strike on their hands which would make their securities worth nothing beyond the pieces of paper they are written on.

I think that third certificate will read somewhat as follows:

"We have investigated the condition of the X. Y. Z. Co.; first, as to questions of fundamental organization, particularly in their relation to the economic and social forces of the day; second, we have examined all questions of personnel such as description of jobs, selection and development of personnel; third, we have investigated questions of rates, amounts and methods of pay; fourth, we have examined questions of attitude toward labor unions, and all forms of association; fifth, we have investigated relations to labor laws, both state and federal, and to court decisions affecting labor; sixth, we have investigated questions affecting the relations of the concern to the public, particularly in matters of safety, sanitation, health and regularity of employment; and we find that the X. Y. Z. Company is giving due attention the the human relations in industry and is not likely to be involved in serious labor trouble or to carry a heavy burden of dissatisfaction cost."

Such a certificate may seem like the wildest dream to a large percentage of employers in the world today, but it will no longer seem so when we can educate ourselves to the point of being willing to move on from some of the outworn political and economic and social theories of our time, and give to these problems some of the thought now given to questions of finance and plant. The manufacturer will then change from the condition of a blind or honestly puzzled employer, clinging to traditions of inherited belief in a worn-out economic and social theory, into a business-like practical sense of the concrete industrial forces and opportunities around him.

In making an audit of this kind-an industrial audit--the first task of the industrial counselor is to get the concern oriented. This means analyzing its organization and finding out whether this organization has effective roots in modern conditions. For example: A concern which is found to be doing nothing toward some form of self-government among the employees can get from me no honest certificate of security against labor troubles.

One of the first things a concern anxious to get headed right must do is to lift its employment department from a subordinate place in some operating department to a level with the manufacturing, selling and accounting branches, and place it directly in charge of a partner or major manager, one of whose chief duties it shall be to develop a perpetual human audit of the kind I am suggesting here. With this personnel branch of its business thus developed at one end of its line of major functions, and some form of internal association among all its members developing at the other end of the line, the concern will become more and more conscious of its real industrial status. From a business point of view no organization of this kind can or should be defended except on the ground either that it pays or that it is necessary in view of existing or imminent law. In saying this I am not for a moment denying to business men other virtues than business virtues; but it is a cardinal point of good business administration, as of ethics, to keep pay and patronage apart.

Don't be led astray by the size of the job when I say that the head of the personnel division of a concern must be actively in touch with economic, industrial, social and political forces of the day; he must be alive to the meaning of trade unionism; he must be able to distinguish between its constructive meaning and its destructive meannesses. He must be equally ready to admit the meannesses of his fellow managers, and anxious about their constructive side. He must be alive to the trend of even the humblest business toward a status in the public service, for the public character that our railroads have taken will be rapidly followed by an effective public interest in the foods we eat and from which we are individually powerless to bar the poison. I am not asking that the personnel manager shall approve of these things. It is not a question of approval or disapproval, but he must be alive to them. So he must be alive to the growth of cooperation, to the real contribution of the trusts, to the growth of consumer's controls, to the backwardness of our educational system as a whole, despite its noble exceptions. He must be alive, still whether he agrees or not, to "votes for women" and the feminist movement. For the personnel manager, to be fit for his job, must be an industrial counselor.

And these are questions which affect your business. And when you go to put them clearly down on paper and to analyze them, you will find them not more numerous or more varied than the problems you face in your selling and manufacturing departments and in you accounting department.

While not more numerous and not more varied, it is true they are more subtle--harder to get a line on, because, just as in physics, you have a number of variables full of different elements. Yet nevertheless it is fairly definite at that end. And at the other end of science you have the whole field of socialism, which is full of the indefinite and intangible, and yet is capable of scientific analysis.

Having charted the situation of the concern in these questions of fundamental organization, the industrial auditor passes on to questions of personnel. What are the fruitful sources of labor supply for the concern? Except at the bottom grades is the concern itself its own best resource? It should be. Roads <u>up</u>, <u>out</u>, and <u>in</u>, should be developed. Its basic discipline should be its own educational system. Its foremen and superintendents should be teachers instead of bosses. Are the jobs clearly stated? The best concern today has criminally wasteful gaps between functions and overlapping of functions. Are the wastes of selecting wrong people for jobs minimized? Is the concern alive with useful counsel one to another? Are individual friction and jealousy seared and withered and cooperative spirit drawn forth by the magnetic power of what the concern as a whole stands for, clearly held in the minds of each individual within it?

The industrial auditor then passes to questions of pay. Is the wage system already beginning to be modified by some form of profit and loss sharing, which, by the way, can only healthfully exist when a concern has at least rudimentary beginnings toward that bogey of the unawakened employer called "share in the management." The verbal bogeys lose their terror before easily installed sane beginnings of self-government. What do the people make by the week, by the month, by the quarter, by the year?

Out of the pay envelope must come the living powers of employee and manager. For both, these questions are vital: purchasing power; savings; insurance against illness, accident, unemployment, old age and death; housing; and such social questions as health, education and recreation. That is what each one in this room is up against, whether he considers it or not. How far may and should the concern efficiently share in these?

And from these more internal questions of organization, personnel and pay, the industrial auditor proceeds to the relation of the concern to labor organizations, labor laws, and public standards. If the concern deals with labor unions, are its dealings merely defensive or are they constructive? Does it take a legitimate hand in seeing that wise laws are framed, or does it fight the principle of a new labor law _in toto_ and stand aloof from details only to be handed later an inefficient statute, a hybrid output of timid politicians and sentimental philanthropists? Are the employees safe from fire and accident? Are conditions sanitary? Is the need of a healthy personnel understood? The shifting force in a large business is, perhaps, the greatest waste of our times from the point of view both of the business and itself and of the community.

The development of the technique of an industrial audit is, of course, in its infancy. But already the constructive power of merely asking these businesslike and practical questions in an ordered and businesslike fashion has been wonderfully fruitful. They open up new horizons to business enterprises. The organization chart of an old time industrial engineer showed a lot of pretty oblongs or ovals connected by interesting lines. Functions and positions held impersonal sway among them. In the new organization chart, the people appear by name; the best paper organization in the world is nothing apart from the men and women who run it. The quality of the personnel is the last and greatest fact in business solvency.

Today when a business concern gets into labor troubles the usual course is for the management to call in their lawyer. As a rule, lawyers have no grounding in the industrial problem; and furthermore, the methods and practices of our courts are not at all the methods and practices proper to the decision of industrial questions. That is one reason why the courts are not the arena in which labor problems can be successfully tried out.

Courts are not equipped either with the knowledge or with the machinery. Many lawyers, of course, as individuals, have gone into various aspects of the industrial problem, and some of them so deeply and skillfully as to have been already in a position of substantially practicing another profession alongside of their legal profession.

The industrial counselor should not be the advocate of either side in a controversy, helping it to put its own ideas across. He should be a master in the growing laws of industry and should have it specifically understood in connection with every service he performs, that his job begins and ends by helping his client to understand and fulfill those laws. Thus he is valuable either to employers, employees, or the public, and whichever is his client, in the sense of paying him, can expect from him only such service as is to the interest of all three parties. No scientific and just service could be built on other grounds. It should be repeated that his job begins and ends by helping his clients to understand and fulfill those laws; and thus he is valuable alike to employers, employees, and the public.

Possible Relations of Scientific Management and Labor Unions

Suppose a manufacturer should say to me, "I wish to start, equip and run a new plant in a certain section of the country." I suppose the ordinary method would be to begin to decide about the size of the plant, what you would make, et cetera. After you had decided what you were to manufacture you would start to consider building the plant and equipping it, and the processes of manufacture and management. And after it was all together you would expect to pick up your labor supply.

The first thing that I would do if I were confronted with such a proposition would be to make a study of the labor situation in that locality before the ground was broken. First I would take up the question of labor supply with all the existing sources of labor supply at that time. I would go to the labor unions and raise all the questions in advance that might be raised afterwards, as far as one could humanly foresee them. Next, I would show that insofar as there were any unions in that vicinity connected with those trades--I should run a preferential shop--I would appeal to the unions for men before I appealed to anybody else. If they could give the men I wanted I would take them in preference to anybody else. Then I would say that I would pay as the piece rate of my wages the union rate in that vicinity, regardless of whether or not the shop were unionized. And any other methods of pay would have to built on that.

Then I should make the union mad by telling them that I would pay a minimum wage in that factory. My great quarrel with the union men is that they have their minds fixed on so much an hour, and they are giving shamefully too little attention to the idea that a week is the shortest unit a man can count on.

I should like to see the union leaders awaken to the job, and see that the ideal of employment is not the week but the year. A year containing the four seasons is the lowest ideal unit of planning which one should engage in. But if one could get industry on a carefully graded weekly basis, instead of the hourly rate, a great step in advance would be made.

When I put that questions to a small group of manufacturers the other day, they came back and said, "Supposing you could not afford to pay the minimum wage in some catastrophic time?" Then I said, "That concern should be declared industrially insolvent, exactly as they do when a man does not meet a note or a company does not meet the interest on its bonds."

Then I would demand that you plan as far as you possibly could for regularity of employment, first by regulating your own business to the greatest extent possible; secondly, by establishing some cooperative relationship with other concerns in other lines of industry, so that when your slack period came against his full period, you could make some shift to the advantage of each; and thirdly, as business men looking after your own interest, by taking some kind of interest in state public work, so the state would not be going into the market when wages were high and business good, but instead would wait until conditions of unemployment were bad.

When I had done those things in regard to the labor situation then I should turn to the side of production, and I should consider there everything that deals with individual capacity in its relation to securing the greatest possible output socially possible at any time. To meet the problem of limitation of output socially possible at any time. To meet the problem of limitation of output, it seems the first thing is to deelop the selling department as nearly as possible to a state of perfection, and study the flow of orders that will come into that plant through proper salemsanship. It has been my experience that frequently the selling side of the business is left to be organized until long after the factory side has been organized. When I had the selling organization completed in this new factory, then I should do all my planning work, and all the system for maintenance of schedule, and all kinds of work analysis. I think before the motion-and-time study people get on the job and task matters are considered, these things should be considered.

Then I would shift the lower costs to the heading called "The rights of the Consumer in the Business"; and there I should lay out the maximum conditions of the business. I should not wait for the law to reach me--I would have no watered stock, restricted dividends, no concealed management salaries---and I would see that the sanitary conditions are good; and then I should say, that it is due to me and to the consumer for me to get my unit cost lower and lower and lower.

If there were some labor union men in this meeting I should take pleasure in saying that where I had arranged to deal with the unions--and this of course would be easier in a perfectly new undertaking, rather than in an old one, although it is practical in both--I could still get by every single thing that a majority of you people in this room would declare to be legitimate scientific managment; that I could get by every single element, because the whole business of relationship between employer and employee would have been shifted from the violent method of adjustment to a constitutional basis, and the whole list of crimes now committed by labor unions and by employers also would have departed.

---

[1] Bulletin of the Society to Promote the Science of Management, November, 1915.

So abundant has become the literature on industrial relations during the past five years that few realize that less than ten years ago that literature was meager, and the voice of Robert G. Valentine was as the voice of one crying in the wilderness. The two papers reprinted here are of historical value and the bulletins in which they appeared, out of print. While the members of the Taylor Society did not agree with Mr. Valentine with respect to many of his views, it has always been a source of gratification to the Society that it had the vision to give him a platform and an audience.

Born West Newton, Mass., November 29, 1872. A. B. Harvard, 1896. Commissioner of Indian Affairs, 1909-12; Chairman, First Mass. Minimum Wage Board, 1913; Industrial Counselor, 1912-16; died September 15, 1916.

An address at the Annual Meeting, December 5, 1914.

THE PROGRESSIVE RELATION BETWEEN EFFICIENCY AND CONSENT[1]

By Robert G. Valentine

Definition of Scientific Management

1. By scientific management I mean those principles of business conduct which are both explicit and implicit in the life and work and writings of Frederick W. Taylor.

2. I mean those principles considered in their purity as principles and considered apart from the particular and local applications of them made by Mr. Taylor.

3. I mean those principles considered as principles very gropingly stated by him and as to statement still in their youth, so to speak.

4. I mean those principles considered as one root of economic life, and to that extent thoroughly sound, but still showing clearly in their present statement that they have not been worked into thorough co-ordination with other equally vital principles of the economic and social world.

5. By scientific management I mean further the attempts to apply the principles as stated by Mr. Taylor as they are applied, for example, in the Tabor Mfg. Company of Philadelphia, the Plimpton Press of Norwood, Mass., and the Link Belt Company of Philadelphia.

And the actual methods of applying the principles at those plants I regard as only indicative of what the real application of the principles as laid down by Mr. Taylor would be. They are sufficiently indicative, however, to furnish the materials for a sketch of an ideal shop run according to the Taylor principles. They further furnish us, I believe, with the basis for the belief that the principles stated by Mr. Taylor, in so far as they are fully applied, furnish the latest word in the progress of the mechanics of industry. For simplicity in this paper, we shall deal with these principles only from the point of view of the mechanics of production.

I am not forgetful of two important facts in connection with Mr. Taylor's life:

1. That many of the impressions he conveyed in describing his ideas did his ideas themselves and his real spirit great injustice.

2. That his own conception of much that is contained in his writings is in many cases fragmentary and apparently short-visioned.

It is, nevertheless, my belief that then the fullest allowance is made for these two facts, Mr. Taylor's contributions to the industrial world will gradually prove themselves to be among the major contributions to human progress. The human limitations of Mr. Taylor's thinking and methods of expression and the crudities of the application of his principles in practice at the present day will weigh little as compared with the revolutionary effects his conceptions will have on the progress of the world when they are thoroughly understood and freed from the short vision and from the ignorant, the merely imitative, or the shyster practitioner.

It should also be noted at this point that much which is being done under the name of scientific management and much of the criticism of scientific management is only serving to give undue importance to the work of the efficiency charlatan, to the loose social thinker, and to the attitude of the half-informed public, all of thich obscures the real issue.

The useful thing to do is for all persons honestly interested in the subject to simplify the problem and to try to solve it in its purity apart from considerations which are not of its essence. It is precisely this which both the most earnest advocates of Mr. Taylor's principles and the most earnest advocates of labor had failed to do up to the time of Professor Hoxie's work. If Professor Hoxie can complete his work through digesting the materials he has gathered, and also through making an investigation of labor in its relation to scientific management as he has made of scientific management in its relation to labor, we shall begin to be in a position where we can get at the question of scientific management in a truly scientific fashion.

Our immediate task together is to see whether we can begin at the present time to get a line on that genuine application of the principles of scientific management which is beneficial to society as against that alleged application which is dangerous to society. I shall try today merely to lay the grounds for the discussion of what I believe to be one basic standard of judgement. If we try to state the problem clearly, I believe that we shall be able to formulate this standard. The standard by which to judge is to ascertain whether any particular application of the principles involves the recognition of a truly independent and organized consent on the part of the workers.

By my statement of the problem I shall endeavor to show that the standard as above stated is a primary standard by which to judge all management.

The Efficient Shop

Let us begin by getting clearly in our minds a picture of an efficient shop as we can easily construct it out of the principles laid down by Mr. Taylor and even out of the present attempts to apply those principles.

I shall picture this shop only in outline because you are all familiar with the details of the picture. I simply want to be sure that we do not lose the proportions of the main outlines in the particular interest which any one of us may have in certain particular aspects of the picture. In my description of this shop I shall, for the moment, ignore the human element entirely as it actually exists in the shop and describe the people handling the operations of which I shall speak as people who, whatever they may be outside the factory, are while in the factory simply animate machines, people who have either been trained or trained themselves, it matters not which for our present purpose, to do their work with all the precision of the most marvellous engine and with all the automatic delicacy and grace and perfect adaptation to environment of the poised bird on the wing.

In such a shop first of all we should find Mr. Taylor's principles applied to the financial and sales ends of the organization. These applications I shall not pause to consider here (because, for simplicity's sake, we shall deal only with the strictly production problem) further than to point out that in any really efficient organization the high spots all along the line must be secured as to their efficiency before the more minute details are highly developed. A great deal of the scientific management in use at the present day, whether in sales, finance, production or personnel, is similar to the situation in which a great deal of money might be spent in curing a person of flat foot who had some disease of the knee which might lead to amputation. This lack of coordination is an excellent illustration of one of the basic inefficiencies which penetrates the whole world today.

Assume, however, that the ideal shop we are picturing to ourselves has avoided these insults to common sense. It will on its production side proceed to organize every single one of its activities in relation to every other activity. That is the essence of the whole matter. That is the essence both of planning and of action in a shop. That is the essence of work analysis, of storeskeeping, of the layout of equipment, of routing, of functionalizing and of costs flowing steadily and thirteen times a year into the profit and loss statement as a by-product of the management practice itself.

In such a process of organization all former standards are revalued, all precedents are fearlessly analyzed; no process which has been improved upon is retained a moment longer than is necessary smoothly to install the better process. The crafts and trades as we have known them are progressively broken up under this process; work is ever more and more specialized and the steady tendency throughout, because of the fact of this specialization, is to need at any particular point of any particular operation the thinking, judging human being less and less, so that the mechanically and easily-trained human being more and more is used, and more and more tends in his turn to give way to inanimate machinery. At the same time that this tendency is going on, the brain of the shop, as has been aptly said, is developing in the planning room until the shop is becoming as perfect an organization of relationships between brain and nerve and muscle as is the human body.

In itself all this is good and but the logical outcome of the introduction of machinery. It means lower unit costs and more wealth. Any force of society which attempts to turn back this progress, or halt or even slow it up is contending with the inevitable. Such a factory as we have outlined is unquestionably the type of the major production method of the near future throughout the world under any form society may take.

Reenter the Human Being

So far we have no problem. But the moment that we substitute in the ideal factory which we have sketched the human being as he exists in the world today, we have our problem. People who have been no less pioneers and discoverers in the field of both general and social psychology than Mr. Taylor was in the mechanics of business organization, have found certain principles as basic as Mr. Taylor's which spring from quite other roots. These equally fundamental principles center in this statement: the days of compulsion--the days of service without consent, are over. In tremendous areas compulsion still exists. We are still conscripted into the world. We are still in great areas of our lives the unconsulted objects of powerful forces. With all our magnificent engineering achievements and somewhat more slowly developing common sense, we are still individually and collectively the apparent sport of earthquake or lightning. When we have once decided to take passage on the sea, we have, so to speak, enslaved ourselves to the possible storms at sea. But in all those areas of life wherein man deals with man, great breaches have been made in the ranks of compulsion. We find, however, slowly and haltingly, through the decades a steadily increasing assertion of the right both of the individual and of the individual in groups to give his consent to that which from any other human quarter he is desired to do.

Consent from the point of view of life in the factory has two main types: individual consent and group consent.

As to individual consent, in some cases it is of the type of the traveler who decides to take ship, abandoning at the factory gate, as the other does at the dock, the right of being consulted by the management as the other does the right of being consulted by the captain. In other cases, continuous rights of consent are still retained.

As to group consent, it is of two kinds: the consent of the factory group by itself, and the consent of the factory group as a part of an inter-factory group.

The most casual study of the whole principle of consent will show that it always tends to strike its roots into wider and wider areas. It is the failure to recognize this principle, for example, which makes the present Rockefeller plan in Colorado a sociological joke and in the future, as in the past, likely to hold a sociological tragedy.

I think there will be little debate among any of us as to the general proposition that a free man--a consenting man--is the more desirable worker. Where we have broken down in imagination is in failing to realize that organized consent as well as individual consent is the basis of a more efficient group. We have been accustomed too much to think of democracy as almost necessarily a mere crude expression of untrained information through votes. Almost nothing has yet been attempted to build up a finer texture of democracy through self-training groups, constantly growing in strength through the consideration of scientifically accurate data.

Another error which we have lazily accepted as a failure of democracy is the idea of life as a fairly static thing. This error is clearest seen in the common statement that certain types of people, certain whole groups of people as well as certain individuals "are not worth any more." The reason they are not worth any more is largely because no adequate educational process has been tried. The theory is disproved by our immigrants when they are given the right chance. It is disproved in the tremendous progress the children in our schools make over the status of their parents. It is disproved above all by the absurd implication that human beings are less the field of the inventive organizer than machinery. More than any other one thing, life is an educational process and it is only when life is artificially restrained, artificially hampered, that, because the educational process is lacking, we wrongly think of life as static and of classes as efficiency castes.

The problem then is to combine, not through failure to come to grips and not through hostilities, but in constructively organized ways, the latest developments of efficiency in production with the latest developments of the science and art of democracy.

A primary standard, then, by which I should judge scientific management would be to consider whether or not the scientific manager and the student of social psychology, who, in shorter terms, might be called "the man of affairs," were jointly addressing themselves to the solution of this problem--the relation between efficiency and consent--in each particular industrial concern; and whether they were recognizing that the ultimate ideal will be the consent of the interfactory group as the only one broad enough on which to build stable conditions of efficiency cooperatively with adequate safeguards to ensure that the human educational process shall not be turned back, stopped, or delayed any more than efficiency shall be turned back, stopped, or delayed. The educational problem is the fundamental problem of statesmanship and it is a minimum demand of that statesmanship that industry shall be a school of citizenship.

Conclusion

Three points emerge clearly:

1. That craftsmanship in the old sense of the term is doomed.

2. That as craftsmanship can no longer furnish the base on which labor organization can grow, unionism, group action, will have to build itself up on a base as broad as the whole educative process itself instead of on the particular educative process of a particular craft. Even today the real strength of unionism is that unions are effective consumers' organizations with a primarily educational interest. As this fact gradually sifts through the minds of employers and managers, they will gradually see that the most inefficient thing they can do is to fail to cooperate with such a great source of energy. The organizations of workers, on their side, can, when once that stand is taken, be counted on to consent to all that makes for efficiency. They will do this because in all legitimate enterprises--which are all enterprises where real service to the public is the test--the workers and the management will be equally concerned in perfecting the service. And at the same time, under constitutional industrial relations, they will contest the share in the management and the share of the product between themselves and with the consumer.

3. That the interrelation of the forces we have outlined--the forces of efficiency and consent--is constantly taking place in the world today in all kinds of crude and unorganized ways. Here and there real elements of interorganization between efficiency and consent appear. But for the most part the labor agreements in operation today are looked upon by employers as a necessary evil and by the workers as steps in their assertion of their rights as consumers and having little detailed relation to production processes. The beginnings of something far better than this are seen in the agreements in the garment trades wherein the manufacturers, the workers and the public are all represented as parties; and in certain kinds of organization which are being worked out in a few business concerns. There is still too little of real accomplishment in this direction to enable us to predicate with any certainty what the course of the development in details of organization will be by which efficiency and consent are made continuously revitalizing agents for each other.

Yet I believe that the point has been reached where it is profitable to attempt to gather together such experience as has been gained and relate it to the probable development of the next few decades.

With this purpose in view, I submit the accompanying chart.

This chart, it should be constantly borne in mind, is neither a dogmatic nor propagandist document. It is merely a working hypothesis by which to test out the facts of business as they occur daily at the desks of managers and at the trade union council tables, or in the occasional assemblages of unorganized labor. The whole aim of this discussion, as I see it, would be falsified if we deluded ourselves into believing that in any seeming array of facts we had found the truth. The only unforgivable thing would be that we, as social scientists, neglect to take into consideration any facts of the moment connected with all the forces that do exist; the only thing that seems to me axiomatic is that when forces do exist, they are better when organized, trained, educated, developed and enlisted in an effective way--anything you like--rather than allowed to play among and upon us blindly.

The picture of these forces submitted in this chart may be summarily commented on, as follows. In every form of factory there are human forces at work which, whether they are organized or not, are of at least equal importance with the forces governing sales, production, and finance. These forces take the two aspects of relationship to a growing intelligence on the part of the managers and a growing intelligence on the part of the employees.

Where these forces are organized they may take the form shown on the chart under the personnel heading at the left end of the factory line and under the cooperative association heading shown at the right end of the factory line. The relation between efficiency and consent is provided for in the form of organization shown, through the relationship between the research department of the education division and the determining boards and wage boards, acting on the scientific facts put before them or the nearest approximation to such facts that can be obtained, sanction the findings in the name of the interests of all concerned.

The facts thus put by the research division before the determining boards and wage boards furnish the material for the whole structure of organization and become an inescapable factor at every debatable point. Thus, if appeal be taken from any findings of a determining board or wage board to the arbitration board shown on the chart, the case is necessarily considered in the light of the best available facts.

Related to the factory, sometimes by formal agreement and sometimes through the entirely unorganized relationships of its individual members, are the local and district unions, or even the mere incoherent thoughts and feelings of unorganized labor. As organization begins to take any shape at all, it begins to crystallize into some form of a shop-union council wherein the interests of the factory and of the local and district unions are to some extent formally organized. In such forms of organizations as the garment trade, the shop union relationship has formally added to it the third relationship of the public.

The questions which come before such a shop-union council divide broadly into questions affecting the conditions of work and questions affecting pay. In the shop-union council's consideration of these questions, the findings of the determining boards and of the wage boards are before it so that here again the best available facts

POSSIBLE RELATIONS BETWEEN FORCES OF EFFICIENCY & CONSENT
Robert G. Valentine

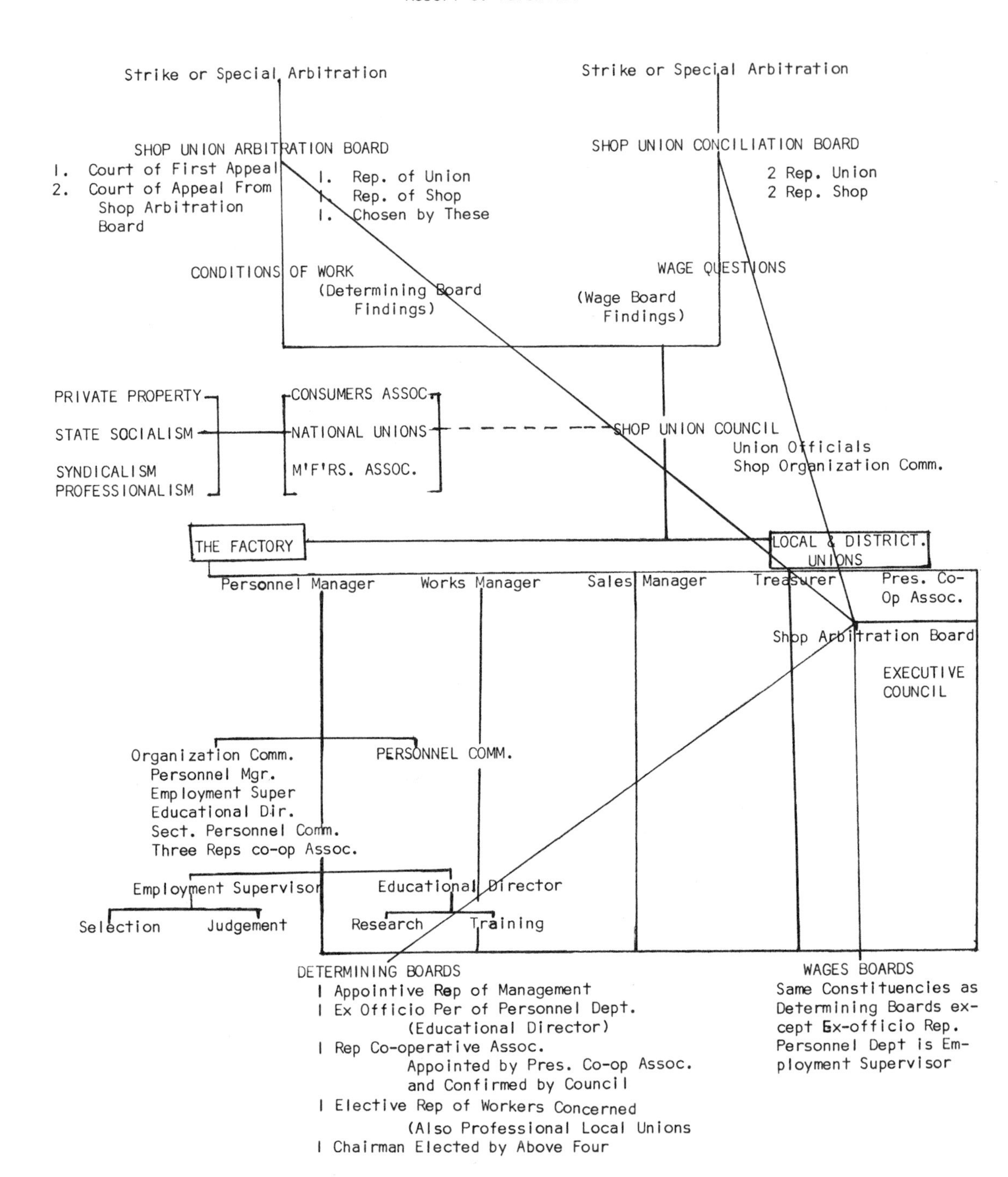

DETERMINING BOARDS
- I Appointive Rep of Management
- I Ex Officio Per of Personnel Dept. (Educational Director)
- I Rep Co-operative Assoc. Appointed by Pres. Co-op Assoc. and Confirmed by Council
- I Elective Rep of Workers Concerned (Also Professional Local Unions
- I Chairman Elected by Above Four

WAGES BOARDS
Same Constituencies as Determining Boards except Ex-officio Rep. Personnel Dept is Employment Supervisor

necessarily form the material of the discussion.

As to conditions of work, experience so far tends to show that all questions are arbitrable; namely, they are capable of being decided by an impartial third party on the basis of the facts presented.

Questions of pay, on the other hand, are still so unsupported by scientific basic facts as to be a matter of conciliation rather than of arbitration.

It will be seen in the chart that appeal lies from the shop arbitration board to either the shop-union arbitration board or the shop-union conciliation board.

At this point, it should be emphasized again that nothing on this chart indicates anything artificial in organization. The attempts that are going on, so far as the chart expresses them, are attempts to strengthen and make saner and sounder the organization of untamed forces which do exist.

This point should equally be borne in mind in the relation of the shop-union council as depicted on the chart to those natural forces which exist in society at large in a more or less unorganized state; namely, consumers' control, whether private or public, the national and international labor unions and manufacturers' associations. These present day forces of social and industrial organization are in their turn more or less crude expressions of three underlying forces shown to us by social psychology, which will in all probability work out between them the society of the future, These three basic drifts appear to be:

1. The fundamental soundness of the principle of private property. This element takes into account the fact that it is a basic instinct of human nature for the individual to desire possession.

2. The force of state socialism. This force takes into consideration the fact that it is equally a basic instinct of human nature to desire to work out things in concert with one's fellows. An excellent example of state socialism at present in practice is the public school system.

3. The force of syndicalism. This force takes into consideration that basic instinct of human nature which leads us to desire to share in the control of the methods of production in which we are concerned and in distribution of the product. An excellent example of this instinct in present day practice is supplied by the whole field of professionalism as seen concretely in medical societies and bar associations.

Such a study as we have outlined here of the forces at work in the world and of our duty to attempt to organize them exactly as the student of electricity has organized that force, makes it the job of the industrial statesman to recognize first of all that there are facts of democracy as well as facts of efficiency, and to see to it, so far as it is humanly possible, that each group of facts is related to the other in organized and efficient ways.

Applied scientific management, then, which does not relate its science to the desires and to the thoughts of all connected with a concern in all their relations, either organized or in process of organizing, is not true to Taylor principles.

---

[1] *Bulletin of the Society to Promote the Science of Management*, November, 1915. An address given at the annual meeting, December 10-11, 1915. See footnote following: Robert G. Valentine, "Scientific Management and Organized Labor," January, 1915.

THE MANAGER, THE WORKMAN, AND THE SOCIAL SCIENTIST[1]

Their Functional Interdependence as Observers and Judges of Industrial Mechanisms, Processes and Policies

By H. S. Person

During the period in which I have acted as your presiding officer, I have purposely refrained from the presentation of addresses and from participation in discussion. I have believed my contribution could be the more effective if limited to the planning of programs and to the continued development on a high plane of the conduct of our meetings. To-night, however, I lift that self-imposed embargo, for the growth in the effectiveness of your cooperation, the intensity of discussion and the influence of this Society has reached a point which, I am convinced, makes it opportune for me to lay before you certain considerations of the deepest importance; certain principles which have governed and should continue to govern the development of this Society.

These principles have manifested themselves particularly in the construction of our programs for the discussion of scientific management. I have been aware of an inquiry in some minds why our programs have consistently provided for the discussion of the social as well as the purely technical aspects of scientific management. I have been aware also of an occasional inquiry how the views of professors and other "theorists" could be of value to an association of "practical" men. In fact, at our last meeting one of the most prominent of industrial engineers, in a perfectly proper and courteous remark interpolated into his discussion of a university professor's contribution, questioned the value of the opinions of theorizing professors of economics. My first reaction was a stirring of my sense of humor by realization of the fact that the distinguished organizer and manager who was speaking is, by virtue of his tendency to search for fundamental industrial principles, the most professor-like of the industrial engineers of my acquaintance. My second reaction was the realization that there had been presented the opportunity to explain the vital principles which have demanded the inclusion in our programs of the discussion of the social aspects of scientific management by workingmen and so-called theorists as well as by practical engineers.

The programs of our meetings were made up at the beginning of discussions of scientific management with no more than passing allusion to its influence on industrial progress. At the last meeting two sessions--the most significant in attendance and enthusiasm--were devoted to a discussion of the effects of scientific management on the individual worker and on industrial progress. During the past two or three years in the development of discussion of problems of particular interest to us, to the point of view of the manager have been added two other points of view--that of the workman and that of the social scientist. By manager I mean any one of that group of executive officers, of higher or lower degree, who are responsible for the organization and operation of a going industrial concern. By workman I mean the individual employee, or any spokesman of organized labor. By the social scientist I mean that group made up of professors of economics and sociology, social workers, editors of surveys and new republics, and so on. While it is true that individuals who have participated in our discussions may have represented points of view which do not fall clearly into any one of these three classes--points of view which are composites of two or of all three; nevertheless, you will agree that there have been these three distinct angles of approach to the discussion of our problems; those of the manager, the workman, and the social scientist.

It is my thesis that no one of these individuals sees the problems of scientific management with an eye which reveals the whole truth; that each is, by some economy manifest in the unconscious organization of persons for the investigation of truth, a functionalized observer of industrial facts and judge of their significance; that each is complimentary to and essential to the other; and that no organization which stands as advocate for one of the latest major contributions to industrial development, as does this Society, can accomplish its purpose if it fails to consider every possible approach to the examination and valuation of the particular contribution which it seeks to promote.

Each of these examining and appraising agencies--manager, workman, and social scientist--in the performance of the common function, possesses advantages and disadvantages not possessed by the other two. What are the principal advantages and disadvantages of each?

The Manager

The manager of a business is one who performs the social service of adjusting the creation of certain utilities embodied in commodities or services, to the demands of individuals for those utilities, in a manner economical of human energy and equipment. The allowance which society makes to him and to his family as a reward for this service should enable him and his family not only to live but also to enjoy certain things which make life to them worth living. The amount of this allowance is determined in most instances (I do not wish to go into refinements) by the degree to which he is economical of human energy and equipment. That economy is popularly called efficiency. To succeed in putting together economically the energy, skill and materials necessary to create commodities or services is no easy matter. In the first place, a very small change in conditions causes the manager's operations to pass from an efficiency which society approves and rewards to an inefficiency which society may not only refuse to reward, but for which it may exact a penalty. In the second place, the elements which the manager must unite in his operations are not stable, and a combination which may be economical at one moment may not be so at the next. There are two results of this instability of elements with which the manager works and of this narrow margin for social approval within which his variations in economy are confined. One is the constant, concentrated attention he must give to the varying elements and their varying combinations--a confinement which deprives him of the opportunity for developing breadth of view. The other is the effort to minimize these variations in elements by standardization of one sort or another, an effort which incurs the danger of his achieving an apparent but unnatural stability which results, without his perceiving the reasons therefore, in maladjustments to the changing industrial world in which he operates.

This simple description of the nature of the manager's function makes it apparent that in valuing industrial mechanism, processes or policies, he suffers disadvantages and enjoys advantages which are unique to him.

There seem to be four disadvantages. First: the fact that the manager's attention is concentrated on the unstable elements of his business--the varying details. I admit that the supervision of many of these details may be delegated, and to the extent that they are delegated the manager frees himself from this limitation. But those who thus free themselves are so few as to be conspicuous. This concentration on technical aspects of the business denies to the manager opportunity to observe the great facts of social and industrial evolution. He may even not keep up with the development of human thought concerning the very service which he performs for society. He has but little time to acquaint himself with the results of investigations of others. He has but little time for books which are the records of the investigations and thinking of others. He has, in fact, but little time for newspapers and other periodicals. Lack of time from business is too frequently as fatal for him as is lack of education for many others; he falls into the habit of accepting statements of facts of industrial evolution which are not true, and opinions of others concerning economic principles which are not sound.

Second: the very nature of his responsibilities compels him to regard and to value all things from the point of view of profits. In most instances he is wholly unaware that there are other standards of valuation of the mechanism, processes and policies, which he is called upon to consider. In those instances in which he may feel there are other standards of valuation, he is too often unable to free himself from the insistent demands which the problems of the ever changing elements of his business crowd upon him, to inquire what those other standards may be. His is a business in which he who hesitates is lost, and he therefore may not stop to work out more than superficial changes; he may not stop to inquire about the fundamental principles of his own managerial activities.

Third: he is subject to the tendency to seek relief from changeability and uncertainty in the elements which he controls by unconscious over-standardization of all of those elements. Some of them--the material elements--by their nature may be standardized, and their standardization brings relief. Others, such as the quantity and quality of demand and the human elements in production, do not lend themselves to the same kind or degree of standardization, but he too frequently fails to perceive distinctions and attempts to reduce these elements to the same kind and degree of control as he applies to others. The result is a mass of new problems added to those with which he is already overwhelmed.

Fourth: he is subject to the danger of regarding all the elements which he directs as commodities, and of failing to recognize that spiritual factors are involved. Particularly, he too frequently fails to recognize that labor as a simple physical force cannot be separated from labor as a distinct and original seat of human intellect, feelings, desires and opinions. Labor as a spiritual force is the most subtle and changeable of all the factors which he combines for the purpose of service through production.

These are the limitations, suffered in various degrees by various managers, which seem to me to render it impossible for them to see the whole truth in estimating new contributions to industrial progress. However, these are but limitations to conspicuous advantages. What are the manager's advantages?

I shall not dwell upon the most significant of his advantages; they are well known and come immediately to our minds. They proceed from superior intelligence combined with experience in the conduct of industrial operations. Most managers are men of great natural ability which is made more effective by technical or other training. Those who have not had the advantage of formal training enjoy perhaps compensating superior natural ability which has enabled them to forge ahead in managerial operations: which has caused them to be set aside by natural selection as industrial leaders. Intellectual ability, disciplined by experience in the industrial field, makes them the keenest observers of industrial facts and renders their judgements in the treatment of industrial problems the soundest. I do not do more than indicate these advantages, dominating as they are, because they are so patent.

His other advantages may be summed up in the statement that the industrial machinery is a result of evolution; that at any one moment it is a complex of numerous finely-adjusted parts; that a slight maladjustment of the parts may bring disaster to many individuals and a major maladjustment may bring disaster to society; that the changes of evolution must be accomplished by small steps and while the machinery is in operation; that the manager himself is a part of this complex machinery; and particularly that he senses all the complexity and delicacy of this industrial machine and the necessity of the avoidance of even slight maladjustment. He senses these facts, even when he does not attempt to explain them, because he has grown up in the midst of them--is of them. He has vast technical information and specially developed faculties which operate in the plane of industrial processes. In the solution of many of his problems, he does not have to rely on the conscious exercise of reasoning powers or the conscious application of rules and directions; he holds sub-conscious intercourse with laws and principles behind his problems, and solves them "on the wing." Otherwise the solution of many of them would be impossible; the opportunity to solve them would vanish before investigation and deliberate reasoning could become operative. As the driver of a motor-bus evolves a sense for velocities and distances, which enables him instinctively to make openings which are to the passenger apparently impossible, so the manager develops special senses which enable him instinctively to estimate the adaptability to industrial processes and the influence on them, of new mechanism, processes or policies. To those not performing the managerial function, this technical information and these special senses are denied. It is possession of this technical information and of these special senses, that makes the manager the "practical" man. The intuitive judgment of the practical man is as reliable and necessary as the consciously reasoned judgement of other men.

These advantages enable him to discern aspects of the truth, in considering the effects of new industrial mechanism, processes or policies, which other judges are unable to see.

The Workman

It has been the traditional opinion, developed through long social experience which it is not necessary to examine here, that the workman, because workman, has no occasion to examine and pass judgment upon new industrial processes or policies. It has furthermore been a traditional opinion that he could not exercise sound judgements in such matters if called upon to do so. The workman has been looked upon as possessing a commodity which he sells to the manager, as the farmer sells wheat to the miller. While it has been recognized that when the workman offers labor for sale he offers not only physical energy but with it a combination of mental and manual dexterity called skill, nevertheless, the traditional opinion has not risen to the conception that labor has any other interest in the transaction than the sale of a commodity. During recent years an entirely different opinion has been developing, and is held not only by working men, but by many social scientists and by an appreciable number of enlightened managers. To attempt to account for the development of this new point of view would take us too far afield. The majority, I imagine, of those who entertain it, qualify it with the condition that while in principle the workman is entitled to examine and pass judgment upon the manager's disposition of his labor, in practice that is impossible because the workman is not qualified by managerial experience to make such examinations and pass such judgements. A minority, on the other hand, advocate the new point of view without such qualification, and assert that labor is entitled to exercise the right of acting under the principle, whatever the degree of skill he manifests in making judgments; that he will learn to make better judgments on managerial matters by experience and responsibility; and that society, even at the cost of a temporary period of less fruitful management (conceded for the sake of argument), should bear the cost of the workman's apprenticeship in managerial responsibility. They assert also that life is more important than industry, happiness more important than profits, and that happiness can be secured only by giving every individual opportunity for the exercise of all his interests and the development of all his faculties, one of which is the faculty of managerial and creative activity. They assert further that the increased technical productivity resulting from the exercise of such a function by workmen, together with the increased productivity resulting indirectly as the result of greater co-operation, will more than compensate for the loss resulting from errors in judgment during the period of labor's apprenticeship in managerial responsibility. Finally they assert that in our society and with our form of government, with labor self-conscious, organized and numerically strong as it is, experiments in the participation of labor in management are sure to be made, experiments which management should anticipate, and in which management should fearlessly and honestly co-operate. Assuming that to be the case, let us ask ourselves what may be the workman's competence to be judge of the desirability of new industrial mechanism, processes and policies.

The limitations of the workman may, I believe, be summed up in the two characteristics: the narrowness of his individual attitude of mind, and the militancy of his organization attitude of mind.

An honest recognition of the facts makes it necessary to observe that, however noble and honorable of character, the great majority of working men have enjoyed neither the education nor the experience to render them broad and sympathetic in their views, informed concerning industrial facts, principles and tendencies, and possessed of trustworthy perspective and sense of values. The truth of this statement is possibly a damning indictment of society, and the fact that occasionally able men and even intellectual giants have risen from the ranks of working men, and that the prospects for all improving, does not make it less so. The average working man has had to leave school at an early age, to begin the long struggle of support of self and family in a regime of the bartering of labor as a commodity, in which the advantages of bartering have been against him. He has had to rise at early hours and put in long days at the factory. He has returned at night weary, thinking principally of the sleep which will restore him for the morrow's work. So it has been, day in and day out. His work has been almost entirely repetitions of more or less automatic operations which have required neither wide contacts nor serious thinking. His function, howsoever socially important, has been a relatively simple one, and has not given him wide acquaintance with persons and things and ideas. His limited education has not given him the impetus, and the weariness of his evenings has not allowed him the inclination to seek contact with things and ideas in the written records of others. Is it surprising, then, that he is not appreciative of the complexity of the industrial mechanism and of the problems of management? Is it surprising that his judgment may not be reliable concerning the immediate and the ultimate consequences of some proposed new mechanism, process or policy? And is is surprising that in the experienced manager's mind the presumption should be against the helpfulness of the workman's judgment of things outside the narrow sphere of his hand or machine craft? Notwithstanding the immeasurable promises of better general and industrial education, the manager's prejudice is not unhuman.

I have suggested that, in the second place, the militancy of the workman's organization attitude of mind is also a limitation to the soundness of his judgment of industrial matters. One would, at first thought, believe that the judgment of the group could not rise higher than the average judgment of the individuals constituting the group. But that is not so, for the influence of the leadership of able minds enters into the calculation. In labor unions are very able individuals who become leaders, and succeed, under certain limitations, in impressing their views upon the group. The group mind should be, and unquestionably is, broader and more sympathetic of the complexity and sensitiveness of the industrial machine, and of the consequences of every proposed policy, than is the individual mind. But is it as much superior, in its actual expressions of itself, as the intellectual ability of group leaders gives us a right to expect and demand?

I believe not, for the reason that the group thinking and action is motivated by a single purpose--a militant effort to achieve class solidarity and class prosperity in the midst of a regime of individual ownership of industrial equipment, managerial control, and bartering for a share of the surplus of productive operations. Other possible aims are neglected for, or subordinated to, or even misused for, this one dominating campaign. Truth in the statement of known facts, and in the search for attainable facts, is not sought for the sake of the truth, be its effect on men's minds what it may. Inaccurate statements are made, and false judgments uttered simply for strategic and tactical reasons. I am not affirming or denying the historical justice of this motive. I am simply stating what seems to be a fact, and suggesting that the fact is a limitation to the reliability of labor's judgment on new industrial mechanisms, processes and policies.

Parenthetically it may not be out of place to observe that here are weighty reasons for management's hearty support of more thorough general and industrial education; and especially for a calm and dispassionate consideration of the possibilities in some other regime than absolute individual ownership, absolute managerial control, and purely individual bargaining.

If these serious limitations to the reliability of the workman's judgment be genuine, what then are the advantages in forming judgments on industrial matters which are possessed by the workman and which support my thesis that his judgment is a necessary complement to that of the manager?

The advantages, as I see them, may be summed up in the statement that workmen in the aggregate are industrial society for the benefit of which industrial operations are carried on; that as participants in industrial operations and beneficiaries of them, in the aggregate and in the long run they sense the ultimate influence of industrial undertakings. In discussing the advantages for forming judgments possessed by the manager, I described certain faculties for intuitive judgment developed in him by experience, which, because his experience is different from that of anyone else, make him able to perceive certain aspects of truth not visible to others. So it is with workmen in the mass. They also, because of their function in industrial operations, have experience which neither managers nor others have, and develop intuitive faculties which neither managers nor others have. They feel the direction of the current of industrial evolution, not because they are carried along in it, but because they are industrial society. Because of this, their intuitive faculties, specialized by their unique experience, sense the immediate and frequently the ultimate influence on the current of industrial progress of specific methods and policies. There may not be convincing reasoning behind their objection to a specific proposal, but there may be something more fundamental than reasoning which guides them.

I am not raising the question of the right of the workman to be called into consultation in determining the desirability of specific industrial methods and policies. I feel that what is right is probably what is, according to social experience, the ultimately socially, expedient. If that be so, what we think and what we do will not deprive the workman of what is his right. I am arguing that from the point of view of industrial management in a regime of private ownership of the materials of production, of managerial control, of the motive of profits, it is expedient to match the workman's judgment against the manager's and the social scientist's, in order to obtain the benefit of the workman's unique advantages for judgment which in an increasing proportion outweigh his corresponding disadvantages.

The Social Scientist

I come now to the last of the trilogy of advisers which the programs of our meetings have called before us to assist in considering the problems raised by scientific management. The unpractical, book-reading, theoretical and dreamy social scientist! as some conceive him to be. What does he know about industry; he who does not do real work for a living? What does he know about management; he who is notorious for his inability to manage? I notice, however, that it is not asked what does he know about industrial evolution? Knowledge of that, so far as it can be known, is conceded to him. To know about the stream of industrial progress, of which manager and workman are atoms, is his specialized function. If that be so, may he not render judgment of some value concerning your practical industrial propositions, especially with regard to whether they are or are not adapted to survive the forces of industrial evolution?

I wish, before considering specifically the advantages and disadvantages of the social scientist for rendering judgments of value to us, to join issue with the implication in the antithesis between "practical" and "theoretical". In making such a contrast one is betrayed by a narrow point of view. The concrete proposition which you make to-day, which you call practicable, may prove to be unworkable next year. Was it really practicable? The theory Professor X proposed today you declare impracticable, but five years from now it may be working. Was it impracticable? The one was practicable for the moment, but it proved not to be for the long run. The other proved practicable in the long run but seemed not so at the moment proposed--possibly in many instances just because you thought it was not and did not support it. In fact, when you say a thing is impracticable, you mean it cannot at once be adopted, and you may be right. But when you say it is theoretical, you should mean that, while at the moment you believe it to be unworkable, it may in the long run be the fundamentally correct thing. There in the contrast you should have clearly in mind. The antithesis is not between "practical" and "theoretical", but between the immediately practicable and the ultimately practicable, between the superficially practicable and the fundamentally practicable, between current practice and principles of future practice.

If the mind of any class of investigators is concentrated on searching out the ultimately and fundamentally practicable, may not their judgments be of great value to the "practical" man who desires to work with the current of the stream which bears him along?

This brief consideration of the conventional error in the use of the words "practical" and "theoretical" suggests the advantages and disadvantages of the social scientist as a competent judge of industrial mechanism, processes and policies.

In the first place, he has not had industrial experience. He therefore lacks technical information concerning materials and men. He not only does not know how a given material will react to a proposed process, but he does not know how human nature will react at a particular time to a particular situation. He has not those intuitive faculties developed by manager and workman in the plane of industrial operations, of which I have emphasized the importance. He acknowledges, in fact formulated, the evolutionary principle that development to be substantial must come by small increments of change. But, because of lack of experience, he is not a judge whether a proposed measure is a small or too great an increment of change. Therefore we too frequently find him advocating measures which the manager's reason or intuitive faculties condemn as impracticable, i.e., too great an increment of change. We too frequently find the social scientist advocating measures which if put into operation, might "strip the gears" of the industrial machine.

In the second place, the social scientist too frequently adds to that disadvantage another: an unconscious assumption that some particular regime of industrial activity towards which he believes society is progressing is nearer than it really is, or is actually present. Possibly this disadvantage is but an intensified and specialized form of the first, but it exists and deserves special attention. It causes bias in the observation and in the interpretation of facts, for what a fact appears to be to an observer is determined in part by the environment in which he believes that fact to exist. For instance, I believe the fundamental error in the so-called Hoxie report on scientific management and labor is of this kind.

There are, to one familiar with scientific management in operation, other conspicuous errors; but the great error is that the committee observed and interpreted facts with unconscious bias. Throughout the report scientific management is judged, not as a step in the evolution of industrial society, not as a reasonable and workable advance on current practice, not as a body of principles and mechanism which must fit into the existing industrial regime. Scientific management is not compared with other current management; it is compared with some form of management which belongs to a regime in which industrial democracy is more fully developed than at present. It is not therefore a reliable report on which to base current individual or state action. But just because it makes us consider scientific management in terms of a possible future industrial regime, it is a great report.

What is the relation of the social scientist to industry which enables him to see aspects of the truth which neither the workman nor the manager can see? It is that relation to industry in which he is not of industry, but is outside it. Both manager and workman are passing judgment with respect to something of which they are a part. The social scientist is passing judgment on something which he examines from without. That is a good principle of investigation and valuation, according to scientific management. The professional industrial engineer is impatient of that narrow-mindedness which prompts a board of directors to declare that no one outside their directorate can tell them about their business. It is just because the industrial engineer comes in from outside that he can see things in their business which they, who are of it, cannot see.

The social scientist, because he looks upon the facts of industry from outside and from a distance, gets the broader view and the larger relationships. The manager, intent on the problems of to-day, is like the person who would attempt to project a curve by two fixed points: the functionalized student of industrial development corresponds to him who establishes three or more fixed points before projecting the curve. Or, to draw another analogy: he is like the military scout on a mountain eminence who searches out the lay of the land to direct the army which is marching through the valleys below. The army below may be defiling eastward through a valley, and every private and company officer believes that to be the general direction of march; the scout and the higher officers who receive and value his advice know that the general direction of the march is intended to be westward. The scout has the advantage of the distant point of view. On the other hand, the officers and soldiers of the marching columns, with their more restricted outlook, are the only judges of where camp should be made tonight and again tomorrow night, for they are the only ones near enough to determine the most advantageous locations of fuel and water. Both the scout and the captain are practical men but they are practical on different planes.

It should be noted also that the social scientist, in his broad survey of industrial development, does not rely entirely upon what he sees for himself. He seeks both the manager's and the workman's observations and opinions, compares them with each other and with his own, and utilizes them in forming his own final judgments.

The social scientist's judgment of the social and industrial value of any industrial proposition is not less valuable than that of the manager and that of the workman. Each is enabled to observe phases of the truth which the other cannot see. An approach to the whole truth is secured by combining and harmonizing their judgments.

That is why a group of men standing for the Taylor philosophy of management should welcome--should insist upon--the widest possible discussion of all phases of scientific management. Especially should they contemplate thorough discussion from the three points of view to which I have given special emphasis. To the manager's point of view should be added those of the workman and of the student of social evolution. Each can contribute something derived from an experience which the others have not had. In this way only can the truth be approached, and the truth is not easy to approach; for scientific management which originated in Mr. Taylor's mind as a method for solving a particular problem of industrial productivity, and developed in his mind into a body of universal principles of management, has finally revealed itself as raising fundamental questions of industrial philosophy.

It is in accordance with these principles of inquiry that the programs of meetings of this Society have been constructed. I wish to give testimony that the membership has responded readily. Inquiry has grown in breadth and intensity, the membership has grown in enthusiastic co-operation, and the Society has grown in importance and influence. That has been due to the nature of the reaction to the plans of the Governing Board. If there is no abatement in the growth of the co-operation of its members, there is no limit which one may place to the ultimate influence of this Society. And one does not fear an abatement of enthusiastic co-operation.

---

[1]*Bulletin of the Taylor Society*, February, 1917. Paper was presented at the Boston meeting of the Taylor Society, March 3, 1917.

MAN MANAGEMENT: A NEW PROFESSION IN THE MAKING[1]

By Meyer Bloomfield

The familiar story of the specializations in modern engineering is illustrative of processes operating today to shape various kinds of human services into recognized and esteemed professions. The record of industrial progress is two-fold; one is the story of applied science, the other of applied man-power. The ancient sense of the term "engineer" was confined to military purposes--to works connected with war preparation and warfare.

When the knowledge employed by military engineers began to be applied to the building of roads--that is to say, to civil purposes--a new branch of engineering started, and the civil engineer took his place alongside the military engineer as a professional man.

The keynote of this departure and specialization was effectively sounded in a sentence found in the charter of the London Institute of Civil Engineers dated 1828, which described the work of its members as the "art of directing the great sources of power in nature for use and convenience of man." No truer characterization of expert service has to my knowledge ever been phrased. Some such purpose underlies all sound industrial practice and guides all intelligent executive direction.

American industrial history, the specialization of technique which have come into it, and the promotion of the professional service--find their explanation in that purpose just quoted.

The First Personnel Problems

All new countries--our own colonial history shows it--are confronted with two typical personnel problems. First, the scarcity of labor; second, the instability of labor. These two are the most ancient of so-called labor problems. They account for the institution of slavery in our history, white as well as black, for indentured and bonded service was kin to the ownership of black workers. Many reasons account of course for the existence of the two labor problems just mentioned, in our early history. The author of American Husbandry (1774) complains that "nothing but a high price will induce men to labor at all and at and same time it puts a conclusion to it by so soon enabling them to take a waste piece of land."

Pioneering

We are accustomed to think of other nations as the great colonizing powers. There has never been colonizing and pioneering anywhere on the scale such as this country in its own development has shown. The United States is the chief example of conquest of wilderness, subjugation of natural obstacles, mastery and peopling of once unsettled territory, expansion, resourcefulness, self-reliance, and creative discontent. These tendencies have left their impress on American character, have given the American type its "set" of mind; and they are as efficacious today as they ever have been, tho less picturesque in manifestation. It is customary for chroniclers of American industrial history to divide our growth into definite periods, the last of these periods being described as that of the disappearance of the American frontier. This took place about 1880 with the end of the free government lands. This period is said to have marked a turning point in our history as indeed it did. With the vanishing of the physical frontier began, however, a series of conquests and developments of a kind as far-reaching as any which preceded. There began an overhauling of our educational system, particularly on the vocational and technical side, science in management began to take shape, and the problems of labor and labor relations began to find expression in contemporary forms of preventive as well as protective legislation, while modern industrial service, modern professional specialization of management as well as of labor organizations, all have started in our time.

The New Frontier

The American is always heading for a frontier. He'll make one if it doesn't exist. The axe and gun may be needed no more, but organizing power, application of science, application of human insight to win the best co-operative human result,--these become the instruments of exploration and mastery. The economic achievements of industrial imagination are as dramatic as have been those of physical courage and perseverance in wrestling with nature. We have sufficient evidence all about us to believe that the service idea creates markets quite as effectively as does manufacturing ability.

Our first personnel problem, as I have already mentioned, was to secure men willing to work. This was typically the problem before the middle of the nineteenth century. The service idea since then applied to labor power has given rise to the question how best to build up and maintain the working force as a stable, reliable and co-operative body.

Shoemaking in Lynn was once carried on, as we know, in the homes. Farmers and fishermen had their little show shops. When the Lynn shoe manufacturer received an order his practice was, as the phrase went, "to issue the tidings." A far different situation confronted the manufacturer when all the labor on his product came to be carried on under one roof. It is of interest to recall the fact that corporations in this country were devised in order to bring together the small savings of the people for purposes of large industrial enterprise.

Our banks and insurance companies started with state encouragement and backing in order to win over small owners of capital. Shares of stock were the device used to attract the small investor. It was a democratic principle which was invoked. The small stockholder believed that he held a franchise with certain rights in the corporation. Common action, as well as individual enterprise, have always characterized our industrial history. It is more than a coincidence that, with the vanishing of those pioneering opportunities to strike out into the wilderness, there began what we might call the forms of contemporary industrial pioneering.

Within our generation these influences have been at work opening up new areas or more fruitful areas of effort such as science in management, applied psychology, vocational training and guidance, industrial legislation, the present-day types of labor organization, programs of labor relations, industrial service within the plant, experiments in joint industrial effort between management and the working force, and new professions connected with the executive, technical and the business direction of the industry.

What do these developments signify? That there lie before us domains of industrial pioneering as large as any we have known. The tools of service and of leadership service based on insight into human nature, and leadership based on the loyalties of men are busily employed in unlocking new resources of human productivity.

Industrial Loyalties

Organization, as the present day industrial executive understands the term, is something vastly different from its older implications. Just as we instinctively favored the volunteer over the conscript in the early days of our war, esteeming the patriotic quality in a man's offering himself through nothing more than moral compulsion, a high sense of duty, so we have begun to recognize that such motives and impulses represent precious assets in industry. The volunteer spirit in an industrial personnel is the most valuable quality which it can possess.

What aims can all our personnel and industrial service projects have if not to release and mobilize productive good will? The personnel which selects you and chooses to work for you will be fully as good as the personnel which, through necessity or chance, has drifted into your shop.

An employment department may do and often does do a most excellent job with this latter class. But if I were an employer I should dread the might of the competition from a rival whose personnel represented a mutual instead of a one-sided selection.

A Profession In The Making

The story of personnel administration during the decade past is a story of the growth of service and leadership maintained on a professional level. The true meaning of personnel activity will not be understood unless we bear in mind the process by which leadership becomes a thing of meaning and secures the key to power.

Leaders are born, we like to say. It is far truer to say that leaders are made--whatever their inborn gifts--made by their followers, made by conditions, by the nature of the effort to be exerted, obstacles to be overcome, opposition to be faced, and by the methods which must perforce be used to win success.

May I dwell a little further on this point and illustrate my meaning? There is a law of evolution which seems to be at work in the realms of leadership. If you watch any movement grow over a period of years, if it really grows and has any vitality and future, you are struck by the changes which take place in the types of the spokesmen, the leaders, the men at the top. Take, for example, our city and town governments. For a long time the good fellow, the orator, the dispenser of easy favors, the champion promiser, holds the center of the stage. There comes a time now and then when managing a city comes to be regarded as a business, financial, or an engineering enterprise. When this connection takes hold of the electorate, there is a chance for the first time to elect a capable administrator, and the speechmaker gives way to the less vocal executive.

The leadership of labor unions shows this evolution of type even more strikingly. From the rough, two-fisted leader of some years ago--the type still extant where conditions favor him--to the skillful negotiator and business agent of today, there is transition full of instruction.

Whatever our views may be as to labor unions and their policies, and I'm not here interested in making out a case for or against them, we may feel certain that the possibility of better leadership for the labor forces or for any other organized human forces, rests largely on the vision and the attitude of all of us. It is in this sense that I insist that leadership is a product and not a self-created thing.

We say nothing new when we maintain that desperation breeds one sort of leadership, lack of confidence another sort, while candor, fair dealing, mutual understanding and reciprocity, bring to the top still another type.

Industry on the whole--or more specifically, industrial management--has much to do with determining what kind of spokesmen and representatives the rank and file shall support. My reason for dwelling on this point is a belief that the most beneficent result of personnel administration is the sustaining of helpful types of leadership both on the side of management and on the side of the men. This result of good personnel work gives it, in my judgment, its fundamental place in modern industry; for it is industry's final guarantee of stability and prosperity.

The Idea Of Profession

I know of no idea which holds out so many possibilities, if we energetically apply it to any vocation, employment, or job, as the idea implied in the word profession. Whoever first thought of management as a profession was a human benefactor.

Whoever first devised a program for training men to do what they had hitherto done self-taught, or not taught at all, made a big contribution to industrial advance.

It was some realization of what had lifted despised and probably menial employments of the past into modern professions which had most to do with the start of the personnel movement as we know it today, and the creation ten years ago of the new vocation of employment manager and personal director.

What is true of the progress of occupations from a menial to a professional level is true of the sciences themselves. They became practical when they became exact. The science of mechanics was harnessed to human service when its laws made prediction possible. Bacon said, "study the laws of nature in order to command by obeying her."

The personnel dictum is; "Study the human nature you deal with in order to win leadership by co-operating with it."

We can get a good sidelight on the rise of a profession of personnel management by recalling briefly what has happened in the growth of other professions.

At the close of the American Revolution only a small proportion of the practicing physicians had any medical degrees. It was not until thirty years ago in this country that legislation began to give the public some protection against incompetent practitioners. Trained lawyers were even fewer in number. Indeed, the lawyer was looked upon with suspicion in some of our colonies.

Until recently the doctor's office was the medical school; the lawyer's office the law school.

In New England, in the early days, the clergyman was sometimes the only physician. Obstetrics was in the hands of dangerously ignorant mid-wives. Physiology, organic chemistry, pathology and surgery, as we now recognize them were unknown. Denistry had to fight for recognition from the medical fraternity.

Pharmacy in this country was once a matter of mere apprenticeship. This is to say, any ignorant boy could dispense death-dealing drugs.

The village blacksmith and the fearful horse doctor were the veterinarians. Much as was the case among the Indians, we good hard-headed, practical people have permitted "enchantment in any form." Educated practice is taking the place of quackery in every form of occupation which has reached the stage of service and leadership; that is to say, the professional idea promotes fitness, training, measurements, standards, a code of ethics, and ideals. These are the dynamic profession-builders and these fundamentals have been unfolding in the personnel field.

When the Boston Employment Managers' Association was started ten years ago, it was with the idea that building up of a working force and dealing with men in their work relations, was a job which had a real professional content. The thought was not a new one, because it came from comparing employment practice in various plants and establishments.

One had only to observe what men like A. Lincoln Filene and Henry Dennison were doing then, what they were interested in working out, to get sufficient stimulus to think along personnel lines.

A few simple principles were back of the formation and the first year's program of the Boston association. The men who came together as members had to do mainly with the hiring of help. It was thought that work of this sort justified a sort of trade organization for exchange of views and experiences. There was none in existence for this type of activity and yet it seemed that the positions which these men held were among the most important and difficult of all executive jobs.

By the fact of association for discussion and common counsel a start in an art of handling men and a science to guide it were made possible. It would be too much to claim that there is an art or a science or a full fledged profession of personnel management today. But the progress during the past ten years towards the goal is unmistakable. Soon after the start of the Boston association the plan was suggested for a course of lectures and a training program in employment management under college auspices. To the Tuck School at Dartmouth College goes the credit for giving the first course in this subject.

Dr. H. S. Person, then its Dean, was the first educator connected with a college school of business to give his warm approval to the plan and capable energies in launching it. In this work he was supported by Dr. E. M. Hopkins, now President of Dartmouth, who was then in a position by reason of his close touch with Dartmouth affairs and his contact with business to make his support decisive. Since then the progress of the training idea for employment and personnel work has been such as to make it now an ordinary feature of the business curriculum in colleges and universities.

Employment and personnel associations spread throughout the country, and four years after the Boston association began, the first national conference on this subject was held.

The man-power problems which were created by the World War and our entering into it marked the turning point of interest in the subject which we are considering.

Inasmuch as this paper is not intended to be a history of the movement itself, or an account of the technique and detailed practice which distinguish it (the literature on this subject is now sufficiently large and familiar), I must pass over many interesting phases and by-ways of the subject. I have been asked to deal with the fundamental conceptions in the movement.

The war record of personnel work has given it a rather dangerous acceleration. The recent business depression, however, has somewhat checked some of its exuberances as well as worked a regrettable sacrifice of valuable efforts. But the fact remains that the movement has grown in some directions too fast for its own good.

It has been the fate of every newly-developed service to attract what Theodore Roosevelt called the "lunatic fringe." The efficiency movement has known it and so has every other specialization of service. Time and a better perspective will weed out undesirable features; familiarity with the best work that is being done, contact with the sound practitioners in this field, more information, more experience, combined with the standards enforced by training courses under university auspices, all these will help lift personnel management to a plane where it will win confidence and support.

There are many unsolved problems in this field, and I am happy to say that there are as yet very few formulas and prescriptions. Much of the work is still in a fluid and provisional stage, as it should be, although the foundations for responsible practice, conscientious service and an acknowledged place in management have been laid. The future is big with opportunities. Whatever technical specializations may grow out of the general conception of personnel management, we need to keep in view that the key to them all is service and leadership.

In view of the tendencies just discussed how should we sum up the growth of the personnel work conception during the ten years past?

In the first place, the personnel movement, as we now know it, grew out of an attempt to institute a sort of professional association among those who were hiring employees. The purpose of the association was, as we have seen, to compare experiences in order to set up standards for good practice. Here was one beginning in the modern art of handling men. There could not be a science until many enlightening experiences were recorded and interpreted.

A technique of man management was thought about. It seemed that if this tendency could establish itself in practice, more real good could be achieved than was possible to the conventional forms of welfare work, which often lacked analysis, self-criticism and human insight. Moreover, the good which the latter work could do was often vitiated by sentimentality, if not self-deception.

An economic argument of great value came for this new movement by the "labor turnover" studies made nine and ten years ago--the phrase "labor turnover" was then coined. There was a telling mass of evidence of human waste made in terms of financial waste. There was also a positive as well as a negative argument early established--the experiences of progressive managements with good employment methods enlarged to the range of a real personnel program showed interesting results by way of teamwork, stability and output.

The movement seemed to be growing into what might well be described--as frequently it was--as Human Engineering. It struck the human note amidst a somewhat mechanical treatment then of organization and production problems.

The professional motive in the movement kept in the foreground the note of service and leadership. The engineering note encouraged the use of systems, records, forms, plant surveys, job analysis and specifications, intelligent selection and helpful supervision.

Sometimes one feature of the movement, sometimes another, predominated--too much sentiment, or too much system. A true proportion could not be expected always. We centralize too much, then decentralize too much, then swing back again, or stand still for a while. Sometimes even we cannot see the men for the forms. But we need not feel disturbed--for all these things are signs of health.

The main point is that personnel work has made its place as an important function of management, that it is on the way to an art and a science of dealing with collective human nature, that such work exacts professional qualities for its success, and that it is so broadening in scope that now it is often a bureau or a division of an Industrial Relations Department. In other words, personnel administration has come to be looked upon as a phase of the whole problem of relationship in industry. At this stage great pioneering opportunities present themselves. Many experiments will be tried; some will fail, some will succeed. But they will be tried because the yeast of the service and leadership idea is now a normal feature of industrial thinking.

Counteracting the tendency to diffuse personnel work into a sort of fog of vague industrial programs there will always be, among clear headed workers in this field, an insistence on sharp definition and clean-cut practice, so far as the technical side of the work is concerned, and a modest, studious and open-minded attitude with regard to the larger opportunities and industrial relations programs which are beckoning. Again, these tendencies are signs of health and a challenge. The only blunder would be, in a time such as ours, to be content with doing nothing, to be a passive onlooker, to grow cynical or hopeless because no perfect or exact solution is in sight.

Somehow, if we expect to hold our proper place in industry--as individuals or organized units--we must take an interest in what is now the supreme personnel problem--that of giving to the personality of the anonymous worker its chance to self-recognition and self-respect, these mainsprings of all big human effort. The job of putting man in management is about as worth while, practical and profitable as any that I know.

When paganism was in flower, with its temples, altars, and wonderfully made idols, there flourished a sort of labor union, a well-organized craft of "Image Makers." These men were supposed to be working for the gods. They were called god-smiths. Presently came Christianity and these idol makers saw that they would be out of a job, if this new movement succeeded. So they offered as stiff an opposition to the coming of a new era as the Founders ever encountered.

It is a great thing to know how to work with the coming good.

The most practical fact in the world is an idea that works. "Every one of these hundred of million human beings," says H. G. Wells, in his _Outlines of History_, "is in some form seeking happiness, is driven by complex and conflicting motives, is guided by habits, is swayed by base cravings, by endless suggestions, by passions and affections, by vague, exalted ideas."

This is the human stuff with which personnel administration is busy trying to make a going organization. We do not intend to repeat the mistake of the god-smiths and fight for idols of our own making. Rather we want to understand the human nature we deal with better, and trust to common sense and our professional equipment and ideals to guide us in our practice, believing that our growing capacity to serve and the loyalties which we win thereby will head us in the right direction.

---

[1]_Bulletin of the Taylor Society_, August, 1921. An address at the Springfield, Mass. meeting of the Taylor Society, February 25, 1921.

SUPERSTANDARDS[1]

Their Derivation, Significance and Value

By Frank B. and L. M. Gilbreth

The value and importance of standards and of standardization as factors and causes of cost reduction is generally acknowledged by all people today, both inside and outside the industries, who have given both the theory and the practice proper investigation and study.

We were convinced of the importance of standards in 1885, but it was not until the late Wm. H. McElwain in 1897 impressed us with the importance of having all minute details of standards put in writing as a permanent record, that we began to put every standard into such permmanent record form.

It was not until 1907, at the beginning of our conference with Dr. Taylor, that we decided to emphasize the fact that the _methods of making_ the standards themselves should be the first thing standardized. This thought was suggested by the fact that we found there were no two standards in his and our practices exactly alike, even where the objects to be attained were identical. We then decided upon and undertook the course of _intensive superstandadization_ and of applying accurate measurement as a prerequisite to making satisfactory standards.

We desire to acknowledge here our appreciation of the great value of the Taylor philosophy, and our emphasis on super-standardization is due in part to Dr. Taylor's emphasis on standardization.

Dr. Taylor's Views on Standards

Dr. Taylor states in "Shop Management": "It would seem almost unnecessary to dwell upon the desirability of standardizing not only all of the tools, appliances and implements throughout the works and office but also the methods to be used in the multitude of small operations which are repeated day after day." He went on to explain the reason for this, and to show that such standardization was profitable from every standpoint, including that of cost. Since that time, authorities of the management world have accepted the value of standardization, though the world outside management is not yet entirely convinced.

We endorse the above statement of Dr. Taylor and we would especially stress the word "methods," for there has been everwhere a lack of appreciation of the fact that methods as well as equipment must be standardized. We would go further and emphasize the great possibilities for profitable standardization of _repetitive components_ of methonds, which methods themselves, as a whole, are not repetitive. _The leisurely examination of components of methods, which is now possible, necessary and most desirable, furnishes a completely new viewpoint and practice in standardization, and offers a completely new, fascinating and profitable field for standardization. This field namely, the leisurely examination of components of methods, covers not only new work, but all old standards that have not been analyzed by the new method_.

Definition of Standard.

Perhaps the best definition of a Taylor standard as so accepted is that given by Mr. Cooke, who says: "A standard under modern Scientific Management is simply a carefully thought out method of performing a function, or carefully drawn specification covering an implement or some article of stores or of product. The idea of perfection is not involved in standardization....

While the above is a most excellent definition of a standard, it embodies a thought that is quite different from that which we are emphasizing in considering the subject of superstandardization, especially as applied to methods. The standard obtained by superstandardization is much more than "simply a carefully thought out method." It is of the essence of superstandardization that it be based on the leisurely examination of errorless records of methods and of use. Much of all activity is performed too fast for the eye to see. Therefore, the standard as resulting from superstandardization is the best method known of performing any activity. It implies use of the best units, methods and devices of research known. To avoid confusion, this new type of standard may be called a "superstandard," tho, ultimately, the old word "standard" must imply the new derivation and use.

Objections to Standards and Standardization.

Occasionally we hear of objections to standards and standardization, and such objections should be considered before proceeding to advocate superstandardization. They have come from those who misunderstood the relation between standards and individuality and monotony. All such objections to standardization have been easily and completely met; not only with accepted theory but also in actual long practice, not only from the standpoint of necessity but also from the standpoint of desirability. While these objections are usually directed against standard methods, they may also be directed against standard equipment or the maintenance of equipment in standard condition.

It is true that there is nothing more monotonous that working under standards that one knows are inferior, and that one can easily improve upon, with no opportunity for making and installing such improvement, or with no recognition for such improvement. Such conditions are ruinous to ambition, to the development of personal and individual expression, and to fostering of the creative instinct and joy in work. They do not exist where standards are adequate and are better than one can oneself devise, and where interest is stimulated and utilized by other parts of scientific management.

Many people are heartily in favor of standardization in principle, but do not themselves practice it. This is especially true of those who have not had wide experience with the simultaneous effects of standardization of method upon large output, lower cost of manufacture, lower cost of living, higher wages and less fatigue. It is not to be expected that anyone will fully appreciate the benefits of standardization who has not studied superstandardization and had the opportunity personally to see and to appreciate the relations between superstandardization, automaticity, fatigue elimination, learning curves, the stabilization of employment, and lower costs. With this knowledge comes a real evaluation of standardization.

We are here advocating the superstandard and superstandardization. Our emphasis has increased, and is ever increasing, because of the value of the actual results of long years of actual experience with extreme standardization of things and methods. We are practicing and advocating an advance in management technic. The principle is the same for all standardization, but the difference in the degree of refinement of method brings about differences in results that are comparable with the expected results of important inventions. To appreciate this difference it is only necessary to review papers and chapters of books on standardization, and to ask: "Is this standard of thing, condition, or method before us the result of guesswork and rule-of-thumb, or is it based upon refined and accurate measurement of the right units?" When examining the printed standards in the literature of scientific management let us not be deceived by beautiful half tones and elegance of printing, efficiency of expression by the editor, or anything other than the measured merit of subject itself. Let us use the method of obtaining the results as a unit of measurement of their value, and rate the work by the fundamental accurately determined facts it embodies. In examining standards of material or equipment, let us note the presence of absence of standards of "practice" as these vitally affect the specifications set down.

The superstandard is a natural development of the standard and a logical part of the growth of management as a science. A superstandard, then, is a standard which is the result of accurate measurement of data relating to the best obtainable, and which embodies the best practice known. It retains all the value of a standard as to means of improvability, but is recognized as the embodiment of the One Best Way extant and a further step toward the discovery of the One Best Way available-at the time. It is well to state here that superstandardization gives special emphasis to fostering and providing temporary, emergency and permanent change toward or from the superstandard, as may be economically wise and desirable. It conserves and develops individuality by the use of the One Best Way Suggestion System, which we have developed with our clients during the last twenty years.

Relation of Superstandards to Standards.

The superstandard supplements and does not necessarily supersede the standard which remains accepted practice during the interim or transitory period. A standard is most useful during the early parts of the installation period, but is developed at the first available moment into the superstandard, which has a far more definite effect upon maintenance, as will be shown later. We desire to emphasize the importance of the relation between superstandardization and maintenance, and to state as our opinion that lack of appreciation and utilization of superstandardization probably is a much greater factor in having installation projects slip back than any other one cause.

Significance of the Superstandard.

The superstandard has great significance from the management standpoint, from the economic standpoint, from the psychological standpoint and from many other standpoints--even from the phychiatric standpoint. From the management standpoint, the superstandard is an indorsement of the philosophy of Dr. Taylor and of the underlying principles upon which scientific management rests. It emphasizes the fact that measurement, not rule-of-thumb, provides the best working methods. It makes clear the point that during these years when scientific management has developed, our belief in standards has continually strengthened, and never for an instant weakened. It indicates that the growing interest in the human element and consideration of the human element has brought out more clearly the necessity for standardization, if the human element is to be conserved and developed. The close and necessary connection between standardization and such development is some times not understood, even by those who have a deep interest in scientific management, and are in the main friendly to it. Therefore, while it may seem elementary and self-evident to management men, it must be continually pointed out and emphasized.

Significance From the Economic Standpoint.

The significance of standardization from the economic standpoint has been recognized ever since the days of Adam Smith and his analysis of the division of labor in 1775. The elimination of waste, that most important of economic questions today, with its effect upon production, distribution and consumption, is vitally affected by the new stress upon standardization. This has been well brought out in the Report of the Committee on Elimination of Waste in Industry, and is underlying thought in the work of the Division of Simplified Commercial Practice of the Department of Commerce, recently established. The economic necessity of production, once questioned, is today increasingly acknowledged. The relationship between increased production and standardization has never been questioned. The economic benefits of standardization and increasing benefits of superstandardization must be self-evident.

Psychological Significance.

The psychological significance of superstandardization is extremely important and must be carefully considered before it is here that possible objections will be found and should be anticipated. There has been an erroneous and widespread impression among those not personally or intensively acquainted with the best forms of Scientific Management as practiced, that standardization has already increased and will continue to increase monotony, dwarfed individuality, prevented the development of individual self-expression, and is disliked by those who work under it. This is not true and never has been, where scientific management worthy the name has been developed. Any intensive knowledge of the writings and practices of Dr. Taylor himself or of those of the best of his co-workers and followers proves that, consciously or not, the human element has developed to a greater extent under scientific management than under any other type of management. Under superstandardization, such conditions and development are not only conserved but increased, for the proponents of the science of management and executives properly trained in the right theory now utilize the findings of the human sciences exactly as they utilize the findings of the material sciences and apply these findings directly in their own fields.

Intensive investigation is applied to the worker, the surrounding conditions and tools, and the methods or motions used. It is thru superstandardization that the more efficient adjustment of worker to work and of method to worker is accomplished. Accurate measurement in the human sciences is leading to a better understanding of human capabilities and possibilities. Superstandardization in industry is leading to a greater understanding of demands and opportunities. The result is not that individuality is stunted, neglected or misunderstood, but, on the contrary, is appreciated and utilized as it never has been, due to an understanding of, and ability to meet individual demands and capabilities.

Presumably because some engineers have been thought to be lacking in training in psychology and other sciences that concern the human element, and because industry devotes so much attention to material output, this point has often been overlooked. When it is realized that the engineer's training is primarily in measurement and that the industries offer opportunities which no other field of activity can offer, a new aspect is given to the entire matter. Those outside industry do not always realize that leaders in psychology and other human sciences are today, and have been for years past, devoting themselves to investigations and installations in the industries, and that psychology is increasingly devoting attention to industrial problems. This is well exemplified by the splendid work of the Institute of Vocational Guidance of Barcelona, which recently acted as host for an International Conference of Psychologists, which discussed many practical aspects of the relation of Psychology of Industry. It is also exemplified by such new publications as the "Journal of the National Institute of Industrial Psychology, Founded in 1921 for the Application of Psychology and Physiology to Industrial and Commerce," which aims, as it states in the first editorial, to "describe in non-technical language the methods and results of applying scientific knowledge to the human aspects of industry and commerce." Those in the industries do not always realize that their strengh lies not in adhering absolutely to tradition but in adapting the new methods and devices at their disposal to meet the increasing demands of the human element for opportunities and development.

Significance From The Psychiatric Standpoint.

Psychiatry, which has so much to do with the study of human likenesses and differences and with adjustment, has a great interest in the development of superstandardization. The phychiatrist has discovered many types in the industries which for one reason or another are mal-adjusted.

This does not mean simply the round peg in the square hole, and does not apply merely to those among the lower grades of employees.

For example, there are two types in the industries differing greatly in some respects from the normal, one of which seems unable, without great difficulty, to acquire automaticity, the greatest of free assets of the normal worker. As a result, he actually has abnormal difficulty in performing an activity twice alike. Another type is that which craves routine and is with difficulty persuaded to attempt to learn or to be changed to another activity, even if such work has better prospects for promotion, or more constant and continuous employment.

Superstandardization of method and of work, or of activity, as some of the modern psychologists prefer to call it, is of greater assistance and value in handling these types. It cannot be too often said that superstandardization, like standardization, aims in no wise to do away with initiative or with individual planning of details in work. It conforms to the principle of separating the planning from the performing, with the best planners in the planning department, and having other who may have to do planning start where the best planners finish. It classifies activity according to the amount of planning that can be done before the activity is started, or according to the amount that must be done during the period of the activity itself. It considers not only all subdivisions of processes involved in the activity down to and including the cycles of motions, but their therbligs. It thus furnishes endless opportunity for investigation of and improvement in detail such as will satisfy the most ambitious inventor, while at the same time it sets aside certain work as within the capability of even those of comparatively low mental calibre, or of abnormal mental activity,and furnishes a market for their ideas, or any self-expression that they may have pertaining to superskill in their narrow fields.

Relation to Fatigue

Superstandardization eliminates fatigue both directly and indirectly. As applied thru Fatigue Study, it measures all those things that have to do directly with fatigue--and standardizes the best available. This covers length of work and rest periods, working conditions, tools and equipment, desks, work benches, chairs, posture--all that effects efficient work from the fatigue standpoint.

As applied thru Motion Study, the improved methods induce efficient habits, reduce to habit all repetitive activites that require no individual decisions, and utilize the finest, most carefully taught type of automaticity. This reduces unnecessary fatigue to the minimum, and leaves time and unwearied attention for those decisions that are necessary and interesting.

Relation to Skill.

Since it concerns itself primarily with elements of motions, as applied to study of methods, superstandardization greatly facilitates the transference of skill. It induces confidence in its results, and determines not only the One Best Way to Do Work, but the One Best Learning Process by which to teach it. This is Vital as it affects the problem of industrial education.

Need for Such Superstandardization.

A most superficial knowledge of present day conditions makes clear the need for such superstandardization. The world in general and industry in particular is going thru a period that is extremely critical. The need for increased production, the need for the maximum elimination of waste, the need for stability are everywhere evident. The relation of superstandardization to stabilization of industry and employment is, perhaps, least appreciated. Only one who has many times gone thru the experience of entering a plant that has absolutely no stability or system, and later seeing the changes that have actually been made by carefully installed standardization, can appreciate its benefits. The effects of superstandardization are similar but more intensive, since the changes made are based upon accurate measurement and are much better founded and carry more weight, as anything known to be absolutely accurate must.

Perhaps the least appreciated benefit resulting from national superstandardization is its effect upon stabilization of employment, for in times of panic manufacturers will be far less timid in manufacturing national standards, knowing that their product will surely be salable at some later date, thus turning their raw stores into assets of greater value, and meanwhile, keeping their labor turnover at a minimum figure.

There has been too much unnecessary and wasteful change in this country based upon nothing but a desire for novelty, and embodying no element of permanence. The losses due to frequent and unnecessary change, for no reason, from one kind of work to another are not realized or appreciated by those who have not had intimate connection with a chart department recording intensive outputs and their causes for fluctuation hourly. The true causes of small outputs, high costs and low wages are never properly known by those who have not investigated the psychological factors affecting change. This does not necessarily mean that there should be no change, or less change, it may mean more change. It means less unnecessary change. Changes cost time and money. They may, under certain conditions, be worth the money, but the fact remains, as Adam Smith emphasized nearly 150 years ago, that the great cost of changing from one kind of work to another is almost universally unappreciated. Superstandardization maintains what has proved itself of greatest value, always aiming consciously at the ideal of the One Best Way, giving it the stamp of approval of permanence, and making changes that are definitely progressive and stabilizing, and that will pay in money or in durable satisfaction.

Much work in standardization has been done both in this country and abroad, but this standardization has not applied to methods and has not had in mind the One Best Way to Do Work. A careful investigation of the work of the Bureau of Standards and of the most excellent publications of the American Engineering Standards Committee illustrates this. It is an import aim of superstandardization to bring to the attention of our research bodies the necessity for standardizing the methods of industry as well as the equipment. There has not been in this country to any such extent as abroad a widespread popular interest in standardization and in the work of those bodies that handle this subject, and it is a second aim of superstandardization to arouse this interest, to foster the work already being done, and thus lead to a more rapid advance in this type of work.

Standardization in Europe.

Europe has made the most astonishing progress in standardization during the past few years because of the realization of the importance of the subject and the general cooperation in its development.

For example, in 1917 the Verein Deutscher Ingenieure, at the suggestion of the German government, organized a central national body, called the Normenausschuss der Deutschen Industrie. Its members are engineering societies, manufacturing concerns, industrial associations and various government departments. The organization, whose purpose is to foster standardization and to promulgate standards, has attached many widely separated fields and published much material, ranging from standardization of lines and letters in the draughting room, to standardization of window frames and sashes for many different types of buildings.

During the last four years, 144 of the standards have been actually endorsed, and hundreds that have been issued as tentative standards are being tested and developed. Each standard is embodied in a separate sheet, if possible, so that it can be used as working equipment by the or purchaser. These standards are supplemented by studies on standardization in all countries that add extensive interest to the intensive information.

Holland has been equally progressive, and the work of the Hoofdcommissie voor de Normalisatie in Nederland is both extensive and intensive. Nothing but a painstaking study of standards issued by these countries can make plain their overwhelming importance. This lies not so much in what they contain, as in what they imply.

Great Britain, Austria, Sweden, Switzerland, Italy,Belgium and Russia, all are at work along these lines.

Europe realizes the necessity of standardization as this country does not. Moreover, other investigators confirm our findings that Teutonic Europe will, partly because of temperament, go into this matter more fundamentally than we of the Anglo-Saxon race will be apt to do, if governed by temperament alone. An unceasing and costly passion for expediency and standards merely for current use has already proved a distinct menace to the development of Scientific Management.

Our one hope lies in superstandardization, in reducing all possible practice to standards based on accurate measurement and on stressing standardization of methods. Here America can be supreme, for it already has the knowledge, the method of attack and the equipment to do the work easily, quickly and inexpensively.

The first thing needed in this country is a change of attitude toward the whole subject. It is vital that the entire nation, and especially those directly interested in industrial management, shall appreciate that our safety lies in superstandardization. We must embody the knowledge of accurate measuring devices and methods at our disposal--measures of both the material and human elements--into standards that can sustain worldwide competetion--and win.

We must reconsider such controversial subjects as the use of the standards of the metric system and of simplified spelling in the light of these facts. But, even more important, we must apply standardization, beginning preferably where there is no disagreement as to its needs.

By express stipulation, and thru strenuous suppression, this presentation before this Society is made noncontroversial. We content ourselves for the present, therefore, by calling for a re-examination of the subjects, methods and results of standardization as embodied in the literature and supposed "best practice" extant, as the final arguement as to the need of superstandardization.

Relation to Maintenance.

An immediate effect of superstandardization is the simplification of the problem of maintenance. The significance of this in scientific management is great. Everywhere, those most intensively acquainted with the problems of management are acknowledging the importance of maintenance of conditions of cumulatively improving standards. They have to do with the relation between the consulting engineer and the resident production manager, and the stability of the work begun by the engineer, after he leaves the plant and the production manager takes over the entire responsibility. If the installation has taken place thru the instrumentalities of superstandardization, provisions is automatically made for the maintenance desired and requisite. The superstandard adequately applied builds up a superstandarized practice that insures maintenance of that which is bes until superseded by proved, better superstandard practice.

Superstandardization in Practice.

Altho founded on a better and more definite theory, superstandardization is no less practical than is standardization. Wherever standards are based on and are the outcome of accurate measurement and are in actual use, superstandardization exists. It has been applied not only in all kinds of industrial work but in many types of outside engineering activities as well. It is important not only where it has shown results in a single type of work or in an individual process, for the results of superstandardization are cumulative and nothing is too small or unimportant to be considered or to be worth while to file for review and possible group installation later. The members of this Society and of similar societies should be encouraged to turn in results no matter how narrow the field of application, in order that these may be filed and available to all and may be built into a standard common working practice. Also, as has been stated, such measured elements make possible skill transference and fatigue elimination.

Value of Definite Examples of Superstandardization.

An important means toward arousing interest and cooperation in superstandardization consists of definite examples of its application. The plant, the industry, the entire population must be made to *think* in terms of standards. They must be made fashionable and fascinating; they must inspire the beholders with a desire to imitate, the user with a desire to exhibit them and extend their use, for personal and national economies and the consequent reduced cost of living and national prosperity.

The standards of method are especially useful here as action is always interesting and leads naturally to imitation.

The cross-sectioned desk, with standard equipment, the standard pencils and supplies rack, the standard rack for inks, the one motion tool room painted white--these have all proved themselves extremely simple, inexpensive thought detonators. Used by many, of general interest, yet seeming to designate no special person as a target for criticism or an example of inefficiency, they furnish admirable starting points as definite concrete examples of superstandards for changing the attitude of an organization toward methods of work, and for making motion study a fascinating game.

Such illustrations, because of their elementary nature, prove that superstandardization is simple as well as profitable, and the results have demonstrated an immediate and also a cumulative value, particularly because they cause all types of individuals to think in terms of the variables of elements of motions.

It is extremely important that examples of superstandards and methods of attack of superstandardization be installed that are available to all office and production departments, that the principles be applied in office and shop alike. It is necessary--yes, vital--that papers and meetings that consider standards unify the interest, experience and problems of purchasing, sales, accounting, and production managers, of "office" and "shop" men, and serve as unifying interests and liaison procedure between the various professional groups.

Relations of Superstandardization to Costs.

Finally, we come to the discussion of the relation of superstandardization to the all-important matter of cost. It must be understood that superstandardization is a method of attack. It need not prescribe a new program. It does not attempt to outline a hard and fixed sequence of installations. It does not necessarily attack present practice in any revolutionary manner. It is in no wise a disorganizing and disturbing element. It is a method of stabilizing and securing results. In first cost, like the accurate measurement upon which it rests, it can compete successfully with the too usual and too customary inaccurate methods. In ultimate cost it need fear no possible competition. Because it is a method of attack, it may be applied first where most needed. Its direct product will be the solution of the immediate difficulties. Its indirect product will be a demonstration of its value as a method of attack and the consequent influence as a teacher, making all members of the organization think along these lines. It is not and never can be the possession solely of one man, of one group of men, of one profession or of one nation. It is not merely for current use. It has no boundaries of time or space. The only boundaries or limitations must be those of knowledge. It accumulates all improvements. It is free and available to all who desire to use it. It is true that knowledge of the proper units, methods and devices of accurate measurement are the greatest tools in effecting superstandardization, but many such tools already exist and are available, and as the demand increases, the supply will increase also. The practice of superstandardization in a special field of management is a problem for intensive investigation by those best trained for the work.

The theory of superstandardization is, or should be, a world possession accepted and increasingly used by everyone everywhere. It is the duty of the management engineer who has had experience with standardization, and now with superstandardization, to explain their benefits and to put his experience at the service of thinkers and doers everywhere toward the solving of today's problems and the stabilizing of today's conditions for the benefit of tomorrow. Moreover, an intensive study of standardization in America shows that unless the management engineer takes his natural place as leader in this work he will lose a great opportunity, perhaps forever.

Recommended Practice.

We believe that superstandardization is the One Best Way for obtaining lower production costs and high wages simultaneously. It is the One Best Way and an immediate way, to reduce the cost of living.

This paper is to be followed by another, giving in detail the recent developments in superstandardization, both the latest practice and the theory on which it is founded, and also taken from data at present being collected by personal investigation in England and on the Continent. This will emphasize more strongly the imperative demand for immediate superstandardization in this country. It will supplement this present argument, based largely on the inherent need by a more extended review of the external competition.

We would summarize the immediate necessities as follows:

1. The evaluation of existing standards, as to:
   a, immediate usability.
   b, place in general plan and development toward perfection,
   c, accuracy,
   d, maintenance and full benefits of that which is installed.
2. The promulgation of superstandards in every field of activity.
3. The instruction of young engineers in the making of standards and of superstandards.
4. The advance of those skilled in standardization into superstandardization.
5. The development of the standard, thru accurate measurement, to that point where the "superstandard" of today becomes the "standard" of tomorrow. We cannot afford to stand still.

---

[1]Bulletin of the Taylor Society, June, 1922. A paper presented at a meeting of the Taylor Society, Philadelphia, March 17, 1922. (Figures referred to in this article have been omitted to conserve space, ed.)

MANAGEMENT AS AN EXECUTIVE FUNCTION[1]

Emphasizing Modern Biology and Psychology as Essential to the Development of a Science of Management

By John H. Williams
Consulting Engineer, New York

The meaning of the term Scientific Management is still in the making. It was coined by Taylor in the early stages of the public announcement of his application of the scientific procedure to management. It met a popular need to express the idea back of the beginning of a new era in management, and was broadly used by people with little or no knowledge of its meaning in the mind of the originator.

In the light of Taylor's own words, it seems to me to represent a personal expression of what he regarded as necessary to correct the deficiencies of the then existing social and economic status of industry. It is comparable in nature, though not in kind, to the present use of the terms liberalism and radicalism with relation to society at large, and is subject to as many different interpretations.

Taylor says, "Scientific Management. . . . . fundamentally consists of . . . . . _a certain philosophy which can be applied in many ways_, and a description of what any man or men may believe to be the best mechanisms for applying these general principles should in no way be confused with the principles themselves." He also says, "I want to tell you as briefly as I can what Scientific Management is. It certainly is not what most people think it to be. It is not a lot of efficiency expedients. It is not the printing and ruling of a lot of pieces of blank paper, and spreading them by the ton about the country. It is not any particular system of paying men. It is none of the ordinary devices which, unfortunately are going by the name of Scientific Management. It may in its essence be said in the present state of industry _to involve a complete mental revolution_, both on the part of the management and the men."

I have always felt that Taylor's selection of the term Scientific Management was unfortunate, because of its inevitable confusion, on the one hand with the science of management and on the other with the function of management, although neither of these latter terms expresses what he most often stressed in what he said and wrote. The absence of accepted terminology which sharply distinguishes these concepts is like a cross roads without sign posts, and has done much to befog an understanding of Taylor's work. Everything he did is clearly definable as either science of management or the function of management and these should be distinguished from his philosophy or state of mind, however much they affected his art and science. His selection of the term Scientific Management is not surprising, however, in that the development of his principles (a science of management) and of himself as an executive managing man (the art of management) had to go hand in hand, and against tremendous odds and misunderstanding, of which none but those who have attempted to pattern their work after his can have any appreciation. It was not unnatural that he coined a term which combined these distinct things as though they had been brought together. With the idealism of a revolutionist he hoped for the merging of the art and science of management, and was impatient of their mutual evolutionary development.

Mr. Oliver Sheldon, in an article in the December, 1923 _Bulletin of the Taylor Society_, refers to "the science of management of which we are beginning to hear so much," but denies the present validity of the term. He speaks of the existence possibly of a "science of bricklaying or a science of chocolate covering, but not a science of management," and goes on to say, "It is the science, the knowledge, the truth, the standards which the bricklayer has to learn. To achieve a science of management therefore, we have to apply the scientific method to the tasks of management, as distinct from the tasks of those whom the management controls. It is fundamental, I suggest, to draw a distinction between operative science (which management, of course, uses) and managerial science, where management itself is the operative."

I believe that it is possible to define certain fundamental principles and rules which will ultimately be entitled to be called a science of management, and even to compile a handbook of standard mechanisms and means consistent with these principles. Taylor in his four principles and in the mechanisms and devices which he originated, went far in this direction, but I do not believe that we know as yet, (and I question whether we ever will) sufficient about man's emotional and intuitive faculties to define laws and principles adequate to constitute a "managerial science, where management itself is the operative."

Mr. Kendall last evening referred to his having spoken, in his earlier paper at the Tuck School Conference, of systematic management and scientific management as representing two different types of management. As I recall this talk, he gave an illuminating description of the distinguishing characteristics of each, but made no reference to the science of management as distinguished from Scientific Management.

The science of management, as I see it, has to do with the determination of the facts concerning the design, selection and operation of means to a given end--in other words, the facts bearing upon a problem of management; whereas management--whether systematic or scientific, whether of a manufacturing or merchandising business, whether of an institution or a government--if it _is management_, and not the _science of management_ is primarily concerned with expediency and leadership, however much it may be tempered by science or system. While every manager should seek to increase the element of fact in the basis of his judgments, the word management does not necessarily imply even a knowledge of the facts concerning the thing managed, and is without regard to effectiveness. It is often spoken of as an art and used synonomously with the executive function of administration. It is preferably used in connection with the direction and manipulation of units of activity, where there are a limited number of opposing objectives, as in a small or simple business or a department of a larger business.

The term administration as a policy determining function is usually exercised by a committee or board of directors, in which case it means something very different from management. Administration in an executive function, however, is very like management and connotes something very different from a science. It is preferably used in connection with the supervision and manipulation of opposing objectives existing in the management of several smaller businesses, or the various departments of a larger business. There is no legitimate difference between it and management except in degree and scope. Either or both may be characterized as systematic, scientific, humanitarian, ruthless or any other of a score of types.

Production is usually considered to constitute one branch of management and selling another, and the adjusting of the opposing elements in these and other branches of a business as still a third. The word management could properly be used to describe the function performed by a person charged with responsibility for production or sales or any other department of a business, or for all of the departments of a business where the business is small enough for them to be handled by one person. But when a business is so large that production, sales, purchasing, finance and other functions are each headed by separate executives, the function of the person charged with responsibility for supervising and manipulating these personalities and coordinating their responsibilities can best be described as administration.

The science of management, or management as a branch of engineering, which I believe to be a more desirable term, should be used by both managers and administrators to determine the facts upon which their policies and decisions are based, but its function as such should stop where the determination of facts ends and expediency begins. However far management as a science may encroach upon management or administration as an executive function through the development of facts bearing progressively upon problems as they arise, there will always be a plane on which the final determination must include things other than facts. If management as a science or branch of engineering hopes for recognition as such, this must always be the place where it stops and management or administration as an executive function begins.

In its present stage of development, management as a science or branch of engineering has hardly gone further than to deal with the mechanics of management, and it is not to be wondered that executives with broad and varied experience in management and administration, in their larger aspects of policies and personalities, resent the sometimes all-embracing counsels of those whose experience is largely confined to the mechanisms of management.

I think it is fair to say that Taylor was the first to collect and formulate the existing knowledge with reference to management into a comprehensive and logical body of principles and practice in any way entitled to be called a science, and for this he is entitled to be called the father of the science of management, although not of management as an executive function. The term Scientific Management implies a certain condescension toward the then existing stage of the art of management which I do not believe was intended by Taylor. His criticism was principally directed at the absence of scientifically determined facts as a basis for management.

When we speak of Darwin as the father of evolution, of Pasteur as the father of modern bacteriology, of Fulton as the father of steam navigation, or of Newton as the father of the law of gravity, we do not imply that they were the first to conceive of these discoveries, or that the last word was said by them. But we do give them credit for being the first to deal with these subjects in a manner sufficiently comprehensive, logical and practical to bring them to the attention of the world. This is the least that can be said of Taylor. In proof of this, I shall cite his "four principles" and show that, although they were developed largely with reference to production, they are fundamental to management in its larger aspects, as is proven by their having been generally adopted by industry at large.

Before referring specifically to the principles, it should be observed that Taylor not only formulated definite principles, but he developed a technique and actually drew all of the necessary forms and standardized the paper work required for their application. More than this, he gave an actual demonstration of all that he advocated in a going, competitive business. Had he done less than this, he would not have received either the recognition or the criticism which has been lavished upon him. The recognition is, I believe, due to the effectiveness of his principles and formulae, and the criticism to an assumption, unwarranted by the facts, that he considered them to constitute the sum and substance of management.

Taylor's first principle was the gathering together of all of the traditional knowledge which in the past has been possessed by the workers, and the classifying, tabulating and reducing of this knowledge to rules, laws and formulae. With reference to production this included roughly: 1, standardization and classification of stores; 2, maximum and minimum requirements of stores; 3, standardization and classification of tools and machinery; 4, product specifications; 5, job analysis and standard route charts; 6, worked material classifications; 7, forms and records.

This, as with all of his principles, is clearly limited to the facts of management and not the executive function. Its soundness is testified to by its counterpart presented by the services performed by the research and statistical department, now quite general in all phases of management.

A second step in his first principle was the development of a science for each phase of man's work, to take the place of the traditional rule-of-thumb method. With reference to production, this included roughly: 1, time study of unit operations; 2, standardization of operations; 3, operation instructions; 4, balance of stores. This has its counterpart in the statistical charts and formulae now almost universally used as an aid to executive judgments.

His second principle was the scientific selection, teaching, development and training of employees. With reference to production, this includes roughly: 1, standards for selection of employees; 2, schools for instruction; 3, standards and records for judging qualifications and efforts; 4, training of foremen, gang bosses, instructors and inspectors. While no reliable tests for the selection of executives have as yet been developed, there is hardly any university of standing that does not include a school of business administration in which it undertakes to prepare young men for the executive function. Is not this a general recognition of his principle with respect to the higher executive function?

His third principle was the cooperation with employees so as to insure all of the work being done in accordance with the principles of the science developed. Notice the use of the words, "the science developed." With reference to production, this includes roughly: 1, informing and educating owner, manager, foremen and employees with reference to plans and methods; 2, central planning and control; 3, comparison of work performed and time consumed with standard, and a bonus reward for satisfactory results achieved. The general application of this principle to the administrative function is easily recognized in the growing use of budgets and accounting methods to see that budgets are conformed to.

His fourth principle was the equal division of work and responsibility between management and labor. With reference to production, this includes roughly: 1, assumption by the management of full authority and responsibility for ways, means and records; 2, relieving workers of all clerical work; 3, determination of sequence and routing of work; 4, supplying workers with proper stores; 5, supplying them with proper tools. This is the forecast of the elaborate organization plans and charts and schedules defining duties and responsibilities, now generally in use in large concerns.

In his application of the scientific procedure to problems of management, Taylor not only gave us a practical beginning but he blazed the way for much that is to come. In this connection I do not feel that any discussion of the evolution and present state of management can be complete without reference to what I believe to be the next step--the inclusion in both the science and the art of management of the use of what has been recently developed in the closely related science of psychology. I do not mean by this what is commonly known by the word psychology, in the sense of the static process of introspection that was taught when most of us went to school, but rather, the fundamental principles of what is sometimes called "the new psychology," with principal reference to what it has to teach us regarding man, the principal factor in both the executive function and the science of management.

Mechanical engineering reached its present high state of development largely through intensive investigation of the materials with which it deals. It did not hesitate to use physics, metallurgy, and other sciences for this purpose. The management engineer has attempted to go forward on the information accumulated by the mechanical engineers, seemingly overlooking the fact that his principal material is man himself, concerning whom he has almost no knowledge.

Can you imagine a mechanical engineer working without a knowledge of physics? With all of his mechanisms, he would be in a pretty plight without a knowledge of the laws of the physical world with which he deals. Why then should we expect more of the management engineer with all of his methods, systems and controls, until he acquires a knowledge of the laws governing the behavior of man, the principal material with which he deals?

The hopeful tendency of today for management as an executive function, and the new and ever increasing opportunity for management as a science to be practiced by those adequately informed and trained for their task is, as I see it, in the rapid development of psychology as a science, and the beginning of its recognition by executives as a controlling factor in management. The growing tendency to consider man's probable behavior on the basis of experience, in place of reasoning according to prescribed rules for behavior, the increasing tendency toward the decentralization of authority, the substitution of clearly defined responsibilities for duties, the keeping of accounts in terms of cost and revenue growing out of responsibilities in place of arbitrary accounting terms--these are all evidences of progress in the right direction.

Whereas we formerly railed at what we chose to call unreasonableness and inconsistency in others, we are now coming to recognize, all unwittingly, but through a better understanding of the dynamics of man, that this unreasonableness and inconsistency is a natural result of differences in nature, environment, and opportunity, and can be adjusted only through changes in environment, opportunity and our own attitude, and that it cannot be adjusted through reasoning or punishment.

Most of us were brought up under the theological traditions of man's essential goodness or badness--the idea that, freed from external influences, man would be good or bad as the case may be. It was thought that he could be reasoned into gratitude, generosity or honesty, even in the face of all opposing influences, and great stress was laid upon the effectiveness of the spoken word. This tradition has done much to befog our understanding of his probable reaction to any given set of circumstances. In our dealings with each other, we have depended upon reason, very much as though it were a law controlling human action.

Modern biology and psychology teach that man is primarily emotional, that he is descended from primitive forms of life, and that his reactions are still influenced and modified by primitive emotions, such as fear, rage, hunger, and desire for comfort. They argue that because he was in a primitive state for millions of years, and has been a reasoning being for only a few thousand years, the first and most powerful influence upon him must necessarily be the old habit reaction of quick emotional response to the primitive fear, rage or love which each situation however subtly may suggest. Only secondarily and after control of his emotional reaction does he become subject to reason and the spoken word.

While these views regarding man's origin and his present state are by no means generally accepted as yet, they have shaken the foundations of the earlier beliefs. Executives are unconsciously beginning to study the probable reactions of those they direct, regardless of the reasonableness of such reaction. Whereas executives used to spend days over the reasonableness of their proposals, and what explanation they might make to justify their actions, they now try to forecast the probable reaction of those they direct, and to adjust things to meet these reactions. Strangely enough, the very men who yesterday flatly denied the theory of man's evolutionary heritage today use its standards in considering the probable reaction to their proposals.

An eminent student of the human mind is quoted by Walter Dill Scott in his "Influencing Men in Business" as saying that most persons never perform an act of pure reasoning, but all their acts are the result of imitation, habit, suggestion or some related form of thinking, which is distinctly below that which could be called reasoning.

Mr. Scott continues: "Our most important acts are performed and our most sacred conceptions reached by means of merest suggestion. Great commanders of men are not those who are best skilled in reasoning with their subordinates or most logical in presenting their truths. In moving and inspiring men, suggestion is to be considered in every way the equal of logical reasoning." And I may add that their unconscious ego and defense trends have now come to be recognized as even more important influences.

James Drever in "The Psychology of Industry" says: "From very early times, speculative philosophy has been greatly interested in that very group of phenomena which constitutes the social province of the science of psychology as we understand it. Thoughts, feelings, desires, emotions were looked upon as manifestations of the mind or soul, a substance quite distinct from the matter of which external bodies consisted. Many of the deepest and most momentous problems were raised by the relations of this mind and this matter to one another. Hence, one of the chief interests of philosophers came to be to interpret both in such a way as to satisfy the demands of the human reason on the one hand, and the needs of the human spirit on the other.

"Thus was created the atmosphere in which the 'old psychology' came into being. It was characteristic of this 'old psychology' that it was either deduced from the supposed nature of the mind or soul, or it was formed by the observation and selection of those facts of experience and consciousness which seemed to support a certain view of the mind or soul, or it was reached partly in the one way, partly in the other. In any case, the old psychology could not in strictness be described as a science. It was the battleground of contending philosophical systems. The truths generally accepted as established principles were submerged in the vast mass of controversial matter in regard to which some held one opinion, some another, according to the philosophical views which required to be supported. As a result, interminable disputes obscured the very real advances in psychological knowledge which were made. Such was without exaggeration, the position of psychology from the time of Plato or Aristotle, or even earlier, until the 18th or 19th centuries.

"It is the application of the method of science in the field of mental phenomena that has given us the modern science of psychology, the so-called 'new' psychology. The 'old' definition of psychology was 'the science of the mind or soul,' or 'the science of mental or conscious processes.' The 'new' definition of psychology is 'the science of the facts of human nature and behavior, or the science of human behavior in its relation to, and dependence upon mental process." There is, indeed, a strong body of opinion among present day psychologists in favor of defining psychology simply in terms of behavior. The new psychologist rightly holds that to define his science in terms of mind or soul is to define it in terms not of facts, but of an inference from facts which might be challenged, and is therefore, entirely illegitimate.

"This new psychology really made a serious start with the application of experimental methods some fifty years ago. A quarter of a century later, when experimental psychology had already made substantial progress, systematic efforts were begun to develop applied psychology in various fields. In all respects therefore, the history of the science of psychology has been that of the other sciences from the time when it first took shape as a definite science."

In his inaugural address to the first meeting of the Industrial Section of the British Psychological Society, in April, 1919, Charles S. Myers said: ". . . . recently another stage in the evolution of psychology has been reached by the systematic study of unconscious processes and of their relation to consciousness. Whereas the earlier philosophical psychology and the experimental school which arose from it, had been mainly intellectualistic, giving undue prominence to the play of reason, this later stage has been characterized by the emphasis it lays on the importance of instinct and the emotions, and by its devotion to the study of unconscious processes.

"As in the case of biology, the results obtained from experimental psychological methods, and indeed, those methods themselves, have begun to be applied to practical purposes--first to Education, next to Medicine, and most recently to Industry, thus creating three applied sciences, those of Educational, Medical and Industrial Psychology; and the British Psychological Society is now instituting three special sections of the Society which are to be respectively devoted thereto.

"Under the application of psychology to management, I include the consideration of the psychological causes of industrial discontent and restricted output, the psychological advantages of different methods of payment and supervision, and other conditions which affect the efficiency and happiness of the workers. During the last few years a flood of light has been thrown on the importance of the emotions and on the changes which they effect and to which they are subject. We now recognize how prone we are to rationalize, i.e., to give an intellectual reason for actions which are really prompted by emotional states, or by subtler influences which are unknown to us or which for good reasons dare not be faced. We now recognize that in order to avoid causing excessive self-depreciation, an emotion may undergo a process of 'projection.' Thus instead of reproaching ourselves, we may attribute the reproach to others; hence arise delusions of suspicion and even persecution. Or, for the same purpose, an emotion may be 'inverted,' e.g., shyness becoming concealed by an affected boisterousness, the desire for a person of the opposite sex by aversion, submissivness by defiance. We understand now more fully the psychological basis of worry and anxiety, the importance of their early treatment, and the psychotherapy of the functional nervous disorders to which, if unresolved, they may give rise. The application of such new advances to the problems of industrial unrest is sufficiently obvious."

I feel that this modern view of man strikes definitely at the barrier which has stood in the way of the development of management as a science. The tendency, whether conscious or unconscious, which I see among executives, to accept the findings of modern biology and psychology as a basis for dealing with man, is the most hopeful sign of the day, not alone for the future of management and administration but for the whole social order.

---

[1] Bulletin of the Taylor Society, April, 1924. Paper reproducing an address presented at a meeting of the Taylor Society, New York, January 25, 1924.

THE BASIS OF INDUSTRIAL PSYCHOLOGY[1]

The Psychology of the Total Situation Is Basic to a Psychology of Management

By Elton Mayo
Research Associate, Wharton School, University of Pennsylvania

I. Methods of Psychological Inquiry

In an address delivered before this Society in April, Dr. H. S. Person examined the existing relationship of psychology and industry. He pointed to the need of a closer relation between the two. He showed not only that industry stands in need of expert psychological investigation but also that the present defects of psychology are largely traceable to the absence of facilities for investigation of the adult mind as it manifests itself in its daily activities. Dr. Person listed four types of psychological methods and their attendant theories. He pointed out the ways in which these approaches had aided or might aid industry. But he also evidently felt that they individually and collectively left something to be desired, for he concluded, "If life be an integral whole, if the behavior of men in industrial relations be in any considerable degree the result of stimuli received elsewhere than in office and facotry, then industrial psychology must have for us a new and larger meaning."

It is the purpose of the present paper to show that Dr. Person's criticism is fundamental not only for industrial psychology but for general psychology as well. It is true that life is an integral whole, and that the worker in the plant and the citizen in the home are essentially the same individual. The actions of any such individual in plant or home cannot be understood as things in themselves; they are incidents to be studied and interpreted as parts of an individuality that is the subject of a continually developing awareness of surrounding. The only adequate basis for psychology, either in industry or elsewhere, is one that will admit this as its essential fact and will work out the implications of this admission in all fields. Such a study we may refer to as a psychology of total situation.

Let me explain what this means more concretely by reference to a single simple instance. A worker was sent to us for observation and inquiry because he was suffering disabilities with respect to his work that he was unable to explain. He was highly regarded by the management, his domestic situation was satisfactory, and the conditions of his work had recently been bettered. We found that for four years it had been his habit, as he worked, to reflect upon his more unpleasant experiences when in fighting line in France. Being a person of average normality, he was able to give up this type of thinking when its dangerous consequences were indicated. And his capacity for happiness and work showed an immediate and remarkable improvement. Now my point is that no investigation of his concentrated thinking would have revealed the situation. He did not concentrate upon these topics at any time; he rather avoided doing so. Nor would any investigation of his adaptation to his job or of his general intelligence have given the correct clue. A psychiatric clinic would probably have discovered what was wrong, but he was not likely ever to have become sufficiently emotional to have been sent to a psychiatrist. This sort of situation is constantly arising in every department of human relations and is not effectively dealt with because there is at present no psychological technique which takes account of the individual's total attitude to life and work. Various methods take account of various aspects of the individual's mentality as if they were things in themselves, and the result is that there is no psychological criterion by which the respective importance of various facts revealed can be adequately assessed. In the case specified above, the worker concerned was adjudged normal by factory and dispensary alike.

Of the various methods at present employed, one may specify three in order to show that they are unsatisfactory in the last resort. One psychology examines the inner articulation of concentrated thinking and makes small effort to discover why an individual should concentrate in this or that direction, or how it is he achieves the mental tension necessary. Another psychology examines the inner articulation of obsessions in a somewhat similar manner. The third type concerns itself with industrial production and limits its inquiry to those aspects of productive activity it considers to be relevant to its problem. All three fail because they have no investigation of total situation to assess and direct their inquiries. They cannot even correlate the different methods they employ.

Directly one takes account of the individual's total situation, a very different result follows. One finds that lesser differences of method are superseded--the one technique is capable of an infinite diversity of applications in factory, school and clinic. In a large factory in the Middle West my attention was recently called to certain interesting illustrations of this fact. Three women worked side by side at a bench; the productive capacity of two suddenly diminished remarkably, the capacity of the third improved. Inquiry showed that the third had recently been very happily married. Of the two whose efficiency diminished, one had had her son arrested by the police for failing to support his family, the other was in process of divorcing her husband. Productive efficiency, like capacity for concentration, is a product or expression of a total mental situation. No mere investigation of productive method or intelligence is enough. In the same factory many other illustrations offered. One girl was in the habit of lying down during the rest periods; her efficiency was much above the average. Certain girl workers were under weight and were put upon a regime which included a fifteen minute period of rest upon a couch in the morning and afternoon. Their productive capacity was greatly increased. Generally it may be said that no psychological method which fails to take account of total situation can hope to be satisfactory either to industry or to psychology itself. What is wanted is a coordinated study of human nature and human behavior capable of being applied in any field.

The question as to what this technique or method should be presents, on the first glance, considerable difficulties. Dr. Person, like the late Dr. Stanley Hall in his last published book, is forced to face the fact that we apparently have not one psychology but many psychologies, not one technique but a diversity of techniques with no obvious common basis. At the very outset of the inquiry, one is compelled to ask the status of these various investigations and especially to ask the nature of the human facts at which each investigation is pointed. Discovery of the relation between the various areas of fact investigated is the only means of discovering the relation between the various methods of inquiry.

There are at present two general forms of psychology in the field --the academic and the medical. I do not propose in this paper to give any special attention to behaviorism in the strict sense, first, because it is an outgrowth of the academic psychology and, second, because it still bears the marks of its physiological origin. In thus discarding it as irrelevant to my present purpose, I must not be supposed to be hostile to or doubtful of the value of physiological investigation. Physiology is at least as important as psychology in the understanding of man; but behaviorism is as yet a physiological rather than a psychological development. At any rate, insofar as behaviorism is psychological, the general outline of my discussion will apply.

II. The Academic Psychology

The academic psychology has been developed mainly in universities, the medical mainly in psychopathological clinics and hospitals. In respect of logic and scientific method, the advantage rests with the academic; in respect of the area of fact surveyed, the advantage rests with the medical. There has been a certain carelessness in the use of words in the clinic; phrases have been admitted to common use which may have a definite reference in case work, but possess no precise logical meaning. On the other hand, the need of dealing with individual situations has forced the clinic to take account of factors which the laboratory can discard. The hope of an adequate psychology must be conceived as dependent on the extension of logical method to cover the whole area of relevant human fact.

The undue restriction of the academic investigation is consequent upon, first, the so-called sensationist tradition in psychology and, second, that limitation of opportunity so well described by Dr. Person. The former of these I cannot do more than mention in this place. The latter is a fact that is becoming increasingly evident and calls for alteration. At no time have clinics and factories been freely open to psychological observation and research. To this alone is due the fact that the demand of the present for expert assistance remains unsatisfied. It is not possible to reproduce in the laboratory normal conditions of human life and work. This the English investigators of industrial "fatigue" have discovered. It was possible to reproduce in a darkened laboratory room the physical surroundings of the coal miner, but it was not possible to reproduce under such artifically contrived conditions and identical mental attitude. By reason of his tradition and his limited opportunity, the laboratory psychologist has tended to take account only of what we may describe as concentrated thinking; his theory implies that concentration is the only form of mental process in which psychology is officially interested. Laboratory experiments have usually demanded not merely concentration but special efforts of concentration; this applies equally to psychological tests and to inquiries such as that of Kraepelin into the nature of mental fatigue. I must not be supposed to deny the high value which such researches undoubtedly possess; my claim is rather that this alone is not enough. That the waking life of the individual is not wholly given to concentrated thinking is admitted by every psychologist of note. There is need that psychology should study dispersed thinking or revery and sleep. Every psychopathological investigation of the past fifty years has tended to the conclusion that the major decisions of a lifetime are made in mental moods of relaxation rather than tensity.

But limited opportunity and laboratory procedure have had another consequence for academic theory. Pierre Janet has shown that capacity for mental tension or concentration consists not merely of a facilitation of the dominant thought process but also of an inhibition of other responses to the existing situation. Capacity to think about the subject of this lecture, for instance, involves not merely a consent and an effort to listen; it involves also a refusal to listen to noises in the street outside, a refusal to reflect upon the nature of the audience, one's personal comfort or discomfort and matters equally irrelevant. Yet one is as conscious of these other things as of the topic of the lecture; the difference is that one refuses to think about them. This distinction between the larger object one is conscious of and the lesser object one is thinking about is unduly neglected by psychology. Description of "mental process" in terms of concentrated attention has led too many psychologists to disregard the wider hinterland of awareness which surrounds, as it were, the dominant thought activity of any given moment. The fact is of course admitted, but its importance as determining the nature of and capacity for concentration has apparently been realized by Janet alone. C. Lloyd Morgan and G. F. Stout mention this wider awareness, then describe it as "subconscious" and take no further account of it. Bosanquet comes much nearer to the truth. He begins by pointing out that the "presentations at the focus" of consciousness are "probably the smallest part of what the mind has present to it." His criticism of sensationism is that sensationist theory takes account only of "the focus" of consciousness--that is to say, of the object of immediate concentration. Yet in spite of this claim, he proceeds to follow the same road as Stout and Lloyd Morgan and fails utterly to develop his assertion that the course followed by any concentrated thought is largely determined by "presentations which are not in focus." He also falls into the trap which the word subconscious prepares for the unwary psychologist.

It may seem at this point that I am deliberately involving myself in unnecessary technicality. I should like to assure my audience that this is not so; my object is to show that laboratory procedure has permitted the academic psychologist to disregard an important fact which hospital practice has made the central thesis and research of medical psychology. One more illustration and I shall have completed this part of my discussion. E. B. Titchener some years ago called attention to the excessive abstractness and consequent falsity of psychological descriptions of consciousness. He was at some trouble, indeed, to name a number of the lesser awarenesses which accompany and coexist with any act of concentration. He would probably have succeeded in re-stating psychological theory but for the fact that he conceived consciousness as a multiplicity of processes rather than a single total awareness. His doctrine is that the consciousness of any given moment consists of a sum of simultaneous processes which run their course in time together. This unwarranted equalization of the various parts of the conscious field involves him in confusion. The dominant thought of any moment is a process, a development of experience and knowledge; the surrounding awareness involves no learning--it is not process in the same sense. In spite of his clearer vision, Titchener is forced by his conception of mental process as the fundamental fact of psychology to attach a superior reality to concentrated thinking. He tries to describe a marginal and inhibited awareness as though it were facilitated; and he fails consequently to see that the fundamental fact for psychology is not mental process but a wide awareness of which the dominant process is a product or expression. He still retains the species of double vision to which his doctrine leads. In a recently republished book he maintains that psychology is the study of mental processes, that mental processes do not intrinsically mean anything and that "meaning is always context." This assertion of what is almost the truth becomes especially interesting when compared with the method and theory of medical psychology.

Generally, it may be said of the academic psychology that, by reason of its tradition and restricted laboratory procedure, it has tended to neglect unduly moods of mental relaxation, to regard concentrated thinking as the only fact for psychological investigation and to disregard the wider awareness, or total situation, of which concentration is at all times the expression or product. The method of medical psychology, imposed upon it by hospital practice, is directly contrary.

III. The Medical Psychology

The two aspects of the medical psychology which I wish particularly to call to your attention are, first, the direction of the inquiry, and second, the method it employs. The direction of the inquiry is especially illuminating in view of what I have said in criticism of the conventional academic method. When a patient is brought into a clinic his thinking is obsessional in character and of value mainly as a symptom. Considered as a dominant thought process after the academic fashion it is chiefly remarkable for its utter irrelevance to reality. Yet it is as unmistakably "there" as any reasoned idea in the normal. Certain instances occur to me in illustration. A girl of 25 was much troubled by the idea that she was "going mad." Two men of my acquaintance "wanted another war." I knew one in a Queensland military hospital, the other in a Philadelphia factory. Both had arrived at this obsession by the same road--long meditations in moods of mental relaxation upon the more ghastly experiences of the war. A professional man took to his bed and refused to get up fearing that he might be "hit by a meteorite." Another professionally trained man constantly expected "an explosion," and was not clear as to whether he or his surrounding was about to explode. All these individuals were in a sense rational; that is to say, they were perfectly well aware of the absurdity and irrationality of the obsessing idea; their complaint was that they were unable to escape thinking it. Now all the various schools of psychopathological investigation proceed on the assumption that these obsessions are the product of long trains of dispersed rather than concentrated thought, originating usually in infancy. An unsuitable environment in infancy has bred an attitude that has persisted into adulthood, long after the infantile surrounding has ceased to be. The obsession can indeed be understood as an adequate response to reality once one knows the patient's intimate history and total attitude to life. Four of the five cases specified above recovered their mental normality comparatively quickly, once their total situation was systematically investigated. This statement of the direction of the inquiry explains the essentials of the method.

The methods--and they are many--employed by psychopathologists are all variants of Pierre Janet's "method of distraction." The methods best known are hypnosis, the hypnoid investigation of Sidis, Jung's association test and Freud's dream interpretation by free association. One might add to the list cyrstal gazing and automatic writing. All these methods are variants of the methods of distraction, because they involve a looking away from the dominant or obsessing idea towards the total situation which has produced it. The early history of the patient, the incidents of his upbringing and education, his adaptation to his surroundings, his dominant trends of revery or day dream in moods of mental relaxation--these items are found to bear an important relation to his total attitude to life at any present time. As compared with the academic, the medical psychology is less logical in method but it has opened up for survey and consideration a much wider area of facts directly relevant to successful thinking and living. In particular, it has drawn attention to, first, the technique of thinking, and second, the content of thinking as affected by the individual's total situation. The chief representative of the former inquiry is Pierre Janet. Janet, working with Charcot, succeeded in demonstrating that the difference between normality and abnormality, rationality and irrationality, may be described as a difference of relation between concentration and dispersed thinking or revery. In the normal person revery illuminates concentration, concentration supplies the material of observation and brings the inspiration of revery to the test of empirical fact. In the abnormal person, concentration and revery are pointed in different directions; the result is that mental condition which is described as divided or alternating personality. In all such cases, there are two or more total situations in the one individual, both defective but each with its distinctive attitude and memory.

The chief representative of the inquiry into the content of thinking is Freud. In the early stages of his investigation, Frued found difficulties with hypnosis and was accordingly led to substitute for it an inquiry into the content of the psychoneurotic mind. He has held at various times three different theories, only one of which, the sex theory, is apparently generally known. The essential of Freudian discovery is the irrelevance of the syntheses which constitute primitive knowledge. The child, the savage and the neurotic do not explicitly criticize the meanings they derive from experience. A soldier suffers cerebro-spinal meningitis and recovers. Subsequently he hears gossip to the effect that a local paralysis will surely follow. After three years of "submerged" meditation upon this he develops a hysterical inability to use his left had and forearm. Instances can be multiplied indefinitely; the magical procedures of savage tribes are as excellent an illustration as any psychoneurotic history. The primitive mind has no logical criterion available by means of which it may sift the reasoned from the unreasoned in its thinking. An African tribesman breaks a piece off an anchor washed up on the beach; subsequently he dies. For generations the anchor becomes a fetish for his tribe. "Irrelevant synthesis" is the chief character of primitive thinking.

The effect of this upon the individual's attitude to life is that all kinds of irrelevant and unjustified meanings are dominant in his total situation. His own capacity to analyze and reconsider is small because he has, for the most part, forgotten the events from which the defective ideas were derived. But there need be no mystery with respect to "hysterical amnesia"; whether normal or abnormal, we all tend to forget events and to retain their meaning. A mathematician demonstrating the binomial theorem would be puzzled to describe the events in which his mathematical knowledge began. As we come to understand, we re-interpret the world about us in the light of our new knowledge. It is the world, or rather our total situation, which carries meaning for us. The events which gave us the meaning are forgotten. For a normal person the world has no terrors; for a hysteric, the world is full of terrors which justify his fearful attitude and behavior. Primitive and neurotic meanings are based upon experiences uncritically interpreted; the psychopathologist seeks to revive and to re-interpret the experiences from which such meanings have been derived.

IV. Conclusions from the Medical Investigation

It is unfortunate that a clumsy and unnecessary terminology should have collected about the researches of the psychopathologist. Terms such as subconscious, unconscious, foreconscious, co-conscious do little but cause confusion and take attention away from the really important aspects of the investigation. If we put all this on one side and look at the facts elicited by clinical research we find:

1. That it calls attention to the existence of four mental states --concentration, dispersed attention or revery, hypnoid states and sleep.

2. That it shows the importance of dispersed thinking in education and in all determination of personal attitudes.

3. That it domonstrates total situation to be the fundamental fact for psychological study.

1. Until quite recently, it was customarily assumed that during the 24 hours of the day, an individual is either awake and conscious or asleep and unconscious. It is now possible to distinguish the four general mental states specified above. The point of chief interest, however, is not that four states are distinguished in place of two; it is rather that the distinction must be stated in terms of attention and inattention. All four are states of consciousness; even sleep must be described as inattentive consciousness. Concentration is the state of greatest mental tensity, sleep is the condition of greatest relaxation. But a passive awareness of the surrounding persists in sleep. This is illustrated by the fact that it is not the intensity of a stimulus--for example a sound --that wakes a sleeper but rather its meaning for him. In the maternity hospital the loud clang and crash of the trolley car outside does not wake the mother, but at the slightest stir in the cot by her side, she sits up in bed. A "shell-shocked" soldier was afraid of the dark but slept well at night if the lights were left on. Directly the lights were turned out, he wakened. Telegraph operators in the country districts of Pennsylvania are allowed to sleep on night duty. They all hear the call

for every station, but all alike develop a capacity for waking immediately when their station is called and for sleeping through other signals. Illustrative facts could be multiplied indefinitely. The whole study of what is usually termed suggestion is a study of the passive responses of dispersed thinking, hypnoid states and sleep.

2. The importance of dispersed thinking is chiefly that described by Janet. The direct relevance of this French psychopathology to factory investigation is astonishing. Janet speaks of neurotic agitation as due to crises of revery; he also points out the difficulty of maintaining mental tensity or concentration, and consequent temporary disintegration, when fatigue has set in. With respect to mental normality as implying a cooperative relation between concentration and revery, it may be said that the same fact is observable in the factory and in business generally. Those whose reveries are relevant to their work are the successful men; the reveries of the unsuccessful men seem to be irrelevant to what they are doing for the most part. This is not, of course, their fault nor are they in any sense to blame.

3. Total situation is the fundamental fact for psychology. Medical researches into the nature of sleep and dispersed thinking give us a new conception of the mental life of man. We have to distinguish between that conscious awareness of, or orientation to, our surroundings which is a steadily persistent character of our mental life, and the act of attention to some particular thing--an active "thinking about" things which is only fitfully present. The conscious awareness of surrounding which begins with infancy persists practically uninterrupted through sleep and waking until the hour of death. Its general character changes slowly as successive experiences or acts of attention establish new meanings or new individual attitudes. But at every point or moment its general character determines the type and quality of the attention or thought that can be given to any aspect of the surrounding. There need be no difficulty with this conception; the same truth holds, for example, of our muscular apparatus. One who has been athletic in youth has established a working relation between his "contractile" muscular fibres which adapt a limb to a new position and his "plastic" muscular fibres which hold that position. Long after he has given up games this relation between muscular contractility and plasticity persists and shows itself in every least or trivial movement. So with our mental attitude; the general significance of the world, determined by earlier thought and education, informs and fixes later capacity for thinking. For every individual the world is primarily meaning derived from former thought and experience. This meaning forms the background against which the particular events of the day, week and year are displayed; it varies with the individual and is perpetually present in his mental attitudes. This is the significance of total situation; we cannot understand why an individual suffers an obsession or leaves his job or, it may be, thinks logically, until we know the background against which for him the events of life are played.

And in considering this it is important to realize that this total attitude is not by any means the product only of concentration or logical thinking. In the average instance, revery--and most frequently revery of an irrational type--has done even more to determine attitude than concentrated thinking. In the total situation of the average individual consequently, both rationality and irrationality play a part. A steady period of work may be succeeded or interrupted by an unexplained flare of emotion, astonishing even to the individual himself. No psychological method can hope to contribute anything to the understanding of incidents of this kind, or to the general understanding of individual attitudes, unless it takes account of total situation. Methods which look only at concentrated thinking or at adaptation to work or at obsessive thinking as if these were facts in themselves are in the position of an engineer who looks at the apex of a pyramid and neglects to examine its base. The apex is supported by its base; every act of concentration is the product or expression of a total mental situation.

Pierre Janet's point is well taken; capacity for concentration, or the explicit perception of realities, or work, is to be understood as capacity for mental tension. Whenever the total attitude is ill-organized or unduly compounded of the irrational products of irrelevant revery, then concentration is difficult or impossible to achieve. And since it is by concentration that we achieve an explicit hold upon the reality about us, it follows that in all such cases the hold upon reality is tenuous in the extreme. Any condition of living which makes for too much revery thinking of an irrelevant type tends to diminish the individual's hold upon reality. Concentration is possible only when supported by a well-ordered total situation. It is the business of total situation psychology in industry to investigate and to eliminate conditions which lead to disharmony in the individual's mental background, and to promote that orientation which alone makes reasoned adjustment to the job possible. Disturbances may originate either in the personal history of the individual or in the present conditions of his work or both at once.

V. The Approach to the Factory

I am well aware that at this point many members of my audience will be asking, perhaps with some alarm, what I propose to do--whether industry is to be asked to submit its entire personnel to the ministrations of the psycho-pathologist. I can at once reassure those who have such questions in mind. There are at present, in every economic organization of any size, personnel managers and psychologists whose business it is to handle the human problems of industry. My whole claim is that such experts should be trained in the type of psychology I have briefly described. The responses of every individual to the associations and opporutnities of the factory or office are, for the most part, determined by causes in his personal history and total situation which lie beyond the immediate control of the management. If the personnel manager or industrial psychologist be trained to take account of his total situation in dealing with an individual, it will involve no more work than at present and the work will be infinitely more effective. There are in particular two reasons why training of this type is becoming increasingly necessary to successful management. The first is that modern methods of industrial organization tend to impose on the average individual long periods of revery thinking. Machine operation, once the worker is habituated to it, does not demand a high degree of concentrated thought. On the other hand, t is impossible for him to concentrate his mind upon anything else. One finds in actual practice, therefore, that the mental mood which accompanies work is very frequently a low-grade revery of a pessimistic order. In one instance, we discovered a worker who, during part at least of his working day, fell into the hynotic somnabulic conditon. Now the danger of this general condition of things both to the individual worker and to industry is obvious to anyone acquainted with psychopathological work. All the authorities agree that an adult nervius breakdown originates in earlier pessimistic reveries--one authority indeed specifies feminine handwork as offering much opportunity for the development of a hysterical mentality. Insofar as this general state of affairs exists and remains uncontrolled, we may expect an increasing condition of emotional unrest manifesting itself in the periodic "crisis of revery" so well described by Janet.

The second reasons why psychological investigation is necessary to industry is that these pessimistic reveries which culminate in disorder and unrest (absenteeism, high labor turnover, strikes) are relatively easily controlled provided that the management has a means of discovering the nature of the cause. It is in respect of this control that the factory differs from thehospital and clinic. A psychoneurotic is little benefited by a change of his conditions of living or working; the relatively normal worker in a factory responds at once to any betterment of his total situation. An individual's occupation is at least half his life: if his occupation is interesting and stimulating, he can support a burden of domestic and private difficulties which would otherwise tend to depress or break him down. Our inquiries seem to show that the usual form which pessimistic revery takes in the factory is that of depressed reflection upon personal and intimate affairs. It is important for management to realize that the conditions of work or occupation can exaggerate or minimize this tendency.

In passing, I should like to call attention to the fact that in discussing these two reasons I have been discussing the vexing question of monotony and boredom as distinguished from physcological fatigue. Monotony in itself is apparently a matter of no great moment; the definition of what consitutes monotony will, in fact, be found to vary with every individual. Monotony becomes a problem for the management of a concern only when it is obviously giving rise to pessimistic revery, not merely in individuals but over wide areas of the personnel.

The psychological approach to the factory, defined as I have defined it, does not involve at the outset any elaborate confusions of card indexing or numerous additions to the office staff. It takes existing problems and re-states them in terms of total situation in individuals and in the factory itself. Its object is better understanding, improved control, and an increase of human happiness.

VI. A Case in Point

I can best explain by an illustration, after which I shall have done. Rather more than a year ago the Industrial Research Department of the University of Pennsylvania was asked to make what contribution it could to the solution of certain problems in a textile mill. The problems, briefly stated, were:

1. A high labor turnover and low productivity in a spinning department;

2. Absenteeism and "eye-strain" in a sorting department;

3. Low productivity in a pickering department;

4. Absenteeism in a winding department.

The only investigation actually proposed to us was that of the high labor turnover in the spinning department; the other problems were discovered as we worked.

1. The spinning-mule investigation has been reported and discussed at length elsewhere, and I do not propose to renew the discussion here. Our findings, briefly stated, were that the conditions of work involved a considerable degree of postural fatigue. This fatigue was complicated and increased by an almost universal incidence of pessimistic revery. To remedy this, the management introduced rest-pauses, four in a ten-hour day, in which the men were asked to lie down and were instructed in the best method of relaxation. Since the institution of this system the labor turnover has become negligible, the evidences of general pessimism have diminished or disappeared, and the productivity of the department has increased by approximately 15 per cent.

2. The sorting of white wool and cotton was done entirely by women of varying ages. There was a tradition in the department that the work caused eye-strain and indigestion. This tradition appeared in the reveries of the workers as an expectation of these ills; every worker in the department gave evidence of such expectation. In this and other departmental investigations, we have had the most excellent backing and collaboration from the Graduate Medical School of the University. Care of the physical welfare of the individual being thus assured, we tried the experiment of interrupting the sorting by six ten-minute rest periods in a ten-hour day. In this instance, as with the spinners, workers were given individual instruction in the best methods of rest. The effect has been to eliminate altogether the periodic emotional crises which used to characterize the work of the department. There have been no complaints of eye-strain or indigestion for six months; absenteeism and evidences of pessimistic thinking have disappeared. There is in this instance no means of measuring productive output, but the management is entirely satisfied that there has been no diminution.

3. The situation in the pickering department has at no time been made the object of active investigation. The management some months ago adapted the procedure in the spinning department to the picker house. Since that time those employed in pickering have earned bonuses of from 5 to 14 per cent. Previously, they had earned no bonuses.

4. The winding department is interesting chiefly because it illustrates a variation of method. Cone-winding is piece-work, and supply is sometimes irregular; workers are therefore unwilling to take regular rest-periods. The workers are women and the relatively high rate of absenteeism was found to be largely due to a tradition of incapacitation by menstrual "cramps." In one month, for instance, one-half the departmental strength absented itself for a day or more for this reason. In this instance, as with the sorters, it was discovered that the tradition of the department appeared as a revery of expectation in the individual. The work involves postural fatigue, the reveries tend to be pessimistic, and the occasional recurrence of the tradition in such reflections acts as what used to be called a suggestion. Investigation was made medically and also by the dispensary

nurse. It seemed entirely possible that physical fatigue might contribute to the causation of dysmenorrhoea. We were somewhat astonished to discover that the physical causes are apparently negligible as compared with the mental, I am expertly informed that the medical help given is not more than "an aid to suggestion;" but the individual attack upon the revery and traditional expectation by the nurse in charge has has the effect of almost entirely removing this cause of absenteeism. In one period of four months, for example, there was no time lost by reason of this ill.

VII. Total Situation and the Individual

This paper would not be complete without some reference, however brief, to our method of approaching the individual and to the content of the pessimistic reveries in particular cases. The individual has to be approached with care, but once he understands that his happiness and well-being are our concern, and that confidences are not divulged to his fellows or the management, he is usually willing to help the investigation. Given this collaboration, our endeavor is to discover:

1. His physical condition and medical history;
2. His personal history, including his dominant reveries;
3. His domestic situation;
4. His adaptation to his work.

This investigation of individual situations is more interesting than the inquiry into general or deparamental situations. It will in the end probably yield more in the way of definite knowledge as to what is happening in industry and in the detail of civilized life. In by far the greater number of cases there is some unsatisfactory circumstance, usually of personal history of private life, which is a habitual topic of dispersed thinking or revery. Any monotony of occupation or unpleasantness in work tends to extend and emphasize this thinking. We have under investigation several hundred individuals of average normality and I give one or two instances which must not be supposed to be specially selected; they are taken more or less at random and are typical.

A girl of twenty-seven has been engaged upon a machine operation for nine years. She began work in adolescence to support her mother and four brothers and sisters after the father's unexpected death. For five years she was the sole support of the family; in the last four years a brother has helped. For seven years she was the best worker in the department; latterly her production has been less. Two years ago a young man wished to marry her and she had, so she says, a nervous breakdown. She is much opposed to marriage; she has developed in revery an expectation that if she marries her adolescent experience may be repeated and a young family require her sole support. Many discussions gave her an opportuinty for expressing her reveries for the first time and her production has recently improved. She is still opposed to marriage.

A clerk in charge of deliveries, approximately twenty-eight, occasionally absents himself from the factory and stays in bed for a day or two. After the war he was unable to work for two years; he suffered what he describes as "neurasthenia." He is happily married and has four children. He is highly esteemed as a worker by the management and as a man by his fellow-workers. He contributes cartoons and humorous columns occasionally to publications and earns small sums thus. He suffers financial anxieties on his children's account. He habitually indulged in anxious or gloomy reflection as he worked until the unwisdom of this practice was pointed out to him. Since then his health and outlook have much improved. He has more intelligence and ability than his work demands; he cannot easily find a quiet corner in his home. His periods in bed are crises of revery; they are diminishing in frequency as he learns how to control revery. He should have more interesting work.

A machine operative of thirty-six is married to a woman much older than himself. They have no children and both regret it. He is highly skilled and is valued by the management. He complains of "neuritis" in his back which his medical attendant cannot diagnose. His wife has spinal curvature.

A man of thirty, married and with several children, is engaged upon a monotonous and unpleasant job. He suffers occasional emotional crises in which he is afflicted with panic for no very obvious reason. These crises were difficult to handle until it was discovered that at the suggestion of the rest he would drop into a condition of hypnotic somnambulism. Inquiry shows that his work has played some part in developing this capacity in him.

A girl in the early twenties is engaged upon a monotonous machine operation for ten hours daily. She partly supports her mother and a large family. The father lives with them but has been demented for some years. A certain proportion of her work time is given to speculation upon the possibility of a similar development in herself.

When individual situations are thus described, I have no doubt that they have an air of being specially selected and unusual. The point I wish to make is that these are fair average samples taken from the several hundred cases we have under investigation. It is only rarely that we discover an individual entirely free from irrational or pessimistic irrelevant revery thinking. There is of course an immense difference according to the suitability or unsuitability to him personally of the work upon which he is engaged. If the conditions of work are good or the work interesting then his job acts as a corrective of any tendency to pessimism or as an antidote to any actual difficulties or problems. On the other hand whenever pessimistic reflection emerges, the effect upon productive efficiency is striking and immediate. This I have illustrated not only by cases taken from Philadelphia but also by those instances of workers in the Middle West cited in my opening paragraphs. Productive capacity, like capacity for concentration, is symptomatic merely of the total situation is adversely affected by any cause whether within or without the factory, a diminished capacity for work will always be one among other symptons.

It is easy, therefore, to exaggerate the effects upon the individual of a traditional discontent within a factory or of so-called "agitation." It is altogether probable that such traditional expressions of emotional attitude have no effect upon individuals except when they afford a means of expressing individual discontents. Our experience with such traditions of discontent has been that the actual individual situation is different in every case; the traditional complaint is no more than a common vehicle of expression.

This type of investigation is not unknown in the United States. The need for it was expressed by Simon Patten of the University of Pennsylvania. The form is should take was explicitly stated by the late Dr. E. E. Southard of the Boston Psychopathic Hospital. In a sense, the work involves an extension of that begun by the pioneer by whose name this Society is honored. Taylor confined his attention, upon the whole, to the problem of irrelevant synthesis or mistaken coordination in our muscular apparatus; there is urgent need to extend this inquiry to discover what irrelevant syntheses of emotions and ideas are imposed upon workers by indifferent education and unsuitable conditions of work. I use the term "workers" here to include proprietors and managers as well as machine operatives. Over the whole field of industry disperesed thinking and emotions bred of revery are making for unrest and breakdown rather than content. Many investigators are needed, but since few opportunities have been offered to the Universities, the inquiry is slow to begin. Industrial psychology is but one aspect of a research into the nature of man. Without such research civilization cannot endure.

---

[1] Bulletin of the Taylor Society, December, 1924. Paper presented at a meeting of the Taylor Society, New York, December 5, 1924.

THE GREAT OBSESSION [1]

A Challenge to Management Engineers and Industrial Psychologists to Join in Establishing A Circular Response Between Employers and Trade Unionists

By Robert W. Bruère
Associate Editor, The Survey

In Harper's Monthly Magazine for July, Elton Mayo, research associate in industrial and clinical psychology at the Wharton School of Commerce and Finance, University of Pennsylvania, psychoanalyzes what he calls the Great Stupidity, vernacular for the Great Obsession, which, in the guise of the Class War between Capital and Labor, bedevils our industrial civilization. In this era of rollicking prosperity, these halcyon days of industrial peace, we in America seem to be taking it for granted that within our happy boundaries the malady of industrial unrest, once the occasion for hysterical alarms, has gone the way of malaria and yellow fever. In spite of the rumblings in the coal fields, in spite of the hepatic depression in the textile industry, in spite of jurisdictional disputes in the building trades where fevered discord between the plasterer and the bricklayers gives a tubercular tinge to contracts apprassed in the millions, we are cheerfully disposed to think of the more malignant phases of industrial unrest as peculiar to the sick civilizations of Europe and the Far East. Who among us has not felt the lotophagic appeal of the benign illusion? So pleasant are its accompanying daydreams that we resent the intrusion even of such great authorities as Mayo cites--biologists, psychologists, economists, historians, political and social philosophers--who, harboring a pessimistic view of the state of our civilization, warn us that there are forces at work among us, feuds, factions, divisions, which are as "the mists of death," symptoms of the "first stages of collapse." Of these, one of the most menacing, they conceive, is the warfare between Capital and Labor, "sometimes active, sometimes passive, but always menacing," child of the Great Stupidity, nursling of the Great Obsession.

Civilizations, like individuals, have their pessimistic reveries, breeders of discord, destroyers of internal harmony. Mayo quotes Machiavelli on the dangers that beset republics as a corrective of our too ready acquiescence in Rousseau's "pious hope that desires and impulses inimical to the general welfare will somehow cancel one another in general discussion or general assembly." Machiavelli, he thinks, is a robuster and wiser counsellor. "Those people," wrote the Florentine sage in the sixteenth century, "who expect a republic to remain without divisions deceive themselves very much; but it is also true that while some injure a republic, others do not. The divisions which injure are those accompanied by factions and feuds, whilst those which do not cause factions or feuds are a benefit to a republic."

In Australia since 1893 the division between Capital and Labor has acquired the morbid quality of factions and feuds. There the industrial issue has been generalized as a political issue. Strikes are more frequent then ever before in spite of the statutory courts of arbitration.

He continues:

> Obsessions are fostered and strengthened by every political event. One of the greatest industrial upheavals of recent years, the Sydney railway strike of August, 1917, was mainly caused by the workers' unreasoning terror of the mere word "Taylorism." The Railway Commissioners attempted to introduce a card system of recording work, with a view to accurate measurement of cost. The trade unions and the Labor Press stigmatized this as an attempt to introduce the "Taylor System" into the workshops. The Railway Commissioners, instead of dealing with the human situation, tried to meet fear with force; they ordered the introduction of the card system. The railway and tramway men at once came out on strike; a few days later coal miners, seamen, wharf laborers, gas workers, butchers, and many other unions ceased work. In some degree the strike spread through all the states of the Australian Commonwealth. This is no solitary instance.

Great Britain seems to be traveling the same road--"the same calamitous road." In the United States, owing to the absence of "class consciousness," the situation, superficially viewed, seems altogether different. Many foreign observers, Australians, Englishmen, Germans, and especially Russians, prophesy that the difference is only one of retarded development, that we too are predestined to travel the same road. The spirit of warfare, they think, has been bred in our bones by ages of the struggle to live until it has become instinctive. There is an inherent economic conflict between the major industrial groups which can only be resolved, they say, by fighting it out. Mayo cites the case of "an otherwise intelligent employer who refused to grant a concession recommended by his executive on the ground that a union in another factory had made a similar request. He did not wish to institute an obviously necessary reform because it was irrationally confused with unionism in his mind." This also is not a solitary instance. Neither American employers nor American laborers are free from the biases, fears, obsessions that dance a mad accompaniment to the warlike spirit when it is aroused, and strive to awaken it with tom-tom rhythm when it sleeps. But they are neverthelesss comparatively free, still so comparatively free that Mayo thinks we may detour the "clamitous road" if we bring to bear upon our situation the analytical and generalizing mind and canalize our latent feuds and factions by inducing employers to deal intelligently with their employees.

How is this to be done?

> If the virtual class-war which obtains in British communities is to be avoided (says Mr. Mayo) it can be avoided only by anticipating the unionization of industry, by making it unnecessary. The first step should be a clear definition of the conditions of the open shop by some association of intelligent employers. . . The second step is even more important. An open-shop policy based on the private opinions and prepossessions of a few employers is utterly valueless.

> What the social situation is in its broader aspects can be discovered only by adequate investigation. Such investigation, like any other, requires experts--in this instance, experts in human research.

No one has penetrated closer to the center of the industrial conflict that Mr. Mayo, no one has more luminously defined its character. The psychological technique of which he is master is as indispensable to the development of a science of human relations in industry as the earlier technique of Frederick W. Taylor has proved to be in the development of the science and art of administration and management. Now it is probable that no one thing has so greatly retarded the indispensable progress of Taylor's scientific technique as the quite unnecessary affront to organized labor and the trade unions which accompanied its early development. Taylor, too, believed that by the intelligent use of the science of management, employers and employers' associations could anticipate the unionization of industry by making it unncessary. Copley, his biographer, voices the opinion "that if Taylor had lived to witness the change in the attitude of many labor leaders since the World War, he would have modified his own attitude towards trade unions."

It would be a tragedy of the first order if a repetition of Taylor's failure rightly to appraise the viability and functional significance of the trade unions should similarly bedevil the introduction of the indispensable technique of modern clinical psychology into the field of industrial relations.

Instead of laying The Great Obsession, the remedy which Mr. Mayo suggests is preeminently calculated to foster and exacerbate it. His proposal in itself might not unreasonably be construed as a concession to that very obsession against trade unions which he deprecates. The danger of such a tragedy is the greater, not only because Mr. Mayo's work has been widely recognized as having much of the pioneering quality of Taylor's, but also because he is research associate at the University of Pennsylvania by virtue of a grant from one of the Rockefeller funds--a fact which in itself is likely to awaken unreasoning prejudice, especially among labor leaders, who are unfamiliar with the policy of scrupulous regard for the scientific detachment and independence of investigators which characterizes the administration of the various Rockefeller educational and scientific foundations.

There is a certain dramatic quality in the circumstance that Mr. Mayo's article appeared immediately after, and indeed was written a few months before a historically significant meeting of the Taylor Society in New York in which disciples of Taylor and representatives of the trade unions joined in removing the Great Obsession from the path of creative cooperation between management and organized labor.

Class war, like war between the nations, may be inevitable. It may be implicit in our present industrial system. It may be inherent in the constitution of human nature. But to drift along on this fatalistic assumption would be to surrender one's faith in the capacity of men to shape their destiny in the light of intelligence, one's faith in the pragmatic reality of science and the healing efficiency of the scientific method when applied to the ordering of human affairs.

To disregard the divergence of economic interest between owners and wage-workers, to play the ostrich with respect to the elements of class warfare that dart like summer lightning through our American industrial and economic life, is asgreat a stupidity as the Jehovah complex of the hard-boiled industrial autocrat or of the radical who dreams of himself as riding the revolutionary whirlwind. But when we have recognized the existence of the problem, the question arises here, as it does in international relations, whether we shall spend our energies girding ourselves for battle, or whether we shall subject the problem to intelligent and objective scrutiny, bring the method of science to bear upon it, and seek the basis for a concert of classes, as of nations, grounded in reason, justice and goodwill. This is what the more thoughtful followers of Taylor, members of the society which bears his name, to whom science is not a catch-word but the breath of life and the hope of peaceful progress, have during recent years, under the leadership of their managing director, Harlow S. Person, been attempting to do.

What is the point of effective concert between Capital and Labor, between management and men? What is the channel of creative cooperation through which the latent division between them, instead of festering into factions and feuds, can be turned to the benefit of the republic? Mayo's conclusion that the happy future of American industry "would seem to depend upon the intelligence of employers and employers' associations" in "anticipating the unionization of industry, by making it unnecessary" seems to me without scientic warrant, a psychologically unsound concession to the still dominant temper of American, and especially pioneering American, public opinion. The same logic, the same inherent functional urge that produces employers' associations, have produced and will continue to produce associations of wage-workers. To ignore this is to fail to take account of all the elements in the total situation.

Employers' associations, like trade unions, are by origin and current policy militant organizations. The same is true of nations. But peace and creative cooperation between two nations is not likely to come about by the adoption by one nation of a policy designed to eliminate the other. If we make our approach to the problem of industrial peace by urging one of the major parties to industry to adopt a policy designed to do away with the self-governing associations of the other, we shall but pour oil on the fires of obsessional irrationality. There are conflicts of interest between them. There are also common interests. The most obvious of these is the elimination of waste through efficient production.

The key to the problem is the objective science of management, where the science concerns itself not only with things, but also with men. The engineering technician holds the key. It is through him that a circular response may be set up between the two parties through which they will achieve, not the elimination of one by the other, or the adjustment of one to the other, but an integration which will yield what Mary Follett calls "the plus values of conflict."

One could feel these plus values emerging at the historic meeting of the Taylor Society to which I have referred. The discussion was opened by Geoffrey C. Brown, consulting industrial engineer, with a paper on Scientific Management and Organized Labor Today--An Example of Cooperation Between Management and Organized Labor Which Indicates One Direction of Industrial Progress.

The speaker was obviously conscious of a certain temerity in what he was about to say. He was uncomfortably aware of the ambiency of the Great Obsession--on the part of scientific management employers against the trade unions, on the part of trade union leaders against "Taylorism." In a foot-note to his rangy title, he hastened to explain that by "scientific management" he did not intend to imply any particular system or group of functions, but rather management conducted in the light of scientific inquiry and knowledge, "management based on facts."

He began by taking note of the accumulating evidence that organized labor is withdrawing from its old attitude of hostility to the introduction of scientific methods into industry. Then he made a statement which hardly ten years ago would have made many of his professional colleagues bristle. Coming from a disciple of Taylor, proclaimed in a meeting of the Taylor Society, it made many of those who heard it sit up and take notice.

> I believe (he said) that those managers are most progressive who now concede the right of labor to organize and to bargain collectively through accredited representatives on questions of wages, hours of work and working conditions. Not to concede this right is, if we reverse the situation, similar to, and about as logical as a refusal on the part of labor to negotiate with management, the accredited agent of an organized group of investors. But if this bargaining or arrangement of terms is to be conducted intelligently and with, as it were, all the cards on the table, labor must comprehend the aims and to a considerable degree the technique of management, while management, in its turn, must be equally alive and sympathetic to the spirit of the labor movement. Otherwise the two are working at cross purposes and any attempt at bargaining degenerates into an effort on the part of each to hoodwink the other.

As an abstract statement, this might have been interpreted by the skeptical as a pious and conciliatory platitude; as a conclusion derived from experience in wrestling with the Great Obsession it acquired the freshness of a new day.

There is probably no group in the industrial world that has been more constant and courageous in devotion to science in management than these disciples of Taylor. They have followed the Great Obsession to its lair; there was a time when they were more or less under its domination; they have wrestled with it; they are well on the way to its mastery. Mr. Brown gave reports of his encounters with the black-winged Apollyon.

In the autumn of 1923, for example, he was called into consultation by the owners of a small New York factory, dedicated to the manufacture of mirrors. He found conditions there which those who have explored American factories of the old individualistic tradition generally expect to find--no adequate stores-keeping, no method of scheduling orders in advance in relation to the plant's manufacturing facilities, no vestige of a cost system. If the owners of such plants found their kitchens in such a state of general confusion and clutter, they would berate their wives for thriftless slatternliness.

Such employers hate to have their habits disturbed. They know their business. They have gotten along well enough for years. They are practical men. Why should they change? When business falls off and they lose money, the fault is not with them but with the ruthlessness of their competitors, the selfishness of the money lenders, with the irrational caprices of nature, especially human nature. Under pressure of adversity they lay off men with little or no notice, cut wages, lengthen hours. Then the walking delegate stalks in upon them--and suddenly becomes the symbol of all the evils by which they are beset. Words are exchanged, the sound of the tom-tom beats through their subconscious memories. Presently both sides act under the irrational influence of the Great Obsession.

This was the situation in Mr. Brown's mirror factory. The problem, as he explained, would not have presented extraordinary difficulties if it had consisted merely in affecting a physical reorganization of the business. It was this psychological obstacle, the emergence of the Great Obsession, that made the path of the investigating engineer a hard and dangerous one to travel. The workmen in this open shop were strongly organized in a trade union affiliated with the A.F.of L. There the union was, as a matter of fact, though the management refused to recognize it. Three times in ten years the plant had been brought to a standstill by strikes. But rather than enter into cooperative relationship with the union, "the management had grown so accustomed to this expensive type of interruption that they frequently referred to it as an unfortunate but inevitable condition of manufacture."

The workers as trade unionists were in a similar state of irrational opposition to change. Anything suggesting "Taylorism" was taboo--immediately evoked the Great Obsession. After Mr. Brown had succeeded in inducing the employers to install a modern cost system, he attempted to introduce a system of scheduling orders in advance through the factory, so that work could be systematized and the machines could be uncluttered. Of course no such system could be made to work effectively until the standard time and cost of each operation had been determined. The workers, too, were creatures of habit. They wanted to be left alone to do their work as they always had done it. They, too, were practical men. If one of these outside experts said that they were doing their work wastefully and inefficiently--well, he was simply a theorist, who would be better off, perhaps, for a little practical experience. But the plant could not be saved from bankruptcy without the accurate determination of the standard-output capacity of each manufacturing operation. This involved time study, and to the ordinary workman time study is "Taylorism," and that is taboo.

Mr. Brown's initial attempts in this direction caused an incipient strike. Under ordinary conditions, this threat of strike would have provoked a lockout; rather than have the union "dictate" to him. The employer would have preferred to shut down the factory, even to liquidate his business. But a consulting engineer had been hired and the problem was turned over to him.

(Here follow excerpts from Mr. Brown's article in the June Bulletin which explain how he secured the cooperation of shop steward and walking delegate and the loca's approval of his investigation.)

Conference, discussion, patent open-mindedness finally prevailed ....(His two years' experience) led Mr. Brown to the conclusion that "the most important single gain lay in the establishment of a spirit of cooperation and what might be termed same relations between management and union." Where such sanity enters in, the Great Obsession flies out through the door.

This record is an interesting sign of the times. Quite as interesting was the response of the members of the Taylor Society and of the old line trade unionists. In the discussion which followed Mr. Brown's paper, a number of management engineers bore similar testimony...... The management engineers are proving that they are practical psychologists as well as masters of materials and machines. But as psychologists they are not experts. Their work needs to be supplemented by the special knowledge and technique in the development of which a small handful of men, among whom Elton Mayo is preeminent, are doing work of as great pioneering importance as that of Taylor himself. It would be a very great tragedy if in the light of the experience of the disciples of Taylor the industrial psychologists should reopen the old breach between the technicians and organized labor. It would be a blessed assurance of industrial peace and sane industrial progress if the industrial psychologists now joined with the specialists in the art and science of management in establishing a circular response between employers and trade unionists through which factions and feuds would be averted, the Great Obsession would be laid, and the conflict between them would be made to yield plus rather than minus values. Is not this the true mission of the technical experts, the trail-blazers and protagonists of the scientic spirit in industry and society?

---

[1]Bulletin of the Taylor Society, October, 1925. Reprinted from The Survey, August 1, 1925.

A SUPPLEMENT TO "THE GREAT STUPIDITY"[1]

By Elton Mayo

Your kindly warning (see "The Great Obsession," Survey Graphic, August, 1925) shows me that there are possibilities of misunderstanding in my Harper article. Since you wish me to define my attitude, to show that I am not an apostle of the forces of reaction, you shall have your way. There is nothing in all you say with which I am not essentially in agreement, even in those places where you become most critical.

I should like you to remember in the first place, however, that in writing "The Great Stupidity," I did not wish to make unwarranted assertions with respect to things American. I am a visitor here for a short term of years; I have been treated with the most extraordinary courtesy and hospitality; facilities for investigation and the extension of my knowledge have been freely offered to me by employers and trade-unions alike. It has seemed to me that it would ill become me to make wide assertions with respect to a situation which I have observed in one small corner of one great city. I have had no wish to add myself to that growing list of visiting wiseacres who give gratuitous advice, based on their mismanagement of their own affairs, to America.

I had hoped it would also be clear that I was not intending, or offering, any sort of general solution of the so-called Capital-Labor difficulty. I believe that all the solutions offered so far have been too general; that the time has come for us to sit down and investigate closely particular situations with all the powers science has added to our equipment. This is, in fact, the method for which I stand, in so far as I stand for anything novel in method. If one takes account of the facts elicited by anthropological inquiry, by psychopathology, by clinical physiology in any industrial problem, difficulties of management tend to clear themselves away before the wider understanding thus achieved. My points--one and two--with respect to the "open shop" were not intended as a recommendation of the open shop. Taking it merely as a fact which had come under my observation, I was concerned to show that an open shop movement which serves to cloak bitterness and enmity cannot do anything but extend and intensify the social disaster. This, at least, one can say from knowledge of what has happened elsewhere, without pretending to any special knowledge of things American. And in saying this I was considering the lesser problem of employers' association, rather than the wider problem of industrial organization.

With regard to this wider problem, anyone acquainted with it has to admit at once the historic necessity and justification of trade-unionism. In England of the early nineteenth century, it was customary to drive little children to work in the mines by making deductions of what they would have earned from their father's already small wages. Once in the mines they were worked for twelve hours a day, harnessed to trucks, half-naked, crawling on their hands and knees. J. L. and Barbara Hammond have made abundantly clear the atrocious neglect and oppression in which trade-unions as agencies of working class defense originated.

These children were the grandparents of the present generation of workers; it is not surprising that the European worker is "class-conscious" and suspicious of the intentions of his employer. In Europe and in Australia (and perhaps in America, too) trade-unions, very much on the defensive, will be an integral part of industrial organization for many years to come--until the traditional memory of this blot upon our history is wiped out. So long as we are content to attempt to work out our salvation by partisan feuds and factions, so long will obsession and irrationality tend to clog and hamper allegedly economic discussions. And for this period, I have no doubt the organization of workers in trade-unions will be needed to insure them against the possible concentration of power in the hands of embittered reaction.

In Europe and in Australia, the existence of trade-unions is nowadays assumed as a matter of course. The first thing that a visitor to this country notices is that here it is not so. And the second thing he notices is that the class-conscious worker, of the European variety, is very rarely encountered in the factory. To such a visitor these are very remarkable facts; they mean that in this country there **is** an opportunity, phrase it as you will, of anticipating the advent of "the great obsession." When I say this I do not mean that every right is to be conceded to employers' associations and that the unions are to be ruled out of court. In our present social condition there must be free organization amongst the workers--the Australian figures I quoted in Harper's show that any blind opposition to this only makes "unionism" stronger. What I do mean is that this country seems to have an opportunity of intelligently anticipating that dichotomy between employer and employed which vexes and has vexed Europe. Where unionism in Europe, however necessary, is often a source of instability and uncertainty, it might be made here a continuing means to stability and security. There are many instances of precisely this in the United States; you quote in your article an instance of how this may come to be.

It was with something of this in mind that I wrote the title "The Great Stupidity" above my Harper article. It was addressed primarily to the present rulers of society. Brooks Adams' contention that the revolutions of history have been due mainly to the stupidity of a ruling class echoes in everything I wrote. Obsessions in those who are ruled matter little and are soon superseded by reason if those who rule are not obsessed.

Machiavelli's sage observations upon Florentine history and the education of princes make an admirable contribution to the study of industrial organization. It does not matter whether one is considering industry under a Russian or an American regime. There must always be skilled executives set more or less in authority over working groups: this is not a political questions, it is a necessity of efficent operation. From what one hears, the Soviet is facing industrial problems of human organization entirely similar to those of England and America. And these problems cannot be solved by power or force or partisan factions, but only by improved understanding. And in this instance, I do not mean an improved mutual understanding between groups, though that is important too. I mean an improved understanding of what is actually wrong, for in any such difference of opinion there is always something wrong; and, as a general rule, neither the employer nor his employees have the least idea what the problem really is. This I hope to illustrate on a future occasion.

There is something then beyond all these questions of group organization and mutual forbearance and understanding. This something is human ignorance and the historical tendency to self-justification and obsession in a ruling class or clique. Only so far as scientific investigation is encouraged-anthropology, psychopathology and clinical physiology as well as economics--is the problem of Machiavelli's Prince likely to be solved. My article was intended to convey my impression that the United States seems to excel other countries in this respect--that it will be well if what is now a tendency becomes an explicit aim.

But I realize that my impression must be subject to correction by those who know the American situation better than I do, better than I ever shall know it. And I welcome correction that will save my comments from being extensively misunderstood.

---

[1]Bulletin of the Taylor Society, October, 1925. Reprinted from The Survey, September 15, 1925.

PURPOSE AS A PSYCHOLOGICAL FACTOR IN MANAGEMENT[1]

A Discussion of the Methods by Which an Integration of Group Purposes Can Be Effected in Industry

By Ordway Tead
Department of Industry, New York School of Social Work

This discussion, however abstract it may seem at times, has a practical intention. A wellknown industrial manager recently remarked, "Industry has been on a war basis. We must try to place it on a peace basis." It is the intention of this paper to consider what line can be followed by managers to get industry upon a basis where good-will is manifested, where cooperation between groups is willing and not enforced, where conflict is a creative and not a destructive force.

I am concerned in the first instance with the conduct of managers both because of their influence and because the activities many of them are now embarked upon indicate that they are concerned to find a better way of confronting industrial conflicts. I do not at all mean to imply that other groups have not equal responsibilities in the same direction.

Much stress has all along been laid upon technique, upon the methods and procedures of executives and of the production they direct. I am here maintaining that the purposes and motives which actuate managers in their work are as important to its true success as their methods. Only when purpose and procedure look in the same direction is the outcome fruitful. In fact, the problem of relations among the several groups in industry--and especially that between managers and the rank and file--will make little progress toward amity unless and until managers consciously strive to change conditions and methods so that the individuals in these several groups can share in and work for the same purposes. Only as the whole complex of policies and practices in industry enables these groups naturally to espouse the same objectives can the possibility of destructive conflict be avoided.

I have thus two related points to emphasize. One is that the character of the purposes of managers is vital to the effectiveness of their behavior. The other is that the purposes of managers--and of all the other groups in industry--change only as all the surrounding conditions allow and require them to change. And this process by which purposes are modified is one of the pivotal points to grasp if managerial behavior is to be affected.

In order to establish the full implications of my thesis, it is necessary to answer a number of questions:

I. What is a purpose; and what effect have purposes on conduct?

II. Where do the individual's purposes come from; and how do they come to be what they are?

III. How do group purposes differ from individual purposes?

IV. What groups participate in the conduct of industry today; and what group purposes are seen manifested in their behavior?

V. Are these group purposes in conflict; and if so,

VI. What is the possibility of establishing and giving effect to purposes which can be shared in and worked for by the different groups participating in industry?

And if there is such a possibility,--

VII. Do any principle and any method suggest themselves from this analysis which will help managers to bring to pass a greater agreement among groups or integration of group purposes in industry than exists today?

Each of these questions will be discussed in turn.

I. Purposes Defined

What is a purpose; and what effect have purposes on conduct? Purposes are of two kinds. There are those which are fundamental and permanent. There are those which are specific and more immediate. The former arise out of basic unlearned needs and desires of the individual; and the fundamental purposes of all persons are therefore qualitatively much the same. And the differences of specific purposes which are found in individuals and groups are those which the surrounding conditions have in part created and fostered. A purpose in either sense is an aim or objective which consciously or unconsciously controls behavior in its direction. A conditioning factor in all purposes is obviously the environment in which action is taking place. Purposes are never without a bearing upon and relation to the conditions at the time--they are, in fact, only intelligible in connection with them. And one element in these conditions which must never be lost sight of is the purposes of those individuals or groups by whom one is surrounded.

The specific things human beings are really striving for are often called their desires. They might also be called their purposes. Desires and purposes may or may not be known for what they are by the individual himself. Often, indeed, the account of the individual as to what he wants is rationalized rather than truly reasoned; and then one only discovers the effective purpose by examination of the kind of conduct which goes forward.

Human purposes are influential--they do direct action which has any element of choice in it. Yet they do not direct it in any independent or arbitrary way. They function in close relation to all the surrounding circumstances of the individual. And the more specific the purpose, the more likely is it to be molded and redirected by these circumstances.

The purposes which motivate human beings thus bear a close relation to the demands which individuals make upon life and to the restrictions which the whole environment puts upon those individuals. Where purposes come from and why they are what they are are thus pertinent questions for further inquiry in any discussion aiming to show the place and importance of purposes in an understanding of the behavior of managers today.

II. The Origin of Purposes

Where do purposes come from; and how do they come to be what they are? Briefly stated, purposes come from (1) the impulsion to satisfy fundamental, unlearned, human tendencies; (2) the impulsion to carry out habits which have been built up out of experience; (3) the pressure and dictation of the social environment; and (4) an imagined conception of some near or remote good which the individual has formulated or has learned and is enthusiastic about (often referred to as an ideal.)

Human beings are typically impelled to conduct along one or another of the following lines: (1) they demand a measure of economic security which means assured provision of feed, shelter and clothing, or access to the means thereto; (2) they demand the opportunity for approval at the hands of those with whom they come constantly in contact; (3) they demand opportunity for the building up of some domestic organization which is controlled more or less by affection and which provides a medium for the upbringing of children; (4) they demand that the activities upon which they are creatively engaged shall be reasonably well harmonized with their capacities, aptitudes and interests; and (5) they demand that the disposition of their leisure time be a matter of self-determination and that its content be satisfying to them.

Habits thus come to be purposes in the sense that by often-repeated experience people find that what they want very much in all sorts of directions is "more of the same." This is probably a more frequently correct explanation of human purposes and desires than any other.

Purposes come also from social pressure, in the sense that what people want to do is built up out of repeated discoveries of "what is expected of them."

And purposes come sometimes from the glamour of a new idea caught from some strong personality, from reading, from imagining some new combination of human elements in experience, that is, some "ideal!"

To ask how the individual's purposes come to be what they are is in effect to inquire what his total experience has been: that is, what has been his ability to realize upon the impulsions which make him the center of continuing activity. His purposes come to be what they are by virtue of the total complex of factors which contribute to forming his personality.

Clearly, then, from this entire discussion the idea is implicit that specific purposes do change and even the manner in which fundamental purposes seek satisfaction may also change. Bearing as they do an explicable relation to the total situation, purposes may be fluid and dynamic. Managers cannot, for example, in an impatient desire to "do something about labor relations," expect to introduce such new features as employee representation and employee stock purchase and expect them to work wonderfully while the executives still cling to the managerial purposes of ten years ago. Also, they cannot expect, having introduced them, that these procedures will leave unaltered the desires of the workers who participate in them. Moreover, experience shows that if they stay in use long enough, these procedures are bound to affect the purposes of the managers who introduce them, by leading them into experiences which are helpfully educational.

Group Purposes vs. Individual Purposes

How do group purposes differ from individual purposes? Group purposes are not different in essence from individual purposes: although there is some difference in certain qualities of the purposes. A group purpose is the desire of the members of the group to secure for themselves by acting together those conditions which will enable them to satisfy certain individual purposes which they consciously have in common. A trade association or a labor union has group purposes in the sense that each is forwarding policies and measures to assure for its members certain things which they desire.

The quality of the group's purpose is likely to be different in a number of particulars. A group tends to keep its specific purposes simpler and more "single track" than an individual. It tends to have them become more intense. And group purposes usually change more slowly than individual purposes, because of the necessity of affecting a considerable number of individuals.

Bearing in mind these qualifications, the specific purposes of a group of employers in one industry organized on trade lines or of a group of craftsmen organized into a union or of a group of foremen in one plant organized into a foremen's council tend to be understandable in the light of their surrounding limiting conditions and of their activity in carrying out their function. Each group necessarily strives for immediate ends which grow out of its own problems. The efforts of employers or of workers or of foremen on behalf of their group purposes are inevitably couched in terms of their respective interests and functional responsibilities.

But the fundamental individual purposes of the members of these several groups--desire for approval, security, creative satisfaction, domestic well-being, satisfying leisure, etc.,--remain much the same, in kind, if not in degree.

In other words, the strife of different groups for the carrying out of their several purposes arises out of certain economic and psychological relationships. The purposes of individuals in the different groups tend to remain essentially constant. Which means that if the different functional groups in industry or politics or elsewhere can possibly construct new specific group purposes of such a character as simultaneously to harmonize with the purposes of other groups, the possibility of a cooperative sentiment growing up among the members of different groups is greatly enhanced--due, of course, to the inevitability of their combining to realize the new purpose.

This truth is stressed because, although there are certain important conflicts of group purposes in economic life today, there is also, because of the possibility of integrated purposes, the likelihood of creating among all the groups participating in economic life an attitude which is, if not beyond conflict, at least partially above it.

IV. Group Purposes in Industry Today

What groups participate in the conduct of industry today; and what group purposes are seen manifested in their behavior? In popular thinking the only group alignment in industrial life is "capital and labor." This is a wholly unrealistic and over-simplified conception. Analysis reveals that there are typically, in specific situations, the following functional groups: (1) the investing group; (2) the managerial group; (3) the manual working group (sometimes sharply divided into skilled and unskilled); (4) the customer group; and (5) the general public group.

The same individuals may participate at different times in sharing the purposes and loyalties of different groups. But the fact of the integrity of different group purposes remains subject to alteration only as the environment or function of the group is modified or for other reasons new purposes are evolved.

The purposes which are typically manifested in the behavior of these groups may be safely generalized upon, if it is always remembered that there are plenty of individual exceptions to the typical case. In fact, it is these exceptions which constitute the hope of the present situation by offering suggestions as to how, by some modifications in purpose, the sentiments of groups have in certain cases been changed.

(1) Typically, the purpose of the investor is to secure as large a return on his investment as is consistent with the security of his principal. The fact seems to be, however, that the size of the typical dividend return in industry today is diminishing as the fundamental risk in the basic industries diminishes. Indeed, in a recent study, Mr. Brookings shows that the return to the investor is becoming a fairly standardized matter, except in new and experimental industries.

(2) It is ususally the purpose of managers to assure that a high yield is earned on the investment, while at the same time the plant is operated in what seems to be technically an effective manner, if this aim can be fulfilled without encountering too great resistance from foremen and workers. Where managers are also owners of stock, their purposes are to that extent made identical with those of the investors. Yet there is room for considerable modification here if they feel that the return can come to them more directly in a higher salary or if their reputation as efficient managers and successful leaders of men is also something of which they are proud. The increasing emphasis upon "professional"status in the managerial world offers, for example, a modification of the typical scheme of managerial purposes.

(3) The purposes of the manual working group are in general to secure as large a share from the enterprise as is possible, consistent with a reasonable expenditure of energy and a reasonable satisfaction to be secured out of the carrying on of the work process itself. Modification of these purposes is a fact of considerable importance in certain experiments going on today of which note will later be taken.

(4) Customers desire to secure an adequate supply of the goods they are demanding, of a sufficiently good quality and at prices which are as low as is consistent with that quality and with ready accessibility to the desired goods.

(5) The general public in its relation to industry functions largely through the administrative and regulative authorities of government bureaus. It may function occasionally through "public opinion in the press and elsewhere. But in both instances the general public is interested in being let alone and being undisturbed in the pursuit of that to which it is accustomed.

V. The Conflict of Group Purposes

Are these group purposes in conflict? Admittedly this statement of the purposes of these several groups is over-simplified. Yet its fundamental truth points to the fact that as these groups confront each other in the economic arena their purposes are in certain important respects in conflict. This conflict is both economic and psychological in origin. Economically, it grows out of the contest among functional groups over the division of a limited volume of national income. Specifically, it arises about problems of the distribution of the return from the conduct of a given business. This means, for example, problems of price, of wages and hours, of the rate of return on investments, of the extent to which surpluses shall be reinvested in the business, etc. No absolute standards are derivable which might entirely remove decisions on these points from the realm of controversy.

Psychologically, the conflict grows out of the fact that the characteristic environment and work of each group almost inevitably breeds attitudes in relation to other groups which are charged with distrust and suspicion, if not with downright antagonism.

There is a resentment between those who work with their hands and those who work with their heads; between those who manage and those who are managed; between those who secure income from investment and those who secure it from direct labor, either executive or manual.

Two practical conditions are to be seen in industry from this point of view of conflict. There are, in the first place, those companies where the aspect of conflict has been allowed to become over-emphasized. And there are, in the second place, those companies where the view is held that there is no real conflict of purposes among the several parties. Both views constitute an inadequate explanation of the real situation. The fact is that there are some interests which investors, managers and workers have very much in common; and these need to be analyzed, stated and emphasized. Constant emphasis and dwelling upon the aspect of day-by-day conflict among the groups is neither wise nor productive. The difficulty is, however, one of emphasis, which can be corrected, especially if the basis of a sound, cooperative, working relationship is understood.

The view that there is no conflict seems to grow out of reluctance to admit the existence of conflict. The idea is "viewed with alarm" because it is feared that conflict may imply violence in conflict, or because of a sincere conviction that conflict is immoral. The notion that this conflict of purposes can become what Miss Follett has called a "creative conflict" and be the means--in fact, the only means--to the evolving of purposes which can be shared is a view which is thus far unappreciated by those to whom the conflict notion is repugnant.

Alternatives to Conflict

An interesting question to raise at this stage of the discussion is: What are the alternatives to admitting the necessary permanence of the element of conflict in industrial life? Miss Follett wisely points out that there are four:

1. The element of conflict can be ignored.
2. It can be denied.
3. It can be assumed that a temporary balancing of interest is all that can be obtained.
4. There can be a successful effort made to create a new working basis which is not a balancing but a sharing and harmonizing of purposes.

Of these four alternatives, only the last two require further discussion. One objection to urging the balance-of-interests view is that it presupposes the existence of a reasonable degree of equality of power on the part of the groups evolved. This equality, however, is not usually achieved in industrial life today. In consequence, attempts to work on the balance-of-interest basis involve some few cases where equilibrium is attained for temporary periods, but many more cases where one or another group is so much superior in power to the others that the basis used for urging settlements is fundamentally a power basis. And from a psychological point of view, the power basis in dealing with adults in another group is not permanently an effective basis.

Consideration of the fourth alternative will take place in connection with the answer to question VI.

Managerial Motives Reviewed:

Before attempting to answer this next major question, it is worth while to particularize a little more about the motive seen in control of the operation of present-day corporations. Even though it is realized that there are different groups involved in carrying on corporate activity, it still is usually assumed that the corporation's aim, especially as exemplified by stockholders and managers, is single, namely, profit-making. And if this is the case, it is easy to see how, economically speaking, customers and manual workers would be in conflict with this purpose.

Such a description of motives is unduly simplified, as a more careful examination of the facts bears out. This problem can best be approached by first raising the question as to why there is economic activity at all. The popular answer is that economic activity takes place because of the desire for profit. The realistic answer is that economic activity takes place also and basically because of the pressure of necessity. Economic activity is today normally a characteristic of people in temperate climates, because they must anticipate their needs for food, shelter and clothing. They are under the necessity of extracting a living from a reluctant and not too bountiful nature. And a true account of the case is that most people work because they have to in order to survive. It is probably further true that human beings in temperate climates derive considerable satisfaction from many of the activities which are typically associated with the conduct of the economic life. The demand for activity as such, both physical and mental, is a dominant characteristic of human beings and much of this satisfaction in sheer activity unquestionably carries over into the economic sphere. People are not only active in industry because they have to be, but because they get considerable satisfaction out of the activity as such.

Examination of particular situations reveals a further interesting variety of motives. It is understood, of course, that profits are, as matters stand, a pragmatic test of economic solvency and commercial utility of an enterprise. Practically speaking, profits are today the accredited device for measuring economic utility; and in the absence of any other universally accepted measure, they have to be reckoned with. But that they supply managers with their sole motive for activity in business would be true in almost no case. And one can find plenty of corporations where profits are thought of as one necessary condition of operation, but not only test of managerial success. A good example of the fact that the profit motive is not inherent in the order of things, but is established by social convention, is seen when one views the purposes at work in the management of public utility corporations, where dividend rates are in effect limited by government.

Profit motivation is, of course, absent also in various economic activities which are governmentally owned and operated.

There are also other corporations not in the two groups mentioned above in which other motives complicate the picture. There are, for example, plenty of managers who are obsessed and controlled by the desire for mere size in business, anxious to build up a volume of business which shall be greater than any other. There are others in which the pugnacious disposition to oust competitors and win out in a fight for markets is a controlling consideration. There are still others where a desire for a serviceable output and the sense of creative accomplishment find outlet through business development. There are plenty of managers who are proud of the traditions of their organization, proud of their trademark, anxious to be known as dispensers of a quality product at a reasonable price.

There is an increasing number of cases, too, where managers take pride, even at the expense of immediate profits, in the goodwill of the employees of the organization, and take pride in fostering in them by practical means a genuine feeling of their essential partnership in the conduct of the enterprise.

Unquestionably, some or all of these as well as numerous other purposes mingle in a bewildering complex in the motivation of managers.

One difficulty has been that the business man has been told so often by the classical economists that he is "in business to make money," that he has himself tended to take this statement as a complete account of the truth about his purposes.

Yet the situation that is disclosed on the managerial side is one where purposes are really plural rather than single, and are likely to be in flux rather than fixed and static. Indeed, before going on to answer the next question, it is of importance to consider why it is in general that purposes change and how they change.

Why and How Purposes Change

Managerial purposes are in practice seen to change for many reasons, of which the following are illustrative:

First: The manager runs into real difficulty and is forced to cast around for some new method of securing his ends. He is likely to find in the course of following a new method that he is also gradually revealing to himself a new purpose. All sorts of illustrations of this simple truth are at hand. A manager believes unit costs in a department are excessive, due to the lack of an incentive method of payment. He decides to change from week work to piece work. The workers in the department make their objections to this change effective by walking out as a body on strike. Perhaps the foremen suggests that if he had taken the matter up with the department in advance and explained that no real reduction in wages was contemplated but rather the opposite, no strike would have taken place. This leads the manager to consider whether he should have some definite method of conference with employees. And thus a purpose of lowering unit costs has become a purpose of improving conference methods with employees.

Second: Change in purposes may be due to the pressure of stockholders.

Third: The pressure of public opinion may bring managers to change their purposes as is true in some cases of employers who have a definite policy to pay a wage equal to the legal minimum wage in other industries, although their own industry may not come under such a legal regulation.

Fourth: Purposes are changed by what someone has well called the "prestige motive." If a manager finds he is playing golf with associates who take pride in a liberal labor policy, for example, his desire for prestige with his associates may lead him to bethink himself of measures in a similar direction.

Fifth: Purposes may change because of the prompting of new desires born of boredom with old desires or started by the acceptance of new ideas acquired from other people or from reading. The active experience of initiating new policies and methods growing our of the willingness to try out new ideas brings with it the actual change of purpose.

In other words, a purpose is not an actuality until it has really affected one's behavior. The actual grip of motor experience upon the individual is the only method by which purposes are changed, for only thus are they wrought into the fabric of the individual rather than being held merely as an opinion.

Indeed, in many cases, the new experience is that which creates the new purpose. As one writer puts it, "On a basis of what has been already experienced, things are desired; on the basis of what has been desired and experienced, new things become desired. This extension and growth of desire take place through the influence of similarity and analogy.

The experience of a considerable number of corporations with safety committees of their employees well illustrates this point. A few years ago many plants undertook to cut down their accident load by appointing safety committees of their employees as points of contact through whom education and preventive work was to be done on the safety question. The purpose of the managers was to reduce accidents. But they soon found that they were discussing notonly accidents and contributory causes with the employee groups, but other common problems. The committee idea was thus naturally extended to the consideration of general grievances and shop problems. From this it was a natural step to the creation of a shop committee which was elected departmentally rather than appointed. Meanwhile the purposes of the managers had come a long way from the initial aim of accident prevention.

Another example is that of a well-known plant in which the managers believed that the inclusion of a certain few key employees in an employee stock-ownership arrangement would be beneficial to company morale. This company had a shop committee which eventually requested the extension of the plan to make all employees eligible. The request was granted. In the course of several years of experience the purposes of the managers as to the holding of stock employees was considerably changed and broadened.

In short, specific purposes do change and evolve, and the manner in which fundamental purposes manifest themselves can be substantially modified. Because people have minds and reflect on experience, and even more because external conditions modify, redirect and restrict experience, their purposes _must_ change. There is an innate craving in human beings for economy in the choice of means to fulfill desires as well as in the choice of desires which can be fulfilled. Purposes, because they help to control activity, help to alter situations and surroundings; and these, in turn, help to re-shape purposes. Thus it is that there exists for human groups which are in conflict the possibility of "integration"--of evolving new purposes to which different groups can subscribe, and in striving for which the genuine desires of all will be realized.

This brings the discussion to a point where it is possible to attempt to answer the next questions:

The Integration of Purposes

What is the possibility of establishing and giving effect to purposes which can be shared in and worked for by the different groups participating in industry? The first answer to this question is that there are already some purposes which can and are being shared in and might be shared in more fully by the groups in industry if they had a full appreciation of the oneness of their interest on these particular matters. A good example here is that of accident prevention work within industry, which, by the creation and introduction of the device of Workmen's Compensation has made it to the definite interest of all groups to work for the lessening of the accident rate. By the simple device of putting upon the employer the burden of paying the premium on accident insurance, efforts at accident reduction have been made a real purpose of managers and investors no less than of the manual workers, because of the possibility of reducing the premium with the reduced accident rate.

Another example is the common interest of investors, managers, and manual workers in a proper program of training within the factory or store. As soon as the management understands that it is common experience for plants which have such a program to cut down the length of the training time by half, to cut down the wear and tear on equipment, the amount of spoiled work, etc., they realize that it is a valid purpose for them to introduce a training procedure. Such a training procedure is highly desirable also from the employee's point of view, since it enables him more quickly to attain a maximum earning power, it shortens the period of awkward inefficiency, it enables him to carry on his work in the least fatiguing and most acceptable way.

These are examples of matters regarding which the same purposes are shared by different groups just as soon as the value of the purpose is clearly realized.

The real problem, however, is in regard to issues where such a commonalty of interest does not seem so obvious. Take, for example, the question of the possibility of employees becoming interested in high productivity at low unit cost. It would seem that the only attempt to make the employees adopt this purpose which has any likelihood of being successful is one in which all the contributing conditions make the employees realize that they have more to gain than to lose by working harder.

They have more to gain than to lose if they earn enough more, if they are not over-fatigued, if they do not more quickly work themselves out of a job, if they can share in the greater gain accruing in profits, if their sense of accomplishment is enhanced, etc. Any plan which will give them assurances on these points has a good chance of their accepting it.

In practice, this realization is actually being obtained by a combination of methods. (1) Some type of incentive payment method is adopted either with or without some differential piece rate under which the employees' rate increases both relatively and absolutely as the productivity increases and as unit costs decrease. (2) Some assurance of regular work or regular income is given so that the employees will not feel that by working hard they are working themselves out of employment. (3) Another requisite is assurance that there will be no rate-cutting unless the character of the job is radically altered.

Given these several procedures for protecting the employees, it has been found possible to bring employees into agreement with the management's purpose of increased productivity. If, however, the employees come with their new experience, to the point of making a careful analysis of the entire economic situation of the company which employs them, they may find that despite all these provisions there is still a rate of profit being made for the stockholders which seems to them unduly high. If, and when, employees feel that by the outlay of their energy on behalf of productivity, even if it is relatively well repaid, they are making unduly large profits for managers and investors, it may still be hard to retain their cooperation--that is, hard to get them to adopt the purposes of these other groups.

Indeed, it is in part because of a sense that such a questioning feeling may possibly arise among employees that certain companies have been led to experiment with the method of stock sale to employees or with profit sharing. Both of these devices aim by the use of somewhat different legal means to effect an identical psychological result, namely: --to make it worth the employees' while to interest themselves in the creation of profits, because they are in turn to be sharers of them.

Another possible step in the employees' experience with an extension of knowledge and power in shop affairs would be (and is already in a few companies) a desire to share in decisions about the major policies of the company because of a realization that such decisions must inevitably affect their group destinies more or less directly. If the logic or pressure of this purpose leads a company to allow the election of one or two employee members to the Board of Directors, this may constitute another step in the direction of integrating and harmonizing purposes. For once a corporation has, for example, a shop committee with some power, an incentive payment plan which is felt to be fair, guaranteed employment or compensation, a sharing of profits by employees through a substantial minority stock ownership, a sharing of ultimate direction by employees,--the result will be that the employees are in a position where they may naturally share in forwarding the same purposes as the investors and managers to a degree which would not today be possible or be safe.

What happens however is not, strictly speaking, that the employees adopt the purposes of investors or managers. For these two groups have at the same time had to modify _their_ typical purposes in order to bring the employees into working agreement. They have had to modify desires to the extent of letting the employees in on a share of the profits, of paying them during periods of idleness, of giving them information heretofore considered confidential, etc. The result is a new purpose or set of purposes satisfactory to all concerned. And they pr ve satisfactory because in the process of experience each group has found the old purposes inadequate to give them what they find they want, and has found that a modification in purpose is not as bad as it might theoretically have seemed to be in advance,--is, indeed, when experience shows it in its true light, desirable and satisfying. And one of the elements in the experience of showing it to be satisfactory is the realization that the purposes of the other groups are also changing.

Whether or not, under the conditions outlined above, the customers and the general public can be in harmony with the shared purposes of these other three groups constitutes at present a real question. And the creating of conditions under which they will share purposes with the three is going to require a good deal of inventive thinking. Much depends on the direction in which the new common purposes of investors, managers and workers become modified. If they virtually conspire in a given case to raise dividends, salaries and wages and take it out of the public in high prices or shoddy goods, there is no possibility of a further integration of such purposes with customers. But if the combined desires of the three primary agents in production look toward rendering public service consciously and willingly on reasonable terms, they will find consumers and everyone else sharing their purpose.

Most emphatically, it is not to be understood that the examples of devices which have been used to illustrate attempts to reconcile the purposes of different groups are here being completely endorsed or recommended as anything like panaceas. They are rather given as illustrations of attempts more or less successful to carry into practice a principle which it is the thesis of this discussion to support and advance for practical application in whatever ways inventive managerial minds can hit upon; the thesis, namely, that the sharing and harmonizing of purposes by managers and workers requires the creation of attendant conditions and terms in a setting where the growth of everyone's purposes is a natural result of the whole experience.

There has been, in short, some slight measure of success already attained in a certain few companies in establishing and giving effect to purposes which can be shared in and worked for by the different groups in industry--or at least, some of them. And it is not difficult to project out of modern tendencies a conception of an industrial republic (of producers) in which our usual notions of democratic organizations have been put into effect and have been reconciled in practice with claims of efficiency, economy and productivity.

This brings the discussion to a point where it seems possible to answer the final question.

A Constructive Principle

Do any principle and any method suggest themselves from this analysis which will help managers to bring to pass a greater integration of the several group purposes in industry than exists today? The answer to this question seems to be in the affirmative. Methods are available, and new ones will undoubtedly be devised, which will create a situation in industrial and mercantile corporations, and perhaps in whole industries, where it will be to the definite interest of different groups to espouse purposes which they could not safely espouse before. These may be purposes of productivity, of profit, of public service, or of some other sort. Considerations of the relative social validity of the different types of purpose is not here in place, although it is probably true that whatever purposes are found to secure simultancously the adherence of the largest number of the affected groups will be socially the most valid.

One important principle is that group purposes cannot be changed solely by exhortation or by appeals to the intellect. Purposes change only in the process of active experience. How the change gets its start has already been shown. It is by the impact of actual events into which the individual or group is more or less inevitably thrust. Let one unsettling suggestion regarding present purposes enter, or one failure to achieve present purposes occur, and a new experience follows, activity is at once either tending to confirm or to deny the validity of some already tentatively influential new purpose. Experience has already tended to suggest a purpose which is more tenable and likely of fulfillment.

A vital corollary of this truth is that individuals or groups do not accept the purposes of others ready-made. One writer has wisely pointed out that for specific purposes to be fully apprehended one must have a share in accepting them as well as in deriving ways and means of realizing them. This should really be axiomatic, since purposes which are taken over and given only intellectual assent have not come through the vivid and vital channel of motor experience, and thus have not the living quality which is necessary to make them influential in conduct. The process of sharing in the formulation of a purpose and in inventing the means of realizing it provides a strong psychological presumption in favor of having it continue to influence action. This fact gives support to the case for the use of the so-called "democratic method" of conducting organizations in a way which can only be mentioned here.

The definite principle to be evoked as the outgrowth of this study is that where the purposes of groups are in conflict, the only way to secure a basis of genuine cooperative activity is to modify the purposes in the direction of others which are acceptable to the several groups; and this modification can come about only by the invention and use of methods and procedures which allow the groups using them clearly to benefit from them and thus to change their purposes.

This principle may not at first glance seem either very illuminating or very valuable. Yet it calls attention to three homely truths about the industrial problem which merit emphasis and which need all the scientific re-enforcement they can get. It calls attention, first, to the impossibility of getting far with industrial peace while the purposes and desires of groups are at odds, limited, narrowly construed, ingrown. Second, it emphasizes the necessity of using the occurance of problem or difficulty as the psychological time to inject new ideas and methods. And third, it calls attention to the necessity for courageous experiment and new insight in the direction of methods and structural arrangements which will be the outward condition and channel for allowing people to manifest goodwill and generous purposes without being imposed upon or exploited in the process.

[1] *Bulletin of the Taylor Society*, December, 1925. Paper presented at a meeting of the Taylor Society, New York, December 4, 1925.

MANAGEMENT'S CONCERN IN RESEARCH[1]

As an Aid in Establishing Operating Procedures, in Making Managerial Decisions, and in Developing a Science of Management

By H. S. Person
Managing Director, The Taylor Society

At discreet intervals I take the liberty of injecting myself into the program of a meeting of this society for the purpose of fulfilling what I conceive to be an official duty; namely, to give the report of a scouting expedition into territory with which management is vitally concerned and into which most of our members are unable to make personal excursions because of the exacting demands of their executive responsibilities. The territory on which I desire to report today is that of research insofar as it concerns management; its importance to management and its methods. The research and the methods to which I shall refer especially are those of the social sciences. The methods of the physical sciences with which management is concerned are well established and well understood, but the methods of the social sciences with which management is now more critically concerned, are not so well established and well understood. And insofar as management is concerned with human beings individually or in groups as consumers and as producers of goods and services, it is a social science.

Research as an Aid to Practical Management

We may feel confident that no one who has had extensive experience in management, or has made serious study of it, will question the value of research to the responsible executive of these days. Therefore our attention to that phase of this report should be primarily for completeness of the record and may be in the form of propositions.

1. Management involves problems relative to purposes, policies, programs, projects, plans and procedures; decisions are made by rational consideration of pertinent facts; the validity of a decision depends not only upon the soundness of the rational considerations, but also upon the completeness and accuracy of the facts.

2. The development of a complicated industrial organization has generated problems of management which are critical, perplexing and exacting in their demands for rational determination on the basis of facts which are numerous, and difficult of ascertainment and valuation.

3. The range of facts required by management in making its decisions is indicated by the following classifications: Facts relating to--

a. Materials: their fabrication and consumer uses.
b. Progress of the arts employed in industry.
c. Organization for and direction of transformative and distributive processes.
d. Human individual and group reactions to organization and direction procedures and relationships.

e. Consumer demand, and the general and particular markets.
f. Industrial tendencies pertinent to long-run planning of policies and programs.
g. Environmental influences such as social customs, government regulation and international relations.

4. It is a large undertaking to procure facts of such a range, and after they are procured the processes of analyzing and evaluating them are complicated. They cannot adequately be procured and evaluated in a casual way, or even in an organized way, by those engaged in executive activities. To meet this situation research organizations to serve executives have come into existence; research units of individual business organizations, cooperative research organizations serving groups of enterprises, independent research organizations equipped to serve industry in a professional capacity, and research units of educational institutions designed to serve industry as well as to train young men in research technique.

5. The conclusion is inescapable that research has become an important function in management, that it is a responsibility of management to stimulate, support and utilize it, and that, for wise utilization, management should keep itself informed concerning undertakings, contributions and methods of research.

Research as an Aid to the Development of a Science of Management

This complexity of the industrial organization, and the consequent complexity of problems of management, has inspired efforts towards what is essentially standardization of elements of the managerial situation of far-reaching importance. In increasing number, enterprises are defining purposes, which is a standardization of objectives; defining policies, which is a standardization of general methods of achieving objectives; and formulating procedures, which is a standardization of particular methods of achievement; the underlying purpose of these efforts being to substitute constants for as many as possible of the variable elements in a managerial situation. Likewise industry as a whole (and this is the significance of the management movement) is attempting to define universally applicable policies and procedures, or at least discover universally applicable methods of defining these in any particular situation; and to this end it is searching for a body of underlying principles, a set of standards, a science of management. Furthermore, recognizing that progress is but a continuing adjustment to an ever changing environment, and that there will always be in industry as a whole and in each particular managerial situation, new elements and new problems, management is striving for principles and methods of solving this succession of variable problems with promptness and with maximum probability of accuracy.

It is inconceivable that progress in this direction can be substantial unless industry recognizes research as one of its functions, and has as much concern in research--its nature and its methods--as in any science or art in which management now has concern. It is for this reason that the Taylor Society inaugurates today a series of sessions on methods and instruments of research.

The Evolution of a Science of Management

Assuming that we do have the beginnings of a science of management, this embryonic science will undoubtedly involve through those stages which, with variations, have been common to the established physical and social sciences. In striking respects the social task of "thinking out" a science is analogous to the individual task of "thinking out" a solution of an individual problem. Either process may be indicated crudely as follows:

I. a. Imagination, or more likely, uncertainty about what action to take in a concrete situation, creates a problem. This establishes the necessity of examining the pertinent facts for the purpose of deriving a conclusion or making a decision; which stimulates--

I. b. Inductive reasoning, or analysis of the facts, which yields general conclusions concerning the facts. The application of these general conclusions to the particular problem, by using them as premises in a process of deductive reasoning, results in--

I. c. Formulation of alternative conclusions or decisions, no one of which is satisfactory because it does not solve every phase of the problem. The most satisfying of these conclusions is adopted as the basis for immediate action; the others stimulate the beginning of a new cycle, as follows--

2. a. Redefinition of the problem, including active exercise of the imagination, and the accumulation of additional pertinent facts; which stimulate--

2. b. Analysis of the more complete facts and derivation of more substantial general conclusions. Deductive application to the problem of these more substantial premises results in--

2. c. Formulation of more positive conclusions or decisions. But new experience discloses the inadequacy of these conclusions or decisions, which stimulates the beginning of a new cycle, as follows:

3. a. Further redefinition of the problem, aided by imagination, and refinement and extension of methods of accumulating additional pertinent facts; which stimulate--

3. b. More intensive and fruitful process of inductive reasoning; more rigid deductive reasoning from more stable premises afforded by the more abundant facts; which stimulates--

3. c. Formulation of conclusions or decisions in the nature of formulae concerning relationships of coincidence, sequence, relative frequency, or cause and effect; the beginnings of a science which permits formulation of standard and dependable procedures in the arts governed by the science.

But new experience, the discovery of new facts, causes questioning of formulated principles, or at least of their completeness, and stimulates the beginning of a new cycle; and so on *ad infinitum*.

It should be realized that this picture of the total process of "thinking out" a problem or a science is artificial in that the elements of the process in actual experience are not so separable. The whole should be conceived as a shuttle motion back and forth between facts and conclusions, of such rapidity that inductive and deductive reasoning become but different aspects of the same integral process.

Students of method are generally agreed that the evolutionary development of method in the several sciences has proceeded, with variations, through these stages:

1. The Deductive Stage: in which emphasis is on the processes of reasoning from facts and not on the quality, quantity or methods of securing of the basic facts;

2. The Qualitative Stage: in which emphasis continues to be on deductive reasoning, but in which attention is given to securing a greater quantity of facts and especially to defining and classifying their characteristics:

3. The Experimental and Quantitative Stage: in which deductive reasoning continues to be the essential final step in the solution of a problem, but in which emphasis is placed on observation of facts under controlled conditions and on analysis and comparison of large quantities of facts.

It is to be observed that in these brief and inadequate statements concerning the development of scientific method, three elements have appeared and reappeared--the accumulation and analysis of facts, imagination, and deductive reasoning. Because imagination can and so frequently does deceive and mislead as by pretending that the results of its processes are established facts or conclusions, we are inclined to underestimate its importance. Because deductive reasoning was highly developed early in our culture, we have become so accustomed to it as to forget its significance. That which we are now inclined to emphasize, because its technique is being enriched every day, is the importance of the processes of accumulating and measuring facts. And it is with this that I am principally concerned in this paper. To be complete and impartial, however, I desire in passing to say a word about imagination and deductive reasoning.

Imagination and Deductive Reasoning

Imagination is one of the outstanding forces in the development of a science. It may play us false when it presumes to tell us what the facts of a case *are*, but it is a great constructive force when it tells us what undiscovered facts there *may be*--what to search for in the wilderness of the unknown. This must have come home to those of you who have read Pupin's autobiography. He speaks with authority on the origin of the electromagnetic theory of light and matter, which has in our day revolutionized the physical sciences. Faraday, stimulated by experiments in his simple laboratory, dreamed about it; Maxwell, the mathematician, the deductive reasoner, proved it must be so; Hertz in his laboratory proved that it is so. Says Pupin: "The general development of this view was due to the gradual development of new physical concepts which were born in Faraday's mind and existed there in a poetical vision;. . . In every creative physicist there is hidden a metaphysicist and a poet. . ."

No industrial organization is complete which does not include one or more dreamer of dreams to originate problems for its research group; no science of management can ever develop without the contributions of those who dream about the management of the future. But these dreamers must know what are dreams and what are facts; they must have that quality of which Pupin says: ". . . in spite of his wonderful imagination and his free use of it, no investigator ever succeeded better than Faraday in drawing a sharp line of division between the new facts and principles which he had discovered and the visions which his imagination saw in the still unexplored background of his discoveries."

Deductive reasoning is the element of total process immediately preceding a conclusion or solution. This method is as all-pervading and essential as is the air we breathe. Facts receive a practical value by treatment in the crucible of deductive logic. Because on occasion its premises or its processes may be wrong is no fault of this process; it is the fault of the user. We should not forget that it is essential, and that is has made some of the greatest contributions to science. Maxwell's contribution to the electromagnetic theory, to which reference has been made, was a _tour de force_ of deductive reasoning in mathematical form; the Einstein theory is also a _tour de force_ of similar deductive reasoning. The scientific world is this year honoring the fiftieth anniversary of the publication of a treatise by Josiah Willard Gibbs, of Yale University, which made thermodynamic chemistry an exact science. "Without his work many phases of modern industry might still be groping experimentally, trying to discuss laws which he set down before they began"--another gigantic contribution of deductive reasoning. In the field of management Taylor's imagination stimulated a line of investigation in which inductive and deductive reasoning by Carl Barth gave us formulae that put the art of cutting metals on a scientific basis and made these readily available through a slide rule in practicing the art.

No industrial organization is complete which does not possess the genius correctly to apply deductive reasoning to the facts of management which are discovered, to make decisions governing actions with the highest probability of success, and to map out lines of investigation with high probability of important discoveries. This is an important function of committees.

The Search and the Re-Search for Facts

In all the sciences utilized by management, particularly in the social sciences and in the science of management itself, the outstanding achievement of recent years has been improvement of the technique of finding and measuring facts. Interest and discussion have been focused on this first important element of the total process of arriving at a decision or solution, rather than the succeeding elements of the total process.

Before there is conscious and highly organized effort to ascertain and measure facts, data are made available by casual observation in experience, and in time of special need by deliberate, conscious observation and by drawing on the intuitions of wise and experienced authorities. Casual observation is unquestionably the most elementary of fact-finding methods, but intuition, which sums up a mass of subconscious casually observed facts, is of great value. It is sometimes indispensable, for intuition frequently discloses master facts, or generalizations from facts of personal experience, which elude capture and measurement by a fact-finding technique and yet may give the key to the solution of a problem. These intuitions may be of service on the one hand by suggesting research for facts by developed techniques, or on the

the other hand, after scientific methods have made their contributions, by stimulating analysis and appraisal along lines which solve the problem.

The qualitative method also is not obsolete. It will always be important. There is no controversy between qualitative and quantitative methods. In fact the qualitative method is essential to the quantitative method. What does the quantitative method count and measure. Try to determine that what without the qualitative method! And after the quantitative method has counted and measured, it is frequently discovered that it has not done so without some uncertainties, and it is with respect to these uncertainties that the qualitative method may again step in and give the key to the solution of a problem.

But it must be emphasized that the quantitative method--the statistical method--is the great achievement of method in the social sciences in recent years. Our sociological and industrial literature is full of it, and its nature and uses are familiar to most executives. It was a great discovery that facts of nature--inanimate and animate--have systematic relationships which may be measured; that these measurements disclose "master facts" not apparent to casual observation--norms, trends, relationships of frequency, coincidence and sequence. Most of the recent progress that has been made in psychology, economics and sociology, in perfecting methods of education, in treating mental and moral defectives, in measuring price trends and relationships, in analyzing consumption and markets, in forecasting industrial tendencies, in establishing budgets and other standards of control, is to be credited to the method of quantitative measurement. However, notwithstanding its importance, in fact because it is so well known and so highly valued, I desire to turn our attention to its principal limitations, which are usually not kept sufficiently in mind.

Limitations of the Quantitative Method

I. The regard for quantity in many instances compels a practical (although not necessarily an intellectual) disregard for exactness of quality, and results in the setting up of more or less unreal units of observation and measurement. A basic assumption of quantitative measurement is that units of a counted and measured group are homogeneous, but many phenomena appear in continuous rather than discrete variation and refuse to conform to that assumption. Furthermore, problems are defined and their factors defined as our conceptions, attitudes and habits discover them. What is a farm; work animal; capital; income; depreciation; surplus; dollar; building; machine; tool; expense addition to capital; raw material; worked material; tubercular victim; criminal; residence; factory building; and so on? The most critical step in a statistical investigation in the social sciences and one of the most difficult, is definition of the unit of observation; and an equally practical difficulty is getting the observed units listed--included or rejected--accurately with respect to the definition. Even those units which we regard as exact--dollars, pounds, feet--may not have great value in the solution of a problem except as they relate to associated qualities which cannot be included in the measurement.

2. Although the method of quantitative measurement reveals facts of relationship such as relative frequency, coincidence and sequence, it is only in exceptional instances, and then not without doubt, that it reveals relationships of cause and effect. Statisticians appear now to place less value on the method of partial correlation than formerly; it is highly suggestive and indicates lines of further investigation, but only when the correlation is very, very high is it regarded as indicative of any dependable cause and effect relationship.

3. Another limitation of the method under discussion is that it is not yet able to measure the data of a problem which are contributed by consciousness, by individuals as original and independent sources of energy, by individual and group "interests." Individuality implies heterogeneity of units. Measurements of this kind are vital in problems involving explanation, prediction and control in the field of managerial activity. For instance, we can after a fashion quantitatively measure the labor turnover in an organization, but we cannot yet measure the emotional stimuli and reactions which are the causes of the turnover. There are intimate and vital controlling facts of managerial relationship beyond the reach of any existing technique of quantitative measurement.

4. Furthermore, a statistical solution is always the determination of a definite, detail question of fact, which is but a fraction of an integral managerial problem. We must remember that it is a process of fact finding, of "master fact" finding. A statistical investigation is a definite, restricted, laborious, time-consuming process. As executive one is confronted by a problem and one requests a statistical staff to ascertain facts within the scope of their technique. But those are not all the facts involved in making a decision. And in the meantime the problem grows with the passing of time, and the quantity and variety of pertinent facts increases. The statiticians contribute their findings, but these are but part of the data from which conclusions must be drawn and on which decisions are based. A science is so vast that total solution by methods of quantitative analysis of specific detail problems is inconceivable.

5. Finally, in the present state of the science and the art of quantitative measurement generally only those phenomena of conduct are quantitatively measurable which represent mass or group habits more or less rigidly fixed. The most magnificent achievements of quantitative measurement have been in the fields of astronomy and biology. Day by day, year by year, century by century each star of a universe of stars runs its appointed course, and measurements made in 1850 will hold good, except for the human errors involved, in 1950. Therefore, we can keep time and predict eclipses to the second. Anatomical and physiological characteristics of species are mass habits which change by such small increments that apparently they do not change. The modal length and the dispersion about the norm of the English sparrow will probably be the same in 1956 as in 1926. There are certain human mass habits having a biological basis--marriages, births and deaths--which change sufficiently slowly to permit valuable statistical measurements. Even mass habits relating to economic activity are profitably measurable, as is evidenced by barometric indexes. Yet here we get on less certain ground, for a sufficient number of mass economic habits, relatively stabilized during a period of relatively stable environmental influence before the war, are

now unstable. Some of the formulae resulting from quantitative measurements made before 1914 are now in doubt.

Management is largely concerned with human conduct and, we are beginning to realize, with elements of conduct of which there is great variability among individuals. We may be able to assume for instance that there will be some sort of standard mass habit reaction to wage payments, but may we continue to assume that the reaction is the same for all classes of wage recipients? We may assume, and we may eventually measure quantitatively, a mass habit reaction to non-financial incentives, but may we assume that all classes of workers react in the same manner or at all? Many critical problems of management are concerned with individual reactions, or group reactions of numerous groups, to stimuli of the managerial environment, and to resolve these we must add to the rich results of quantitative measurement equally rich results of other methods of research.

Other Methods of Research in Management

In the physical sciences investigators are imaginative and bold. Investigators should be not less bold and imaginative in the social sciences--and in the development of a science of management. Too frequently scientists concerned with the industrial field hesitate to attack many important problems for fear the results will not be definitive as results and as tests of method, with the outcome that they are inclined to neglect the difficult and attack the easy problems. Some one has said that to discover incomplete information about an important matter is a greater service than to secure complete information about an unimportant matter. It is quite possible to carry along side by side researches which yield their important results by testing and validating methods, and researches which yield important results in new although incomplete information. If scientists will indicate a willingness to attack some of the difficult problems of management for which there is not as yet an adequate research technique, if they will utilize methods not yet perfected and perfect them by use, if they will conceive, experiment with and validate new methods, it is probable that industry will respond by offering the necessary facilities. It is true that industry also must be more imaginative and bolder than it now is, but the scientists should take the lead. In the matter of research industry cannot be expected to respond to experts who are timid and doubtful. There was no timidity about Taylor when he attacked the problem of measuring a day's work--even his brother engineers declared it could not be done. The results of this boldness have been enormous in practical results and in influence on industry's mental attitude towards scientific investigation of problems of management.

There are four methods of research which I should like to see utilized more in investigations of problems of management. One, if we may call it a method, is the reconnoissance. Men of affairs, business as well as military leaders, value exploratory investigations. More investigations of a thorough nature would find support and be undertaken were their probable value pre-determined by reconnoissances. Reconnoissance, in fact, pertains to determination and definition of the imagined problem.

The second, if we may for convenience also call this a method, is that of the clinic. The clinic is in principle much like the reconnoissance; the former is a preliminary investigation of a problem restricted in scope; the latter is a preliminary investigation of a problem extended in scope. The clinic explores a problem pertaining to an individual or a small group of individuals such as the reason for low morale and low production in a spinning room, and may lead to dependable investigation of the experimental order; the reconnoissance explores a problem of social nature, such as the reasons for labor unrest in an entire industry, and may prepare the way for an intensive quantitative investigation. It is quite possible that there could be established in an industrial plant something with the essential characteristics of the clinic of a hospital, but without the latter's formal organization and equipment. Has not every executive who maintains "a close personal contact with his workers" established an embryo clinic?

Another method is the interview, which will secure attention in the paper to follow, by Miss Van Kleeck. It is a method which has not been adequately tested, perfected and validated. It should be, for it is the best method available for discovering a certain class of important facts--those relating to mental and emotional reactions to managerial stimuli. Achievements of the interview method in psychiatry, and the similarity to or identity of its problems with many crucial problems of management, justify a plea for its more serious use in management research.

The fourth method which I have in mind is the experimental method. It has been highly developed in the physical sciences and in academic psychology. The method should be utilized in industrial plants in study of problems of management. We have heretofore limited our quantitative researches pretty much to investigations of chance conduct. This throws light on what we as industrial cooperators have come to be under the influence of uncontrolled environmental forces. We should experimentally vary our managerial environment and under controlled conditions record and measure the consequences. This might throw light on what we can make ourselves come to be as industrial cooperators under the influence of controlled environmental forces. It may be that we can make ourselves masters of our managerial fates. For, while we are undoubtedly individual and group bundles of fixed habit patterns, there is apparently a section of each bundle in which the habits are plastic rather than fixed, and may be susceptible to molding influences. Many a time when some new procedure is advocated by an executive, his associates will exclaim that it cannot be done--"it is contrary to human nature." A decision to try it out proves that it can be done. Too much had been assumed concerning human nature. I feel that utilization of the experimental method in investigation of managerial problems would yield rich results.

How Industry May Cooperate

This paper has been addressed primarily to industrial executives. It may be that some are convinced of the necessity of promoting research in industry, may desire to meet their responsibility in the matter, and may ask in what practical ways it can be done. I shall in conclusion answer this question briefly and sufficiently for our purpose.

1. Firm histories or logs, would be an important contribution. Such records would have to be very carefully devised, and professional assistance should be utilized in devising them. In the large they would consist of statistical data and of data concerning policies, plans, programs, procedures, and so on, including reasons--the genuine reasons--for decisions. Such logs would after a period of years constitute a great reservoir of valuable information.

2. The trade associations of the various industries might well keep, to the great profit of industry, histories, or logs, of the respective industries. Whereas the firm log would emphasize internal experience of a particular firm, the trade log would emphasize experience common to all the firms of the trade, including general industrial conditions affecting the industry.

3. Many a firm might profitably establish a research unit, a functionalized individual or department within the organization, commanding the resources of scientific method and continually engaged in investigation of problems of management as they are perceived by the executives. The logs and results of firm researches should be available as a social service to investigators of repute and dependability.

4. Groups of firms may cooperate in research concerned with common problems. The research may be planned and supervised, and with respect to some problems carried on in detail, by a special organization like the well-known Retail Research Association, or it may be planned and carried on by representatives of the cooperating firms, meeting as a research group, as in the Manufacturers' Research Association of Massachusetts, about which you are to hear in detail at this meeting.

5. Managements might profitably utilize, more than they now do, the services of independent professional research organizations, such as the National Bureau of Economic Research. There are organizations of this kind which command the highest quality of research ability and render service on a high professional plane.

6. Managements should utilize and support, more than they now do, the research facilities of higher educational institutions. The research laboratories of engineering schools and of the departments of the physical sciences are now being utilized, although not to the extent to which they should be; and similar use of facilities of schools of business administration and of industrial engineering departments of engineering schools should be made. I believe a firm could not make a more profitable investment than to establish in such a school an annual fellowship of say $500, which would give it for each academic year the use of a keen young man for investigation of one of its problems under its own and outside expert research direction.

7. Finally, industry should, by financial support and at least by offering the necessary laboratory of normal managerial processes, encourage research which is carried on by students of method for the purpose of discovering and validating methods which will become the tools of research generally. With respect to this contribution of management to research, the justification of the contribution should not be the immediate and direct practical value of research results, but the ultimate, indirect practical value of discovery and validation of methods to serve industry in the development of a science of management.

---

[1]*Bulletin of the Taylor Society*, December, 1926. Paper presented at a meeting of the Taylor Society, New York, December 10, 1926.

INDUSTRIAL PSYCHOLOGY[1]

Its Progress in the United States--Psychology as Science, as Point of View and as Method

By W. V. Bingham

Director, Personnel Research Federation, New York

In what directions and to what extent has the science of psychology influenced industrial thought and practice in the United States? What influences have operated to bring industrial problems to the attention of psychologists, and to bring psychological doctrines to bear on the thinking and practice of business executives, industrial engineers, labor managers, trade union leaders, and students of social science whose primary interest centers in industrial relations? How keenly are the masters of American industry aware of the problems of individual and social psychology that have been brought into the spotlight of inquiry as a result of mass production and minute division of labor, with the resulting tendencies toward repetitive processes, shorter hours, better wages, modification of many skilled trades, demand for highly specialized, non-transferable skills, and decreased need of mere physical strength in the worker? What help have the practitioners of scientific management or the administrators of personnel policies received from the science of psychology?

No damage will be done through frank admission at the outset that the significant and constructive contributions of industrial psychology in America have been meagre. Psychology is a rapidly growing but still youthful science. It has been absorbed in the task of putting its own house in order. Within the past generation it has had to win the co-operation and respect of its elder sisters, the biological sciences. New techniques of research have had to be devised, new hypotheses formulated and put to the acid test of controlled experiment. Efforts in these directions have met with such success that there has been a wholly unprecedented and disproportionate demand for the services of psychologists as instructors in university and college courses in psychology. Then, too, the applications of psychology to problems of elementary and secondary education have absorbed a large share of the energies of the most brilliant of American psychologists. One need only mention the names of such leaders of psychological research as Thorndike, Terman, Judd, and G. Stanley Hall, to illustrate the fact that careers in educational psychology have attracted some of our ablest men. And today, if industry is to bring it to pass that the attention of eminent psychologists shall be focussed on the problems of human relations and conditions in factories and offices, it must be prepared to compete not only with the instructional budgets of the universities and the considerable financial rewards that accrue, through publication, to those who greatly improve techniques of public education; it must compete as well with enticing research opportunities now opening up to psychologists on problems arising in the fields of political science, law, criminology, child guidance and social betterment.

Not only have psychologists been under pressure to bend their efforts toward non-industrial problems; they have been content to see large areas of psychological inquiry in industry pre-empted by capable investigators whose training has been primarily other than that of the psychological laboratory. Many of the best contributions to the study of industrial fatigue, accidents, illumination, and simplification of work, have been made not by psychologists but by industrial engineers and specialists in scientific management. A canvass of the contributions of Frederick W. Taylor and his associates, for example, reveals numerous studies in the subject matter of industrial psychology. Hence an unwarranted tradition has prevailed, to the effect that questions of time and motion study, incentives, factory training, and the design of tools, machines, benches and chairs to fit the requirements of the worker, are exclusive prerogatives of the engineer. Theoretically it has been recognized that each of these subjects has its psychological aspects, to which it might be presumed that a psychologist could contribute. Practically, the management engineer has known these problems so much more intimately in their industrial setting that the psychologist unversed in factory practice has for the most part preferred to turn his energies in other directions. Indeed, it may be confessed that certain forays by amateur industrial psychologists into this territory have been ludicrous enough in their outcome to lend emphasis to this unfortunate tradition. Industrial executives must share in part the responsibility for these fiascos. Over and over again they have engaged as psychologist a novice whose claim to the title was that he had studied elementary courses in college, or perhaps had been an assistant in routine psychometric work in the Army or in a child guidance clinic. One cannot help smiling at such choices, made by business men who would never for a moment think of putting a complicated problem of mechanical development or chemical research on the shoulders of an inexperienced or half-trained engineer.

But enough by way of apology and explanation. What benefits, if any, have accrued to industrial relations in America because of the work of psychologists?

Some of these benefits we shall find are broad and general. Some are specific and detailed. They can best be envisaged after we have listed the chief industrial problems which are primarily psychological or which present psychological aspects.

Psychological Problems of Industry

Psychology is variously described as the positive science of conduct, the science of behavior, the science of experience. Whatever the limitation of scope implied in any such definition, the fact is that one finds today in any systematic volume on psychology, a wealth of fact and generalization with respect to human nature. Those problems of industry may be considered psychological which involve questions of human nature.

Foremost are the problems which have to do with the <u>worker in relation to his work</u>. Many such problems arise in helping the worker find the simplest, easiest, most natural ways of doing his work; conserving his energy; reducing fatigue; increasing quality and quantity of output; eliminating personal injuries and lost time due to accidents; removing unnecessary fears and irritations connected with the work; reducing unrest, discontent and dissatisfaction with the job and with the working conditions surrounding it; and increasing the laborer's store of contentment, pride and satisfaction in his accomplishment. These are all basic practical problems of industrial management, most of them capable of at least partial solution through the application of shrewdness and common sense, but all of them offering a challenge to the psychologist to apply his science and to supplement common sense by analysis, objective measurement and experimentation. Common observation of the behavior of workers engaged in heavy labor or in work requiring close attention, might well have suggested to any sensible supervisor the economy of insisting upon appropriate properly spaced rest periods; but the fact is that this device has rarely been employed except where science and controlled experiment have first demonstrated its worth and indicated the optimal distribution of rests for the particular tasks in hand. Scarcely more than a good beginning has been made in the scientific understanding of rest periods in relation to fatigue, monotony, workers' reveries, outbursts of temper and radicalism. Here, as in other aspects of the job in its relation to the individuality of the worker, the psychologist has significant opportunities for industrial application of his science.

A second group of psychological problems arises out of the <u>relations between a worker and his fellow workers</u>. How to harness the impulse to competition, and insure a healthy rivalry for high quality of output or freedom from accidents; how to eliminate the conflicts, irritations and jealousies which sometimes clog the human machinery of the factory; how to prevent loss of working time in idle banter while supplying on appropriate occasions ample opportunities for good fellowship--these are questions which are ordinarily left to chance or to common sense. More basic is the best means of developing a substantial group solidarity, a ready helpfulness, a willingness of experienced workers to take new employes in hand and teach them the practices and ideals of the shop. Then, too, workers sometimes tend to teach each other various fears and notions leading to conscious restriction of output. They may spread an apprehension of layoff or of piece rate cutting, when no genuine basis for it exists in reality. Here the problem arises as to how such unwholesome influences of workers on one another can be minimized, or replaced by influences which make for better mutual education and co-operation. These are complicated problems of practical social psychology.

Yet, a third group of problems centers in the <u>relations of the worker and his immediate supervisor</u>. These relations may be harmonized by making sure of the reasonableness of work requirements; by making work assignments and instructions clear and definite; by introducing an equitable routine procedure of distributing work and materials, to do away with the possibility of partiality or favoritism in these regards; and by making the supervisor a skillful instructor and an understanding helper of his men, as well as a fair and just disciplinarian. The psychological aspects of these processes are sufficiently obvious.

No less psychological in essence are many of the problems arising out of the worker's relations to the management. Consider, for example, the assurance of steady employment. This has often been made possible through improved market analyses, business forecasting and careful scheduling of production. The effect produced on the worker by relief from the overshadowing fear of layoff is a psychological fact of major importance. So, too, with many questions of wage rates, methods of payment, and policies regarding stock ownership, insurance, pensions, housing, loans, vacations, facilities for education and recreation, and the like. The adequacy of the machinery provided for airing and prompt adjustment of grievances reflects the management's grasp of practical industrial psychology. The same may be said of its success in providing suitable recognition of merit and competence, not so much through resort to non-financial rewards and recognition (although these have their value and are often prized), but rather through proper payment by results, and adequate provision for advancement. Many economists are prompt to insist today that the problem of wages has its psychological aspects.

Group relations of workers and management have presented continuing problems whose psychological aspects are sometimes almost as perplexing as their more obvious economic phases. The reader need only remind himself of the misunderstandings, the mutual suspicions, the conflicting preconceptions and unyielding prejudices which too often have beclouded the thinking of workers' representatives and employers alike, when collective versus individual bargaining, trade union versus shop committee organization and similar issues of joint relations have been brought forward.

Both parties have at times resorted to espionage in their fact finding, a practice as unsound in its psychology as in its ethics. Both have been prone to color their inquiries with preconceived conclusions. Better methods of ascertaining the truth about actual and imaginary grievances, and the purposes and practices of employer and employe alike, will tend to bring about more wholesome industrial relations. The duty of undertaking to improve these techniques of fact finding is one which the psychologist must not hesitate to accept. Already J. D. Houser, B. V. Moore, L. L. Thurstone and others have made a promising start in this direction.

The psychology of leadership requires clarification. It is not implied that there is any need for more argument or pooling of opinion as to the personal qualities which make for effective leadership within the ranks of labor or of management. What the psychologist demands is first of all a new, minute, comprehensive description and analysis of what the real, successful industrial leaders do. When this factual foundation has been properly laid, the drafting of better plans for discovering and developing the leaders of the future will not seem so complicated. Opportunity and reward for exercise of constructive leadership and originality by workers and executives of whatever status will probably then seem a most natural policy. If channels are open for the flow of ideas and ability from one department or level of the organization to another, if real leadership wherever revealed is given its chance, both individual and group relations may be expected to benefit.

Relations of workers and management are already profiting from the studies which psychologists and educators have made regarding the development of leaders. Consider the function of an executive as a trainer of men. Studies of the technqiues of teaching particular skills, habits, attitudes and items of essential information have led to many generalizations with reference to the processes of training. Excellent methods have been evolved for making the necessary preliminary analyses of work to be done, difficulties encountered, items to be taught. Procedures have been developed for determining the content and outlining the successive steps in a training program. Practicable techniques for giving preliminary instruction and for training on the job have been evolved. Investigations have even been made as to the difficulties met in getting executives themselves to learn and to use these improved techniques of teaching their subordinates, and as to the best ways of overcoming these difficulties. In such ways the methods of research are being profitably applied to educational problems of industry and business. As the results of such researches gradually find their way into the practice of supervisors and executives, relations of workers and management cannot fail to profit thereby.

One now hears more than formerly about the psychological importance to industry of yet another group of relations, those of the worker to his family and, indeed, _to the entire circle of contacts_ outside as well as inside the factory gate. Psychologists with a psychiatric background have properly been reminding management that careless accidents, temper, trouble making, insubordination, absenteeism and other sorts of objectionable behavior often have their roots in worries traceable to conditions far from the immediate setting. Intensification of these worries during periods of excessive fatigue has been demonstrated. Attention has been called to the damage suffered by certain temperaments as a result of pessimistic reverie during the course of long continued monotony. One obvious implication is that a sound industrial psychology must reckon not only with temperamental differences between workers and their relative susceptibility to the effects of different sorts of repetitive or taxing labor; it must know not only the conditions in the plant predisposing to monotony or fatigue; it must realize also the influence of the varied conditions that modify the employe's anxieties and hopes, his fatigue and recuperation, both during and _after_ working hours.

But it is one thing to recognize the importance of the total situation in determining a worker's inner feelings and outward behavior, and quite another matter to infer that, therefore, wise personnel practice will seek to inquire into intimate personal and private circumstances in order better to be able to help make suitable adjustments. There must be no trespass on the worker's independence and self-respect. It is a neat problem of practical psychology, how to mold conditions so as to effect a maximum of well justified contentment and willing efficiency, without risk of wrecking the whole morale through resentment against uninvited paternalism. Mr. Ford marched up this hill, and then marched down again. The practical solution reached by some executives has been to leave with the workers themselves the opportunity for initiative in such matters, and for management to stand ready to move only when, as, and if needed and invited so to do.

The psychological problems of industry have now been surveyed as they present themselves to the student of the worker in his relation to his job, to his fellow workers, to his immediate supervisor and to the management of the industry in which he is engaged. Not only his relations as an individual employe have been considered, but also his relations as a member of a group which, as a group, has vitally important relations both with the management of the particular concern which gives him employment and with the industry as a whole. While there is little doubt that the most varied and intriguing psychological problems arise in studying the worker in relation to his own work, there is no question that the psychological aspects of the situation are of vital importance in considering each of these other relations also. In what ways has the science of psychology influenced industrial thought and practice with reference to these industrial relations?

How Psychology Has Influenced Industry

Industrial relations in America have been influenced by psychology in three ways. Industry has responded to psychology as science, as point of view and as method.

Psychology as Science. Psychology as a science consists of a systematized body of facts and generalizations about human nature. Foremost among the industrially significant facts of modern psychology are those which reveal the enormous range and variety of differences between people. Scarcely a generation ago American thought and practice was still somewhat under the influence of the political doctrine of equality which had been held most fervently at the time when the nation was born. To be sure, no one had seriously contended that all men are created equal in talent; but scarcely anyone had realized how vast are the differences in native endowment and capacity for achievement until Cattell, Boas, Thorndike and other exploring the trail originally blazed by Sir Francis Galton, found ways of quantifying and measuring individual differences. They gave graphic and mathematical expression to these measurements.

While studying the wide range of differences which people exhibit in their capacity to discriminate colors, sounds, extent of arm movements and other sensory data, they also carried forward investigations in reaction times which showed how greatly people differ in motor capacity. After many of the relatively simple processes had been examined, differences in types of attention were observed. Other investigations were centered on the measurement of differences in ability to localize sounds, to perceive spacial relations, to remember, to manipulate and construct.

The discovery of the possibility of devising units and scales for use in measuring such differences of ability was an epoch making invention. Its application was rapidly extended to the measurement of achievement in school work and has had a profound influence on educational practice. Meanwhile procedures were devised--following the pioneer work of Binet and Simon--for measuring the rate and extent of mental development. Concepts of mental age and the intelligence quotient became current. Convenient means for examining large numbers of persons at the same time were perfected; and during the war, data were secured which revealed in spectacular relief the vastness of the spread of human abilities as well as their proneness to cluster about the central tendency of mediocrity.

Differences between individuals not only in abstract intellect but also in social and mechanical abilities were studied. Certain trade tests, for measuring proficiency in different occupations, were standardized. People's interests were made the subject of inquiry, and techniques were developed for quantifying differences in mental attitudes, likes and dislikes, occupational preferences and personal tastes. More recently the ambitious task has been undertaken of measuring the strength of volitional tendencies. Character, as well as intellect and temperament, has come within the range of quantitative measurement; and while the reliability of the methods so far developed for measuring character is so low that few psychologists will venture as yet to draw practical inferences from them, it is nevertheless significant that the idea of mental measurement has now been extended until it comprehends the entire personality.

Partly as a consequence of these researches, it is recognized, more clearly than formerly, how much individuals differ from each other in originality and initiative, in output of energy, in tact or in social sensitivity, and in self-control, as well as in general intelligence, and in a long array of specific abilities. All these facts, tersely put by Cattell and Thorndike and emphatically reiterated in public address and in semi-popular writings by Walter Dill Scott, Munsterberg, Goddard, Terman, Hollingworth and many others, have influenced the thinking and practice of industrial leaders.

Many industrialists of today, it may be recalled, were themselves students of elementary or advanced psychology in college when individual differences were first stressed. Later, in positions of business responsibility, some of them recognized acutely the need of personnel procedures which give due emphasis to these facts of human nature. Functional organization of personnel activities in factory and office, and development of techniques for personnel classification, transfer and promotion, job analysis, employment interviewing, placement, training, and follow-up, probably proceeded somewhat more rapidly because of what psychology had done to make more evident the nature and extent of individual differences.

Of practical moment also have been the findings of psychology regarding the relationship between various abilities. For instance, the law of compensation has been found inapplicable. Common belief had held that the person who is greatly superior to his fellows in some regards is probably inferior to them in others--that if he is very talented in mathematics, for example, he is probably something of a dullard in athletics or in art. The facts have been found to be quite the opposite. Persons who are found to be highly superior in one ability are more often than not above the average in any other desirable trait. In other words the correlation between favorable traits is quite generally positive. At the same time, the correlation is in most instances low. Psychologists have often been surprised to find how slight is the association between abilities apparently very simular. It as Spearman and others contend, there are certain _general factors_ characteristic of a person's make-up--call them intelligence, energy, perseverance or what you will--it is certain that there are also a great number of quite specific abilities, very largely independent of one another.

These findings have lent emphasis to the need for the employement interviewer to be very cautious in inferring future accomplishments from fragmentary data, whether these data are in the form of impressions gained in conversation, mental test performance, school record, or reports from former employers. He needs all the information he can get. He especially needs to find out which items are really significant, under the conditions of work which prevail in his own plant and in the local labor market.

Another inference from these facts regarding the specificity of abilities has to do with the nature of industrial training. There is sound warrant for the tendency toward better training on the job rather than toward more formal training of a general sort.

To precisely what extent industrial practice in the United States has been modified by the body of psychological knowledge regarding individual differences and the correlation of abilities, who shall say? It is obvious that the tendencies of the past twenty years in employment, training, supervision, transfer and other personnel functions have been in the direction of greater recognition of and provision for wide differences in endowment. Public school practice has also been modified in many ways which have made it possible for multitudes of young people more easily to effect a satisfactory adjustment with the working world. Such changes might conceivably have taken place, even though psychologists had not been measuring, analyzing and comparing so many aspects of so many people. It seems reasonable, however, to suppose that the findings of these kinds of psychological research have directly as well as indirectly had a real influence in industry.

Much the same might be said regarding the generalizations from research in educational psychology. One outstanding characteristic of man is his educability, and psychologists have steadily been prying deeper and deeper into the laws of learning. Principles governing the formation of habits, acquisition of skills, mastery of technical knowledge, elimination of gross defects of personality, development of social effectiveness, modification of likes and dislikes, and inculcation of ideals and attitudes--all these are applicable in offices, stores and factories as well as in school or college. Some of the best data regarding effects of practice and of fatigue on the work curve have come from experiments in psychological laboratories.

The doctrines of interest, and of attention and distraction, have had their application where safety devices were to be invented and installed; where jobs were to be classified according to their psychological requirement; where workers and students were to be advised with reference to their future vocational plans. The psychological theories most prevalent a dozen years ago regarding instincts and the fundamental drives which motivate human conduct, have influenced the thinking of industrial leaders regarding financial and nonfinancial incentives, group spirit, the damage done by fear and the value of insuring to manager and worker alike his sense of self-respect and his belief in the worth-whileness of his labor. Writers like Robert Valentine, Carleton Parker, Ordway Tead, Z. C. Dickinson, Robert Bruere, H. C. Metcalf and Whiting Williams interpreted these doctrines for economists and engineers, bridging the gulf that too often divides the psychologist from the industrialist.

Perhaps enough has been said to illustrate the way in which the subject matter of psychology has tended to affect industrial practice.

A single case, more concrete than those already mentioned, will serve as a sample of repeated instances in which the discoveries of the psychological laboratory have found useful application.

For many years Professor C. E. Ferree in the psychological laboratory of Bryn Mawr College concentrated his research on problems of the efficiency of the eye under varying conditions of illumination. He developed new apparatus and precise procedures for measuring the fatigue of vision. Using these methods, he worked out the principles which must apply to all determinations of the relative effectiveness of different intensities and distributions of light. He compared the merit of direct, indirect and semi-indirect systems. When his conclusions were first announced they ran counter to the tenets currently held by engineers; but today they are commonplaces of illuminating engineering practice. Thousands of factory employes, now doing their work under more favorable conditions of illumination, will never know that they have in part to thank a research psychologist for their relief from the annoyances of unnecessary glare, distraction and eye strain.

Psychology as point of view. Less tangible than the effects of these concrete products of psychological research, but none the less real, has been the influence on American industry of what may be called the psychological point of view. In essence this point of view consists in a more than ordinarily tenacious belief that human experience is understandable, that human behavior is not a spiritual mystery but a natural phenomenon like other phenomena of the organic world. Such a belief leads to the persistent attempt to understand one's fellows, to appreciate their motives and ambitions, to comprehend their shortcomings and their possibilities. It makes one impatient of superficial explanations of unsatisfactory employe behavior as due to "carelessness" or "laziness" or "pure cussedness." One asks, "Why was this motorman careless?" and proceeds to get the facts about his previous training on the job, his treatment by supervisors, his length and distribution of working hours, his health, his eyesight, his scope of attention, his worries and tendencies to reverie. Then such a vague blanket trait term as "carelessness" drops out of one's vocabulary. Moreover, the psychological point of view prevents an executive from letting his personal feelings warp his judgment. It helps him to be at once more objective and more intelligently aware of points of view other than his own.

The psychological point of view is that of the scientist trained to focus the searchlight of inquiry on every puzzling problem of human adjustment. It is identical with the point of view of scientific management in so far as scientific management concerns itself with the human problem of industry. If there has been any vital difference in point of view between industrial psychologists and management engineers, it is with reference to their primary purpose. The industrial psychologist has wanted first of all to help the worker, in simplifying his methods of work, bettering the conditions under which his work is done, improving his training, and developing personnel techniques which will facilitate his adjustment to the occupation in which he will find the most satisfaction. Incidentally the psychologist may believe that these services will perhaps benefit the industry, the management and the social order also. The engineer has similar objectives but is ordinarily thought of as placing first the economic stability, prosperity and usefulness of the enterprise.

The personal satisfactions accruing to competent, well paid, well trained employes are his secondary objectives.

While this contrast in points of view of psychologist and management engineer may have some historical warrant, particularly in England, it cannot be said to hold universally in America. The writer knows personally Taylorites who seem to him to place considerations of human betterment first, and to regard the industry which they plan for or manage merely as a means to the self-realization of the workers and supervisors who constitute its personnel. He also confesses an acquaintance with psychologists as well as engineers both in America and in Europe who have shown themselves willing to place their talents as the disposal of employers with a single eye to profits.

This difference in attitude and primary interest is not inherent in the science; it is a personal matter. It may depend on temperament, or on the social philosophy one holds.

The question of priority of objective might be a matter of more grave concern at this point, if it were not that the farsighted investigator--be he psychologist or management engineer--sees clearly that he must travel much the same road in either event. After all, there is a considerable identity of interest of employes, managers, owners and public. An industrial psychologist in a chocolate factory recently stated his objective as follows: "The purpose of the psychologist is to see that the workers leave the plant at night neither fatigued nor irritated nor nervous." He showed not a trace of interest in increasing the owners' profits. But when I asked the president of the corporation why he had this psychologist in his factory, the prompt and decisive answer was, "I find it pays."

Psychology in America has contributed to the point of view that it pays in the long run to attempt to understand the deep-lying motives and ambitions of people, and to work with the current of human nature rather than counter to it. It has made this point of view explicit in its application to problems of vocational adjustment, including placement and training, in conformity with the individual's proclivities and talents. In other directions, also, the psychological point of view is coming to be more frequently taken, with promise of leading to better mutual understanding and more co-operative relations throughout industry.

Wholesome as such a point of view may be in approaching questions of human relations in industry, it will not carry the manager far toward practical solutions of his difficulties unless he has at hand the necessary appropriate techniques for problem solving. This brings us to the third way in which psychology has influenced American industry; through its method.

Psychology as method. The main methods of psychological research are two: experiment and statistics.

The task of any natural science may be stated in most general terms as the determination of the relationship between variables. The variables with which psychology deals include the environmental forces and conditions which influence behavior, as well as the innate capacities, habits and attitudes of individuals in interaction with the world in which they work and live.

It is sometimes said that the biological sciences, of which psychology is one, differ radically from the physical sciences in that the variables with which they have to deal are more numerous, complex and difficult to control. Wherever all the variables, or all but one, can be controlled, the ideal method is that of experiment. Here the ingenious investigator can test his hypothesis by setting up a crucial situation and making observations or measurements which are decisive as to the manner in which the independent and the dependent variables are related. If, however, there are independent and uncontrollable variables which make impossible the resort to experiment, the scientist has recourse to the method of statistics. This is a method which, thanks to Pearson, Spearman, Thorndike, Kelley, Thurstone and others, has been developed extensively in its application to psychological data. It has proved to be an invaluable complement to the methods of the experimental laboratory.

The refinements of statistical procedure evolved in connection with psychological research have been slowly finding their way into industrial personnel studies. If, before the war, one talked to American business men about correlations, scatter diagrams, regression lines, central tendencies, standard deviations, or measures of reliability and validity, they listened with amused tolerance, if at all. Today these concepts are fairly well recognized as a necessary part of the mental furniture of anyone who undertakes to deal precisely with the data of human behavior. They have found their place in the thinking and writing of many who are undertaking to understand the more fundamental aspects of human relations as they exist in industry.

The method of the controlled experiment on the other hand, although simpler to understand and often more decisive in its findings, has unfortunately not been as generally adopted by industry. To be sure, there have been innumerable so-called experiments tried in industrial relations. But most of these have not been carried out according to the canons of science. A manager has decided, for example, to try the experiment of changing his method of remuneration. In place of an hourly wage he has introduced a straight piece rate; or instead of piece rate he has tried one of the currently popular task-and-bonus systems. But in most instances he has introduced at the same time several other variables. He has changed foremen, or improved the routing of materials, or insisted on a more thorough coaching and follow-up of new employes, or installed a better ventilating system. So when, after several months, his accounting department reports a decided lowering of unit labor costs, it is still a matter of opinion whether these economies are to be credited to the new method of payment by results. Industrial management cannot hope to reap the full benefits of the scientific method as applied to the study of the human problems of the factory, until it is ready to make a larger number of genuinely scientific experiments.

Psychology has demonstrated the usefulness of the methods of experiment and of statistics in solving some of the complicated problems of human relations. It has developed refinements of technique which are readily carried over into industrial research. Responsibility rests with the individual investigator, however, to furnish the penetrating insight and the ingenuity which alone can formulate brilliant and industrially significant hypotheses for scientific study.

Psychological techniques have sometimes been borrowed by industrial engineers, as in the case of recent fatigue studies, earlier investigations having failed because the effects of suggestion were not controlled. In other instances, the psychologist has been borrowed as well as the technique, as when Thorndike helped carry out the research of the New York State Ventilation Commission, which established the primary importance of air movement. The Society for the Promotion of Engineering Education has repeatedly called into its councils such psychologists as Seashore and Thurstone. And so the general methods and specific techniques of psychology, as well as its point of view and its subject matter, are gradually being appropriated by industrial engineering.

Agencies for Furthering Industrial Psychology

A sketch of the influence of psychology on fundamental relations and conditions in American industry would not be complete without mention of certain agencies which have been carrying forward psychological research and slowly spreading throughout the texture of business and industry some familiarity with psychological content, method and point of view.

Chief among the agencies which have been furthering psychological developments are the universities. Every university has its psychological laboratory for research. It also offers courses of instruction which are taken by great numbers of students. While many of these courses are general in nature, some of them treat specifically the psychological problems of business, such as advertising and selling, and also touch upon applications of psychology to vocational selection, learning, fatigue, incentives, group relations in industry and other problems of management and of individual adjustment. These courses of instruction in applied psychology are for the most part elementary, and broad in scope rather than intensive. During the past twenty years they have served to introduce many thousands of young people to the basic principles of industrial psychology as first outlined by Munsterberg and as formulated from time to time in the books of Scott, Hollingworth, Poffenberger, Swift and others. Such books have had some circulation among mature business men as well as students. Unfortunately the readers have often, especially since the war, been so intrigued by the chapters dealing with mental tests and other devices for the measurement of individual differences that they have overlooked the relatively more fundamental psychological considerations which alone can give to mental test procedures their true significance.

In a few universities there exist also centers for advanced training and research in industrial and commercial psychology. Among the foremost at the present time are the University of Michigan in Ann Arbor, the University of Pennsylvania in Philadelphia, Columbia University in New York, and the University of Chicago. Stanford University in California, Northwestern University in Evanston, the University of Pittsburgh, the University of Minnesota in Minneapolis, the University of Iowa in Iowa City, the University of Ohio in Columbus and some of the other state universities are hospitable to such research. Promising developments are now taking place in the Harvard Graduate School of Business Administration in Boston, and in Yale University in New Haven.

Curiously the emphasis in many of these centers has been on the psychological problems of commerce rather than of industry. Curiously, too, the great engineering schools of institutes of technology have completely neglected psychological research. The outstanding exception to this sweeping generalization is the Carnegie Institute of Technology in Pittsburgh, where was established under the writer's direction in 1915 the first Division of Applied Psychology in any American Institution, and later, the first Bureau of Personnel Research, and where, for eight years, a notable group of psychologists were engaged in research on problems of importance to co-operating industries and business concerns. Ke gy and Yoakum's book on "Selection and Training of Salesmen," Strong and Uhrbrock's "Job Analysis and the Curriculum with Special Reference to the Printing Industry," and Craig and Charters' "Personal Leadership in Industry" record some of the more enduring products of these studies. One outgrowth of this movement at Carnegie Institute of Technology was the establishment in 1917 of the Research Bureau for Retail Training. This Bureau, now permanently endowed and affiliated with the University of Pittsburgh, has recently published a summary volume covering ten years of continuous psychological, economic and educational research. The influence of its work on personnel practice in department stores has not been limited to the local constituency but has been felt throughout the nation.

That competing firms have co-operated in support of such investigations is significant. That the findings have in large part been passed on to other firms for the benefit of all and for the public good is evidence of broad mindedness. It well illustrates the growing conviction in American business and industry, that the ancient practice of maintaining trade secrets wherever possible is sometimes an unprofitable if not a ludicrous form of selfishness.

Such limited psychological research as has been carried forward by individual corporations has likewise for the most part been open to the inspection of any visiting scientist or personnel manager. A few street railway and taxicab companies with laboratories of their own for investigating individual susceptibility to accidents and related psychological problems of transportation, have not hesitated to exchange methods, data and results. Among such firms as the Eastman Kodak Company, the Western Electric Company, the General Electric Company and the American Telephone and Telegraph Company there has been free exchange of specifications for psychological laboratory equipment and of other technical information.

Several of these companies contribute to the support of the Personnel Research Federation which maintains a clearing-house for the exchange of research information, as well as a staff for consulting work and for carrying forward specific studies. Among its current investigations is one regarding the effects on accident reduction of individual attention to workers who are found to have a susceptibility to accidents. Another investigation, designed in the end to facilitate the flow of correct information from workers to management, consists of a study of the technique of the personal interview. In this task of jointly furthering the scientific approach to the human problems of industry, a number of government agencies, university departments and independent research organizations likewise co-operate. The Engineering Foundation, the National Research Council and the American Federation of Labor initiated this co-operative movement which signalized a definite recognition of the need for co-ordination of research plans and extensive stimulation of sound research developments in industrial psychology and related aspects of personnel science. The Personnel Journal, now in its seventh volume, furnishes the record of accomplishment to date.

The establishment of the Personnel Research Federation followed upon the research developments at Carnegie Institute of Technology already mentioned, and other undertakings which had received an impetus from the widespread interests in applied psychology awakened by the military accomplishments of psychologists and personnel managers during the war. The Scott Company, for example, with Walter Dill Scott as its guiding spirit, for four years operated as a firm of personnel consultants to large business concerns, and made familiar to American industry a number of psychological concepts, principles and techniques recorded in the volume, "Personnel Management," by Scott and Clothier (1923). The immediate stimulus toward the establishment of the Personnel Research Federation, however, came from two sources. One was a series of significant investigations as to the value of the psychiatric approach to industrial problems, made by the late E. E. Southard, M.D., at the request of the Engineering Foundation. The other was a recognition by the National Research Council, of which James R. Angell was then the head, and by its Division of Anthropology and Psychology, of which the writer was Chairman, that the problems of industrial psychology were of increasing importance and that there was some danger of duplication of research effort unless there existed an agency to facilitate exchange of information, to survey the field as a whole, and to plan constructively in the light of known needs and facilities for research.

The National Research Council, which represents mainly the physical and biological sciences, has continued its efforts to further practical psychology, for example in its applications to problems of highway safety. More recently the Social Science Research Council has come forward, and as one of its activities is helping to plan and to finance selected investigations in industrial psychology. Both of these Councils also offer each year certain fellowships for advanced students of psychology, and a few of these investigators have chosen as their topics for study problems in industrial psychology and related aspects of personnel science. The Psychological Corporation, founded by J. McKeen Cattell in 1921 as a means of making the services of American psychologists conveniently available to industry, has served useful purposes, not least of which has been to inform inquirers as to who and where the real psychologists are, in contradistinction to the dilettantes, charlatans, character analysts and pseudo-scientists who prey upon the public in America as in Europe.

The readiness of business firms to co-operate for the advancement of knowledge in the common interest, may again be exemplified by their support of such national associations as the American Management Association and the Taylor Society (an international association to promote the science and the art of administration and of management). Both of these organizations have from time to time encouraged discussions of psychological problems and of psychological research before their membership. It is a wholesome sign that the participation of psychologists in the work of these associations has grown somewhat during the past four years.

Papers of industrial significance are occasionally but all too rarely presented before the American Psychological Association. These most often are related to problems of vocational selection and placement, since American psychologists have concerned themselves with determination of interests and abilities by means of various techniques of testing, rating and individual appraisal, more often than with problems of the simplification of work, industrial fatigue, monotony, incentives and similar practical problems of the factory.

One exception to this indictment is Mrs. F. B. Gilbreth, who years ago had a clear vision of the problem. She worked jointly with her husband to spread among industrial engineers some understanding of the psychological point of view, especially with reference to fatigue, and to develop ingenious techniques for use in motion study and work analysis. In her private institute she has continued to introduce each year a few engineers to this point of view and to the refinements of these techniques. Another exception is C. S. Yoakum, whose contacts with the automotive industry and with business concerns have enabled him to formulate specifically problems of personality study, work histories, personnel accounting and measurement of the effects of management policies, and whose psychological researchers in vocational guidance are basic. Elton Mayo, to mention yet another, has brought the findings of psychopathology and the doctrines of Janct stimulatingly to bear on problems of irritation and irrationality in the factory. A number of younger psychologists are engaged in work which has its industrial bearings, and the temptation is strong to touch upon their individual contributions. Our generalization would, however, apply to the most of them, namely, that they are more often interested in employment psychology than in the psychology of the worker at work.

This paper, already too long, must be brought to a close with a word about industrial psychology in relation to government agencies. It may surprise European readers to learn that the federal government of the United States has never established an agency for research in industrial psychology, such as the Industrial Fatigue Research Board of Great Britain. Admirable research, to be sure, has been done by the Bureau of Mines in co-operation with the Public Health Service. The Department of Labor and the Federal Board for Vocational Education have published many studies on topics related to industrial psychology. But the research work, at least so far as the writer is aware, has been done for the most part by economists, educators, physicians or engineers, rather than by investigators whose training has been primarily in psychology. Only one agency of the national government has on its staff a well known psychologist; L. J. O'Rourke, of the U. S. Civil Service Commission. In a strategic position, he is changing for the better the character of the postal service and other government offices, by judiciously applying the techniques of psychological science to the procedures used in selecting and placing government employes. A few municipal and state governments are similarly benefiting by psychological research, and this movement is being fostered by the Bureau of Public Personnel Administration.

And so, in conclusion, it is admitted once more that psychology is influencing industrial relations and conditions in the United States most directly--through its contributions to vocational selection and the understanding of individual differences. Within other equally important areas of inquiry, the influences of psychological content, methods and point of view have been more indirect, and probably less potent than they will be after labor and management come to a clearer realization of the essentially psychological nature of many of their difficulties, and after more psychologists, in turn, have had opportunity to come to grips with these difficulties, not as they are defined in books, but as they crop up in the daily relationships of factory operation.

---

[1] Bulletin of the Taylor Society, October, 1928. Part of an American report on Fundamental Relations in Industry presented at the First Triennial Congress of the International Industrial Relations Association, held at Cambridge, England, July, 1928.

PART FIVE

SOME IMPORTANT AND TIMELY COMMENTARIES
--A POTPOURRI--

This section contains but six selections each of which serve to illustrate the concern of individuals and groups in the direction of development of management theory and practice, the employment of our human and natural resources, and the problem of equity in income distribution. The authors include a past president of the United States and a successful engineer, a past president of the American Federation of Labor, a social and managerial philosopher, a college professor and a past managing director of the Taylor Society, and a French engineer.

Hoover's article "Industrial Waste" is an address to the misallocation and nonallocation of resources within the economic system of the United States. The student will recognize the concepts of system, of comparative economic advantage, of some of the causes of economic fluctuations, and the need for seeking solutions to industrial labor strife. The author calls upon the engineering profession for leadership in the analysis of these problems and for the proposing of remedies.

The second article and the one which is most readily recognized by students of management is Follett's, "The Illusion of Final Authority." In this discourse the author, whose training and education was in the fields of philosophy, political science and law, first raises many of the questions which are still not settled almost a half a century later--the relationship of the concepts of power and authority in organization structures and how do they affect the attainment of individual and organizational goals. To Follett, coordination holds a unique position as a function of management in that without it cooperative effort is not possible. As a management philosopher she holds a unique position in that unlike those who sought her advice she was not a practicing manager. With Gantt she helped to build the bridge to a more enlightened scientific management based more on the needs and aspirations of those individuals who contribute their labor and who make organizations work.

The third article on Henri Fayol is included because of its contribution to the tapestry of scientific management, to the understanding of the contributions of France, and lastly because Fayol's "administrative function" parallels the work of Taylor but at a higher (more inclusive) level. It is interesting to note in de Freminville's article that Fayol as well as Taylor's critics in this country got tangled up in Taylor's functional foremanship as being a violation of the concept of Unity of Command. Unlike the critics, however, Fayol after having had the idea explained to him saw that he had been too fast to find fault.

The next two articles by William Green, then President of the American Federation of Labor, gives organized labor's views on two pertinent topics--management and industrial waste. In "Labor's Ideals Concerning Management" Green indorses the private enterprise system and indicates a keen awareness of the problems and motivations of management. He espouses the need for managers to recognize the role of the worker bargaining collectively for his own betterment and that rather than being a descriptive social force organized labor is a stabilizing force in society and industry. Labor, Green notes, recognizes that success in management means success of labor and that labor can and will contribute to the solution of industrial problems.

In his second article, "Labor's Interest in Industrial Waste Eliminations" Green states that labor's interest is to secure higher wages and enjoy improved conditions of employment. Other areas of concern to organized labor include industrial safety, instability of employment, and the treatment of workers to achieve conditions of high morale. Green in both of these articles speaks as a labor-management philosopher of the first order in that he bridges the gap between idealism and pragmatism without sacrificing either.

Concluding this part is Harlow S. Person's article on "The Call for Leadership." This is a timely reminder that leadership whether in the managing of a nation or a corporation is generally in short supply. In developing his thesis that forceful, imaginative, resourceful leadership is required in situations of crisis the author starts with a categorization of leadership into two classes. This is followed by noting the rarity of crisis leadership and the incapacity among us as citizens for followership. Some insights into today's related problems are discussed in a section on "The Nature of the Call," and the article concludes by posing a challenge to business. Although written at a time of economic depression and adjustment (1933) the article provides much food for thought and argument.

INDUSTRIAL WASTE[1]

By Herbert Hoover

The Federation of Engineering Societies has been brought about solely that we might secure for public service the collective thought and influence of 100,000 to 200,000 of our professional engineers. This great body of men in administrative and technical service penetrate every industrial avenue and thus possess a unique understanding of many of our intricate economic problems and an influence in their solution not equalled by any other part of the community. Wanting nothing from the public either individually or as a group, they are indeed in a position of disinterested service. This Federation has initiated services to the public in many directions.

I propose to deal with only one measure of this service today. Your Council has organized a preliminary survey of some of the weaknesses in our production system. This survey will attempt to visualize the nation as a single industrial organism and to examine its efficiency towards its only real objective,--the maximum production. In a general way this inquiry will bear upon the whole question of deficiency in production--industrial waste in a broad sense.

The waste in our production is measured by the unemployment, the lost time due to labor conflict, the losses in labor turnover, the failure to secure maximum production of the individual due either to misfit or lack of interest. Beyond this again is a wide area of waste in the poor coordination of great industries, the failures in transportation, coal and power supplies which re-echo daily to interrupt the steady operation of industry. There are again such other wastes due to lack of standardization, to speculation, to mismanagement, to inefficient national equipment and a hundred other causes. There is a certain proof of deficient production by comparisons of our intense results in 1918, when, with 20% of our man-power withdrawn into the army, we yet produced 20% more commodities than we are doing today. We are probably not producing more than 60 or 70 per cent of our capacity; that is, if we could synchronize all national effort to maximum production, we could produce 30 or 40 per cent more commodities and service. Our national machine is today doing worse than usual, as witness the 3,000,000 idle men walking our streets. One part of the human measure of this shortage in production is the lack of necessities or comforts to them and their families, and their anxieties as to the future.

No one will ever suppose that it is ever possible to bring national productivity up to the full 100, but the whole basis of national progress, of an increased standard of living, of better human relations, indeed of the advancement of civilization, depends upon the continuous improvement in productivity. While we currently assume that great advances in living standards are brought about by new and basic invention, yet in fact even a greater field of increasing standards lies in the steady elimination of these wastes. The primary duty of organized society is to enlarge the lives and increase the standards of living of all the people--not of any special class whatever. We are therefore proposing to make a preliminary examination of the volume of waste in certain industries, the proportions that lie in each field of fault. And no engineering report is worth the paper it is written upon without constructive suggestions in remedy.

There is ofttimes a superficial dismissal of this subject of maximum production on the assumption that there are positive limits in production due to over-supply. Such assumption has no proper foundation in the broad view of industry as whole. Too much economic thought on production has delimited its boundaries by the immediate volume of demand of a given commodity. There is no such things as the nation over-production, if it produces the right commodities. The commodities or services produced by the whole nation are capable of absorption by the whole nation if they are of the right character. In other words, if we could attune the whole industrial machine to the highest pitch, agriculture as well as manufacture, an increasing production would mean a directly increasing standard of living. When ten men or one hundred million men divide their united output, they can by doubling their output have twice the amount to divide. The problem in doubling output is to direct it to commodities or services that they can use. There is no limit to the increase of living standards except the limitations of human strain, scientific discovery, mechanical invention and natural resources.

It is true enough that any particular commodity or service can be over-produced, for each will reach a saturation point in demand when all the members of the community have been supplied. The absorption of increased productivity lies in the conversion of luxuries of today into necessities of tomorrow, and to spread those through the whole population by stimulation of habit and education. Wheat bread, railways, good roads, electricity, telephones, telegraphs, automobiles and movies were once luxuries. They are still luxuries to some parts of the population.

It is but a corollary that certain commodities can better be produced for exchange for commodities from outside our boundaries of more appropriate character to our needs. Today we have capacity for production of some commodities not only in excess of our home need, but even beyond export demand under present financial conditions. As a matter of practical remedy, we must either reorganize these financial relations or alternately abandon some part of this kind of production and turn our idle men to making things of which we are not yet fully supplied.

To put the matter in another way, there is no limit to consumption except the total capacity to produce, provided the surplus of productive power is constantly shifted to new articles from those that have reached the saturation point of demand. For instance, we have the productive capacity wasted today that would improve the housing conditions of our entire people to the level that perhaps only fifty percent of them enjoy--and at the same time not entrench upon our established necessities. I am not suggesting that the forces of production can be shifted by imperial direction. The practical thing that can be done is to eliminate some of the wastes and misfits in our production, and depend upon the normal processes of business and human desires to absorb them.

The largest area of waste lies in the large periods of slack production and unemployment, due to the ebb and flow of economic tides between booms and slumps. The ideal would be steadily increasing production--an ideal of no likelihood of exact realization because of inability to ever guage the advance in growth consumption or the approach of saturation. On the other hand, there are certain possibilities of stabilization worth consideration. For instance, we can classify labor into that engaged in production and service from this equipment. Our studies of industries as a whole show that we usually expand our equipment just at the periods of maximum demand for their products instead of doing our plant expansion during periods of slack consumption. We thus make double demands on labor and we doubly increase unemployment in periods of reduced consumption. That is indeed one of the factors in our great unemployment today. Every-one knows that for our normal productivity, our transportation facilities are today inadequate. We know that we are insufficiently housed, insufficiently equipped in our public roads and our public utilities; that we need an entire revision of our power supply, that we need expansion of our water ways and yet armies of idle men are walking the streets. The reasons why this occurs are not far to seek, in that it is at times of high productivity that capital is most easily obtained. It is then that the necessity of increased equipment most impresses men's minds and it is the high hopes of these periods that lead them into the adventure of expansion. Nor is it possible to expect that all industry could be so stabilized as to do its capital construction in periods of depression in commodity demand. Nevertheless, there are some industries that could, by cooperation of the government and cooperation amongst themselves, be led in this direction. More particularly does this apply to railways, telephones, telegraphs, power supplies and other public utilities, and to the expenditure upon our state, municipal and national public works.

Another variety of intermittent employment, and thus great waste, lies in certain industries now operating upon an unnecessarily wide seasonal fluctuation, as for instance the bituminous coal industry. This is today one of our worst functioning industries. Those mines operate seasonally and erratically. They proceed from gluts to famines, from profiteering to bankruptcy. As already determined by our engineering bodies, the men who mine our coal find work only seventy per cent of their time. In other words, there are thirty per cent more equipment, thirty per cent more men, attached to this industry than are necessary if it were stabilized to continuous operation. The mining engineer have already pointed out the directions in which remedy lies, through storage, through railway rate differentials and other remedies. Through constructive action, an army of men could be released from this industry of necessity to convert some luxury into a necessity of tomorrow. This is no plan to control prices or profits, although through it both the producer and consumer in coal could be placed upon a sounder basis than today. The interest of the consumer and producer, is, however, even less important than relief from the intermittent employment and unemployment within this industry that today brings a train of indefinite human misery and some of our lowest standards of living.

The second largest area of waste in productivity is the eternal amount of labor friction, strikes and lockouts. The varied social and economic forces involved in this problem need no repetition here. Fundamentally this is not alone a struggle for division of the results of production between capital and labor, but there is also a loss greater from strikes and lockouts in the element of purely human friction and loss outside the area of dispute on wages and hours. The growth of industry into large units has destroyed the old mutuality of interest between employee and employer. Our repetitive processes have tended to destroy the creative instinct and interest in employees; at times their efforts sink to low levels indeed. We will yet have to reorganize the whole employment relationship to find its solution. There is great promise in this field during the past two years, and the progress in this matter is one of the subjects under our inquiry.

Yet another variety of loss lies in the unnecessarily faulty distribution of our labor supply due to seasonal and to shifting demands. An adequate national employment service is indeed the first need to reduction of these wastes.

Probably the next largest fraction of waste in productivity lies in a too high degree of individualism in certain basic products and tools. In other words, a standardization of certain national utensils makes for economy in distribution, in operation and in repairs. The necessity of maximum production during the war opened a great vista of possibilities in this direction. Such standardization as car couplings, or wheels, and cars generally, represent real progress in this direction. These possibilities lie in a hundred directions. There are all sorts of cases from sizes of chains to the size of automobile wheels. Today dozens of different sizes are placed in the market by manufacturers and entail not only special equipment and skill to produce these many varieties, but also great stocks are required in distribution and losses are entailed due to lack of interchangeability. It is certain that there are a great many articles of every day use in which the manufacturer would indeed be glad to undertake some cooperation in standardization, from which the saving in national effort would be interpreted not into millions but into billions of dollars. This does not mean that we stamp the individuality out of manufacture or invention or decoration; it means basic sizes to common and every day things.

Another type of waste lies in our failure to advance our industrial equipment. The Super-Power Board will demonstrate the saving of 25,000,000 to 50,000,000 tons of coal annually by the electrification of our eastern power supply. The St. Lawrence Waterway Commission will demonstrate the saving of five to ten cents a bushel to the farmers of fifteen states by unlocking the lakes to ocean going vessels. Nor will this added efficiency to our national transport injure our present systems of canals and waterways, for we have ever found that the prosperity of an industry blesses them all.

Nor do we believe it is necessary to effect these things by the government. The spirit of cooperation that has been growing in our country during the last thirty years has already solved many things; it has standardized some things and is ripe for initiative toward cooperation of a wide-spread character. The leadership of our Federal government in bringing together the forces is needed. No greater field of service exists than the stimulation of such cooperation. The first stop is sane analysis of weakness and sober proposal of remedy. If the facts can be established to an intelligent people such as ours, action is certain even if it be slow. Our engineers are in unique position for this service, and it is your obligation to carry it forward.

---

[1] *Bulletin of the Taylor Society*, April, 1921. Abstract of an Address delivered before the Executive Board of the American Engineering Council, Federated American Engineering Societies, of which Mr. Hoover is President, Syracuse, N. Y., Feb. 14, 1921.

THE ILLUSION OF FINAL AUTHORITY[1]

Authority Must Be Functional and Functional Authority Carries with It Functional Responsibility

By Mary P. Follett
Author of "Creative Experience"

When writers on business management speak of "ultimate authority," and "supreme control" as two of the functions of administration, I think that expressions are being used which are a survival of former days. These expressions do not seem to me to describe business as conducted today in many plants. Business practice has gone ahead of business theory. So much goes to contribute to executive decisions before the part which the executive head takes in them, which is indeed sometimes merely the official promulgation of a decision, that the conception of final authority is losing its force in the present organization of business. This is as true of other executives as of the head. Here, too, final decisions have the form and the force which they have accumulated. I have seen an executive feel a little self-important over a decision he had made, when that decision had really come to him ready made. An executive decision is a moment in a process. The _growth_ of a decision, the _accumulation_ of authority, not the final step, is what we need most to study.

The most fundamental idea in business today, that which is permeating our whole thinking on business organization, is that of function. Every man performs a function or part of a function. Research and scientific study determine function in scientifically managed plants. I think a man should have just as much, no more and no less, authority as goes with his function or his task. People talk about the _limit of authority_ when it would be better to speak of the _definition of task_.

If, then, authority is derived from function, it has little to do with hierarchy of position as such, and in scientifically managed shops this is more and more recognized. We find authority with the head of a department, with an expert, with the driver of a truck as he decides on the order of deliveries. The despatch clerk has more authority in despatching work than the president. I know a man in a factory who is superintendent of a department which includes a number of subdepartments. He tells me that in many cases he says to the head of a sub-department, that is, to a man in a subordinate position to his, "With your permission, I do so and so." This is a decided reversal of the usual method, is it not? In the old hierarchy of position the head of the subdepartment would be "under" the superintendent of the department; the "lower" would take orders from the "higher." But my friend recognizes that authority should go with knowledge and experience, that that is where obedience is due, no matter whether it is up the line or down the line. Where knowledge and experience are located, there, he says, you have the key man of the situation. If this has begun to be recognized in business practice, we have here the forerunner of some pretty drastic changes in our thinking on business management.

A moment ago I used the word "under." Perhaps it may seem advisable sometime to get rid of the words "over" and "under." I know a chief executive who says he does not know whether he is at the head or at the bottom, and he wishes there was some way of making out a chart that did not put the president at the top. I was interested last summer in England, in meeting the head of a large business, to find that one of the chief difficulties in his thinking was concerned with this question. He said he didn't like all this matter of some being "over" others, yet he knew it was necessary--as we all do. What is the way out of this dilemma?

Two years ago my nurse in the hospital said to me, "Did you notice that operating nurse? Didn't she look black? I wonder what has happened this morning"? I innocently said, "Perhaps one of the surgeons has reprimanded her for something." To which my nurse replied, "Why, he couldn't. The doctors are not _over_ us. They have their work and we have ours." At first I did not like this, it seemed like chaos indeed. I thought the old way much better--of the doctor's having full responsibility, of his giving all the orders and seeing to it that the nurses obeyed his orders. But I asked several doctors about it, and they told me that there is a marked tendency now in this direction, and while it obviously has drawbacks, there may be a good side to it; it may indicate on the part of the nurses a greater interest in their work and a willingness to take more responsibility.

It seems to me that the word "over" represents something perfectly proper and something not proper. The thing it should not mean I can best illustrate by the wife who said with pride: "John has seventy in his department that he's boss over." But there is much that is hastening the disappearance of the word used in this way, notably newer methods of dismissal. Dismissals made after consultation with the psychologist may come in time to be looked on in the same way as when a doctor says a man's heart is too weak for a particular job. That decision does not mean that the doctor is "over" anyone. It is only capricious firing, firing that is unfounded, that makes a man over another, and that kind of firing is disappearing.

The conception of authority that we are considering this afternoon, the conception of authority as belonging to function, should do away with the idea widely held that the president "_delegates_" authority. A writer on this subject says: "The chief executive should define clearly each staff executive's responsibility and its relation to general purposes and plans and should grant each staff executive adequate corresponding authority." But is that exactly what happens in business? Is not this a matter of fact decided by the plan of organization? The duties, authority and responsibility of the staff executives are inherent in the plan of organization. Whatever formality is necessary on the part of the president _is_ more or less of a formality.

This phrase "delegated authority" assumes that your chief executive has the "right" to all the authority, but that it is useful to delegate some of it. I do not think that a president should have any more authority than goes with _his_ function. Therefore, I do not see how you can delegate authority except when you are ill or taking a holiday. And then you are not exactly delegating _authority_. Someone is doing your job and he has the authority which goes with that particular piece of work. Authority belongs to the job and stays with the job.

The view that the "_right_" to all authority lies with the head, but that he delegates some of it to others comes, I think, from what one might call the historical outlook on leadership rather than the analytical. We look back and see that when a business begins in a small way the head has many duties which after a while, as the business grows, are given to others. This has made people think that these duties by right belonged to the head, but that he has found it convenient to delegate some of them while, as a matter of fact, the convenience is just the other way round. There are in business certain separate functions; the smallness of a business may make it convenient for one man to perform them all, but they are still separate functions. For instance, in a small bank, the head, in addition to his many other duties, looks after new business. In a large bank, a separate man has the responsibility for new business, exchange, deposits, credit loans, etc. But the _separation of function does not mean the delegation of authority_. The unfortunate thing in writing on business organization is that our language has not caught up with our actual practice. As distribution of function has superseded hierarchy of position in many plants, delegation of authority should be an obsolete expression, yet we hear it every day.

I say that authority should go with function, but as the essence of organization is the interweaving of functions, authority we now see as a matter of interweaving. An order, a command, is a step in a process, a moment in the movement of interweaving experience, and we should guard against thinking this step a larger part of the whole process than it really is. There is all that leads to the order, all that comes afterwards--methods of administration, the watching and recording of results, what flows out of it to make further orders. If we trace all that leads to a command, what persons are connected with it, and in what way, we find that more than one man's experience has gone to the making of that moment--unless it is a matter of purely arbitrary authority. Arbitrary authority is authority not related to all the experience concerned, but to that of one man alone, or one group of men.

The particular person identified then with the moment of command--foreman, upper executive or whoever it may be--is not the most important matter for our consideration, although of course a very important part of the process. All that I want to emphasize is that there _is_ a process. A political scientist writes, "Authority coordinates the experience of man," but I think this is a wrong view of authority. The form of organization should be such as to allow or induce the continuous coordination of the experience of men. Legitimate authority flows from coordination, not coordination from authority.

Another corollary from this conception of authority as a moment in interweaving experience is that we have not authority as a mere leftover. We cannot take the authority which we won yesterday and apply it today. That is, we could not if we were able to embody the conception we are now considering in a plan of organization. In the ideal organization authority is always <u>fresh</u>, always being distilled anew. The importance of this in business management has not yet been estimated.

Of course, you will understand that in all this I am speaking of business organization in the more progressive plants, but they are as yet far more organized under the old doctrines.

Let us now ask ourselves what there is in the present organization of business which seeks to diffuse rather than to concentrate responsibility. First, management is becoming more and more especialized; the policies and methods of a department rest on that department's special body of knowledge, and there is a tendency for the responsibility to be borne by those with that special body of knowledge rather than by a man at the top because of his official position.

I saw the statement recently that the administrative head should hold frequent consultation with the heads of departments, and from the facts thus gained make his final decisions, construct his policies. But it is a matter of everyday knowledge to business men that their heads of departments pass up to them much more than mere facts. They give interpretation of facts, conclusions therefrom, judgments, too, so that they contribute very largely to final determination, supreme control, even to what has been called administrative leadership. In fact, both as to the information and the conclusions handed up from the executives, it is often not possible for the head to take them or leave them. These conclusions and judgments are already, to a certain extent, woven into the pattern, and in such a way that it would be difficult to get them wholely out. Hence, while the board of directors may be theoretically the governing body, practically, as our large businesses are now organized, before their decisions are made there has already taken place much of that process of which these decisions are but the last step.

Another indication of the view of authority which I am considering this afternoon, is that the planning department provided in so many plants is passing from a <u>tool</u> of management to a <u>part</u> of management, a part of a functionalized management. To be sure, the planning department is still so much of a novelty that there are many different ideas in regard to its place in the plant. It may be asked for only statistical information. In the case of a decision pending for the sales department, for instance, it may be asked for a record of past sales with analysis in regard to volume, localities, etc. Usually, however, it is asked for more than this, for the probable future development of certain localities, what the future demand will probably be, the probable effect of the raising of price. By the time this has all been passed up to the head his decision is already largely predetermined.

Whatever our exact idea of a planning department, I think we shall agree that functional management means that authority goes with function and not with a certain position at the top of the chart. There is hardly a staff official, is there, who provides merely material on which some line official bases his decision? Take the industrial relations manager. He is usually given a staff position. His work is largely research and planning, but in the presentation of results there is advice, either given openly as advice or suggestion, or else veiled under his general conclusions. If this official does not issue orders, does not exercise authority in the usual sense, he has as real an influence as the line official who issues orders and who influences his subordinates by direct contact with them.

Still another evidence of the diffusion of authority is the tendency in present business practice to solve problems where they arise, to make reconciliations at the point where conflict occurs, instead of the matter being carried "up" to someone. This means that departmental heads are being given more and more authority within their own units. Of course, all methods of decentralization tend to weaken the significance of "final" authority, and the tendency today is to decentralize. The administrative head is not the man in whom all control is centered, but the leader of many men with specific control.

I say that the tendency is to decentralize. I have heard it said twice at this conference that the tendency is to centralize. Both statements are true, for centralization and decentralization are parts of exactly the same thing.

Instead then of supreme control, ultimate authority, we might perhaps think of cumulative control, cumulative authority. I am indebted to Mr. Dennison for this phrase which seems to me to have implicated in it one of the most fundamental truths of organization.

Mr. Filene says: "I think some day we are going to recognize that this idea of one leader in a business is a fallacy, and that a composite general manager will develop." What the Filenes, and other firms too, have done is to make their formal organization coincide with a decided tendency in business practice. They found that there was power, leadership, all along the line. They recognized the existing. They sought to take advantage of it, to make this scattered power cumulative and hence more effective. There is nothing academic about the recent reorganization of business plants. There is nothing self sacrificing either. The upper executives have not given up anything. They have gathered into the management of their business every scrap of useful material they could find.

That business men are facing this undoubted fact of pluralistic authority, that modern business organization is based to some extent on this conception, is very interesting to me, for I have been for many years a student of political science, and it seems significant to me that now I have to go to business for the greatest light on authority, control, sovereignty--those concepts which have been supposed to be peculiarly the concepts of political science. For instance, in the last book I read on government, a recent one, the writer speaks of a "single, ultimate centre of control," but I do not find that practical men are much interested in ultimates. I think that with political scientists this interest is a survival from their studies in sovereignty. The business man is more concerned with the _sources_ than with the _organs_ of authority. Moreover any _over_ emphasis on ultimate control disregards one of the most important trends in the recent development of thinking on organization: "central control" used to mean the chief executive; now it is a technical expression of scientific management indicating the points where knowledge and experience on the matter in question are brought to a focus. This is very significant.

I should like, however, over against the statements made by students of government, to give some words of a practical administrator. In Franklin Lane's report to President Wilson on leaving the Cabinet, in suggesting that the heads of departments should be the advisors, the constructors of policies, he said: "In a word, we need more opportunity for planning, engineering, statesmanship above, and more fixed authority and responsibility below." This is interesting as taking away some of the pomp and circumstance which one attached to the word authority and making it a part of routine detail. Indeed authority seems to be becoming a humbler virtue.

And as it is the idea of pluralistic authority which is dominating progressive business organization today, so the crux of business organization is how to join these various authorities. Take the purchasing of materials. The authority for this should be assumed by the purchasing agent and by the department which gives its specifications to the purchasing agent. If the purchasing agent thinks that some of these specifications could be changed and cost thereby reduced without decreasing quality, he should discuss this with the department in question. While I realize that much can be accomplished by friendly relations between individuals, I think that organization should have for one of its chief aims to provide for a joint authority in those cases where combined knowledge is necessary for the best judgment.

This problem is being solved in a number of plants by a system of cross functioning. In one factory I know, they are trying to build up a structure of inter-locking committees. This is perhaps the most important trend in business organization. I don't mean committee government when I say that--that may or may not be the best way of meeting this problem--but the trend toward some kind of cross functioning. Let me take the New England Telephone Company as providing an example of this trend, although of course there are many other companies which would do equally well for illustration. Here we find the four departments--traffic, engineering, commercial and plant--conferring with one another or all together. These conferences are often informal but are expected of all officials. Each department is supposed to get in touch with certain others. The district traffic manager asks the wire chief from the plant department to talk the matter over with him, or if it is a commercial matter, he calls in the commercial manager of that district, or if it is a question of blue prints or costs, he asks the engineering department if they will send a man over. They may settle it among themselves. If not, the traffic manager puts it up to the division of traffic, and he may consult the division superintendent of plant and commercial departments. Here, you see, we have a combination of going both across and up the line. When the Main exchange in Boston was cut into two last summer, the question came up whether to cut thirty five a day or five hundred in a blanket order over night. This affected all four departments--traffic, engineering, commercial and plant. They agreed, after discussion, on the blanket order. If they had disagreed, they would have taken it up to the general superintendent of each department--*up* the line, note. Then the four superintendents would have consulted--here a cross relation. If these had agreed the matter would have ended there. If not, it would have had to go to the General Manager--*up* the line.

This combination of across and up exists, as I have said, in many plants today, and I have found it an interesting thing to watch, interesting because significant perhaps of a change in the accepted principles of organization which will eventually change not only business, but government as well. And it is noteworthy, in connection with this point, that the Telephone Company does not have, and does not seem to need, any special coordinating department, because there is a "natural" continuous coordinating inherent in their form of organization.

The chief weakness in business organization is lack of coordination. Yet I hear more talk of coordination than of anything else. Why then do we not get it? One reason is that the system of organization in a plant is often so hierarchical, so ascending and descending, that it is almost impossible to provide for cross relations. The notion of horizontal authority has not yet taken the place of vertical authority. We cannot, however, succeed in modern business by always running up and down a ladder of authority. Moreover, cross functioning seems often to be conceived of as useful only when difficulties arise, or when it is obvious that joint consultation on some specific problem would be desireable. But as such consultation is necessary all the time, some machinery which will operate continuously should be provided. And this is now recognized.

Of course, one difficulty about a degree or a manner of working together which hides individual effort comes from the egotism, the perfectly natural and to some extent justifiable egotism, of the persons concerned. Each executive wants his special contribution to get to the ears of the boss.

Another difficulty about coordination, and one of the greatest, is that it is not sufficiently recognized that coordination is not a culminating process. You cannot always bring together the _results_ of departmental activities and expect to coordinate them. You must have an organization which will permit interweaving all along the line. Strand should weave with strand, and then we shall not have the clumsy task of trying to patch together finished webs.

The chief reason, however, that we are not more successful with this problem is that we do not yet fully comprehend, I think, the essential nature of coordination. Coordinated control, or what I have called the field of control as distinct from any one factor in it, is more than a mere addition of specific controls. I should like to spend the few moments I have left in considering this point further.

In any situation the control is complex, not single. Consider Italy at the present moment. While the most interesting thing about that situation is that one man is such a large factor in it, yet to understand the Italian situation we have to get together _all_ that is influencing Italy, all that has gone to give Mussolini his power. In the same way, in attempting to solve a business problem it is essential first of all to find out what are all the factors which constitute that problem. And yet that is not enough, to get together all the factors; we have not found what I call the field of control by saying that it is composed of A plus B plus C plus D. The field of control is determined not only by these constituents but by their relations to one another.

This means, among other things, that if one factor is withdrawn or added to a situation, you have then not that situation minus or plus that factor, for all the rest will be changed. You see it on a Board of Directors. One man leaves and all the rest become a little different. The influence of that Board of Directors as a total is not the same as it was minus that man's influence, because his withdrawal, by changing slightly every other man, has made the total a little different. You all know that a President in relation to one Board of Directors may be very different from that same President in relation to another Board.

An organization consultant called in to find why a certain department in a business was not keeping pace with the rest of the business, told me he found that the solution of the problem lay not in changing any one thing or any two or three things in that department, although that was what the Board of Directors had expected him to do. But what he suggested to the Board was certain changes in the relation between the factors of which that department was composed. In the language I am now using he found that the important thing in that particular field of control was not some one or another or all of the constituents, but the relation of these to one another.

All that I am saying is a matter of everyday experience to the business man. It happens to be considered by certain scientists the most important thing in present scientific thinking. The most interesting thing in the world to me today is the approachment I see between progresive business thinking, as well as various tendencies in business practice, and certain recent developments in the thinking of scientists, philosophers and psychologists. Men working quite independently of each other, working in quite different fields, too, are coming to agree on a very fundamental principle, perhaps the most fundamental principle the human mind has yet caught sight of. This principle is involved in the very nature of unities. It is that the essential nature of a unity is discovered not alone by a study of its separate elements but also by observing how these elements interact. Such biologists as Henderson and J. S. Haldane (Henderson is a biological chemist), such philosophers as Whitehead, such physiologists as Cannon, such psychologists as the whole _Gestalt_ school, are coming to agree on this point. They say that every organization has a form, a structure, and that what that organism does, its unified activity, depends not on the constituents alone, but on how these constituents are related to one another.

As I am saying the same thing of a total of control; namely, that a field of control is not a mere aggregation of specific controls, it was not quite accurate, or rather did not tell the whole story, when I spoke of cumulative authority, unless you understand cumulative authority as integrated authority, as interweaving controls, an expression I also used. Biologists speak of the "system of control" in an organism meaning exactly this, the self-direction, self-regulation, which an organism has in virtue of the way its parts behave together. This parallel in thinking between academic men and business men is enormously significant. If I were speaking modestly, I should say that I think we may be pretty sure we are on the right track if we find such confirmation as this from scientists and philosophers. If I were speaking not modestly but as I really believe, I should add to that, that I think they also might feel that they are on the right track because we in these associations studying business management can from our experience confirm what they are saying.

The possible examples from business management of the working of this fundamental principle are innumerable. Take a situation made by credit conditions, customers' demand, output facilities, and workers' attitude. They all together make a certain situation, but they constitute that situation through their relation to one another. If you change one, usually some, if not all, of the others are changed.

Or take the way sales policy, production policy and financial policy influence one another. When they join to form a genuine unity, we have no mere aggregation. Each has been somewhat changed in the process of joining. And the whole, or general policy, is different because of this change in the parts. This is, it is not the aggregation but the integration of these parts which constitutes the field of control. This is the point we forget, and forget to our disaster, over and over again in business management. The awareness of what the field of control actually is in a given situation is essential to successful business management. Perhaps that is what hunch is--recognizing the field of control, but we cannot consider hunch this afternoon. All that I want to emphasize is that whether we do it unconsciously, as in hunch perhaps, or consciously and deliberately, the first approach to every business problem should be the question, "What is the field of control?" and the realization that that field of control is constituted not by certain elements alone, but by certain reciprocal activities.

I should like to say incidentally that if democracy means only all taking part, I do not believe in democracy. It is organization we want, the relating of parts, cofunctioning organic interactivities. The great weakness of the English Labor Party is, in my opinion, that it does not see this.

If the first step in the understanding of a business problem is an understanding of what constitutes the field of control, the second is an understanding of the process of passing from one field of control to another. Perhaps no one thing will have a greater effect on business management than a realization of the importance of this, for then anticipation will not mean forecasting alone; it will mean far more than predicting the next situation. It will mean more than <u>meeting</u> the next situation, it will mean <u>making</u> the next situation. One of the largest manufacturers in Milan said last July that he and a number of other Italian manufacturers were making a thorough study of American methods of scientific management so that they would be ready to deal with the industrial situation when Mussolini's hand should be withdrawn. This means in the language we are using this afternoon that when that field of control is broken up, they are going to have a hand in making the next. This kind of anticipation goes far beyond forecasting, but the consideration of anticipation not as prediction but as control would take us beyond the limits of this paper. I have given this hint here because back of everything I ever say or write on business management there is always the idea of control as the self directing power of a unity. A genuine coordination or integration gives you control. That is why coordination is the most important point in organization.

A few weeks ago I was having a talk with a small group of people. Two of the men were philosophers, one was a consulting expert on industrial relations. The question was asked by some one why business men were doing so much thinking nowadays, thinking on abstract questions. My answer to that was that all of us, including business men, are accepting more fully perhaps than ever before in the world, the idea that we can control our activities. In our individual lives the tendency is no longer to submit to fate, inheritance or even environment. We see this same trend of thinking in the social sciences. Roscoe Pound, a jurist, writes of conscious control. John Maynard Keynes, an economist, says that we are now entering on an era of stabilization in which the doctrine of laissez faire must be abandoned in favor of deliberate conscious control. In business, too, it is the dominant thought. Why are we studying the business cycle? Why are we now studying unemployment instead of accepting it as inevitable? What is all the study of management but just an indication of this? Moreover, the real reason that we have personnel work, the study of human relations in industry, is because we have waked up to the fact that the human as well as the mechanical side of industry can be studied, and much learned thereby to give us control of the situations between executives and workers or between executives themselves.

In short, business is coming to be considered not so much a speculative undertaking as a social enterprise, resting on scientific knowledge, controllable by further and further developments in scientific methods. The dominant thought of the twentieth century, the contribution which the twentieth century is giving the world, is a richer idea of the meaning of control than we have ever had before, and it is among business men that we find those who are doing perhaps more than anyone else to give that thought reality.

---

[1] *Bulletin of the Taylor Society*, December 1926. Paper presented at a meeting of the Taylor Society, New York, December 10, 1926.

HENRI FAYOL[1]

A Great Engineer, a Great Scientist and a Great Management Leader

By Charles de Freminville
Consulting Engineer, Schneider et Cie, Paris

Foreward

We desire to express to M. de Freminville, on behalf of the readers of the Bulletin, their appreciation of his kindness in preparing, by request, this interesting statement concerning Henri Fayol and his doctrine. The Fayol doctrine is in many respects identical with and in many more respects complementary to the Taylor doctrine. Fayol focused his attention on organization and control of general administration; Taylor focused his attention on organization and control of shop operations. But although they started from opposite points of the compass, they so set their courses that it was inevitable their doctrines should come together. The life and doctrine of Fayol should be inspiring and helpful to the American executive as the life and doctrine of Taylor have been to the French executive. (Editor).

A year ago the management world lost one of its eminent leaders in the sudden death of Henri Fayol, who had remained full of life and energy despite his great age. His life, turned from the beginning toward the highest ideals, was of such magnificent simplicity that its history can be given in a few words, though the task accomplished is of immense value.

After graduating from the Ecole des Mines de St. Ettienne in 1860, he was engaged by the Mining and Metallurgical Sté de Commentry Fourchambault, in which he was to spend his whole engineering life. He was general superintendent from 1888 to 1918, when he retired from his executive position to become Director of the Board of the same company.

In public life he was a member of the most important committees in Mining and Metallurgy and a member of the Conseil de Perfectionnement du Conservatoire des Arts et Metiers, as well as an officer of la Legion d'Honneur.

His research on the technical problems involved in coal mining as well as his scientific contribution to the study of the formation of coal fields have become classics. In these studies some of the greatest geologists cooperated with him. Some of his papers were published in the Bulletin de l'Academie des Sciences.

He gave a great impetus to research in special steels at the laboratory of the Imphy works of his company, where such men as Chevenard and Ch. Ed. Guillaume completed their studies. The latter was the recipient of the Nobel prize for 1921.

The full story of his own executive work is included in the following short statement: In 1888 he assumed the responsibility of the management of the Societe de Commentry Fourchambault et Decazeville, that company being then in the most critical position, and in 1918 he was able to hand it over to his successor in a splendid financial situation and, still more important, with a staff of exceptional ability.

His remarkable attitude toward the work he had accomplished is shown by his statement that this astounding success ought to be attributed solely to the method he had followed: "With the same mines, the same plants, the same amount of capital, the same market, the same board of directors and the same staff, simply because of the new system of management, the company experienced an ascending prosperity to be compared only with its previous downfall." And he was anxious to make evident that by simply planning and acting with a little method and order anyone could have done what he had done.

His friends in the scientific field were struck with the unflinching faith in "method" which was apparent in all his works, and the great professor, Termier, the savant, the poet and highly religious man, speaking of the discoveries of Fayol, said: "I wonder whether one of the discoveries or the method which led to the discoveries must be most admired," and Fayol goes on; "It is not the theory of 'coal mine fires' which led to the 'theory of deltas'; neither 'geology' which led me to 'administration'; it is not the 'problem of administration' which led me to the 'problem of life.' The whole thing sprang up before me as the result of 'Method,' the one 'Method,' the universal 'Method' of which we must make use in all things and in everything, everywhere."

In the year 1900 he began to disclose his thoughts on management at the International Congress of Mining and Metallurgy and still more forcibly in 1908 and 1916, when he presented his great paper "Administration Industrielle et Generale," which has been termed a catechism for the chief executive's education.

"It is evident," said Sainte Claire-Deville, an eminent mining and metallurgical engineer, "that 'administration' and 'organization' have existed for a long time, but the great merit of Fayol is carefully to have observed during his long career a number of experimental facts in relation to organization, to have deducted from them a very few simple principles that he put into a very clear form. These are so simple and so clear that one is inclined to say: All that is old, is known, is evident! To be sure it is. But if any one of us is sincere he will confess that while he had known, or thought he had known, Fayol's principles, he had disregarded them, willingly or not."

Fayol came that we might understand better what a leader in state or private business management, an administrator, ought to be. He made us realize what were the essential qualities of the great Roman colonial administrators, of the great managers of state affairs, of which France has had several; one of the greatest, if not the greatest, being Colbert, who, like Fayol, began with the management of private affairs before assuming charge of those of the country.

The Administrative Doctrine of Fayolism

"The Administrative Doctrine," says Fayol himself (Second Congress of Administrative Sciences, Brussels, 1923) "is a body of principles, rules and processes aiming at helping the management of any undertaking, be it big or small, in industry, commerce, politics, or even an undertaking with a religious or other aim."

1. Essential Functions.
   All the functions in any undertaking are contained in the six following groups:

   a. Technical (producing, manufacturing, transforming)

   b. Commercial (buying, selling, exchanging)

   c. Financial (finding and managing capital)

   d. Safety (protecting property and persons against casualties)

   e. Accounting (inventory, cost accounting, balance, statistics, etc.)

   f. Administrative (planning, organizing, commanding, coordinating and controlling)

The administrative doctrine deals only with this last group, therefore it does not include the whole government of the undertaking. Governing is conducting the undertaking towards a certain goal, trying to make the most of the resources at its disposal. It is looking towards the accomplishment of the six essential functions. Administration is one of the six functions trusted to the care of the government, but it takes such a great place in what the highest executive has to do that people may sometimes think that his task is purely administrative.

The administrative function consists essentially of foreseeing, organizing, commanding, coordinating and controlling.

Foreseeing is forecasting the future and planning action.

Organizing is building the material and social frame of the undertaking.

Commanding is bringing the staff and force into action.

Coordinating is linking, uniting and harmonizing every act and effort.

Controlling is seeing that everything goes on according to the established rule and issued orders.

Therefore, administration is not the exclusive privilege of the chief executive or directors of the undertaking; it is a function which is distributed, like any other of the essential functions, between the head and limbs of the social body.

The technical function is not limited to the workman or the engineer; it extends upward to the chief executive. Conversely the administrative function is not an exclusive attribute of the chief; it extends downward to the lowest executive. But the share of each class of executive in discharging any of these functions is largely different from any other class, to such an extent that there is no comparison between the capacity--technical, administrative, or of any kind--in a man on the first step of the ladder and the capacity of the same denomination of the chief executive.

The essential capacity of the lowest executive is that professional capacity which is most important for the undertaking considered, and the essential capacity of the chief executive is the administrative capacity.

Through foreseeing, organizing, commanding, coordinating and controlling, the administrative function has a part to play in the accomplishment of every other function. Therefore, when the administrative function is well discharged it is very likely that the other will be equally well discharged.

To be a good administrator the chief executive must be able: first, to foresee, organize, command, coordinate and control; and second, to have a sufficient competency in that special function which is characteristic of the undertaking.

The other qualities and knowledges that should be found in every highest executive are: health and physical vigor; intelligence and intellectual vigor; moral qualities, will; energy and if needed, audacity; courage in assuming responsibilities; a high sense of duty and due regard for general welfare; strong general culture; general knowledge of all essential functions.

2. Administrative General Principles.

The administrative capacity has its foundation to a certain extent in natural gifts; but it has a foundation also in a thorough understanding, acquired from actual experience, of the principles and rules of the Administrative Doctrine, which can be summarized as follows:

Division of work; authority coupled with responsibility; discipline; unity in command; unity in management; general interest first; equitable remuneration of work; centralization (more or less according to circumstances); equity; stability of staff (small turnover); initiative; cooperation ("l'union fait la force," better than "diviser pour regner").

Such are the fundamental principles put in practice under the "Administrative Doctrine." To carry out these principles, it is necessary to set on foot a _planning or budgeting provision_ for the future based on a thorough understanding of the past and present life of the undertaking; an _acting program_ or schedule safeguarding unity and continuity in acting; an _organization chart_; _annual_, _monthly and weekly reports_; and _proceedings of the committee of executives_, of the greatest importance for cooperation.

When Fayol published his book "Administration Industrielle et Generale" in 1916, he said: "I have been busy at it for half a century. Should some of the ideas it contains come to be of current use in conducting business, after another half century, my time would not have been lost." Today 15,000 copies of the book have been printed and the demand is very great.

His Missionary Work

But, in his own mind, Fayol had merely given a start to an important movement. To keep his friends in contact he founded a "Center for the Study of Administrative Science" freely opened to all interested. Courses in the Science of Administration were created at the Ecole des Hautes Etudes Commerciales, Ecole de l'Intendance de l'Armee, Ecole du Commissariat de la Marine, Ecole de Guerre, Conservatoire des Artes et Metiers, etc.

Above all he wished to bring about a change in the methods in use in state administration and to show that what is absolutely necessary in conducting industrial businesses is still more necessary in conducting state business, where it seems to be absolutely ignored. To that end he made a thorough study of the working of the Post Office Department and other industrial state departments, and even of the working methods of the Board of State Ministers, where he wished to establish more responsibility and continuity in work concerned with national policy rather than with departmental administration. He succeeded in attracting attention in such quarters, and he saw the dawn of the practical application of his principles in state administration. The greatest accomplishment of that kind has been in Belgium and Holland. His books have been translated into many languages and his doctrine is known the world over as Fayolism.

Fayolism and Taylorism

Some people think of Fayol as opposed to Taylor; of the French spirit contrasting with the American spirit. This view does not lead to a fair appreciation of these great men.

Both had an absolute faith in scientific method, but circumstances were such that they made different use of it. They started as if from opposite quarters of the horizon to join in the conclusion of their work. Both were pioneers and reformers in quest of the good of all concerned in industry, of the welfare of their country and of the world at large.

The chief difference is found in the place where the first studies of the one or the other were made; Taylor started with the man at the bench or the lathe and built upward; Fayol, more concerned with the task of the chief executive and even of the board of directors, followed the consequences of their conduct all the way down to the working man.

Both of them were men of intellectual culture and high ideals, and they were fighters to the same extent, never satisfied with a more or less benevolent approval. Nothing but the actual practice of the principles they had brought forward could please them. Both encountered more opposition than praise.

While Taylor was misrepresented as trying to drive the workmen, to which practice he was absolutely opposed, Fayol was accused of leading industry towards the obsolete and unpopular methods of the great public administrations of his country, which he was really fighting with the greatest energy. It may be said that Fayol was evoking the work of the great French pioneers in management of public affairs, whose spirit had been corrupted by their successors, and that Taylor was striving to bring the industrial world to a better understanding of and more effective and humane use of the equipment which had been developed to such an extent in the United States. Both were acting as reformers of the evils they were accused of fostering.

Again, both of them had to hear people saying that there was nothing new in the work they had done, that their so-called principles were known to everybody. What everybody knows is simply wonderful, but it is no less wonderful that everybody makes such little use of what he knows; that it requires a great leader and a lifetime work to bring him to do it.

Taylor had departed when Fayol began his missionary work. But at that time Fayol made a thorough study of Taylor's work, to check up, as it were, his own ideas and principles. Like Taylor, he was far more concerned with finding what was true than what could be termed new. At first he was startled with the idea that he did not agree with Taylor. Being anxious to find out how this could be, he came to me in 1916 to discuss the matter, and from that year we were friends.

The confusion came from Taylor's opposition to the omniscient and omnipotent foreman of old. This at first appeared to Fayol as a disregard of the principle of "Unity of Command," which he considered essential in good management. He was not immediately convinced by my argument that Taylor was calling on the management to fulfill completely its own duty--it may have been because I did not put the thing clearly enough before him at that time. This misunderstanding came to an end at the opening of the International Scientific Management Congress in Burssels in October, 1925, when, after arguing once more on the point, I told him that it could be said without the smallest hesitation, that Taylor was absolutely the man who made efficient, even to the smallest operation in the workshop, the "Unity of Command," the method in use being closely controlled by the management. This was a state of affairs which had not existed at all before him; through the functional foreman, functional unity was secured in the whole system.

Then Fayol saw clearly that it could be said that, actuated by the same spirit and guided by the same method, Taylor and himself, starting from opposite directions, had met halfway to reinforce their actions.

No general planning can give its best without a thorough analysis and complete preparation of the smallest operations, whereas, to proceed securely with the organization of the work in the shop it is necessary to forecast the future according to Fayol principles. This pleased Fayol immensely and he told me that, when I should precede him in speaking at the opening meeting of the Congress, I must make such a statement, and that he would enlarge upon it and declare that men like Taylor and himself, moved by the love of truth, could not be in opposition as formerly he had feared. That he did in a spendid manner, and before he died very suddenly, a few days later, he declared repeatedly to his friends that this had been the greatest joy he had experienced for a long time.

---

[1] Bulletin of the Taylor Society, February, 1927.

LABOR'S IDEALS CONCERNING MANAGEMENT[1]

Labor's Attitude Toward Industry and Industrial Processes Is Changing--

Understanding and Cooperation Will Serve the Best Interests of All

By William Green
President, The American Federation of Labor

Introductory Remarks of Henry S. Dennison, Presiding

I am here to introduce. May I not take the job literally and really attempt to make known the Taylor Society to William Green and William Green to the Taylor Society.

The Taylor Society believes that the managing of business is an activity capable of supporting the severest demand for professional behavior which may be put upon it; that the profession of management is taking form and must continue to develop as business units grow big and stock holdings scatter. Even when hired by capital--as is as yet most often the case--it is not capital; and though working hourly in the shop or mill with labor, it is not labor. "The Management," as the Taylor Society must conceive it, is not simply "The Old Man" or the Old Man and his staff--but that whole group of men and women who must devise such ways for keeping the whole organization going as will most efficiently compound the varied motives and meet the complex desires of consumer, dealer, investor, supplier, laborer and staff worker.

The Taylor Society knows that business management can never properly be said to be managing, much less be accorded the respect due a profession--unless it recognizes the bald fact that business, besides bringing materials into new relations with each other and so making, as we loosely say, new commodities--brings human beings into active relations to each other and so makes new men. The Society knows, therefore, that true management cannot suffer the obsession of production or dividends, but must see both of these and plenty more of the possible fruits of a healthy organization in their true proportions.

Management must see and know the areas of common interest and the areas of conflict among the half dozen great classes of live men and women with which it deals, and as it casts off its chains of ignorance, will know how increasingly well to integrate them. It must, moreover, learn how to enlist their powers more fully in its service--how to gain discrimination from the consumer, cooperation from dealer, constructive suggestion from supplier, and real interest from workers. And it alone can hope so to inspire and to integrate because--(and only so long as)--its own chief interest is in the joy of a great job well done.

Recognizing dispassionately these natural areas of mutual and of conflicting interest, management could not do else but acknowledge the appropriateness and the many social values of association among them.

It expects to find and to deal with associations among consumers, dealers, supplying trades, financiers, and workers; to learn from them to hold clearer views of their fundamental needs; and to find them seeking their own share of social progress most intently.

Any man reading history unblinded by his prejudices must be grateful for what associations of workingmen have done during the past one hundred years. They have saved, I believe, the dignity of human labor. Yet no man caring for the future of his kind would on that account absolve unions of any social wrong they may commit; to ack-knowledge the past is to challenge the future.

The dispassionate student, seeing some near-sighted employers of yesterday and today, may expect an answering irritation from workingmen tomorrow; but in all professional honesty he must nevertheless point out its ill effects and work to allay it. To remove the causes of such irritation the Taylor Society has always striven. Up until tonight, Mr. Green, we have, indeed, confined our tender ministrations to the employer. And if I myself am known beyond the broadcasting range and outside the special wave lengths of our Dennison advertising department, it is as none too charitable to the employer when his responsibilities and opportunities are in question. But on this fortunate and deeply valued occasion the Taylor Society expects to give the poor chap an earned respite.

So much for the Taylor Society. It stands, in a word, for the high destiny and unlimited responsibility of business management to inspire and coordinate the finest efforts of all parties to our economic undertakings towards the broadest advancement of mankind. Strife it accepts, but in the insistent faith that growing wisdom can raise the planes of strife.

And, ladies and gentlemen of the Taylor Society, may I make known to you William Green--miner, district president and then treasurer of the United Mine Workers of America; state senator and author of Ohio's Workmen's Compensation Law; vice-president and now president of the American Federation of Labor. His works have acclaimed him a lover of strife upon the highest planes, a believer in the great opportunities of business management, a friend of our faith with whom we can hold fruitful consultation in scientific mood. And with all his titles and honors, we tonight shall regard him chiefly as the very human leader of some millions of very human friends of ours, and as our honored and respected guest. Mr. Green--

Address by William Green

The marvelous growth and expansion of American industry is due to the stimulating influence of private enterprises and personal initiative. The call of industry meets with a most hearty response from adventurous men, for there is something fascinating and attractive about industry which appeals to their genius and imagination. Hope of financial reward and material gain may be the incentive which inspires action, but risk and uncertainty always cast their shadows over the establishment and progress of every business experiment.

These uncertainties are offset by the qualities of personal initiative and confidence in the ability and resourcefulness of the human factors involved. Faith and confidence in humanity form the basis upon which industrial progress rests. Invention and experimentation contribute to material prosperity but intricate machinery and arduous research are of no avail if personal skill and technique are lacking.

Modern industry represents the development of an important phase of our civilization. Its contribution to the welfare and happiness of the people bears tribute to the worth and soundness of our civilizing processes. With all its imperfections the so-called capitalistic administration of industry is the best of any thus far devised. Under the present form of industrial administration a high degree of perfection has been attained, but even greater and more effectual progress can be made if the owners of industry and those who exercise financial control over it are sagacious enough to sense the trend of public thought and the attitude of the public toward industry.

There are many manifestations of a prevailing public desire to improve upon our present system and methods through the development of a higher degree of coordination and cooperation among all the units of productivity. There is no evidence of any disposition on the part of the people to invade the field of hazardous uncertainty by substituting some other system for the one we now have. They want improvement, not retrogression. They believe this can be accomplished through the elimination of abuses which have crept in and through the correct solution of the industrial problems which are faced by all those associated with industry.

This leads us to a consideration of the numerous factors associated with industry. They are varied, each contributing to the exigency and to the success of the endeavor. The three important factors are capital, labor and management. The others are of minor importance and of lesser consequence.

Not until recently was management considered of great importance. Formerly capital and labor were regarded as the only essential factors. This view prevailed during the period when the relationship between employers and employees was of a more personal character. It must be relinquished because financial changes have taken place until now, through the diversified ownership of corporations, management control has supplanted personal ownership control. This brought with it the formation of new relationships and the assumption of new responsibilities.

Labor is intensely interested in this changed relationship because it is directly affected by it. It is facing the facts which this change has brought with it in a spirit of goodwill. It hopes and believes that this changing process will result in industrial improvement and human betterment.

The primary purpose of management in industry is to control and direct the forces of production in such a way as to secure the highest returns possible upon the capital invested. The methods through which this objective may be realized have been the subject of universal study. Originally it was assumed by employers that the only way by which earnings could be maintained on a satisfactory level was through the establishment of low wage scales. Financiers held that high wages and fair dividends were incompatible; that earnings could be increased only through reductions in wages. This concept has been forced to give way under the searching analysis of modern thought and study.

No longer do we accept this wage theory. Instead it has been shown that production costs may be reduced while wages are being increased. Management is very largely responsible for this achievement, not altogether, perhaps, because there are other factors in industry which contribute in full measure to the accomplishment of this result. Each and every factor deserves full credit for the part it plays in lowering costs and increasing wages.

The power of decision and direction in the formulation and execution of policies lies with management. It is the agency which is charged with responsibility and is held accountable for success or failure. The degree of success which may be attained depends very largely upon the training and ability of management. A full measure of success can only be attained through the harmonious cooperation of all the productive forces in industry. To bring this about is one of the problems of a successful manager.

The great creative force in industry is labor. Machinery, money and other equipment are of very great importance and are essential to industrial success, but these instrumentalities are made forceful, effective and active only through the service and activity of labor. This fact directs attention, in a most direct way, to the relationship of labor and management and to the functions of each with reference to production and development. All of this involves a fundamental, sound, human relationship. The establishment of confidence and understanding between management and the workers, faith in each other and a firm belief in the integrity and honesty of those human forces is of immeasurable value and contributes very greatly to the success and welfare of industrial undertakings.

All of this requires a proper regard for the rights of labor and management. It requires even more. There must be an understanding of human nature, of human qualities and of those inspirational forces which move men who are engaged in serviceable action.

Management must deal with labor collectively and because this is true the means and methods through which it may be done most effectively are questions of supreme importance. Experience has shown that the most effective way, the most practical way, is through trade unions, organized, maintained and administered by the workers who compose them. This method insures to the workers independence, freedom of expression, a free choice in the selection of their spokesmen and a forum wherein they can consider and discuss managerial and industrial problems.

The trade union is an institution originated by the working people. It is composed of members voluntarily associated together for mutual helpfulness and self-development. The workers are the architects who designed the trade union structure and they are the builders who erected it. The members who compose it are thoroughly conscious of its potential and active powers and regard it as the agency through which the economic and intellectual powers of the workers may be developed to the highest point.

For many years both managers and owners in industry wrongfully regarded trade unions as destructive forces which should be repressed and completely annihilated. Much of the time and energy of ownership was devoted to the consideration and execution of plans and policies designed to crush and destroy trade unions. This was attended by waste of a most inexcusable kind because much money represented in the earnings of the concern was used in the attacks upon the establishment and growth of trade unions.

Such policies of trade union opposition have always been productive of losses which cannot be properly measured in the terms of dollars. These losses are represented in an absence of goodwill, of cooperation, and of a high standard of service, and in the unfavorable psychological condition which is created among the workers.

There are many evidences that these policies are giving way to a newer concept, to the belief that trade unions are firmly established in our industrial life. In fact they have grown in spite of opposition until they constitute a part of America's institutional life. It is known they are now regarded as a necessity, an essential, stabilizing force in society and industry. Men of thought and vision understand that the destruction of trade unionism would be a most serious blow to our economic and industrial life. Indeed, many believe it would be the most severe blow which industry could sustain.

Trade unions may give to industry and to management service of great value. The intelligence, the knowledge and the training which comes through trade union affiliation may be utilized to the benefit of industry and to those associated with it. It is for management to understand how this may be done and through such understanding to enlist the full support and cooperation of the officers and members of trade unions.

People find it very difficult to break the bonds of primitive thought and rise above an intolerant policy which has long been followed. So it is with some employers and some managers. Their constitutional and fundamental objection to trade unions has led them to accept substitutes therefor in the form of company unions and employees' representation plans. Having sensed the instinct for organization among the workers they endeavor to satisfy it through the organization and development of company-controlled organizations.

These company unions may resemble the trade union. The difference between them is in substance rather than in form. The inspiration of the company union comes from without and that of the trade union comes from within. The company union is restricted in its resources, its independence and its vitality. The power of veto, of domination and of control lies within the employing group. The members of company unions cannot deal with management upon an equal basis. The company unions are not trade unions.

Because of the insecure foundation upon which the substitute for trade unionism rests the company unions would collapse and cease to exist at the will of the employer. The toleration of their existence must ever be contingent upon the maintenance of independent trade unions.

The purpose of management which fosters the organization of company unions is clear and easily understood. The motive behind their action is a selfish one. It represents the desire for autocratic control and managerial domination. They seek to maintain the form of collective bargaining without its virtues or its spirit of independence. They seek control rather than cooperation. They exert the power of compulsion instead of inviting the voluntary cooperation of their employees. While there may be some managers who are sincere in their attempts to deal with company organized unions, they are unconsciously responsible for wrong to labor and disservice to industry. They are attempting to build an industrial structure upon a wrong principle.

The disposition of management, in some instances, to establish a system of production out-put so that the worker serves in a mechanical capacity is both unwise and unprofitable. It is in cases of this kind where standardization is over-done. It carries with it a form of speeding-up against which workers everywhere have protested. The net result is to destroy personal initiative, to make work monotonous instead of interesting and to cause a large and uneconomic labor turnover.

It is becoming increasingly clear that management must face facts. Management must either deal with trade unions organized by the workers, free and apart from outside influences, or deal with their workers individually. Company unions may serve some temporary purpose but they cannot function permanently or successfully. No substitute plan of workers' organizations can fill the place of bona fide trade unions.

It is conceded that industry is complex in that there are blended into operation and activity numerous elements all having to do with quantity and quality of production. Chief among these elements are finance, marketing facilities, machinery, raw materials, standards of production, skill of management and the mental and physical power of labor. Of secondary importance are large scale organization, the adoption of economic and modern methods and machinery, the elimination of waste and the elimination of duplication of effort.

While labor is not responsible and has no voice in the selection or employment of management it is vitally and directly interested in the quality and character of management.

Labor realizes that the success of management means the success of labor.

For that reason labor is willing to make its contribution to assist management and to bring about the right solution of problems dealt with by management.

Some of these problems are regularization of employment, fluctuation in prices, standardization of output, healthful and sanitary conditions of employment and the ever-pressing problem of unemployment. Safety of life, the prevention of accidents and continuity of employment make for economy in production costs and promote efficiency in service. These are questions of prime consideration. Industry sustains great losses from intermittent employment because of the lowering of workmanship morale and the consequent deterioration in the character of service rendered. It may be difficult to define the reasons for lowered morale and deterioration of service but the facts are that intermittent employment produces that result. Injury to workers through accidents is another cause of lowered morale and waste. Not only does the worker who is the victim of industrial accident suffer intense mental and physical pain but the depressing effect of such suffering is clearly evident among all groups employed in the vicinity where the accident occurs.

The great problem of unemployment is ever with us and constantly pressing for solution. It is one of the direct sources of waste. It is demoralizing in its influence and lies at the base of social unrest causing much human suffering. The problem of unemployment is a challenge to industry. It must be met--not in the spirit of toleration or resignation, but in the spirit of determination to conquer and control.

In touching upon Labor's ideals concerning management we are conscious of the fact that we have been and are now passing through a period when changes are taking place. These changes affect human relationships in a most vital way. Many of our older concepts are giving way to the newer and more progressive points of view. The relationship of management to labor is changed and is changing. The mental attitude of labor toward industry and industrial processes is undergoing revision and readjustment. Management is understanding more and more that economies in production can be brought about through the cooperation of labor and the establishment of high standards rather than through the autocratic control and exploitation of labor. Labor is understanding more and more that high wages and tolerable conditions of employment can be brought about through excellency in service, the promotion of efficiency and the elimination of waste. It is becoming more clearly understood that high wages and a high standard of efficiency in industry are correlated and the industry that is best managed, most economically controlled, where workmanship of the highest order under satisfactory conditions is maintained, is the industry that can pay the highest wages.

Labor entertains many ideals concerning management. The attendance of labor's spokesmen at meetings of this character is an evidence of this fact. We invite most sincere reflection and most careful consideration of all the ideals which labor holds concerning management. The serious-minded, thoughtful spokesmen of labor are not optimistic enough to believe that labor's ideals concerning management will be immediately realized. An ideal may be properly regarded as an unrealized peak of perfection to which we may aspire. In this respect it is visionary, serving as an incentive to effort and to achievement. Even though these ideals may be for the moment unattainable they are so practical in character and so fraught with spiritual and material possibilities as to urge us forward in an earnest endeavor to realize them.

Management holds a most strategic position. Its activities and its policies touch the very life, wellbeing and happiness of the workers. Chief among the ideals of labor is the development of cordial relations between the workers and management. The workers believe that through understanding and cooperation the best interests of all those associated with industry can be served.

It is the hope and desire of labor that management will respond to this lofty sentiment so that in the consideration of policies management may seek to understand not what it might compel the workers to do but instead what the workers may be able and competent and willing to do.

Through such understanding all the associated productive powers of industry can be mobilized into an economic, sustained, impelling force through which economy in production may be completely accomplished. Through the development of a cooperative spirit and the establishment and maintenance of a frank relationship the rewards of the efforts of all those associated with industry can be equitably distributed.

The wisdom of such a policy will be made manifest in a high standard of workmanship, in increased industrial earnings, in waste elimination and in the personal contact between management and the workers which is free from suspicion, antagonism and hatred.

It is an ideal of labor that management shall formulate and follow such wise policies as to bring to the workers the realization of high living standards as this condition would be of benefit to both owners and workers in industry.

Organized labor looks most earnestly toward the establishment of such an industrial relationship. It stands ready to do its full share in bringing about the consummation of these ideals. We ask that employers and management join with us in this noble and inspiring work.

---

[1]*Bulletin of the Taylor Society*, December, 1925. Paper presented at a joint meeting of the Taylor Society and the Management Division of the American Society of Mechanical Engineers, New York, December 3, 1925.

LABOR'S INTEREST IN INDUSTRIAL WASTE ELIMINATION[1]

Four Papers Presented Before a Conference on the Elimination of Waste in Industry, Held Under the Auspices of the Central Labor College of Philadelphia, April 9 and 10, 1927

LABOR AND WASTE ELIMINATION

By William Green
President, American Federation of Labor

Time and experience have developed a new conception of the vital problems which affect industry. Our viewpoint and understanding of the effect of industrial processes upon the welfare of all associated with industry have undergone a most revolutionary change. We now find that the line of separation cannot be drawn between any group or groups either interested in or connected with the producing forces of industry. There is no point which can be definitely fixed where the interest of one group begins or ends. The interests of all are so inextricably woven together as to preclude a diversion of effort or objective. One group cannot permanently prosper at the expense of the other nor is any one group immune from the evil consequences of uneconomic industrial operation. Industry is made profitable and the rewards of industrial efforts are increased in proportion to the co-operation established between employers, employes and management.

The exploitation of the workers on the part of employers and management cannot be defended by those who believe in justice and fair dealing. Driving processes are regarded as unscientific and inhuman. The successful employer inspires and leads men and women to give their best service and to do so freely and voluntarily.

The workers understand, as never before, that high wages depend upon the degree of efficiency developed among individual workers and the collective productivity of all who are employed. The basis of successful management as well as the basis of our modern wage structure has been changed.

Modern industry requires management to formulate plans, adopt methods and utilize every reasonable and honorable means at its command to promote economic production. Wages very largely depend upon successful management and the sustained service of the workers, made possible through the creation of opportunity for personal initiative and group activity.

There may have been a time when working people did not regard industrial waste as pertinent or important. They felt that it was no concern of theirs but that it was a problem belonging to management. Working people were chiefly concerned with wages, hours and conditions of employment. When conferences were held between the representatives of the workers and management discussion was limited by management to those questions. If the workers suggested changes or improvements in industrial methods or processes as an argument in favor of higher wages such suggestions were resented as an intrusion upon the prerogatives of management. Industrial waste, duplication of effort, increased efficiency and productivity were questions which were considered outside the limit of conference discussion between employers and employes.

Because of this mental attitude on the part of employers and employes no joint effort was made to seek a remedy for this condition of affairs. Where the wage schedules and conditions of employment were formulated and posted by employers without consultation with their employes there was no opportunity for a joint discussion of the questions of management and labor. Under such conditions management assumed full responsibility for industrial success or failure. It autocratically fixed wages, hours and conditions of employment and all other questions connected with the operation of industry were regarded as belonging to managerial control and determination. This state of affairs still prevails in some industries.

The working people were keenly alive to the injustice which they suffered under this form of industrial management. They arrived at the definite conclusion that their position in industry entitled them to recognition. They understood clearly that the losses of industry through mismanagement and waste fell heavily upon them. They were conscious of the fact that they could make a larger contribution to industrial expansion and development than they were giving through skill, labor and service and it was out of this state of mind that the demand for the broadening of collective bargaining grew.

There was no other way through which individual and collective expression could be given to the feelings, opinions, ideas and desires of the workers. They insisted upon the right of their representatives to meet with the employers and management upon this common plane of understanding and equality. They believed this to be one of the inherent rights of mankind. It is the recognition of the American principle which served to develop a free discussion of public grievances and public questions.

Back of all the collective skill, strength and power of all the working people of our nation are the soul and mind which give inspiration and impetus to all their physical powers. These unseen forces must be given an opportunity to function in concert with the strength and brawn of labor. From this co-ordination of all the workers' power of production there follows the establishment of a standard of excellency in service which ultimately reaches a maximum of efficiency.

If all the older as well as the newer problems arising out of industrial activities are to be grappled with and dealt with by employers and employes, who in the last analysis, are jointly affected, the machinery of collective bargaining must be more generally and universally utilized and strengthened. Management can do a great deal to prevent waste and further the elimination of waste. On the other hand, labor can assist management not only in dealing with the problem of waste but also in dealing with other industrial problems if given an opportunity to do so. Labor is willing and ready to do its share in the performance of this important work. The trade union is an agency through which this character of service can be rendered.

Waste in industry may be divided into three classifications--material waste, human waste and spiritual waste. Labor has given most careful thought to each of these classifications putting emphasis upon the human and spiritual rather than upon the material classification.

Material waste in industry, however, greatly affects the economic life of the workers. As waste detracts from the earnings of industry so it detracts from the wages of employes. The value of the services of employes may be completely destroyed through the operation of wasteful processes and the experience of an industry may be changed from a losing venture, because of waste, to an earning enterprise, because of the elimination of waste.

The difference between industrial success and industrial failure is many times found in the wasteful processes which often attend industrial operations. The unwarranted destruction of raw materials, natural resources and finished products, the uneconomic use of means of productions, negligence in the care of machinery and mechanical devices, indifference to the saving and protection of property and the failure to utilize all facilities available which make for economic production fall within the category of material waste. Furthermore, labor realizes that indefensible waste takes place when labor's industrial efforts go for naught or are unnecessarily duplicated through the failure of management to systematize and intelligently direct the working forces of industry. Practically all of this character of industrial waste can either be prevented or materially reduced. It is not a problem impossible of solution. A joint study supplemented by joint efforts can overcome this destructive evil.

The desire of labor to interest itself in the problem of waste is based upon its wish to secure higher wages and to enjoy improved conditions of employment. So long as industry is only partially efficient labor believes that the wages paid can be substantially increased through an increase in industrial efficiency and the elimination of waste. By the same process the cost of manufactured articles to the public can be materially reduced.

The most tragic feature of our industrial development is connected with the loss of human life and the mental and physical suffering caused by industrial accidents and unemployment. It is particularly deplorable because it strikes the bread-winner and, in addition to increasing the expenses, stops the income upon which the family depends for sustenance and life. Much of the loss of life caused by industrial accidents is morally indefensible and criminal.

For instance, science has demonstrated the fact that mine dust explosions which result in the loss of hundreds of lives could be avoided through the simple process of rock dusting. Notwithstanding the fact that we are in full possession of this scientific knowledge it is not used except to a limited extent, consequently an appalling loss of life occurs in the mining industry through gas and coal dust explosions. The death rate from accidents is considerably higher in the mining industry of our country than it is in the mining industry of any other nation in the world.

While industrial accidents cannot be absolutely eliminated the fact is that both fatal and non-fatal accidents can be greatly reduced. In this respect alone there is great opportunity to prevent human waste. The injury to society cannot be measured by the loss of earnings sustained by a breadwinner through an industrial accident. There is no standard by which we can measure the bodily suffering, deprivation and mental anguish experienced by the workers, their wives and children who are victims of these industrial tragedies. Human life is so potential, so sacred and so valuable that all scientific knowledge should be used and all practical means and methods employed for its conservation and protection.

Labor has rendered great service through the development and support of legislation for the protection of the lives and limbs of workers in industry. It will serve in every way possible in the furtherance of practical plans for the conservation and protection of the lives and bodies of all who are employed in industry.

One of the most difficult problems associated with industry is the problem of unemployment. It is of such grave consequences as to demand the best of our thought and judgment in trying to find a solution. We cannot evade it or ignore it. We must face it frankly and courageously. When acute it is a menace to society and if permitted to continue over a wide-spread area it serves to threaten the security of government. Reasonably steady, regular and continuous employment creates a happy state of mind, removes the spectre of want, hunger and misery, begets a feeling of confidence and permits workers to make orderly planning for the future.

Surely a stabilized, continuous policy of employment is within the range of human possibilities. Unemployment is waste of the most vicious kind. It constitutes a waste of human opportunity, of effort and of human creative capacity. It is a lamentable state of affairs when industrial plants fully equipped, modern and up-to-date in every respect are idle and many working people are suffering from unemployment. The trade and commerce of entire communities become stagnant and the financial strain imperils the existence of banks and all lines of business. We could render no greater service to the people of this generation than to find the solution of the problem of unemployment.

When we consider spiritual waste we deal with values which are most sacred and precious. We cannot estimate their worth or appraise their importance. Their maintenance is essential to the success of industry. The highest and best type of service is rendered where the workers are enabled to labor under favorable conditions, in a satisfactory environment and where the exercise of the right to organize for mutual helpfulness is freely conceded. This is true of both skilled and unskilled labor.

The success of industry requires the maintenance of a high morale and that sort of spirit which is inspired by a zeal and enthusiasm for service. Management should inspire and encourage the development of the moral and spiritual powers of the workers by paying high wages, creating opportunities for leisure and recreation, and by consultation with the workers, through their chosen representatives. Low wages, intolerable conditions of employment, excessive hours of labor and autocratic management dull the intellect, break down morale, crush the spirit and chill the interest of working people.

Treatment accorded workers by a management which classifies them as mere machines and which bestows upon them certain benefits, in a paternalistic way, tends to bring about a decline in spiritual and moral values. Management should recognize the right of the workers to develop their spiritual, intellectual and moral powers. They should be accorded the fullest and freest opportunity to do so. If the workers can help themselves and build up their intellectual, spiritual and economic powers through association in their trade unions they must be given the opportunity to do so.

Our nation cannot maintain its industrial supremacy among all the nations of the world unless it fosters and nourishes those spiritual and moral values which contribute so much to the efficiency of the American workers.

---

[1] _Bulletin of the Taylor Society_, June, 1927.

THE CALL FOR LEADERSHIP[1]

A Challenge to Business and to Politics

By H. S. Person
Managing Director, Taylor Society, New York

It appears unnecessary to undertake a comprehensive discussion of the nature of leadership. It may be assumed that we have a common understanding of its nature sufficiently definite to serve the purpose of the evening. Yet because reference to a call for leadership implies that the type of leadership in mind has not been realized, it is desirable to specify what that type is.

Types of Leadership

For our purpose we may first divide leaders into two classes:

1. Leaders of research and thought.

2. Leaders of action as distinguished from leaders of research and thought. The cry today is for leaders of action who can catch up with leaders of thought.

Then we may divide leaders of action into two classes:

1. Those numerous leaders who are essential to carrying on the conventions and customs of life. Such leaders are never wanting, although their qualities may vary greatly. Social processes could not go on without them. Every institution must have its leader; every group its leader. Some of these leaders simply serve to co-ordinate the divided labors through which established patterns of activity are carried on. Others among these, and they are many, lead the way to improvement or at least change of conventions and customs. Industry has its Fords; retailing its Woolworths; politics its La Follettes; education its Deweys; religion its Fosdicks. Many of these leaders are noteworthy also as leaders of thought; some of them may start forces which in the long run profoundly modify institutions. Their aggregate influence is enormous. Yet we are not this evening concerned with the type of leadership which leads only with respect to conventional and particular aspects of culture.

2. Those occasional outstanding leaders of action who arise in times of social crisis involving collective aims, morals and the direction of the cultural trend of an entire society--Caesar, Charlemagne, Napoleon, Bismark, Lenin and Ghandi, Washington and Lincoln. Such are the leaders who appear at a time of dislocation of the secular trend; geniuses of action who perceive the nature of the dislocation and are able to gather

up the scattered fragments and reassemble them into a new, functioning, organic whole which utilizes the very forces that had caused the secular break. It is with leadership of this type that we are concerned tonight because it is for leadership of this type that there is a call in the United States today.

Assuming for the moment that the state of our affairs constitutes a call for such leadership, let us ask ourselves why a leadership is so slow in responding to the call; why perhaps affairs must become worse and the call stronger before the necessary leadership emerges.

Rarity of Crisis Leadership

Crisis leadership is rare the world over, but in the United States it is particularly difficult to produce, and one may fear that this difficulty is increasing. There are undoubtedly many reasons for this, among which the following may be noted:

1. A century dominated by pioneering, opportunistic exploitation of the vast resources of a continent has indicated one consistent major line of policy and conduct for the United States. Only one real crisis has heretofore appeared--the conflict between a feudalism and a nascent industrialism which culminated in the Civil War. This conflict found its leaders who performed their tasks and disappeared. Since then the trend has been one of easy development of the new industrialism, in which because of no call for its exercise, the capacity for crisis leadership has atrophied.

I am not unmindful of Woodrow Wilson, the greatest among our leaders since Lincoln, but the crisis through which he led was minor compared to that which confronted Lincoln or that which now confronts us; and in its later stage of intensification following the armistice new phases of the crisis presented problems too difficult for this exhausted leader to solve.

2. The relatively high standard of living realized by all social classes as a result of this appropriation and exploitation of abundant resources has led to an intellectual and moral softness, a complacent satisfaction with things as they are, which dims the capacity for perception of the significance of trends and even for perception of a cultural crisis during the early stages of its appearance.

3. The size of the United States, the diversity of resources, and the regional characteristics of its basic livelihood activities have tended to focus individual attention on local interests and problems instead of on national interests and problems, and few of us have become able to think on a scale comparable to the scale of the forces which have led to crisis.

4. The influence of political democracy has been against the emergence of leaders. We are the first great democracy in history, and we are politically young and inexperienced. We have not yet learned how to adjust democracy to our developed, complicated needs, and among other

things to our need for leadership. In our democracy so-called leadership has come generally to consist in ascertaining the trend of mass emotion and uninformed opinion and then assuming a position of "leadership" of such trends. While leadership cannot go against mass trends, it is not genuine leadership if it merely follows and is distinguished only because it has run out in front; like the dog which is always ahead of its master but also always has a weather eye for the direction in which its master intends to go. True leadership must <u>risk</u> possessions and limbs and life in persuading the mass to modify its course, whereas our so-called leaderships are chiefly concerned with <u>protecting</u> possessions, limbs and life. We observe a humiliating illustration of this in connection with those sectors of our problem pertaining to war debts, and to modification of policy concerning the manufacture and sale of intoxicating liquors. Attention has recently been called to the fact that Senator Cummins at the time of the first loan to our allies pleaded that it be made an outright contribution and not a loan; that there were moral grounds for making it a contribution and practical grounds for not making it a loan. He prophesied that a loan would eventually come back to plague us. In the face of fulfilment of his prophesy we appear no wiser than we were then, and present a case of increasingly stupid ineptitude.

5. The political institutions of the United States, especially our particular type of federal government, tend perhaps even more than democracy <u>per se</u> to deprive us of real leadership on the national plane. Our form of federal government, in contrast for instance to the Canadian, emphasizes the rights of states. This on the one hand intensifies localism of interests, as has been already noted. On the other hand, it affords entrance into the national area and access to opportunities for national leadership only when one has first come to identify himself with local interests and leadership and has become crystallized in that respect. Furthermore, continuance of service and of opportunity in the national area is contingent on continued representation of local interests and viewpoints. We elect none of our national servants at large; even the President is chosen by discovering who can best convince the greater number of localities that he will represent their respective particular interests. And in the organization of the legislative and executive branches of the government we have set up a system of checks and balances which stifles leadership. How through such political channels can we secure leaders who have a truly collective point of view?

6. The nature of our industrial institutions has become such as to render almost impossible the emergence from that source of leadership with a collective point of view. The corporate form of organization has become dominant, and huge corporations have become numerous. When a young man enters into the service of a corporation he enters into a bureaucracy which has institutional ideals, aims and purposes; and a powerful though perhaps unwritten institutional code. Generally he realizes little opportunity for individuality and self-expression except insofar as these conform strictly to the institutional aims and bureaucratic code. The consequence is that few individuals in the service of corporations can, while they are still young and plastic, break through

the restricting shell and stand forth as leaders unrestrained by particular interests. Nevertheless, before I am finished, I shall suggest that we must first look to industry for leadership at the present stage of our crisis.

7. The educational system of the United States has not been such as to promote that type of leadership which we have been describing as desirable in a democracy. At the present moment, however, there is some sign that the product of this system is becoming more realistic and independent in its thinking than has been the case in the last half century. The chaotic state of the environment in which the young and intellectually plastic find themselves in ever increasing numbers is perhaps producing its effects. There are evidences of questioning and of change in educational methods which may in turn result in the vision to lead.

The task of educating the whole population in this country had become so enormous and the influence of certain groups so important that education, like industry, was put on a mass-production basis. The result of this has been to develop the rubber-stamp, "me too" type of personality which conforms to a pattern instead of showing the boldness and initiative in thinking that are essential to both leadership and followship. The leadership which we need and seek can be generated, discovered and given its opportunity only by a group that records and analyzes its experience and defines its objectives on that basis. After the group has defined its objectives it must also have a sense for the means of obtaining them. In other words, it must be able to see in individuals those qualities of perception and definition which make possible the working out of the means of accomplishment of desired ends. There is today evidence of the emergence of an adult-education movement which should help to develop these group qualities.

Incapacity for Followship

I have considered at some length, although not exhaustively, why national leadership is so difficult to find in the United States. Another reason, so important that I consider it by itself, is a general incapacity among us for followship. There can be no leadership without followship; a leader can be a leader only if he represents--is inspired and sustained by--a following group. Before we can have really <u>national</u> leadership the people of the United States must become capable of thinking <u>nationally</u>, and of rallying behind one or another leader who sees the collective nature of our problems and of their solutions.

Few of us are capable of thinking nationally. A diagnosis of the reasons for this would be essentially identical with our diagnosis of the reasons for scarcity of leaders. In fact, it is highly probable that if we as individuals had capacity for followship, leaders would automatically emerge when needed, for the conditions which promote effective followship likewise promote leadership. For reasons of convention I have set out to talk about the call for leadership when what I should have done was to label my address "The Call for Followship."

Perhaps we can get first our followship and then, as a by-product, our leadership, if more of us can be persuaded to recognize how real is our need.

The Nature of the Call

Without trespassing upon the discussions of the closing session of our meeting on Friday evening, December 9, to which this opening session is distinctly related, it is desirable to say something about the crisis which constitutes a call for followship and leadership.

There is warrant for believing that we are experiencing not merely a cyclic depression, which itself establishes a need for strong and able leadership, but also the beginnings of a prolonged disturbance resulting from a break in the secular trend. It is the latter that establishes the need for wise and heroic leadership. This break in secular trend is comparable in its dangers to that which seventy years ago culminated in open conflict between two sections of the Union. What makes the call for followship and leadership today so urgent is the plain fact that we must remove the risk of a future conflict which although perhaps different in form might be similar in essential nature.

Several new forces in our national development have come to focus during the past decade and the resultant combined force has caused what we call a break in the secular trend.

The first of these new forces relates to population. The closure of our doors to immigration has made significant the fact that we have for some time been experiencing a declining rate of increase of population, and are confronted by the prospect of a stationary or declining population which may be realized during the lives of the younger among you in this audience. At the same time the production of social income has been increasing at a rapid rate, and the potential production with available equipment is far beyond anything we have yet realized. This requires enormous readjustments in order to maintain the circular flow of production-consumption forces; such as equalization in the domestic distribution of social income; or rapid development of foreign markets; or radical restriction in agricultural and industrial production; or some composite of these. This is a problem which challenges the wisest and boldest of leaderships.

The second of these new forces relates to international finance and commerce. We have been a debtor nation. Recently fate has been apparently unkind enough to make us a creditor nation. If we elect to remain a creditor nation what has been called a favorable balance of trade will have become unfavorable and what has been called an unfavorable balance of trade will have become favorable. To make the necessary readjustments will be a shock to our business structure as now organized. If we elect (and are able) not to be a creditor nation and therefore put obstacles in the way of the loan of surplus capital abroad, then we shall have forced its investment in upon our domestic market, the distribution channels of which are already clogged with a productivity which they cannot carry under present conditions. Or we may devise some way not now formulated of directing this investment upon the market in such a manner that it will not clog the channels of distribution, but that premises a policy and procedure which would be revolutionary. Here is a second problem which challenges the wisest and boldest of leaderships.

The third of these new forces is the most perplexing of all and is the major cause of dislocation of the secular trend. We have within fifteen years added a new increment of technology which has so enlarged the means of utilizing Nature's powers in production that in many trades old standards of measurement of the relations of the individual to productivity have become obsolete. We still distribute social income among the low-income classes, which purchase more than three-fourths of consumer goods and services, on the assumption that each should receive in proportion to his productivity before the day of high-powered production. As a matter of fact, the actual productivity of the high-powered equipment which he tends multiplies many times the productivity realized under the earlier conditions. The consequence is an increasingly uneven distribution of social income and savings; investment in productive equipment more rapidly than effective purchasing power is built up; technological unemployment; obsolescence of capital goods; a creaking and grinding of the commercial and industrial mechanism; and periodically a complete breakdown with consequent distress and misery and psychiatric disturbances of the collective mind. This problem is a challenge for the wisest and boldest of leaderships.

And there are other problems of a secondary nature. Many of the accustomed mechanisms of commerce and industry are functioning badly under the complicated conditions of modern business and increase the dislocation caused by the major forces. Our currency, banking system and control of credit are no longer suitable: the corporation as a legal form of organization has so evolved that it is unmanageable as a social institution; even our concept of private property, which from one point of view is a social mechanism, requires revision and redefinition to fit the present stage of industrial evolution.

These major and minor problems are all *parts of a great composite problem*; and together they constitute a challenge for the wisest and boldest and most energetic leadership to a *solution as comprehensive as is the range of these related elements of the problem*.

The Present Challenge to Business

The present challenge is to *business* to find us the needed leadership. The absence of any present collective leadership in business and the nature of past provincial leaderships in business are largely responsible for the present dislocation in the cultural trend. It is the responsibility of business to atone for past sins by establishing a socially-minded, constructive leadership. Even if the only way out is what may shortsightedly be believed to be a cost to business the responsibility remains to lead us to a stabilized, dynamic society characterized by that plenty which it is technically possible for us to create and enjoy.

The obstacles to leadership to which we have called attention in the political area make it highly improbable that such wise and bold leadership as is required will soon arise out of that department of our life. Apparently effective political leadership can be expected in a democracy only when affairs have reached that stage of confusion when the very existence of the State is at stake. Fortunately, we still far from the stage of confusion.

Although, as we have indicated, the bureaucracy of corporations has been an obstacle to the development in industry of creative collective leadership, yet if we consider as a group in our society those particular individuals who now occupy positions of power in industry, there is in that group a collection of natural abilities, a fund of experience, a knowledge of commercial and industrial technique, and a homogeniety which, had it the vision and the will to do, could give us the leadership for which we call. It could provide the leadership and automatically the nucleus of a followship. So great is the respect and admiration of American citizens for the past century of accomplishment of American business, that were our business leaders to provide the nucleus of a followship headed by a strong leadership, that nucleus would be joined by a great mass of citizens who sense our difficulty and are patiently waiting for the signal.

However--and here is involved both the vision and the will to do--that leadership must be distinctly in the general and not in any special interest. It must not look toward restricted production, price maintenance and other related devices aimed to conserve at any cost the equity values which have been unwisely permitted to be built up. The leadership we picture carries with it sacrifice rather than immediate advantage; immediate sacrifice for the sake of the ultimate advantage of not having to experience still greater sacrifice in the future.

It is difficult to understand why business should not accept this particular challenge, in view of the fact that it has given so many hostages in the nature of invested savings and has so much at stake. Its stake could be in danger of forfeit were confusion permitted to become more confounded, and discontent to become fatalistic, overt opposition to the police power of established society, in which case really effective and ruthless political leadership would surely come to the front.

---

[1]Bulletin of the Taylor Society, April, 1933.

PART SIX

DEVELOPMENT OF SCIENTIFIC MANAGEMENT ABROAD

This concluding section represents but a small sample of the literature available on the introduction and development of "scientific management" abroad. After having perused the record of accomplishments of such enterprises as the Soho Foundary in England of 1800, managed by the sons of James Watt and Mathew Boulton, it can be convincingly argued that many of the mechanisms associated with the scientific management movement had at least been conceived of and in some cases developed in countries other than the United States. Whether the ideas that were implemented were continued over a long period of time, and whether these techniques were known or employed by others, the record is far from clear. Another foreign precursor of "scientific management" techniques abroad would be Charles Babbage part of whose accomplishments are recorded in his "On the Economy of Machinery and Manufactures" (1832). Babbage notes such factors of managerial importance as the need for work specializations in reducing the time required for a worker to learn a technique or process, the use of timing an operation to determine a fair day's work, and many other managerial techniques which would have to wait many years to be "discovered." Other notable foreign contributors whose efforts preceded the American development would include the French engineer Charles Dupin's "Discours sur le sort des ouvriers," and the Prussian general Karl Von Clausewitz's treatise on "Principles of War" (1832).

Another facet of the discussion of the introduction of scientific management abroad is concerned with the transmission of ideas from one country to another. In regards to the writings of Taylor the correspondence between Taylor and Mr. Le Chatelier[1] indicates that Taylor's paper "On the Art of Cutting Metals" was translated and published in France in 1907 and his "Principles of Scientific Management in 1912. Japanese, Italian and Lettish translations of Taylor's "Principles" were also made in 1912. In the correspondence referred to, Taylor notes that not all translations were accurate in that the translator took upon himself the task of re-writing the ideas of Taylor with the result, inferred from Taylor's comments, that the publications were in part incorrect. Without dwelling unduly on this aspect of foreign knowledge and employment of scientific management it should be noted that as time went on many foreign visitors coming to the United States sought out these promulgators of the gospel of efficiency. Foreign visits by practitioners and theorist of scientific management often included addresses and conferences to foreign learned societies and groups of industrialists who were eager to hear the latest developments or to raise questions as to their value and appropriateness to other than American industry.

Turning to the articles chosen for this section; the first one entitled "What Lenine said about the 'Taylor Society' " is an excerpt from Pravada shortly after the successful communist overthrow of the Kerensky government of Russia. The article despite it being a harangue and jumping from one topic to another and back again has a not too subtle message for its audience "to be successful revolutionaries we must learn how to organize Russia economically and the first order of business is to restart industrial production. To do this we need the knowledge of the bourgeois capitalists--the latest word is the Taylor system." Lenine's insistence upon the need to study and teach the "Taylor system and other progressive measures of capitalism" is interesting in that he, like most of the "consultants" of the scientific management "era", were eager to pick up and exploit the short run gains of employing the scientific mechanics but was unable to see or perhaps to philosophically assume the burden imposed by an acceptance of the philosophy of scientific management.

Slonim's "Russian Scientists in Quest of American Efficiency" is an account of Russian progress in installing the "Taylor Method" in Russian industry during the 1920-22 period following the revolution. The author describes the most salient points in a memorandum prepared by the "Presidium" of the Central Institute of Labor. Among the accomplishments noted in the memorandum was the establishment of an organization known as the "Central Institute of Labor" with the stated goal "to implant into the character of the peoples of Eastern Europe and Siberia, the searching, daring, persisting American energy." The author quoted, from the same memorandum, a passionate appeal by Russian scientists to the "American patrons of science" to help them in "the plowing up of the tired out Russia". The author ends with a number of observations as to how the institute got started and the problems faced by the organizers.

Mary Van Kleeck's article "Observations on Management in the Soviet Union" is a lengthy discussion of the goals and accomplishments of the Soviet five year plans between 1928 and 1932. Although the author seems to mistake the mechanics for the philosophy she does note that since the application of knowlege and being restricted through private ownership as in the United States the Soviet Union with its socialized control of industry have given "Scientific Management in that country a scope which is new in the history of modern industry."

The next article by Oliver Sheldon gives an Englishman's observations and appraisal of management in Great Britain. In "The Art of Management" Sheldon does what the overwhelming majority of past and present practitioners and writers fail to do--after quoting Taylor as to what scientific management is or is not--to abide by that definition in discussing his scientific management philosophy. His succinct discussion provides the reader with a most notable philosophical treatment of the spirit of scientific management. He concludes with a brief discussion of the progress being made in the implementations and teaching of scientific management in Britain.

The last selection by Ethel Dietrich should be of interest to both the student of management as well as the student of economics. The discussion is primarily of de Freminville's study of the writings of the French engineer Perronet and the probable employment by Adam Smith of Perronet's example on the manufacturing of pins in Smith's book "The Wealth of Nations".

---

[1]"Frederick W. Taylor to Henri le Chatelier," Bulletin of the Taylor Society, October, 1928, pp. 206-14.

WHAT LENINE SAID ABOUT THE "TAYLOR SOCIETY"[1]

Peace temporarily having been obtained, the duty of the Soviet Republic is to concentrate for a time on the most important and difficult problem of the revolution--the problem of organization. The respite which has been granted must be utilized to cure the wounds which have been received by the whole social and economic organization of Russia. In that way only shall we be able to offer further resistance to bourgeois opposition, and particularly to aid social revolution in the West, delayed for a number of reasons.

The negative work--the destruction of feudalism and monarchy--was performed by the bourgeois revolution of Kerensky. The organization it effected was but a continuation of bourgeois minority control. On the other hand the Socialist revolution of October 25, 1917, is confronted by the problem "of establishing an extremely complex and delicate net of newly organized relationships covering the systematic production and distribution of products which are necessary for the existence of tens of millions of people. . . . The victory of the Socialist revolution will not be assured unless the proletariat and the poorest peasantry will manifest sufficient consciousness, idealism, self-sacrifice and persistence. . . . The main difficulty is the economic domain--to raise the productivity of labor, to establish strict and universal accounting and control of production and distribution, and <u>actually to socialize</u> production."

"We are now confronted by the problem which is the most urgent and which characterizes the present period; to organize the <u>management</u> of Russia. We the Bolshevik party, have <u>convinced</u> Russia. We have <u>won</u> Russia from the rich for the poor, from the exploiters for the toilers. It is now up to us to <u>manage</u> Russia. . . . For the first time in the history of the world the Socialist party has succeeded in completing, essentially, the task of winning power and suppressing the exploiters, and in coming <u>close</u> to the problem of management. We must prove worthy of this. . . .We must not fail to see that besides the ability to convince and win in civil war, successful management depends on the ability for <u>practical organization</u>."

<u>A New Phase of the Struggle</u>

"Were we to attempt now to continue the expropriation of capital with the same intensity as heretofore, we would surely be defeated; for our work of the organization of proletarian accounting and control has. . . . not kept pace with the work of the direct 'expropriation of the expropriators.' If we will now turn all our efforts to the work of the organization of accounting and control we shall be able to solve this problem, we shall overcome our shortcomings and shall win our 'campaign' against capital."

". . . it is becoming urgent for the proletarian state authority to make use of the bourgeois specialists for the purpose of replowing the soil so that no bourgeoisie could grow on it. . . . Without the direction of specialists of different branches of knowledge, technique and experience, the transformation toward socialism is impossible, for socialism demands a conscious mass movement toward a higher productivity of labor in comparison with capitalism and on the basis which has been attained by capitalism. . . the best organizers and the biggest specialists can be used by the state either in the old bourgeois way (that is for a higher salary), or in the new proletarian way (that is by creating such an environment of universal accounting and control as would inevitably and naturally gain the submission of and attract specialists)."

"Let us assume that these greatest 'stars' must be paid twenty-five thousand rubles each. Let us assume that this sum (25,000,000) rubles must be doubled (supposing premiums granted for particularly successful and rapid accomplishment of the most important tasks of organization and technique) or even made four times as large (supposing that we must get several hundred better paid foreign specialists). Well, then, can this expenditure of 50,000,000 rubles a year for the reorganization of the work of the people according to the last word of science and technique be considered excessive or unbearable for the Soviet Republic? Of course not. The vast majority of the conscious workers and peasants will approve such an expenditure, knowing from practical life that our backwardness compels us to lose billions, and that we have _not yet_ attained such a high degree of organization, accounting and control which would cause the universal and voluntary participation of these 'stars' of the bourgeois Intelligentzia in _our work_."

"Of course, there is another side to this question. The corrupting influence of high salaries is beyond dispute--both on the Soviets (the more so, since the swiftness of the revolution made it possible for a certain number of adventurers and crooks to join the Soviets, who, together with the incapable and dishonest among certain commissaries, would not mind becoming 'star grafters') and on the mass of workers. But all thinking and honest workers and peasants will agree with us and will admit that we are unable to get rid at once of the evil heritage of capitalism; that the Soviet Republic can be freed from 'tribute' of fifty or a hundred million of rubles (a tribute for our own backwardness in the organization of _universal_ accounting and control _from the bottom up_) only by organization, by increasing the discipline among ourselves, by getting rid of all those who 'keep the traditions of capitalism,' i.e., of loafers, parasites and grafters. If the conscious advanced workers and peasants will succeed, with the help of the Soviet institutions, to organize and discipline themselves, and to create powerful labor discipline in one year, then we will in one year do away with this 'tribute' (which may be reduced even earlier) depending on the measure of success attained in creating labor discipline and organization among the workers and peasants. The sooner we ourselves, workers and peasants, will learn better labor discipline and a higher technique of toil, making use of the bourgeoisie specialists for this purpose, the sooner we will get rid of any tribute to these specialists."

"The center of gravity of the struggle with the bourgeoisie is shifted to the organization of accounting and control. This must be taken into account in order to determine correctly the urgent economic and financial problems with regard to the nationalization of the banks, monopolization of foreign trade, state control of currency, the introduction of a satisfactory--from the proletarian standpoint--wealth and income tax, and the introduction of obligatory labor service."

"A socialist state can come into existence only as a net of production and consumption communes, which keep conscientious accounts of their production and consumption and economize labor, steadily increasing its productivity and thus making it possible to lower the working day to seven, six or seven less hours."

Higher Productivity of Labor

"In every socialist revolution, after the proletariat has solved the problem of winning the power, 'the problem' is in the main and fundamentally a problem of the creation of a higher-than-capitalism social system--to raise the productivity of labor, and in that connection, and for that, to effect its higher organization. . . ."

"To increase the productivity of labor we must first of all secure the material basis of a large industry; the development of the production of fuel, iron, machinery and of the chemical industry. The Russian Soviet Republic" possesses "collossal stores of ore (in the Urals); fuel in Western Siberia (coal), Caucasia and the southeast (petroleum) and Central Russia (peat); vast resources of lumber, water power and raw materials for the chemical industries, and so on. The exploitation of these natural resources by the latest technical methods will furnish a basis for an unprecedented development of production."

"Higher productivity of labor depends, in the first place, on the improvement of the emotional and cultural state of the masses of the population. This improvement is now taking place with unusual swiftness, thanks to the Soviet organizations; but it is not perceived by those who are blinded by the bourgeois routine and are unable to comprehend what a longing for light and initiative is now pervading the masses of the people."

"Higher productivity of labor depends, in the second place, on higher discipline of the toilers, on higher skill, efficiency and intensity of labor, and on its better organization. . . . The most conscious vanguard of the Russian proletariat has already turned to the problem of increasing the labor discipline. For instance the Central Committee of the Metallurgical Union and the Central Council of the Trade Unions have begun work on appropriate measures and drafts of decrees. This should be supported and advanced by all means. We should immediately introduce piece work and try it out in practice. We should try out every scientific and progressive suggestion of the Taylor System. . . . .To learn how to work--this problem the Soviet authority should present to the people in all its comprehensiveness. The last word of capitalism in this respect--the Taylor System--as well as all progressive measures of capitalism, combined the refined cruelty of bourgeois exploitation and a number of most valuable scientific attainments in the analysis of mechanical motions during work, in eliminating superfluous and useless motions in determining the most correct methods of work, the best systems of accounting and control, etc. The Soviet Republic must adopt valuable and scientific technical advance in this field. The possibility of socialism will be determined by our success in combining the Soviet rule and the Societ organization of management with the latest progressive measures of capitalsim. We must introduce in Russia the study and the teaching of the new Taylor System and its systematic trial and adaptation."

"While working to increase the productivity of labor, we must at the same time take into account the pecularities of the transition period from capitalism to socialism, which requires, on the one hand, that we lay the foundation for the Socialist organization of emulation, and on the other hand, requires the use of compulsion" through a dictature of the proletariat.

Organization of Emulation

"Among the absurdities which the bourgeois is fain to spread about socialism, is that Socialists deny the significance of emulation. In reality only socialism, destroying classes, . . . for the first time opens the road for emulation on a really mass scale. And only the Soviet organization, passing from the formal democracy of a bourgeois republic to the actual participation of the toiling masses in management, for the first time puts emulation on a broad basis."

"Let us take publicity as a means for the organization of emulation. . . We must systematically endeavor that. . . work should be carried on to create a press which will not amuse and fool the masses with spicy political trifles, but will bring to the attention of the masses and will help them to study seriously, the questions of everyday economics. . . . . The press should serve as a weapon of socialistic instruction, giving publicity in all details to the successes of the model communes, studying the principle of their success and their methods of economy, ... so that a comparison between the results of the enterprise of different communes would become a subject of general interest and study. . . "

Efficient Organization and a Dictature

"It would be the greatest stupidity and the most absurd opportunism to suppose that the transition from capitalism to socialism is possible without compulsion and dictatorship. . . . In the first place, it is impossible to conquer and destroy capitalism without the merciless suppression of the resistance of exploiters;. . . in the second place, every great revolution, and especially a Socialist revolution, even if there were no external war, is inconceivable without an internal war. . . .and a state of greatest uncertainty, instability and chaos. . . . all elements of decay of the old order. . . . cannot fail to 'show up' during such a profound transformation. . . . These elements of decay cannot 'show up' otherwise than through increase of crimes. . . . It takes time and an iron hand to get rid of this."

"This historical experience of all revolutions. . . was summed up by Marx in his brief, sharp, exact and vivid formula: 'The Dictature of the Proletariat.'. . . . But 'Dictature' is a great word. And great words must not be used in vain. . . . There is lack of appreciation of the simple and obvious fact that, if the chief misfortunes of Russia are famine and unemployment, these misfortunes cannot be overcome by any outburst of enthusiasm, but only by thorough and universal organization and discipline. . . ."

"Every large machine industry--which is the material productive source and basis of socialism--requires an absolute and strict unity of the will which directs the joint work of hundreds, thousands and tens of thousands of people. This necessity is obvious and has always been recognized. . . . and we, the Communist Party (the Bolsheviki), which gives conscious expression to the aspiration of the exploited masses for emancipation, ... should be in the front ranks of the weary masses which are seeking a way out and should lead them along the right road--the road of labor discipline--harmonizing the problem of holding meetings to discuss the conditions of work with the problem of absolute submission to the will of the Soviet director, dictator during work."

"The 'meeting holding' is ridiculed and more often wrathfully hissed at. . . . But without the 'meeting holding' the oppressed masses could never pass from the discipline forced by the exploiters to conscious and voluntary discipline. 'Meeting holding' is the real democratism of the toilers, their straightening out, their awakening to a new life, their first steps on the field which they themselves have cleared of reptiles, and which they want to learn to put in order themselves, in their own way, in accordance with the principles of their, Soviet, rule."

"Our aim is to attract every member of the _poor_ classes to practical participation in the management, and the different steps leading towards this end (the more diverse the better) should be carefully registered, studied, standardized, verified on broader experience and legalized."

---

[1] _Bulletin of the Taylor Society_, June, 1919. Abstract in the form of quotations from the principal parts of an article by Nikolai Lenine, entitled "The Urgent Problems of the Soviet Rule," translated from _Pravda_ of April 28, 1918.

RUSSIAN SCIENTISTS IN QUEST OF AMERICAN EFFICIENCY[1]

By S. Slonim

There recently appeared in several newspapers of the United States a cable dispatch from Europe as follows:

> <u>Special Cable Dispatch</u>
> Copyright, 1922, by Public Ledger Company
>
> Berlin, Aug. 22.--The Soviets are introducing the Taylor Efficiency System in Moscow factories. The Central Workers' Institute located at Gastew employs sixty professors to teach instructors how to introduce the system into factories and the Soviets are underwriting the Institute.
>
> In addition to the efficiency methods borrowed from the United States, psychological and physiological workers tests, based on the French and German plans have been introduced.
>
> The Soviets, however, are encountering the same difficulties of the American capitalists who found the workers unwilling to be "efficiencyized" although members of the school maintain the higher class of workers support them.
>
> A considerable part of the funds for founding the efficiency system were raised in America and Herbert Hoover, through the head of the Russian department, M. Slonim, expressed interest in the plan. The school has applied to him asking for assistance to purchase instruments.

Believing that the members of the Taylor Society would be interested in an authoritative statement concerning the facts alleged in this dispatch, the editor consulted Mr. S. Slonim, at present with the American Relief Administration, and Mr Slonim kindly prepared the statement printed below.

It appears that there is as yet no general introduction of Taylor methods in the factories of Russia, but that a central institute has been organized for the purpose of experiment, in general with respect to scientific methods in industry, and in particular with respect to Taylor methods. This institute, located in Moscow and with branches elsewhere, is not merely a research organization; it has interested factories where production operations are actually carried on, and where Taylor methods are applied in accordance with Russian interpretation of them and to the extent that limited available equipment makes experimental operations possible.

These efforts are at present crude--for want of proper equipment some experimental machines are being made of wood! But the mental attitude seems to be sound; it is scientific and its motive is the regeneration of Russian industry.

Many appeals for equipment have come to the American Relief Administration, but the nature of the assistance requested does not properly fall within the field of its operations. Mr. Slonim suggests that members of the Taylor Society may find in this situation the opportunity for a practical international cooperation; one member may have a machine he can spare, another a stop watch, another a piece of photographic apparatus, others precision tools of one sort and another, others organization charts, sets of standing orders and forms; and so on. The value of a moderate contribution from each of a hundred firms or individuals in the United States to this fundamentally sound movement in Russia, he states, cannot be estimated. It might eventually prove to be one of these imponderables so influential in determining the course of international commercial relations. (Editor.)

From the wreck and ruin of the old order left by the disastrous war and revolution, a crippled and much-battered Russia is gradually emerging with a new viewpoint.

First to arise from among the ruins of old Russia, as it was natural to expect, were the scientists and engineers. It was to them that the by this time sobered-up bolshevik politician and sadly-awakened proletarian are looking for guidance--for the word of wisdom and hope.

What tragic trials the Russian men of science went through is already well known to the world and need not be repeated here.

The first indication that the creative forces of Russian scientific thought are beginning to assert themselves was when at the offices of the American Relief Administration in New York, a memorandum prepared by the "Presidium" of the Central Institute of Labor of Moscow arrived by mail from Moscow. In that somewhat lengthy document, the most characteristic parts of which are quoted below, the executive committee, or the "Presidium" of the Institute, as they call themselves, after stating their aims and aspirations, seek to engage the good offices of the A.R.A. to present the case of the Institute before the American patrons of science, in expectation that the patrons will make a "gesture worthy of the builders of the New World." (In Russia the words America and the New World are synonymous.)

According to the memorandum, the idea of establishing an Institute of Labor in Russia is quite an old one. The first attempts in that direction were made in the year 1889, when the so-called "Social Museum" was opened in Moscow, as a result of the resolution passed at the International Exhibition in Paris in 1889. But under the old czarist regime, the words social and political were synonymous, and that was sufficient for the authorities to look with suspicion upon the "Museum" as an institution with political aims.

It was natural that the Russian Revolution, by pushing the laboring class to the forefront of the social arena, by making labor the centre of social gravitation, should give also an impetus to questions of efficiency--of greater production, of social engineering. After the Revolution, during the years 1917-1920, a number of engineering and labor organizations repeatedly raised the question of the necessity or organizing an institution devoted to the study of labor in all aspects.

Only in 1920 a small group under the patronage of the "All-Russian Central Council of Professional Unions" succeeded in forming an organization, not only for the scientific study of the processes of production, but for the immediate introduction of the most efficient methods into the industries as well. The organization which undertook this thankful, but enormous and responsible task, is known in Russia as the "Central Institute of Labor." Its goal, as the leaders of the Institute express it in their memorandum, is "to implant into the character of the peoples of Eastern Europe and Siberia, the searching, daring, persisting American energy."

According to the program, as outlined by the Presidium, the work of the Institute runs along four main lines: Technical, Biological, Economical and Pedagogical. The pre-eminent line of research is technical. In this the Institute sounds a note of triumph for the instrument of precision, the machine; the victory of the strictly defined "mechanical gesture." By these means, by "mechanical onrush and relentless mechanical energy" the Institute expects to rejuvenate industrial Russia.

The Institute does not intend to confine its activities within the limits of purely research work; it wants to get into the thick of life. The Institute has already shown its influence in the biggest Russian industrial plants, in the large economic organization. In a word the Institute wants to become the standard bearer of the "culture of efficiency" in Russia; it wants to create the psychological atmosphere of stern colonizers, fighters for a healthy, able-bodied efficient generation.

The personnel of the Institute consists of men who are imbued with the ideal of European and American methods of production. They would become the proclaimers to the Russian masses of a new era of productive and remunerative labor, but--

And here we come face to face with that fateful "but," which has always played a tragical part in Russian life, whether czarist or bolshevik. The only difference between the "but" of today and the "but" of the czarist times, is that in czarist Russia they could but they wouldn't, and in bolshevik Russia they would, but they couldn't.

Czarist Russia had all the opportunities to organize institutions and laboratories and equip them with the latest devices for the study of labor productivity from both material and human points of view. But not only was the czarist Russia not interested itself in the establishment of such institutions, it looked with great suspicion upon any initiative in that direction.

On the other hand, the bolshevik government is frantically trying to raise the productivity of the country which industrially is literally devastated, but lacks the means. An institute of the calibre and aims of the Central Institute of Labor needs large means for its efficient development.

Hence the cry for help addressed to America through the medium of the American Relief Administration. "We need," writes the Presidum of the Institute, "laboratories, shops, machinery and apparatus, but to our regret, we have not got them."

"We appeal to you;" runs the same memorandum, "your capital can create monuments of culture. We know that the best American institutions, laboratories, bureaus of research, universities, the best institutions of learning, have been created by your milliarders. We know that the Chicago University is the pet child of Rockefeller; we know that Carnegie has heaped his gold on the American Libraries, that in Pittsburgh and in Washington he founded scientific institutes, where industry and science blend into an overwhelming synthesis. . . We know that America is covered with societies for the rationalization of the economic life, and we know that as the culmination of all this grandiose work there has appeared that super-structure, 'The Federation of American Engineering Societies,' and finally we know also that a committee has been appointed for the study of 'Elimination of Waste in Industry.' We know that the man who is marching at the head of this triumphal procession is Herbert Hoover, he, who wants now to Americanize Europe. . ."

"We ask the American patrons of science to make the gesture worthy of the organizers of the New World, help us to start our Institute; send to us across the Atlantic a few of your technical, psycho-technical and photo-technical laboratories, present to us a few of those values which you so ably give for the development of your forever-searching energetic country."

"We will readily inscribe on each thing sent to us not only the word "America," but we will make these gifts to be memorials to the name of the Society or the individual who will thus work with us on the plowing up of the tired out Russia."

Such is the eloquent--if not the impassionate--appeal of a group of Russian scientists who are impatient to push ahead their work, from which years of revolution and privation have kept them back.

And that is why when a glimmer of light is at last beginning to penetrate the darkness which had enveloped Russia for so long a time, the soul of the Russian scientist, which was during all that time at its lowest ebb, suddenly became all a quiver and now passionately appeals to the world for a helping hand.

When in the year 1920 it became known that an institute dedicated to the study of modern methods of production was going to be opened in Moscow, tens of organizations and hundreds of professional people in Russia offered their services. But it was only on the spur of the moment. The enthusiasm aroused at first died away when it became evident that the work of building up the Institute required great sacrifices, since there were no instruments, no machinery for experimentations, no food for the workers, no fuel for heating the shops. Finally it sifted down to a group of about sixty people of the highest attainments in their respective professions. And they began to work. "It was," as the Director of the Institute, Alexsey Gasteff, wrote in one of his letters to the writer, "by sheer will power and enthusiasm that we decided to go against the elements. And where we have needed metal, we have supplanted it by wood. In this manner we created a scientific "Robinsoniada--all of its own. We made wooden models, wooden apparatus, etc. And all this in the hope that the day will come when our wood will be transformed into metal."

As outlined in the program, the work of the Institute was planned on a broad scale worthy of an endowment by a Rockefeller or a Carnegie foundation, but as it stands today there is "little powder in the magazine."

The Institute consists of six laboratories:

1. Cinematographic.
2. Technical.
3. Bio-Technical (mechanics of work movement).
4. Physio-Technical (energy of the working body).
5. Psychotechnical (psychology of the workmen).
6. Pedagogical (the study of work discipline).

And at the top of all--the study of methods for scientific organization and management of various undertakings (Chart I).

Notwithstanding the almost insurmountable difficulties which the Institute had to overcome during the short two years of its existance, it has succeeded in founding a publication, "Organization of Labor," which would do honor to any society of the same kind in any civilized country. Already three issues of about 200 pages each have appeared. Besides this publication, which is the official organ of the Institute, there have been published a number of text-books and monographs, pertaining to a number of diverse subjects on labor efficiency. It may be of interest to the American reader to get a glimpse of the contents of this official organ of the Institute. In the first number of the publication appear such articles as: "Our Problems," by A. K. Gasteff; "Fundamental Principles of the Management of Undertakings," by A. L. Fest; "Concerning the Taylor System," by M. V. Pionlukovsky; "Concerning the Question of Classification of Labor," by C. G. Strumilin; "The Study of Work Movements by the Method of Ciclograms." The bibliographical part of the organ glitters with exhaustive reviews of kindred foreign literature, among which the American literature on the subject occupies the first place.

Since the war America occupies the uppermost place in the Russian mind. American progress in a remarkably short time; her ingenuity, initiative, daring; the enormous sweep of her undertakings; these fire the imagination not only of the average Russian, but of its politicians and scientists as well. That ardent desire of every Russian to see as quickly as possible the comeback--the material reconstruction of Russia--inevitably forces the attention of all Russia upon America. Of all the countries in the world Russia understands that it is from there that some day in the near future the men and the means will come, who will lead Russia out of the wilderness of desolation. The names of Taylor and his American followers in questions of industry and production stand today on the same plane of authority in Russia as the name of Lenine in the world of Russian politics.

---

[1]Bulletin of the Taylor Society, October, 1922.

OBSERVATIONS ON MANAGEMENT IN THE SOVIET UNION[1]

By Mary Van Kleeck
Director of Industrial Studies, Russell Sage Foundation, New York
Associate Director, International Industrial Relations Institute

The completion of the first four years of systematic and integrated national planning would make 1932 in the Soviet Union a time of absorbing interest to students of the science of management, even if there were to be no second Five Year Plan. Given the added fact that during these months the State Planning Commission--the Gosplan--has been actively at work in the day-to-day details involved in the making of the next plan, the value of the present as a moment for observation of procedure and method is more than doubled. The main purpose of my presentation is indeed to point out to you, as management engineers, the importance of studying the planned economy of the Soviet Union during this period of industrialization. Impressive as are the statistics of achievement, and important as are certain weaknesses and maladjustments which the administrators themselves are the first to recognize, the significant questions for the scientific management movement center, I believe, less in the actual facts regarding successes or failures than in the methods of making and administering a plan.

To narrow the question to a sharper focus, the process of making the second Five Year Plan and the changes in procedure as compared with the first, show what has been learned by experience since the five-year period began in the autumn of 1928. This kind of learning by experience is surely of the essence of progress in the science of management. More fundamental, however, than the method of planning, which is, after all, only one of the main functions of management, is the question, "How is socialized industry administered?" The making of a plan for a specified period in the Union of Soviet Socialist Republics is only a subdivision of that larger task of administration to which the Soviet Union committed itself when it adopted its new economic system.

At the risk of posing a question far too wide in scope even to outline superficially in a half hour after dinner, it is necessary to define my subject in these large terms, for in the United States, obviously, scientific management has had its rise and development and has achieved its results in the shop. When it has extended over a series of shops, it has nevertheless been limited to a single industry and to that part of a single industry which is under homogeneous ownership. It is significant that Mr. Sanford E. Thompson, in his presidential address this evening, on the influence of Scientific Management in American industry, has quite properly taken as his unit for inquiry the separate company or establishment.

If there were no contrasting scheme of management extending over all the industries of a nation, as in the U.S.S.R., this limitation to a single ownership in the United States would be so obvious as to require no comment. In the early days of development it has not been recognized as a severe limitation upon the work of the management engineer. It has been hoped that the Scientific Management movement would spread from shop to shop until finally it should dominate American industry. But note Mr. Thompson's report that in the present situation answers to his inquiries show that the emphasis is shifting from the management of production to "the science of marketing." Yet it is evident that when the single establishment approaches the problems of marketing it finds many factors in the situation which are quite beyond its control. In fact, of the four principles of Scientific Management--research, setting up of standards, control over application of standards and co-operation--the only one which can completely be applied to problems of distribution would appear to be research, and it must be research into what exists and has existed, rather than facts directed toward control of a predetermined procedure toward an accepted end.

By a curious coincidence, this distinction between research into the past and research directed toward a planned and controlled future is almost an exact quotation from the remarks of one of the officials in the central statistical office of the Soviet Union. That office has the title, Central Board of National Economic Accounting. Its chairman is V. V. Ossinsky, who headed the Soviet delegation at the World Social Economic Congress at Amsterdam in 1931. One of his staff explained to us that economic accounting there was for the purpose of providing a basis for a plan, whereas, as he expressed it, the statistical service of a capitalistic country confines itself to collection of facts about things as they are or have been.

The planned economy of the Soviet Union is different from the management of an individual enterprise, not merely in its extent but in its essence. Management in the U.S.S.R. is responsible for the harmonious functioning of the total national economy shaped toward a definite social end. The end may be defined as the creation of a new collective society based upon the socialization of industry. Thus by what may appear to management engineers in the United States as a paradox, management in the U.S.S.R. is not to be observed primarily in the workshop nor even in a series of workshops, but first in the sum total of the national economy and secondarily in the separate local units of operation. The whole is primary in the sense that the human body is primary and the cells secondary. One cannot fully understand the functioning of the human body, except as a whole, though one makes ever so minute analyses of the separate cells, one by one. But while defining the whole as primary, it is not to be understood that the local industrial unit in the U.S.S.R. is unimportant. On the contrary, the understanding of the whole gives greater rather than less importance to the cells or units of which it is composed.

I went to the Soviet Union with the idea of discovering whether the principles of American Scientific Management appeared, in the light of Soviet experience, to be universal or whether they belonged to the American scene, or at most to the characteristic forms of control and private ownership which have so far been associated with modern industry. It is always difficult to disentangle what are universal principles in distinction from their applications in the habits or practices peculiar to a particular environment. In the natural sciences laboratory experiments are familiar, in which certain conditions are varied in order to discover constant elements. In accordance with the same method, today, with two economic systems existing in the world, it is possible to observe, as in the laboratory, which elements in economic life are inseparable from a given system and which appear to possess the quality of universality.

Here again, however, the paradox must be emphasized from another angle. The management engineer from the United States who goes to Russia will naturally think that the place to study management is the shop. Yet in a sense he cannot find the essence of Soviet management there. Indeed, as you have probably been told by technical engineers returning from Russia, shop management has many weaknesses in the Soviet Union today. Those who know how long it takes to develop Scientific Management in any workplace and how slow has been the process of gaining recognition for the movement in the United States, can only be surprised that so great progress has been made in shop management in the Soviet Union in the brief period of fifteen years since the revolution, with the first ten of these disorganized by civil war, the intervention of western nations and the aftermath of these events. But more important is the fact that management in the U.S.S.R. is not to be studied in the local unit but in the total national economic life.

It is the subject as a whole, then--"How is socialized industry administered?"--that I must emphasize. But I have advisedly taken the title, "Observations on Management in the Soviet Union," in the laboratory sense of the word "observations." I give you, so to speak, a batch of notes in the hope that you will continue these notes either through first-hand observations in the Soviet Union or through critical and discriminating study through the reports of others. And let me urge that you apply to the reports of those who are writing on this subject today rigid tests of accuracy, for management in the Soviet Union has reached a stage of experience where the mere cursory inspection by travelers without experience in research or in management cannot discover the significant facts.

In seeking to make observations on the procedure of developing the second Five Year Plan, I narrowed the question further to the coal industry because I had had some opportunity in the past to observe conditions in the coal industry in the United States. Moreover, the theme which had been the center of interest in our studies in the coal industry, and to some degree in other industries, in the United States was "labor's participation in management," and in the U.S.S.R. this question as to the extent of centralization or decentralization and the share of the workers in the making and administration of a planned economy had an important place in my inquiry. In other words, I wanted to know where authority rests in the management of industry in the Soviet Union. Who makes decisions, and upon what basis of fact and knowledge?

Let us begin with these questions not in the offices of the Gosplan in Moscow, but in the mining region of the North Caucasus, in the Donetz Basin, which was expecting to produce 60 per cent of the coal required by the second Five Year Plan, or more than double the production planned for this region in the past five years. Following inspection in the mines and talks with the miners underground and in the communities where they live, we met in conference the chief engineer of the coal trust of the North Caucasus, representatives of the labor department and the planning department of the trust, the president of the trade union of the region, and the director and the chief engineer of the nearest mine. These were administrators, not planners; but as administrators they have a definite function to perform in assisting the State Planning Commission in gathering the material necessary for planning the coal industry. The regional administration which they represented is responsible directly to a division of the Council of People's Commissars in Moscow which has to do with the All-Union administration of heavy industry, including fuel. This All-Union administration functions through some eighteen trusts. Each trust has a chairman with one or two assistants constituting the board, and each is divided into several sections, including (1) planning, (2) industrial technique, equipment and the like, (3) labor, with a director in charge of each section.

The labor department has three main divisions: the first, the economic section, has to do with all questions of personnel, including selection of workers, wages and costs of production; the second has to do with what are called technical norms, including standards of output, length of working day, and all such questions as those involved in piecework, bonuses and the like; the third deals with housing and cultural matters, sanitation and the food supply.

The trust deals directly with the local industrial unit, which may be a single mine; or two or more mines near together may constitute a unit. Each local industrial unit has a director and a chief engineer. The North Caucasus trust is composed of eleven industrial units and a department for development of mines for future operation. It supervises also the management of a plant for manufacture and repair of underground equipment. Each industrial unit has a labor department with parallel functions to those already indicated for the labor department of the trust. The trust reaches only to the industrial unit and its board. Local mine management is the responsibility of the director and the chief engineer; that is, it rests in the local unit.

The relation of the local labor department to the labor department of the trust works two ways. Norms of output which are developed as standard must of course be applied under the constantly changing conditions involved in the digging of a mine. It is in the local industrial unit, and indeed in each pit, that norms or standards are first formulated. The labor department of the trust gathers them up in written form. There are textbooks or manuals which embody them. These then become the guidance of the local units, which, however, through the local labor department of the mine must see that they are maintained. Sometimes a condition arises which is not covered in the standard procedure, and in that event a staff member is sent from the labor department of the trust to deal with the miner at work underground and the labor department of the mine. The director of the local industrial unit corresponding to the superintendent of a mine in the United States, who, as already indicated, is appointed by the director of the trust, appoints all local directors, including the chief of the pit or the mine foreman. The director of the trust is in turn appointed by the board of the trust, who in turn are appointed by the administrative officials responsible to the Council of People's Commissars.

It was the president of the trade union who answered our question as to the relation of the trade union to the labor department. He described the structure of trade unions in the U.S.S.R. They are divided industrially. All workers around the mines belong to one union. The trade union has its regional or "rayon" headquarters, and each mine or industrial unit has its own trade-union committee. The workmen in the mine are divided into groups known as brigades, and each brigade has its own representative in the trade union.

Each local union or trade-union committee in a mine has sections which correspond to the labor department of the trust and to the labor department of the industrial unit, thus enabling the trust and the local management to function with the trade union on the following subjects: (1) planning and administration of wage rates and standards of output; (2) protection of living and working conditions, including management of central dining rooms and other matters having to do with the standard of living, in which the union either takes full responsibility or acts as a constant critic of the administration and a stimulus to its improvement; (3) cultural provisions; such as organization of "Red Corners" for reading and discussion, libraries, classes, and in general the activities of workers' clubs. A committee on conflicts deals with disputes. It includes two representatives of the union, a representative of the trust, and a direct representative of the workers, elected by them.

The function of the trade union in relation to all of these labor standards, in the words of its president, is "control." To one concerned with Scientific Management in the United States, this idea of control, voiced by the trade-union president in the exact meaning of Taylor's principles, was of great interest. He told us that the setting up of standards was regarded by the workers as a technical problem for experts, but that control in administering standards was a function in which the trade union had a responsible part. If workmen in a mine cannot agree regarding the application of standards set up by the technicians, an industrial conference is called, which includes the workmen involved, and they endeavor to reach an agreement. If this is impossible, the dispute goes to the conflict committee, and it may go higher if settlement at that stage is impossible. The next steps would be through national officials of the union on the one hand and representatives of the administration of heavy industry on the other hand, and possibly representatives of the Communist Party if the issue were of great importance.

Later in our conference, among the first questions put to us about American conditions was an inquiry by the president of the trade union, who asked: "In America, who controls standards of work or norms in the mines?" Those of you who are familiar with the sad lack of true Scientific Management in our mines and with the recent collapse of those methods of negotiation whereby the trade union participated in the application of standards, will readily understand the difficulty which we had in answering this question.

Of course all regional arrangements are subject to policies and conditions adopted for the industry as a whole in all regions. For instance, basic wage payments are determined by national agreement to which the trade union is a party. Labor laws administered by the Joint Commissariat of Labor set standards which must be observed in regional administration.

All of this information relates, of course, to the actual management and administration of the mines, not to the planning of the coal industry. We turned at this point to planning, and particularly to the role of the workers in it. How much do they share, for example, in the decision to more than double the output in the North Caucasus in the second Five Year Plan?

It was the trade-union president who immediately answered the question, followed by the chief engineer of the trust. The president of the union told us that the Five Year Plan is made by the working class itself. In each mine a temporary control committee is named, consisting of a representative of technicians, two representatives of the planning division of the administration, two representatives of the trade union, and six workers selected directly by the miners. This committee in each mine discusses what that mine can do in the next Five Year Plan and sends to the regional trust a report which in turn is conveyed by the trust to the State Planning Commission.

It may be a matter of interest to know the answer to our question as to what were the main outlines of the second Five Year Plan as actually suggested by these committees in the North Caucasus region. The plan at that moment was in the process of development. The representative of planning of the North Caucasus trust answered the question, describing three main points of emphasis for the second five years:

1. In opening new mines, a kilometer of coal might formerly be left between two shafts. Pits in this region are now to be constructed so that 25 kilometers of coal will be worked out in the course of 60 to 65 years. By forecasing the amount of production per year, an equation can be worked out which determines the most effective area of coal to be taken out through one shaft, and hence the distance between shafts is estimated.

2. Mechanization is to be pushed as rapidly as possible, first, in order to solve the problem of shortage of labor, and secondly, in order to get the mines equipped for a permanently adequate rate of production. In this region at the present time the work of undercutting is 62 per cent mechanized; the conveyor or loading system, 40 per cent; and underground transportation, including emptying of cars at the tipple, only 3 or 4 per cent.

3. The main task is improvement of quality and utilization of by-products. In the first Five Year Plan in mining, as in other industries, quantity was the point of emphasis. To deal with the quality of coal, a new plant has been planned for preparation of coal, with the aim of handling six to eight million tons a year.

Incidentally, it may be said that the by-products of coal are richest in the Siberian mines, and work is going forward on such methods of preparation as will conserve them. In the North Caucasus region an experiment is under way to make gas by direct burning of coal in the ground, without extraction. Obviously in these two directions the work of research may at any moment result in far-reaching changes which will directly affect current plans for coal production. But these circumstances would be dealt with by the institutions of planning.

So much for the administration of the coal industry in the locality and the region and the relation of these administrative units to planning. It may be the clearest procedure now to shift the point of view to the offices in Moscow where the plan is made and administered for the Union as a whole. Before making that shift, however, it should be pointed out that the State Planning Commission has its regional representatives in the county or region planning office of the North Caucasus in Rostov, which is nearest to the coal mines visited by us. In that office the plans for the whole region for the mines and all inter-related industries, including agriculture, are studied for submission to the State Planning Commission in Moscow. The next unit of planning is the republic. For example, the Ukranian Republic makes for its own area a plan which must take account of the plan made for that portion of each industry, such as coal, which is within the boundaries of the constituent republic. These plans, both for the region as a unit and for the republic, are based upon the needs of their respective areas and represent the contribution of the area to the All-Union plan.

On the administrative side, as already pointed out, the coal trust is part of the Commissariat of Heavy Industry under the Council of People's Commissars, but the coal trust of the North Caucasus region, like every other trust, and its constituent industrial units have also been included in the conference called by the State Planning Commission in the preparation of the second Five Year Plan. This twofold task of administrative units acting as advisers in planning is an interesting aspect of management in the U.S.S.R. They act as advisers with reference to planning and then as administrators in carrying out the plan. They have a relationship and a scheme of organization and procedure which is functional for the industry as a whole for for related industries comprehended in the term "heavy industry," while at the same time they form part of all plans of locality, region and republic in which the constituent units of the mining undustry are situated. A notable feature of the second Five Year Plan is this functioning of the smallest unit of operation in the making of the plan.

We may now trace the administration of the coal industry, including its advisory relation to planning, back to the offices of the Main Fuel Administration, which is part of the Commissariat of Heavy Industry existing only as an All-Union commissariat with no corresponding commissariats in the different republics. It is interesting to note that the administration of light industry is a joint union and republic responsibility. The immediate preoccupation of the Main Fuel Administration is not so much with the Five Year Plan as with yearly and quarterly plans within the Five Year Plan, and their fulfillment. The Fuel Administration deals not only with coal but with other types of fuel, including oil and its by-products, peat, wood and other combustibles. Other enterprises inform the Fuel Administration as to their need for coal. Daily telegrams keep the Moscow office informed of actual current needs for different kinds of quantities of coal in different industries; and daily reports from the mines give information as to output and transportation.

The relationship of the Main Fuel Administration to the State Planning Commission for the second Five Year Plan is twofold. First, general directives, showing the relation of the coal industry to other industries, are laid down by the Gosplan. Then the Main Fuel Administration and its trusts and local units work out the specific application of these general directives throughout their own operations. In conference in Moscow, the results of the work of these administrative units are brought together. Then the Gosplan makes the total plan and issues it as instructions, subject, however, to counterplans which are again brought in by the Main Fuel Administration and its trusts and local units and represent discussion all the way down the line to the local shop or mine committee of workmen and technicians. Finally, the Gosplan makes a formulation, "balancing" the industries in their inter-relationships and determining the investment of capital and other aspects of a unified financial plan. The last step is the adoption of the plan by the All-Union Congress of Soviets.

How this has worked with reference to the second Five Year Plan, was more clearly seen in the offices of the State Planning Commission in Moscow, which has a fuel division. Obviously, coal is only a part, though a vital one, of the whole planned economy. Here is illustrated a fundamental difference in concept as between planning as it is administered in the Soviet Union and as it is discussed in the United States. Planning conceived merely as a technique, can be carried out in different branches of industry and in different establishments. This, however, does not constitute a planned economy, which, in the nature of the idea, is a total and integrated whole. All branches of industry in the Soviet Union are planned at the same time.

Considering coal within this framework, the main object of a plan for fuel is the development of the metal industries. When this is adopted as the main objective, all other uses of fuel fall into place in terms of their relative importance. Their importance is determined in the light of the planned economy. The immediate objective is industrialization. Metal occupies the central position in this development. It does not take the major supply of coal, but the plan for coal is made after acceptance of the figures given by the metal industries.

This, then, is the first factor as to how much coal is required for industrialization (namely, how many tons of pig iron are needed and how much coal it takes to make them). The second factor is transportation. The third is development of electric power. These three are looked upon as the primary factors determining the need for coal.

Time does not permit elaboration of the various factors which must be considered in determining the total quantity and the regional distribution of production in an industry like mining. Suffice it so say that it involves, of course, technical questions, mechanization and productivity of labor on the one hand, and on the other hand housing and community development. It also involves consideration of location of contributing industries, location of consuming industries, and decision as to what is the most economical relationship between all these points of production and distribution and how much transportation is available.

Knowing the main directives which determine the need for coal and the limiting factors in producing it, the question them is, "Who reaches decisions?" We have noted the process of negotiation between the trust and the trade union in the region of the North Caucasus. Having worked out their conclusions as to what the different mines of the North Caucasus could produce, representatives of administration, of trade unions and of workers came to Moscow for an All-Union fuel conference which was held early in July, 1932. The purpose was to accumulate ideas and recommendations from all over the country for the second Five Year Plan. The number participating was 666, of whom 361 were engineers and 113 economists. Women in these two groups numbered seventeen. Fifty of the conferees were workers, all of them so-called shock brigaders or leaders who are stimulating production out of loyalty to the Communist Party and the socialist state. The remaining 142 were from miscellaneous groups. On the basis of this material, a first evaluation of the second Five Year Plan for fuel in general was in process of being made at the time of my interview.

These details, however, represent a balance which is not to be taken as fixed. In the words of the chief of the coal division of the Gosplan: "These balances are not fixed, because we grow, and growing we break the limits. The balance is simply the estimate." Three steps are involved in striking the balance, as already shown. First a prospective figure reflects average possibilities. In order to increase these possibilities, a second step is taken, in the form of a yearly plan which is always higher than the Five Year Plan; and to increase this yearly plan, a third step is taken, in so-called counterplanning, which began in 1930. These counterplans are made at the workplaces, where possibilities of increase are more clearly seen than at the Gosplan. Thus the maximum production is not ordered from Moscow, but planned by the miners underground and the technicians with whom they are associated. It is they who are eager to accomplish more than the quotas which represent the average figure from the State Planning Commission. It is in this process of administration, involved in the carrying out of an estimated plan, that frequent changes occur which are sometimes misunderstood as indications of errors in advance estimates. To a management engineer, however, they are rather a reflection of the fact that the carrying out of the plan is a living process and not a mere record on paper.

The conference in connection with the coal industry was one of twenty-four held in Moscow during the summer of 1932. It is worth while to quote here decree No. 429 of the Council of People's Commissars, dated March 25, 1932. It begins thus:

> The successful fulfilment of the work connected with the preparation of the second Five Year Plan demands the active participation of all state trade unions and social organizations. It is necessary to draw into this work the widest masses of the workers and of the members of collective farms. In the drafting of the second Five Year Plan it is necessary to provide for the widest participation of all eminent scientists and engineers and scientific research organizations of the U.S.S.R., such as the Academy of Sciences, the Communist Academy, the Lenin Agricultural Academy, etc.

The Council of People's Commissars then decreed the steps to accomplish this purpose, which may be briefly summarized as follows:

1. The State Planning Commission was to supply outlines and methodological instruction to the All-Union commissariats, to the constituent republics and to the most important regions not later than April 1.

2. The All-Union commissariats were to present preliminary drafts of the control figures of the second Five Year Plan to the State Planning Commission in accordance with the outlines furnished by the Commission, not later than July 10, while constituent republics were to present these

materials not later than July 20. On the basis of these materials, and the work of conferences to consider separate problems, the State Planning Commission was to present unified control figures to the Council of People's Commissars not later than August 20.

3. After these control figures had been considered by the Council of People's Commissars, the State Planning Commission was to prepare detailed instructions and quotas concerning the control figures for 1933 and for the second Five Year Plan. These were to be forwarded to the All-Union commissariats, republics and regions not later than September 1. The detailed figures for 1933 were to be prepared by the All-Union commissariats not later than October 20 and by the republics not later than November 1, while the preliminary plan for the development of the national economy was to be presented by these bodies to the State Planning Commission by the latter part of November.

4. Finally, the State Planning Commission was to present the plan for 1933 for the approval of the Council of People's Commissars of the U.S.S.R. by December 1, and the entire second Five Year Plan by January 1, to be formally adopted by the All-Union Congress of Soviets.

The special congresses and conferences referred to in these instructions were twenty-four in number, covering the following subjects:

1. Allocation of productive forces
2. Electrification
3. Fuel
4. Chemistry and its application in the national economy
5. Development of geological and geodetic work during the second five-year period
6. Mechanization of difficult labor processes
7. Water economy
8. Specialization and co-operation in the machine-building industry
9. Organization of repair work and mechanical shops for the major branches of national economy
10. Reconstruction of the lumber industry
11. Technical reconstruction of the food and consumers'-goods industries
12. Reconstruction of transport
13. Transport, other than railway
14. Mechanization of agriculture
15. Feed cultivation, vegetable and fruit growing and the utilization of these products
16. Livestock breeding and utilization of products
17. Reorganization of construction work
18. Electrical communication
19. Trade turnover and its material base
20. Labor and personnel
21. Reorganization of municipal construction, city housing and living conditions
22. Problems of health preservation and proper utilization of leisure
23. Development of scientific research work in connection with the second Five Year Plan and the organization of a network of scientific

research centers

24. Cultural work and the creation of the material base for the cultural revolution

Three sections of the decree then describe the procedure for co-operation with the State Planning Commission by the commissariats and by the republic and local planning organizations. For instance, each commissariat was to name one of its vice-commissars to supervise the work. The commissariats would receive outlines and instructions from the State Planning Commission and in turn transmit them to their subsidiary organizations, the industries, trusts, factories, etc., and the suggestion was made that the All-Union commissariats might call special conferences, drawing into these conferences scientific institutions and social organizations. The planning organizations of republics and regions were called upon to plan the economic and cultural development for their geographical areas, and they were charged with laying special stress upon plans "for the development of large cities." Finally, stress was laid upon the importance of labor's participation. The last two paragraphs of the decree are as follows:

1. All State, trade-union and social organizations are urged to start in immediately to draw the wide mass of workers into discussing and proposing solutions for problems connected with the second Five Year Plan.

2. The State Planning Commission, the All-Union commissariats and the Council of People's Commissars of the constituent republics are instructed to assure the wide participation of the All-Union council of trade unions, the central committees of trade unions and local trade-union organizations in all stages of the work in the preparation of the second Five Year Plan.

Thus it becomes clear that the procedure described to us in the North Caucasus as actually under way in the mines, is the standard procedure for all industries. Space does not permit an account of how this applies in agriculture or in factories, but the whole idea may be summed up by saying that management in the U.S.S.R. has for its goal an all-inclusive purpose to establish a new society; that the new society is to be a collective economy; that all who are able are expected to work, and that when the class divisions of the old economy have been eliminated through the process of socialization of industry all who are able to work will be expected to fulfil their function in the economic system, while in turn each will share in the collective goods and services; that the whole process is grounded in the Hegelian philosophy that the rational is the real and that the real is rational, and hence procedure and administration and all decisions connected with organized economic life must be based upon facts and a knowledge of natural law.

To a group of management engineers it hardly needs to be said that decisions, to be effective, must proceed from knowledge. Once the task has been accepted of developing a rational, planned economy, knowledge becomes the master for the reason that no other master could make a plan which would work. This delicate balancing of one industry in relation to another, this constant watching of results, cannot be accomplished by writing down figures representing decisions of one person. As one of the administrators in the State Planning Commission expressed it, all parts of the national economy are interdependent, but not from a single hand. Each decision creates the necessity for the next decision, and each must be in harmony with reality and rational because based upon natural law. Gradually the dictatorship of a revolutionary period gives place, through the administrative process, to the authority of knowledge which is the fruit of science.

Thus far, no analysis has been given of the political institutions within which planning and administration of socialized industry are carried on. This also is a very interesting aspect of the new economic system in the Soviet Union. As the primary purpose of the Communist state is the organization of economic life, the political forms must be adapted to the administration of socialized industry. The nucleus of the new political organization is the Soviet or council or shop committee. In the smallest local unit the workers elect delegates to the Soviet, and thus step by step is built up the central authority, the All-Union Congress of Soviets, which is directly composed of the workers' representatives in the different branches of industry. Out of the Soviet grow the institutions for planning and administration.

Of course it is known that the Soviet Union is made up of constituent republics, just as the United States consists of states, with relationships to be worked out between federal and state governments. In the U.S.S.R., the administrative organization is centered in the Council of People's Commissars, under which function commissariats of three main kinds: the People's Commissariats of the Union, with no corresponding bodies in the constituent republics, such as the Commissariat of Heavy Industry; the republic commissariats with no corresponding All-Union bodies, such as Education and Health; and the Joint Commissariats, such as Agriculture and Light Industry. In these plans of administration and in the distinction between what is regional and what is of All-Union importance, is another field of study of great interest in management research.

Of course a planned economy must be a record-keeping economy. Reference has already been made to the Central Board of National Economic Accounting. It centralizes control and planning of statistics, but much of the actual task of collection is in the different administrative agencies in the trusts or the republics or the regions. Moreover, in factories and mines everywhere one finds records of accomplishment, many of which are individualized, showing not only the output of a given department and its relation to the quota, but also the progress record of individuals.

These progress records of individuals are of course part of the whole subject of incentives. Naturally the purpose of building a new society which is to be a workers' republic is in itself an incentive for the workers. Added to this general motive, however, is the reward given to individuals who make notable contributions. For example, we visited the agricultural machine factory in Rostov just after it had completed a heavy task of building the required number of combines or reaper-thresher machines. After a tremendous spurt of energy which finished the task, the workers took their vacations. All workers in Russia have vacations with pay. The plant newspaper, of which we received a copy, when I took it home and had it translated was found to contain a decree signed by Joseph Stalin as Secretary of the Communist Party, naming out of the mass of 17,000 workers, individuals who deserved rewards and describing their particular achievements. Sometimes the reward may be a scholarship for study, and sometimes it is a group reward, such as the building of a workers' club. On the other hand, slackers may be held up to derision. One finds, for example, in the Park for Culture and Rest in Moscow bronze busts commemorating the contributions of individual workers to economic progress, while also there are caricatures of those who have obstructed progress. Thus humor is included among the incentives.

It would of course be pertinent in observations of management in the Soviet Union to analyze the actual figures of output under the first Five Year Plan. Among the many illustrative figures which are available, probably the most significant is the fact that 81.5 per cent of the national income in 1931 was derived from the socialized sector of industry, as compared with 52.7 per cent in 1928, and that 1932, when finished, will probably be found to have 91 per cent of the national income from socialized industry. During that period there has been an increase in the national income. Measured in billions of rubles at 1926-27 prices, the national income in 1931 was 38.1 as compared with 26.8 in 1928, with an estimated figure of 49.7 for 1932-33.

First, these figures reflect the fact that the Soviet Union is accomplishing its industrialization by the accumulation of its own capital for production. Naturally this is achieved by self-denial. Attention has had to be concentrated upon production goods. The people have had to do without many consumption goods. There is not enough food. The peasants have more money than ever before to spend, but goods which they wish to buy are not in the market. The difficulties are great, but the important point is that all of these are problems to which the institutions of administration and planning are giving attention. The second Five Year Plan will aim to increase consumers' goods and to eliminate inefficiencies in distribution, while continuing emphasis upon industrialization.

The second fact of great significance, the fact that so large a proportion of the national income is derived from the socialized sector, is important in any study of management. Management in the Soviet Union has the responsibility and the power to control this proportion of the national income and to direct it as an instrument of the economic plan. This power to distribute the national income enables the Soviet Union to determine what the standards of living of its people shall be, and to raise them as productive capacity increases.

The universality of the principles of Scientific Management emerges as one observes their applicability in the new economic system of the Soviet Union. The outstanding difference is that in the United States limits are set to the application of knowledge because the area of control through ownership is not comprehensive enough to plan and control the relationships of factors which are essentially inter-related. The extent of the socialized control of the Soviet Union has given to Scientific Management in that country a scope which is new in the history of modern industry. It will take time to perfect its application in the Soviet Union to the lowest industrial unit with the completeness and precision already attained in the best managed shops in the United States. But meanwhile the range of problems which is being presented in the U.S.S.R. by this large-scale integration of industries reaches far beyond the widest stretch of the imagination of the management engineer in America. Here

Scientific Management is tied to a hitchingpost, when it should be free to follow as far as electricity can carry it.

Returning to the United States, I found among my books a pamphlet which I had previously overlooked. It was a speech made by Lenin in Moscow in 1918, entitled "The Soviets at Work," in which he said: "We, the Bolshevik party, have convinced Russia. We have won Russia from the rich for the poor, from the exploiters for the toilers. And now it is up to us to manage Russia."

Lenin considered the political organization of a workers' republic insufficient. The workers must learn to manage and must base their management on "universal accounting and control of production and distribution." And he declared: "We should try out every scientific and progressive suggestion of the Taylor system. Successful management depends on the ability for practical organization."

---

[1]Bulletin of the Taylor Society, April, 1933. Presented at a meeting of the Taylor Society, New York, December 8, 1932.

THE ART OF MANAGEMENT
FROM A BRITISH POINT OF VIEW[1]

By Oliver Sheldon

It would be both ungracious and untrue to deny that, in recent years, a very strong impulse towards more efficient industrial management has come to us in Great Britain from the United States. Fresh breezes have crossed the Atlantic, bearing new ideas and scattering old ones. Most cordially I, for one, acknowledge the service which Mr. Taylor and those of his compatriots who worked with him or have since faithfully carried out his great principles have performed to the world at large, and, after the United States, to this country in particular. Wherever manufacturing is carried on, this acknowledgment is due.

Much water has, however, flowed under the bridges since the first beginnings of the new era in management. Scientific management has now come to claim its capital S and its capital M, and has been awarded its inverted commas. With increasing study and a wider and constantly wider circle of readers, teachers, critics and experimentalists, the basic principles have become overlaid and difficult to distinguish. Much knowledge has conduced to obscure the main issues. There are so many trees that one often fails to discern the outline of the forest. There are false prophets to mislead the unwary and confuse the student. A vast enthusiasm to run has made some careless of the goal towards which they are running. The impetuosity of youth has overwhelmed the judgment of age. The quick glance of eagerness has seized upon tangible forms and not penetrated to the underlying spirit, as a man who reads the anecdotes of a book but skips over the conclusions.

Scientific management has accordingly suffered in the process, and has been, as it were, obscured beneath a mask. This applies in a greater degree the further one is from the source. Scientific management has been largely presented to this country in a distorted form. Its mechanisms have been everything; its philosophy nothing. It has come flushed with superficial enthusiasm, equipped with hidebound contrivances, glowing with ethereal promises, and pointing airily towards "short-cuts," along rosy primrose-strewn paths. It has accordingly evoked cynicism, sarcasm and the "cold shoulder." Yet beneath it all, it was patent to those who cared to pierce the spangled cloak that here lay a message of immense portent; and, even to those who scarcely paused to think, the mechanisms themselves suggested some facets of the truth. In general, however, I think one may fairly say that "Scientific Management," frilled out complete with capitals and inverted commas, accompanied by its profligate pursuer "Efficiency," similarly bedizened, has, in externals at any rate, received in this country a chilly reception.

Those who have witnessed its presentation cannot be surprised that this should be so. Day-to-day experience of industry is a fully adequate preventive against the deceptions of the industrial conjurer. Efficiency, as a term of industrial significance indicating a multitude of systems of specious appearance but of dubious value, has consequently come to be the outcast of our industrial vocabulary. The phrase "Scientific Management," though saved from a similarly degrading fate, has become one to be expressed with caution and reservations.

It is vastly important, therefore, if the great principles of scientific management are to become part of the web and woof of our industrial philosophy, that every effort should be made to tear away the glittering garments and reveal the real body which stands behind. When we speak of "scientific management," what is it that we mean? Is it a set of mechanical contrivances, like so many Meccano toys? Is it a transportable system of things, like a ready-made suit of clothes, that one dons and becomes a different being? Is it a complete and definite theory, or is it a general attitude to things? Is it something one installs, or is it a means which one employs? Is it an object to be attained, or is it an attitude of mind to which one must school oneself? I postulate these queries, not wholly in childish innocence, but rather because I am convinced that the future of scientific management in Great Britain depends upon the answer.

Let me digress for a moment. On the morning of October 8th, 1923, readers of the Public Ledger of Philadelphia were confronted with the intriguing headline--"Scientific Management Unknown in Great Britain. Scientists know nothing of business and business men know nothing of science." To a British reader this must have conveyed the sense that one was amongst the ranks of the "great unwashed"--a grimy urchin playing in the dirty puddles of an industrial back-yard. Yet one could not but be struck by the glint of truth in an ambiguous title. After all, one said to oneself, where can one point to any unadulterated application of time-study, functional foremanship, standardization, planning, instruction cards, and task-work? Not here; not there; indeed, anywhere? Perhaps, there, just in one or two isolated instances. Truly, the gloom is darker than a moonless night of winter. Yet, for all that, one felt that there was something--some struggling hands, some forward-looking impulse of many scattered minds, some jerking, spasmodic, tense activity, hardly to be called a movement, yet eminently buoyant on the tide of progress--which gave the lie to all that the headline implied. And, after all, it resolved itself into the fundamental question--"Well, what do you mean by scientific management?"

Let us go back to the words of Mr. Taylor himself. "Scientific management," he says, "fundamentally consists of . . . a certain philosophy which can be applied in many ways, and a description of what any man or men may believe to be the best mechanism for applying these general principles should in no way be confused with the principles themselves." And again he says, "I want to tell you as briefly as I can what scientific management is. It certainly is not what most people think it to be. It is not a lot of efficiency expedients. It is not the printing and ruling of a lot of pieces of blank paper and spreading them by the ton about the country. It is not any particular system of paying men. It is none of the ordinary devices which unfortunately are going by the name of scientific management. It may in its essence be said in the present state of industry to involve a complete mental revolution, both on the part of the management and of the men."

Such statements as these indicate the breadth of vision of Mr. Taylor in a way which no amount of explanation can. They entirely rule out of court those who assess the presence or absence of scientific management by the presence or absence of certain mechanisms. Primarily, scientific management consists of a certain attitude to industrial problems. He, in fact, is an exponent of some branch of scientific management who deals with his factory problems by the scientific method. The scientific method may be described as a series of definite stages, culminating in a "law" or a "standard." The first stage is the accurate, systematic and wide examination of the facts. The basis of all science is fact, truth. The scientist collects his data from as many sources as possible, in as great an amount as he can command. Dispassionately he reviews them--singly and collectively. He then classifies his facts, groups them and re-groups them. Finally, from this accumulation of fact, he derives a principle, a law, or a standard. In order that his facts may be properly grouped and carefully weighed, he insists throughout upon exact measurement and the accurate definition of every tool he uses, be it a fact, a word or a measure. Scientific management, then, is the conduct of the work of management according to the scientific method--investigation, classification, definition, measurement and standardization.

If this conception of scientific management be correct, then it follows that it can be applied to the management of any enterprise, whether large or small, and to any section of an enterprise. The main work of Mr. Taylor was devoted to the application of this general philosophy to operative work and to the immediate supervision of operative work. But he himself fully realized the universal applicability of his principles. Indeed, the recent work of the Taylor Society on sales management and on the higher direction of a business by a chief executive are instances of the scientific method being used in fields somewhat remote from the factory floor. One is applying the scientific method whether, after exhaustive investigation, one determines the standard figures to be supplied to the chief executive or the standard output to be expected from the workman.

Before returning to our main theme, moreover, I think it is vital to distinguish between scientific management and the "Science of Management," of which we are beginning to hear so much. It is the difference between the scientific method as an instrument by which management arrives at certain standards, and the standards themselves. A science is the codified knowledge acquired as a result of the use of the scientific method. If, therefore, the management has applied the scientific method to some operative process--let us say, laying bricks or covering chocolates--the outcome is a science of bricklaying or a science of chocolate-covering, but not a science of management. It is the science, the knowledge, the truth, the standards which the bricklayer has to learn. To achieve a science of management, therefore, we have to apply the scientific method to the tasks of management as distinct from the tasks of those whom the management control. It is fundamental, I suggest, to draw a distinction between operative science (which management, of course, uses) and managerial science, where management itself is the operative. We need standard methods of control, standard managerial procedures, scientifically determined, as well as standard methods of operation. Just as we investigate operative processes, so should we investigate managerial processes. We should investigate precisely how the work of management is performed, sift it into its primary elements, and then reconstruct it into a new set of standard methods. It is, as we know, just as possible to have standard methods of engaging employees, of compiling plans or of routing orders, as of laying bricks--and these constitute the essential science of management. I submit, therefore, that the management has the dual task of formulating a science for every branch of operative work it controls and of formulating a science, by the same methods for every branch--direct and indirect--of that control. The two are, of course, interdependent. The standard methods of management will depend, to a great extent, on the standard methods of operation, as for instance, functional foremanship is a necessary outcome of the setting of operative tasks. But it is important to realize, firstly, that the scientific method is applicable to the work of operative and manager alike; secondly, that the outcome, in both cases, is a science to be learned, and thirdly, that the one science is something distinguishable from the other. Scientific management, therefore, knows no limits, and its object is not only to determine how best to perform operative tasks but also, and of greater importance, how best to control their performance and carry out the many varied activities auxiliary to that control.

It is an easy step from this line of argument to the realization that management is an art. To elaborate a science of chocolate-covering and of all the activities concerned, directly or indirectly, in the control of chocolate-covering is one thing; but to apply and make use of this fund of knowledge is quite another thing. The application of knowledge is an art, and not everyone who knows can successfully apply his knowledge. Even if, therefore, our science of management were as exact as that of law or of medicine, there would still be required the skilful exercise of human faculty, the art, of the manager. But it is clear, I suggest, that management can never be reduced in its entirety to a set of scientific laws. What Mr. Church has described as the "determinative" element in management must always be beyond all scientific standardization. It can be rendered immensely easier, by providing for it a scientific "administrative" element, but it cannot, of itself, be subjected to laws or principles. Neither can the human side of management be reduced to a science. Broadly, management is concerned in two primary elements--things, in the sense of machines, methods and systems; and men. The former is susceptible to scientific treatment, the latter is not. We may set up the most scientific standards of output, the most carefully designed organization of duties, the most elaborate system of planning, but these will be of little avail unless we have the rare human faculty of inducing men to work according to our systems and up to our standards. This is beyond all science. We may have scientific selection of men, we may have admirably devised systems of remuneration, we may establish the most just systems of rating, but when all is finished, there still remains the throb of human interest, enthusiasm, cooperation which along can set in operation the carefully adjusted wheels of our machine. With a broad basis of tested knowledge, the manager has the means to obtain the very best results--but only, if he himself has that intangible capacity to make use of his knowledge and inspire his staff to apply it. There may be a science of costing, of transportation, and of operation, but there can be no science of cooperation. That is dependent not on scientific principles but on ethical principles. It is a question of ideals, not of systems. It must always remain a problem of mentality and of the spirit. One concludes, therefore, that valuable as is indeed the elaboration of scientific principles, laws and standards to govern the methods by which management may achieve certain ends, there must be added to this a spirit of leadership, based on a fundamental belief in the purpose of industry, and conducing to the utmost cooperation between all the various grades engaged in a common enterprise. The happy union of the two--science on the one hand and what we may call ethics on the other--is essential to the complete realization of one's dream that industrial management is one of the greatest arts which ever existed to benefit and uplift mankind.

I have very briefly emphasized and explained the two points above--the fact that the science of management is something distinguishable from the science of operative work, and the fact that management is an art, calling for leadership, cooperation and human skill as much as for a broad basis of science--because I believe that, without an understanding of these two ideas, one cannot fully appreciate the progress which the art of management is making in this country. Owing to circumstances which would take far too long to discuss in this paper--circumstances arising out of the exceptional mentality of Labor, the form in which the social consciousness has developed, and, still more fundamentally, the particular temperament of Britishers generally--the developments of recent years in industrial management have been and are still rather in the two directions indicated above than in the direction of what one may call "material" science. There is far more being done, more thought being applied to, firstly making management efficient as distinct from making the worker efficient, and secondly, the human relations of industry, than to either the application of the physical sciences to industry or the study of operative processes, as exemplified by the work of Taylor, Gilbreth and many others in America. The progressive British employer is more impressed with the fact that management is a synthetical art than with the equally true fact that it is founded on analytical study. His attention is, therefore, much more drawn to problems of higher organization on the one hand and problems of human association on the other than to the broad basis of operative efficiency on which these must be founded. One finds, therefore, much thought and experiment applied to wage systems, profit-sharing schemes, the question of unemployment, the application of Christian principles to industry, copartnership, industrial welfare, Works Councils, etc., arising from his concern in the problems of human leadership and association. One finds again considerable attention given to such questions as the relation of production to sales, the duties of the higher officials, the training of executives, the organization of control, the use of committees, etc., arising from his concern in the efficiency of his managerial organization. But one finds slow progress in the use of time-study, motion study, the application of science to materials, or the standardization of operative processes. Progress there is, of course--probably more than one hears of--but it is not moving with the same assurance in this as in other directions.

The comments of Mr. Herbert N. Casson--the writer above whose name the Ledger of Philadelphia inscribed such startling headlines--may perhaps appear more comprehensible in the light of what has been said. He writes:

> Naturally, the British business world is packed full of exceptions and contradictions. Everywhere you go, you will see patches and makeshifts. There is virtually no such thing in England as "scientific management" outside of half a dozen exceptional firms. . . .
>
> An Englishman rejects the scientific method, not because he fails to appreciate its advantages, but because he values still more highly the human element in his business. He does not regard his workers as automatic and never will. He will break up any scheme of improvement to make it fit a foreman or a sales manager. . . .
>
> He does not put output first. He cannot understand mass production. He persists in making exceptions that destroy the efficiency of any plan of increased production. . . .
>
> There is a spirit of give and take in Britain which many people think is carried too far in business life. . . .
>
> (The English) regard science as only one of the factors that must be considered in the solution of any practical problem. . . .

In the main, these are comments to which I can subscribe, but they do not in any way damp my belief that the art of management in Britain is on the move forward. This movement may not be just on the exact track which it is following in the United States, nor is the movement so rapid. But it is movement, growth, development of an unmistakable kind. As will be gathered, in some directions we are only just beginning, but in others I think we have, at any rate, passed more than a few milestones. Management is certainly in the midst of its "growing pains." Beneath the somewhat hard and weather-beaten skin, there is every evidence of growth. There is a reaching after new ideas, a deeper delving after facts, a more deliberate founding of policy upon scientifically won data, a closer examination of detail, a wider appreciation of costs and measurements of one kind or another, and, perhaps, most significant of all, a slowly developing search for the underlying purpose of industry--a search stimulated by the wide understanding of the need for the human milk of cooperation.

This stirring in the camp of management is singularly unobtrusive. One has to look for it; it does not force itself into the open to be seen by all. Here, we find a firm with a singularly exact costing system; there, a firm which has a carefully developed planning scheme; this firm with a successful profit-sharing scheme; that firm with an effective council system. Yesterday, there was perhaps a conference on foremanship; today, maybe, a conference on salesmanship. Here is a firm developing a carefully devised organization of its higher staff; there is a firm undertaking detailed research into processes. Quite generally, there is an increasing tendency to employ a certain proportion of university and similarly qualified men for the managerial work which, in a decade, has vastly increased in complexity.

Then, apart from the activities of individual firms, beginnings are being made on a more corporate basis. An Institute of Industrial Administration has been begun. A similar body, studying allied problems in a different sphere, is the Institute of Public Administration. The Institute of Industrial Psychology is a very flourishing body of recent growth. The British Association (contrary, I suggest, to Mr. Casson's comment that "the scientific men made no pretense of being of service to the world of trade and commerce") has established a Psychology section which is largely concerned in the industrial application of the science, in addition to its Economics section which again cannot be regarded as a sphere alien to industry. The Industrial Welfare Society has a large membership, and is becoming recognized as the headquarters of the so-called "welfare" work--a branch which administrators, I submit, cannot fail to regard as an integral part of management. A Sales Managers Association has been formed. The Industrial Fatigue Research Board is conducting research of immeasurable potentiality. Some twenty odd research associations have been set up under the Department of Scientific and Industrial Research. The London-Cambridge Economic Service is another recent venture, bringing economics into close touch with administration. Other societies indirectly helping to promote a higher standard of skill in management are the Institute of Chartered Accountants, the Institute of Cost and Works Accountants, the Chartered Institute of Secretaries and various engineering and statistical societies.

Furthermore, this activity is being reflected in the expansion of the curricula of some of our universities. The Manchester College of Technology is not only conducting research work, but is setting up an educational standard in industrial administration and the application of various sciences to industry. London University now includes business administration in its curriculum, and as a part of its economic degree. Leeds and Birmingham Universities are promoting similar study.

Again, in the development of the art of industrial management, one cannot by any means disregard the activities of such societies and bodies as the Industrial League and Council, the Labour Copartnership Association, the National Alliance of Employers and Employed and the Workers' Educational Association, to take a few prominent examples. In promoting the study of the human side of industry and of the problems relative to the place and functions of industry in our social commonwealth, such societies as these are definitely contributing to a wider basis of knowledge, an encouragement of experiments and a higher standard of managerial skill. That these activities are carried on in happy cooperation with Labor is an indication of what Labor may yet contribute to the promotion of the art of management.

All this activity, inchoate as it may appear, indicates a very real stirring in the life of industry, and, more particularly, in all that concerns its direction and management. Unconsciously almost, there is a spreading appreciation of the fact that industry is vastly more complex than it was some years ago, that the difficulties are greater, and, perhaps most of all, that Labor is a mare far more difficult to guide. Consequently, there is a corresponding appreciation, on the one hand, of the increasing need for the application of science to industry and the use of the scientific method in management, and, on the other hand, of the great human responsibility of management and the need for relating that responsibility to some dominant ideal and purpose, some code of ethics which shall be applicable wherever industry is carried on. Management is beginning to feel the intricacy of its task and the weight of its responsibilities. Slowly, with painstaking effort, by cautious experiment, and in a somewhat haphazard fashion, a new management is emerging--a management with new ideals, new methods and new personnel. The tips of its fingers peep out here and there through the old encrusted surface, breaking new ground in this direction and in that. Progress is truly slow. For those who look only for the application in practice of definite systems and recognized mechanisms, there is practically no progress at all. But for those who are prepared to look a little deeper and scan the wider horizon, for those who regard management not only as the function elaborating scientific methods and standards but also as the function charged with the high task of leadership and the pioneer in the development of our daily shifting social order, there is a stir of life which tells unmistakably of the passing of the old order. That this advance will come in conformity with the traditional British caution, use of compromise, and regard for continuity one may be certain. But of its coming, all the stars of heaven are singing, if we could but hear them.

What is lacking in this growth of our art of management is a corporate feeling. Each business is feeling its own way; each society or institute is ploughing its own lonely, rather narrow furrow. There is little which the manager in one plant would regard as linking him in any way to the manager of another plant. There is, indeed, often enough no live appreciation of any professional bond linking together the various branches and grades of the management within the confines of one single plant. There is little articulate feeling that all who practise any part of the art of management are capable of being bound together in a common profession, based on a common technique, employing a common method, and pursuing a common purpose. That method--the scientific method--is not yet by any means being generally practised. That purpose--the common purpose of management--has not yet by any means been generally adopted. Consequently, the practitioners of management have not yet come to feel any strong and vivid corporate relationship. There is comparatively little corporate organization, therefore little corporate research or corporate literature. We lack our Taylor Society. We lack that free interchange of experience and information between individuals and businesses which, in the United States, has been carried some way and is an essential of all-round progress. We lack, further, that literature on management which forms a practical link between every reader. These will and must come--practical expressions of a corporate feeling. We have our beginnings but they are nothing more. They contribute comparatively little to the leavening of the whole. But I regard the formation of some definite corporate organization, representing the thought and mentality of management--viewed as the guiding partner in industry, welded together in a professional association as the next great step to be taken. It is high time that the dividing walls were razed to the ground, the shutters which hide us from each other, taken down, and all our experiments, experiences, information, standards, practices and plans brought together for the good of the whole. Then truly might we look to management, as a body, achieving a professional status, actuated by a corporate motive and applying to all its problems the proven methods of science.

---

[1]Bulletin of the Taylor Society, October, 1923.

EARLY STEPS TOWARD SCIENTIFIC MANAGEMENT IN FRANCE

By Ethel Barbara Dietrich
Mount Holyoke College

Among the leading west European industrialists is M. Charles de Freminville, the president of the Conference de l'Organization Francaise and the consultant of Le Creusot, the largest steel works in France. Throughout his seventy years he has been connected with the French iron and steel industry and has watched its growth from the small forge period. His point of view is historical; and his approach to modern industrial problems is that of the scholar as well as the practical engineer. Though probably no one has done more to stimulate the application of the management methods of Taylor and Fayol to French industry, he has made also an interesting contribution to the history of economic thought in a recent study of several engineers, especially Perronet.

As early as 1717 l'Academie des Sciences drew up a questionnaire, in which there was a demand for sketches showing the attitudes taken by workmen during their work. Various *memoires* were prepared in response to the request, using as the basis for investigation the manufacture of pins at Laigle, "les plus renommees du royaume," but none, according to M. de Freminville were in any sense equal to those of a young engineer from Alencon by the name of Perronet, who published two memoirs: *Explication de la facon dont on reduit le fil de lait on a differentes grosseurs, dans la ville de Laigle, en Normandie* (1739) and *Description de la facon dont on fabrique les epingles a Laigle*, en Normandie (1740). Unfortunately for the fame of Perronet in economic history the publication of his *memoires* by l'Academie in a collection of studies made by its members since the end of the seventeenth centure which was begun in 1761, was preceded by the publication of *La Grande Encyclopedie* of Diderot and d'Alembert in 1755. In it there was a description of the manufacture of pins at Laigle with sketches by a M. Delaire, a learned philosopher with no practical experience, which according to M. De Freminville was unmistakably based on Perronet's earlier studies "sans en nommer l'auteur qui etait alors inconnu." In 1760 Perronet sent his two *memoires* to Diderot who published them both *in extenso* following the article of M. Delaire in the second edition of *l'Encyclopedie* (1783).

These articles were preceded in *l'Encyclopedie* with the following statement, showing that the chief interest in them at that time was the application of the principle of the division of labor:

"Ces deux descriptions faites aves soin par deux excellents physiciens qui voient bien et raisonnent ce qu'ils voient, doivent tourner au profit de l'art et feront sans doute excuses les repetitions necessaires des memes procedes, qui sont d'ailleurs presents dans un ordre et avec des developpements differents que nous ne nous sommes pas cru en droit d'alterer ou de changer."

M. de Freminville feels that there is little doubt that Adam Smith's classic description of the manufacture of pins as an illustration of the principle of the division of labor was based on these two studies of Perronet. Smith had, of course, developed his theory of the division of labor in his Glasgow lectures, which was based on de Mandeville's "Fable of the Bees"; but, instead of using de Mandeville's examples from the production of clocks and watches, he mentions the manufacture of pins as divided into eighteen operations. As Smith had reviewed at considerable length l'Encyclopedie in his letter in the second number of the Edinburgh Review, published in January, 1756, there is every reason to suppose that he had read M. Delaire's article on the manufacture of pins and thought the illustration more up to date. It is quite possible, moreover, that later when he was in Paris consorting with the physiocrats, he might have learned of the two manuscripts of Perronet which were then in Diderot's hands, as the question of the division of labor seems to have been a matter of interest according to the statement quoted above. In "The Wealth of Nations," Smith speaks of the trade of pin maker as "one in which the division of labour has been very often taken notice of"; and, though he claims to have visited a "small manufactory of this kind where only ten men were employed," he seems familiar with studies of "some manufactories" where eighteen distinct operations were performed by different workers. How responsible the latter were for his selection of the pin industry as an example of the advantages of the division of labor is a question. But at least there are now records of two excellent studies on the division of labor in the manufacture of pins thirty-six years before his classic example appeared.

Perronet's claim to an important place in the history of scientific management is perhaps more easily established, as he became a famous builder of bridges and founded the Ecole des Ponts et Chaussees de France, the predecessor of the Ecole Polytechnique. M. De Freminville describes his method in the two memoirs as follows:

"Il s'attache au prix de revient, qu'il note pour chaque operation elementaire, tout en observant la facon dont le travail humain est utilise, la mesure dans laquelle la production est limitee par la fatique, etc."

Besides these two studies, many of his plans have been preserved in Les Oeuvres de Perronet (1788) which contain careful detailed studies of elementary operations, scientific co-ordination of the different tasks and wage studies, based on the work performance which would have delighted Taylor. Furthermore, to quote again from M. de Freminville, ". . . . il est impossible d'avoir pousse plus loin qu'il ne l'a fait l'art de prevoir." All his plans were completed in the minutest detail before any work was commenced, as for instance the bridge of Louis XVI which it took five years to construct.

The following quotations from Les Oeuvres de Perronet illustrate the method as well as the resourcefulness of this scientist:

> Specifications for the construction of the bridge Louis XVI.
>
> Par. 137: The work of each chaplet (of the pumps for draining) will be done by twelve laborers, four of whom will

work together at their winches. An equal number will relieve them every two hours without discontinuance, day and night, so that the work of each man will be reduced to eight hours out of twenty-four. Only three men will be needed on each relay when the rise of the river is only two feet above the low water mark because the water will then be four feet less in depth than when it comes from the higher drain pipe at the head of the chaplet, which will make a diminution of nearly one-fourth of the depth of the column of water from the whole chaplet.

Par. 138: The workmen employed at the pumps will be paid for so many turns of the winch and not by the day as is the custom, and for this purpose there will be placed at the head of each chaplet a suitable machine to count the turns of the winch according to a model which will be given.

Par. 145: Enough pile drivers will be employed so that the work can be carried on night and day without interruptions. The workmen will be paid by the piece.

Thus the rediscovery of Perronet by M. de Freminville adds a bit of possible evidence with regard to the sources of material used by Adam Smith and at the same time gives to "scientific management" a hitherto unknown alien ancestor.

---

[1]A review of *Evolution de l'Organisation Scientifique du Travail a propos de Congres International de Bruxelles* by C. de Freminville. (Paris: Revue de Metallurgie, Vol. XXII, April and May 1926. Pp. 199-208, 269-276.) Reprinted from *The American Economic Review*, Vol. XVII, No. 3, September 1927. Pp. 490-493. Bulletin of the Taylor Society, December, 1928.

Appendixes

Index to the Taylor Society Bulletins
(Name-Title-Date)
1914 - 1934

Adams, Charles P., Scientific Marketing of a Perishable Product, April, 1926.

Andersen, Robert Julius, Why Systems Fail, August, 1925.

Anderson, D. R., Cost Accounting as a Tool of Management, June, 1932.

Anderson, O. A., Rhythm in Repetitive Work, August, 1930.

Ansiaux, Maurice, Under-Consumption, October, 1932.

Archbald, Hugh, The Need of Better Management in Mining Operations, April, 1920.

Ashcroft, A. G., An Outline of Organization for Quality Control, April, 1931.

Babcock, George D., Production Control, December, 1924.

Babcock, George D., and James C. Heckman, Some Organization Lessons of the War: addresses at the session of Friday evening, October 3., December, 1919.

Barber, Joseph H., Coordination of Sales and Production, June, 1924.

Barber, Joseph H. (Closure of), What are the Controllable and the Uncontrollable Factors in Management?, February, 1930.

Barnum, C. L., How the Division of Simplified Practice Plans Conferences with Organized Trade Bodies, October, 1924.

Barnum, C. L., Preserving Ideals in Solving Practical Problems, April, 1926.

Barth, Carl G., Labor Turnover Formulas: a mathematical discussion, April, 1920.

Barth, Carl G., Dwight V. Merrick, Robert T. Kent, Morris L. Cooke, Thomas W. Mitchell, Reynold A. Apeath, Frank B. and L. M. Gilbreth, Stop-Watch Tim Study: A Symposium, June, 1921.

Bates, W. W., Personnel Activities of the Delaware and Hudson Railroad, April, 1

Benedict, Howard G., Performance Ratings and Bonuses for Salaried Employees, Au 1922.

Berger, George G., Who is Responsible for Buying Power?, June, 1933.

Berger, George G., A Method of Measuring and Rating Management, August, 1929.

Bergen, Harold B., How Personality Influences Selection and Placement, June, 19

Beyer, Otto S. Jr., The Technique of Cooperation (Part I of Union-Management Cooperation in the Railway Industry), February, 1926.

Bingham, W. V., Industrial Psychology, October, 1928.

Haskell, L. W., The Application of Time Study to Shop, June, 1928.

Haskell, L. W., The Production Study as a Check, June, 1928.

Hathaway, H. K., Premium and Bonus Plans, April, 1923.

Hathaway, H. K. Standards (concluded), December, 1927.

Hathaway, H. K., Field of Activity of the Society, January, 1916.

Hathaway, H. K., Maintenance of Machinery and Equipment as a part of the Taylor System of Management, May, 1917.

Hathaway, H. K., Standards, February, 1920.

Hathaway, H. K., Standards, October, 1927.

Hathaway, H. K., Scientific Management in Japan, August, 1929.

Hathaway, H. K., Incentive Wage Systems, October, 1929.

Hathaway, H. K., Cost-Accounting Methods Developed by Frederick W. Taylor and His Associates, June, 1932.

Hathaway, H. K., IV Periodic Financial Reports and Their Uses, April, 1933.

Hathaway, H. K., V. Accounting as a Tool of Management, June, 1933.

Hathaway, H. K., Applied Scientific Management-I. Introduction: Its Applicability to All Areas of Management, October, 1932.

Hathaway, H. K., II. Organization and Classification, December, 1932.

Hathaway, H. K., III. Organization: Functions of Major Executives, Especially the General Manager, February, 1933.

Hathaway, H. K., Methods Study, October, 1930.

Hathaway, H. K., Wilfred Lewis, February, 1930.

Hemmerly, William D., Balance of Work, June, 1920.

Henderson, Charles, Some Experiences in Managing During the Past, February, 1931.

Henderson, Fred, The Economic Consequences of Power Production, October, 1933.

Henderson, P. E., Translation of A French Opinion by Charles De Freminville, April, 1930.

Henderson, P. E., Introduction to a Case of Production Planning in a Very Small Organization, August, 1931.

Herrmann, Milton C., A Case of Production Planning in a Medium-Sized Organization, October, 1931.

Herrmann, Milton C., Management of an Industry, August, 1933.

Hines, Walker D., Planning in a Particular Industry, October, 1931.

Holcombe, John M., Jr., A Case of Sales Research: report on first steps in a study of the selection of life insurance salesmen, June, 1922.

Hoover, Herbert, Industrial Waste, April, 1921.

Hopf, Harry Arthur, An Interpretation of a German View of Scientific Management, October, 1926.

Hopf, Harry Arthur, Problems of Bank Organization, April, 1927.

Hopkins, Ernest M., The Function of the Supervisor of Personnel, January, 1915.

Hopkins, Ernest Martin, The Industrial Problem, August, 1920.

Horwitz, Harry B., Harry A. Wembridge and Herman J. Hutkin, Statistical Compilation: Some of Its Uses as a Function of Scientific Management, February, 1923.

Hotchkiss, Willard E., Business Cycles and Unemployment, April, 1924.

Houser, J. David, Measuring Consumer Attitudes, April, 1932.

Hovey, Floyd F., Cost Accounting and Budget Making, April, 1931.

Hovey, F. F. and C. E. K. Mees, Cost Control with Fluctuating Production, August, 1929.

Hudson, Ray M., Washington News Letter, April, 1923 - June, 1923.

Hull, Hayden E., The Responsibility of the Individual for His Own Unemployment, June, 1933.

Hull, E. Hayden, A Technique in Employment for Subexecutive Positions, April, 1929.

Hull, E. Hayden, Management Psychology a Joint Responsibility, April, 1928.

Hunt, Edward Eyre, Notes on Social and Economic Surveys, February, 1928.

Hunt, Edward Eyre, Scientific Management and World Economics, June, 1927.

Hunt, Edward Eyre, Taylor a Scientific Revolutionary, February, 1925, Part II.

Hutkin, Herman J., Harry B. Horwitz, and Harry A. Wembridge, Statistical Compilation: Some of Its Uses as a Function of Scientific Management, February, 1923.

Odencrantz, Louise C., International Industrial Welfare Congress, October, 1925.

Ogilvie, Paul, The Futility of Lockouts and Strikes, December, 1923.

Ogara, J. E., Vehicular Accident Prevention, October, 1928.

Parmenter, O. A., Selecting Element Times, June, 1923.

Perris, Norris M., Distribution Costs, February, 1930.

Person, H. S., The Call for Leadership, April, 1933.

Person, H. S., A Four-Plank Platform, June, 1931.

Person, H. S., The Development of the Policy of the Taylor Society, February, 1932.

Person, H. S., Introduction to Round-Table Conference on Cost Accounting, June, 1932.

Person, H. S., Is Your Organization a Group?, August, 1924.

Person, H. S., Management's Concern in Research, December, 1926.

Person, H. S., The Manager, the Workman, and the Social Scientist, February, 1917.

Person, H. S., The New Challenge to Scientific Management, April, 1931.

Person, H. S., On the Contribution of Scientific Management in Industrial Problems, June, 1923.

Person, H. S., The Opportunities and Obligations of the Taylor Society, February, 1919.

Person, H. S., The Relations of the Chief Executive to His Principal Associate Executives, April, 1926.

Person, H. S., Scientific Management, October, 1916.

Person, H. S., Scientific Management, October, 1919.

Person, H. S., Scientific Management, October, 1928.

Person, H. S., Scientific Management and Economic Planning, December, 1932.

Person, H. S., Scientist of Work, February, 1925, (Part II).

Person, H. S., Shaping Your Management to Meet Developing Industrial Conditions, December, 1922.

Van Kleeck, Mary, A French Labor Leader Interprets Scientific Management, February, 1930.

Van Kleeck, Mary, The Interview as a Method of Research, December, 1926.

Van Kleeck, Mary, The Social Meaning of Good Management, December, 1924.

Walker, Q. Forest, What Interest Has the Investment Banker in Scientific Management?, April, 1928.

Warner, Edward P., Emergency Measures for the Relief of the Present Depression, April, 1932.

Watson, Earl E., Unit Times vs. Overall Times, June, 1928.

Webb, Sidney and Arnold Freeman, Some English Observations on Scientific Management, June, 1919.

Welch, Emmett H., Purchasing Power and Wage Policy, October, 1932.

Welch, Emmett H., Reply to Purchasing Power and Wages, A Critical Review of Mr. Welch's Article in the October (1932) Bulletin, February, 1933.

Weld, L. D. H., The Cost of Marketing, April, 1933.

Wellman, Harry R., The 1923 Model Sales Machine, June, 1923.

Wembridge, Harry A. with Harry B. Horwitz & Herman J. Hutkin, Statistical Compilation: Some of Its Uses as a Function of Scientific Management, February, 1923.

Whalen, Grover A., National Planning, February, 1932.

White, Jerome C., Scientific Management in the Coal Industry, April, 1927.

Williams, H. H., Comparison of Time Measuring Mechanisms, August, 1931.

Williams, H. H., High Wages and Prosperity, February, 1928.

Williams, John H., The Ways and Means of the Chief Executive, April, 1923.

Williams, John H., The Applicability of Industrial Cost-Accounting Practices to the Electrical Utility Field, June, 1932.

Williams, John H., Management as an Executive Function, April, 1924.

Williams, John H., The Budget as a Medium of Executive Leadership, August, 1928.

Williams, John H., Is There an Optimum Size of Organization? (Control and Size in Management), February, 1930.

Williams, John H., On the Index as A Factor in Industry, July, 1916.

Williams, John H., Top Control, October, 1926.

Williams, LeRoy D., and Alfred B. Holt, Cost of Living in Relation to Wage Adjustments, October, 1919.

Williams, Whiting, Industrial Relations-A Survey of the Problem, June, 1930.

Wittwer, Eldon, Sales Costs, June, 1933.

Wolf, Robert B., Individuality in Industry, August, 1915.

Wolman, Leo, The Bearing of Industrial Equilibrium on Regularity of Operations and of Employment (Industrial Equilibrium in A Business Economy), February, 1930.

Woodbridge, C. K., Methods of Compensating Salesmen, August, 1921.

Yates, Claude T., The Qualifications of a Purchasing Agent, October, 1924.

Yoakum, C. S., Experimental Psychology in Personnel Problems, June, 1925.

Fiftieth Anniversary of A.S.M.E., April, 1930.

Industrial Code Committee, June, 1930.

Industrial Code Committee of the Taylor Society, Industrial Employment Code, February, 1931 & October, 1931.

Japanese Industrialists Visit the United States, October, 1930.

Joint Committee of the Taylor Society and the National Association of Credit Men, Balance Sheets of Management, April, 1931.

A New Honorary Member--Major-General William Crozier, December, 1930.

Scientific Management in the Program of the United Textile Workers of America, October, 1930.

The "Taylor System" in French War Industries, June, 1919.

APPENDIX NO. 2

The Taylor Society[1]

This brief statement of the founding and development of The Taylor Society (originally the Society to Promote the Science of Management) was prepared by Dr. H. S. Person, the Managing Director of the Society.

The Background. In 1886 Henry R. Towne presented the paper The Engineer as Economist before the A.S.M.E. Thereupon followed in that society a series of papers relating to management, chiefly on wage systems, ending with Taylor's A Piece Rate System in 1895. Then followed seven years of no papers on management before the A.S.M.E. In 1903 and 1904 several papers were presented, among them Taylor's Shop Management. In 1906 Taylor's On the Art of Cutting Metals was presented before the A.S.M.E. followed by one paper on a phase of management in each of the years 1907,1908, 1909, and 1910. In 1911 the A.S.M.E. had no paper on a management subject.

The group of young engineers associated with Mr. Taylor felt during this period that it required a struggle to get a paper on management before the A.S.M.E.; that each time a paper of significance was presented (Towne's in 1886, Taylor's in 1895 and 1903) consideration of the subject was stimulated, but the interest soon waned; that the dominant group in the Society did not believe management subjects should engage its attention and put obstacles in the way of such attention; that there was in the Society possibly hostility to the Taylor theories and methods and that they could not receive adequate consideration; and that in general the A.S.M.E. was not giving adequate attention to the subject of management as compared with the growing public interest.

On the following page is a tabulation of the number of items relating to management by years, and whether presented before the A.S.M.E It has been prepared from Scientific Management; a list of references in the New York Public Library, compiled by Walter D. Brown, Technology Division, N. Y. Public Library, 1917.

This group therefore decided that to secure a discussion of management problems to an extent warranted by the importance of the subject and public interest in it, a forum other than the A.S.M.E. would have to be found.

The Founding of the Society to Promote the Science of Management. On November 11, 1910, a meeting was held at the Athletic Club, New York, to consider the matter. There were present Morris L. Cooke, Frank B. Gilbreth, Robert Kent, Conrad Lauer (representing Charles Day), and Wilfred Lewis. Mr. Gilbreth was the host.

It was decided to organize a society for the discussion and promotion of scientific management. A formal organization was not effected, but from then on James M. Dodge presided at meetings and Robert Kent acted as secretary-treasurer. For two years, with such informal organization,

---

[1] Presented during Management Week October 16-21, 1922 and at the Annual Meeting, New York, December 4-7, 1922 of The American Society of Mechanical Engineers.

	Year	Presented before A.S.M.E.	Not presented before A.S.M.E. Published in periodicals such as *Engineering Magazine* and others
Towne's The Engineer as Economist	1886	2	0
	1889	1	0
	1891	1	0
	1893	1	0
Taylor's A Piece-Rate System	1895	1	1
	1896	0	1
	1897	0	4
	1898	0	2
	1899	0	10
	1900	0	12
	1901	0	24
	1902	0	17
Taylor's Shop Management	1903	5	20
Taylor's On the Art of Cutting Metals	1904	1	22
	1905	0	17
	1906	3	17
	1907	1	22
	1908	1	46
	1909	1	30
	1910	1	57
	1911	0	219
Committee Report, The Present State of the Art of Industrial Management	1912	1	165

meetings were held approximately once each month, usually at Keene's Chop House, where management subjects of live interest were discussed. The membership during this period increased to some twenty-five or thirty.

As a result of the increasing public interest resulting from the Eastern Rate Case Hearings (winter of 1911-1912), it was decided to make the organization more formal and to make more of the society. Accordingly a meeting was held at the Hotel Astor, November 7, 1912, and a formal organization effected. The Society was named The Society to Promote the Science of Management. James M. Dodge was elected president and Robert Kent, secretary. Meetings were thereafter held less frequently (three times a year) but were more carefully planned. The place of meeting was usually New York, Philadelphia, or Boston. In 1913 H. S. Person was elected president, and succeeded himself annually until 1919. In December, 1914, was begun the publication of a small journal for members called Bulletin of the Society to Promote the Science of Management. By 1917, when the United States had entered the war, the membership had increased to about 110.

<u>During the War</u>. During the war the activities of the Society were in abeyance, the officers and over fifty per cent of the members of the society having been absorbed into the war organization of the United States.

<u>Reorganization and Change of Name to Taylor Society</u>. Immediately after the armistice in 1918, members of the society in Washington and the vicinity held a meeting to consider the resumption of activities of the society. It was felt that the society should undertake more serious work, in view of the probable larger public service possible during reconstruction, and it was decided to establish a central office with a salaried executive. The name of the society had been changed in 1916 to Taylor Society, in honor of Frederick W. Taylor, who had died in 1915; an office was established April 1, 1919, in the Engineering Societies Building, New York; H. S. Person was chosen the managing director, and John Otterson, Winchester Repeating Arms Co., was elected president. Mr. Otterson was succeeded by Henry S. Dennison, and Mr. Dennison by Richard A. Feiss, who is president at the time of this writing, August, 1922.

The objects of the Society as stated in the Constitution are, through research, discussion, publication and other appropriate means:

1. To secure an understanding and intelligent direction of the principles governing organized effort, for the accomplishment of industrial and other social purposes for the mutual benefit of
    a. The Community
    b. Labor
    c. The Manager
    d. The Employer
2. To secure the gradual elimination of unnecessary effort of of unduly burdensome toil in the accomplishment of the work of the world.
3. To promote the scientific study of teaching of the principles governing organized effort, and of the mechanisms of their adaption and application under varying and changing conditions.

4. To promote general recognition of the fact that the evaluation and application of these principles and mechanisms are the mutual concern of the community, labor, the manager and the employer.
5. To inspire in labor, manager, and employer a constant adherence to the highest ethical conception of their individual and collective social responsibility.

APPENDIX NO. 3

The National Association of Corporation Training

The National Association of Corporation Schools was organized on January 24, 1913, to formulate a definite and constructive educational program for firms engaged in industry and commerce. Its officers and directors were drawn from representative firms including: The New York Edison Company; Burroughs Adding Machine Company; General Electric Company; The Pennsylvania Railroad Company; The Curtis Publishing Company; Yale and Towne Mfg. Company; Consolidated Gas Company of N. Y.; Dodge Manufacturing Company; National Cash Register Company; and the Westinghouse Electric and Manufacturing Company.

At the first meeting of the Executive Committee, an Educational Committee was appointed "to devise couses and recommend best how to teach: salesmanship, advertising, manufacturing, transportation, accounting, financing, purchasing, general office work, stenography, clerical work, filing, correspondence, physical efficiency, hygiene, sanitation, recreation, exercise and the elements of psychology. The general purpose was to assist firms having established educational work, or about to start such work. Through reports, members were informed as to what others were doing and what they might and should be doing.

For the first three years the emphasis of the work of the Association was directed toward preparing the new employee for his first working duties. In 1916 the scope was enlarged to develop employees old in point of service. By 1917 the work had broadened to include "all of the activities classified as human relations." This meant that the Association was definitely in the personnel field. In 1919 it was declared that the Association "has become a great clearing house for all authentic information on the subject of Employee Relations in Industry."

In 1920 it was believed that the Association faced a crisis brought on by the increased service being rendered and rising costs. A plan of reorganization was therefore developed providing for incorporation. The name of the organization was changed to The National Association of Corporation Training. The object was stated to be "the founding of an organization that shall contribute in every way possible to the mutual benefits of all concerned in industry and commercial enterprises; to develop the efficiency of the individual employee and to coordinate his best interests with those of employers; to develop the highest standards of efficiency in industrial operations; to have the courses in established educational institutions expanded to meet more fully the needs of industry and commerce; and to encourage all branches of literature, science and art, or any of them that pertain to industry and commerce." Three classes of members were provided for:

A--Commercial, industrial, transportational, financial, or governmental organizations

B--Any employee of a Class-A member

C--Individuals not eligible as a representative of a Class-A member, or as a Class-B member.

However, this reorganization did not modify appreciably the work of the Association, which continued until May 20, 1922, when the plan of merger with the Industrial Relations Association of America into the National Personnel Association was approved.

APPENDIX NO. 4

The Management Division of the A.S.M.E.

The Management Division of The American Society of Mechanical Engineers was organized in July, 1920. In the first annual report, the following definition of management was given:

"Management is the art and science of preparing, organizing and directing human effort applied to control the forces and to utilize the materials of nature for the benefit of man."

Interpreting the thought of that definition into a program, the same report stated the purpose of the Division to be:

"Inasmuch as the problems of management are of the utmost complexity and difficulty, the Management Division of The American Society of Mechanical Engineers in seeking to render disinterested service therefore declares its purpose to be the formulation and declaration of the fundamentals of management, both regulative principles and accepted practice, and the dissemination of Management knowledge.

"In working toward this object, the Management Division can thus not only be of service to the other Professional Divisions of the Society, to the individual members of the Society and to other societies of like aim, but also to all who are in responsible charge of human effort, and therefore, through them can benefit society at large.

"In carrying out such a broad purpose the activities of the Management Division will vary with changing need, thus no comprehensive listing can be made to cover the present or the future. It is only possible to suggest a few already in project, namely:

"The standardization of management terminology, units of measurement, the improvement and development of management education; the elimination of management wastes in industry; the elimination of unnecessary fatigue in industry and engineering; and lastly, management research."

Almost from the start, the membership of the Management Division has exceeded that of any other Professional Division. It now (September, 1922) numbers 1740.

APPENDIX NO. 5

The Society of Industrial Engineers

In May, 1917, the Western Efficiency Society held a national convention in Chicago on The Importance of the Human Factor in Industry. On the day following the close of this convention, a group of engineers and executives met to discuss the human factor in preparedness and to consider the part which the expert could play in winning the war. At this meeting the Society of Industrial Engineers was organized. Before this meeting, the Council of National Defense had strongly urged the organization of such a national society and had indicated how such a body could assist the Government in the emergency of war. In June, 1917, the chairman of the Aircraft Board invited the directors of the society to a conference in Washington. As a result the society was called upon to gather through its members information on the personnel, financial and industrial resources of Ordnance Bureau of the Army. Until the armistice, the activities of the society were devoted to furthering the carrying on of the war. T wo-thirds of the first board of directors filled positions in Government service; a majority of the members were engaged in organization and production work incident to the war.

During this period the activities of the society were devoted to the first object for which it was founded: "To furnish a vehicle for bringing together in closer relationship persons who are actively engaged in promoting efficiency in business and for making the training and ability of such persons available in the emergency arising out of the present war."

At the close of the war the second object became the guide for society work:

"To furnish a medium for bringing out original contributions to the science of management.

"To provide an organization through which persons who are applying scientific methods to the solution of the problems of production and distribution may exchange views and coordinate their efforts.

"To cooperate with other societies.

"To codify and standardize professional principles and practice.

"To develop the professional standards of the industrial engineer.

"To promote efficient, energy-conserving management.

"To enhance the efficiency and prosperity of American industry."

In July, 1910, the board of directors put into effect a plan of functional organization which has continued in force. The membership (September, 1922) is 1032, divided into six classes: patron, professional industrial engineers; professional technical engineers and accountants; managing executives of commercial and industrial activities; educators in engineering economics, psychology and other lines associated with management; juniors and students.

APPENDIX NO. 6

The Industrial Relations Association of America

This brief statement of the founding and career of the Industrial Relations Association of America (originally the National Association of Employment Managers) was prepared by Mark M. Jones, the first secretary and a director of the organization.

Sporadic attempts to organize the relationship between manager and men, rendered impersonal by the division of labor and the introduction of automatic machinery, can be traced as far back as the 80's. At first the development of this management function was slow. Somewhat later the number of specialists in the personnel field increased. It was not made up entirely of persons specializing on employment management. The growing importance of the whole problem of industrial relations had much to do with the formation of this association and while the majority of the members were specialists in the personnel field, a large number were either in the general management field, or outside of industry but directly interested in industrial relations.

Between 1910 and 1917 other local organizations for the discussion of employment problems developed in New York, Philadelphia, Chicago, Pittsburgh, Cleveland, Newark, and Rochester.

The inter-city aspect and the beginning of the national movement dates back to 1914, when men responsible for hiring held a meeting in Minneapolis for the purpose of exchanging ideas. The success of this small meeting was such that it resulted in a second meeting in the same city in May, 1915, which was attended by persons from a much wider area.

In May, 1916, a general meeting was held in Boston, and in the same month of 1917 a conference at Philadelphia was attended by several hundred.

At this Philadelphia meeting it became apparent that some medium for cooperation, a clearing house for the experience of local groups, was needed, and a committee of ten was appointed to consider the advisability of forming a national association. The committee reported that it believed the time inopportune for such action but recommended that a national committee be created for the purpose of arranging an annual convention, as well as continuing the study of the desirability of a permanent national organization. Adoption of this recommendation resulted in the creation of the National Committee of Employment Managers' Associations.

A meeting was immediately planned for Cleveland, Ohio, to be held during the following year. The war situation, however, caused a change in plans. The National Committee arranged to hold the convention in Rochester, in May, 1918, in recognition of the pioneering work of Rochester University in graduating the first class of employment managers trained under a special course for the United States Government.

An attendance of over 800 men and women at the Rochester convention was evidence of the need for a more formal national agency, and after considerable discussion it was voted to organize a national association. An organizing committee was elected for the purpose of so

When the National Association got under way during the closing months of 1918 it was mainly an organization of organizations. Its control was in the hands of rèpresentatives of local associations, for while there were three other classes of members, the group members representing local employment managers' associations held the balance of power and determined the policies of the National Association of Employment Managers.

The task of the National Association when first organized was stated as follows:

1 To arrange and manage an annual convention
2 Issue a bulletin
3 Promote the organization of local employment managers' associations
4 Assist local employment managers' associations then in existence
5 Operate a free employment service which would assist specialists in the personnel field to secure positions
6 Establish and maintain a central clearing house for employment information
7 Conduct such research work and surveys within the employment field as might be approved by the Board

The first convention after the formation of the National Association of Employment Managers was held at Cleveland, Ohio, in May, 1919. An attendance of 2000 was an indication of the stimulus to the movement provided by the war.

As the result of a widespread demand arising out of the widening scope of the employment manager, with the result that his activities comprehended many more functions than could be described through use of the word "employment," the name of the National Association was changed on March 1, 1920, to The Industrial Relations Association of America. It was under this name that the first peak in the movement was reached. The annual meeting in Chicago, in May, 1920, attended by 5000, was one of the very great national conventions of that period.

Soon after the 1920 meeting the change in the business situation was reflected in the personnel field and a decline in interest and support set in. As personnel work had in many cases been the last addition to specialized management functions, there was a widespread belief that it would be the first to be discontinued. Experience has since indicated that such apprehension was not well founded. There were but few cases where that policy was applied in retrenching or where intemperate action destroyed a sound piece of work. Personnel work was decreased greatly, but not often to the same extent as other management functions. Wherever a severe reduction took place it came more as a result of individual work than an inherent weakness in the idea or plan.

In the first discussions of a national organization there was present a small group which was anxious to decentralize the unit of association membership to the utmost by placing membership on an individual basis. The majority did not look with favor upon this departure, and the concentration of power and control in a group membership was the result. The experience of the organization ultimately established the fact that the group basis could not be entirely satisfactory. It did not provide the foundation for cooperation which was necessary if the Association were to make a real contribution to the progress of its members. It required many months, in fact, several years, for the advocates of individual membership to prove their case. However, at the 1921 convention of the Industrial Relations Association of America, held in New York City in November, a committee, widely representative of the whole country, presented a report which strongly advocated reorganization on an individual basis. The problems of the individual members of the National Board of Directors were so numerous, however, that they had little opportunity to apply themselves to the problems of the association.

Finally, the Board of Directors recognized the need for a considerable alteration in the structure of the Association and decided that the way might be cleared for the most expeditious action if the Association were dissolved and an organization established along the lines suggested to the convention by the Reorganization Committee. The necessary steps to that end were taken and the Industrial Relations Association of America ceased functioning on December 31, 1921.

An organizing committee for the new association was then at work, and out of the whole situation a merger with the National Association of Corporation Training was arranged. This crystallized in the formation of the National Personnel Association in April, 1922.

APPENDIX NO. 7

The National Personnel Association

The National Personnel Association was formed to take over the activities of the National Association of Corporation Training and the Industrial Relations Association of America. The possibility of such a union was discussed informally at a joint meeting of the Executives Club of New York and the New York Chapter of the National Association of Corporation Training, held on February 17, 1922. On the following day a letter of invitation was drafted and signed by 20 men who supported the suggestion of union, requesting attendance at a meeting to be held on March 9. On that day 34 persons were in attendance out of about 100 invited.

It was unanimously decided to form a national organization devoted to employment or personnel activities, provided the two existing organizations could be combined. A committee was appointed to consult with the officers of these two organizations and report a plan.

This committee reported on April 7, submitting a plan for the new association and providing for an organizing committee to put it into effect. This committee was appointed and met on the same day. Anticipating this action, the officers of the I.R.R.A. had secured authorization to enter the merger. An expression of opinion from Class-A members of the N.A.C.T. was overwhelmingly in favor of the union.

On April 21 the articles of incorporation were completed and signed, putting the union into effect and bringing the National Personnel Association into existence. Its purpose is:

"To advance the understanding of the principles, policies and methods of creating and maintaining satisfactory human relations within commerce and industry.

"1 By assisting administrative executives, those engaged in personnel work and others who are interested in problems of personnel administration through providing opportunities for conferences, cooperative research, and exchange information among members.

"2 By studying the problems of personnel administration, including employment, training, development, health, employee service and cooperation.

"3 By assisting established educational and other institutions to interpret the personnel needs of commerce and industry by maintaining reciprocal relations with them."

Two kinds of members are provided for: individual and company. The membership is (September, 1922) 500 individuals and 120 companies.